In this major new work Alice Harris and Lyle Campbell set out to establish a general framework for the investigation of syntactic change. Systematic cross-linguistic comparison of changes in syntax across a wide variety of languages is used to construct hypotheses about the universals and limits of language change more generally. In particular, the authors seek to determine the range of causes of syntactic change, to develop an understanding of the mechanisms of syntactic change, and to provide an understanding of why some languages undergo certain changes and not others. The authors draw on languages as diverse as Pipil and French, Georgian and Estonian, and their insightful analyses of these data are one of the book's great strengths.

Rigor and precision are combined here with a great breadth of scholarship to produce a unique resource for the study of linguistic change, which will be of use to scholars and students alike.

CAMBRIDGE STUDIES IN LINGUISTICS

Historical syntax in cross-linguistic perspective

HISTORICAL SYNTAX
IN CROSS-LINGUISTIC
PERSPECTIVE

ALICE C. HARRIS

Professor of Linguistics and Anthropology, and Chair of
Department of Germanic and Slavic Languages,
Vanderbilt University

LYLE CAMPBELL

Professor of Linguistics,
University of Canterbury

CAMBRIDGE
UNIVERSITY PRESS

Published by the Press Syndicate of the University of Cambridge
The Pitt Building, Trumpington Street, Cambridge CB2 1RP
40 West 20th Street, New York, NY 10011–4211, USA
10 Stamford Road, Oakleigh, Melbourne 3166, Australia

First published 1995

Printed in Great Britain at the University Press, Cambridge

A catalogue record for this book is available from the British Library

Library of Congress cataloguing in publication data

Harris, Alice C.
Historical syntax in cross-linguistic perspective / Alice C. Harris, Lyle Campbell.
    p.   cm. – (Cambridge studies in linguistics 74)
Includes bibliographical references and index.
ISBN 0 521 47294 6 (hardback) – ISBN 0 521 47881 2 (paperback)
1. Grammar, Comparative and general – Syntax. 2. Historical linguistics. I.
Campbell, Lyle. II. Title. III. Series.
P291.H25 1995
415 – dc20   94–15013 CIP

ISBN 0 521 47294 6 hardback
ISBN 0 521 47881 2 paperback

LTL

This work is dedicated to Georgia Harris and to Richard and Cleo Campbell

Contents

Preface

This volume is intended primarily as a work for specialists and advanced graduate students. It is not an elementary textbook or introduction, and it does assume some knowledge of syntax, of historical linguistics, and of basic issues in diachronic syntax. Our main purpose in this work is to present a comprehensive and cohesive approach to diachronic syntax. It is a basic work in the sense that we view it as a standard reference or handbook. It is likewise basic in the sense that it reexamines fundamental issues and attempts to contribute to a resolution of them. We view it as foundational; while all academic work of course has predecessors, this approach is not built directly upon previous work.

For readers who do not have the background that we assume, it may be helpful to read (or reread) chapter 3 after chapters 4–6, inasmuch as chapter 3 is entirely theoretical and purposely avoids detailed discussion of examples. Many basic examples that contribute to making the theory more accessible are provided in chapters 4–6. Readers not familiar with discussions of word order during the last two decades may find it helpful to read chapter 8, or at least its Introduction, before chapter 6.

As discussed in chapter 1, this work is based upon cross-linguistic data. In addition to the Indo-European languages, which we assume will be familiar to many readers, we especially include many examples from the language families with which we are most familiar – Finno-Ugric, Kartvelian, North East Caucasian, Mayan, and Uto-Aztecan. The general appendix provides a family tree of each of these.

A reviewer of a manuscript version of this book encouraged us to expand upon many points discussed in this work, but everything cannot be covered in a single work, and Cambridge University Press has encouraged us to shorten it. For the same reason we were unable to follow up on many of the reviewer's suggestions for discussing one or another of our examples with respect to phenomena that were not directly relevant to the points we addressed.

Chapter 9 is based on Alice Harris' article, "Alignment typology and diachronic change," in Winfried Lehmann (ed.), *Language typology 1987:*

systematic balance in language. We are grateful to John Benjamins publishing company for permission to use this article.

We would like to express our sincere appreciation to a number of friends and colleagues who provided assistance with various languages – to Silke Albright and Hans Schulz for judgments on modern German, to Jaklin Kornfilt on Turkish, to Larry Crist on Old French, to Antonina Gove on Russian, to John A.C. Greppin on Armenian word order, to Dodona Kiziria on Georgian, to Annie Lloyd on American Sign Language, and special thanks for a great deal of work to Christine Ebel on Old High German, to Seija Tiisala on Finnish, and to Joseph Harris on Old English and on runes. We thank Dee Ann Holisky for discussion about English compounds and James V. Staros for commentary on biological evolution. We have presented parts of this work in several forums, and we would like to thank members of those audiences, especially the members of the 1991 Linguistics Institute course Aspects of Historical Syntax, at which a preliminary version of this book was presented. We are grateful, too, to many colleagues in historical syntax who have read and commented upon portions of this manuscript. Of course, any remaining problems are our responsibility.

This material is based upon work supported in part by the National Science Foundation under Grants No. BNS–8419143, BNS–8419447, BNS–8712111, and BNS–8712240 and by the National Endowment for the Humanities under a Fellowship for University Teachers. Any opinions, findings, and conclusions or recommendations expressed in this publication are those of the authors and do not necessarily reflect the views of the supporting organizations.

Abbreviations

A	agent; adjective
ABL	ablative
ABS(L)	absolutive case
ACC	accusative
ADP	ad position
ADV	adverbial case
AFFIRM	affirmative
ALL	allative case
AOR	aorist
ASP	aspect
ASS	associative
AUX	auxiliary
CAUS	causative
COL	collective
COMP	complementizer
COP	copula
DAT	dative
DEF	definite
DEM	demonstrative
DET	determiner
DIMIN	diminutive
DO	direct object
DS	different subject marker
E	empty
EMPH	emphatic
ERG	ergative
EXCL	exclusive

F(EM)	feminine gender-class
FOC	focus
FUT	future
GEN	genitive
HSP	Heaviness Serialization Principle
IMPERF	imperfective
INCL	inclusive
INCOMP	incompletive
INDIC	indicative
INF	infinitive
INST	instrumental
INTERJ	interjection
IO	indirect object
ITER	iterative
LOC	locative
M	masculine gender-class
N(EUT)	neuter gender-class
NAR	narrative case
NEG	negative
NMLZR	nominalizar
NOM	nominative
O(BJ)	object
OBL	oblique
PART	partitive
PASS	passive
PERF	perfective
PER(S)	person
PFCT	perfect
PL	plural
POSS	possessive
POSTP	postposition
PREP	preposition

PRES	present
PRET	preterit
PRO	pronoun
PRT	particle
PTCPL	participle
QUES(T)	question particle
QUO(T)	quotative particle
REDUP	reduplication
REL	relative
RHET	rhetorical
S(UBJ)	subject
SBV	subjunctive
SG	singular
SRP	subject-referring pronoun
SUBOR	subordinator
SUF	suffix
TOP	topic
TRANSL	translative case
UNIV	universal (unmarked) tense
V	verb
XP	phrase with head of category X (variable)

Old Georgian data from the Gospel of Matthew (Mt.) are cited from Blake 1976, those from Mark (Mk.) are from Blake 1974, and those from John are from Blake and Brière 1950. "Ad." indicates the Adysh or Adiši codex, AD 897; "A" the Opiza codex, AD 913; "B" the Tbet'i codex, AD 995.

1 *Introduction*

This book is about historical syntax in general. Although syntactic change was an important part of the comparative linguistic tradition, and while the past fifteen years or so have seen a significant increase in attention to the topic, the study of diachronic syntax is still largely disorganized and unfocused and lacks the sort of consensus enjoyed, for example, by historical phonology. This book is aimed at remedying this situation in so far as this is possible at the present time. It is intended as a basic treatise on diachronic syntax. Some might claim that the present state of the field is too fragmented and overwrought with conflicting claims to offer much optimism for achieving our goal, which is to establish a general framework for syntactic change. This state of affairs, however, does not render the task impossible, just more important, exciting, and more urgent.

1.1 Goals of a theory of diachronic syntax

Recent work in diachronic syntax has been chiefly of three sorts: (1) studies of particular changes in individual languages; (2) research on specific kinds of change (e.g. word order change, grammaticalization); and (3) explorations of the diachronic implications of particular formal approaches to grammar, often given more to championing the particular theory of syntax than to actually accounting for linguistic changes[1] (for details, see chapter 2). The approach followed in this book differs from these. Rather than focusing on particular changes in individual languages, we investigate changes cross-linguistically. Rather than limiting attention to individual kinds of change (or single mechanisms of change), we establish commonalities in changes across languages and determine what mechanisms lie behind them and how they fit into the overall explanation of syntactic changes. While this has not been done heretofore, several have recognized its importance and have called for such research; a sense of how the field is viewed and of the importance of this task is seen in the following statements:

> We should work to enlarge the pool of well-grounded and accessible empirical data available for discussions of syntactic change; to translate informal and intuitive notions of the nature and causes of change into explicit proposals that can be scrutinized for their adequacy.   (Langacker 1977: 100)

> Zu den Aufgaben der historischen Sprachwissenschaft gehört die Feststellung und Klassifizierung von Typen der Sprachveränderungen . . . Eine umfassende Typologie des Syntaxwandels gibt es nicht.   (Ebert 1978:10.)

> To the tasks of historical linguistics belongs the establishment and classification of types of language changes . . . A comprehensive typology of syntactic change does not exist.   [Our translation, ACH/LC]

While in principle the study of syntactic change should both inform and be informed by general linguistic theory, too often rigid devotion to a particular theory of syntax has limited rather than magnified insight into diachronic processes. Our findings clearly have relevance for general theories of syntax; however, we take as our starting point the actual changes themselves, rather than the predictions and constraints of any existing theory of syntax (this procedure is justified in chapter 3).[2] Our interest is primarily in the nature of syntactic change, rather than in the form of the theory of such change (see Moore and Carling 1982; esp. p. 3).

Specifically, in our study we have attempted (1) to investigate syntactic changes in a number of languages and language families, (2) to compare these to determine what are possible syntactic changes and what the commonly recurring types of changes are, and (3) to frame a general approach to syntactic change based on the results. Our goals, then, for this book are: (a) to characterize the class of possible changes in the syntax of natural languages; (b) to determine and state formal constraints on syntactic change; (c) to attempt to explain (at least some aspects of) syntactic change; and (d) to show how an understanding of the nature of syntactic change can form the basis for syntactic reconstruction. Our findings provide the foundation for a theory of syntactic change, which includes (1) mechanisms of change (limited to three: reanalysis, extension, and borrowing), (2) a set of general diachronic operations, and (3) a set of general principles that interact with these operations (see chapter 3).[3]

1.2   Orientation to the organization and contents of the book

In chapter 2, on the history of diachronic syntactic study, we survey the treatments of syntactic change throughout the history of linguistics. This contributes to our general goal of framing an adequate approach to historical syntax, since whatever proved wrong or impractical in the past must be abandoned, while true achievements and empirical findings must be accommodated and incorporated in any adequate treatment. By including the insights and avoiding the errors of previous work, we make large initial strides towards our ultimate goal of framing an appropriate framework for historical syntax.

In chapters 3–6 we begin to develop a framework for diachronic syntax and closely examine three mechanisms of syntactic change – reanalysis, extension, and borrowing. The basic components and fundamental assumptions of the framework we propose are laid out in chapter 3, and these are presented, exemplified, and defended in detail in chapters 4–6.

Reanalysis (chapter 4) has been the single most important mechanism for most attempts to explain syntactic change throughout the history of linguistics. Reanalysis depends upon surface ambiguity or the possibility of more than one analysis. It changes structure, and we examine examples of change through reanalysis of (i) constituency, (ii) hierarchical structure, (iii) category labels, (iv) grammatical relations, and other aspects of underlying structure.

Extension generalizes a rule. It is a mechanism which results in changes in the surface manifestation of a pattern and which does not involve immediate or intrinsic modification of underlying structure. It is the subject of chapter 5, dealt with together with constraints on its operation.

Syntactic **borrowing** and the consequences of language contact are treated in chapter 6. This is a neglected and abused area of diachronic syntax. We determine the role of borrowing and language contact in a theory of syntactic change and we evaluate hypothesized universals concerning grammatical borrowing.

In chapters 7–10 we deal with the cross-linguistic ("intersystemic") comparison of diachronic systems and their contribution to the overall framework we propose. We apply the methods of "Intersystemic Comparison" (described below) to four areas of diachronic syntax. Although some of these areas have been very much discussed in the literature, we believe that we succeed in taking a fresh approach to the problems and in discovering some previously undetected regularities.

Chapter 7 describes processes that simplify biclausal structures and states shared characteristics of these processes. Chapter 8 deals with the role of word order change, both chronicling the failure of certain approaches to word order change and contributing to an understanding of how word order changes and of the effects of other grammatical changes on word order harmonies. Chapter 9 treats changes in alignment, i.e. the distribution of the morphosyntactic markers or characteristics in ergative, accusative, and active typological patterns.[4] Here we discuss the origins of alignment changes, a constraint on changes in alignment, and the question of typological consistency in alignment. In chapter 10, we deal with the origins of and changes in complex constructions, and their relevance to the general framework of syntactic change.

On the basis of findings in the earlier chapters, the overall nature of syntactic change is addressed in chapter 11, and in particular disputed aspects of explanation, prediction, and causation are explored. There we discuss some of the persistent problems of diachronic syntax, including regularity and directionality. Our views on these issues contribute to developing an approach to establishing correspondences and reconstructing earlier stages of syntax. We argue that syntactic change is rule-governed and orderly. We pull together a variety of evidence to show that while several types of change that have been claimed to be unidirectional are not, the sorts of changes known as grammaticalization proceed in a single direction, with infrequent exceptions.

Chapter 12 in a sense develops a practical application of the framework developed here. It deals with the establishment of syntactic correspondences and with syntactic reconstruction. Various assumed obstacles to syntactic reconstruction are discussed and prospects for successful syntactic reconstruction are demonstrated. The chapter shows exactly how correspondences in syntactic pattern can be established, though some have claimed that this cannot be done. These correspondences are the first step in reconstruction, and the remainder of the chapter shows how the established principles of reconstruction (both internal and comparative reconstruction) can be successfully applied to syntax.

1.3   On the relation to synchronic syntax

We take the position that the syntax of natural languages is constrained by natural laws and that there are definable principles of syntactic change, some of them not derivable from the characteristics of the class of possible grammars. We suggest that it is not enough that input, output, and transitional stages be sanctioned by general (synchronic) linguistic theory. In an adequate theory of change, specific shifts must be characterized as lawful or unlawful for natural language. Such characterizations are stated in this work, especially in chapters 4–6 and 7–11. These characteristics include constraints on the changes from one possible syntactic system to another.

Some recent approaches to diachronic syntax have explored the implications of one or another theory of (synchronic) syntax for diachrony. We consider the results of these studies relatively unproductive and unrevealing of the real nature of syntactic change. Instead, we have tried to explore the nature of syntactic change first and then consider the implications of these facts for a comprehensive theory. We are therefore interested in discovering what characteristics of a given change are shared across languages, and what characteristics are language-particular. We are interested in specifying what changes and what stays the same in a given diachronic process, and ultimately in explaining why and how changes take place. Our primary concern is not with how these facts can be accommodated within current theories, but we are attentive to the question of what these historical properties can tell us about linguistic theory. In this sense, our approach is not theory-driven, but data-driven.

1.4   On prediction

Absolute prediction of change is not, as sometimes suggested, the major goal for diachronic syntax, or indeed for any retrospective science. It is sometimes objected that prediction is necessary for explanation, and that theories of linguistic change which do not predict are therefore inadequate. For example, from this point of view, it might be objected that a theory that recognizes reanalysis of a syntactic construction in the face of surface ambiguity (or multiple possible analyses, see chapter 4) cannot predict when such a change will take place or what exact form it may take, or when it may fail to take place even though the appropriate condition of multiple possible analyses holds. The quick but accurate answer to this objection is that prediction is not necessary for valid explanation. Evolution by natural selection is recognized as scientifically legitimate explanation in spite of the fact that it permits no prediction of the evolutionary changes it is almost universally acknowledged to explain.

A longer and perhaps more satisfying answer is that both explanations of evolution/biological change by natural selection and of various reanalyses and certain other syntactic changes do permit certain predictions within the limits described below. The matter of prediction, with the closely associated concerns of causation and explanation, is considered at length in chapter 11, and therefore we only introduce the topic here.

Attempting to predict that some change will occur or which change will take place in a language is akin to attempting to predict that someone will speak or predicting what they will say. A synchronic theory should state the limits on what a speaker can say, in the sense that it will characterize the grammatical utterances of natural languages. This, however, is very different from predicting a specific utterance. Similarly, it should not be an aim of a theory of language change to predict that a particular change will occur. It is, however, appropriate that such a theory should predict the limits of such change, by characterizing the possibilities of change.

Perhaps for some the view that a theory should predict change stems from the belief that change takes place "only when necessary" (Lightfoot 1979a: 124).[5] Romaine (1981: 287) points out that the view that change takes place "only when necessary" is falsified by the existence of any two closely related languages which differ syntactically (see chapter 2 for additional discussion of this point). If two languages (or dialects) exist, they differ; one or both must have changed with respect to the pattern(s) wherein they differ. According to the claims in Lightfoot (1979a), this change must have been triggered by specific conditions, which made the shift "necessary." But if the dialects differ only with respect to a single syntactic pattern, the conditions which are seen as triggering the change existed in both dialects; the change was thus "necessary" for both, but only one underwent it. In his later publications (see Lightfoot 1988a, 1988b, 1991), Lightfoot concedes that syntactic change does not occur solely when "necessary." He says:

> These environmental changes, on the other hand, typically do not result from the genetically determined acquisition process, whereby something triggers some structural property with systematic effects [i.e. sets a parameter]. Rather, they are induced by contact with other languages and dialects or introduced for stylistic reasons . . . For such environmental changes we have no systematic explanations, and as far as grammarians are concerned they may as well be attributed to chance.
>
> (Lightfoot 1991: 169–70; see also Lightfoot 1988a: 319)

If a particular (perhaps "environmental") syntactic change is not necessary, it follows that change cannot be predicted.

While a theory of language change cannot predict that a particular change will occur, it can be predictive in the sense that we can state to an extent what the course of a particular change will be if it does occur, according to the universals. From general principles, once they are stated, one should be able to deduct the characteristics of a particular change that falls within the parameters of a well-understood type.

That the fact of change is not fully predictable does not entail either that change is random or that the limits of change cannot be stated. We discuss the latter of these first, returning to the question of randomness below. We believe that while the fact of change cannot be predicted, the bounds on change can be stated. It is neither possible nor desirable that linguistic theory predict that a particular syntactic change will occur; it is both possible and desirable that a theory sanction changes that do occur and rule out those that do not, and that it characterize the mechanism(s) possible in such a shift. Examples of ways in which a theory can differentiate changes that may occur from those that may not are given in the chapters that follow, especially chapters 7–10; examples of characterizations of the mechanisms possible in particular changes are also given there.

1.5   On explanation

Explanation of linguistic change has been a hotly contested matter in the linguistic literature. We take up the issues in detail in chapter 11, where, hopefully, we contribute to understanding explanation in syntactic change, but also to epistemology in general with regard to linguistic change. In the present chapter we merely introduce the topic of explanation to indicate our general orientation in this book. Explanation can take many forms. Many approaches have been criticized in recent literature as not offering "true" explanations, even those that increase our basic understanding of some phenomenon. We embrace a variety of strategies that advance an understanding of diachronic syntax, among these are an examination of causes of syntactic change (see chapter 11), scrutiny of the mechanisms that implement syntactic change (chapters 3–6), relating a change in one language to a parallel change in another and relating these to a more general type of change (both in chapters 7–10). Causation, argumentation, and explanation in diachronic syntax are discussed in several places below, and in considerable depth in chapter 11.

1.6   Characteristics of a theory of syntactic change

Previous work has resulted in a partially shared set of assumptions about diachronic syntax, but there has not been an integrated theory or framework for research in this field. A number of scholars have put forward hypotheses about the nature of specific changes, but these are not necessarily mutually consistent (see chapter 2). Some hypotheses that have been proposed have been formulated in such a way that they are too vague to be tested, while others are simply inherently untestable. A hypothesis that is untestable is without value. A theory should have empirical consequences; it should provide for hypotheses that are testable; and it should define a set of facts which, if discovered to be true, would disprove the hypotheses. Clear statements of hypotheses and testing of them are essential to the further advancement of the field; however, it is also necessary to value philosophical and historical understanding of the issues. In the last fifteen years some very negative views have been expressed in the literature on the very possibility of doing diachronic syntax, variously questioning or denying the possibility of identifying syntactic change, doing syntactic reconstruction (see chapter 12), and of formulating a theory of language change.

In order for the field to advance further, a single overarching framework at least for diachronic syntax is needed, with a set of hypotheses that make clear statements about the limits of change. A complete theory of syntactic change should do at least the following:

(a)   describe the range of causes of a change from A to A';
(b)   provide an understanding of the mechanisms that carry out a change from A to A';
(c)   characterize the set of changes that languages undergo and those they cannot;
(d)   provide an understanding of why languages undergo certain changes and do not undergo others;
(e)   characterize the source of new structures, including both old patterns that spread to new domains and patterns that are entirely novel in the language.

Naturally, it is too soon to meet any of these goals in a complete way. However, these should be long-term goals of the field, and the theory should continue to evolve, taking into consideration new findings on particular changes. This book attempts to draw nearer to meeting these goals.

1.7   The method employed

The method we have used involves the cross-linguistic comparison of changes in the syntax of different languages. This permits us to make hypotheses about universals of change in the areas examined. Of course, many other researchers have used cross-linguistic data in the search for linguistic universals, but the approach we follow has not been employed in diachronic syntactic research.

First, we have concentrated on comparing changes that a number of unrelated or distantly related languages have undergone. Changes that recur in language after language are subject to study, generalization, and, at least in some instances, explanation. Second, we have looked at details of these changes, rather than concentrating exclusively on the grand schema. For example, in the area of complex sentences, we have not been exclusively interested in the issue of whether these originate in parataxis, but have examined subtypes of embedded clauses, linking individual types to differing types of assertions. By studying individual types we can provide a more accurate and detailed picture of origins of embedded clauses. Third, in addition to looking at details, we have examined broad categories of change: for example, we have not focused our attention exclusively on a common individual change such as an independent modal verb becoming an auxiliary, but have compared this with other independent verbs that have become auxiliaries, and have examined all these in the still larger category of the elements of biclausal structures becoming a variety of grammatical words, clitics, or affixes. Fourth, we have examined the parts of structures in the context of complete structures. For example, we have not been content to consider the fate of modal verbs, but have taken into consideration the complete change of structures containing independent modal verbs into structures containing modal auxiliaries.

This method may be termed **Intersystemic Comparison**.[6] "Intersystemic" should be understood as denoting a number of ideas simultaneously. The "comparison" is among languages cross-linguistically. At the same time, "intersystemic" refers to the (sub)systems involved in broad categories of change. The term emphasizes that it is whole syntactic systems that must be compared, not isolated facts. Finally, it refers to the fact that we must take into consideration all styles and registers of language – literary language, oral literature, conversation, and others.

We use these data from a wide variety of languages to formulate generalizations about syntactic change. These generalizations are hypotheses about the very nature of syntactic change, and as such they are subject to testing, verification, and revision.

1.8   The syntactic framework

We have attempted to approach the data with as few assumptions as possible, primarily restricting those made to ones shared by many or most investigators. We assume that the structure of a clause includes information about (i) constituency, (ii) hierarchical structure, (iii) category labels, and (iv) grammatical relations. To the extent possible, our discussion does not rest upon assumptions concerning which characteristics of clauses may be present in underlying levels of structure and which may be derived or assigned by other rules. We do assume that the syntactic structure of a clause may contain more than one level.

No *a priori* assumption is made concerning the basis for the generalization of cross-linguistic diachronic facts; that is, we look for generalizations in terms of any one of the elements of clause structure listed above or in terms of others. We have found that assuming just this much provides a framework within which we can make comparisons of specific structures cross-linguistically, while not encumbering ourselves with theoretical problems which would make comparison impossible.

1.9   The evidence

The problems of obtaining evidence for diachronic studies in syntax have frequently been addressed (see, for example, Lightfoot 1979a, 1981a; Allen 1980[1977]; Faarlund 1990b; Joseph 1983). Often cited are the lack of a native speaker's intuitions, accidental gaps in the corpus, the need for philological skills and thorough knowledge of the languages under investigation, and the small number and variety of languages attested over a long period of time. We believe that the collaboration of scholars versed in languages of different families, each attested over a long period, can help to overcome the last two problems cited.

Attested evidence of changes must be considered the single most reliable source of data on language change of any kind. Yet various aspects of the attestations are sometimes unclear. A case in point is *do*-support in English. This construction originated in Middle English, so in theory it should be possible to identify clearly its Old English source and to trace the development of its present distribution, given the abundant documentation for the history of English. In fact, however, there is no consensus as to whether it resulted from contact, developed internally from causative *do*, or developed from aspectual *do* (see Garrett 1992 on the last and on summaries of other recent proposals), or concerning how it achieved its current distribution. Thus, attested evidence of change, while it is the most reliable data we have, is not without its problems.

It has been suggested that there is so much disagreement about changes in English and, to an extent, other European languages only because there are so many linguists with different views working on these languages, while there is sometimes more consensus about change in more exotic languages precisely because there are only a few linguists working on those issues. Lightfoot (1988a: 316–17) urges this view strongly and very critically; he has even given it a name:

> the "data" do not lie prestine [*sic*] pure in a well-organized supermarket awaiting collection by a conscientious scholar. Often it is not enough simply to go to the handbooks and look up the facts, as if they exist independent of interpretation, analysis, and debate. In the case of illuminating changes, things are rarely that simple.
>
> This commonplace idea, unfortunately, is less well entrenched amongst historians of language than what I have dubbed the "Ebeling Principle" (Lightfoot 1979b): the more exotic a language and the fewer the linguists who have analyzed it, the more tractable and self-evident its grammar. This powerful and damaging principle has misled historians.

Here Lightfoot is talking mostly about reconstruction and the failings of historical studies of word order, but his point is aimed at all diachronic linguistic work.[7] He cites his Ebeling Principle right after going through examples from Middle English and Spanish. However, English and Spanish are notoriously messy. This may be due in part to Lightfoot's notion that it correlates with the number of linguists who have analyzed these languages, but certainly other factors are also involved. The messiness of English and Spanish historical grammar is due no doubt at least in part also to influence from contact with other languages and dialect borrowing (see, for example, Posner 1985: 184; Samuels 1987; Toon 1987). German, some of the Slavic languages, Finnish, and Georgian, however, are examples of languages which have been somewhat less influenced than English and Spanish by other languages and dialect borrowing,[8] have an extensive literature, and have been investigated by a large number of linguists. In the historical grammar of these languages most changes are well documented and well understood. Also, both synchronic and diachronic analyses of languages with more morphology than English are often more straightforward than those of English. In particular, the origin of a construction may be more apparent because of more morphology.

In 1979a Lightfoot first introduced the Ebeling Principle in the context of criticizing other scholars of diachronic syntax for imprecise analyses of the exotic languages they discuss. As we stated above, only a precise hypothesis can be tested, and a clear statement, even if it ultimately proves to be wrong, may be valuable to the field for the advances in true understanding that it helps to promote. However, even an imprecise or intuitive idea, such as the Transparency Principle, may sometimes have value in advancing the field, due to the discussion it generates.[9] Examples from diverse families are valuable in a different way; they offer confirmation of the generality of a change or principle and are at least indicative of the limits of variation.

As the primary evidence in our study, we have taken well-studied cases with written documentation attested over a considerable length of time, from the solidly attested Indo-European languages, especially Germanic and Romance, and from Georgian and Finnish. The latter two each have extensive traditions of philological and linguistic investigation not well known to linguists outside the language families they represent. This evidence is supplemented with less studied cases with rich written documentation, including Mayan, Nahuatl, and Pipil. These languages have colonial grammars and extensive texts attested for over 450 years.

In a recent work on diachronic syntax, Faarlund (1990b: 16–18) points out that for some well-attested dead languages we have something approaching the negative data that synchronic syntacticians depend upon. There are some kinds of evidence that may be taken as indications that certain constructions were impossible. Among these is what Faarlund refers to as "missed opportunities." If a modern language regularly uses a particular construction in a certain environment, and if the ancient language from which it is descended regularly does not use the construction in that environment, we may assume that the construction in question did not exist in the ancient language; this is more likely to be the case if the construction is obligatory or nearly so in the stated environment in the modern language. We feel that most text-based studies of attested change, including our own, make the assumption of this sort of negative data. The present explicit recognition of that assumption seems sufficient to cover the routine use we make of it in this book.

A fruitful and often overlooked source of reliable data in diachronic syntax is found in dialect differences. It has not been widely recognized that use of dialect data can overcome some of the specific difficulties enumerated above. In living dialects one can have access to native speakers; there need be no accidental gaps, since one is not limited to a finite corpus. Attention to dialect differences broadens the database for a study such as ours.[10] Because dialects are generally relatively close, the constructions being compared often differ minimally and for this reason may constitute an ideal object of study. In addition, the direction of development is sometimes more obvious between dialects or closely related languages, often clearly documented in written attestations. Thus, the relative tractability of syntactic changes in compared dialects provides both more solid circumstances in which to test assumptions about syntactic change and relevant evidence from any language with dialects that differ grammatically. This being the case, we have not neglected this exciting laboratory for the investigation of syntactic change; examples of use of syntactic differences among dialects are found in every chapter, beginning with chapter 4.

Changes involving reconstructed stages of a language must be used judiciously, but we believe that they should be included in the database of any investigation of diachronic syntax. The validity of these data clearly depends on the reliability of the reconstruction. Some reconstructions are so well supported, at least in broad outline, that there is little disagreement about them: for example, within the Daghestan (North East Caucasian) family, reconstructing the existence of a gender-class system (in broad outline) is not controversial, since some languages in every subgroup preserve gender-class agreement, the markers are phonetically similar across the family, and the functions they serve are the same or similar in different languages. Because this is widely accepted and richly supported for the proto-language, the loss of this system in Lezgi, one of the languages lacking gender-class agreement, constitutes a legitimate datum for the study of the loss of agreement. On the other hand, some other aspects of reconstructions are often not (yet) well understood and may be controversial, and changes based on these are unlikely to be reliable data for comparison. Some scholars have criticized analyses that rely on reconstructions,[11] but carefully selected, such data significantly extend the range of examples and supplement attested instances. We have used well-known cases based on comparative reconstructions, where the changes and their directions are well understood, such as the development of Indo-European infinitives out of deverbal nouns in one or another oblique case, and the development of Finnic cases. We have also made use of our own reconstructions, making reference to the full discussion and documentation of these elsewhere, for instance Harris (1985) and Norman and Campbell (1978). (See chapter 12 for more discussion and other examples.)

Creole languages are widely assumed to undergo the same sorts of changes other languages undergo, but to be able to do so more rapidly. We do not disagree with this but consider it an empirical question. First one must discover separately the nature of syntactic change in creoles and that in other languages, and then one must compare these to determine whether they are essentially the same.[12] Nevertheless, judiciously used, data from Creole languages can supplement the database for diachronic syntactic studies.[13]

We have taken into consideration traditional philological and linguistic approaches – such as Delbrück (1893–1900) on Indo-European, K'iziria (1982) on Kartvelian, and Hakulinen (1968), Ikola (1959), and Itkonen (1966) on Finno-Ugric languages – as well as material treated in terms of more contemporary orientations – such as Lightfoot (1991a) and Breckenridge and Hakulinen (1976), to mention just two. In order to broaden the base of our investigation as much as possible, we have supplemented our database with information on a wide variety of languages on which we ourselves have not done original research. Nevertheless, in order to minimize the problems of incomplete appreciation of the context of the entire syntactic system, we have relied most on the language families we know best, Indo-European, Uralic, Uto-Aztecan, Mayan, Kartvelian, and North East Caucasian.

Although some will find flaws with the approach we take, we strive for precise statements of generalizations, but in those chapters where they appear for the time being to be impossible, we do not eschew statements of near-universals and generalizations that are not yet in a testable form. We try to balance the need for precise analyses with the need for breadth of evidence when discussing putative universals.

2   The history of historical syntax: major themes

2.1   Introduction

The long history of the study of syntactic change is characterized not by major breaks in tradition, but by a few persistent themes.[1] Most recent claims are not new, but were anticipated in the past and are the continuation of lines of thought which have endured in the history of linguistics. This view of the history of diachronic syntax contrasts sharply with that held by some scholars today: for example, Lightfoot argues that little insightful work on syntactic change was achieved in the past (197a: 7–41; 1988a: 305–7). We disagree with his interpretation of linguistic history; as will be seen, it is not the case that "the nineteenth-century [and earlier] linguists . . . made no attempt to posit general principles of syntactic change," nor that "certainly there was no tradition of work on syntactic change, and, despite isolated discussions, it was not until the 1970s that syntactic change became an area of communal work among linguists" (Lightfoot 1988a: 305). While Lightfoot has articulated this view clearly, numerous other contemporary practitioners of diachronic syntax imply in their work that they hold a similar view.[2]

In section 2.1 we show just the opposite, that the tradition of work on syntactic change is important to understanding and explaining syntactic change today. We point out that a number of nineteenth-century linguists did "posit general principles of syntactic change," including the Agglutination Theory (section 2.2.1.2), the Growth Principle (section 2.2.1.3), Meillet's statement of grammaticalization (section 2.2.1.4), several general principles of word order, including Wackernagel's Law, Behaghel's Laws, and principles enunciated by Herder, Fulda, and others (sections 2.2.2.2–3), functionalist principles proposed by Scaliger and others (section 2.2.4), and the development of hypotaxis out of parataxis (section 2.2.5). Some of the principles named here, such as the Agglutination Theory and Wackernagel's Law, were originally formulated for Indo-European only, but they assume a universal underlying principle. We argue that there was indeed a "tradition of work on syntactic change," which included the following recurrent themes and lines of analysis: (1) development

14

of grammatical categories, the Growth Principle, and grammaticalization (section 2.2.1), (2) word order (section 2.2.2), (3) a functionalist perspective (section 2.2.4), (4) the development of complex sentences (section 2.2.5), (5) child language acquisition (section 2.2.6.2), and (6) reanalysis (section 2.2.6.3) and borrowing (section 2.2.6.4) as mechanisms of syntactic change. We do not attempt to present an exhaustive history (see Campbell, in press a), but instead emphasize work in the nineteenth and twentieth centuries that continues and elaborates the tradition out of which aspects of our own work (and other later work) grows.

As mentioned in chapter 1, work in diachronic syntax since 1957 has been chiefly of three sorts: (1) studies of particular changes in individual languages (e.g. Traugott 1972; Ebert 1978; the papers in Fisiak 1984); (2) research on certain kinds of change, such as word order or grammaticalizations (e.g. Li 1975; Hawkins 1983; Heine and Reh 1984; Traugott and Heine 1991a); and (3) the exploration of the diachronic implications of a particular theoretical approach to grammar, often given more to championing the formal theory of syntax than to actually accounting for the individual changes or to attempting to discover the real nature of syntactic change (e.g. Lakoff 1968; Greenberg 1978; Lightfoot 1979a, 1991). In section 2.3 we examine some of this work that has been most influential. The chapter as a whole serves to place these kinds of work in their historical context and to appraise both the richness of the explanations and the empirical findings from the past, which must not be neglected in research efforts today.

Our primary purpose in undertaking the research that is reported in this chapter was to examine the history of the study of diachronic syntax for what it can contribute to our general goal of framing an adequate approach to historical syntax. Whatever proved wrong or impractical in the past but is still currently under consideration in theoretical discussions must be abandoned, while true achievements and empirical findings must be accommodated and incorporated. By including the good and eliminating the bad from previous work, we implicitly argue for the accuracy of our framework, since it is developed to capitalize on past successes and to avoid pitfalls identified in former work.

2.2 Foundations of the diachronic study of syntax

2.2.1 Grammaticalization, reanalysis, and their forerunners

Grammaticalization is a topic of extensive current interest, and its roots are to be found in the ideas discussed here. (For definition and more discussion, see section 2.2.1.4.) Reanalysis is another topic that reaches back into antiquity and yet continues to be influential today.

2.2.1.1   The earliest tradition

Grammaticalization and reanalysis are among the many continuing themes of linguistics that began with the Greeks: [3] for example, Aristotle (384–322 BC) reduced the finite verb to a nominal (participle) plus copula, e.g. interpreting *ánthrōpos badízei* ("[the] man walks") as *ánthrōpos badízōn estí* ("man walking is," i.e. "the man is a walker / walking one") (Stankiewicz 1974: 159). This reduction was later interpreted as a historical claim, and from it stemmed the long-standing debate concerning the priority of nouns versus verbs and the discussion of the development of grammatical categories in general (see Stankiewicz 1974).

Arabic grammatical practice, which had its roots in the Greek tradition, continues some of the themes that remain important in the later tradition. Although Arabic grammarians considered Arabic immutable, "the language in which God chose to reveal His word, enshrined in the Holy Qur'ān" (Owens 1988: 22), some earlier grammatical change was recognized (e.g. by Ibn Fâris, died 1004): for example, for the Tamîmî tribe *mâ* is a simple negative (not governing any case), while for the Ḥijâzî it is a sentence negator governing an accusative, as the verb *laysa* "be not" does:

(1)   (a)   Tamîmî
        mâ   zayd-un   darîf-un
        NEG Zayd-NOM kind-NOM
        "Zayd is not kind."

       (b)   Ḥijâzî
        mâ   zayd-un   darîf-a
        NEG Zayd-NOM kind-ACC
        "Zayd is not kind."

Compare (in the dialects of both tribes):

       (c)   laysa zayd-un   darîf-an
        be.not Zayd-NOM kind-ACC
        "Zayd is not kind."   (Owens 1988: 26)

This analysis constitutes a very early example of the discussion of reanalysis (see section 2.2.6.3 and chapter 4); the "reanalysis" of *mâ* in the Ḥijâzî dialect is based on the grammatical properties of *laysa*. As will become evident below, reanalysis as a mechanism of syntactic change was recognized early and repeatedly throughout the history of linguistics.

2.2.1.2   The Agglutination Theory

Inspired by universal grammar (particularly Leibniz's *grammaire ration-elle*) and by the Dutch etymologists, who separated stems and roots (*Grundbegriffe*) from affixes (*accessorische Begriffe*), Franz Bopp (1816, 1833–52, I) assumed the Agglutination Theory, that Indo-European endings were derived from formerly independent elements attached to verb roots. One of Bopp's main goals was to show that a one-to-one correspondence between morphological and semantic elements could be established more widely in the Indo-European parent language by comparative reconstruction (Kiparsky 1974a: 332).

Bopp's approach was followed by many. It is illustrated in his treatment of verb endings, where Bopp's reconstruction of "first person singular" in Indo-European was -*ma*, "second person singular" -*tva*, with reconstruction of the rest of the system based on semantic components. Plurals were derived from combinations of these, with "first person plural" -*ma-tva* and "second person plural" -*tva-tva*; other plurals were formed from the repetition of singular endings, the middle by repeating active endings. Thus for Curtius (1871), extending Bopp's scheme, plural middles were reconstructed for "first person plural" as -*ma-tva-tva* and for "second person plural" as -*tva-tva-tva*; for Schleicher (1861–2 [1871]), these were -*ma-tva-ma-tva* and -*tva-tva-tva-tva*, respectively (Curtius 1870, 1871; Kiparsky 1974a: 334). This sort of treatment was later abandoned with the Neogrammarian criticism of Glottogonic Theory (see below).

2.2.1.3   The Growth Principle and its rejection

A number of basic claims revolve around the notion of growth of grammatical categories (often connected with development of cognitive processes). Since early times, a very frequent explanation of syntactic change has involved the belief that grammatical change is characterized by a principle of growth in which change moves from littler to bigger, and from more concrete to more abstract. For example, Sanskrit grammarians had a Root Theory for the development of grammar, deriving all words ultimately from verbal roots. The theory that roots were historically prior to bound morphemes was an important assumption through the nineteenth century.

Just as grammarians and etymologists considered the structurally simple word to be historically prior, philosophers of language in the seventeenth century assumed a historical order of ideas or meanings, that simple ideas were prior to complex ones, and ideas of things were prior to ideas of relations, i.e. nouns preceded verbs historically.

The littler-to-bigger view is seen, for example, in Vico's (1948 [1744/1725]) theory that gesture > interjection > monosyllabic root > bigger words/constructions, where similar views were repeated for the next 150 years or so. Adam Smith's (1761) language typology had similar attributes; his "flexional" (uncompounded) languages were connected with more concrete ideas; his languages exhibiting "composition" showed more abstraction.[4] The growth view is reflected in the evolutionary views of the development of Indo-European grammar espoused by Bopp, Humboldt (1836 [1988]), Schleicher, and many others.

This "glottogonic" or growth view was forcefully denied by the Neogrammarians (see above); it is instructive to see why. August Schleicher's (1861-2) *Compendium der vergleichenden Grammatik der indogermanischen Sprachen* is T H E acknowledged synthesis of nineteenth-century historical and comparative linguistics for its time (Koerner 1983: xvi; cf. Schleicher 1848, 1983 [1863], 1983 [1865]). Schleicher expounded the view that languages evolve from isolation to agglutination (with affixes derived from lexical roots) and go on to flexion, with gradual progress in the direction from simple to complex forms. However, for Schleicher, "growth" (through agglutination) took place only in the prehistoric phase, when languages were still young and capable of word-building (the period of *Sprachbildung*), whereas only changes of "decay" (by sound change and analogy) took place in the later historical period, after the growth process had entirely ceased (in the period of *Sprachgeschichte*) (Müller 1865: 331; Schleicher 1869: 31; 1983 [1865]: 82; Christy 1983: 35; Maher 1983: xxvi–xxviii; Bynon 1986: 131, 142).

The Neogrammarians rejected Schleicher's (and others') "growth process" as a primary example of "glottogonic speculation" – the principal distinction between the Neogrammarians and their predecessors. Brugmann rejected this separation of stages (Osthoff and Brugmann 1878). For him, the same types of language change apply to all phases of linguistic history (cf. Paul 1920[1898]: 174; Weinrich, Labov and Herzog 1968; Christy 1980, 1983: 74–5; Hock 1986: 629); analogy was needed at all stages (A. Davies 1986: 154). This reflects the impact on linguistics of Sir Charles Lyell's (1830 [–1833]) uniformitarianism ("that all past events – yes, every single one – could be explained by the action of causes now in operation. No old causes are extinct; no new ones have been introduced" [Gould 1987: 105]).

Here it is instructive to contrast Brugmann's Neogrammarian (uniformitarian) treatment of verbal endings with that of Bopp, Schleicher, and Curtius (see above), who viewed personal endings as having developed from pronouns (or other roots) which became attached to the verb. That is, at stake here are fundamentally different views of language typology and of the nature of grammatical change, views which influenced the course of modern linguistic thinking. Schleicher (1861–2 [1871]) had reconstructed *ma* for the "first person singular active pronoun" in Proto-Indo-European; he postulated that it was (1) weakened to *mi* (e.g. Sanskrit *ásmi*, Greek *eimi* "I am"; Sanskrit *bhárāmi* "I carry"); (2) was lost in Greek *phérō* "I carry"; (3) lost its *m* in the Greek perfect *léloipa* "I have left" (assumed to be from *léloipma*); (4) lost the *a* of Greek *épheron* "I was carrying" (with -*m* > -*n*); and (5) lost both the *a* and the *m* in the Greek "aorist" *étupsa* "I beat" (assumed to be from *étupsama*). However, none of the "sound changes" necessary to derive these (save -*m* > -*n*) is found in other Greek forms. Brugman[n] (1878), in contrast, reconstructed four different first-person endings: -*mi* and -*ō* for "present" (in different verb classes); -*m* (-*m* > Greek -*n*) and *m̥* (postconsonantal, which became Greek -*a*) for "past"; and -*a* for "perfect." (Sanskrit *bhárāmi* [< *bherō*] he held to be due to contamination of the -*ō* and -*mi* class verbs.) Brugmann's motivation for this reconstruction was the principle of exceptionless sound changes; in this way the attested forms are accounted for without postulating otherwise unattested sound changes. The result is that some of the reconstructed pronominal endings show no clear similarity to the independent pronouns; therefore, according to Brugmann, it is not warranted to assume that personal endings were necessarily independent pronouns in origin (A. Davies 1986: 157). The processes of change (sound change, analogy) were the same from the proto-language onward, and there was no need to assume independent lexical roots lying behind grammatical endings. This struck at the heart of pre- or non-Neogrammarian notions of typology, origin and evolution of grammatical categories and morphology, and of the very nature of language in general. The glottogonic view of language development was dismissed (Delbrück 1901: 47; 1893 [1880]: 66, 77).

2.2.1.4   *Grammaticalization*

Meillet (1912: 132) introduced the term "grammaticalization" with the sense of "the attribution of a grammatical character to a formerly independent word" (though, as we have shown here, the notion is much older than its name in the history of linguistics):

> L'affaiblissement du sens et l'affaiblissement de la forme des mots accessoires vont de pair; quand l'un et l'autre sont assez avancés, le mot accessoire peut finir par ne plus être qu'un élément privé de sens propre, joint à un mot principal pour en marquer le rôle grammatical. Le changement d'un mot en élément grammatical est accompli.   (Meillet 1912: 139)

> The weakening of the sense and the weakening of the form of auxiliary words go hand in hand; when both are rather advanced, the auxiliary word can end up being nothing more than an element deprived of its own

> meaning, attached to a main word to mark its grammatical role. The change
> from a word to a grammatical marker is complete.
>
> [Our translation, ACH/LC]

By this he meant an original independent word with independent meaning (*mot autonome*) develops into an auxiliary word (*mot accessoire*) and ends up as a grammatical marker (*élément grammatical*). This process is characterized by a concurrent weakening of both the meaning and the form of the word in question (Meillet 1912: 139, 148). Kuryłowicz's (1965: 52) much-cited definition is: "Grammaticalization consists in the increase of the range of a morpheme advancing from a lexical to a grammatical or from a less grammatical to a more grammatical status, e.g. from a derivative formant to an inflectional one." (See also Hoenigswald 1963: 34; Heine and Reh 1984: 15; C. Lehmann 1984: 36, 1986: 3.) Grammaticalization phenomena have been discussed in regard to such partially overlapping concepts as "semantic bleaching/weakening," "reanalysis," "syntacticization," "univerbation," "condensation," and "reduction" (see Kuryłowicz 1964, 1965; Benveniste 1968; Traugott 1982; Langacker 1977a: 103; Givón 1984; Heine and Reh 1984; DeLancey 1985; C. Lehman 1986; Heine, Claudi, and Hünnemeyer 1991; Traugott and Heine 1991). As in the earlier "growth" literature (above), some refer explicitly to the output of grammaticalization as being "more abstract" than its input (e.g. Traugott 1980: 46, 1990; C. Lehmann 1982: 128).

Many of the views held earlier concerning the development of grammatical categories represent, in effect, early versions of "grammaticalization."[5] For a very clear example, grammaticalization is illustrated by the very common nineteenth-century belief that "the personal inflections of the verb [in Indo-European] are simply personal pronouns that have lost their independence" (Sweet 1900: 53, 113). Much of the literature on "growth" and the "origin of language" was presented in ways akin to current treatments of grammaticalization, though some of the "growth" literature appears to have tolerated a higher degree of speculation. There were indeed excessive, sometimes even ridiculous, proposals in the past. For example, all of the following claims for changes were made with a certain frequency: individual imitative sounds > roots > isolating verbs or nouns > compounding > agglutination > inflection.[6]

Examples of grammaticalization are important in the broad database of grammatical changes, and instances occur in most of the subsequent chapters of this book. As will be seen in those chapters, however, we find that grammaticalization cases can be explained adequately by the other mechanisms of syntactic change (see chapters 3 and 4), and we therefore attribute to grammaticalization no special status in our approach.

2.2.2 Word order

Some of the more important claims throughout the history of linguistics with respect to syntactic change have involved attempts to deal with word order. These were often related to typology and notions of the growth of grammar and origins of parts of speech (grammatical categories).

The Growth Principle is embodied in the often-repeated principle of word order that shorter constituents come before longer constituents. This notion was present in the Greek and Roman traditions as an implicit principle of ordering in both rhetoric and grammar which placed the increasingly longer elements more towards the end of the sentence (Scaglione 1972: 30), akin to Behaghel's Law of Growing Members (see below).

It was stated clearly by Richard Sherry (1550) as a rule of preferred sentence composition, who warned against "puttynge a weaker word after a stronger [one], but that it styl go upward and increase" (Scaglione 1972: 155). Related are Jespersen's (1894: 57) Principle of Relative Weight: "Lighter elements can be placed near the center, while heavier ones are relegated to more peripheral places," and, in particular, Behaghel's Law of Growing Members (see below). This all sounds surprisingly similar to Hawkins' (1983) formulations of his Heaviness Serialization Principle, which is intended to explain both historical and universal aspects of word order, and it is reflected in work on "grammaticalization," as well.

In the Arabic tradition, Ibn Khaldûn (1332–1406) observed the change wherein fixed word order was substituted for case inflection in order to distinguish "agent" from "object"; he pointed out that Classical Arabic's VSO order (where S and O bore case suffixes) had changed to SVO order in the dialects, which lost case endings (Owens 1988: 270). He (as others before) attributed this change to foreign contact (Ibrahim 1987: 103).

In Europe, attention to word order change came from the comparison of the ancient languages, particularly Latin, with modern descendants, as in the school practice of rearranging the "inverted" word order of classical texts into "natural (logical) order," e.g. as required in French translations. Aarsleff (1988: liii) speaks of "the centrality of the problem of inversion in the linguistic thought of the eighteenth century." Some seventeenth- and eighteenth-century French grammarians distinguished the ancient type (with free word order) from the modern type (with word orders they took as representing the true natural sequence of thoughts), e.g. Le Laboureur (1669). Gerauld de Cordemoy (1668), invoking child language acquisition, claimed natural word order follows the order in which children learn, first things (subjects), then qualities, and then actions, and finally the objects of such actions (Scaglione 1972: 227). Bernard Lamy (1675) noted that in French fixed word order functions to replace lost inflectional endings (Scaglione 1981: 41), a functionalist view echoed by, for example, Martin Harris (1978). Condillac (1746 [1971]: 238) hypothesized that nouns appeared before verbs because in gesture language humans first pointed at the objects of their desire, then named these objects, and later gave names to the desires. Thus, the natural order was to place the grammatical object first, then the verb (Scaglione 1981: 41).

The issue of inversion separated the rationalist universal grammarians from followers of Locke (Aarsleff 1988: liii). For Locke, language was essentially a human invention (Plato's convention), thus with no god-given or natural order to be expected. The rationalists, with their correspondence between words and thoughts, held that word order would parallel the order of thought (said to be natural, as in logic). Thus, Antoine de Rivarol (1784) argued for the superiority of French due to its direct or "logical" word order (SVO), as opposed to Latin's "inverted" order (SOV). Herder (1772) supposed that language may have had such word order in its primitive stage, but that it developed orders more suited to newly evolved social and political organizations, to become more poetic and sensual, thus creating new "inversions" (deviations from fixed or "logical" order). Humboldt repeated with enthusiasm Joseph-Dominique Garat's sentence, in seeming echoes of Herder, that "languages with inversions favor clarity because they offer more means of expression" (Aarsleff 1988: xliv, cf. liii). Herder also had a "functionalist" perspective, asserting that the adoption of fixed word order avoids structural ambiguity, ambiguity being related to the limitations of inflection. French, for example, had to offset this deficiency with fixed word order so that subject could be distinguished from object (Scaglione 1981: 53, 74; cf. Sweet 1900: 42).

Adam Smith (1761), as mentioned above, explained the development of fixed word order in general as the result of a reduction in the case system, which in turn was due to language mixture. Friedrich Carl Fulda (1777–8) introduced a principle of ordering which became very influential, particularly among Indo-Europeanists (see below): the *Bestimmende* (determining/qualifying/ modifier) precedes the *Bestimmte* (determined/qualified/modified), for example adjective before noun, and adverb before adjective (Scaglione 1981: 81). Fulda's generalization became for Adelung (1781, 1782b) the *Grundgesetz* (basic law) that the less determined always precedes the more determined. He asserted that this law was universal, "that it can be taken as original in all languages," and that it is only in language's later development that exceptions are found (Scaglione 1981: 82, 85).

The interpretation of word order changes became more formal, and hence for us more interesting, with Berthold Delbrück's work. Delbrück

(1878), the foremost Neogrammarian authority on syntactic change, postulated that "originally the verb must have come at the end of all types of IE clauses [SOV], therefore also of dependent clauses," and he suggested that the shift to second place in main clauses had to do with stress, similar to Wackernagel's (1892) famous solution, discussed below (see subsequent Indo-Europeanist reconstructions: Brugmann 1904 [OV]; Winfred Lehmann 1974, 1980 [OV]; Vennemann 1974a; Friedrich 1975 [OV]; Watkins 1976 [SOV]; etc.).

Otto Behaghel (1878) argued that SOV was original for Germanic; his evidence included compounding. He observed (Behaghel 1878: 283):

> Ein Compositum wie *du übertreibst* ist also nur denkbar, wenn es eine Zeit gab, in welcher das Adverb seinem Verbum nicht wie heute nachfolgte, sondern vorausging. Diese durch unsere Composita verlangte Worstellung ist aber genau diejenige, die uns noch heute im Nebensatz vorliegt, und wir erhalten somit den wichtigen Satz: DIE URSPRUNGLICHE DEUTSCHE WORTSTELLUNG IST NICHT DIE DES HEUTIGEN HAUPTSATZES, SONDERN DIE DES HEUTIGEN NEBENSATZES.

> A compound like *du übertreibst* ["you exaggerate"; *über* "over," *treiben* "push/drive"] is only thinkable if there was once a time when the adverb did not follow its verb as it does today, but rather preceded it. This word order, which is required by our compounds, is exactly the one we find today in subordinate clauses, and we maintain thereby the important statement: the original German word order is not that of today's main clauses [i.e. SVO], rather that of today's subordinate clauses [i.e. SOV].   [Our translation, ACH/LC]

That is, originally there was Noun + Adverb + Verb (e.g. German *er, der die Nacht durch schlief* (he who the night through slept) "he who slept through the night," which changed to *durchschlief* (slept-through) (Scaglione 1981: 121). A similar claim was made by de Saussure (1949: 247) concerning the shift from adverb through "preposition" to preverb, and more recently, Craig and Hale (1988), based on cross-linguistic findings, have proposed that positional preverbs develop from postpositionals which become cliticized to the following verb, as in Behaghel's example ([*die Nacht durch*] [*schlief*] > [*die Nacht*] [*durch-schlief*]). Behaghel (1892), however, later attempted to explain the verb-final order of German subordinate clauses by appealing to the impact of humanistic Latin from the Renaissance, which he said caused the verb to shift to the right only in subordinate clauses, arguing for Proto-Germanic SVO order.[7]

Wackernagel (1926–8: 5), in accord with many others since Fulda (1777–8), maintained that one of the most important laws of word order in the Indo-European languages is that the "determining [modifier]"

(*Determinierende*) precedes the "determined [head]" (*Determinierte*).
Moreover, Wackernagel's Law, that clitics tend to appear in sentence second
position, is one of the firmest discoveries in the history of syntactic change
(see Sweet 1900: 43).

The history of more recent treatments of word order is not dealt with here,
but rather in the chapter on word order change (chapter 8).

2.2.3   Behaghel's Laws

Behaghel's influential "laws" involve both the notion of "growth" and the issue
of word order. Among Behaghel's (1923–32, IV) several general claims were
his five "laws." (1) Where units of equal status are conjoined (or contrasted) the
longest comes last in the sequence. This is known as "Behaghel's Law"
(Behaghel 1909: 139) (*das Gesetz der wachsenden Glieder* [the Law of Growing
Members]). (2) Differing degrees of sentence stress explain different patterns
of element order. (3) What belongs together (in a mentalistic sense) is placed
together. (4) Of two linked elements, the more important comes second. Or,
more fully, an element which picks up preceding information stands before
one which does not: so the "given" precedes the "new" (a principle of discourse
analysis "rediscovered" in recent years, e.g. Chafe 1976; Givón 1984: 263).
Article-before-NP illustrates this law. (5) A differentiating element precedes
the element which it differentiates. This last law, so often repeated since Fulda
(1777–8), is exemplified by the sequences Adjective–Noun, Genitive–Noun,
Adverb–Adjective (see Collinge 1985: 241, see also below).

2.2.4   Functionalist perspectives

While functionalist explanations of grammatical change are very popular
today, often linked with notions of grammaticalization and typology through
discourse analysis (e.g. M. Harris 1978, 1981; Givón 1984; Heine and Reh 1984;
Hopper and Thompson 1984; Claudi and Heine 1986; Heine and Claudi 1986;
Hopper 1987; Comrie 1988; Craig and Hale 1988; Heine, Claudi, and
Hünnemeyer 1991; and the papers of Traugott and Heine 1991), they are by no
means new: for example, Ibn Khaldûn (1332–1406) observed that Arabic word
order was substituted for lost case endings in order to distinguish "agent" from
"object" (Owens 1988: 270). Similarly, William of Conches (*c.* 1080–1154)
claimed that everything in structure was put there to serve communicative
functions, which resulted when prehistoric people assigned words to signify
particular meanings and devised linguistic structure. Modistic practice in
general had a functionalist tinge to its logical/semantic orientation.

J. C. Scaliger (1540), in a functionalist version of the Growth Principle,
believed that cases emerge because of ambiguity, to make clear the role of

nouns in a sentence, since, he believed, nouns originally lacked inflection (Breva-Claramonte 1983: 62). Lamy (1675) observed that French fixed word order has the function of replacing lost inflectional endings (Scaglione 1981: 41). Herder (1772) also held the view that the adoption of fixed word order avoids structural ambiguity, ambiguity being related to the limitations of inflection. Herder, too, cited French fixed word order as an example, also believing that it functioned to distinguish subject from object (Scaglione 1981: 74). Meillet (1916 [1970]: 100) presented a view held by many: "The progressive reduction of inflection . . . in Germanic . . . has brought about the use of word order as a means of grammatical expression, as well as the use of auxiliary words." (Other functionalist notions abounded; some were mentioned above in the discussions of word order, typology, and the Growth Principle.)

It will be important to keep functionalist perspectives in mind in the framing of an explicit account of syntactic change.

2.2.5   The development of complex sentences

Related to the origin of grammatical categories and word order change (discussed above) is the persistent theme of the development of complex sentences, particularly of relative clauses. A belief repeated with great frequency has been that hypotaxis (subordination) developed from parataxis (juxtaposition, coordination). The issue of whether Indo-European had *Nebensätze* (subordinate clauses, i.e. hypotaxis) or only main clauses (parataxis) was addressed by most who dealt with Indo-European grammar and is still an important topic (e.g. W. Lehmann 1974, 1980; Watkins 1976; Bednarczuk 1980; C. Lehmann 1984: 365; Hock 1986: 341).

An early example not untypical of many subsequent treatments is Friedrich von Schlegel's (1808) belief that hypotaxis evolved from parataxis, that "primitive" languages just juxtaposed independent clauses from which subordinate clauses gradually evolved. Heinrich Bauer (1833), who helped to propagate Fulda's and Adelung's *Bestimmende*-before-*Bestimmte* Principle of word order, was among the earliest to put forward the parataxis-to-hypotaxis thesis. He believed that "primitive" languages merely juxtaposed independent clauses which were logically, but not formally, linked; he saw the development of conjunctions as an evolutionary advancement in language (Scaglione 1981: 7, 105). Ernst Windisch (1869: 205) concluded for Indo-European that "the simple sentence was developed already before the languages split up, but not complex sentences (*die Satzgefüge*)." Delbrück was also in favor of the notion that hypotaxis developed from parataxis and that "there was once a time in which only principal clauses existed" but that by Proto-Indo-European times things had developed further so that sentences "probably contained relative and adverbial clauses" (Delbrück 1893–1900 [1900]: 412–13; Jolly 1873; W. Lehmann 1980: 114). Brugmann (1925: 8) held that the sequence of two or more sentences which stood in a closer relationship to each other was nearly as old as the simple sentence, developing coordinate and subordinate relations; conjunctions developed in time. He considered many sorts of shifts in syntactic structure to be the result of the boundary between main and subordinate clause being broken (compare Langacker's [1977a] boundary shifts). For example, for Brugmann, the shift of a main-clause pronoun to the following logically dependent clause had its origin in Proto-Indo-European times; e.g. "I saw that; he slept" changed to "I saw that he slept" (*ich sah, daß er schlief,* based on/derived from *ich sah das, er schlief*) (see Paul 1920 [1898]: 299). In this example, then, it is reanalysis (see chapter 4) that is taken to be the mechanism whereby subordinate clauses develop, i.e. by which paratactic constructions become hypotactic.

A major issue in the development of complex sentences dealt with the origin of relative clauses and their status in Proto-Indo-European – many doubted that they existed in Proto-Indo-European (see Windisch 1869; Jolly 1873; Tomanetz 1879; Hermann 1895; Brugmann 1925; cf. Scaglione 1981; Christian Lehmann 1984: 365ff.; etc.). On the other hand, after investigating possible subordinate structures, Meillet (1922: 377) concluded that "the relatives are the only subordinates for which we have factual reasons to believe they were Indo-European." Hirt (1934–7) also maintained that Proto-Indo-European already had relative clauses, the oldest dependent clause.

Frequently, Indo-European scholars linked speculation on the origins of agreement (concord) with their claims concerning the development of complex sentences. For example, Brugmann's (1925: 7) definition is typical: "Words which stand in a particular syntactic relation to each other, for which no other means of expression such as word order or intonation exists, are used where possible in formal agreement with each other." He believed agreement developed as a result of the generalization of certain suffixal elements with more special relationships to the noun, pronoun, and verb; agreement in case originated through apposition (cf. Brugmann 1925: 148). As Sweet (1900: 59–60) put it:

> In primitive language permanent attribute-words [later adjectives] were naturally put in juxtaposition with the substance-words [later nouns] they qualified.
> Many languages then found it natural and convenient to bring out more clearly the connection between head-word and adjunct-word by repeating the

form-words or inflections of the former before or after the latter as well, the result being grammatical concord. Thus in *I bought these books at Mr. Smith's, the bookseller's*, the repetition of the genitive ending serves to show more clearly that *bookseller* is an adjunct to – stands in apposition to – *Mr. Smith's.*

In chapter 10 we examine the origins of complex sentences, taking into account all these claims. As will be seen there, traditional approaches were not very sophisticated in dealing with changes that can result in subordination and complex sentences, though many of the examples discussed are useful.

It is interesting that syntactic change has been claimed to affect main clauses before subordinate clauses (if at all) (Biener 1922a, 1922b), and that this view is still maintained by many. Thus, some scholars think that subordinate clauses are less subject to syntactic change than are main clauses because they exhibit a more restricted range of morphosyntactic trappings due to their backgrounding function in discourse (Givón 1971, 1984; Hopper and Thompson 1984). The general idea involved is the belief that change starts in main clauses and may or may not ultimately come to affect subordinate clauses, but that it does not begin in subordinate clauses, later reaching main clauses. In any absolute version, this claim is clearly falsified by numerous examples, such as the Estonian change from participle to a finite verb form meaning "indirect (reported speech)," which began first in lower clauses and later spread to main clauses (see section 5.2.1 and Campbell 1991 for details).[8]

2.2.6   Modes of explanation and paths of change

Among the modes of explanation that have been proposed for syntactic change throughout history we find many different claims and approaches. In this section, several of these are surveyed.

2.2.6.1   General claims

While many general claims concerning grammatical change are found in the pre-Neogrammarian literature (see Campbell, in press a), we begin discussion with the Neogrammarians because their general claims were part of their well-articulated and integrated theory.

Delbrück (1888, 1893, 1893–1900 [1900], 1901) was the acknowledged Neogrammarian leader in syntactic change; his thinking dictated the direction of most subsequent work on historical syntax, though he confessed his major inspiration to be Paul (1920 [1880]). Thus, following Paul, he maintained that "all explanation of linguistic phenomena must proceed from research on the competence (*Sprachthätigkeit*) of individual persons" (Delbrück 1893: 70). That is, much like modern generativists, he was a mentalist, seeking largely psychological explanations involving the individual's linguistic knowledge (see below).

One important claim made by Paul (1920 [1898]: 251) concerning change was that "there is in language no precaution at all against defects [*Übelstände*] entering, rather only reaction against what is already present." This has been reasserted in recent research on grammatical change (by scholars who perhaps were unaware that Paul had already framed the position they espouse); Lightfoot's (1979a: 123) slogan, "languages practice therapy, not prophylaxis," taken apparently from Kiparsky (1974b: 328; 1982: 190; see also Langacker 1977a: 96; Samuels 1987; see below) is essentially the same claim.

Wackernagel (1926–8, I: 5) dealt with three kinds of "relationships" in historical syntax. His first was aspects of language which are part of human nature and widely found in languages (i.e. universals and typology). He cited as an example "one of the most important laws of word order in the Indo-European languages," that the "determining [modifier]" (*Determinierende*) precedes the "determined [head]" (*Determinierte*) (see above). His second was inherited relationship. For example, in Greek when two gods are called, the first is in the vocative, while the second is in the nominative case with *the* after it. This was one of the oldest Indo-European relics, since the same arrangement is found in the Rigveda, where the second god is followed by the cognate form *ča*. German's verb-last word order in subordinate clauses is another example, which Wackernagel compared to the "law" of Latin word order and with "the same rule" in Old Indic prose. Thus, in spite of often expressed doubts about the reconstructibility of syntax (see discussion in chapter 12), Wackernagel successfully demonstrated with these examples that certain aspects of syntax can be reconstructed (see chapter 8). Wackernagel's third relationship was that of similarity having to do with borrowing (see chapter 6).

Wackernagel's (1892) Law is "one of the few generally accepted syntactic statements about IE . . . that enclitics originally occupied the second position in the sentence" (Watkins 1964: 1036). Wackernagel argued that in Old Indic the verb was originally in final position (SOV) and unstressed in independent clauses (though stressed in subordinate ones), leading the short, unstressed verb forms to be treated as enclitics and thus to be moved to second position, attaching themselves to the first word of the sentence. This law has had a significant impact not only on Indo-European studies and historical syntax in general, but in recent typological studies as well, though not always remembered under Wackernagel's name (Wackernagel 1926–8, I: 46; Collinge 1985: 217; cf. Steele 1975, 1977).

2.2.6.2 Language acquisition and grammatical change

Language acquisition plays a central role in most recent and current approaches to syntactic change, and discussion of the role of language acquisition in grammatical change has a long history. Cordemoy (1668), for example, proposed explanations for word order based on the order in which little children learn language, first things (subjects), then their qualities, followed by actions, and finally objects of the actions (Scaglione 1972: 227). Child language acquisition and the origin of language were also linked. Vico (1948 [1744/1725]: 137) called upon empirical observations of children's language to explain several of his claims about change, including "Last of all the authors of the languages formed the verbs, as we observe children expressing nouns and particles but leaving the verbs to be understood." A.H. Sayce (1880: 107–8) related several prevalent nineteenth century themes to each other and to child language acquisition, for instance that language originated as onomatopoeic imitations resulting in simple roots, that society progresses through unilinear evolutionary stages (savagery to barbarism to civilization), that language evolution is also unilinear and progressive (from isolating [radical/root] to agglutinative to inflectional), and that this language evolution is correlated to the social evolution of the language's speakers (hence the "primitive" languages of "savages" retain vestiges of earlier stages of human language in general), all mirrored in child language acquisition: "What still goes on in the nursery was a general procedure in the childhood of mankind . . . if we are to infer anything from the habits of the nursery, and of those savage tribes which best represent the infancy of mankind, onomatopoeia must have played a large part in the formation of language."

Child language acquisition directly or indirectly played an important role in the Neogrammarian mentalistic outlook on language change (see Fick 1881: xxviii and Wackernagel 1926–8, I: 47). Hermann Paul (1920 [1898]: 115), probably the foremost Neogrammarian authority, saw analogical creation and divergence in use in children's language as a main cause of change. In our terms (see chapter 3), Paul utilized the notions of both extension and reanalysis. His view is a clear forerunner of modern approaches (see below). Meillet also called upon principles of child language acquisition to explain grammatical change. He explained semantic simplification (part of "grammaticalization") as the result of language acquisition. To take a specific example, he cited the observation that the German *Imperfekt* ("simple past"), as in (a) *der Hund bellte* [the dog barked] "The dog barked" (the simple past), appears late in the speech of children, and is rarely used, while periphrastic forms (e.g. the "compound past"), such as in (b) *Der Hund hat gebellt* [the dog has barked] "The dog barked," are more common in children's speech (Meillet 1909 [1951]: 152). Meillet (1909 [1951]: 155) believed that the periphrastic forms, such as (b), are morphologically more conspicuous and therefore are easier to handle ("plus commode à manier") than the more irregular non-periphrastic forms, such as (a).[9]

Since the advent of generative grammar, child language acquisition has had a central role in the theory of syntactic change; this is taken up in some detail below.

2.2.6.3   Reanalysis

Reanalysis, usually related to aspects of child language acquisition, has been perhaps the single most important factor in modern treatments of syntactic change (e.g. Ebert 1976, 1978; Parker 1976; Haiman 1977; Langacker 1977a; Muysken 1977; Lightfoot 1979a; Allen 1980 [1977]; Timberlake 1977; Romaine 1981; etc.; see chapter 4), and in our framework it is one of but three basic mechanisms of syntactic change. To this point in the discussion we have encountered a number of examples of reanalysis in the history of linguistics. In one general view, languages may undergo reanalysis when some surface construction permits two or more different interpretations, and the grammar changes to include interpretations that were not formerly found. That is, faced with a construction which is ambiguous on the surface, a language may opt for more than just its original function or meaning. In this view, the circumstances – multiple interpretations available for some construction – need to obtain, but the language is not necessarily obliged to change. A different, but related, view is that languages undergo reanalysis precisely to avoid developing opacity, surface ambiguity, or perceptual complexity, often to favor ease of processing, to rectify learning difficulties.[10] (See Lightfoot 1979a as the best-known representative of this later view.)

In linguistics, change has also often been seen as a function of competing tendencies, for instance towards "signal simplicity" vs. "perceptual optimality" (Langacker 1977a), or of the application of the "system" to alter the "norms," and of "abduction" (Andersen 1974; Haiman 1977; Timberlake 1977; Coseriu 1978 [1957], 1985; M. Harris 1978). A significant difference is that for Neogrammarians and their followers innovations originate in "performance" (Paul's *Sprachusus*, de Saussure's *parole*), while in modern approaches innovations arise in "competence" (individual psychology/cognition). Reanalysis (restructuring) takes place in the language acquisition process, to produce more efficiently the same output as adult grammars which may no longer be optimal due to changes added during the speaker's adult life. While its connection to formal theory may be new (as asserted by Lightfoot 1979a), the concept of reanalysis has significant historical antecedents.

An early example of reanalysis is Bopp's (1816) treatment of the infinitive, which has been taken as the beginning of historical syntax by some (see Delbrück 1893: 45). Bopp showed that the infinitive was originally a nominal form, but abstract, and thus in time was reinterpreted as part of the verb system (see Disterheft 1980).[11] Today, this may be understood as an early demonstration of syntactic reanalysis.

Paul's (1920 [1898]: 115) treatment of reanalysis sounds surprisingly current. He presented examples of "divergent reanalyses" (*abweichende Neuerzeugung*) as a principal mechanism of change, for him a part of analogy, found in children's acquisition and use of language. A good example is found in the "pronouns" or "particles" which belong to the main clause, but were reinterpreted and merged with a subordinate-clause-introducing particle, e.g. German *daß* (like English *that*): *ich sehe, daß er zufrieden ist* ("I see that he is satisfied") from original *ich sehe das: er ist zufrieden* ("I see that; he is satisfied") (Paul 1920 [1898]: 299; cf. Brugmann 1925: 8; our chapter 10).[12]

Brugmann's (1925: 7) three paths of grammatical change also include reanalysis. These were: (1) Shift in syntactic structure (*Gliederung*): "Parts of groups are combined with parts of other groups to form a new group, and through this . . . new construction types develop." (2) Two constructions used simultaneously become mixed so that a third results which contains components of both. (This, called "contamination," was an often proposed explanation of change, see Paul 1920 [1898]: 160; section 5.5). (3) "Words which stand in a particular syntactic relation to each other, for which no other means of expression such as word order or intonation exists, are used where possible in formal agreement with each other" (*Kongruenz*)(see p. 26 above).

All three involve reanalysis, and Brugmann's (1925: 148) explanation of "agreement" offers a particularly clear example thereof. He thought that agreement in case originated through apposition, where repeated constituents came to be presented only once, e.g. Old Indic *bhrátara, várunam á: vavrtsva* "to brother Varuna turn," originally "to brother, to Varuna turn." The outcome was a reanalysis with an attributive adjective ("brother") agreeing in case (the dative in this example) with a head noun (Varuna).

For a more tractable and extremely telling example, Wackernagel (1926–8, I: 47) stressed "a not unimportant point" which today would be called reanalysis:

> Gelegentlich wird etwas nur darum festgehalten, weil es in einem spätern Sprachzustand umgedeutet werden kann . . . Das Englische möge hier ein Beispiel liefern. Der heutige Engländer sagt z.B. *the King was offered a seat*: "Dem König wurde ein Sitz angeboten." Hier ist auffällig, dass bei

Umsetzung des Verbums *to offer* ins Passiv nicht der angebotene Gegenstand im Subjekt genannt wird, sondern der Empfänger. Dies widerspricht durchaus der herkömmlichen Bedeutung des Verbums *to offer*; trotzdem ist *the King* für das englische Sprachgefühl Subjekt. Nun hat die geschichtliche Forschung erwiesen, dass man im ältern Englischen in solchen Sätzen nicht *king*, sondern *kinge* sagte, und das war eine Dativform, und der Satz bedeutete einfach: "dem Könige wurde angeboten ein Sitz." Aber nachdem durch phonetischen Schwund der Endung Dative und Nominativ zusammengefallen waren, war *king* . . . nur als Subjektsnominativ zu Verstehen.

Occasionally something is maintained only because a new interpretation can be given to it in a later language state . . . English may provide an example. The present-day Englishman says for example, "the King was offered a seat". . . It is striking that with the conversion of "to offer" in the passive, the object does not get named subject, rather the recipient. This thoroughly contradicts the original meaning of the verb "to offer"; nevertheless, "the king" is the subject in English *Sprachgefühl*. Historical research has shown that in older English in such sentences one said not *king* but *kinge*, and that was a dative form, and the sentence meant simply: "(to) the King was offered a seat." However, after the dative and nominative had fallen together due to phonetic loss, *king* was . . . to be understood only as the nominative subject.

[Our translation, ACH/LC]

Wackernagel (1926–8, I: 48) asks, "what are the actual factors in the restructuring of syntactic use [*Neuschöpfung syntaktischen Gebrauchs*]?," answering that both logical and psychological factors are involved.

It is remarkable how very similar Lightfoot's (1979a) influential view of syntactic change turns out to be to Wackernagel's, even to the extent that Wackernagel's example, cited here, is one of Lightfoot's principal cases (see Lightfoot 1979a: 229–39; 1981a: 225). Thus, Lightfoot is mistaken when he asserts that work neither of the distant nor of the recent past has provided much insight on syntactic change. From the above we see that it is simply not so that "the nineteenth-century linguists . . . made no attempt to posit general principles of syntactic change" (Lightfoot 1988a: 305).

2.2.6.4   *Language contact and syntactic borrowing*
Language contact, together with social, political, and economic factors, has been a popular means of explaining grammatical change throughout history. These "external" explanations existed long before they were given new credibility through modern areal linguistics and sociolinguistics. In particular, language contact and syntactic borrowing have been important in the history of linguistics and are fundamental to an encompassing account of

syntactic change (see chapter 6).

In the Arabic tradition, Ibn Ḥazm of Cordova's (died 1064) explanations for linguistic change were divine inspiration, human convention, and natural instinct, including geographic and climatic factors, with the suggestion that language diversity was due to social and political conditions more than anything else (Breva-Claramonte 1983: 90). Bibliander (1504–64) (1548) listed the causes of linguistic change as: the mixture of peoples and languages, political and social change, neglect and education (Arens 1969: 71). Humboldt's (1836) opinion was very similar; he lists as causes the lapse of time, migration, mixture, and political and moral conditions such as to alter national identity (Hoenigswald 1974: 350).

To take a more specific example, Adam Smith (1761) explained the development of fixed word order as the result of reduction in the case system which was due to language mixture (section 2.2.2) – when adults are forced to learn a foreign language with complex and irregular inflections, they fail to reproduce some of the forms:

> Their ignorance of the declensions they would naturally supply by the use of prepositions [*ad Roma* or *de Roma* instead of *Romae*; similarly *io sono amato* instead of *amor*]. And thus, upon intermixture of different nations with one another, the conjugations, by means of auxiliary verbs, were made to approach towards the simplicity and uniformity of declensions . . . The place, therefore, of the three principal members of the phrase is in the English, and for the same reason in the French and Italian languages, almost always precisely determined.   (quoted in Diderichsen 1974: 288)

Turgot (1756), in his modern-sounding and very influential article, explained language change as involving language contact and internal variation. Kraus (1787) also distinguished between genetically shared traits and borrowing (*gemischte Sprachen*). Gyarmathi (1799) was perhaps the first to document syntactic borrowings convincingly; for example, he noticed that Estonian, but not Finnish, Lapp, or Hungarian, has possessive adjectives, and attributed them to German influence. August von Schlegel's (1820) typological thinking included also pure vs. mixed languages, with the origin of "analysis" being from foreign influence, although he also allowed for development through internal means, as well. One of Wackernagel's (1926–8, I: 8) three types of syntactic relationships in language was that of foreign influence; he cited several examples of syntactic borrowing from Vendryes (1968 [1921]).[13]

Today, there can no longer be any serious doubt concerning the existence of or the possible extent of syntactic borrowing and change due to language contact (see Thomason and Kaufman 1988; our chapter 6).

To this point in the discussion we have observed how traditional views of typology and language evolution have persisted in the history of linguistics, and we have seen how this history contains valuable insights with respect to the treatment of word order change, the development of complex sentences, and the mechanisms lying behind syntactic change in general. Moreover, with the advent of the Neogrammarians we find a well-articulated general framework of linguistic change, with syntactic change embedded in it. This paradigm had a cognitive orientation (relying on notions akin to child language acquisition and modern competence) and utilized modes of explanation of syntactic change, e.g. reanalysis and borrowing, which we find highly visible in current approaches to syntactic change. These are central also to our own model.

We now turn to more modern approaches.

2.3   Historical syntax since 1957

The study of syntactic change in the latter half of the twentieth century has been dominated by general linguistic theories which entail particular views of language change. In particular, generative grammar has been extremely important, though many studies also acknowledge inspiration from other general orientations to linguistic change, e.g. Coseriu (1978 [1954], 1985), Andersen (1973), Anttila (1972), Givón (1984, 1991), and Traugott and Heine (1991). Most of these approaches share a strong psychological orientation, associating language change with aspects of child language acquisition. Since aspects of this recent history have been discussed repeatedly (Timberlake 1974; Ebert 1976, 1978; Muysken 1977; Lightfoot 1979a; Allen 1980 [1977]; Hawkins 1983; Joseph 1983; Lenerz 1984; Faarlund 1990b; Campbell, in press a), we do not recite it here again in detail, but rather concentrate on particular issues of importance for a general understanding of syntactic change. Since these more recent studies influence current views concerning syntactic change, in this section we not only report them as part of the historiography of linguistics, we also critically evaluate the more important claims in the interest of arriving at an adequate framework for the treatment of diachronic syntax.[14]

2.3.1   The generative paradigm

Most specific work in the latter half of the twentieth century on diachronic syntax stems in some way from the outlook of generative–transformational grammar. Early generative work on syntactic change depended directly on generative grammar's view of linguistic change in general. This view was introduced by Halle (1961, 1962, 1964), elaborated by Kiparsky (1965, 1968, 1971), and later by King (1969) and others. It holds that linguistic change is grammar change; that is, it is what happens in the transition of grammars from one generation to the next. Child language learners presented with the output of the adults' grammar must construct their own grammar, whose internal structure need not necessarily coincide with that of their adult models, though the output produced by both the older and younger generations' grammars will match relatively closely. However, after learning an optimal grammar as children, adults later in life may add changes which are not integrated optimally into their grammars. Later, children hearing the output from such a non-optimal adult grammar will restructure their own internal grammars to be more optimal (simple) to achieve the same output. (See Faarlund's [1990b: 18] description of this basic assumption.)

To take a more-or-less hypothetical example, suppose an earlier generation had learned a grammar with the rule that the pronoun *who* requires an object case marking (*whom*) when it occurs as the object of a verb or a preposition, and then as adults these speakers added a rule that just deleted the object marking. The next generation of speakers would hear only *who* and would simply learn *who* in all contexts, in effect eliminating the two adult rules. That is, the adults' non-optimal grammar would have two rules, R1 to add case marking (*whom*) in relevant environments, and R2 to convert *whom* to *who* (deletion of case marking). The child language learner, hearing only the output *who*, would learn neither R1 nor R2, and thus would construct his or her grammar with simpler internal structure but with the same output as that of the adult models.[15]

Central to the generative view of language change is the notion that linguistic change in general, and therefore also syntactic change, takes place in the language acquisition process and in the transition of grammars from one generation to the next. As seen above, such a view was already held by Paul (1920 [1898]) and the Neogrammarians; it is central to almost all post-1957 approaches. Early generative applications to historical syntax include Klima (1964, 1965, 1969), Traugott (1965, 1969, 1972, 1973), King (1969), and R. Lakoff (1968). While each offered relevant insights in its time, all share an orientation (to a greater or lesser degree) of championing a particular version of generative theory and selecting (or squeezing) the data of syntactic change to fit the theory. Rather than discuss each of these individually, we concentrate on evaluating Lightfoot (1979a) as the best-known representative of the application of generative grammar to diachronic syntax. (Later we take up Lightfoot's more recent work.)

2.3.2.1   Lightfoot and Extended Standard Theory
Lightfoot (1979a; see also 1974, 1980, 1981a, 1981b, 1981c, 1983) has attempted the most ambitious and best-known generative treatment of diachronic syntax, based on the Extended Standard Theory (EST). The main thrusts of Lightfoot's work were: (1) to argue for the Extended Standard Theory (and later for Government-and-Binding theory, see Lightfoot 1988a, 1988b, 1991, see also below) by illustrating how this formal theory might contribute to understanding diachronic syntax; and (2) to propose and defend the Transparency Principle (TP), "a rather imprecise, intuitive idea about limits on a child's ability to abduce complex grammars" (Lightfoot 1981b: 358). For Lightfoot the TP means that the elimination of excessive opacity is the explanatory principle behind certain far-reaching syntactic reanalyses. His goal, then, was to characterize "the limits to the permitted degree of exceptionality or derivational complexity," and in so doing to predict change and when it will occur (Lightfoot 1979a: 122). As argued by Romaine (1981), Lightfoot's Transparency Principle is never presented precisely enough to make it clear how it might be tested.

Lightfoot approaches syntactic changes from the standpoint of a formal theory of syntax, from which perspective the theory decrees how syntactic changes are to be interpreted. His is a top–down approach.[16] Loosely stated, Lightfoot's scenario for the explanation of syntactic change is that grammatical complexity builds up gradually in a language (through minor changes) until a sudden catastrophic and far-reaching restructuring of the grammar takes place, eliminating derivational complexity – that is, the TP applies, ridding the language of foul opacity and restoring transparency.

Lightfoot's approach has received heavy criticism from various directions. We take up just a few of the more crucial issues for illustration's sake (but see Aitchison 1980; Fischer and van der Leek 1981; Romaine 1981; Warner 1983; Allan 1987).

The major mechanism in Lightfoot's TP is reanalysis, which it shares with other views of syntactic change (see above, and our chapter 4).[17] Lightfoot, however, claims that reanalyses happen only when necessary (see Lightfoot 1979a: 124); this claim is clearly overstated (for counterexamples, see our chapter 4). Romaine (1981) points out that if this were true, closely related languages (and, we add, dialects of the same language) would not undergo different changes, as they do. (We take up the issue of necessity in section 4.3.1.)

Perhaps the major difference between Lightfoot and others is Lightfoot's emphasis on just those reanalyses which he sees as catastrophic, with far-reaching effects on the overall grammar. As Romaine (1981) points out, however, Lightfoot has no principled means of distinguishing the catastrophic changes, which he sees as the result of the operation of the TP to restructure the grammar, from the gradually accumulating less significant changes, which he later sometimes refers to as "environmental" changes.

Another major aspect of Lightfoot's (1979a) treatment of syntactic change is the central and deterministic role given to autonomous syntax. He claims that syntactic change (and indeed syntax in general) is autonomous; therefore reanalyses depend exclusively on the surface structure configurations and take place independently of semantic relations, pragmatic considerations, or discourse functions. That is, for Lightfoot syntactic rules (and syntactic changes) operate independently of considerations of meaning and use. In this, Lightfoot follows Muysken (1977), who had previously emphasized the autonomy thesis for syntactic change (see Muysken 1977: 171). This, however, is one of the most heavily criticized aspects of Lightfoot's theory (see Romaine 1981; Fischer and van der Leek 1987; Breivik 1989; Faarlund 1989, 1990a: 60; cf. Comrie 1988). As Romaine (1981) pointed out, contrary to his claims, Lightfoot's approach in fact goes beyond autonomous syntax. For Lightfoot the TP operates in unison with perceptual mechanisms to define "less highly valued" grammars; that is, the autonomous TP still interacts with perceptual processes, but these are beyond autonomous syntax. It cannot be the case that the TP, the operative aspect of syntactic theory, autonomously "explains" change, while change is held at the same time to be therapeutic to make languages more transparent: if syntactic change is governed by autonomous syntax – unaffected by use – then how can any change in it ever be seen as therapeutic or adaptive (for better use)? In short, syntactic rules cannot be assumed to operate independently of meaning, use, pragmatics, sociolinguistic value judgments, foreign-language influence, etc., and even Lightfoot acknowledged that at least therapeutic changes and perceptual strategies play a role (Lightfoot 1979a, 1981a, 1981b).[18]

Faarlund challenges the autonomy assumption on logical grounds, referring to two common kinds of explanation: in one something is subsumed under a generalization; in the other it is related to something in a different domain. He points out that in the case of syntax "if we never depart from the domain under study to find explanations [which Lightfoot's autonomy thesis in fact prevents], we end up with a circular system where pure formalisms become explanations" (Faarlund 1990a: 60–1).[19]

2.3.2.2   *Lightfoot and the Principles-and-Parameters approach*
Here we address Lightfoot 1991 as the most accessible representative of the Government-and-Binding (or Principles-and-Parameters) approach to

syntactic change in lieu of a review of the disparate variety of other recent works which utilize this approach. In some ways Lightfoot's 1991 (also 1988a, 1988b) approach is different from that of Lightfoot 1979a. For example, Lightfoot (1991: 77, 166) seems to have modified his earlier approach to include, at least in principle if not frequently in practice, a broader, more cross-linguistic perspective on syntactic change, of the sort we have advocated:

> By undertaking this kind of comparative study, one may expect to learn something about the status of triggering experiences and about how parameters are set.
>
> (Lightfoot 1991: 77)

> Nonetheless, languages do not change in completely arbitrary ways; many changes recur in one language after another. Despite the role of nongrammatical factors and chance, some changes and the manner in which they arise can be explained and they occur as a matter of necessity, reflecting new parameter settings and often being somewhat catastrophic in nature.
>
> (Lightfoot 1991: 166)

Since cross-linguistic variation is an essential aspect of research on parameters, it follows naturally that Lightfoot 1991 would make a bit more room for a cross-linguistic perspective than Lightfoot 1979a did with its emphasis on the autonomy thesis. While this change can only be seen as healthy, the range of languages considered in Lightfoot 1991, though broader than 1979a, will still be seen as scant by those who study languages outside the Indo-European family (cf. Comrie's 1989 [1981] criticisms). Thus the main examples of linguistic change in Lightfoot 1991 are still from English, with representatives from other Germanic languages, primarily Dutch, but also Scandinavian languages and German, with reference also to examples from Latin, Italian, Brazilian Portuguese, Spanish, and creole languages (with some discussion of Kru and Ijo in connection with creoles). Some Chinese data are discussed, but no examples of syntactic change in Chinese, even though it is essentially the only non-Indo-European language touched upon. In short, Lightfoot 1991 may profess to have a cross-linguistic spirit, but in actual practice there is little cross-linguistic meat on the 1991 book's bones.

While Lightfoot 1991 repeats many of the examples from the 1979a book, their treatment has been modified to some extent to accommodate criticisms of his earlier work. For example, it is now admitted that certain changes were not so nearly contemporaneous as he had claimed (see our chapter 7 for examples and discussion). The principal new proposal is degree-0 learnability – that children's parameters are set essentially only by evidence from matrix clauses (plus a bit; see our chapters 7 and 10). However, as we shall see, there are very few substantive changes in the basic assumptions about syntactic change, and much of the 1991 book is essentially a translation of EST and TP terminology into that of Principles-and-Parameters, with parameter settings. Lightfoot still seeks to explain key aspects of syntactic change through the language acquisition process – exposed to a range of "linguistic expressions" (the triggering experience), and mediated by principles of universal grammar (UG), children acquire a grammar, the basic aspects of which are mostly fixed by about the age of puberty. However, syntactic change is still viewed largely as before, as first the gradual accumulation of less important changes followed by catastrophic reanalyses of the grammar, where parameter setting plays the role formerly performed by the TP:

> The picture of language change that emerges is one of "punctuated equilibrium." Languages are constantly changing gradually and in piecemeal fashion, but meanwhile grammars remain in equilibrium, unchanged in their structural properties. From time to time, however, they undergo more radical, catastrophic restructuring, corresponding to new parameter settings . . . what is interesting about linguistic change of this type is that it requires a particular kind of explanatory model: one couched in claims about the genetically determined makeup of part of our cognitive capacity and about the way language acquisition proceeds. It is the definition of the parameters that accounts for the shape of the catastrophic changes. A coherent notion of what kind of linguistic experience sets these parameters will account for the timing of the structural changes. (Lightfoot 1991: 173)

On this view, changes may also take place during adolescence and middle age, and these changes are not determined by the language acquisition process and UG (i.e. by the setting of new parameters). These piecemeal and gradually accumulating changes are typically due to other factors:

> languages sometimes undergo a period of particularly rapid change, then settle into a time of relative stasis. From the perspective adopted here, it is natural to try to interpret such cascades of changes in terms of a new setting for some parameter, sometimes having a wide variety of surface effects and perhaps setting off a chain reaction. Such "catastrophic" changes . . . are quite different from the piecemeal, gradual, and chaotic changes which constantly affect the linguistic environment.
>
> These environmental changes, on the other hand, typically do not result from the genetically determined acquisition process, whereby something triggers some structural property with systematic effects [i.e. sets a parameter]. Rather they are induced by contact with other languages and dialects or introduced for stylistic reasons . . . For such environmental changes we have no systematic explanations, and as far as grammarians are concerned they may as well be attributed to chance: they are unlikely to tell us much about the nature of grammars, grammatical theory, or trigger experiences.

(Lightfoot 1991: 169–70; see also Lightfoot 1988a: 319)

In this regard, the extremely damaging criticism that held for Lightfoot 1979a still holds for 1991, that Lightfoot has no reliable basis for distinguishing the "catastrophic" changes (seen in 1979 as due to the operation of the TP and in 1991 as due to new parameter settings) from the gradually accumulating "environmental" changes. Moreover, while Lightfoot (1991) considers many changes to be reanalyses and equates them with the setting of a new para-meter, in several of these changes it is not at all clear that anything remotely "catastrophic" has taken place: for example, Lightfoot goes so far as to see a change which is limited to single lexical items or to the determination of the meaning of individual lexical items as due to the setting of a parameter (see Lightfoot 1991: 19–20). This is a particularly telling flaw in Lightfoot's theory, since its mode of explanation depends crucially upon being able to identify accurately when new parameters are set:

> the point at which parameters are set differently illustrates the limits to at-tainable grammars... An individual's grammar may differ significantly from that of her father; that constitutes a new parameter setting. If changes over time can inform us about the limits of grammars, the study of diachronic change can show how idiosyncratic properties may be added to a grammar without affecting its internal structure, and diachronic study may show what it takes to drive a grammar to reanalysis, with a parameter set differently. Ex-amining historical reanalyses illuminates what kinds of triggering experi-ences elicit grammatical reanalyses and what kinds are not robust enough to have that effect.   (Lightfoot 1991: 172)

Lightfoot (1991: 162–3) comes close to admitting the difficulty of distinguish-ing his two types of change:

> So gradualness exists: triggering experiences may change gradually, lexical classifications may change gradually, and new parameter settings may gradu-ally permeate a speech community. Much of this gradual change may have no immediate effect on the setting of *structural* parameters, which are reset only when the triggering experience has changed in some critical fashion.

However, Lightfoot does address the issue of distinguishing the two types of change, if only indirectly. Based on his treatment of "six new parameter set-tings in the history of English,"[20] Lightfoot specifies "distinctive characteris-tics" of new parameter settings (Lightfoot 1991: 166), which we evaluate in turn.

His first such distinctive characteristic is that "each new parameter setting is manifested by a cluster of simultaneous surface changes" (Lightfoot 1991: 167). This, however, begs the question: how can an accidental clustering of changes with no inherent connection among themselves be distinguished from others which may be causally connected and therefore reflective of the sort of major reanalysis Lightfoot sees in his new parameter settings? Also,

Lightfoot (1991) mentions some new parameter settings which are isolated, not connected with any cluster of other changes. Such isolated parameter-setting changes would be very difficult to distinguish from individual changes that do not set parameters.

Lightfoot's (1991: 167) second characteristic is that new parameter settings may "sometimes set off chain reactions," but this is not a very clear diagnostic criterion. If new parameter settings do not necessarily set off chain reactions (of later but related changes) and if it is not always possible to distinguish later changes which are related in this manner from those which have no connection, then this characteristic proves to be no strong help in distinguishing the changes which are due to new parameter settings from the other "environmental" changes Lightfoot finds relatively uninteresting.

The third characteristic is that "changes involving new parameter settings tend to take place much more rapidly than other changes, and they manifest Kroch's S-curve" (Lightfoot 1991: 167; cf. Kroch 1989a,b). While we find this to be an interesting point, it, too, is not sufficient to distinguish formally the two kinds of change Lightfoot insists are so different. This has to do with the issue of gradualness, which Lightfoot discusses at length, and which we take up in chapter 3. Briefly, there are several practical and logical problems with seeking rapid, S-curve changes (i.e. that start slowly, then suddenly increase rapidly, then taper off again more slowly) as diagnostic of new parameter settings. First, one needs fairly extensive and accurate documentation in order to establish the S-shaped trajectory of a change's history; this sort of information will be unavailable for the vast majority of linguistic changes. Second, how rapid is rapid? How do we distinguish a faddish change that catches on fast from the setting of a new parameter which may take a bit more time? That is, as Lightfoot (1991: 168) acknowledges, in a community some children may set a new parameter while others have not yet done so, and "the first people with the new parameter setting would produce different linguistic forms, which would in turn be part of the linguistic environment for younger people and so contribute to the spread of the new setting." While this may allow for the abruptness of grammar change in individuals of different generations, there is nothing in this cognitive model which requires the spread about which Lightfoot speaks of a new parameter setting throughout a speech community to be rapid or S-shaped. Even Lightfoot's description seems to reflect gradually increasing environmental pressure towards triggering a new parameter as more and more individuals produce more and more of the different forms which would trigger the change in those acquiring their grammars later.

Lightfoot's (1991: 168) fourth characteristic is that "obsolescence [of structures] manifests new parameter settings." He asserts that a novel form may be introduced for expressive reasons (i.e. change which is not the result of a new parameter setting), but that:

> a form can hardly drop out of the language for expressive reasons or because of the influence of another language . . . On the contrary, obsolescence must be due to a structural "knock-on" effect, a by-product of something else which was itself triggered by the kind of positive data that are generally available to children.   (Lightfoot 1991: 168)

But, why not? Why can a language not have two alternative means or stylistic options for expressing some grammatical notion where gradually over time one is favored for expressive or other reasons so that it ultimately replaces the other? For example, many varieties of Spanish have both the morphological future (e.g. *Juana come-rá* [Juana eat-Fut] "Juana will eat") and the periphrastic or analytic future (*Juana va a comer* [Juana goes to eat] "Juana is going to eat"), but in colloquial varieties of Mexican and Central American Spanish, the analytic option has essentially completely displaced the morphological future, which is not used and is considered archaic and affected, not part of the local dialect. It is difficult to see the obsolescence of the morphological future as due to any new parameter setting exhibiting rapid change consequences, as defined by Lightfoot's characteristics.

The fifth distinctive characteristic is that "any significant change in meaning is generally a by-product of a new parameter setting, for much the same reason that the obsolescence of a structure must be the indirect consequence of a more abstract change" (Lightfoot 1991: 168–9). Again, why? Can some structure not have more than one meaning, one of which gradually fades, without that fading being necessarily due to a new parameter setting? Lightfoot cites his example of "psych-verbs" (e.g. *like*, which formerly had NP[Dat] *like* NP[Nom], e.g. roughly "to Jane please the pears," i.e. "the pears give pleasure to Jane"; after the change it came to be NP[Nom] *like* NP[Acc], e.g. "Jane likes the pears," i.e. "Jane derives pleasure from the pears"), saying:

> Such changes affecting the thematic roles associated with particular NP positions could hardly arise as idiosyncratic innovations that somehow became fashionable within the speech community. It is hard to see how the variation could have been introduced as a set of independent developments, imitating properties of another language or serving some expressive function through their novelty. Rather, such changes must be attributed to some aspect of a person's grammar which was triggered by the usual kind of environmental factors – in this instance the existence of only structural cases.
> (Lightfoot 1991: 169)

Again, why? Grammars frequently have more than one option (or construction) for particular verbs or verb classes, particularly with psych-verbs. For example, Spanish has:

(2)   (a) se   me   olvid-ó   el libro
            REFLEX me.dat forget-3RD.PRET the book
            "I forgot the book." (literally: "the book forgot itself on me")

        (b) olvid-é   el libro
            forget-1ST.PRET the book
            "I forgot the book."[21]

German has had such options as (3a) and (3b) since Old High German times (Bennett 1979: 852, 854):

(3)   (a) mich hunger-t
            I.ACC hunger-3RD.PERS
            "I am hungry." (literally: "it hungers me")

        (b) ich   hunger-e
            I.NOM hunger-1ST.PERS
            "I am hungry." (literally: "I hunger")

Why could variation, such as in these Spanish and German examples, not be introduced as something "fashionable," based perhaps on analogy with other patterns in the language, and then gradually, perhaps through slow lexical diffusion (see chapter 5), replace the older pattern? It is logically possible for a new parameter setting itself to come about as an acceptance of fashionable variation.

Lightfoot's sixth "defining property of new parameter settings" is that they "occur in response to shifts in unembedded data only" (Lightfoot 1991: 169). This is Lightfoot's main thesis, that children are degree-0 learners, meaning that essentially only material from matrix clauses (plus a bit) is relevant to their setting of parameters. Regardless of the accuracy of this claim, this can hardly be useful for distinguishing Lightfoot's two sorts of changes, those reflecting new parameter settings and the "environmental" changes, since both kinds can take place in matrix clauses.

In short, just as with the 1979a version, Lightfoot 1991 relies crucially on a distinction between two major kinds of changes, here changes due to new parameter setting vs. the accumulating or environmental changes, but is unable to distinguish these in any clear or formal way.

The failure to distinguish these two kinds of changes is just one instance where Lightfoot's approach suffers seriously from a dependence on concepts which are not defined clearly enough to achieve the goals intended for them within the approach. The issue of "robustness" is another. In this approach it is believed that when children are exposed to appropriate "trigger experiences" (or "primary linguistic data"), this causes parameters to be set in their emerging grammars (Lightfoot 1991: 10). For the data to trigger the parameter setting it must be "robust" – sufficient to trigger the setting – but, unfortunately, it is not at all clear when exposure to certain data is sufficient or insufficient to cause a parameter to be set. Given that it is uncertain just how much or what kind of relevant data is needed to constitute the robustness necessary to trigger a parameter setting, it is difficult to accept some of Lightfoot's claims that certain changes are the result of new parameters being triggered based on his interpretation of the robustness (or lack thereof) of the data upon which the change depends. That is, there is a pernicious circularity in these cases: whether the data were robust enough or not is determined by whether or not a certain sort of change is perceived, but at the same time the change is said to take place because the primary linguistic data were deemed sufficiently robust. Thus, we might ask, for example, why Lightfoot's examples from Dutch and English seem to behave so differently in this regard. Lightfoot (1991: 52–5) sees what appears to us to be rather strained and marginal evidence of OV in Dutch matrix clauses as sufficiently robust to set OV as the underlying order in the face of the overwhelming majority of VO expressions the Dutch child hears. However, in the case of the English psych-verb change (e.g. *like*, see above) such evidence as case-marked pronouns (e.g. *him likes the queen* "He likes the queen") and discrepant number agreement (*the king like the pears* "The king likes the pears/The pears please the king"; *the kings likes the pear* "The kings like the pear/The pear pleases the kings") is seen as insufficiently robust and consequently English changed as a result of a parameter having been set which was unfriendly to the analysis these conflicting but insufficiently robust data would require (Lightfoot 1991: 129–36).

Some differences between the 1979a and 1991 approaches are perhaps matters more of emphasis than of substance. In 1979a Lightfoot insisted on the autonomy of syntax, that syntactic rules (and syntactic changes) operate independently of considerations of meaning and use, though, as pointed out above, this was not strictly followed in his own practice, and in any event it is shown inaccurate by facts from numerous cases. In 1991, Lightfoot seems to allow much more room for "external" or "environmental" factors beyond sheer syntax, and yet, there still seems to be some carryover of the autonomy thesis in several of the explanations offered. For example, this seems to be behind Lightfoot's (1991: 148) denial that semantic factors could be involved in the origin of English modals, which ignores the fact that many languages have created a category of modals involving verbs with these meanings, but which lack the particular configuration of morphological and syntactic traits Lightfoot finds so important to the change in English (see, for example, Dik 1987; Givón 1984; M. Harris and Ramat 1987; and our chapter 7). Lightfoot's strong anti-functionalist stance, even when the functionalist explanation is from Chomsky (Lightfoot 1991: 153–4), appears to have the same autonomy background. He also sees change in meaning as generally a "by-product of new parameter setting" (Lightfoot 1991: 168), rather than ever causally involved in the change, and this too would appear to be a holdover from the 1979 autonomy thesis.

While in the 1991 book the interplay of chance and necessity are not as visible as in 1979, the sentiment that reanalyses (or new parameter settings) take place out of necessity is still to be found (e.g. Lightfoot 1991: 166). As seen above (and in chapter 7), this claim is shown inaccurate by a number of counterexamples.

2.3.3   Formalism versus functionalism

The post-1950s approaches discussed so far all have a cognitive, psychological orientation which emphasizes the role of language acquisition mediated by linguistic universals in their attempts at explanation of linguistic change in general and of syntactic change in particular. This raises important, fundamental questions both about the nature of language and about language change, and about how linguists may explain these. In the generative approaches, exemplified here particularly by Lightfoot's work, all universals are taken to be part of the human biological endowment, hard-wired in the brain of the child language learner and therefore very important in regulating syntactic change. However, a major competitor of this formal approach is the more functionalist orientations found overlapping each other in work on typology, discourse analogy, and in particular on "grammaticalization" (see for example, Givón 1984, 1990a; Heine and Reh 1984; Hopper 1991; Traugott and Heine 1991). In these views, change is understood as not necessarily a consequence of the transition from generation to generation, explained by child language acquisition, but rather as the result of language fulfilling its discourse and communicative functions. When these two orientations (neither completely homogeneous as practiced by their various adherents) are contrasted with one another, we are led to ask, must all linguistic universals be innately available to the child language learner, part of the biological endowment hard-wired in the infant language learner's brain, or do some universals stem from the function of language independently of the speaker's genetic mental make-up? Several have challenged the hard-wiring interpretation of all universals (e.g. Givón 1984, 1990; Aitchison 1987: 14–18; Faarlund 1990b). The answer will have telling consequences for how syntactic change is viewed. We need to ask, are there universals which result naturally in any case due to the functioning of language and conceivably need no direct biological foundation for their existence?[22]

We conclude that a fully adequate theory of syntactic change cannot afford to neglect either the innate (with attention to child language acquisition) or the functional (with attention on discourse functions) motivations for language change. In our approach we address both. The autonomous syntax hypothesis is inadequate, while the attempt to explain all change on the basis of biology, the genetic endowment, is too restrictive and unnecessarily unrealistic.

Finally, we do not treat the post-1950s word order studies or grammaticalization separately in this chapter, but rather deal with these more directly in individual chapters of the book (see especially chapters 4, 5, 7, and 8).

2.4   Conclusion

Most topics of current interest in historical syntax are not new; many have a distinct and distinguished history. Perhaps the most significant difference is in the more recent attempts to integrate them into formal theoretical frameworks – time alone will tell whether this amounts to advancement in understanding. In any case, as we have argued, what has been learned from the study of syntactic change in the past is important and should play a role in framing an adequate approach to diachronic syntax. We discover from past treatments elements which should be included in such a framework and others which should be abandoned. We mention what should be included by way of setting the stage for the framework which we defend in this book (see especially chapter 3).

Reanalysis has been and continues to be an extremely important mechanism of syntactic change (seen in the examples from Arabic grammarians, Bopp, and especially Delbrück, Paul, and those who came after, including generative grammarians and others). Extensions were also observed in Paul's scheme of things, though only cursorily (see chapters 4 and 5).

The role of language acquisition (and the cognitive orientation in general) has proven productive and is extremely important, together with what is understood of linguistic universals. Nevertheless, we must avoid the excesses of the autonomous syntax thesis and the compulsion to deny *a priori* any form of explanation not related to a genetically endowed version of universal grammar. In short, empirical issues are at stake here. The fact that certain existing formal theories of syntax do not address certain functionalist matters is by no means evidence that the unaddressed issues are insignificant to the understanding and explanation of syntactic change in general. On the other side, while we must recognize both the value of functionalist explanations, of explanations which rely heavily on typology and discourse, including grammaticalization, we must also recognize their limitations and avoid the pitfalls seen in the lack of rigor and the excessive speculations on the part of some in the past and in the present, as well. (See chapter 11.)

As we have seen, the importance of language contact and syntactic borrowing for a theory of grammatical change was fully recognized and demonstrated by many in the past, and this makes borrowing and language contact important in current attempts to explain syntactic change generally. (See chapter 6.)

The studies throughout history that have contributed to word order change, the development of complex sentences, and the origin of and change in grammatical categories (and grammaticalization in general) must receive considerable attention in any attempt to draft a theory of syntactic change. Minimally the syntactic changes that they accurately describe in these areas constitute an important part of the database, and any attempt at a theory of syntactic change can and should benefit from taking these into account, and, what is more, an account of these changes provides a minimal test of adequacy for any such proposed theory. Such a theory must be able to account for these changes, which are part of our linguistic scholarly heritage, which provide rich resources, and which are, as part of the existing linguistic literature, never out of view on the drawing board where linguistic theories are constructed and tested.

Other specific aspects of this history are taken into account in the other chapters of this book.

3 Overview of a theory of syntactic change

In this chapter we begin to lay out a theory of syntactic change. In order to develop such a theory it is necessary to address what the entity upon which change operates is, what the forces of change are, how those forces act upon that entity, and what – if anything – constrains those forces. This chapter introduces our theory of how syntax changes over time, defines some basic terms, and presents some claims about syntactic change that are treated in detail in subsequent chapters.

3.1   Basic assumptions about language change

Views of language change have assumed that:

(a)   human beings are genetically endowed with aspects of universal grammar which regulate how infants acquire languages and hence determine what constitutes a possible language;

(b)   child language acquisition is *(in large measure)* responsible for linguistic change;

(c)   change is abrupt since change occurs in the construction of a new grammar by child language learners which may differ in its internal structure from the grammar of adult models (whose grammars may no longer be optimal due to additions or modifications later in life).

We evaluate each of these in order to make clear the relationship of these assumptions to our own theory. Let us take up the claimed abruptness of syntactic change ((c) above) first. (We take up the issue of gradualness in detail in this context in section 4.4.) There is growing evidence that it is not useful to consider syntactic change in terms of a dichotomy between gradual vs. abrupt, and syntactic change may be considered gradual in a number of respects: for example, Timberlake (1977) has shown that syntactic change through reanalysis is often gradual in the sense that as the grammar adjusts to the new situation, additional, less far-reaching changes occur. These "actualizations" may be considered micro-changes, part of a larger macro-change. Chung (1977: 4) has argued that "syntactic change is actualized for sentences that undergo superficial rules before it is actualized for sentences that undergo major cyclic rules," and the same phenomenon has been found in another, very different case (Harris 1985: 345–6). Some syntactic phenomena spread from lexical item to lexical item (with change in the grammatical properties of these lexical items) and in this sense are gradual (for example, Naro and Lemle 1976; Aitchison 1980; Naro 1981; Warner 1982: 117–23; Fischer and van der Leek 1987; Goossens 1987). Extensions are often gradual in the sense that they apply to one word or one small group of words at a time (see section 5.3). Further, extensions may remove one exception, then another, and another, so that the overall effect is of gradual progression (e.g. section 5.3.2). Most extensions also proceed gradually in the sense that they produce variation; at first both the older norm and the newer form are used, sometimes interchangeably, sometimes corresponding to more formal vs. more casual usage (section 5.4). The frequency of a phenomenon may increase gradually (Kroch 1989a, citing Ellegård 1953; Hiltunen 1983: 145 and elsewhere), such that the innovation often comes to be used with increasing frequency. For these reasons, syntactic change gives an overall impression of proceeding gradually. A change may be gradual either in the grammar of a single individual in his or her life time or across different grammars through time.

The notion "discrete" is also helpful in explicating what goes on when a language changes its grammar. That is, there clearly is a discrete aspect to many changes as seen in the language acquisition process with the transition of grammars from one generation to the next, where the grammar is constructed anew by each individual. As we understand it, reanalysis itself is a discrete process, though the actualization process through which it meshes with the grammar is more gradual. Thus syntactic change has both discrete and gradual aspects.

This brings us to (b) above, the claim that child language acquisition is mainly responsible for change. There is evidence that grammatical change is not always limited to the language acquisition process. The grammar of an adult can change; evidence to support this claim comes both from variation in texts by one author or speaker over a period of time, and in longitudinal studies of speakers of various languages, including non-literary ones (such as in Fox, see Goddard 1988; cf. Brink and Lund 1975, 1979; Labov 1982: 67–9). These facts show that the grammar of an adult is best viewed, not as an inflexible completed object, but as an adaptable, constantly growing set of generalizations. It is true that children learning a language have a special role to play in furthering linguistic shifts, and it may also be true that the possible changes adults may make in their grammars may be highly constrained by the form of the grammar they acquired as children.

Nevertheless, in light of the evidence, it is necessary to revise our views of assumptions (b) and (c).

The role of (a), biologically endowed universals, in syntactic change is very important. Language universals provide the most extensive constraint on syntactic change. It is possible to modify the view of language evolution to accommodate the updated versions of assumptions (b) and (c), without challenging the basic validity of (a).[1] It is to this task that we now turn.

3.2   Outline of a theory of syntactic change

Our theory is based upon the existence of:

(1)   only three **mechanisms** of syntactic change;
(2)   a set of general diachronic **operations** implemented by means of one of these mechanisms;
(3)   a set of **general principles** that interact with these operations; and
(4)   a set of **syntactic constructions** which are part of universal grammar, in the sense that they are always available to be drawn on for alternative expression.

Each of these is discussed briefly in the sections below, and in greater detail in the chapters that follow.

3.3   On mechanisms of syntactic change

3.3.1   Definitions

Alteration of syntactic patterns takes place by means of specific mechanisms of change. We hypothesize that there are only three basic mechanisms: **reanalysis**, **extension**, and **borrowing**. All three have been much discussed in the literature on diachronic syntax (see chapter 2). Our proposal differs in that we claim that no other mechanisms exist, and that others that have been suggested, such as rule addition and loss, lexical diffusion, changes in phrase structure (PS) rules, grammaticalization, contamination, etc., are really just specific instances or consequences of one or a combination of these mechanisms.

We begin by defining informally what we mean by each of these terms. Many examples are given in the three chapters that follow this, in which each of these mechanisms is discussed in considerably greater detail.

Reanalysis is a mechanism which changes the underlying structure of a syntactic pattern and which does not involve any modification of its surface manifestation.[2] We understand **underlying structure** in this sense to include at least (i) constituency, (ii) hierarchical structure, (iii) category labels, and (iv) grammatical relations. **Surface manifestation** includes (i) morphological marking, such as morphological case, agreement, and gender-class, and (ii) word order.[3] Reanalysis has also been termed reinterpretation, and we make no distinction between these two terms; **rebracketing** and **restructuring** are specific kinds of reanalysis. As discussed in greater detail in chapter 4, reanalysis depends upon a pattern characterized by **surface ambiguity or the possibility of more than one analysis**.

Extension is a mechanism which results in changes in the surface manifestation of a pattern and which does not involve immediate or intrinsic modification of underlying structure. As demonstrated in chapter 5, extension is not limited to morphology, as sometimes supposed, though it may be more common and easier to identify in that domain than in more abstract syntax. Extension is not the same as analogy, though extension might be seen as part of analogy as traditionally defined in the linguistic literature. Since the term analogy has been used to cover so many different sorts of phenomena, we choose to avoid the term altogether. We speak here rather of "analogues," by which we mean a condition where a structural similarity exists between two (or more) items, or classes, or constructions, etc. The existence of the analogue often stimulates change through extension, but it may also prompt change through reanalysis or through borrowing; it is not, however, necessary for any change to occur. As used here, analogues are not themselves processes or mechanisms of change. In this sense, then, an analogue is similar to contact and to surface ambiguity (or multiple analyses); each is a frequent cause or stimulus of change, but not, itself, a mechanism of change.

The definition provided above for extension may seem quite broad and general, but we argue in chapter 5 that in fact this mechanism is highly constrained.

Though the terms **language contact** and **borrowing** are sometimes used interchangeably, we distinguish between them. By **language contact**, we mean a situation in which the speakers of one language are familiar in some way with another. That is, language contact is a situation; while it often leads to change through borrowing (one language otherwise influencing another, possibly reciprocally), contact itself is not change. Language contact is often a catalyst to change through reanalysis or extension, while borrowing, of course, can come about only through language contact. We use the term **borrowing** to mean a mechanism of change in which a replication of the syntactic pattern is incorporated into the borrowing language through the influence of a host pattern found in a contact language.[4] Many things that are often labeled "borrowing" in the literature should, we believe, more properly be considered "language contact," since they involve other mechanisms of change which happen to be triggered by the contact language.

It must be pointed out that many of the cases we see as a single change are the result of more than one of these mechanisms in operation in a particular instance. A single change can involve the operation of a single mechanism independently or multiple mechanisms acting either in unison or sequentially. This should come as no surprise, since we are accustomed to the idea that a single syntactic pattern often results from more than one synchronic process; for example, a simple content question such as *what did she eat?* involves (in approaches accepted by many) *do*-support, subject–verb inversion, and movement of the w h-word. Examples of changes involving more than one mechanism are given in chapters 4 and 5.

3.3.2   Observations and claims about these mechanisms

Borrowing is an **external mechanism** of change, involving motivations towards change from outside the affected language; reanalysis and extension are **internal mechanisms**. Reanalysis and extension are complementary processes; the first affects the underlying structure but not the surface manifestation, while the second affects the surface, not the underlying structure. These two mechanisms have certain other complementary features, but in other respects we believe them to be quite different.

Only reanalysis and borrowing can introduce an entirely new structure into a language, and in this sense they can produce more radical change than extension can. Examples of reanalyses that bring about radical change by introducing an entirely new structure to a language are discussed in sections 4.2.3 and 4.2.4. Numerous examples of borrowings that introduce entirely new structures are among those discussed in chapter 6. The closest parallel for extension involves the further deployment of a structure in an entirely new area of the grammar of a language. Some word order changes have begun in one or another aspect of sentence structure and through the mechanism of extension have virtually overhauled the word order structure of the language; examples are discussed in section 8.5.2.1. Other examples of relatively extensive change through extension have taken place in case marking in the Kartvelian languages (Harris 1985: 297–8, 371–80). Nevertheless, by definition, extension cannot introduce an entirely novel structure.

Reanalysis often creates irregularities which are then "smoothed over" by subsequent changes, which include extensions and other reanalyses. (This is discussed in greater detail in chapters 4 (section 4.4), 5, and 11.) From a longer time perspective, these often look like a single change; however, on closer examination, if the change is attested, we can see that a number of independent **micro-changes** have resulted in a single **macro-change**.

Borrowing can introduce change in underlying structure and surface manifestation at the same time. Whether or not morphemes from the donor language are borrowed with the borrowed syntactic pattern, morphemes can be combined in ways that produce a novel or extended surface structure.

It has often been observed that language cannot change so rapidly that speakers of immediately succeeding generations lose the ability to communicate; communicability must be preserved (see, for example, Weinreich, Labov, and Herzog 1968). The independence of the processes of reanalysis, operating on underlying structure, and extension, operating on surface structure, contribute, together with other factors, to preserving communicability. Borrowing, we suggest, makes it possible to change underlying and surface structure at the same time because it makes reference to an outside system. In syntactic borrowing, introduction of an exotic construction will be recognized by speakers and identified with the donor language; it is this that makes it possible to change underlying and surface structures in a less constrained way through borrowing (see chapter 6, Borrowing).[5]

3.3.3 Mechanisms and the causes of syntactic change

The causes of syntactic change are in effect the same as those of other types of language change. There is increasing evidence that most changes in language structure have multiple causes, and often these are quite complex.

Language contact, surface ambiguity, and analogues can all be among causal factors in changes and are not limited to that mechanism (as just discussed above) with which they have been most closely associated. That is, while language contact is a necessary condition for borrowing to take place, as surface ambiguity (or the possibility of more than one analysis) is for reanalysis, and analogues for extension, these conditions are often part, but only part, of the cause of a particular change of some other type. For example, Joseph (1983: 179–212, especially 186) shows that language contact within the Balkan *Sprachbund* (where the languages have eliminated infinitive constructions altogether, or have only highly restricted ones) was one cause of the loss of the infinitive in Rumanian (as also in other languages in the *Sprachbund*); however, this change in Rumanian took place through internal mechanisms. Avoidance of surface ambiguity may be one cause of an extension, and analogues can play a role in reanalysis. While each of these three factors may be a cause of a particular change, they do not offer a complete explanation of syntactic change.

A tension between the speaker's need for concise expressions and the hearer's need for redundancy and more elaborated expressions is often credited with causing change (see, for example, Langacker 1977a; Birnbaum 1984), and this is true for syntactic change, just as for phonological or morphological change. Note that a single mechanism – reanalysis – is responsible for reduction in formal structure and, as described in section 3.4 below, also responsible for elaboration of formal structure.

3.4   On universally available syntactic constructions

We recognize a set of universally available syntactic constructions from which any language may draw for alternative syntactic expressions. Such expressions may turn up spontaneously a single time, but sometimes they recur and at times become part of the grammar of a language. The development of these **exploratory expressions** and the way they interact with reanalysis are discussed in greater detail in chapter 4. In this section our purpose is, rather, to characterize the set of constructions that may be exploited as exploratory expressions and to indicate the role they play in syntactic change.

One respect in which syntax differs from phonology and morphology is that syntactic patterns allow for far greater creativity. We suggest that isolated creative, exploratory expressions are made constantly by speakers of all ages. Such expressions may be developed for emphasis, for stylistic or pragmatic reasons (to facilitate communication as in changes to avoid ambiguity or to foster easier identification of discourse roles), or they may result from production errors. The vast majority of such expressions are never repeated, but a few "catch on." Only when the expression is used in additional contexts and is generalized (by means of one of the mechanisms described above) may we speak of a grammatical change having taken place. The basis for proposing such a set is the observation that in many languages where a particular device or construction is not part of the grammar, it may nevertheless come to be used in a marginal way. Constructions of this type may be judged ungrammatical, stylistically odd, or foreign, but will nevertheless be understood. Under appropriate circumstances a native speaker might use one of them as a poetic expression, as a periphrasis motivated by the desperation of not finding a more appropriate means of expression, as a way of deliberately producing stylistic oddity or foreign flavor, or for other stylistic reasons or communicative needs. From our point of view, exploratory expressions are important because they sometimes become part of a grammar.

A simple example of such a construction, an example discussed in greater detail in chapter 4, is that of negation through use of an "expression of minimal value." In French (and many other languages present similar examples) an inherited marker of negation (*ne*) was combined with a noun referring to something of minimal value; dozens of such combinations are attested (Möhren 1980). Some of these were grammaticalized, with *ne . . . pas* becoming the most neutral negation (see M. Harris 1978: 23–9; Winters 1987). We hypothesize that French (together with languages like it) differs from other languages, such as English, only in that the former grammaticalized this, while the latter did not. That is, we hypothesize that the construction is available for exploitation by languages. The construction is found in English in *not a whit, not a bit, not a lick*, etc.; but these have the status of idioms, rather than of neutral expressions or of grammaticalized categories of the language.

A second example is the use of a case or adposition meaning "from" for the periphrastic expression of the genitive or the partitive. This is the origin of the postnominal *of*-genitive in English (*of* meaning "from" originally) and the *von*-genitive of German (e.g. *das Auto von Frau Meyer* "Mrs. Meyer's car"), which is currently in the process of progressively replacing the morphological genitive (e.g. *das Auto der Frau Meyer* [the car the.FEM.GEN.SG Mrs. Meyer]). Also, the *de*-genitive of Romance languages has replaced the Latin morphological genitive; *de* meant "from," as it still does in other contexts in, for example, French and Spanish.

Similarly, partitive constructions develop from ablative or genitive constructions. For example, while English has no true partitive, it has the somewhat archaic sounding partitive construction (not so truly grammaticalized as the partitives of many other languages), as in *he ate of my bread and drank of my wine.* We hypothesize that periphrasis using comparable elements is universally available to be used by any language. This development is attested in several languages: for example, in Latin, the periphrastic genitive had a partitive function; one finds *bibō dē aquā* [drink.I from water.ABL] "I drink (some) water" along side of *bibō aquam* [drink.I water.ACC] "I drink (the) water" (M. Harris 1978: 77–8). In the French partitive construction, as in *j'ai mangé du poisson* "I ate (some) fish," the partitive marker *de* (*du* from *de* "from" + *le* definite article) developed from the periphrastic genitive described above. The Baltic languages use the genitive for partitive objects, as does Russian (where original Indo-European ablative and genitive have merged) (see Timberlake 1974). The partitive case of Balto-Finnic languages, illustrated by Finnish (1), also developed from an ablative:[6]

(1)   Söin omena-a
         ate.I apple-PARTITIVE.SG
         "I ate (some of) the apple," "I was eating the apple."

In Old High German there was a partitive genitive which indicated that the object was only partially affected:

(2)   ich will   im   mînes   brôtes   geben
                 I   want   him.DAT my.GEN bread.GEN to.give
                 "I want to give him some of my bread."   (Ebert 1978: 52)

The use of "from" is likely to be related to the closeness of the meaning of this adposition/case to that of the genitive and partitive. (See section 12.4.1.)

Another example of a universally available syntactic construction is the focus (*it-* or WH-) cleft. While not every language has clefts, it is likely that such constructions are easily added to grammars. The focus cleft may be so widely available because it is structurally equivalent to a copular clause with a relative clause modifying one of its constituents (see section 7.2.5.1).

The set of syntactic constructions we are proposing may be compared with the creation of secondary color terminology. Many, perhaps all, languages use a comparable description as the basis of (non-basic) color terminology. In English we have expressions of the form *sky blue, periwinkle blue, fire engine red* beside ones of the form *fuchsia, aqua, jade.*[7] The former construction is also productive and may compare the color of any familiar object to that of an object not known to the hearer; *my new hat is clip-board brown.* We assume that the color construction is so widely available because human beings create metaphors relating the unfamiliar to the familiar.

It may be useful to compare the role of exploratory expressions in reanalysis with the role of mutations in biological evolution, for they are similar, though not identical. Biological evolution occurs only when a mutation has introduced in an organism a feature that differentiates that organism from most others of its species. The changes introduced by mutations are random (constrained only by the properties already present in the organism's genetic make-up). Most mutations affect only a few organisms and thus do not induce evolutionary change. But if a mutation gives an organism an important advantage over others of its species, often due to some change in its environment, it (and others with the same mutation) may have an advantage for survival and therefore for reproduction, while others of the species lacking the adaptive advantage may not survive, that is may not be as successful at producing offspring. Offspring of the mutants who inherit the same mutation are more likely to live and reproduce with more offspring which have the mutation. In this way, a mutation can be perpetuated. The mutations themselves are random; however, environmental circumstances determine which mutations will have an adaptive advantage for the survival of the organism and its offspring which also exhibit the change.

Syntactic constructions from the universally available set, like biological mutations, may be introduced as exploratory expressions to a given language by the productive grammar. While exploratory expressions are not entirely random, it appears that they are often introduced for reasons that have little to do with the reasons for which they survive (if indeed they do). Most exploratory expressions occur in only a few instances (sentences) and thus do not induce grammatical change; but some eventually become fixed, often because they fulfill a need, such as reinforcing a marker that has become inadequate through attrition of form. Biological mutations are transmitted through genes, while linguistic mutations are not, but rather result from the differential language learning of succeeding generations. The one important parallel is that in both cases many mutations are produced but few are perpetuated.

3.5   On universal principles

The universal principles we propose are of several kinds and are discussed in various places in chapters 4–11. We suggest that there are constraints on mechanisms and in section 5.3 we formulate a specific constraint on the mechanism of extension: Extensions always proceed by removing conditions on the rules extended. We also propose constraints on specific operations (see sections 7.5, 8.5, and 9.4).[8] Thus, particular changes may be governed both by a general constraint on the mechanism of extension and by a specific constraint on an operation. In chapter 8 we describe examples of extensions of word orders that are constrained both generally and specifically, and in chapter 9 we adduce examples of alignment extensions involving both general and particular constraints.

3.6   The role of operations in an account of syntactic change

There exists a set of informally recognized diachronic changes which are seen to recur with frequency across the world's languages, and which are derivable from the mechanisms of syntactic change, the set of available constructions, and the general principles governing syntactic change. We propose to call these *operations* to give them a more specific name. These operations do not necessarily apply in every language or even when the conditions for their application are met. Rather, they constitute a set or inventory of changes which have been observed in the history of a number of unrelated languages, changes whose shared characteristics are best seen as somehow universally available because of their apparent naturalness.[9]

In universal grammar it has often been proposed that there exists a set of synchronic operations. The nature of the operations naturally varies according to the theoretical paradigm adopted. We may cite passivization and movement of relative pronouns as examples of such operations. Taking the latter as a further example, we may point out that linguists are led to posit a universal set of synchronic operations on the basis of two kinds of observations. First it is observed that there exists a regular relationship between sentence patterns such as those illustrated in (3a) and (3b).

(3)   (a)   Mary can play "The Moonlight Sonata"
       (b)   (the sonata) which Mary can play

Second, it is observed that the same relationship exists between similar sentence patterns in many other languages, many of them unrelated. On this basis it is hypothesized that a rule relating (3b) to (3a) exists in universal grammar. Other rules are observed in a similar way, and it is hypothesized that a set of such processes exists.

In a parallel way we hypothesize a set of universally available diachronic operations, based on observations of an analogous sort. For example, first it is observed that there exists a regular **diachronic** relationship between the pattern illustrated in (4a) and that illustrated in (4b):

(4)   (a)   ic wille mid flode folc   acwellan
             I wish with flood people to.kill
             "I want to kill people with (a) flood."

                                        (Genesis 1296, cited by Visser 1969: 1677)

       (b)   I will kill people with a flood

Second, it is observed that this same diachronic relationship exists (between the lexical verb "want" and a later grammatical morpheme "future") not only in English and in most or all of the Balkan languages and in Armenian, but also in completely unrelated languages, such as Laz, a language of the Kartvelian family, and many others.

Identification of a change/operation that has taken place in many unrelated languages provides us with the opportunity to study and compare the individual transitions, analyzing what it is that changes and what remains constant, what it is that is common to all changes of a particular type and what it is that is different. In some instances it is found that the shared traits of a change of a particular type, such as the "want"-future illustrated in (4) (see Bybee and Pagliuca 1984, 1987; Bybee, Pagliuca, and Perkins 1991), is also common to a broader spectrum of changes, in this instance all changes which derive an auxiliary from a higher verb. In this instance the diachronic change closely parallels an abstract synchronic analysis that has been proposed, and the other operations discussed in chapter 7 similarly involve structures with higher verbs. In chapters 8–10 we discuss other types of diachronic operations, for most of which synchronic parallels are unlikely to be proposed.

The purpose of studying single operations is to find out more about the limits of such changes – what can happen and what cannot happen. We hope in this way to be better able to understand the individual change in a particular language, the individual operation, and diachronic syntax as a whole.

It is not our intention to suggest that all, or even most, syntactic changes fall into the category of one of the operations discussed here.[10] There are many syntactic changes that require such specific circumstances that the same change is unlikely to occur often. However, even with these it is possible that future research will discover more abstract parallels, with shared features that can profitably be identified.

3.7   Why this theory?

In the paragraphs above we have provided an outline of a theory that is elaborated in the rest of this book. This theory provides an approach to the problems of diachronic syntax as a whole and a framework for the analysis of the history of the syntax of particular languages and language families. Often the real data of syntactic change appear to be random, messy, and even chaotic; the framework proposed here provides a way of making sense of these data (see section 4.4, and chapter 12). The theory, however, does much more than that. It solves some long-standing problems and offers explanations of hitherto poorly understood phenomena.

First, by identifying reanalysis and extension in the way that we do, we offer an account of why a language goes through a stage at which a construction has properties of multiple structures. After reanalysis, typically extension alters one aspect of the surface manifestation before others. At this point, a surface structure has some of the structurally ambiguous aspects that it had before reanalysis, but also one (newly extended to it) that is unambiguously characteristic of the new analysis, and often at least one that is characteristic of the old. For this reason, speakers must be able to see both analyses at once. It is this that explains, for example, the fact that clauses containing modals in English retain aspects of a biclausal structure, which have led to proposals of biclausal underlying structure, as well as aspects of a monoclausal structure, which have led to competing linguistic proposals (for further discussion, see sections 4.3.1 and 4.4.3).

Second, the mechanism of extension as defined here permits us to account for the gradual nature of syntactic change while maintaining the concept of a grammar as a set of specific rules. Early treatments of diachronic phenomena within generative grammar described changes in rules, with the implication that (for some scholars the direct insistence that) such changes must be abrupt.[11] However, a great deal of evidence has built up that syntactic change is – at least much of the time – gradual (see discussion and references above).[12] The mechanism of extension offers an account of this gradual aspect of syntactic change, while tightly constraining the ways in which it may proceed (for further discussion see chapter 5 and section 4.4.3).

Third, the mechanism of reanalysis as defined here enables us to identify the origins of certain kinds of gradual change and the constraints on those origins. Several important recent papers have provided careful records of the gradual implementation of particular changes (Naro and Lemle 1976; Naro 1981; Fischer and van der Leek 1987; Kroch 1989a). What these studies do not identify clearly is the mechanism that gets these processes started and constraints on that mechanism.[13] It has been pointed out (Campbell and Mithun 1980) that typological analyses of word order change claim that word order, too, over time becomes typologically consistent, but that these analyses have not shown how, under these circumstances, a new order could ever gain a foothold. The mechanism of reanalysis is shown to set off a number of changes of this sort, as discussed in greater detail in chapter 4 and in chapter 8.

Finally, the system outlined above provides a framework and guidelines for identification of syntactic correspondence sets and for reconstruction based upon them. The difficulties associated with the transfer of these notions from diachronic phonology and morphology to the realm of syntax have been articulated by Campbell and Mithun 1980, Lightfoot (1979a: 8), and others (see further discussion and citations in chapter 12). Recognition of the elements discussed above permits the development of these notions for syntactic reconstruction, while providing sufficient checks on the method to insure that reconstructions are answerable both to the data and to the universals.

4 *Reanalysis*

4.1 Introduction

In this chapter we define reanalysis, provide a number of examples in order to convey some understanding of the variety in and limits on this mechanism, and show in detail how reanalysis works. We investigate its relation to grammaticalization and actualization, and we show how it fits in our overall view of grammar change. Reanalysis has been the most important concept for most attempts to explain syntactic change throughout the history of linguistics and especially in the last thirty years or so (see chapter 2).[1] Langacker (1977a: 57) might well be speaking for the field in general when he says: "not all diachronic developments in the domain of syntax involve reanalysis . . . but this is clearly a major mechanism of syntactic evolution which we must understand in depth if we wish to understand how and why syntactic change occurs." It is also of central importance in our approach, and we attempt here to define it rigorously and characterize it in detail.

Reanalysis, as defined in chapter 3, is a mechanism which changes the underlying structure of a syntactic pattern and which does not involve any immediate or intrinsic modification of its surface manifestation. This definition is intended to isolate one part of a process for further discussion; it is not intended as a claim that changes involving reanalysis cannot additionally involve some modification of surface manifestation (though such modifications necessarily involve mechanisms other than reanalysis). Indeed, as discussed in section 4.4, such a modification is very often a part of the process of change, subsequent to the reanalysis itself. While the surface structure is not directly affected by reanalysis, underlying structure is.

Reanalysis directly changes underlying structure, which we understand to include information regarding at least (i) constituency, (ii) hierarchical structure, (iii) category labels, (iv) grammatical relations, and (v) cohesion (defined below).[2] A given reanalysis may primarily affect any one of these aspects of structure, and examples of each are given below. Semantic change is involved also in many of these reanalyses.

(i–ii) *Constituency and hierarchical structure.* Examples of reanalysis in which constituency and hierarchical structure have changed are familiar in the historical literature on changes, in Germanic languages in particular. For example, the English complementizer construction with *for* + *to* is the result of the reanalysis of a former construction in which the *for* + Noun Phrase belonged to the main clauses, as in (1):

(1)   [it is bet for me] [to sleen my self than ben defouled thus]
       "It is better for me to slay myself than to be violated thus."
                                        (Chaucer; cited from Ebert 1978: 12)[3]

In this example, although *me* is part of the surface constituent *for me*, it functioned as coreferential to the logical subject of the infinitive (*to sleen*); later *for* + Noun Phrase + Infinitive was reanalyzed as a constituent, as seen in Modern English (2), where the whole constituent can be preposed:

(2)   [For me to slay myself] [would be better than to be violated thus]

Similarly, the German infinitival construction *um zu* + Infinitive, it has been argued (by Paul and Behaghel, cited by Ebert 1978: 12, 30), is from a similar reanalysis. Formerly such sentences had the prepositional phrase structure which is illustrated in (3):

(3)   [er ging aus um Wasser] [zu holen]
       he went out for water   to fetch
       "He went out for water, to fetch (it)."

Originally in such sentences the nominal (*Wasser* in this case) was governed by the preposition (*um*). However, the nominal came to be understood as the logical object of the infinitive (e.g. *Wasser zu holen*) and these were reanalyzed as such in the infinitival construction, where *um* in such environments lost its former locative meaning and came to be understood as the introducing morpheme for the structure, as illustrated in (4):

(4)   [er ging aus] [um Wasser zu holen]
       he went out   for water   to fetch
       "He went out (for) to fetch water."[4]

After this reanalysis, *um zu* began also to appear optionally without any object (e.g. *Wasser* in the examples above), for example:

(5)   Esopus gieng umb ze suchen
       Aesop   went for   to search
       "Aesop went to look for (it)."   (Steinhöwel, cited by Ebert 1978: 30)[5]

Other examples primarily involving constituency include the Nuclear Micronesian noun incorporation, discussed in section 4.2.3, and Georgian relative clause structure discussed in section 4.2.4. More complex examples of changes in constituency are discussed in chapters 7 and 10.

(iii) *Category labels*. The reanalysis of a verb in a serial verb construction as an adposition, together with the accompanying reanalysis of the dominating node as an adpositional phrase (PP), is an example of a change that primarily affects **category labels**. Lord (1973: 274) gives the example of the Twi verb *wɔ* "be at," which has been reanalyzed as a preposition *wɔ* "at," as well as other examples from African languages. Here the category label V is reanalyzed as Prep, and VP (or S) as PP. Constituency and word order remain unaffected, but grammatical relations are affected. (Several other similar examples are found in Heine and Reh 1982.)

A further example of category change comes from Li and Thompson's (1974a, 1974b) treatment of word order change in Chinese. According to their analysis, ancient Chinese had a word order pattern S *bǎ* O V O, where *bǎ* is the verb "take hold of." Because this was a serial verb construction, two verbs and objects were permitted in the pattern. In this pattern, *bǎ* was reanalyzed as an object marker and consequently the pattern was reanalyzed as S O V.[6] As a consequence of that reanalysis, the basic word order of the language and the rules that effect that order in individual sentences were radically altered; at the same time, the actual order of the pattern did not change at all. Put differently, the actual words continued to occur in the same order; what changed was the grammatical functions of those words.

(iv) *Grammatical relations*. In the loss of the inversion construction in English, it is surface **grammatical relations** that are primarily affected. In Old English a rule of inversion made initial subjects indirect objects, in examples such as the familiar *me thinks*, traditionally referred to in English studies as the impersonal construction. This rule, apparently always optional, began to apply less and less frequently. Due in part to the weakening and eventual loss of case marking on nouns, the effects of the rule, when it did apply, became less apparent, and the construction was reanalyzed; the surface object (underlying subject) was reanalyzed as surface (and underlying) subject (see section 4.4.3.2 and sources cited there). (Other examples that include reanalysis of grammatical relations are discussed in chapter 9.)

(v) *Cohesion*. By **cohesion** we mean the status of a linguistic sequence as a fully independent word, a clitic, an affix, or an unanalyzable part of a larger unit. In many changes, the four statuses form a continuum; an element that is at one time a fully independent word may become a clitic and then an affix, ending up as an unanalyzable part of another word, no longer having the status of morpheme. It is clear that independent words are manipulated by the syntax and that unanalyzable parts of words are not. Information regarding cohesion must therefore be available in underlying structure. Cohesion, in this sense, is also related to surface phenomena, including stress, and this issue is further discussed below. (Cohesion may be viewed as concerning boundary type: word boundary, morpheme boundary, no boundary.)

An example is found in changes in varieties of Nahua (a branch of Uto-Aztecan) where constructions with *nemi* "to live, to walk" have changed so that *nemi* has lost its status as an independent word. Comparative evidence from Nahua dialects and from related languages confirms that *nemi* was originally an ordinary verb meaning "to live, to walk (around)." In Tetelcingo Nahuatl, Michoacan Nahual, and North Puebla Nahuatl, a construction has developed in which *nemi* has lost its independent status, and has become a verb clitic meaning "go around doing" (e.g. Verb-*ti*-*nemi* [-*ti*- "CONNECTIVE," -*nemi* "AMBULATIVE"]), as illustrated in the North Puebla Nahuatl example (6):

(6)   čoka-ti-nemi
         cry-CONNECTIVE-AMBULATIVE
         "He/she goes about crying."
                    (Brockway 1979: 156; cf. also Sischo 1979: 355, and Tuggy 1979: 110;
                                                see also Langacker 1977b: 147)

Huasteca Nahuatl has developed further, reanalyzing the clitic *nemi* as a "habitual" marker and moving it into the preverb-root morphological position occupied by directional morphemes, as illustrated in (7):

(7)   ki-nen-palewiya
         her-HABITUAL-help
         "She helps her continually."   (Beller and Beller 1979: 279)

(-*nen*- ‹ *nemi*; *nen* is a regular allomorph of *nemi* in certain phonological environments, as seen in, for example, *nen*(-*ki*) "he/she lived/walked"). In these cases the verb *nemi* has lost its independent status, exhibiting a change in cohesion.[7]

In the appendix to this chapter we discuss another example of two changes in the status of a linguistic element from word to clitic and from clitic to affix, in the context of reanalysis. In section 4.2.1 we describe a transition from affix to a synchronically unanalyzable part of a larger morpheme. (Langacker [1977a] presents other examples which we define as cohesion, and much of the grammaticalization literature is concerned directly with this process.)

In the descriptions above, most of the examples we have selected for purposes of illustration primarily involve just one aspect of underlying structure. However, many instances of reanalysis involve more than one of these aspects of underlying structure at once.

4.2 Examples of reanalysis

The purposes of this section are (a) to provide some examples for further discussion of important issues related to reanalysis, and (b) to give an idea of the scope and limits of reanalysis. At the same time we illustrate the potential complexity of reanalysis in general; in even the simplest examples several abstract elements may be affected by a single reanalysis.[8] A longer example involving reanalysis and its interaction with extension is presented in the appendix to this chapter.

4.2.1 French

The development of Modern French yes/no questions provides two interesting examples of reanalysis. (Our discussion follows M. Harris 1978: 30–6; see also our section 7.2.3.1.) Old French used intonation together with inverted word order as a device for marking questions: Verb Subject . . . In question inversion, the entire verb inverted with the entire subject; thus in Old French we find:

(8)   est morte m'amie?
        is   dead my.friend
        "Is my friend dead?"   (*La Chastelaine de Vergi*; Foulet 1930: 233)

From the fifteenth or sixteenth century, a biclausal structure came to be used in yes/no questions. Development of this structure may have been influenced by the preference for a clefted structure for a content question, with a similar pattern (see M. Harris 1978: 32), for instance:

(9)   est-ce que mon amie est morte?
        is it   that my friend is dead
        "Is it [the case] that my friend is dead?" "Is my friend dead?"

The matrix clause continues the special question word order: Verb Subject . . .

The matrix clause in the preferred yes/no question pattern in (9) has been reanalyzed as a sentence-initial question particle. That it functions as a particle is shown by the fact that the former verb can no longer occur in the full range of tense/aspect forms available for "be," but occurs in the invariant form *est*. As a particle *est-ce que* is attached sentence-initially to a sentence which otherwise has the form of a simple declarative; for example, the order of constituents following *est-ce que* is the ordinary order of a simple declarative: Subject Verb . . ., as in (10):

(10)   Est-ce que l'homme voit la femme?
           QUESTION the.man sees the woman?
           "Does the man see the woman?"   (M. Harris 1978: 32)

The colloquial language has adopted an additional question particle, *ti*, whose origin and development provide another clear example of reanalysis. In the mid fifteenth century, French forms such as (11) contrasted with ones such as (12), in which the verb ends with a *t*.

(11)   aime il? "Does he love?"
(12)   dort-il? "Does he sleep?"
           est-il? "Is he?"
           aimerait-il? "Would he love?"

Note that both sets of forms have the special question word order, with the subject, *il* "he," following the verb. Final *l* was eroded in the pronunciation of colloquial speech, leaving the forms of (12) ending in [*ti*]. This *ti* came to be reanalyzed as a marker for questions involving third person masculine pronoun subjects, and then later was extended, gradually becoming a general interrogative particle, as in:

(13)   les filles sont ti   en train de dîner?
           the girls are QUESTION in way of to.dine
           "Are the girls eating dinner?"

(14)   tu vas ti?
           you go QUESTION
           "Are you going?"   (M. Harris 1978: 33; Bennett 1979: 858)

4.2.2   Udi

The next example comes from fossilized gender-class agreement in Udi, a language of the Lezgian group of the Daghestan (North East Caucasian) family. This example is more morphological than syntactic and is included in part to demonstrate the scope of the mechanism of reanalysis. In the proto-language verbs agreed with the subjects of intransitive verbs and with the direct objects of transitive verbs, that is with nominals in the absolutive case. Agreement was marked by means of prefixes on finite verbs, and markers indicated the gender-class of the nominal. For Proto-Lezgian, class markers of the singular are reconstructed with the forms *w (Class I, masculine), *r (Class II, feminine), *b (Class III, other living things), *d (Class IV, non-living) (Xajdakov 1980: 186ff.). The verb structure is reconstructed in part as (15).

(15)   CLASS MARKER + Vowel + VERB STEM

The vowel that occurs in (15) and in Daghestan languages that maintain reflexes of this system was not originally part of the verb. Jeiranišvili (1956) and Schulze (1982: 148) have shown that in Udi, as part of the process of its losing the old gender-class agreement system, a number of verb stems of the form (15), more specifically *b + Vowel + VERB STEM, were reanalyzed as a simple verb stem. That is, *b*- no longer marked the "other living-things" class, but was simply regarded as part of the verb root, i.e. $b+ak$ > bak. Examples include the verb stems $b+a+k$ "being, birth, possibility," $b+o+q$' "love, want," and $b+o+x$ "cook by boiling." It is likely that before reanalysis, the agreement classes had been reduced in number, perhaps to two as in Tabassaran, and then possibly to an opposition of only *b*- to a zero marker. This is part of a general tendency in Lezgian languages towards neutralization of gender-class oppositions in the inherited system (see Schulze-Fürhoff 1992).[9] In the course of this reanalysis, the surface manifestation did not change, but the morpheme boundary was lost.

4.2.3   Nuclear Micronesian

Noun incorporation in Nuclear Micronesian provides another example. M. Hale (1991) shows that in Proto-Nuclear Micronesian, as in many Western Austronesian languages today, definite direct objects are obligatory topics, while indefinite direct objects cannot be topics. Topicalized objects were moved outside the VP to clause-final position; the three clause types may be schematized as (16) (after Hale 1991: 29–30):

(16)   Proto-Nuclear Micronesian
    (a)   intransitive clause [V (Adv)]$_{VP}$
           transitive clause
    (b)   indefinite object [V N (Adv)]$_{VP}$
    (c)   definite object [V + Pro$_i$ (Adv)]$_{VP}$ [NP$_i$]$_{TOPIC}$

Verb forms were eroded phonologically from the right, reducing the root in the intransitive and in the transitive with indefinite object; the shape of the transitive with definite object, however, was protected by the pronominal copy, which however was itself eventually eroded to nothing. This erosion of verb forms is quite likely what conditioned the subsequent reanalysis. The indefinite object structure schematized in (16) was reanalyzed in at least some Nuclear Micronesian languages as noun incorporation, while the definite object construction continued to be treated as involving an independent noun. Adverbs are included in the schema in order to show how the presence of intervening material could help native speakers analyze these clause types in this way. Examples (17) illustrate the two types in Ponapean, where incorporation is obligatory for bare noun objects with non-specific reference (Hale 1991: 3).

(17)   (a)   I kang-ehr wini-o
              I eat$_{tr}$-DIR medicine-that
              "I have taken that medicine."

        (b)   I keng-winih-er
              I eat$_{inc}$-medicine-DIR
              "I have medicine-taken."

In the incorporated example, (17b), the directional affix attaches to the V + N complex, while in the unincorporated example, (17a), it attaches to the verb.

4.2.4   Georgian

A change in Georgian in historical times provides the last example for this section. In Old Georgian, which dates from the fifth century AD, one type of relative clause followed its head and was formed with a clause-initial relative pronoun, *romel-* "which," *vin* "who," etc., which agreed in number with the head noun. Canonically the case of the relative pronoun was determined by its grammatical relation within the relative clause, and the case of the head was determined by its grammatical relations within the matrix clause. In Georgian case assignment is also based on the class and series of the verb form, and here, too, it was the verb form of the relative clause that was relevant for determining the case of the relative pronoun, and the verb form of the matrix clause that was relevant for determining the case of the head, in canonical examples. However, Old Georgian also has several examples of regressive "case attraction," a construction in which the head noun reflects the case of the relative pronoun, as in (18). (The functions of cases in Georgian cannot be accurately characterized with the names used in other languages; the traditional case names are used here but should be interpreted as merely arbitrary.)

(18)   q'ovel-i,   romel-i   xitxovs,   miiγis
        all-NOM   which-NOM   s/he.ask.it s/he.receive.it
        "All who ask will receive."   (Haemet'i Mt. 7: 8; cited by Dondua 1967: 24)

The canonical form of (18), without case attraction, would be instead (19), since the verb *miiγis* requires Nar(rative) case for its subject.

(19)   q'ovel-man, romel-i   xitxovs,   miiγis
        all-NAR   which-NOM   s/he.ask.it s/he.receive.it
                                (Haemet'i Mt. 7: 8; cited by Dondua 1967: 25)

Under regressive case attraction, the case of the head noun was determined by that of the relative pronoun, rather than by its own grammatical relations within the matrix clause. In some examples the relative clause is followed by a resumptive pronoun, fulfilling the same grammatical role as the head noun and marked in the case determined by the matrix clause; this is illustrated by (20):

(20) mama-y   igi   šen-i,   romel-i   xedavs   daparul-sa,
      father-NOM the.NOM   your-NOM   which-NOM   s/he.see.it secret-DAT

      mogagos   **man**   šen   cxadad
      he.reward.you **he.NAR** you   openly

      "Your father, who sees in secret, will reward you openly."
                                    (Mt. 6: 6 Ad.; cited by Dondua 1967: 26)

Without case attraction, the form of (20) would be as in (21), since the verb *mogagos* governs the narrative case for its subject, "your father."

(21) mama-man man   šen-man,   romel-i   xedavs   daparul-sa
      father-NAR the.NAR your-NAR   which-NOM   s/he.see   secret-DAT

In (20) the resumptive pronoun, *man* "he," is in the narrative case, as though to compensate for the fact that the real subject *mama-y igi šen-i* "your father," with which the resumptive pronoun is coreferential, is not in the "correct" case, but in the case governed by case attraction, the nominative case of the relative pronoun *romeli* "which."

The *-i* form of the nominative case is an innovation, and the older zero form also occurred in Old Georgian manuscripts. Old Georgian relatives of the type in (20) thus had the structure in (22), (HN is the head noun, RelPro the relative [declinable] pronoun, RC the relative clause, and RP the resumptive pronoun); here both the head and the relative pronoun optionally have the older zero form:

(22) mama(-i)   [romel(-i)   xedavs   daparulsa]$_{RC}$ mogagos   man
      father-NOM which-NOM   he.see.it secret.DAT   he.reward.you   he.NAR

      HN   RelPro   RP

Of course, there were also examples in which the head noun and the relative pronoun happened to have the same case independently of one another. After reanalysis we find the structure in (23), where N is the noun relativized (no longer the head), and RelPrt is an invariant relative particle (no longer a declinable pronoun):

(23) [mama(-i) romel(-i) xedavs daparulsa]$_{RC}$ man mogagos
      N   RelPrt   RP

The *-i* form of the nominative case is shown on the relativized noun in (23), since the zero form was lost about the same time; however, both the *-i* form and the zero form could appear in both structures, (22) and (23). In (23) the relative has become a headless relative of the type called the non-reduction strategy (or head-internal type). Once it was reanalyzed as a head-internal relative clause, it was no longer necessary for the relativized noun to be first in the clause. The head-internal type is still found in Modern Georgian, in examples such as (24):

(24)   minda, betania-ši rom k'olmeurnoba-a,   is   vnaxo
        I.want.it Betania-in that collective.farm-it.is it.NOM I.see.it
        "I want to see the collective farm that is in Betania."

(Cited in Vogt 1971: 51)

In an additional later change, the invariant relative particle, *romel-*, underwent reduction to *rome* (attested), before becoming *rom*, and in many dialects, *ro*. The old relative clause structure formed with relative pronouns, including *romeli* "which," continues to exist beside the newer relative clause type.

The reanalysis of the pattern in (22) as that in (23), like the reanalyses in (1)/(2) and (3)/(4) above, includes **rebracketing**.[10]

4.3   Preludes to reanalysis

4.3.1   Is ambiguity a prerequisite?

Timberlake (1977), in his insightful discussion of reanalysis, has suggested that ambiguity is necessary for reanalysis to take place. What, then, *is* ambiguity? On one common understanding of ambiguity, a sentence is ambiguous if it has two meanings. Consider again the noun incorporation example from Nuclear Micronesian, discussed in section 4.2.3. It is not clear that structures such as (16b), before they were reanalyzed, had two meanings. Recall that indefinite objects could not be topics, and that non-topicalized objects could only appear in the position shown in (16b). There seems to be no evidence of more than one meaning here.

Another understanding of (structural) ambiguity involves necessarily that each of the possible readings is a structure that is *otherwise available in the language*. Favorite linguistic examples, such as (25), have two possible structures, one corresponding to the meaning "relatives who visit . . ." and the other to "to visit relatives . . ."

(25)   Visiting relatives can be dangerous

Crucially, each of these readings (different underlying structures) is found in unambiguous contexts, such as in (26) and (27), respectively; neither of the readings/structures of (25) is found exclusively in ambiguous examples.

(26)   singing children . . .
(27)   doing homework . . .

If the structure of (26) or of (27) did not exist in English, (25) would not be ambiguous. Yet it is known that reanalysis can introduce *a brand-new construc-*

tion, one that has not previously been available in the language. Consider again the change in relative clause structure in Georgian, described in section 4.2.4. The attested sentence pattern (20) had the structure (22) in Old Georgian. That it had a second potential structure, (23), is shown by the fact that it was indeed reanalyzed as (23). Nevertheless, no relative clause like (23) existed in the language before; it was the reanalysis that introduced it. If this is ambiguity, it is an ambiguity of a sort slightly different from the usual understanding of it.

While it is essential that two analyses be possible, it is important to stress that *opacity* it not a prerequisite to reanalysis.[11] For example, through reanalysis, postpositions have developed from nominals which bear certain case endings in Finnish; these, however, need not involve opacity. In Finnish, for instance, *lapse-n rinna-lla* has two possible readings, the original, "on the child's chest," and the innovative postpositional reading, "beside the child":

(28)   lapse-n   rinna-lla
        child-GEN chest-On
        "on the child's chest"

(29)   lapse-n   rinnalla
        child-GEN POSTPOSITION
        "next to the child"

There is absolutely nothing opaque about (28), the original and literal reading, which would require the inception of (29). The lack of opacity can be clearly seen in the fact that (28) is still perfectly valid, alongside innovative (29). That is, *-lla* continues to mean "on" in other environments and *rinna-* (underlying *rinta*) continues to mean "chest" in other environments. A speaker has all the information needed to make the analysis in (28), yet the construction was nevertheless also analyzed as (29).

Babby (1987) has shown that Old Russian NPs were reanalyzed in spite of the fact that the case marking clearly revealed their structure. In Old Russian, quantifiers were the heads of NPs and bore the case marking determined by the syntax of the clause in which they occurred; quantified nouns were dependents and were marked with the genitive. Thus in Old Russian an NP such as *pjat'* (NOM) *butylok* (GEN.PL) "five bottles" had the same structure as an NP like *korzina* (NOM) *jablok* (GEN.PL) "a basket of apples." In spite of the clarity of the case marking of this structure and in spite of the parallel with the pattern *korzina jablok*, the structure of NPs containing quantifiers was reanalyzed, such that in Modern Russian the quantified noun is the head, according to a number of criteria, including case marking and agreement (see Babby 1987 for details).[12] Thus reanalysis does not depend upon opacity or upon a lack of evidence supporting the old analysis.[13]

While not necessary for reanalysis to take place, opacity (in the form of ambiguity) can trigger grammatical changes. This is the main focus of some work on syntactic change (e.g. Lightfoot 1979a) and is discussed further in section 4.4 (see also chapter 2).

In order for reanalysis to occur, it is not essential that every token of the structure in question be open to multiple analysis: for example, it is known that in Old Georgian the examples with case attraction, which provided the basis for reanalysis, were in the minority; the canonical pattern with the case of the head noun determined by the syntax of its own clause, as in (19), was more common. As example (11) shows, in the middle of the fifteenth century, not all third person masculine questions in French used [t]; yet [t] of verbs was reanalyzed as part of a question marker for questions with third person masculine subjects (later to become the general question marker). Thus reanalysis, innovation of structure, can take place even while examples that unambiguously show the old structure are clearly available. We refer to the patterns which have the potential for multiple structural analyses, and which thus provide the input to reanalysis as the **basis of reanalysis**. For example, the pattern in (12) was the basis of the French reanalysis of *ti*, the pattern in (20) was the basis of the Georgian reanalysis, and the pattern in (16b) was the basis of reanalysis in Nuclear Micronesian. (See also Campbell 1986, 1988.)

To summarize, the conditions necessary for reanalysis to take place are that a subset of the tokens of a particular constructional type must be open to the possibility of multiple structural analyses, where one potential analysis is the old one (applicable to all tokens) and the other potential analysis is the new one (applicable to a subset). We understand that the new potential analysis may be entirely new to the language or only new to this context or environment.

4.3.2   The role of the productive grammar: exploratory expressions

In every language certain phenomena develop which in some cases lead up to change. It is only in retrospect that these are recognized as preludes to change, since in many instances no change occurs and the phenomena in question simply disappear. It must be emphasized that exploratory expressions are not in and of themselves instances of change, but rather are produced by the productive grammar; their importance here is that they sometimes lead to reanalysis. Exploratory expressions were introduced in chapter 3 and their overall role was discussed there; in this section it is our intention to focus on how they develop and how they interact with reanalysis.

By **exploratory expressions** we mean expressions which are introduced through the ordinary operation of the grammar and which "catch on" and become fixed expressions and eventually are grammaticalized. Such expressions may originally be introduced for emphasis, for reinforcement, for clarity, for exploratory reasons, or they may result from production errors or after-thoughts. It appears that most initial exploratory expressions are made by applying the rules of grammar in a regular way, but it may be that some perhaps also involve ignoring (breaking) existing rules of grammar. The vast majority of such expressions are never repeated, but a few will come to be used frequently, will gain unmarked status, and will be grammaticalized. It is only when the exploratory expression has been reanalyzed as an obligatory part of the grammar that we may speak of a grammatical change having occurred.

A simple example of such an expression comes from the development of the French negative expression *ne . . . pas*, introduced in chapter 3. In Old French, negation was expressed by *ne* with a verbal expression (or by *non* when not accompanied by a verbal expression). Exploratory expressions were introduced to emphasize or reinforce the negative content of the unstressed particle. These reinforcements were originally nouns such as *pas* "step," *point* "point,"[14] and their initial introduction into sentence structure did not involve any change, just as the reinforcer *bit* may be used in English expressions such as *I don't care a bit* or *I didn't sleep a bit*. In French the change occurred, not when the reinforcers were introduced by the productive grammar, but when they were reanalyzed as a necessary part of the negation itself. In particular, *ne . . . pas* was reanalyzed as the neutral, or unmarked, negativizer.[15]

In Old English, verbs of ordering and wishing occurred with complements expressed in the subjunctive, as in (30):

(30)   Ic   ðe   lange bæd   þæt ðu   þone   wæl-gæst
        I.NOM you.ACC long ask.PRET that you.NOM that.ACC body-ghost

        wihte ne   grette. . .
        at.all NEG approach.SUBJ

        "I long asked you that you not approach that spirit at all . . ."
                (*Beowulf* 1994b–1995, cited by Visser 1963–73, II: section 869)

The verb *shal* began to be added in the complement as an exploratory expression, apparently to strengthen the sense of obligation of the predicate of the subordinate clause.

(31)   he   bisohte   þat heo   him   solde   helpen
         he.NOM beseech that they.NOM him.DAT should.SUBJ help
         "He begged that they should help him."
                           (Layamon 6595, cited by Visser 1963–73, III, part 1: section 1546)

In the complement *shal* was put in the subjunctive form, *solde/shulde* "should," according to the existing rules, and its own complement was in stem form, as in (32):

(32)   shulde "should" + VERB STEM

This pattern could be produced by the preexisting rules, since *shulde* is ultimately the subjunctive of *shal*, and was therefore in the form preferred with the matrix verb of ordering or wishing. Thus, in Middle English the MODAL + VERB STEM pattern itself was just one realization of the VP, produced by regular rules of the grammar. The exploratory expression with *should* became a popular way of strengthening the subjunctive mood with verbs of ordering and wishing; when the *should* lost its force through frequent use, (32) became a fixed expression in this linguistic context.

(33)   prescribing . . . that he **should lie** in bed all day
                           (Virginia Woolf, *Orlando*, cited by Visser section 1546)

Exploratory expressions, then, are expressions which can optionally be produced by the productive rules of a grammar as it exists at a given time. Such expressions may at a later time be reanalyzed to become part of the formal grammar. Thus, exploratory expressions do not require a change in the grammar for their initial appearance, but they sometimes lead to one.

It is convenient to be able to refer to different stages of the process of introduction of exploratory expressions and their possible reanalysis, although there are no breaks in the grammar to mark these stages. We will refer to the initial stage as **introductory**; at this point the expression has only been used a few times. Among these, a few will "catch on"; at this point they may be widely used, yet the full impact of the novelty of the construction may be felt. We refer to these as **popular** expressions. In the early months of 1992, the innovative negation with postsentential *Not!*, as in, for example, *He's a good student – Not!* (meaning roughly, "He's not at all a good student"), was at this stage in the United States. A few introductory exploratory expressions become **fixed**, regular manners of expressing an idea. At this point these have become unmarked; they no longer have their full impact. It must be emphasized that these three "stages" are nothing more than a convenient way to refer to the beginning, middle, and end of a continuum; in this sense, these three "stages" are a descriptive fiction.

Let us clarify the relation between exploratory expressions, the mechanisms of reanalysis, and change. The *introduction* of an exploratory expression does not, in and of itself, involve change in the grammar because, by definition, these are expressions that can be produced by the existing grammar. The *fixing* of an expression is produced by the mechanism of reanalysis. Thus exploratory expressions are not a mechanism of change, but are sometimes the *basis for* reanalysis. Here we have given some simple examples of changes involving exploratory expressions; in chapter 10 we consider some more complex examples.

Because those who handle and control language are human beings, in language change sociological, biological, and psychological factors play a central role. Exploratory expressions may be introduced because they provide novelty, because they are fun, because they link the speaker with a social group with which he or she wishes to be associated, etc. Sometimes such innovations take hold for social reasons, as Labov (1981, 1982) has shown for phonological change (see also Coseriu 1978 [1957]; H. Andersen 1980, 1989). Functional efficiency or the needs of discourse may be a driving force in the adoptions of other changes, as many are prone to claim (see Langacker 1977a; Givón 1984, 1990a). A third circumstance, similar to the second, that may favor an exploratory expression is areal influence. Detailed research has shown that often an areal phenomenon originates in the various languages of the area in completely different ways (Steever 1981; Joseph 1983). Some areal phenomena apparently develop through the fixing of exploratory expressions (for an example, see Harris 1985: 289–91).

4.3.3   The role of change in other parts of the grammar

A reanalysis may be preceded by (and in some cases even triggered by) a change in the surface form: for example, in French, the loss of word-final [l] preceded and may have been a facilitating factor in the reanalysis that produced the question marker, *ti* (see section 4.2.1). In the Nuclear Micronesian example it appears that phonological erosion of the verb forms preceded reanalysis, since before reanalysis the material that was eventually lost would have been word-final, but not after reanalysis. Nevertheless it is not possible to determine whether reanalysis followed this erosion immediately, in which case they would be in a real sense part of the same change, or whether there was a significant intervening period. Even in an attested change it may not be possible to determine the precise order of events, in part because the change in the dialect represented in one manuscript does not necessarily occur at the same time as change in a dialect represented in a different manuscript.

Another example comes from the change in the Cakchiquel aspect system, whereby the adverbial particle *tan* "now" + the aspect markers were reanalyzed as tense morphemes. Modern Cakchiquel has verb tenses, although its relatives in the Quichean subgroup (and most Mayan languages) lack tense markers, having for the most part only aspectual systems. In fact Old Cakchiquel also had only aspect markers, and the change to tenses is attested in the abundant colonial grammars and other sources (see for example, Anonymous 1720 [1692]). Unanimously these present Old Cakchiquel with the aspect system:

       ‹x-› (/š-/) "completive aspect (perfect)";
       ‹t-› (/t-/) "transitive incompletive aspect";
       ‹c-›/‹qu-› (/k-/) "intransitive incompletive aspect."

A "present" sense could be indicated in the incompletive aspects by the particle *tan* "now," for example, *tan t-in-ban* [now INCOMP.ASP-1ERG-do] "Now I am doing it," *tan ti-v-oqueçeh* [now INCOMP.ASP-1ERG-believe] "Now I believe it." This pattern, introduced as an exploratory expression, was reanalyzed as a fixed expression of present tense. In time this combination of particle and incompletive aspect markers underwent phonological and semantic changes:

(34)   *tan* + *t*-Verb > *tan* + *d*-Verb > *nd*-Verb (> *n*-Verb in some dialects);
        tan + *k*-Verb > *tan* + *g*-Verb > *ng*-Verb (> *(n)y*-Verb in some dialects).

That is, the *t*- and *k*- aspect markers (for transitive and intransitive verbs, respectively) were voiced after the final -*n* of the *tan* particle, which itself was cliticized to the verb, then phonologically reduced, and ultimately grammaticized as present-tense markers, *nd*- or *n*- (with transitives) and *ng*-, *ny*-, or *y* (with intransitives). The changes in (34) are phonological and semantic changes, actualization of the reanalysis of *tan* + aspect. Two further reanalyses, which resulted in the modern tense system, were also part of actualization (see below): the old completive aspect marker, *š*-, was reinterpreted as "past," since actions that are completed typically occur in the past; the former incompletive *k*- with no preceding particle came to be reinterpreted as "remote past" (from "[was] on-going action" to "remote past action," i.e "was going on a long time ago"). All of these stages are attested in Cakchiquel documents since the mid 1500s (for details, see Campbell 1977: 126, 1990b).

In the literature there are many examples of phonological changes which make syntactic reanalyses possible, perhaps even triggering them in certain instances.[16] Among these are the changes in case endings in Lardil (discussed in Klokeid 1978), in Finnish (discussed in Anttila 1972; Breckenridge and Hakulinen 1976; Timberlake 1977; Campbell 1986; 1989, 1990a), in Artašen (discussed in Harris 1985: 385–9, 422–3).[17] Morphological changes, too, can create the conditions which lead to reanalysis; an example of this is the reduction described above in the gender-class system of Udi, prior to reanalysis of the class marker *b-*. Several other similar examples are discussed in Langacker (1977a), and Heine and Reh (1984).

4.4   Reanalysis and actualization

Timberlake (1977: 141) has shown the importance and utility of distinguishing reanalysis from actualization. He defines reanalysis as "the formulation of a novel set of underlying relationships and rules" and actualization as "the gradual mapping out of the consequences of the reanalysis." As Timberlake shows, if it is assumed that reanalysis applies only *after* a number of changes in the surface structure, those surface changes are themselves unmotivated. On the other hand, if reanalysis is seen as *preceding* those surface changes, the latter are explained; they bring the surface into line with the innovative underlying structure. We recognize the correctness of this argument and the importance of the distinction between reanalysis and actualization, and we build upon this concept below.

Note that taking the approach that reanalysis is followed by actualization raises the question of what motivates the reanalysis. This question is answered in part in section 4.3 above, where a number of different causes of reanalysis are discussed (see also chapter 11).

4.4.1   Actualization

Old Finnish had a rule of subject-to-object raising (see Breckenridge and Hakulinen 1976; Timberlake 1977) which treated underlying subjects of certain participial clauses as objects of the matrix verb. As objects, they bore the marking appropriate for objects – either the accusative, partitive, or nominative case under specific well-defined circumstances. An example with the accusative object is:

(35)   seurakunna-n   hen lupasi   pysyueise-n ole-ua-n[18]
        congregation-ACC he   promised lasting-ACC be-PART-ACC
        "He promised the congregation would be long-lasting."

However, the original accusative singular *-m* and the genitive singular *-n* fell together through phonological change (final *-m* > *-n*). This syncretism permitted and perhaps led to the reanalysis of the object of the matrix verb as the genitively marked surface subject of the participle through the reinterpretation of the accusative singular *-n* for object marking as a genitive singular *-n* marking the subject of the participle. Only singular nouns provided the basis for the reanalysis, since in pronouns and plural nouns the accusative and genitive remain distinct. Examples (36)–(37) contrast Old Finnish examples (the (a) forms; the (a') forms show the Old Finnish examples in Modern Finnish orthography) having object case markings (accusatives or partitives), with their present-day counterparts (the (b) forms), which have genitive subject markings; this demonstrates that a change took place:

(36)   (a)   ia   hen neki heijet   hädese   souta-ua-n. (1642)

        (a') ja   hän näki hei(d)ä-t hädä-ssä souta-va-n
              and he   saw they-ACC danger.in row-PART-ACC

        (b)   Ja   hän näki heidä-n   hädä-ssä souta-van
              and he   saw they-GEN danger-in row-ing
              "And he saw them rowing in danger"

Notice in (36) that the pronoun *heidä-t* (they-ACC) in the accusative is no longer permitted in this construction in Modern Finnish.

(37)   (a)   ihmedhen . . . io-ij-ta   eij-kengen kuullut
        (a') ihmei-den . . . jo-i-ta   ei-kenkään kuullut
              wonders   which-PL-PARTITIVE no-one   heard

              tule-va-ta
              tule-va-ta
              come-PARTICIPLE-PARTITIVE

        (b)   ihmeiden . . . joi-den   kukaan ei kuullut tule-van
              wonders   which-GEN.PL no.one no heard come-PARTICIPLE
              "wonders which no one heard were coming"

In Modern Finnish the partitive *joita* is no longer grammatical in the construction in (37) (Breckenridge and Hakulinen 1976: 51).

(38)   (a)   huomasin molemma-t   miehe-t   palan-neen
              noticed.I both-PL.ACC man-PL.ACC return-PAST.PARTICIPLE

        (b)   huomasin molemp-i-en mies-ten   palan-neen
              noticed.I both-PL.GEN man-PL.GEN return-PAST.PARTICIPLE
              "I noticed that both men returned/had returned."
              (See Hakulinen 1968: 463–8)

As analyzed by Timberlake, actualization of this reanalysis consisted of the following further changes:

> (i) all nominals – not just singular nouns – have come to be expressed in the genitive; (ii) the participle no longer agrees like an adjective in case and number with its underlying subject, but has adopted an invariant [-n] form; (iii) instead, the participle has innovated a limited kind of subject–verb agreement, so that when the matrix subject and the subject of the participle are

identical, the participle is inflected with a possessive affix agreeing in person
and number with its subject.   (Timberlake 1977: 148)

(Change (iii) is considered further below.)

The view that reanalysis is distinct from and must precede actualization is
supported by two sorts of additional evidence. First, in some changes it is
clear that a structure must be reanalyzed in its existing context before it could
be extended to a new context. A particularly clear example is Tibeto-Burman
ma "not" which initially occurred in two types of disjunctive yes/no question,
the A-not-A structural type is illustrated from Cantonese in (39):[19]

(39)   nee zek-mu-zek   iň ah?
        you smoke-not-smoke *iň ah*
        "Do you smoke?"

The second disjunctive structure was a sentence-final negative tag; see
Thurgood (1983: 257–8 and 1984: 341–2) for details. In many Tibeto-Burman
languages the negative *ma* in structures of both types was reanalyzed as a
marker of yes/no questions and functions now in that capacity. Some languages made the additional change of extending the yes/no question marker
to content questions. Two facts show that the reanalysis of negative *ma* as a
yes/no question marker must have occurred before the extension of this marker to marking content questions as well. First, only a proper subset of the languages that made the reanalysis also made the extension. Secondly, *ma*
could not logically have been extended to content questions in its original
function of negative; it must first have been associated with questions. Both
facts show that the reanalysis and extension occurred at least partially independently and in this order.[20]

A further sort of evidence for making a distinction between reanalysis and
actualization is found in the abundant examples of reanalyses that have not
(yet) been followed by the sorts of actualization that the grammar of the particular language would lead us to expect. A particularly clear example of this
comes from Gã. The comitative verb "be with," used in a serial verb construction, was reanalyzed as "and," a simple NP coordinating conjunction; today it
has the form *kὲ* in Gã, as illustrated in (40):

(40)   kòfí kὲ ámà tsὲ   dzí ówúlà ágó
        Kofi and Ama father is Mr. Ago
        "Mr. Ago is the father of (both) Kofi and Ama."   (Lord 1973: 288)

Because *kὲ* has been reanalyzed as "and,"[21] we would expect certain kinds of
behavior of the NPs conjoined by *kὲ*, but in fact we find that several of the
rules of the grammar have not (yet) been extended to them. First, since Gã
distinguishes subject pronouns from object pronouns, we would expect

subject pronouns when the NP *kὲ* NP complex functions as subject, and object pronouns when that complex functions as object. However, regardless of the function of this complex in the sentence, the NP that precedes *kὲ* must be a subject pronoun and that which follows it must be an object pronoun. For example, in (41), *mì* "I" is the subject form, and *lὲ* "him" is the object form, even though the conjoined phrase, *mì kὲ lὲ* "I and him" is the subject:

(41)   mì kὲ   lὲ   tá
        I   and him sit.sg
        "He and I sit."   (Lord 1973: 288)

Second, since Gã has number agreement with subjects, when the NP *kὲ* NP complex is subject we would expect plural agreement. But in fact this rule has not been extended to NPs conjoined with *kὲ*, and they take the singular form instead, as in (41). In (41) the subject, even though it is semantically plural, takes the singular form, *tá*, rather than the plural, *ìrà*. For additional phenomena which do not yet treat NP *kὲ* NP as a coordinate phrase see Lord (1973: 286–9). The change in meaning from "be with" to "and" (see example (40) above) provides evidence that the Gã construction has been reanalyzed; the fact that four rules of the grammar have not been extended to treat these coordinate NPs in the way expected of this grammar shows that actualization has not been completed.[22]

These considerations provide evidence for treating reanalysis as distinct from actualization.[23]

4.4.2   Is extension actualization?

In this subsection we further characterize the process of actualization, asking whether it is the same thing as extension.

Examining a number of instances of actualization of reanalysis, we have found that each example of change under actualization was itself either an extension or an additional reanalysis. In the Finnish example, the changes under actualization are extensions. For example, (i) the rule which after reanalysis assigned the genitive case to singular nouns was extended to apply to all nominals; the resulting rule could be stated as (42):

(42)   Subjects of participles are marked with the genitive case.

Similarly, the rule which assigned possessive suffixes was extended to the participial construction (Timberlake's (iii)). To understand this change, we need some background. The genitive case on nouns signals possession (as well as subject of participle, in the example just seen); pronominal possession is signaled by possessive suffixes on the possessed nominal (rather than by

the genitive suffix on the possessor, as is the case with nominal possessors).
Compare, for example, (43) and (44):

(43)   Ritva-n   koira
       Ritva-GEN dog
       "Ritva's dog"

(44)   koira-ni
       dog-1ST.PERS.POSS
       "my dog"

(One can say *minu-n koira-ni* [my-GEN dog-my] "my dog," but the genitive
minu-n is totally optional.) Given the functional equivalent of genitive for full
nominals with possessive suffixes for pronominal possessors, the change was
extended, and the noun–modifier agreement pattern was replaced in the
case of pronominal subjects of the participle with a rule which marks the participle with a possessive suffix according to the person and number of its
pronominal subject. This suffix is shown after actualization in (45):

(45)   usko-n   näke-vä-ni   poja-n
       believe-I see-PARTICIPLE-1.PERS.POSS boy-ACC
       "I think that I see the boy."

The extension involved generalizing to the subject of the participle the
pattern with possessive pronominal suffixes, as in (45).[24]

   Phonological change may also be part of actualization. An example is
found in the Georgian change described in section 4.2.4. The Old Georgian
relative pronoun *romel(-i)* was reanalyzed as a relative particle as part of a reanalysis of the whole structure of the relative clause; as part of the actualization, *romel(-i)* was reduced to *rome*, then *rom*, and is currently undergoing
further reduction to *ro*.

   In other examples of reanalysis we have examined, actualization includes
both extension and reanalysis in morphology, syntax, or lexical items.[25] Just
as actualization may involve changes other than extension, extension may
occur other than as a response to reanalysis (see note 3 in chapter 6 for examples of contact-induced extension). Thus, while actualization often consists of
extensions, the two are not coextensive.

4.4.3   Multiple analyses during actualization
During the period of actualization, a single input structure continues to have
multiple analyses in the grammar of the individual speaker. For descriptive
purposes it is convenient to recognize three stages to reanalyses:

> *Stage A, Input*: The input structure has all of the superficial characteristics of
> the input analysis.

> *Stage B, Actualization*: The structure is subject to multiple analysis; it gradually acquires the characteristics of an innovative analysis, distinct from that of Stage A.
>
> *Stage C, Completion*: The innovative structure has all of the superficial characteristics of the innovative analysis.

Reanalysis is the transition from Stage A to Stage B. Stage B is the period of actualization, and the speaker makes both (or many) analyses, which may be related to each other in different ways at different times. Stage B typically consists of multiple changes, reflecting the characteristics of the particular construction in the particular language. It may be noted that the gradualness of change is due in part to the duration of actualization in some changes. Some reanalyses may not reach Stage C; they are never completed, in the sense that all the characteristics of the innovative analysis may not be acquired.

It has often been assumed, especially in the description of change in individual languages, that in reanalysis the period of multiple analyses is only transient, and that the innovative analysis rapidly *replaces* the earlier analysis. There are at least three kinds of evidence that multiple analyses continue to be available in individual grammars for some time, though that time of course is different for different changes. Evidence comes from the possibility of multiple reflexes, from variation and conflicting data, and from the possibility of reversibility of change.

4.4.3.1   Multiple reflexes

In chapter 7 it is shown that in English the *have* perfect, as in (47), developed through reanalysis out of possessive *have*, the construction in (46) (see Traugott 1972: 94); that is, in stage A, there existed only structures comparable to (46), with the possessive meaning.

(46)   Sarah has the finished report
(47)   Sarah has finished the report

It would be perfectly possible in such a change for the innovative structure, (47), to have replaced the input structure, (46); but in fact the two coexist. In this example a single input, illustrated by (46), came to have two reflexes, (46) and (47).[26] Another example is that presented above, (28)–(29), of the coexistence in Finnish of a postposition alongside of its original nominal source.

Another example of multiple reflexes from a single input comes from the change in Georgian described in section 4.2.4. The older structure, (22) with a postnominal relative pronoun, was reanalyzed as (23), a head-internal relative clause, and the two structures continue to coexist today. During the period of actualization, the reduction of *romel(i)* to *rome*, then *rom* and *ro*, distinguished the surface structure of the two types.

The existence of two (or more) reflexes from a single input, as in these examples, shows that after reanalysis (that is, in stage B), more than one analysis is available and must continue to be if more than one reflex is to survive. In instances of this type, after the additional changes of actualization one analysis comes to be associated uniquely with one set of surface characteristics, while another analysis is associated with another set.

Chapter 7 gives a number of additional examples involving biclausal structures coexisting with their reanalyzed counterparts, and multiple reflexes seem to be very common.[27] Nevertheless, in many reanalyses there is a single reflex. For example, as discussed in section 4.2.3 above, the reanalysis of Nuclear Micronesian transitive verbs with indefinite objects as noun incorporation has, in some languages, a single output – the noun incorporation construction. Because this change is not attested, we cannot be sure that there were not originally two reflexes, the second lost during stage B or even in stage C. The study of a number of attested changes suggests that in all reanalyses there are multiple analyses available during at least a part of the actualization. As an example, in chapter 7 it is argued that the modal verbs of Old English were not, in fact, at first replaced by modal auxiliaries as is often assumed, but rather that the two coexisted for a time during the actualization of the reanalysis of the biclausal structure as monoclausal. (See also the Finnish example cited above.) The question of whether all reanalyses proceed in this way requires additional research.

4.4.3.2 Conflicting data: variation

The recognition that a speaker uses multiple analyses during the period of actualization provides a natural account of the apparently contradictory data that are found in real changes. Change in the affective so-called impersonal verbs[28] (henceforth inversion verbs) of English provide an example of such data. One of the constructions of these verbs characteristic of the Old English period is illustrated in (48).

(48)   þam   wife   þa   word   wel licodon
       the.DAT woman.DAT those.NOM words.NOM well liked.PL
       "The woman liked those words well."   (*Beowulf* 639)
       Pattern: dative experiencer, nominative theme

It is characteristic of this construction that (i) the experiencer was in the dative case, (ii) the theme was in the nominative, and (iii) the verb agreed with the theme, or if none were present, was in the third person singular. (The same verbs occur in other constructions.) In Middle English this is replaced by a construction in which (i) the experiencer is in the nominative case, (ii) the theme is in the object case, and (iii) the verb agrees with the experiencer, as in (49); case and agreement are, of course, retained only to a very limited extent:

(49)   þe lewede men   likede him   wel
         the ignorant men.NOM liked him.OBJ well
         "The ignorant men liked him well."
                              (*Piers Plowman*, A Prol. 69, cited by van der Gaaf 1904: 68)
         Pattern: nominative experiencer, objective case theme

Some of the inversion verbs also occur in other, lexically governed patterns; these are discussed in some detail in section 5.3.3.2. Our analysis follows van der Gaaf (1904) in many ways. We have elsewhere proposed a specific analysis of inversion in Old English and of the transition in Middle English.[29] Not all of our analysis of inversion in Old English is relevant to the discussion here, and our view of the transition has changed as a result of the present more comprehensive study of cross-language syntactic change. What is important here, and what we argue for in this section, is that during actualization, two analyses coexisted. On one analysis, referred to here as analysis I, the inversion analysis, the experiencer was object and the theme was subject. On analysis II, the experiencer was subject, and the theme direct object. The inversion construction, illustrated by (48), is an ancient construction, which, for some verbs, coexisted with (49) in Old English and was later replaced by it, for most verbs.[30] Loss of pattern (48) occurred at different times for different verbs, but for most it was rare by the sixteenth century in the work of most authors (van der Gaaf 1904, Visser 1963–73, I: 35); some dialects retain the inversion pattern for some verbs (van der Gaaf 1904; see also section 4.4.3.3). We assume that the pattern was reanalyzed, with the experiencer as (surface) subject and the theme as (surface) object.[31] During actualization the general (structural) patterns of the language were extended to the reanalyzed NPs, including extension of nominative to the experiencer as reanalyzed subject, extension of objective case (dative and accusative having fallen together) to the theme as reanalyzed object, and extension of the privilege of conditioning agreement to the experiencer as reanalyzed subject. Some details of this actualization are discussed below. The cause of the change was primarily attrition of markers of case and agreement, but van der Gaaf (1904: 28–39) discusses a number of other factors that may have been instrumental in the change.

We assume that word order in Old English was "free" and that unmarked order was SOV (see chapter 8). As word order in general gradually became fixed in English, and as the unmarked order changed from SOV to SVO, the order of constructions with the inversion verbs also did. Allen (1986: 396) shows that in the thirteenth century there was an increase in postverbal positioning of the experiencer, as would be expected on analysis I. According to Allen (1986: 397–8), if the theme is pronominal, at this period it is nominative when it is clause-initial, and objective case when it occurs after the verb. The former pattern (nominative theme in clause-initial position) is consistent with analysis I, while the latter pattern (objective case theme in clause-final position) is consistent with analysis II. Overall, this variation in case assignment is consistent with the claim that reanalysis occurred and that part of its actualization was the increasing positioning of experiencer and theme according to their reanalyzed grammatical relations. The covariation of case marking and word order supports the view that two analyses were available during this period of actualization.

Apart from the occurrence of so many case patterns and the fact that (48) and (49) overlap in time, the account of this change is complicated by the fact that during the actualization the characteristics of the two basic constructions may be mixed. Examples showing the verb agreeing with a dative experiencer are plentiful, as in (50):

(50)   sum men þat han suche likynge wondren what hem   ailen
                                            what them.DAT.PL ail.PL
        "Some men who have such pleasure wonder what ails them."
                                    (*The Chastising of God's Children* 103, 15)

Less common, but also occurring, are examples where the verb still agrees with the theme or is third person singular in its absence, but where it is the experiencer that is in the nominative case.

(51)   preieþ þanne first for ʒouresilf as ʒe   þenkiþ moost spedeful
                            you.NOM.PL think.SG
        "Pray first for yourself as you think most beneficial."
                   (*The Chastising of God's Children* 224, 20; cited by Butler 1977)

In (51) ʒe is plural but does not condition plural agreement, even though it is in the nominative. Thus, examples such as (50) and (51) mix the characteristics of the old construction with those of the new. Note that (50) and (51) are from the same source, and other examples of both types are from approximately contemporary sources. Additional examples are cited in Butler (1977), van der Gaaf (1904: 69), and Visser (1963–73: 31). Once it is recognized that during the period of actualization multiple analyses are available to the speaker, it is possible to account in a natural way for the variation shown in (50)–(51). In (48) both case marking and agreement are based on analysis I. In (50), case marking makes reference to analysis I, while agreement is extended to *hem* on the basis of analysis II. In (51) this relationship is reversed, with agreement based on analysis I, and nominative case marking extended to *ȝe* on the basis of analysis II.

During the actualization, the case marking characteristics of the two constructions can also be mixed. In example (52), both arguments are ambiguously dative or accusative. Note that no combination of dative-experiencer and dative-(accusative-)theme occurs in any of the canonical patterns;[32] examples such as (52) do not occur frequently and are limited to the transitional period. (For further details on this construction, see Allen 1986: 397–8).

(52)   so wel us   lyketh   yow
        so well DAT-ACC like.3.SG DAT-ACC
        "We like you so well."
                                        (*Canterbury Tales*, E 106, cited by van der Gaaf 1904: 68)

The availability of multiple analyses in the internal grammar of individual speakers makes it possible to account for sentences such as (52). We assume that the experiencer here is marked according to analysis I, while the objective case is extended to the theme on the basis of analysis II.[33]

Lightfoot (1991: 136–7) proposes to account for the case variation in terms of diglossia. The English situation does not have two of the defining features of diglossia, namely that one variety be "high" and the other "low," and that each variety have a distinct social function. Further, in introducing the notion of diglossia originally, Ferguson specifically notes that "diglossia is not assumed to be a stage which occurs always and only at a certain point in some kind of evolution, e.g., in the standardization process" (1959 [1972]: 233). It seems clear that the term "diglossia" was intended to distinguish the relatively rare examples of distinct social functions for distinct language varieties (each with its own linguistic properties clearly defined as distinct in the differing language varieties) from the much more common kind of variation found in this English example.

If Lightfoot wishes to extend the notion of diglossia to the common sort of variation illustrated above, he will have to have not only two, but many, grammars. Just to include the variation in agreement illustrated above, we would have to resort to tri- or tetraglossia. When we consider that at the same period there was variation in numerous other constructions, such as *do*-support,[34] a single speaker would, on Lightfoot's approach, have to control quite a large number of grammars.

Not only does the diglossic account lead to a plethora of grammars, without further complications, it is unable to account for sentences such as (50)–(52) above.[35] Lightfoot's specific proposal for a diglossic account is as follows:

> A grammar with oblique case would generate "impersonal" forms like (1c)–(1g) [similar to our (48)]. Lexical entries would be along the lines of [(53)], and NPs assigned a lexical case would not surface with a structural case, as I have indicated. A grammar lacking morphological dative case. . .would also lack oblique lexical cases. Therefore the lexical entries would specify no D-structure cases. As a result, NPs would have to acquire cases structurally, under government of some case assigner. No dative experiencers would be generated, but these verbs would occur with NPs in the objective case.
>
> (1991: 136–7)

> [(53)] (a) hreowan: experiencer-dative; (theme-genitive)
>   (b) lician: experiencer-dative; theme   (Lightfoot 1991: 131)

If we assume that Lightfoot's two grammars generate complete sentences, neither grammar nor the combination of the two can generate sentences such as (50)–(52). Only by recognizing two analyses *within the same grammar* can these sentences, with properties of both analyses, be generated during the transitional period. Under Lightfoot's assumptions, a diglossic account could be made to account for these sentences in either of two ways. First, it could incorporate into the "grammar with oblique case" the multiple analyses argued for here. If this is done, the second grammar, the "grammar lacking morphological dative case" would then be an unnecessary complication. A different approach would be to permit diglossic grammars to "collaborate" on a single sentence. This is only a variant of the approach advocated here, since it locates multiple analyses in different grammars, which, however, would have the property of generating sentences in much the same way a single grammar does.

Sentences such as (50) and (51) are infrequent and occur only during the transition; they appear to represent a combination (van der Gaaf's "blending") of elements of the two major constructions at once. This blending is evidence of the continued existence of multiple analyses through the period of actualization. A satisfactory analysis must account for attested phenomena such as these, as well as for the canonical patterns.

We have provided a specific account of the loss of inversion in English (with some further aspects of this change to be discussed in section 5.3.3.2). The main thrust of our argument, however, is for only one feature of this account, namely that from late Old English through the sixteenth century, dual analyses were present in the grammars of speakers. (Towards the beginning and end of this period fewer speakers had dual analyses, while in the middle most speakers must have had this.) There are numerous other accounts that provide for multiple analyses, but any approach that does not recognize multiple analyses during this transition is inadequate.

4.4.3.3   Reversibility

It appears to be uncommon for a change to reverse itself, but this does occur, and reversals provide further evidence of continuing multiple analyses in actualization. A lexical example occurs within the change discussed in the preceding section. Like other inversion verbs in English, *seem* occurred in the inversion construction, illustrated above in (48).

(54)   hit   semit   me   for certayn
           it.NOM seemed.3.SG me.DAT
           "It seemed to me for certain."
                                       (*Destruction of Troy* 198, cited by van der Gaaf 1904: 23)

This verb also participated in the variation cited above, as illustrated by (55) and (56):

(55)   me-seem   my head doth swim
           me.DAT-seem.1.SG
           "(It) seems to me my head swims. . ."
                                       (*Damon and Pythias*, 79, cited by Butler 1977: 158)

(56)   do as ye   seems   best
           you.NOM.PL seem.3.SG
           "Do as seems best to you."
                                       (*Generydes*, 6007, cited by Butler 1977: 166)

In both examples, characteristics of the Old English construction are mixed with those of the construction that occurs in Modern English for most verbs. In (55) the experiencer is in the dative, as in analysis I, but it governs agreement as required by analysis II. In (56) the experiencer is in the nominative, as in the newer construction, but does not govern agreement. Thus, in terms of the stages stated above, *seem* had entered Stage B, with the rules of case marking and agreement extended to a new analysis, as in (55) (cf. (50)) and (56) (cf. (51)), respectively. What makes *seem* different from other verbs of this type is that it, in effect, reversed the change. Other inversion verbs in English went on to a Stage C in which a single analysis exists, with the experiencer in the nominative; *seem* did not.[36] Instead, for *seem* the original construction was continued. Like other datives, the dative marking the experiencer of this verb was replaced with *to* + NP; the theme continues to be in the nominative, and the verb continues to agree with it, just as in the older construction: *he* (Nom) *seems* (3.Sg) *intelligent to me* (continuation of dative).

The change to the dative experiencer construction could be analyzed as a change entirely independent of the fact that *seem* had previously occurred in that construction and independent of the fact that most of the verbs that had occurred in that construction had changed to the nominative experiencer construction. However, it is far more plausible that these changes were related, and that the change of *seem* to the dative experiencer was indeed a reversal of the change it had earlier begun. This is most naturally accounted for through the concept of the continuing dual analysis of this construction, with the observation that for other verbs analysis I was later lost, while for *seem* analysis II was lost.[37]

4.5 Some kinds of change that may be effected by reanalysis

In this section we look briefly at some of the types of change that reanalysis may bring about. These types are not necessarily mutually exclusive, nor do all examples of reanalysis fit into any one of these types.

4.5.1 Innovative and preservative reanalysis

Reanalysis may introduce a radical new structure to a language, or it may preserve and renew existing structures, and accordingly we distinguish **innovative reanalysis** from **preservative** (in essence structure-preserving reanalysis). In preservative reanalyses, a structure is reanalyzed as conforming in a new way to already existing elements of the language; in innovative reanalysis, the structure introduces a new structure, which may coexist with that which was already in effect. The reanalysis of the English noun *while* "a portion of time" (e.g. *he sat for a while*) as a complementizer introducing an adverbial clause (Pasicki 1983) is an example of a preservative reanalysis, since English already possessed adverbial clauses with complementizers in clause-initial position. (That is, an N became a Comp, and an NP became an S'.)

A more complex example of preservative reanalysis is seen in the development of several new case endings from postpositions (and by the combination of other case suffixes into new cases) in various Balto-Finnic languages, where other case endings previously existed before the change which resulted in the new additional cases. Cases develop from postpositions when the postposition is felt to be so closely connected to its attribute noun that together they are reinterpreted as one word; semantic and morphophonemic changes (e.g. vowel harmony) often take place which conceal the word boundary and change the status of the elements, resulting in new case suffixes. In Balto-Finnic languages the fusion in several instances was so late that corresponding postpositions are still found alongside the new cases. We can compare Estonian *poja-ka* (orthographic ‹poja-ga›) (boy-COMITATIVE) and Finnish *poja-n kanssa* (boy-GEN with), both meaning "with the boy." In fact, Finnish dialects illustrate the intermediate steps in the development which led from the original postposition (as in the Finnish form) to the new case ending (as in Estonian). Standard Finnish has the postposition *kanssa* "with," e.g. *lapse-n kanssa* (child-GEN with) "with the child." In several dialects, however, this has developed into a "comitative/instrumental" clitic (and in some dialects into a case suffix), of the form *-ka(h)*, *-ka:n*, e.g. *isän-ka* "with father" (*isä* "father"), *koiran-ka:n* "with the dog" (*koira* "dog") (Kettunen 1930: 29; Oinas 1961). The documented history of Estonian attests the gradual development of this postposition into the *-ka* case suffix.[38] (See Laanest [1982: 174–5], Oinas [1961], and Campbell [1990a: 63–5] for details and for many other similar cases.)

The introduction of an entirely new construction, that is, innovative reanalysis, is discussed above in section 4.3.1, where it is shown that the Georgian relative clause, described in section 4.2.4, was an entirely new structure created by reanalysis of the old relative clause with introductory relative pronoun.

4.5.2   Transfer of meaning/function

The transfer of meaning (or function) involves one or two processes of reanalysis. A good example (presented above in section 4.3.2 above) of this is that of the development of negation in French, where it was shown that the exploratory expression *ne . . . pas* was reanalyzed as the unmarked expression of negation, formerly *ne* alone. The French example illustrates the transfer of function, but in addition clearly shows this as a two-step process, for in the spoken language *ne. . . pas* has been reanalyzed, such that *pas* alone indicates negation, and *ne* is an optional added emphasis, still also recognized as an obligatory part of negation in the literary dialect.[39]

A set of examples that involve a larger structure is that of the cleft-to-highlighter changes discussed in chapter 7. In these changes the function of a biclausal structure, a cleft, is transferred to a particle that functions in a single clause.

4.5.3   Meaning change in reanalysis

In many examples of reanalysis, the meaning is changed, but in subtle ways. When we speak of meaning here, we are referring to the meaning of the whole sentence in which the affected pattern occurs, not necessarily to the meaning of the affected pattern itself. Let us look at some types of meaning change. In the reanalysis of French *ne . . . pas* as the unmarked expression of negation, the emphasis previously afforded by *pas* "step" was lost; the meaning change was the loss of emphasis. In fact, any time an emphatic construction is reanalyzed as unmarked, the meaning that was associated with the marked aspect is lost.

It is commonplace for changes of tense, aspect, or mood to accompany reanalysis. An example is the reanalysis of a copula construction with an adjective-like stative past passive participle as a passive, frequently with loss of the stative element of meaning. For example, older Finnish had a copula construction with a subject and a past passive participle, as in (57), transliterated in (57') in the modern orthographic equivalent:

(57)   nyt kijnni ote-ttu ole-t ja pan-du sijtte-i-sin (1642 Bible)

(57')   nyt kiinni ote-ttu   ole-t   ja   pan-tu   siitte-i-siin
         now stuck take-PTCPL   are-2.SG and put-PTCPL   shackles-PL-INTO
         "Now you are captured and put into shackles."

The meaning of this construction was stative and focused on the result of the action (Ikola 1959: 43–5). This element of the meaning is emphasized in the translations of the examples in (58):

(58)   (a) työ   on teh-ty
             work.NOM is do-PTCPL
             "The work is done." "The work is in a state of having been done."

        (b) seinä-t   o-vat   maala-tu-t
             wall-NOM.PL are-3.PL paint-PTCPL-PL
             "The walls are painted." "The walls are in a painted state."

The pattern in (57) and (58) has been reinterpreted as a passive (perhaps better called an impersonal verb form, since no overt agent/logical subject can be expressed with this construction), and now has the additional meaning "the work has been done," "the walls have been painted." While the older stative result meaning is still available, a newer meaning of process (with an implied but non-specified agent) is also possible for this construction.[40]

Reanalyses do not always change meaning, however. For example, there is no apparent change of meaning in the Georgian example described in section 4.2.4. Even the meaning elements named above do not necessarily change, even when the construction that expresses them is the object of reanalysis: for example, while the analytic *iq̇o-* passive in Georgian has an attested origin similar to that described above for Finnish (and for English in note 40), the stative meaning originally associated with it has never been changed (see Harris 1981: 203–4).

4.5.4 Reanalyses as grammaticalization

In our approach, the process of grammaticalization involves reanalysis in the sense defined above.[41] Grammaticalization is one type of macro-change, consisting minimally of one process of reanalysis, but frequently involving more than one reanalysis. Two related sorts of processes are typically the focus of study in the grammaticalization literature. One is the lexical-item-to-grammatical-morpheme model, which usually involves some kind of phonological reduction and often a change in status from an independent word to a clitic and/or affix. The second is the discourse-structure-to-morphosyntactic-markings model, which deals with the fixing of discourse strategies in syntactic and morphological structure (see Traugott and Heine 1991: 2). Grammaticalization is often associated with "semantic bleaching," and this "bleaching" is the result of reanalysis or, perhaps better said, it is the essence of the reanalysis itself. Grammaticalization may involve reanalysis of a complex structure as a simpler one or reanalysis of category labels. These aspects of grammaticalization are here considered reanalysis because the structure is altered, while the surface manifestation may remain the same: for example, when English *will* (originally "want") became semantically bleached and was grammaticalized as a future marker, initially the surface was essentially unaltered, only its grammatical status changed (see Bybee and Pagliuca 1987; Bybee, Pagliuca and Perkins 1990, 1991).

An example from the Kartvelian languages, given in detail in the appendix to this chapter, serves to illustrate why we consider reanalysis to be an important part of the process that is termed grammaticalization; at the same time it illustrates the semantic aspect of grammaticalization. This reanalysis, a change in category with a concomitant change in meaning, is part of the macro-change of grammaticalization but is partly independent of the other micro-changes in the sense that they are not simultaneous. We assume, in addition, that the reanalysis does not entail the other micro-changes. Although the semantic consequences of reanalysis involve an ongoing series of changes, evidence from a small set of archaic verbs shows that the semantic change does not take place at the same time as the phonological erosion. Since changes of these two sorts frequently occur in parallel, it is clear that they are related, though not the same change. We take this example to be typical of grammaticalization, except that all relevant parts of it are attested and for this reason give evidence concerning timing.

4.6 Summary

In this chapter it has been our purpose to paint a more complete picture of reanalysis. We have provided examples, some extensive, some brief (some cases referred to are discussed elsewhere in this book), and have discussed in some detail the kinds of situations that may lead to reanalysis, the relationship between reanalysis and its actualization, and a few of the kinds of change that may be effected by reanalysis.

While most researchers on diachronic syntax agree that reanalysis exists, there are some differences of opinion. First, there is some divergence of opinion with respect to the question of whether and in what sense ambiguity is a prerequisite for reanalysis. We have discussed this issue in section 4.3.1, arguing that multiple analyses must be available, and that opacity is not required. Second, while some have claimed that phonetic change cannot trigger morphosyntactic change, we have argued in section 4.3.3 that this is not so, summarizing or citing examples from several languages.

A third question is at what point reanalysis applies. According to the definition accepted here, the effects of reanalysis *per se* are not directly visible, and identifying the point at which it occurs presents a very real problem. Some scholars have taken the position that what they call reanalysis (defined differently) applies relatively late, with many small changes leading up to it (especially Lightfoot 1979a). We have argued in section 4.4 (in part following Timberlake 1977; see also chapter 2) that such an approach leaves the small changes unexplained and that locating reanalysis earlier in the process provides an explanation for those changes. Explanation for reanalysis itself is discussed in section 4.3 (see also chapter 11). This line of argument is continued in the next chapter, where extension is treated in greater detail, and in section 7.4.1, where one particular example is discussed at some length.

Finally, there is some disagreement among scholars concerning whether multiple reflexes may coexist, that is, whether the source of a new construction can continue to exist alongside of a reanalyzed new construction based upon that source. It is sometimes assumed (for example, Lightfoot 1979a: 81–115) that in reanalysis a new structure replaces the old. While this is true in some instances, there are also many instances in which the two continue to coexist for centuries (see section 4.4.3.1).[42] This is closely related to the question of whether variation is best accounted for through the existence of multiple analyses, already recognized as a prerequisite for reanalysis, through so-called diglossia, in the extended meaning of multiple grammars, or through other means (see section 4.4.3). While we have presented arguments to support our positions in this chapter, much additional evidence is presented in subsequent chapters.

Appendix: Preverbs in Kartvelian

In Kartvelian languages, as in many others, adverbs have become directional preverbs. Crucial parts of the change are attested. The entire macro-change involves all parts of the grammar and consists of the following parts: category change from adverb to preverb, constituency change (the adverb began to form a constituent with the verb), word order change, meaning change, change from independent word to proclitic to prefix, phonological reduction.

In Svan there are two kinds of so-called preverbs. One type occurs as independent words, as in (59).

(59)   ačad   sga
        s/he.go inside

> (*Svanskije teksty na laščhskom narečii*, cited by Deeters 1930: 17
> from A. Oniani's 1917, tale no. 7)

The structure in (59) represents the earliest attested stage in the development of the preverbs described below. The same elements that may follow the verb in the structure in (59) may alternatively be proclitic to the verb, as in (60), where *sgāčad* is from *sga=ačad* "in=went."

(60)   sgāčad
        in=s/he.go   (cited by Deeters 1930: 15 from the same source)

Even in preverbal position, *sga* is a proclitic in Svan, not a prefix, as shown by the fact that it may be separated from the verb by one or another particle. This is illustrated in (61), where *sgāy* is synchronically from *sga=i* "in=again."

(61)   (a) sgāy   ačad   dāv-í. . .
             in.again s/he.go devi(mythological being)-NOM
             "The devi went in again . . ."   (cited by Topuria 1967: 60)

        (b) sga ud   etqǝrix   yērbat-s. . .
             in   again they.implore God-DAT
             ". . .again they implore God . . ."   (cited by Topuria 1967: 61)

While *sga* "in" and three other elements – *ži* "up, on," *ču* "down, under," *ka* "out, from, thither" – may still occur as independent adverbs, as in (59), or may cliticize to the verb, as in (60), there are four other preverbs in Svan that have undergone the further process of affixation; *an* "hither," *ad* "thither, away from," *es* "thither," *la* "in, thither." The four adverb/proclitics are distinguished from the four prefixes by the following behaviors: (i) the former may occur independently, as in (59), while the latter cannot; (ii) a particle may intervene between the proclitics and the verb, but not between the prefixes and the verb; (iii) while elements in both sets undergo a number of phonological changes, it is all and only those of the prefix set that undergo umlaut when followed by stem-initial *i* in the verb, e.g. *ä-xw-i-t* (← *an-xw-i-tii*) "I mowed it for myself," *ät-šixan*

(← *ad-i-šixen*) "you burned," but *ču izbi* "s/he ate it" (Topuria 1967: 56, 60); (iv) the ad-
verb/proclitics can serve as an affirmative answer to a yes/no question, but the prefixes
cannot, as in (62):

(62)   Proclitic *ka* "out"
         kācäd   mo? – ka
         out.s/he.go QUES – out
         "Did s/he go out?" – "Yes."

Thus, the adverb/proclitics are clearly distinguished from the verbal prefixes.

One set of adverbs in Svan – *sga* "in," *ži* "up, on," *ču* "down, under," *ka* "out, from,
thither" – were reanalyzed as optionally separable elements of the verb, contributing to
the meaning of the verb. Frequently, but not always, they occurred immediately before
the verb or separated from the verb by one other element, as in (61). Phonological change
made these elements proclitic to the verb when immediately pre-verbal, as in (60).
Earlier the same changes had taken another set – *an* "hither," *ad* "thither, away from," *es*
"thither," *la* "in, thither" – along the same path from adverb to verbal proclitic.[43]

The further development of preverbs is best seen in Georgian, a sister language. As
part of a later reanalysis, the directional meaning of some preverbs was reduced in
some environments: for example, *da-* originally "down" (Šaniʒe 1973: 261), has almost
entirely lost this directional sense, as shown in examples such as *da-c̣era* "s/he wrote it"
(cf. *č̣a-c̣era* "s/he wrote it down"). Other preverbs, such as *a-* "up" (Old Georgian *aɣ=*)
fully retain their directional sense in some verbs (e.g. *a-vida* "s/he went up"), retain it in
some meanings of another verb (*a-iɣo* "s/he picked it up, took it, received it"), and do
not retain it at all in others (e.g. *a-c̣era* "s/he described it"). Another part of the reanalysis is that preverbs, while retaining their directional or reduced meanings, took on the
function of marking perfective aspect.

In Old Georgian the directional preverbs have already become proclitic to the verb,
but like the Svan directionals in (61), they permit other clitics to intervene (tmesis). They
are already closely associated with the verb, in the sense that particular verb stems occur with particular (sets of) preverbs. But in the Old Georgian data, the preverb does
not yet mark perfective aspect, though it has already begun to occur more often with
perfective forms.

These preverbs have also been affected by gradual phonological erosion: for example, Old Georgian *aɣ=* "up" became Modern Georgian *a-*, *gan=* "out, from" became
ga-, and *c̣ar=* "away from" became *c̣a-*. The semantic change is partly contemporaneous with the phonological erosion, but even in Old Georgian the proclitics did
not always have strictly directional meaning: for example, *aɣ=c̣era* already had the
meaning "s/he described it" in Old Georgian.

A small set of verbs reveals some interesting facts about the overall change. While
the older forms *aɣ=*, *gan=*, and *c̣ar=* were fully replaced by the shorter forms in most
verbs, a few verbs have retained the original forms beside the new ones and have developed a contrast between the new and the old. Examples of this are provided in (63)
(from Šaniʒe 1973: 249):

(63)   Newer form   Older form
        a-zrda "raise (of people, animals,   *aɣ-zrda* "educate"
            or plants)"
        a-dgoma "stand up, get up"   *aɣ-dgoma* "arise from the dead, be
                                                  resurrected (in a religious sense)"
        ća-suli "gone"   *ćar-suli*[44] "past (of time)"
        ga-axleba "renew, make (like) new,   *gan-axleba* "renew, make (like) new,
            renovate"   restore, begin again"[45]

Generally the verb with the new (reduced) form of the preverb has a more general or literal meaning, while the form with the older form of the preverb has developed a more specialized or metaphorical meaning. The change in form appears to be partly independent of the change in meaning because the meaning difference in the pairs of verbs cited above is not directly connected with the meaning of the preverb. For example, the root *-axl* means "new," and the original directional meaning of *ga(n)-* "out" seems equally irrelevant to both forms cited above.[46] The root *-dg-* means "stand," and the original directional meaning of *a(ɣ)-* seems equally relevant to the meaning of both forms above. If the change in form and the change in meaning had occurred together or were directly connected, we should see the directional meaning in the older form, but not in the newer. A second reason for believing that the two changes are not directly related is that the older form had both the general, literal meaning and the specific, metaphorical meaning before the two forms became associated with different meanings. For example, in Old Georgian *aɣ=zrda* meant both "raise" and "educate" (*aɣ-zrda* "raise [plant]" in Psalms 103 [104]: 28 A, "educate" in Acts 22: 3); *aɣ=dgoma* meant both "stand up" and "arise from the dead" (*aɣ=dgoma* "get up" in Mt. 2: 13, "resurrection" in Mt. 22: 28); and *ćarsrul* (later *ća(r)suli*) meant both "gone" and "past (of time)" (*ćarsrul* "gone" in Šušanik" IV, 19, "past [time]" in Mk. 6: 35 AB).[47] If the change in form were part of the change in meaning, then one of these meanings would not have developed until later when the preverb took on its new shape.

5   *Extension*

5.1   Introduction

Extension is one of the three basic mechanisms of change in our approach. We defined extension in chapter 3 as change in the surface manifestation of a syntactic pattern that does not involve immediate or intrinsic modification of underlying structure. Many aspects of extension are discussed in chapter 4, especially in section 4.4. This chapter is devoted to a more detailed description and presentation of examples. The central purpose of the chapter is to state a constraint on extension.

It has often been said that diachronic change simplifies the grammar; yet it has often been pointed out that if that were always so, grammars would become noticeably simpler in the course of time.[1] In the realm of syntax, it is clear that reanalysis often can introduce complexity to the grammar (though it can also result in simplification, as well), while extension can eliminate exceptions and irregularities by bringing the new analysis into line with the rest of the existing grammar. The constraint on extensions, formulated below as (39), makes concrete the observation that extension always plays this role.

Extension is a mechanism that operates to change the syntax of a language by generalizing a rule, and in section 5.2 we give two examples of this. The constraint which we discuss in greater detail in section 5.3 below states minimum observed limits on the application of extension in general. There are still stronger constraints, which seem to operate on individual aspects of grammar, and these are discussed in chapters 7–9. Thus, although extension may occur, it is certain that it does not apply without constraint. We show in section 5.3.3.1 that syntactic change discussed as lexical diffusion is a type of extension, and we discuss a means of modeling lexical extension in section 5.3.3.2. In section 5.4 we discuss one course an extension may follow, with variation and a change in markedness. Section 5.5 is an excursus on two notions of traditional diachronic syntax and an explanation of how we account for them.

5.2   Some examples of extension

In Chapter 4 we have provided examples of extension in our discussion of the distinction between reanalysis and actualization. In this section we provide additional examples, with the emphasis now on the extension. Others are also presented later in the chapter.

5.2.1   Estonian reported speech

Balto-Finnic languages have a number of participial constructions and some of these have changed in Estonian (and Livonian, as well, though it is not discussed here) to "reported speech" forms.[2] Estonian created an "indirect" or "reported speech" form through reanalysis of former participle endings in subordinate constructions, and later extended this new morphosyntactic marker to main clauses. We state first abstractly the changes that took place, which are made more understandable by the further discussion and examples which follow.

The change involves two alternative complement structures with essentially the same meaning. These structures were used with speech-act (SAV) or mental-state (MSV) main verbs. In stage 1, two constructions were available:

(1)   (a)   Main.verb(SAV/MSV). . . [*et* . . . Finite.verb]
          (b)   Main.verb(SAV/MSV). . . [. . . verb-Active.Participle].

The (a) construction makes use of the complementizer *et* and a finite verb form; the (b) construction uses no complementizer and an active participle, one of the non-finite verb forms. The active participle of (b) was reinterpreted as a finite verb form associated with "reported" speech, called "indirect":[3]

(2)   Active participle formant > indirect marker

Beside the new analysis it retained the old analysis, i.e. active participle (cf. section 4.4.3.1. on multiple reflexes). Note that this is considered reanalysis because the category of the active participle changed to finite verb + indirect marker; at this point there has been no change in the surface. The reanalysis in (2) made it possible for the reinterpreted form, like other finite forms, to occur in construction (1a), yielding, in Stage 2, the following three constructions:

(3)   (a)   Main.verb(SAV/MSV). . . [*et* . . . Finite.verb]
          (b)   Main.verb(SAV/MSV). . . [. . .Verb-Active.Participle]
          (c)   Main.verb(SAV/MSV). . . [(*et*) . . . Finite.verb-Indirect]

Examples of (3a–b) are given in (4) and (5), respectively:

(4)   sai kuul-da, et   seal üks   mees   ela-b
           got hear-INF that there one.NOM man.NOM live-3.PRES.INDIC
           "S/he came to hear that a man lives there."

(5)   sai kuul-da seal   ühe   mehe   ela-vat
           got hear-INF there one.GEN man.GEN live-PRES.ACTIVE.PARTICIPLE
           (same meaning as (4))

The innovative construction (3c) is seen in (6) and (7).

(6)   sai kuul-da, (et) seal üks   mees   ela-vat
           got hear-INF that there one.NOM man.NOM live-PRES.INDIRECT
           "S/he came to hear that (they say) a man lives there."

(7)   isa   ütles poja-le, (et) ta sõit-vat   homme
           father said boy-To (that) he travel-PRES.INDIRECT tomorrow

           linna
           town.Into

           "The father told the boy to travel to town tomorrow."

Examples (6) and (7) show that the verb + indirect marker (which was reanalyzed in (2) from earlier Verb + Participle) has changed further, undergoing an extension, because the surface has now changed. Before the extension the indirect interpretation had only been possible in pattern (3b), its original domain, and there had not been a surface configuration like that in (3c), its extended domain. In (3c) it occurs optionally with the complementizer *et* and its subject now takes nominative case (e.g. *üks mees* in (6)), rather than the former genitive (as seen in *ühe mehe* in (5)). Thus, the indirect verb forms were extended to occur in finite clauses.

In Stage 3, the reinterpreted active participle, now an indirect form of a finite verb, was further extended to main clauses, as in (8)–(10).

(8)   ta   tege-vat   töö-d
           he.NOM do-PRES.INDIRECT work-PARTITIVE
           "They say he is working."

Forms with the former Past Indirect (from the Past Participle) are more common:

(9)   ta   tei-nud   töö-d
           he.NOM do-PAST.INDIRECT work-PARTITIVE
           "They say he worked."

(10)   naabri   perenaine ole-vat   linna
        neighbor.GEN lady.NOM is-PRES.INDIRECT town.Into

        sõit-nud
        travel-PAST.INDIRECT
        "They say the neighbor lady (lady of the house) has traveled to town."

Thus, through reanalysis of a former participle construction, Estonian has
created an "indirect" modality marker employed with finite verbs. The new
"indirect" forms which originated in complement clauses came by extension
to be employed also in main clauses (as in (8)–(10)).[4]

5.2.2   Case marking in Laz

An example of extension of case marking comes from Laz, a language of the
Kartvelian family. In Common-Georgian-Zan, there were two complex sets
of case-marking rules, one for clauses containing a verb form in one of the
tense–aspect–mood (TAM) paradigms constituting the set referred to as Series I, and another for clauses containing a verb form in one of the paradigms
of Series II:

(11)   (a) If the verb is in Series I,
        (b) the subject is marked with the nominative case,
        (c) the direct object is marked with the dative case,
        (d) the indirect object is marked with the dative case.

(12)   If the verb is in Series II,
        (a) (i)   and if the verb is a member of Class 1 or 3,
             (ii)   the subject is marked with the narrative case,
             (iii) the direct object is marked with the nominative case,
             (iv)   the indirect object is marked with the dative case;
        (b) (i)   but if the verb is a member of Class 2,
             (ii)   the subject is marked with the nominative case,
             (iii) the indirect object is marked with the dative case.[5]

There are simpler, more general ways of writing these rules, but this way
enables us to see more easily the effects of the rules on individual arguments
of the verb.

The effects of rule (11) can be seen in examples (13)–(15) from Mingrelian,
where the roman numeral in the gloss represents the Series, and the arabic
numeral indicates the verb Class.

(13)   k'oči   ʔviluns ɣe-s
        man-NOM kill.I.1 pig-DAT
        "The man kills a pig."

(14)   baɣana   ʔude-s   skidu
            child.NOM house-DAT stay.I.2
            "The child stays at home."

(15)   baɣana   ingars
            child.NOM cry.I.3
            "The child cries."

The complexity of rules (11) and (12) may be seen as an incentive to some sort of change, though exactly this system is still retained in both Georgian and Svan. In Laz, but not in its sister languages, rule (12) was extended to Series I, and is responsible for case marking in examples such as (16), (17), and (18) (contrast with (13)–(15)).

(16)   k'oči-k   q'vilups ɣeǰi
            man-NAR kill.I.1 pig.NOM
            "The man kills a pig."

(17)   bere   oxori-s   doskidun
            child.NOM house-DAT stay.I.2
            "The child stays at home."

(18)   bere-k   imgars
            child-NAR cry.I.3
            "The child cries."

The change in the surface pattern of cases in Series I can be summarized as in table 5.1. Like other extensions, this one results from a reanalysis; because it is complex and not directly relevant to this discussion of extension, we do not describe it here (but see Harris 1985: 363–70). This is considered extension because the surface pattern changes; previously this pattern of case distribution had not occurred with verbs of these TAM categories (so-called Series I).

5.3   Towards a constraint on extension

As defined above, extension is a broad, powerful mechanism of change. In fact, however, extension in natural language produces changes that are considerably less varied than this would suggest. The basic observation is that the process of extension is systematic, and the environment into which a rule may be extended is restricted by the nature of the rule in the particular language. Observed extensions generalize to a natural class based on categories already relevant to the sphere in which the rule applied before it was extended. For example, in the Estonian example the indirect marker was extended first from a narrow class of subordinate clauses (complements of SAV or MSV without complementizers) to a

Table 5.1 *Series I case marking*

	Subject of Class 1, 3	Subject of Class 2	Direct Object
Common Georgian-Zan (13)–(15)	Nominative	Nominative	Dative
Laz (16)–(18)	Narrative	Nominative	Nominative

broader class (now with or without complementizers), then from subordinate clauses to matrix clauses. In each extension, the old domain and the new domain together form a natural class within the context of Estonian grammar. In the Laz extension described in section 5.2.2, the case marking system of one set of tense–aspect–mood categories (traditionally called "Series II") was extended into another (called "Series I"). In the grammatical system of this language, the area into which the case marking was extended (Series I), together with the area from which the case marking was extended (Series II), forms a natural class, namely all non-evidential verbs.[6] The kind of extension which seems not to exist, but which is logically possible, would generalize to categories that fail to form a natural class with the categories in which the rule applied before extension. For example, we would be very surprised to find a language like Estonian except that indirect marking were extended *only to matrix clauses with animate objects.* Animate objects have nothing to do with the application of the rule before extension, and we do not expect new *kinds* of conditions. We would not expect to find a language which had the case-marking rules of (11)–(12), and which then extended the narrative case to mark subjects of Class 1 and 3 verbs in Series I, *but only if they were plural.* Number of the nominal to be marked has nothing to do with the rule before extension, and we observe no examples of new *kinds* of condition being placed on a rule in extension.[7]

In the subsections below we discuss informally certain aspects of the changes extension brings about in the form of a rule.

5.3.1   Conditions on rules

In the examples discussed above, the type of extension that actually occurs could be characterized as *removing a condition from a rule.* By **condition** of the rule, we mean here a requirement that must be met in order for a rule to apply; the conditions specify the precise environment in which the rule applies. In this sense a condition on a rule may well be stated as an inherent part of the rule, the structural description: for example, if we formulate passivization as a rule that promotes a direct object to subject, the presence of a direct object is, in this sense, a condition of the rule. We distinguish three types of conditions on rules. **General conditions** are ones that may be stated in terms of structures, grammatical relations, or categories; they may be stated in a way that is broadly applicable, without listing lexical items. A general condition is a positive statement as to what must obtain in order for the rule to apply. **Exceptions** to rules are also conditions on rules; they are statements that the rule may apply just in case the condition is not met, just in case the exceptional circumstance does not obtain. Exceptions may be stated in a general way – on the basis of structures, on grammatical relations or categories, or on semantic categories – or they may involve a lexical listing. General conditions and both types of exceptions are discussed in greater detail below in this section.[8]

Let us look at the examples above in this light. Before it was extended, the Estonian indirect form had two conditions placed on its occurrence: (i) it occurred only in the complement of a SAV or a MSV; (ii) it occurred only in non-finite environments, that is, if that complement were not introduced by the complementizer *et* and if its subject were in the genitive case. Both conditions were removed through extension of the rule, and now the construction is not limited to non-finite contexts or to complements.

In the Kartvelian example in section 5.2.2, "If the verb is in Series II" is one condition for the application of rule (12), and this condition was removed in the extension of this rule. That is, the series of the verb ceased to be one of the conditions that had to be met in order for the rule to apply.

5.3.2   Exceptions as conditions on rules

We noted above that exceptions may be stated in a general way – on the basis of structures, grammatical relations or categories, or on semantic categories – or they may involve a lexical listing. Both types are illustrated in this subsection.

An attested change in Finnish provides an example of extension as the removal of exceptions. In Standard Finnish, verbs of obligation take genitive subjects; if fully affected direct objects are present, they are in the nominative case.

(19)   minu-n täyty-y   ostaa omena
        I-GEN   must-3RD.PRES to.buy apple.NOM
        "I have to buy the apple."

This class of verbs and constructions of obligation includes a sizable number (e.g. *tulee* "must," *tulisi* "should," *pitää* "must," *pitäisi* "should," *täytyy* "must," *on*

VERB+PRES.PASS+PTCPL "must" [e.g. *on men-tä-vä* "have to go"], *on pakko* "it is necessary that," etc.). Other verbs in Standard Finnish (SF) take subjects in the nominative; direct objects are in the accusative when fully affected.

(20)   minä   osta-n   omena-n
        I.NOM buy-1ST.SG apple-ACC
        "I (will) buy the apple."

In Western Finnish dialects, however, the general pattern of (20) has been extended to verbs of obligation. In these dialects verbs of obligation no longer take genitive subjects (and nominative objects, when a fully affect object is present), but rather nominative subjects, with which the verb agrees (and accusative objects when fully affected, partitive objects when partially affected), for instance (see Saukkonen 1984:184):

(21)   (mä)   täydy-n tehdä⁹   (sä)   pidä-t   mennä
        (I.NOM) must-I to.do   (you.NOM) must-You to.go
        "I must do (it)."   "You must go."

The Western Finnish grammatical change is regular, since it did not change randomly in only one or a few of the obligation forms, but rather regularly changed the entire pattern, shifting from former genitive marking for subjects to the nominative case with verb agreement in each of the verbs and compound constructions involving obligation (with fully affected objects marked accusatively). It illustrates the elimination of a construction that is lexically governed by a set of verbs that may be characterized semantically. The genitive-subject construction may be considered an exception in the sense that it is a minority construction, that is, it is less generally used than another. This example with a regular extension of the more general pattern for the non-obligation verbs contrasts with another Finnish example, which follows, where the extension of the regular pattern for non-motion verbs is governed by individual lexical items.

In Finnish, non-finite complements of motion verbs differ from those of non-motion verbs. Motion verbs, such as "come" and "go," govern the so-called third infinitive illative, as in *tulee anta-ma-an* (comes give-3RD.INF- ILLATIVE) "comes to give" and *menee teke-mä-än* (goes do-3RD.INF- ILLATIVE) "goes to do." A few non-motion verbs, such as "strive" and "start," also govern the third infinitive; for example, *pyrkiä tekemään* "strive to do," *ruveta tekemään* "start to do." Other non-motion verbs, such as "must," "try," and "begin," govern the first infinitive, as in *pitää antaa* "must give" and *pitää siivota* "must clean," *pitää tehdä* "must do," *yrittää tehdä* "try to do," *alkaa tehdä* "begin to do." We may give a rough representation of the rules governing these as (22) and (23):

(22)   (a)   Use the first infinitive form in the complement
      (b)   except where the matrix verb is a motion verb, and
      (c)   except where the matrix verb is among the set {*joutua, pakottaa, pyrkiä, pystyä, ruveta,* . . . *sattua*} (glosses given below).

(23)   (a)   Use the third-infinitive illative form in the complement
      (b)   in other instances (i.e. with motion verbs)

Historically, rules (22)–(23) were regular, since the verbs listed in (22c) were formerly motion verbs; through semantic change they have lost their original motion connections, as summarized below:

> *joutua* "to get involved in, to end up in": in dialects and closely related languages this means "to hurry to, to arrive, to have time, to come at last."
> *pakottaa* "to force, to compel, to coerce": in older stages of the language and in dialects this means "to drive (away), to attack."
> *pyrkiä* "to strive, to try" (earlier "to hurry to do"): in dialects and closely related languages "to ask permission to leave, to hurry, to ask/call to one's presence, to allure/tempt/entice to, to fetch."
> *pystyä* "to be able to, to have the ability to": in dialects and closely related languages "to get/come dislocated, to come/get out of joint" (related etymologically to "to stick into, to stab, to get stuck into, to be placed into").
> *ruveta* "to begin": in Older Finnish, dialects, and in closely related languages "to stick onto, to adhere to, to settle into, to spread/for a disease to be contagious."
> *sattua* "to happen, come to pass, take place by chance, to occur, to touch, to hit (target)": in Finnish dialects this means "to touch, to make sore, to move something, to fit, to insult/injure"; in sister languages it means "to reach/catch up with, to become part of, belong to." [10]

In Vermland and Häme dialects the rules governing the use of first infinitives have been extended to include some of these verbs which formerly were exceptions under (22c): for example, some of these dialects have *pyrkiä tehdä* "strive to do," with the first infinitive. The Vermland dialect has the same construction, as well as *ruveta tehdä* "start to do." (For details and other cases of verbs changing their grammatical cooccurrence patterns, see Saukkonen [1984: 182–3].) In Vermland, the dialect which has regularized most the use of the two infinitives, the extension may be stated as the removal of the exception condition, line (c), from rule (22). It is clear, too, that after extension the domain of application of each rule is a natural class: (22) applies, before extension, but has exceptions; (23) applies after extension to the natural classes of motion verbs (third infinitive illative) and non-motion verbs (first infinitive). In some dialects, not every verb in the set named in line (c) of rule (22) is regularized; in these dialects the entire condition is not eliminated, but the number of exceptions is reduced. At this point in these dialects, the domain of application of neither rule is a natural class: with a few non-motion verbs, (22a) fails to apply, while (22c) does apply. In situations such as this, extension has not yet established a natural class as the domain in which the rules apply; nevertheless, after the extension the natural class is more complete than it was before.[11]

We cannot fail to note that an equivalent way of stating (22)–(23) is as in (24)–(25):

(24)   (a)   Use the third infinitive illative form in the complement
        (b)   if the matrix verb is a motion verb, or
        (c)   if the matrix verb is among the set {*pyrkiä, ruveta, joutua, pakottaa, kyetä, pystyä, . . . sattua*}

(25)   (a)   Use the first infinitive form in the complement
        (b)   in other instances.

If the rules are stated this way, we must say that (25) is extended when the condition in line (c) is removed from rule (24). This way of stating the rule makes the point that exceptions may be seen simply as options, often, as here, lexically governed ones. The extension then eliminates the variation.

Very often exceptions are lexically governed, as in the second Finnish example above. The elimination of the third infinitive with illative from certain non-motion verbs involves the gradual elimination of lexically governed exceptions.

Notice that both Finnish examples are in keeping with the general observation that extension is systematic, and that the environment into which a rule may be extended is restricted by the nature of the rule in the particular language. Although both examples involve elimination of exceptions, in the sense defined above, in each instance the new environment is a natural class within the categories recognized by the language. In the first change, obligation and non-obligation verbs, the categories recognized by Standard Finnish, are combined into one category in the western dialects. In the second, the extension makes a simpler opposition: motion verbs vs. non-motion verbs.

5.3.3   Lexically governed rules and lexical extension

5.3.3.1   Lexical diffusion – the context

Some scholars argue that some sound changes spread gradually through the lexicon, one or several words at a time (Wang 1969, 1977; Wang and Cheng 1977; Labov 1981). These linguists suggest that sound change may be *phonetically abrupt* (discrete, proceeding by perceptible increments), but *lexically gradual* (spreading word by word through the lexicon).[12] While there may be good reasons why this notion is so controversial in phonological change, there seems to be much agreement in syntax that some syntactic changes involve lexical diffusion.[13]

The view that at least some syntactic changes proceed via lexical diffusion has frequently been entertained in studies of diachronic syntax (see examples below). Since sound change is associated with the actual physical form of utterences but syntactic change is more abstract and not physically constrained in the way sound change is, the two may well operate differently with regard to spread through the lexicon. In synchronic syntax, unlike phonology, we are familiar with the concept of rules and patterns being lexically governed. This is especially true of various aspects of complementation. For example, in English verbs like *hate* may take the *for. . .to* pattern, but verbs like *expect* cannot:

(26)   I hate for you to leave early

(27)   *I expect for you to leave early

Given these synchronic differences among verbs, it is not at all surprising to find variation over time in just which verbs govern which patterns. It does not surprise us, for example, that *bigynne* could occur with *for. . .to* in Middle English (Warner 1982: 123), though only with *to* in Modern English.[14] This small change is one kind of diachronic lexical diffusion of syntactic patterns.

The notion of lexical diffusion has been discussed in a wide variety of syntactic changes, though in some of the sources cited below it is not referred to by this name.[15] Many changes that involve complementation in one way or another spread through the lexicon; numerous examples of this are discussed in Ard (1975),[16] Disterheft (1984: 101), R. Lakoff (1968),[17] Warner (1982 *passim*, e.g. 116–17, 123–4, 142, 146, 171), and section 5.3.2 above.

Joseph (1983) documents lexical diffusion of the loss of the infinitive in Greek and in other Balkan languages. One example will serve here to illustrate the process. In Classical Greek a large number of verbs governed infinitives in a variety of contexts, and these were gradually replaced with finite verb forms with a particle or complementizer. For example, *thélō* "want" originally governed an infinitive when the subject of *thélō* and of the infinitive were identical. Joseph (1983: 53) notes that by the first or second century AD this verb could take either the infinitive, as in (28a), or a finite form with *hína*, as in (28b).

(28)   (a) tê:i   epaúrion   e:théle:sen   ekseltheîn eis   tè:n Galilaían
              the.DAT next.day   wanted.3SG   go.out.INF into the Galilee.ACC
              "The next day, he wanted to go out into Galilee."   (John 1: 44)

    (b) thélousin hoi Ioudaîoi   hína phoneúousin autón
         want.3PL the Jews.NOM PRT kill.3PL   him.ACC
         "The Jews want to kill him."   (*Acta Pilati* 11.2.5)

Thus *thélō* "want" was added to the list of verbs taking the construction with the particle *hína* and a finite form.[18]

Other areas of the grammar in which lexical diffusion has been discussed include the syntax of agreement rules (Naro and Lemle 1976; Naro 1981), the coding of attributives (Plank 1980: 307, citing Wackernagel 1926–8, I: 296), the so-called impersonal construction (Fischer and van der Leek 1987), and word order (see chapter 8).

5.3.3.2   Modeling lexical diffusion

In the context of a general discussion of the gradualness of syntactic change, Lightfoot (1991: 159–60) discusses variations on one way of modeling lexically governed gradualness of change, namely the use of lexical features. Approaches of this sort have been used for some time, and Fischer and van der Leek (1983, 1987) propose such an approach to describe lexical variation in the loss of the so-called impersonal (henceforth inversion) construction in English (see also section 4.4.3.2). Lightfoot says of systems of lexical features:

> Such models, with fairly unconstrained systems of features, permit accurate codifications of what occurs in the historical texts at any period. However, they cannot be construed as representations of a person's mature linguistic capacity, because they are demonstrably not attainable. This can be seen particularly clearly in cases of obsolescence, where the loss of a construction with some verb is codified by a new lexical feature on that verb. The problem is that this new feature is a response to the *absence* of some syntactic form, and there is no reason to believe that children set grammatical parameters on the basis of negative data . . . Although they can be made to be observationally accurate, systematizing what is recorded in the texts at an arbitrary time by ever-changing lexical features, these models characteristically offer no explanations for the changes being recorded.   (Lightfoot 1991: 159–60)

As we see, Lightfoot raises three objections to this approach: (i) there is no agreed-upon, constrained set of lexical features; (ii) children cannot set parameters on the basis of negative data; (iii) lexical features offer no explanation of change. In Lightfoot's description of his own approach to gradualness (1991: 160–2), he does not specifically address the sort of lexically governed gradualness found with inversion verbs, but he does propose that "lexical items may be categorized differently, and this recategorization may affect some words before others, progressing gradually" (1991: 161). His proposal for dealing with the inversion construction relies on "diglossia," which he uses to mean the presence of two grammars, such that one grammar generates sentences with dative experiencers (see (48) of chapter 4), while the other generates parallel sentences with nominative experiencers. Problems with this approach are raised below in this section and in section 4.4.3.2.

Lightfoot's first objection, that the set of lexical features is unconstrained, is a very real problem. An enormous number of characteristics are relevant to various phenomena in various languages. Our feeling about this, however, is that the large set of lexical features is just the way it is out in the real world of languages; that is, these features describe observed facts about language, which linguists must analyze and come to terms with, rather than reject out of hand.

Throughout his 1991 book, Lightfoot takes the position (a) that children have no access to negative data and (b) that such data would be necessary to set parameters in instances such as that cited above. Yet it has been argued that children *do* have access to a kind of indirect negative evidence, in that they take note of the absence of a particular syntactic pattern in an environment in which it might be expected (Chomsky 1981: 9). Further, there is evidence that direct negative evidence is not necessary for language acquisition (Baker 1979; Wexler and Culicover 1980, Lasnik 1981; all cited by Chomsky 1981: 9). Thus, while Lightfoot objects to a lexical features approach on the basis of a claimed lack of negative evidence ((ii) above), there is certainly no unanimity of opinion on this matter among the linguistic community.

As a third problem Lightfoot asserts that the lexical feature approach offers no explanation (1991: 136) and further that this is characteristic of all such approaches (1991: 160). Fischer and van der Leek assert that this approach is explanatory (1987: 112). As we show in chapter 11, there are many kinds of explanation. Fischer and van der Leek's account, in our view, "explains" primarily in the sense that it provides the means for an accurate description of case variation as it occurred for various verbs over time.[19] Lightfoot's account "explains" in the sense that it relates the facts concerning the reflex of the inversion construction to his analysis of other phenomena (1991: 137). However, Lightfoot's approach, while accounting for the two major options available for the language as a whole, provides no way to describe – accurately or otherwise – observed differences among verbs in this change.

Consider the range of lexical differences in case marking in constructions with inversion verbs. Inversion verbs are those that occur with (i) the experiencer in the dative case, (ii) the theme in the nominative case, (iii) the verb agreeing with the theme. This is illustrated by (29):

(29)   þam   wife   þa   word   wel licodon
        the.DAT woman.DAT those.NOM words.NOM well liked.PL
        "The woman liked those words well."   (*Beowulf* 640)

The first kind of variation is that in Old English some, but not all, inversion verbs could also occur in the nominative experiencer pattern. *Lician* "like" of (29) is an example of an inversion verb that did not occur in the nominative experiencer pattern in Old English; this verb first occurs with the nominative experiencer pattern in 1340 (see (35)) (van der Gaaf 1904: 68).[20] A second kind of variation is that, some, but not all, inversion verbs could substitute the accusative for the dative in marking the experiencer in the inversion construction. An example of a verb that could substitute the accusative for the experiencer is *hreowan* "pity, grieve, rue," illustrated in (30) (compare (38a), below, where the experiencer is dative):

(30)   hreaw hine   swiðe
        grieve him.ACC so
        "It grieved him so . . ."   (*Genesis*, 1276, cited by van der Gaaf 1904: 6)

A verb that does not occur with an accusative experiencer in the inversion construction is *lician* "like." A third lexical difference is that some, but not all, inversion verbs also occur with the theme in the genitive; this is possible in both the inversion construction and in the direct pattern (that is, in the pattern with nominative experiencer). An example of a verb that may take the genitive to mark the theme is *hreowan* "pity, grieve," illustrated below in (38a, b). Recent discussions of inversion have treated this genitive as an isolated fact about the inversion verbs (Anderson 1986; Fischer and van der Leek 1983, 1987; Lightfoot 1991), but in fact certain other verbs in Old English take genitive objects. An example of a non-inversion verb that regularly takes genitive objects is *bīdan* "await":

(31)   gif þū   Grendles   dearst . . . bīdan
        if you.NOM Grendle.GEN dare.2.SG await.INF
        "If you dare await Grendle. . ."
                            (*Beowulf* 527b–528, cited in Anderson and Williams 1935: 128)

Other verbs that lexically determine genitive objects are listed in Anderson and Williams (1935: 128).[21] Finally, some, but not all, inversion verbs could take the theme in a prepositional phrase; a verb that may occur in this construction is *langian* "desire, long for":

(32)   ða   ongan hine   eft   langian on his cyððe
        then began him.ACC again long   on his home
        "Then he began to long for his home again."
                            (*Blickling Homilies* 113/15, cited by van der Gaaf 1904: 6)

Thus there are at least four lexically determined variants for marking one or another of the arguments of inversion verbs in Old English.

A lexical feature approach provides a way to describe the synchronic lexical variation of all four types, as well as the lexical diffusion of syntactic change: for example, for a synchronic description of Old English the entry for *lician* "like" would specify that it requires inversion (with dative marking of the experiencer and nominative marking of the theme following automatically), while for *hreowan* "rue, grieve" that construction was optional.

(33)   OE *lician*   Inversion
        hreowan   (Inversion)
                         (Theme: Genitive)[22]

Both the optionality of inversion and the optional marking of the theme with genitive, rather than with nominative, are indicated in lexical entries of this sort. The other variations described above can be specified in the same way. Changes over time are also indicated with lexical features:

(34)   OE *lician*   Inversion
        ME *liken*   (Inversion)

That is, while *lician* required inversion in Old English, by Middle English it had become optional, as shown by (35), which illustrates this verb in the nominative-experiencer pattern.

(35)   Of this mirie meting wel may þou   lyke
        of this merry meeting well may you.NOM like
        "You may like this merry meeting well."
                         (*Gestes of Alisander* 873, cited by van der Gaaf 1904: 68)

So, the two patterns in (29) and (35) were available for *liken* in Middle English. Lexical differences in rates of change can also be indicated in this way. Van der Gaaf (1904: 68, 70) indicates that the first occurrence of *liken* with the direct (non-inversion) construction in the written record is 1340, while for *list(en)* "like" it is "in fact quite half a century earlier." Of course, these dates cannot be taken as reflecting the first occurrences of this construction in the spoken language, but we may assume that *list(en)* did begin to use the direct construction significantly before *liken* did so. This lexical difference in time of change may be indicated in the form used above, making use of van der Gaaf's dates as approximations.

(36)   OE   *lician*   Inversion
        1340   *liken*   (Inversion)

        OE   *lystan*   Inversion
                            Experiencer: Accusative
        1290   *list(en)* (Inversion, Experiencer: Accusative)

According to the last entry, the inversion construction becomes optional for *list(en)* by 1290, with accusative marking of the experiencer in this construction. Dialectal variation by verb can be indicated in a parallel way.

Lightfoot's (1991: 131) sample lexical entries, quoted in (37), provide for lexical determination of the genitive theme, but not, apparently, for the other types described above and in other sources:

(37)   (a) *hreowan*: experiencer dative; (theme genitive)
        (b) *lician*: experiencer dative; theme

Without lexical features, the additional variation described above is not easily included in lexical entries such as (37) (in any one grammar).

The multiple-grammar (diglossia) approach advocated by Lightfoot is predicated upon the assumption that all inversion verbs in English manifest both dative and nominative experiencer constructions. Anderson (1986) suggests that *hreowan* "pity, grieve," which he notes in the three different patterns in (38), is representative of other inversion verbs; and Lightfoot agrees (1991: 134).

(38)   (a) him   ofhreow   ðæs mannes
             him.DAT pitied.3.SG the man.GEN.SG
             "He pitied the man."
             Pattern: dative experiencer, genitive theme

        (b) se mæssepreost   ðæs monnes   ofhreow
             the priest.NOM.SG the man.GEN.SG pitied.3.SG
             "The priest pitied the man."
             Pattern: nominative experiencer, genitive theme

        (c) ða   ofhreow   ðam munece   ðæs hleoflian mægenleast
             then pitied.3.SG the monk.DAT.SG the leper's   feebleness.NOM.SG
             "Then the monk pitied the leper's feebleness."
             Pattern: dative experiencer, nominative theme
             (Anderson 1986: 170–1; the fourth line, indicating the *pattern* is our addition.)

That is, in essence Lightfoot denies that there is lexical variation regarding nominative vs. dative marking of experiencers (making the differences instead properties of different grammars), though the lexical entries he proposes recognize lexical differences regarding genitive vs. nominative marking of the theme (1991: 131, quoted as (37)). Other anglicists, however, have not assumed that existing gaps were accidental (for example, van der Gaaf 1904

and Allen 1986:387, citing also Elmer 1981: 145 in the same regard). The inci-
dence of "missed opportunities" in patterns of richly attested verbs, such as
the absence of the nominative experiencer pattern with *lician* "like" before
1340, is evidence that some verbs could not occur in the full range of patterns
illustrated in (38).[23] It would seem to be consistent with Anderson's and
Lightfoot's reasoning to assume that all of the variation described above
characterizes all inversion verbs in Old English, even though each type is
attested only for a proper subset of them. If this assumption is indeed made,
the diglossic approach would presumably require additional "diglossic"
grammars for each of the additional patterns described above (see section
4.4.3.2 on proliferation of grammars). If, on the other hand, it is assumed that
"missed opportunities" for richly attested verbs represent genuine lexical
differences among verbs, then some sort of lexical feature representation will
be necessary to represent the reality of these verbs and the changes they underwent. In this and numerous other changes, it has been shown that different lexical items (here, different inversion verbs) undergo changes to the surface
manifestation (actualization) at different times, and this can be represented
with lexical features.

   The model we propose for this change thus involves both multiple analyses
(which is typical of reanalyses; see section 4.4.3) and lexical features of the general type proposed by Fischer and van der Leek. As shown in section 4.4.3.2,
Lightfoot's analysis cannot account for the kinds of anomalous sentences that
are found during change, such as examples (50)–(52) of chapter 4. As shown
in the present subsection, only an analysis with lexical features or something
equivalent gives an accurate description of the process of change in this and
other instances involving lexical diffusion.[24]

5.3.3.3   *Lexical extension and the constraint on extension*

Lexical diffusion, in the sense discussed above, satisfies our definition of
extension since it is change in the surface manifestation of a syntactic pattern
that does not involve immediate or intrinsic modification of structure or of
the category label of a constituent. Because lexical diffusion is one kind of
extension, we refer to it here as **lexical extension**. Syntactic rules that are lexically determined must make reference to a specification of governing lexical
items; this reference is here termed the **prerequisite** of a rule. A prerequisite is
a specification of which lexical items (if any) govern a process; it may take the
form of a general semantic, syntactic, morphological, or phonological characterization of lexical items, or a listing of otherwise unrelated verbs, or both.
Prerequisites are a condition on a rule, in the sense that they state a situation
that is necessary, though not sufficient, for a rule to apply.[25]

Exceptions are statements of the conditions under which a rule does not apply; prerequisites are statements of the conditions under which a rule does apply. They are two sides of the same coin. We showed in section 5.3.2, using Finnish as an example, that a given set of rules can be written with an exception, as in (22)–(23), or with a prerequisite, as in (24)–(25), with the same effect in each instance.

At the beginning of section 5.3, we observed informally that extension is systematic and that the environment into which a rule is extended is restricted by the nature of the rule in the particular language. In addition we noted that extensions generalize to a natural class based on categories already relevant to the sphere in which the rule applied before it was extended. While the latter is generally true, in changes involving lexically determined rules, the extended class may not include some members of the natural class. For example, in the Finnish example involving the first infinitive and the third infinitive illative (section 5.3.2), in the Häme dialect some of the exceptional verbs in the non-motion semantic class still do not take the first infinitive. However, while the concept of natural class does not always apply, we can informally state the observed constraint making reference to conditions on rules of the three types discussed above.

(39)   *Constraint on extension*
    Extension of a rule R is limited to removing a condition from R.

Because exceptions, as shown above, are one kind of condition on a rule, (39) includes the removal of exceptions, either *en masse* (as was done with genitive subjects in Western Finnish dialects, section 5.3.2) or individually (as was done with non-motion verbs taking the third infinitive illative in the Häme dialect). Since prerequisites are equivalent to negative exceptions, it is likewise included in (39). Thus, (39) is the equivalent of the following statement: extension of a rule R is limited to removing a condition from R or a lexical item from an exception condition to R or by adding a lexical item to a prerequisite of R.

We note in addition that it is possible to write rules differently, even within a single framework, and that what is written as a condition in one version may not be a condition in another. Speakers, too, may formulate rules differently. We assume that the constraint above applies to any part of a rule that can, in some version, be stated as a condition.

Finally, (39) is the statement of the outside limits on extension and is not intended to imply that extension of a rule necessarily involves any change in that rule. In some instances an extension apparently takes place, following a reanalysis, without any change in the rule itself. For example, following the reanalysis of NPs containing quantified nouns in Russian one finds the following change in the surface manifestation:

(40)   (a)   Old Russian
       toju   pjat'ju   butylok
       that.INST.SG.FEM five.INST.SG.FEM bottles.GEN.PI

       (b)   Modern Russian
       temi   pjat'ju   butylkami
       those.INST.PL   five.INST bottles.INST.PL

       (a) and (b) "those five bottles"   (Babby 1987:106)

As described briefly in section 4.3.1, following the more extensive discussion in Babby (1987), in Old Russian, quantifiers were the heads of such phrases, while in Modern Russian the quantified noun is the head. As a result of this reanalysis, in (40a) *toju* "that" occurs in the feminine singular to agree with *pjat'ju* "five," which was feminine singular; while in (40b) the demonstrative is in the plural in agreement with the new head, *butylkami* "bottles" in the plural. This change in the surface manifestation is an extension of the rule of NP-internal number agreement, yet between Old and Modern Russian there was no change in the rules of NP-internal number agreement themselves (Babby 1987:106). Rather, the extension was the result of applying the existing agreement rule according to the new analysis that resulted from reanalysis. Thus, extension does not require any change in the extended rule. The constraint in (39) states the limits on extension, not a requirement on such a change.

5.4   Variation, markedness, and "S" curves

In investigating the nature of extension, we need also to consider what happens in the domain into which a rule is newly extended. In changes where the relevant data are available, we have found that when a rule is extended, at first no other change is made, and the rule which has been extended and the rule which formerly governed this domain coexist, with resulting variation, until the latter ceases to apply in this domain. In the Laz example discussed in section 5.2.2, data are available that show that this was the path the change followed.

The Maxo dialect of Laz permits variation in the marking of the subject (but not of the direct object) of a verb in Series I; the subject of a Class 1 or 3 verb may be in the narrative, as assigned by the extended rule, or in the nominative, as assigned by (11), the rule that formerly governed the domain of Series I. Application of the extended version of (12) and of (11) are illustrated in the (a) and (b) sentences, respectively; (41) illustrates a Class 1 verb, and (42) a Class 3 verb.

(41)   (a)   usta-k   oxori   k'odums
               carpenter-NAR house.NOM build.1
               "A carpenter builds the house."

        (b)   usta   oxori   k'odums
               carpenter-NOM house.NOM build.1
               "A carpenter builds the house."   (Čikobava 1936b: 2, 1-2)

(42)   (a)   monč've-k k'lyuxums
               hen-NAR cluck.3
               "A hen clucks."   (Čikobava 1936b: 5:2)

        (b)   monč'a k'roxams
               hen.NOM cluck.3
               "A hen clucks."[26]   (Čikobava 1936b: 2,21)

The Maxo dialect retains the extended version of rule (12) and lines (a–b) of rule (11); the two rules together produce the variation in the marking of subjects shown in (41) and (42). We assume that other dialects of Laz likewise passed through a stage at which variation according to rule (11) and the extended version of rule (12) was tolerated in the domain of Series I, that speakers gradually applied (11) less and less often, until it occurred so infrequently that a new generation of speakers failed to learn it. This, then, is one source of variation in language.

In some variation, one variant may be marked, the other unmarked (though this is by no means always the case, since often enough none of the variants is marked or considered odd by speakers, but rather all are treated as more or less equal alternatives). In cases of inequal variants, as an extension begins, the old pattern, no matter how illogical it may have been, is comfortable to speakers, and the innovative pattern is felt as something different, marked. Gradually the innovative pattern becomes more familiar, and the older pattern comes to be perceived as an oddity, since it inevitably no longer fits with the general (extended) pattern of the language. The older pattern eventually comes to be felt as archaic, as a highly marked pattern, and then is lost. This path of spread through the community describes the S-curve documented in recent work by Kroch (1989a,b) and Ogura (1993). Drawing on data collected by Ellegård (1953), Kroch showed that *do*-support spread through English in this manner. Our interpretation of these data is that *do* was reanalyzed early as a supporting auxiliary, and subsequently *do* began to be used in environments appropriate for support (originally including affirmative declarative clauses).[27] The S-curve itself, then, represents the actualization of this reanalysis, and the change in markedness occurs at the mid-point of the "S," as speakers begin to expect *do* in the environments where it may occur.

5.5   Blending and contamination

In this section we make a brief excursus to consider two related notions from traditional approaches to diachronic syntax in order to show how we account for the phenomena described by these terms and to establish their place in our approach.

Blending has already been mentioned in section 4.4.3.2, where it was noted that van der Gaaf (1904) used this term to describe an aspect of the syntax of inversion verbs in Middle English. In this instance van der Gaaf showed that the inversion construction (his "Type A") of Old English, in which certain verbs occur in construction with dative experiencers and nominative themes, was replaced by the direct construction (his "Type D"), in which experiencers have all the properties of subjects and themes of inversion verbs have all the properties of objects. The patterns he refers to as blends combine properties of the inversion constructions with properties of the direct construction: for example, in (52) of chapter 4, the experiencer is in an objective case (ambiguously dative or accusative), as in the inversion construction, while the theme is also in the objective case, as in the direct construction. Those patterns referred to as blends by van der Gaaf never become common and do not endure. We account for such patterns by recognizing that multiple analyses continue to exist for an extended period of time after reanalysis, and by making it possible for an individual rule (here assignment of objective case) to extend in the way described in section 5.4.

The term "contamination" has sometimes been used to describe the origin of a new construction based on two partially similar constructions. Contamination is defined by Paul as follows:

> Kontamination ist Mischung zweier Konstruktionen, die entsteht, indem sich zwei sinnverwandte Ausdrucksformen gleichzeitig ins Bewußtsein drängen.
> (Paul 1949: 427)

> Contamination is a mixing of two constructions, which originates through two semantically related expressions simultaneously forcing themselves into the consciousness.   [Our translation, ACH/LC]

The notion was frequently employed by Neogrammarians and their followers in more traditional treatments of the history of several Indo-European and Finno-Ugric languages (see chapter 2). Ebert (1978: 16) cites the following examples of contamination from Paul (1920 [1898]). In German, both (43a) and (43b) are normal ways of expressing possession:

(43)   (a)   das gehört   mir
                that belongs me.DAT
                "That belongs to me."

        (b)   das ist mein
               that is mine

According to Paul, (44) develops out of the mixing or contamination of these:

(44)   das gehört mein
        "That belongs to me," literally: "That belongs mine."

Similarly, out of (45a) and (45b), in the same meaning, (45c) develops.

(45)   (a)   ich freue mich   deines   Mutes
               I   please me.ACC your.GEN   courage.GEN
               "I rejoice in your courage."

        (b)   mich   freut dein   Mut
               me.ACC   please your.NOM   courage.NOM
               "Your courage pleases me."

        (c)   mich freut deines Mutes

(For other examples, see Paul 1920 [1898]: 160–73.)

While (44) and (45c) were never fully accepted, the Neogrammarian notion of contamination has been used also to account for sentence patterns that became fully productive: for example, in Estonian (above), (3c) was said to be based on (1a) and (1b). One property of (1b), namely the active participle, now reanalyzed as the indirect form of a finite verb, is extended into the domain of (1a), embedded clauses introduced by *et* "that" and containing a finite verb form. In fact, Ikola (1953), following Neogrammarian influences and especially Paul (1920 [1898]), characterizes this change in Estonian as "contamination" (see Campbell 1991: 289). All examples of "contamination" that we know of are analyzable as examples of extension, often including the reanalysis that precedes it, just as in the Estonian example. Thus, the traditional notions of both blending and contamination are straightforwardly accounted for in the theory developed here.

5.6   Conclusion

The purposes of this chapter have been to provide examples and detailed description of extension, as defined in chapter 3, to examine the conditions under which it applies, and to state a constraint on its application, (39). In addition we have pointed out that lexical diffusion in syntax is one type of extension (section 5.3.3.1), and we have proposed a model for it (section 5.3.3.2).

We have discussed "S" curves as a representation of extension, noting its relation to variation and markedness. Finally, we have examined the relevance of some traditional notions to our approach and our account of them.

6   *Language contact and syntactic borrowing*

Es gibt keine Mischsprache.

(Max Müller 1871: 86)

Es gibt keine völlig ungemischte Sprache.

(Hugo Schuchardt 1884: 5)

6.1   Introduction

As set out in chapter 3, syntactic borrowing is one of the fundamental mechanisms in the approach to syntactic change developed in this book. In this chapter, we evaluate universals (and general claims) that have been proposed in the linguistic literature concerning borrowing, we illustrate various aspects of syntactic borrowing and other changes induced by language contact, and we show how these fit in to our approach in general.

Syntactic borrowing is perhaps the most neglected and abused area of syntactic change. Excesses in the past are well known and require little comment here; more disturbing is that such problems persist even to the present day. Current views range from the extremes on the one hand, that syntactic borrowing is either impossible or is very rare, to on the other hand fanciful explanations that all otherwise unexplained syntactic eccentricities in a language may be due to foreign influence. This notwithstanding, grammatical borrowing was generally regarded as respectable and important in the history of linguistics (see chapter 2). In this chapter it is our hope to put syntactic borrowing in balanced perspective and to determine the role it must be allotted in any theory of syntactic change. We approach this task in the following way. First, after evaluating hypothesized general claims and universals which have been proposed concerning grammatical borrowing, we consider selected case studies of grammatical borrowing, chosen because they illustrate points we wish to emphasize with respect to syntactic borrowing, from which we draw some general conclusions. We end with the implications of syntactic borrowing for theoretical interests in syntactic change; we argue that these are considerable.

In spite of a long tradition of study and many clear examples, several scholars have expressed what seem to us to be too strong aversions to grammatical borrowing. For example, Meillet (1914: 86–7) was of the opinion that:

> Il y a aussi des emprunts grammaticaux; mais, comme les emprunts de phonèmes qu'on vient de voir, ils sont liés à des emprunts de mots, et ils concernent ce qu'il y a pour ainsi dire de moins grammatical dans la grammaire. Il n'y a pas d'exemple qu'une flexion comme celle de *j'aimais, nous aimions* ait passé d'une langue à une autre; on n'emprunte une chose de ce genre que si l'on emprunte tout le système d'un coup, c'est-à-dire si l'on change de langue.
> (Meillet 1921 [1914]: 86–7)

> There are grammatical borrowings; however, like the borrowing of phonemes that we have just seen, they are linked to borrowings of words, and they have to do with what within the grammar, so to speak, is least grammatical. There are no examples where an inflectional pattern like that of *j'aimais* ["I loved," imperfect], *nous aimions* ["we loved," imperfect] has passed from one language to another; something of this sort is not borrowed unless the whole system is borrowed en bloc; that is, unless the *langue* [language system] is changed.　　　　　　　　　　　[Our translation, ACH/LC]

Sapir, in his well-know quibbles with Boas over the prospects for distinguishing borrowed from native material in efforts to work out genetic relationships among Native American languages, came to make some particularly negative pronouncements concerning grammatical borrowing; for example, in the chapter entitled "How languages influence each other" in his influential book *Language* he declared: "nowhere do we find any but superficial morphological interinfluencings" (Sapir 1921:203). And elsewhere:

> Such examples as these [e.g. English -*ize* and -*able*] are hardly true evidences of a morphological influence exerted by one language on another. Setting aside the fact that they belong to the sphere of derivational concepts and do not touch the central morphological problem of the expression of relational ideas, they have added nothing to the structural peculiarities of our language.　　　　　　　　　　　　　　　　　　　(Sapir 1921: 202)

And again:

> An examination of such cases [languages which took on structural features owing to the suggestive influence of neighboring languages], however, almost invariably reveals the significant fact that they are but superficial additions on the morphological kernel of the language. So long as such direct historical testimony as we have gives us no really convincing examples of profound morphological influence by diffusion, we shall do well not to put too much reliance in diffusion theories.　　　　　　　　　　　(Sapir 1921: 206)

Sapir's view had considerable impact in shaping opinion, particularly in

America, but similar opinions were also reflected in the thinking of a number of influential European scholars (see Sommerfelt 1960a, 1960b; Vachek 1972: 221–2). In fact, we still find strong doubts concerning the possibility of syntactic borrowing, for example: "Borrowing is generally regarded as a weak tool for explanation. This certainly holds for borrowing at the sentence level, since . . . no convincing example has ever been presented" (Gerritsen 1984:118).

While the terms **contact** and **borrowing** are often used interchangeably, we make a distinction between them. By **contact** we mean a situation in which the speakers of one language are familiar in some way with another. That is, contact is a situation; contact often leads to change through borrowing (one language otherwise influencing another, possibly reciprocally), but the contact itself is not change. Contact is often a catalyst for changes through reanalysis or extension, and borrowing takes place only through contact. We use the term **borrowing** to mean a change in which a foreign syntactic pattern (either a duplication of the foreign pattern or at least a formally quite similar construction) is incorporated into the borrowing language through the influence of a donor pattern found in a contact language. Many things that are often labeled "borrowing" in the literature should, we believe, more properly be considered "contact," since they involve other mechanisms of change which happen to be triggered by contact with another language.[1]

In what follows we attempt to present a more balanced view of the role of borrowing in syntactic change than that reflected in the history of the study of syntactic change. We begin with an assessment of general claims and proposed universals of borrowing.

6.2   Proposed universals (and other general claims) concerning grammatical borrowing

Given that grammatical borrowing has received little rigorous attention within the study of syntactic change, particularly recently,[2] it might seem surprising that universally applicable statements regarding grammatical changes due to borrowing have been proposed at all. Borrowing involves externally motivated changes and is not among the internal factors so popular in recent theories of syntactic change – particularly those that rely on language acquisition and constraints in universal grammar to explain grammatical change (see chapter 2). Nevertheless, several general claims and universals concerning grammatical borrowing have been put forward and we evaluate some of the more significant of these now.

6.2.1 The structural-compatibility requirement

This claim is suggested in a variety of very similar forms. Meillet (1914: 84, 87) thought structural borrowing was rare and that grammatical borrowing was possible only between very similar systems, such as those found in dialects of the same language. Perhaps the claim is best known in a form made for phonological structure by Jakobson (1938 [1949/1962]: 54): "La langue n'accepte des éléments de structure étrangers que quand ils correspondent à ses tendances de développement" (Jakobson 1938 [1949/1962]: 241). This became more generally familiar from Weinreich's (1953: 25) quotation of it: "One might therefore say, with Jakobson, that a language 'accepts foreign structural elements only when they correspond to its tendencies of development.'" Weinreich (1953: 25) supposed further: "Since such latent internal tendencies, however, by definition exist even without the intervention of foreign influence, the language contact and the resulting interference could be considered to have, at best, a trigger effect, releasing or accelerating developments which mature independently." (See also Haugen [1954: 385–6], who reaffirms this claim with respect to bound morphemes.) For a version of the structure-compatibility constraint more specifically concerned with syntax, Allen's (1980 [1977]: 380) formulation is explicit: "As a hypothesis, we would expect syntactic influence only when the two languages had a good deal of syntactic similarity to begin with."[3]

Others who hold such a view include Ebert (1978: 16–17):

> Syntaktische Entlehnungen sind oft schwer zu erkennen, weil die fraglichen Konstruktionen häufig "vom System zugelassene Möglichkeiten" (Coseriu) darstellen . . . Lehnsyntax kann auch quantitativ sein: eine an sich heimische Konstruktion wird unter dem Einfluß einer fremdsprachlichen Fügung häufiger gebraucht.
>
> Entlehnungen werden in verschiedenem Grade assimiliert und sind oft daran zu erkennen, daß sie nur in einer gewissen Art von Texten, in einem Stil, in einem geographischen Raum oder im Sprachgebrauch gewisser sozialer Schichten vorkommen.

> Syntactic borrowings are often difficult to recognize, because the constructions under consideration often represent "possibilities permitted by the system" (Coseriu). Loan syntax can also be quantitative: a native construction is more often used under the influence of a foreign-language construction.
>
> Borrowings are assimilated to different extents and are often recognizable from the fact that they occur only in a particular type of text, in one style, in one geographical region, or in the linguistic usage of particular social strata.
>
> [Our translation, ACH/LC]

(Cf. similar statements by Aitchison [1981: 121], Bickerton [1981: 50], and others.)

Common sense suggests that the structural-compatibility proposal – in some form – is aimed in the right direction, since in principle it ought to be easier to borrow constructions that are similar to existing ones (or at least do not conflict with the borrowing language's basic structure) than structures that go against the structural grain of the borrowing language. However, the claim has counterexamples, and therefore any insistence that grammatical borrowing happens only in situations of shared structural similarity is simply wrong.

Many examples involve grammatical borrowing from typologically divergent languages, including non-similar constructions formerly unknown in the borrowing language which often are quite at odds with the basic typology of the borrowing language. A few such counterexamples are: (a) Ethiopian Semitic, with wholesale overhaul of word order typology in several of the languages due to Cushitic influence (Leslau 1945, 1952; Hetzron 1972; Little 1974; Campbell, Bubenik, and Saxon 1988); (b) syntactic borrowings in the South Asian linguistics area, including, for instance, the infinitive suffix -*na* in Gondi borrowed from Hindi-Urdu, relative clause formations with finite verbs in all literary Dravidian languages borrowed from Indo-Aryan (as opposed to native Dravidian participial relative clauses), passive constructions from Sanskrit and English in Dravidian (see discussion below), etc. (Gumperz and Wilson 1971; Nadkarni 1975; Sridhar 1978; Emeneau 1980; Appel and Muysken 1987: 158–9); (c) Media Lengua (Muysken 1981), a variety of Quechua which exhibits considerable syntactic change due to Spanish influence, including the introduction of prepositions, conjunctions, complementizers, word order changes, and the subordinator *ndu* (from Spanish participles ending in -V*ndo*); (d) Chinookan dialects, which have adopted the tense–aspect systems of their neighbors, with "simple taxis and aspect distinctions on the Pacific Coast," as in Salishan languages, but with "multitense (morphosyntactic paradigm) distinctions in the southern Plateau," as in neighboring Sahaptian languages (Silverstein 1974); etc. (For other examples, see Appel and Muysken 1987: 158–62; Campbell 1980; Comrie 1981; Dawkins 1916; Gair 1980; Gołąb 1959; Fujii 1985; Heath 1978; Hill and Hill 1986; Hyman 1975; Jacobsen 1980; Lehiste 1988; Leslau 1945, 1952; Li 1983; Masica 1976; Oswalt 1976; Pray 1980; Rédei 1970; Sandfeld 1930; Thomason 1980; Thomason and Kaufman 1988; Vendryes 1968 [1921]; Weinreich 1953.)

Given the importance attributed to this claim, we cite the case of American Finnish which has borrowed a number of constructions from English which show that grammatical borrowings need not be compatible with native grammatical trends. We present only one example here, but for others see Campbell (1980). Standard Finnish does not permit infinitival complements of nouns or adjectives with subject raising; however, American Finnish borrowed such a construction from English:

(1)   tämä oli ensimmäinen kerta mei-lle mennä tä-llä   laiva-lla
          this   was first   time us-For to.go   this-On ship-On
          "This was the first time for us to go on this ship."

A Standard Finnish equivalent of (1) would be (2):

(2)   tämä oli ensimmäinen kerta, kun   oli-mme matkusta-neet
          this   was first   time   when had-We travel-PAST.PTCPL

          tä-llä   laiva-lla
          this-On ship-On

Another sentence illustrating this is (3):

(3)   oli aivan liian kauan häne-n   odottaa
          was really too   long he-GEN to.wait
          "It was entirely too long for him to wait."

These are entirely impossible in Standard Finnish.

Appel and Muysken's (1987: 159) notion of "resyntactization" perhaps fits in this context; they have in mind examples such as the replacement of the relative clause rule in Konkani grammar by a structurally very different type of relative rule from Kannada, an example of grammatical convergence in the Indian linguistic area.

Such examples as those presented here show that the structural-compatibility requirement in any absolute sense is incorrect. It is as a general tendency or preference that we may expect the claim to hold, but how is it to be framed? To be very useful in a theory of change, it would require an explicit notion of what "shared syntactic similarity" is and how one determines it. Essentially at stake here is how social factors can overcome structural resistance to borrowing (see Thomason and Kaufman 1988: 15).

6.2.1.1   *Fit with innovation possibilities of the borrowing language*

A variant of the structural-compatibility requirement suggests a slightly broader outlook which anticipates the language's future based on its current structure. It is claimed that borrowed material must fit the system of possible modifications in the receiving language; that is, the "innovation possibilities offered by the receiving system" (Vogt 1954: 372). This is much like Coseriu's (1978 [1957]) approach, stating that changes happen only where the "norms" of the language (the patterns and forms actually used) do not fully match the "system" (predicted by the rules and patterns of the language, though not necessarily actually deployed in the "norms"); only changes in the "norms" which conform to possibilities already in the "system" are permitted. If this claim were strictly true, a language could never change its typology as a result of foreign influence. This, however, is quite false, as will be seen in examples mentioned above, those presented below, and others (e.g. those treated in Campbell 1987; Campbell, Bubenik, and Saxon 1988; cf. Thomason and Kaufman 1988: 18–19). For example, syntactic borrowings in American Finnish produced typological changes in the language which are quite at odds with the "system" of Standard Finnish, as for example those just mentioned above, the loss of case endings together with the imposition of rigid grammatical word order to indicate subject and object roles of NPs (contrasted with Standard Finnish's cases and flexible word order) (Campbell 1980; Sahlman–Karlsson 1976: 104–7).

We illustrate this last point in greater detail with examples of grammatical borrowings in Pipil from Spanish (Campbell 1987). Pipil, like most other Mesoamerican languages, has relational nouns (possessed noun roots functioning as locatives, e.g. *i-tan ne kwawi-t* "under the tree" (*i-* "its," *-tan* "under," *ne* "the," *kwawi-t* "tree"), rather than prepositions or postpositions. Under Spanish influence, some Pipil relational nouns shifted both form and function to become true prepositions of the Spanish type. The relational noun *-(i)hpak* "on, upon, over, on top of" now occurs frequently as the remodeled preposition *pak*:

(4)   pak kal "on top of the house"

(5)   pak me:sah "on the table"
        (contrast former *i-hpak ne me:sah* [it-on the table])

(6)   mu-sa:luh   *pak* i-kechku:yu
        REFLEX-stuck on   his-neck
        "It stuck on his neck."[4]

A periphrastic genitive equivalent to Spanish *de* "of" has developed from the relational noun *-pal* "possession" (e.g. *nu-pal* "mine"), becoming a true preposition. The possession of one noun by another in former times was shown only by the pattern, e.g. *i-pe:lu ne ta:kat* "his-dog the man" for "the man's dog." Some examples of the new preposition are:

(7)   kinekit   kikwat ne nakat, ne ihyak   nakat **pal ne masa:t**
        they.want they.eat the meat, the stinking meat *of* the deer
        "They want to eat the meat, the stinking meat of the deer."

(8)   tik nu-ma:taw ohombrón plastas *pal* **turuh** wi:ts
       in my-net   big   cowpies *of* cow   come
       "What came in my bag were big plasters of cow."

Similarly, the relational noun -*wan* "with" (previously always possessed, *i-wan* "with her," *nu-wan* "with me") has now become a preposition *wan* "with":

(9)   nin ni-nemi nu-chan tise:nnemit   *wan* **se: nu-amiguh**
       here I-am   my-house we.together.are *with* a   my-friend
       "Here I am at my house, sitting together with my friend."

(10)   ta-ta:wilua   *wan* **i-espehuh**
       REDUP-shine *with* his-mirror
       "He shines with his mirror."

(11)   mas ka tiyu:tak wi:tsa-ya   *wan* **ne i-tapak**
       more in evening come-IMPERF *with* the her-wash
       "Later in the evening she was coming with her wash."

The borrowed category "preposition" is totally at odds with the former "system" (not just the "norms"), and is not "structurally compatible" with the typological grain of the language. (Central Mexican Nahuatl also presents similar examples of grammatical borrowing; see Suárez 1977; Hill and Hill 1986.)

   As examples such as those considered here show, syntactic borrowing and contact-induced grammatical change are not necessarily restricted to the "innovation possibilities" (even if these could be clearly defined) of the borrowing language.

6.2.2   Borrowing as replacement, as "morphological renewal"

One of Weinreich's (1953: 31–7) claims, as reformulated by Heath (1978: 73), is that the borrowing of a morpheme usually involves the replacement of a native morpheme by one from another language rather than the creation of a new morphological category filled by a borrowed morpheme – "morphemes are usually borrowed in such a way that they replace an old morpheme, formally renewing rather than creating a category." This is a variety of the "structural-compatibility" principle. Thomason and Kaufman (1988: 54) present a similar scenario: "In morphology and syntax it seems likely that most interference, except in cases of heavy influence, will involve either new means of expressing functional categories already present in the receiving language or (for morphology) loss of previously existing categories." Sommerfelt (1960a: 311) held a very similar opinion: "The usual form of grammatical influence from language on language inside a cultural area is not one of direct borrowing of elements but an adaptation of native elements to correspond to the model of the language which exercises the cultural influence." However, Weinreich and Thomason and Kaufman may include the wholesale borrowing of foreign morphemes, while Sommerfelt appears to mean only the adapting of existing material under foreign influence. An example which illustrates the notion of "morphological renewal" is the borrowing of English *-s* "plural" in Welsh, acceptable according to the claim since Welsh already had a category of "plural." Counterexamples, however, are abundant, several presented by Heath: for example, a formerly unattested category of "ergative" was created by diffusion in a number of languages of Arnhem Land (Heath 1978: 75–7).

Appel and Muysken's (1987: 159) notion of **resyntactization** is related but deals with syntactic rather than morphological matters. It differs, however, in that it deals with cases which involve general types of constructions which already exist in the language, say "passive" for example, but which explicitly do not preserve structural compatibility, as for example the structurally rather different relative clause rule borrowed from Kannada into Konkani, which replaced the native Konkani rule – involving a Dravidian structure (compatible with SOV languages) which was basically incompatible with the Indo-Aryan typology of Konkani, though both the original and the borrowed were kinds of relative clauses. Many borrowings and reanalyses which are due to language contact result in structures which were not formerly part of the language, for example the Pipil prepositions and the American Finnish subject raising with infinitives mentioned above, show that contact-induced change is by no means limited to resyntactizations, reformulations of existing categories and constructions.

We therefore conclude that morphological renewal due to borrowing and language contact and resyntactization are possible, perhaps even quite frequent, and that such changes are in no way limited only to such renewal.[5]

6.2.3   Claim: grammatical gaps tend to get filled through borrowing

Quite in opposition to the spirit of the structural-compatibility hypothesis, and yet akin to it in many ways, is the claim that some languages borrow precisely because they lack otherwise useful syntactic categories or constructions which they encounter in other languages with which they come into contact. More precisely, it has been claimed for several languages that they borrowed conjunctions and/or various subordinating devices only after and because they came into contact with other languages already possessing these things, seen as "gaps" in the grammars of the borrowers, thus explaining why they set upon acquiring the new material so rapidly when the notions became familiar to them from contact languages (see K. Hale 1971; Karttunen 1976; Heath

1978: 115–16; Mithun 1980; Campbell and Mithun 1981, Hill and Hill 1981; Campbell 1987). Thus, as the claim in such cases goes, it is precisely the lack of shared structural similarity which stimulates the borrowing, though "gap" seems to suggest no structural incompatibility. Needless to say, the notion of filling structural gaps is controversial and not supported by all scholars (see, for example, Brody 1987: 508).

Heath's (1978: 115–16) functional constraints on borrowing include a version of the gap-filling view: "Only those morphemes have actually been diffused which contribute something to the borrowing language which was previously lacking . . . morphemic borrowing is viewed in its therapeutic aspect. Borrowings are interpreted as devices to fill functional gaps." Heath cites as examples (a) the borrowing of ergative markers in Ngandi, which serve to distinguish the subject and object of transitive verbs, formerly easily confused, and (b) the borrowed noun class prefixes useful in discourse for cross-reference and anaphora in languages of Arnhem Land.

Vachek (1972: 221–2) seems to combine both the structural-compatibility constraint and the filling of grammatical gaps in his claim that: "The influence of external factors upon the development of the structure of language could only assert itself because its assertion was in harmony with the needs and wants of the structure exposed to that influence."

An example of such gap-filling was proposed for changes in Pipil complex sentences (see Campbell 1987). Formerly the language had very limited and perceptually none-too-salient resources of coordination and subordination (e.g. Ø [that is, juxtaposition]) for coordinate clauses, *i-wan* (relational noun, "its-with") "with" for coordination of nominals, and *ne* for most kinds of subordinate clauses, relative clauses included). This state of affairs was not as efficient for the hearer to process as a grammar with different overt conjunctions for varied kinds of clauses. The changes in Pipil (through the borrowing of Spanish conjunctions and the reshaping of certain relational nouns to function as conjunctions) were motivated, it is hypothesized, to fill the "grammatical gaps" recognized in contact with Spanish. Pipil acquired a variety of coordinate conjunctions:

pero, pe:roh	but	(Sp. pero)
ni, ni ke	neither nor, nor	(Sp. ni, ni que)
sino	but	(Sp. sino)
y	and	(Sp. y)
mas bien	rather	(Sp. más bien)
o	or	(Sp. o)
wan	and	

Wan now appears as a full coordinate conjunction "and," having lost the relational-noun requirement of occurring only with possessive pronominal prefixes; it had previously functioned to conjoin only nominals, such as *Juan i-wan Maria* (John her-with Mary) "John and Mary" / "John with Mary," but in its new form it also serves to conjoin clauses, such as:

(12)   ne ta:kat k-itskih   ne mich *wan* ki-kwah
         the man   it-caught the fish   and it-ate
         "The man caught the fish and ate it."

(13)   k-ali:ka-t ne ye:y pipiltsitsín   se: in-mihmichintsitsín *wan* ne se:yuk
         it-take-PL the three boy.PL.DIMIN one their-fish.PL.DIMIN   and the other

         k-ali:ka se: i-tapahsul ne wi:lutsin mareño.
         it-take a its-nest the bird   mareño
         "The three little boys bring some little fish and the other brings a
         small mareño bird's nest."

This change, coupled with the borrowed Spanish conjunctions, has altered Pipil from a language of limited coordination with no true coordinate conjunctions.

Pipil had very few subordinate conjunctions, but has added several additional kinds of subordinate constructions through the borrowing of Spanish *ašta* "until," *porké* "because," and *tay ora* "when" (*tay* "what," *ora* "hour" [Sp. *hora*]), plus developing *pal* "in order to, so that" from the relational noun *i-pal*. Historically the "generic" subordinator *ne* was used for all of these. Pipil relative clauses have also changed, due to Spanish influence, to provide a variety of relative structures (for details, see Campbell 1987). The combined effect of the changes in coordination, relative clauses, and other subordinate constructions makes a rather large variety of complex sentences more distinguishable (more like Spanish), with discourse functions that are easier to perceive and process. (See also Boas [1930] and Hill and Hill [1986] for extensive discussion of the similar Central Mexican Nahuatl case.)

While we have no particular objection to the view of language contact and borrowing leading to the filling of so-called "structural gaps," we suspect the general notion requires much further investigation. Nevertheless, however this ultimately comes to be viewed, it seems quite clear that contact situations can and quite frequently do result in the acquisition of new clause types, involving both subordinate and coordinate conjunction, which constitute more extensive resources and discourse options than were available before the contact-induced changes and borrowings took place.

6.2.4 Claim: free-standing grammatical forms are more easily borrowed than bound morphemes

Along these lines, Weinreich (1953: 41) suggested a more sympathetic constraint on borrowing: "In the interference of two grammatical patterns it is ordinarily the one which uses relatively free and invariant morphemes in its paradigms . . . which serves as the model for imitation." Heath's (1978: 72) reformulation of Weinreich's view is: "An unbound (free) morpheme is likely to replace a more bound one." Aitchison's (1981: 120–1) claim that detachable elements are most easily borrowed is akin to this, as is Maher's (1985) that enclave languages tend to replace synthetic constructions by analytic or periphrastic ones. On a broad level, this suggests that when typologically distinct languages are in contact, the one with the most isolating and non-flexional typological structure should win out and be the source of influence on languages which are less clearly of this structural type. It also suggests that when grammatical subsystems are at stake, the direction of influence will be from the more "syntactic" (isolating) one to the more "paradigmatic" or morphological one. (See Hill and Hill [1986: 233–334] for positive examples of the development away from "synthetic" towards "analytic" structures in convergence.) Again, there are clear counterexamples to this claim if it is taken as anything more than a tendency. Probably social factors and the intensity of contact play a stronger determining role with respect to which will borrow from the other than strict linguistic typology.

Among the counterexamples, Heath (1978: 73, 98–100) himself documented the borrowing of a negative suffix from Ngandi which replaced the original unbound negative particle in Ritharngu. Li (1983) presented the case of Wutun (Chinese) borrowing from Anduo Tibetan, for example, a causative suffix instead of resultative compounds. Similarly, Ma'a (Cushitic) has taken on a "rather full Bantu grammar that includes much inflectional morphology and even some allomorphy" (Thomason and Kaufman 1988: 20). (See also Carranza Romero 1986.)

6.2.5 Claims of borrowability based on rankings of grammatical categories

A variety of claims range from a more simple form that some particular grammatical category (say "verbs" or "conjunctions") cannot be borrowed to more complex claims that maintain that some categories rank highest in terms of borrowability, others lowest if borrowable at all. The spirit of this claim is found in Whitney's (1881) view: "Whatever is more formal or structural in character remains in that degree free from the intrusion of foreign material" (quoted in

Haugen 1950: 224). Deroy's (1956: 66) outlook was similar: "Plus l'élément est lexical, plus il est empruntable, mais plus il est grammatical, moins il est empruntable." Haugen (1950: 224) spoke of this in terms of a "scale of adoptability," while Vočadlo (1938; Haugen 1950: 225) had a "scale of receptivity."

Coteanu (1957: 133), for example, claimed that prepositions, conjunctions, and articles, to the extent that they are used grammatically, can be borrowed from one language to another only with great difficulty – though this is clearly not the case, as seen in the typical borrowing of conjunctions and other discourse particles from Spanish into a large variety of Indian languages of Latin America (as in the Pipil changes cited above; for abundant examples see Boas 1930; Suárez 1977, 1983: 135–7; Brody 1987; Campbell 1987; see Carranza Romero 1986 for much borrowed Spanish morphology in Quitaracza Quechua, including the Spanish infinitive marker -r on native verbs).

In the extensive diffusion among Aboriginal languages of Arnhem Land, Heath (1978: 105) divided morphological categories into those that were readily borrowed and those that were not. Under "diffusible" he listed: case affixes, number affix, noun class affixes, diminutive affix, derivational verbal affixes, negative affix, other postpositions, inchoative verbalizer, etc.; under "non- diffusible": independent pronouns, bound pronominals, verbal inflectional affixes, demonstrative stems, demonstrative adverbs. However, he does not intend these observations as universal constraints, noting different borrowing patterns in some European languages. Rather, he attempts to delve deeper, seeking functional and structural reasons for this pattern of borrowed vs. non-borrowed morphological categories (see below).

In brief, while some grammatical categories may typically be more resistant to borrowing than others, an absolute ranking will provide little real satisfaction. The circumstances of each borrowing situation may lead to violations in individual languages of any proposed borrowability scale.

6.2.6   The principle of local functional value

Another of Weinreich's claimed restrictions on borrowability is restated by Heath (1978: 72) as: "A morpheme whose grammatical function cannot be understood except in the context of a broader morphosyntactic environment is unlikely to be diffused." Related to this, Haugen (1956: 67) held that "function words, which only occur as parts of utterances, are seldom borrowed." Heath (1978: 73) is inclined to accept Weinreich's claim as valid; however, while it is headed in the right direction, counterexamples exist, for example in the case in several Mesoamerican Indian languages of the borrowed discourse particles, relative clause markers, adpositions, etc., taken from Spanish (see Suárez

1983: 135–7; Brody 1987; Campbell 1987). For other counterexamples, see Thomason and Kaufman (1988: 91–5, 100–9, 215–330).

6.2.7   The reduction-of-allomorphy claim
Heath (1978: 72) restated another of Weinreich's views as a claim involving the situation where one language has a single allomorph of some particular morpheme while another language with which the first is in contact has multiple allomorphs for the same morpheme; the claim is that there is a tendency for the single allomorph of the former to replace the multiple allomorphs of the latter. (See also Maher's 1985 claim concerning enclave languages that they tend to reduce the number of allomorphs compared to non-enclave versions of the same language.) For counterexamples, see Heath (1978: 73).

6.2.8   The structural simplification claim
Related to the last claim is another, that structural borrowing results in simplification; that is, in the reduction of variants and of constraints or conditions on the employment of the borrowed material, or in the reduction of the grammatical subsystem of the borrowing language where the borrowing is employed. Vogt's (1948: 39) version of this claim is: "On observe souvent qu'une langue, ou un patois, perd des distinctions formelles, dans des circonstances qui rendent l'hypothèse d'influence étrangère assez naturelle. Mais la création de nouvelles catégories morphologiques au sens étroit du mot sous l'influence d'un autre système semble se présenter assez rarement." Coteanu (1957: 143) stated the claim as: "Eviter les complications morphologiques est une caractéristique de l'évolution des langues mixtes." While as a broad tendency this claim is to be recommended, there are clear counterexamples, such as those discussed in the filling of structural gaps (above), usually resulting in complications rather than simplifications. (See also examples in Thomason and Kaufman 1988.[6])

6.3   Moravcsik's universals of borrowing
Moravcsik (1978) made several quite explicit proposals for universals of grammatical borrowing, the more salient of which we take up now.

1 No non-lexical property can be borrowed unless the borrower already includes borrowed lexical items from the same source language (Moravcsik 1978: 110). With this, Moravcsik claims that grammatical morphemes are not borrowed until after some lexical morphemes have been borrowed first. This

is probably true, but trivially so; that is, there is no apparent principle of language which would require this to be the case. Since lexical items are easily borrowed, they would normally show up first, and then after more intensive contact, grammatical loans might occur, if borrowed at all. However, there would seem to be no inherent connection between prior lexical borrowings and grammatical loans – and hence no theoretically significant implications, even if this claim should prove true. In many Latin American Indian languages, for example, Spanish conjunctions (grammatical morphemes) were borrowed very early and easily, since the languages often lacked such conjunctions or had a very limited number. For a possible real exception, see the rather extensive Finno-Ugric structural influence on Russian and Slavic languages in the relative absence of lexical loans (Thomason and Kaufman 1988: 43, 242–50, cf. 20–1).

2 No member of a constituent class whose members do not serve as domains of accentuation can be included in the class of borrowed properties unless some members of another constituent class are also so included which do serve as domains of accentuation and which properly include the same members of the former class. This proposed universal is intended to exclude cases where "bound morphemes" such as clitics, affixes, and parts of compounds are borrowed, but no free forms of which they are a part are borrowed (e.g. *-ette* of *kitchenette* exists only because *cigarette* and *statuette* were borrowed containing *-ette*).

While counterexamples may be rare, they are not unknown. Clear cases of borrowing of bound clitics (not accented) are attested from Finnish to Lapp; the Finnish enclitics *-han/-hän* "emphatic," *-pa/-pä* "emphatic," *-kä* "negative clitic," *-ko/-kö* "question," and *-kin* "positive orientation, also," *-kaan/-kään* "negative orientation, neither" have all been borrowed in various Lapp dialects. There is no evidence to compel us to believe that these were first borrowed attached to some host noun or verb. It has also been claimed that some Balto-Finnic clitics were borrowed into Latvian and Lithuanian, though this is controversial. (See Laanest 1982: 293–4; Nevis 1985.)

For this claim it should be noticed that its domain is largely limited to morphology (with clitics being between morphology and syntax); the claim is ultimately not very "syntactic." Notice also that in principle there is no reason why a language could not borrow some semantically very salient affix without concomitant borrowing of some particular word containing the affix. For example, it should not be surprising to find a language which formerly lacked derivational-morphological means for signaling ordinal numbers, but which borrowed a bound affix from a neighboring language that derives ordinals from cardinal numbers, attaching it to native numerals to produce new ordinals. Examples of borrowed aspect markers on native verbs and of borrowed noun classifier systems with native nouns are known (see the cases cited by Thomason and Kaufman 1988 and others mentioned below) – could these systems be borrowed in relative absence of their host verbs or nouns in the donor language? Since verbs are rarely borrowed, the possibility exists.

3 A lexical item whose meaning is verbal can never be included in the set of borrowed properties. By this Moravcsik intends to deny the existence of a language that has borrowed a symbolic association of a verbal form and a verbal meaning. This proposal, as stated, is clearly false. This may be aimed in the right direction: it is clear that nouns are borrowed most easily, and other categories with more difficulty, which makes borrowing of verbs rarer. While some languages may borrow only nouns, and far fewer have borrowed verbs as verbs, clearly verbs can be borrowed as members of the syntactic category of verbs. Examples are not difficult to find: Nahuatl *pašalua* "to have fun" (from Spanish *pasear*); English loans from Latin, French, Yiddish, e.g. *perceive, acquire, desire, chase, maneuver, schlep*, etc.; Finnish from Swedish, English, Russian, etc. (e.g. *Kommunikoi-* "communicate," *kopioi-* "copy," *tykkää-* "to like" (Swedish *tyka*), *snaja-* "to know" (Russian *zna(ju-* "[I] know"), etc.

Moravcsik also proposes that no lexical item that is not a noun can belong to the class of properties borrowed from a language unless this class also includes at least one noun. That is, according to this claim, nouns are borrowed first and foremost, and non-nouns are borrowed, if at all, not until after some nouns have been borrowed. Again, this seems accurate, though not a very exciting discovery. Since nouns name things, prototypically refer to visible, concrete objects, and are the first to be acquired in language acquisition (see Givón 1984; Hopper and Thompson 1984), it is unsurprising that nouns would typically be the first acquired also in language contact. Nouns also tend to have fewer morphosyntactic markings than verbs, making loans easier to assimilate in this category.

4 No inflectional affixes can belong to the set of properties borrowed from a language unless at least one derivational affix also belongs to the set. This universal would exclude a language that has borrowed inflectional affixes but no derivational ones.[7] While this may usually be the case, this proposal is clearly false in an absolute sense, since counterexamples exist: for example, Bolivian Quechua has borrowed *-s* "plural" (inflectional) from Spanish, but apparently without any borrowed Spanish derivational affixes. It may be significant that this proposal involves morphological material, and much of inflectional

morphology is "supplied" in some way by rules of the grammar in most contemporary theories of syntax. Perhaps a more revealing way to look at this claim would be in terms of the semantic content of the borrowed affix – it is unlikely for semantically weak or redundant affixes to be borrowed (e.g. verb agreement), but affixes with a clear semantic content (e.g. "plural," "gender," "genitive," and most derivational morphemes) might in appropriate circumstances be taken over by a borrowing language. For other counter-examples, see Heath (1978) and Emeneau (1980).

5 A lexical item that is of the "grammatical" type (which includes at least conjunctions and adpositions) cannot be included in the set of properties borrowed from a language unless the rule that determines its linear order with respect to its head is also so included. As stated, this proposed universal would exclude a language which borrows the form and the meaning of a preposition but uses it in postposed position, or borrows the form and meaning of a postposition which it uses preposed, or borrows a clause-initial conjunction and uses it in clause-final position or vice versa. This amounts to a claim that such forms are borrowed only in accordance with their original word order arrangements. In some ways this claim seems counterintuitive, since it suggests that regardless of the borrowing language's word order typology, it could borrow such forms only if it takes at the same time the word order arrangements of the donor language. This amounts to a claim that languages of different word order types either cannot borrow such forms at all from one another or may do so only by opposing their native word-order patterns. Surprisingly, however, counterexamples to this claim are not as readily available as one might expect (see Dawkins [1916], Thomason and Kaufman [1988: 242–6] for some apparent exceptions; see chapter 8 for related discussion).[8]

6.4   Word order and borrowing

In this section we take up word order borrowing; as will be seen, cases of borrowed word order bear serious implications. We consider a variety of examples, basing our discussion primarily on the word order universals of Greenberg (1963) and particularly of Hawkins (1983), drawing heavily from the discussion and examples in Campbell, Bubenik, and Saxon (1988).[9]

6.4.1   Borrowed word order
A rather large number of cases have been reported in which basic word order patterns have been borrowed (see Moravcsik 1978: 102–3; Comrie 1981: 200–3),

and "the effects of diffusion . . . seem to be particularly pervasive in the area of word order" (Dryer 1992: 83). For example, it is argued that Ethiopian Semitic borrowed from Cushitic (see below). Ahom (Thai) is reported to have borrowed Modifier–Head order from Assamese (Indo-European) or some Tibeto-Burman language. Munda languages, it is claimed, borrowed Modifier–Head order from Dravidian. Evidence has been presented that some Kwa languages (Nupe, Yoruba, Ewe, Igbo) borrowed Noun–Genitive order from Bantu. Pipil, Xinca, and Copainalá Zoque all apparently borrowed VOS from neighboring Mayan languages. (See Hyman 1975; Campbell 1987; M. Harris 1978, 1984; Campbell, Kaufman, and Smith-Stark 1986; Campbell, Bubenik, and Saxon 1988; Comrie 1988). M. Harris (1978, 1984: 193) argues that the topic-initial phase of French is due to Germanic influence.[10]

Thus, it is well established that basic word order can be borrowed or can change due to language contact. In fact Smith (1981: 52) has asserted that word order changes are due above all to language contact, while the other causal factors which have been proposed are of negligible importance. This is an extreme view, in our opinion, but it does reflect the fact that indeed many attested word order changes have been brought about by language contact and borrowing.[11]

6.4.2   Word order borrowing and universals

Our main message in this section is that contact and borrowing play a special role in word order typology.[12] It will be shown that certain of the word order types (see Greenberg 1963; Hawkins 1983:288) come to exist only through foreign influence. Thus, contact and borrowing have important consequences for proposed universals of word order and even for the very definition of universals in general.

We begin with the example of type 19 and type 20 languages (as defined by Greenberg and Hawkins). In Hawkins' (1983) expanded sample, type 19, with the orders SOV, Preposition–NP (Prep), Genitive–Noun (GN), and Adjective–Noun (AN), has only two languages illustrating it. Such a small number of exemplifying languages makes type 19 suspicious. Hawkins' two languages are Amharic (Semitic) and Old Persian (Indo-European). While the word order descriptions of these languages are accurate, it is clear that their word order cooccurrence patterns are due to borrowing (or areal diffusion). It is instructive to examine these cases more closely.

Amharic has borrowed extensively from Cushitic languages, which are typically SOV and postpositional (see Leslau 1945, 1952; Hetzron 1972; Little 1974; Ferguson 1976). While it is clear that Amharic has changed its word order under Cushitic influence, it should be noted that it is not the only one of the

Southern Peripheral Semitic languages (Diakonoff 1965:12) which has digressed from the Semitic prototype of SVO/Prep/NG/NA, that is, Hawkins' type 1. Rather, these languages vary significantly in their word order patterns, evidencing differential responses to Cushitic impact. For example, Geʔez of Ethiopia (extinct) represents the Semitic pattern, type 1. The northernmost Ethiopian Semitic language, Tigre, combines the orders SOV/Prep/NG (as in Semitic) with AN (as in Cushitic), thus representing type 18, a type without representatives in Hawkins' (1983:288) sample. Amharic moved one step closer towards the Cushitic type 23 by acquiring GN as well. As observed by Greenberg (1980: 233), GN order with a prepositional possessive is very unusual (it is found also in Pashto, see below). The southernmost Semitic languages of Ethiopia, such as Gafat and Harari, were so completely "cushiticized" that they belong to type 23: SOV/Post/GN/AN.

In sum, Amharic appears to be half-way between the Semitic type (type 1) and the Cushitic type (type 23). Chart 1 of Cushitic influence on Southern Peripheral Semitic languages is revealing:

type 1	VSO	Prep	NG	NA	Geʔez (Semitic type)
type 18	SOV	Prep	NG	AN	Tigre
type 19	SOV	Prep	GN	AN	Amharic
type 23	SOV	Postp	GN	AN	Harari, Gafat (Cushitic type)

Clearly, then, Amharic's word order (type 19) is due to Cushitic influence. Apart from Amharic, Old Persian is the only other representative of type 19 in Hawkins' sample. We suggest that the Old Persian pattern is also due to contact/borrowing; however, what one means by "Old Persian" must be specified carefully, since three varieties are distinguished: (a) "Gathic" – that of the Gathic hymns, composed in eastern Iran by Zoroaster himself, (reflecting an older stage of Old Persian, *c.* 900 BC); (b) "Old Persian" – the language of the cuneiform inscriptions of western Iran from the sixth to the fourth centuries BC; and (c) "Younger Avestan" – the variety used in western Iran in the composition of the Younger Avestan hymns during the fifth and fourth centuries BC.

We will take up Gathic in more detail below; it is this variety which Hawkins lists as representing type 19. Old Persian (of cuneiform inscriptions) has the word order patterns (where, following Friedrich's 1975 convention, the more dominant orders are represented in capital letters, and non-dominant, alternative orders are in small letters): SOV/svo, AN/na, GN/ng, POSTP/prep, and reln/NRel (type 23). Younger Avestan shows SOV, an/NA, gn/GN, postp/PREP (type 17). Friedrich (1975: 46) argues that Younger Avestan's combination of a verb-final pattern with other head-initial orders is the result of contact/borrowing from the Mesopotamian *Sprachbund*. Other reasons for this otherwise unusual combination of word order patterns, according to Friedrich, may have to do with Greek bilingualism and the influence of Aramaic. This order, type 17, remains in Modern Persian.[13]

The language of the Gathic hymns shows the patterns: SOV, PREP/postp, GN/ng, an/na, NRel/reln – that is, Gathic would represent type 19 if AN is basic or type 20 if NA is basic. Friedrich (1975:44) considers it impossible to determine whether NA or AN was dominant in Gathic, though there is a slight dominance of GN over NG (cf. Campbell, Bubenik, and Saxon 1988: 217).

Regardless of whether Gathic's basic word order can be resolved as type 19 or type 20, it is important to point out that other Iranian languages appear to represent both types (although type 20 had no representatives in Hawkins' sample): for example, Pashto, a modern Iranian language, has SOV/GN/AN, but both prepositions and postpositions. Shafeev (1964: 51–2) lists seven prepositions and ten postpositions; these are typically used at the same time, that is as "circumfixes." Greenberg (1980: 240) argued that "circumfixes" arise in the transition from a prepositional to a postpositional language (though this may not be the only source of circumfixes; see Campbell, Bubenik, and Saxon 1988: 218). This view is supported by historical evidence from Pashto. A century ago, Trumpp (1873: 91) listed alternative dative forms, such as "to a chieftain":

(14)   *va malik* (with preposition)

(15)   *va malik* (*va*) *tah* (with circumfix)

(16)   *malik* (*va*) *tah* (with postposition)

In contemporary Pashto, only the latter two constructions are possible; the preposition option has been eliminated (Shafeev 1964: 18). If we take type 19 to be any language which has SOV/GN/AN with prepositions (as part of circumfixes or not), then Pashto would exemplify type 19. The same view, but with postpositions, would make Pashto a representative of type 23.

Tajik, like Modern Persian, has been classified as a type 17 language (SOV/Prep/NG/NA). In northern Tajik dialects, however, the Persian genitival construction NG is being replaced by the Turkic GN, the result of widespread Uzbek–Tajik bilingualism there. Northern Tajik is thus characterized by SOV/Prep/GN/NA, type 20 (with no representatives in Hawkins' sample).

In summary, the Iranian languages considered here and their basic word order patterns are given below:

type 17	SOV	Prep	NG	NA	Younger Avestan,
					Modern Persian, Tajik
type 20	SOV	Prep	GN	NA	Northern Tajik, Gathic
type 19	SOV	Prep	GN	AN	Gathic (?), Pashto (?)
type 23	SOV	Postp	GN	AN	Old Persian, Pashto (?)

Neither Pashto nor Gathic is a clear-cut example of type 19; the only clear case, Amharic (above), owes its word order to contact/borrowing from Cushitic. Northern Tajik, the only clear representative of type 20 known, has borrowed from/been influenced by Turkic.

The question is, then, what the relationship is between contact/borrowing and word order universals, and specifically whether it is possible for types 18 (as in Tigre, above), 19, and 20 to develop without external influence, given that the only known examples are the result of the influence of borrowing or language contact.[14] This question has important implications for the relationship of universals to borrowing, and for the general definition of universals.

Universals are neither accidents nor mysteries, but have explanations. Several pragmatic explanations have been offered for principles of word order. Thus, the Cross-Category Harmony Principle, that modifiers either all tend to precede their heads or all tend to follow, has been related to processing, to the need to distinguish heads of phrases from non-head modifiers (Hawkins 1983: 97–8; 1985: 573).[15] If in a language modifiers consistently precede their heads, or alternatively, consistently follow, then processing is facilitated; heads and modifiers are distinguished and identified based on the strategy of the consistent relative position one to the other.[16] A similar pragmatic explanation is offered for the Heaviness Serialization Principle (Hawkins 1983: 98–106), which defines a preference for "lighter" modifiers to occur leftward in their respective phrases, while "heavier" modifiers tend to be placed rightward (see Hawkins 1985: 573). Preposed long modifiers make it more difficult to determine the head; once the head has been identified, a following long modifier (e.g. relative clause or adjective phrase) is more easily processed. Thus categorial harmony and heaviness shifts aid language users to unpack the constituent structure.

In an efficient language, the word order patterns are arranged to make processing easier, thus establishing universals of word order. However, absolute adherence to these principles is neither expected nor required; a language which does not conform would not be impossible, merely less user-friendly. All else being equal, we expect greater cross-categorial harmony, more conformity to the word order universals, and we expect word order changes often to be in the direction of ease of processing.

It has been argued that some universals can have exceptions when external, sociocultural factors are at play (Campbell 1980; Chung and Seiter 1980; M. Harris 1984: 177, 181; Harris 1985: 425). Notice that in such a case, a proposed universal does not cease to be a universal simply because it may have a few culturally determined exceptions, but rather, it becomes a statistical universal (see Greenberg 1975). The important questions all remain the same. We still want to know why the trait occurs in all or nearly all languages and why only one or a few languages depart from the otherwise universal norm. Perhaps the degree to which a universal can have exceptions (i.e. be statistical rather than absolute) is correlated to the strength of its underlying explanations: for example, perhaps the perceptual burden is so great on a potential language with only consonants that no language could conceivably violate the universal that all languages have vowels. But languages with non-conforming word order patterns are unlikely to be constrained to the same degree, making some externally motivated exceptions more possible and hence more likely.

Borrowing and language contact are the primary external factors in these instances; they can sometimes motivate exceptions to otherwise exceptionless universals (see Campbell 1980; Smith 1981; M. Harris 1984).

Taking this position on universals, we conclude that there is something unusual, almost illegitimate, about types 18, 19, and 20. That is, clearly some few languages have come to share the configuration of word-order patterns that make up these types, but usually (perhaps always) this appears to be due to borrowing/language contact. Therefore, we suggest that word order universals should be framed first on the basis of the patterns which have more solid internal motivation, not based on the more marginal types such as 18, 19, and 20. We permit the universals to be statistical where necessary, but with the stipulation that exceptional languages, at least in all the cases known to us, fail to conform because borrowing or language contact has been involved.

This view correlates the possibility of exceptions with the degree of disruption to efficient functioning/processing such exceptions would engender in languages not conforming whole-heartedly to the universal. We are interested in the general principles of language – how the pieces interrelate, and how they may change. Some of these principles have been considered to be absolute (exceptionless) universals, others near (or statistical) universals. Still others have not been associated to universals, but rather with typological connections. The general principles of language are all at play in each of these three kinds of patterning. The more efficient the language (i.e., not permitting borrowing or language contact to motivate departures from principles), or the greater the value of the universal for facilitating language processing, the more likely it is that absolute conformity will be found.[17]

6.5   Case studies

We now turn attention to selected cases of syntactic borrowing and grammatical change due to language contact, from which we will draw conclusions about implications for syntactic change in general. We have selected the cases dealt with here both because they are generally revealing, and because of their typological and geographical diversity.

Some of these cases are well documented in the literature. If these had received the acknowledgment they merit, it would not be necessary for us to reassert the arguments we present here. These include the following.

1 Ethiopian Semitic has borrowed from Cushitic SOV/POSTP/AN/RelN/, suffixing, compound verbs, negative copula, distinct present tense for independent versus subordinate clauses (Leslau 1945, 1952; Hetzron 1972, 1980; Little 1974; Ferguson 1976; Greenberg 1980; cf. Campbell, Bubenik, and Saxon 1988).

2 Balto-Finnic and Slavic languages have borrowed syntactic constructions from one another (see Timberlake 1974; Thomason and Kaufman 1988: 238–51). For example, Timberlake (1974: 220) demonstrates that the employment of objects in the nominative case in certain syntactic environments in North Russian, Lithuanian, and Latvian dialects, particularly with impersonal verbs and with verbs of obligation, arose as a syntactic borrowing from language contact with some West Finnic language(s). The geographical contiguity of these Russian dialects with West Finnic, the structural similarity of the usage, and the fact that this innovation is limited to these dialects, speak in favor of this analysis.

Compare, for example the Russian construction illustrated in (17) with the Finnish construction in (18):

(17)   voda   pit'
         water.NOM   drink.INF
         "[It is necessary] to drink water."

(18)   täytyy juoda   mehu
         must   drink.INF   juice.NOM
         "It is necessary to drink the juice/one must drink the juice."

Finnic was the model for the Russian construction (as well as the corresponding one in Latvian and Lithuanian dialects) in this case. In another example, Latvian and Lithuanian (Baltic languages) share with Estonian and Livonian (Balto-Finnic languages) the so-called "modus obliquus" (also called "relative mood") verbal aspect, that is, a reported (or indirect) speech marker, acquired by Baltic languages under influence from Balto-Finnic (see section 5.2.1). Russian's partitive construction (called second genitive) is due to Finnic influence (Timberlake 1974; Comrie 1981: 154; Thomason and Kaufman 1988: 243–5).

3 There has been considerable syntactic convergence among languages in the Balkan linguistic area. This includes, among other things, the development of postposed articles, periphrastic future, periphrastic perfect, lack of infinitives, and syncretism of the dative and genitive (Schaller 1975; Joseph 1983, 1987; Comrie 1989[1981]: 204–7).

4 Chinookan dialects adopted the tense–aspect systems of their neighbors due to language contact:

> Corresponding to linear geographical extension from west to east, the "tense" category shows increasing development into an articulated morpho-syntactic paradigm. The end points of the geographical area both fit into local patterns, simple taxis and aspect distinctions on the Pacific coast [as in neighboring Salishan languages], multitense distinctions in the southern Plateau [as in neighboring Sahaptian languages].   (Silverstein 1974: 49)

5 There are many cases of grammatical diffusion in the South Asian (or Indian) linguistic area. Emeneau (1980), Gumperz and Wilson (1971), Nadkarni (1975), Sridhar (1978), and others list abundant examples, such as: the loss of negative-incorporated forms in major Dravidian languages, replaced by analytical negative constructions due to Indo-Aryan influence; the infinitive suffix -*na* in Gondi borrowed from Hindi-Urdu; the Pengo borrowing of the Oriya genitive morpheme; borrowing of finite relative clause formations in all literary Dravidian languages from Indo-Aryan; the passive constructions from Sanskrit and English in Dravidian. Gair (1980) documents the borrowing in Sinhalese of a focus construction (similar to cleft sentences in English) from Dravidian neighbors.

6 Cases of borrowed switch-reference constructions are documented by Jacobsen (1983:172-4) in western North America and by Austin (1981b: 329–32) over a continuous area in various languages of Australia.

7 Media Lengua (Muysken 1981) is a variety of Quechua which has undergone extensive lexical borrowing from Spanish and exhibits considerable syntactic change due to Spanish influence, including the introduction of prepositions,

conjunctions, complementizers, word order changes, the subordinator -*ndu* (from Spanish participles in -V*ndo*), etc.

8 Baonan, a Mongolian language, has been highly influenced by Chinese. Some examples include the borrowing of resultative compounds ("call-come" = "call someone with the result that he/she comes"; "hit-faint" = "hit someone with the result that he/she faints"), and the borrowing of Chinese clause-medial copula (e.g. former *habíb dèfu o* [Habib doctor be] "Habib is a doctor"; borrowed *habíb sị dèfu* [Habib be doctor]; Northern Mandarin comparative construction; etc.) (Li 1983). Li also discusses other cases of grammatical borrowing in the area. These include Wutun, a Chinese language influenced by Tibetan (Li 1983: 32–4), and Hui, another Chinese language, heavily influenced by so-called Altaic languages (Li 1983: 36–8).

9 There has been much diffusion among the Australian aboriginal languages of Arnhem Land (Heath 1978). Heath documents extensive borrowing and areal convergence in particular among Ritharngu, Ngandi, Nunggubuyu, and Warndarang. In morphosyntax, Heath found direct borrowing of case affixes (e.g. ergative markers, instrumental, ablative, genitive–dative–purposive, comitative), number affix, noun class affixes (with discourse functions of reference and anaphora), diminutive affix, derivational verbal affixes, negative affix, postpositions, inchoative verbalizer, among others. Among "indirect borrowings" (by which he means instances where a language changes "its inherited words and morphemes under the influence of a foreign model, so that structural convergence results" [Heath 1978: 119]), he finds changes which innovated enclitic pronominals, convergence in type of subordinated clauses, verbal inflectional categories, case suffixes, verbal aspect, etc.

10 Much influence from English and Western languages on the syntax and discourse functions of Japanese subjects has been documented (Fujii 1985).

6.5.1   Laz

We take up in somewhat more detail a few cases which contribute to the general understanding of the nature of syntactic borrowing. The first is the case of two apparently borrowed constructions in Laz (with comments on other borrowings of a similar nature), which illustrate (a) that syntactic borrowing is indeed possible, and (b) that new constructions (*contra* Lightfoot) can be due to borrowing.

Laz has developed a number of constructions which are attributed to Turk-

ish influence by Georgian linguists (Jikia 1967). The construction illustrated
in the following example is unlike anything in Laz's sister languages:

(19)   oxorǰa   qʼona-ša   idu   var-idu-ya-ši
       woman field-ALLATIVE she.went NEG-she.went-QUOTATIVE-GEN
       "when the woman went into the field . . . / as soon as the woman
       went into the field . . ."

Two aspects of this are attributed to Turkish. First, the use of a case to mark a
clause meaning "when," as in Turkish:

(20)   kadın   tarla-ya   git-tiğ-in-de
       woman field-DATIVE go-GERUNDIVE-3.SG-LOCATIVE
       "when the woman went to the field"

Interestingly, while Laz has several deverbal nouns similar to the Turkish ger-
undive of (20), in the construction in (19) Laz attaches the case marker -*ši*
instead to a finite verb form, having both tense and agreement. Second, the
use of an affirmative verb form, followed by a negative verb form, to mean
"when," such as Turkish:

(21)   kadın   tarla-ya   gid-er   git-me-z
       woman field-DATIVE go-AORIST go-NEG-AORIST
       "as soon as the woman went to the field"

While in Turkish these two features mark temporal clauses, they are not used
together; in the Laz example, they are employed together, with both meanings
(as in Turkish examples (20) and (21)).

   While such Laz examples may be quite limited, the use of the ending -*ši*
with a finite verb form in one or the other of these two meanings is common.

   Next, a Laz question construction also appears to show the results of Turkish influence, for instance:

(22)   k-ye-xt-u-i   va   ye-xt-u-i
       AFFIRM-up-come-3SG-QUEST NEG up-come-3SG-QUEST
       "Did it come up?"   (Čikobava 1936a: 119)

While the question pattern "A-not-A" is not typologically unknown in other
languages (e.g. Mandarin), these lack the question particle, which Laz
employs. This is parallel to the Turkish construction:

(23)   kadın   tarla-ya   git-ti-mi   git-me-di-mi
       woman field-DATIVE go-PAST-QUEST go-NEG-PAST-QUEST
       "Did the woman go to the field (or didn't she)?"[18]

Thus Turkish borrowing seems to be involved in these two Laz constructions.
   It is interesting to note that Laz (and Mingrelian) apparently have borrowed

the particle *kə/k*-from Armenian (where it has a solid etymology, now used with all present indicative forms). It is glossed AFFIRM in Laz, as in example (22). Similarly, Asia Minor Greek has borrowed the question particle *mi* from Turkish (as in example (23)). An example from Asia Minor Greek is:

(24)   nó   o dékum to so do peí s   *mi*
        FUTURE it we.give it to the son your QUESTION
        "Shall we give it to your son?"

6.5.2   American Finnish

The next case we discuss is that of American Finnish. The Finnish spoken in North America provides striking examples, since the original forms before the changes are clearly known in every case, and hence the direction of change is not in question. Also, the explanation of these changes is very evident: the primary cause is clearly influence from English. We consider only a few examples.

1   passives – see above;
2   object of infinitives – see above;
3   subjects for second infinitives.

The Standard Finnish so-called "second infinitive" is a gerundial form which permits no overtly specified subject. On the English model of appositive gerunds in *-ing*, a change in American Finnish permits such subjects, even when they are not coreferential with the subject of the main clause:

(25)   vainaja   syntyi   Duluthi-ssa, vanhemmat oll-en
        deceased was.born Duluth-In   parents   be-Ing
        "The deceased was born in Duluth, his parents being

        Mr. ja   Mrs. Matt Salo
        Mr. and Mrs. Matt Salo
        Mr. and Mrs. Matt Salo."

(26)   entinen Hilda Paavola ja   Frank Anderson vihi-ttiin,
        former Hilda Paavola and Frank Anderson marry-PAST.PASS
        "The former Hilda Paavola and Frank Anderson were married,

        pastori Mänttä vihki-en   heidä-t.
        Pastor Mänttä marry-Ing they-PL.ACC
        Pastor Mänttä marrying them."

In each of these changes it is clear that Standard Finnish represents the older, original form from which American Finnish has innovated due to influence from English, the dominant language in this bilingual setting. Clearly, then, language contact is one potential cause of syntactic change. Moreover, the very close relationship (and short time of separation) between the two varieties, American Finnish and Standard Finnish, coupled with the marked syntactic differences just presented, illustrates both the degree of remodeling a language can undergo due to borrowing and language contact, and the short amount of time actually required for such changes to be perpetrated.[19] In each instance, the origin is found in Standard Finnish and the nature and direction of the American Finnish changes are absolutely clear. The history of American Finnish provides rich examples for the study of syntactic changes, most of which owe their explanation to language contact. (See Campbell 1980.)

6.5.3   Pipil

The final case we consider is that of a number of syntactic changes in Pipil which are due to borrowing from Spanish.[20] Pipil is like many other Latin American Indian languages in showing strong influence from Spanish. Unlike many others, however, Pipil has documentation and its history is quite clear from before the time when the effects of contact were felt on this language. (For details see Campbell 1987.)

The Pipil comparative construction has been borrowed directly from Spanish, employing the Spanish loanwords *mas* "more" (from Spanish *más*) and *ke* "than" (from Spanish *que*):

(27)   mu-manuh   mas   bibo   ke   taha
         your-brother   more   smart   than   you
         "Your brother (is) smarter than you (are)."

(28)   ne   siwa:t   mas   galá:na   ke   taha
         the   woman   more   pretty   than   you
         "That woman is prettier than you (are)."

Compare (28'), the Spanish equivalent to (28):

(28')   esa mujer es más linda **que** tú

Pipil had several different comparative expressions, like those of Classical Nahuatl (see Andrews 1975: 349–53; Langacker 1977b: 118; Campbell 1987), before its contact with Spanish, but these have been eliminated and now it has only the comparative construction borrowed from Spanish.

As mentioned above, clause coordination is another construction borrowed directly from Spanish. Proto-Uto-Aztecan (PUA) had no reconstructible coordinate conjunctions, only Ø (simple juxtaposition) for conjoined clauses, though a postposition meaning "with" may be reconstructible for conjoined nominals (Langacker 1977b: 159–60). Proto-Nahua (PN) continued this pattern, as did Pipil, though later the postposition developed into a relational noun (see below). While both these constructions are still found in Pipil, they are rare and new forms with true coordinate conjunctions either borrowed from Spanish or brought about by Spanish influence are much more frequent (see above).

As shown in Campbell (1987), Pipil subordinate clause structure has also been considerably changed under Spanish influence. We cite only one of the several kinds, the case of relative clauses. Relative clauses in Proto-Nahua were essentially as in Classical Nahuatl, where relativization was signaled in one of two ways: with markerless juxtaposition, i.e. ∅ (no subordinating element), or with the "generic" subordinator *in*, for instance:

(29)   ∅-type
        yo-ni-kin-ta   miekeh tla-tlakah pihpinawah
        PAST-I-them-see many   PL-man   were.ashamed
        "I saw many men who were ashamed."

(Example from modern Malinche Nahuatl [Hill and Hill 1981: 90].)

(30)   *in*-type
        in paʔtli   in   o:nimitswa:lnotkilili. . .
        the medicine SUBOR I.you.brought
        "The medicine that I brought you (honorific) . . ."
                                        (Garibay 1961: 142; cf. Langacker 1977b: 181.)

Pipil relative clauses show considerable change in the direction of Spanish. The first type, juxtaposition (∅-marker), has been almost completely eliminated. The second type, introduced by *ne*, the reflex of the Proto-Nahua "relative clause introducing particle" (and generic subordinator) **in*, still exists, though is now rare in occurrence. However, other types have been innovated and the relative clauses with *ke* (a borrowing of the Spanish relative marker *que*) are much more frequent:

(31)   ki:sa se: animál *ke*   yehemet k-ilwia-t "tsuntekumat"
        leave an animal *that* they   it-say-PL "skull"
        "An animal appears which they call (the) 'Skull.'"

The addition of new relative markers and the near elimination of ∅-marking has made relative clauses clearer by providing a means for distinguishing them more clearly from other subordinate clauses which were also introduced originally by ∅ or **in* (in Pipil *ne*).

The combined effect of the changes in coordination and relative clauses makes a rather large variety of complex sentences more distinguishable and hence more like Spanish in their actual deployment.

Another example is that of the periphrastic future. The former future suffixes in Pipil are extremely rare today, unused and almost unknown for the most part. Usually future meanings are given in periphrastic constructions, e.g. *ni-yu ni-k-chiwa* (I-go I-it-do) "I'm going to do it." In this, Pipil corresponds to local Spanish, where the periphrastic forms, e.g. *lo voy a hacer* "I'm going to do it,"are the most typical, with future forms such as *lo haré* "I will do it" (cf. archaic Pipil *ni-k-chiwa-s* [I-it-do-FUT]) very rare and stilted. The Pipil future suffixes are *-s* "singular" and *-s-ke-t* "plural," e.g. *ni-panu-s* "I will pass," *ti-panu-ske-t* "we will pass." Some examples are:

(32) Na ni-yawi ni-mu-kwepa   ni-k-ilpia
      I   I-go   I-REFLEX-return I-it-tie
      "I'm going to tie it up again."

(33) n-yu ni-mitsin-ilwitia
      I-go I-you.PL-show
      "I am going to show you (pl.)."

Another case is the development of prepositions (see above). (See Campbell 1987 for several other examples of Pipil syntactic changes due to borrowing.)

(For additional cases, see Nevis 1985: 118–24; Smith, Robertson, and Williamson 1987; Lehiste 1988: 16; Thomason and Kaufman 1988.)

6.6   Explanations and conclusions

How are these various borrowed changes to be explained, and how do they relate to theoretical claims about syntactic change? Do the theoretical claims render these changes more understandable? Are the changes more instructive about the value of such theorizing? In changes cited here the overwhelming causal factor has been contact with other languages. This may be distressing to those who maintain that language contact and syntactic borrowing as an explanation of change are usually insignificant or wrong. The cases surveyed here mean, however, that borrowing must be accorded a significant position in the ranks of mechanisms of syntactic change.

Several proposed universals and general principles of grammatical borrowing were surveyed, but not surprisingly, most of these do not hold true in any absolute sense. The moral for would-be constrainers of grammatical borrowing, then, is that given enough time and intensity of contact, virtually anything can (ultimately) be borrowed. Thus we conclude with Thomason and Kaufman (1988: 14) that "as far as the strictly linguistic possibilities go, any linguistic feature can be transferred from any language to any other language." This being the case, it is safer to think of these proposed universals and principles of borrowing as general tendencies, and not as absolute constraints. It may be a sobering but necessary realization for some that grammatical borrowing can be a very powerful force that must be reckoned with in framing theories of grammatical change.

We also saw that, contrary to opinions expressed by many, borrowing and language contact can introduce structures to a language which are not harmonious with existing structures. This can lead to rather striking typological changes in a language, and, in particular, studies of word order change and word order universals must pay particular attention to language contact and borrowing (see also chapter 8).

Of course, not all changes due to borrowing wreak havoc on the structure of a receiving language – probably the majority do not. For example, for some theorists, the syntactic changes due to borrowing and language contact in the Pipil case may seem dull in that they reflect little of the sorts of change so favored in recent theoretical discussions of syntactic change. One perceives no telling typological shift or drift (W. Lehmann 1973; Vennemann 1974a; M. Harris 1978, 1984), no salient abductive reinterpretation of otherwise ambiguous or unclear surface patterns (Andersen 1973; Timberlake 1977; M. Harris 1978), and no therapeutic grammatical overhaul in the wake of phonological and morphological decay (M. Harris 1978, 1984; Lightfoot 1991). One finds no compelling reanalyses in defense of transparency, ridding the language of foul opacity (Langacker 1977a; Lightfoot 1979a). In the Pipil changes presented here there are no significant instances where the applications of the "system" (of grammatical possibilities) has led to alterations in the "norms" (the actually realized grammatical forms) (Coseriu 1978 [1957]). In short, most of the more popular current claims about the nature of syntactic change are by and large simply irrelevant in many of these cases of change due to borrowing. The inescapable conclusion is that borrowing itself must be recognized as an independent mechanism of syntactic change.[21]

7 Processes that simplify biclausal structures

7.1 Introduction

Our goal in this chapter is the presentation of universal characterizations of some of the diachronic processes that turn biclausal constructions into monoclausal ones. We approach this goal first by describing one such process from the point of view of several languages, then generalizing about the form of this process. We then examine a different process, and make generalizations about its form. Finally we analyze a large category of processes and end the chapter with a statement of general principles governing all the changes examined within the chapter.

To this end, section 7.2 discusses processes that derive from cleft clauses containing pragmatic markers. In section 7.3 we describe the transition from quotation constructions to structures involving a quotative marker. A process that derives a variety of periphrastic expressions of verbal categories is discussed in section 7.4. All three processes considered here are types of reanalysis; in section 7.5 we state general principles governing changes of biclausal to monoclausal structures.

7.2 Highlighting constructions

We examine in this section cross-linguistic evidence concerning one origin of **highlighting** – the use of particles to mark focus or topic.[1] This is not an exhaustive inventory of sources of such markers;[2] instead we deal in some detail with a single common pathway of development, derivations found in a wide variety of unrelated languages.

7.2.1 Previous proposals
A number of language-specific treatments, some of them referred to below, have dealt with this topic, but we are aware of only two discussions of the universals of this phenomenon. Givón (1979: 246–8) claims that focus cleft constructions develop out of loosely constructed paratactic constructions

containing relative clauses, and that focus fronting develops out of the cleft through loss of the copula. This analysis, based on synchronic Kihung'an data, is somewhat speculative, since the diachronic relationships among the five constructions involved are not truly recoverable.

Heine and Reh (1984: 109–10, 147–82, 249–50) have shown that focus particles often come from cleft constructions. Their proposal is best summarized in the three stages they discern:

> *Stage I:* There is a cleft structure something like
>
> $$\left\{ \begin{array}{c} \text{NP} \\ \text{PP} \end{array} \right\} \text{copula - subordinate clause}$$
>
> This structure serves to foreground new, asserted information, expressed by the sentence-initial constituent, the presupposed part of the sentence being encoded in the subordinate clause.
>
> *Stage II:* The copula is desemanticized to a focus marker. This structure is exploited to optionally emphasize WH-words. This stage is characteristic of most weakly grammaticalized systems.
>
> *Stage III:* The focus construction undergoes functional shift, i.e. it is no longer possible on synchronic grounds to derive it from the cleft construction, its source. At the same time, WH-words are obligatorily marked for focus (1984:181).

We have found no counterexamples to the stages described here. In section 7.2.5 below, we provide a more specific proposal, distinguishing universal aspects of this development from language-specific ones. In section 7.2.2.1 we clarify relevant aspects of the structure of the input construction. In the rest of section 7.2.2 we provide examples of the cleft-to-focus construction pathway, and (in section 7.2.2.3) discuss some problems of argumentation that these examples raise. In section 7.2.3 we explore the use of focus in questions, and in section 7.2.4 we describe a similar development of a cleft-like structure into a topic marker.

7.2.2   Focus

7.2.2.1   The synchronic structure of clefts

We use the term **cleft** here to include both the construction called cleft (often *it*-cleft in English) and that termed pseudo-cleft (or WH-cleft). Some of the controversial aspects of the structure of clefts are not relevant to our discussion, and we concentrate on those aspects that play a role in the diachrony of this process in universal grammar. The synchronic characteristics of this structure always include the following:

(1)   The cleft (a) consists of a superordinate clause (S_1) and a subordinate clause (S_2),[3] (b) the former containing a copula, and (c) the latter having the structure of a relative clause.

Characteristic (1a) is straightforward; the remaining defining characteristics are discussed below, together with some other characteristics frequently found.

It is well known that many languages, such as Arabic, do not use an overt copula in equational sentences, while others, such as Russian, do not use the overt copula in certain tenses. It is expected that in the cleft the copula would be present or absent under the same conditions as in equational clauses. Thus, criterion (1b) is intended to include a zero copula in those languages where a zero copula is in general use.

Generally, in a cleft construction the subordinate clause has the structure of a relative clause (Keenan and Hull 1973b; Schachter 1973). Universally there are a variety of strategies available for formation of relative clauses (for example, Maxwell 1979; Keenan 1985), and we assume that any one of these can be used in a cleft. The types of marking available for a relative clause include a relative pronoun or a relative particle, which may occur in any of the positions available to complementizers; these markers are referred to here as **relativizers**. Since zero marking is also a possible relative clause strategy, it too is available for use in the formation of clefts. Generally, in a cleft a language uses one or more of the relativization strategies that are in current use for relative clauses in that language, but the possibility exists of using relative clause strategies not in use for relative clauses in that language. Universally relative clauses are characterized by an NP (or some other constituent[4]) that is represented by a gap, a relative pronoun, or an anaphoric pronoun. Thus, the subordinate clause of the source construction contains a constituent, referred to here as the **clefted constituent**, which is represented by a gap, a relative pronoun, or an anaphoric pronoun. This constituent may fulfill any grammatical role in the subordinate clause, though some languages place language-particular constraints on this role.[5] The analysis presented here is independent of any assumption that the clefted constituent is present in deep structure and later deleted, or absent at all levels. In the discussion of clefts below, the clause that does not contain the copula is referred to as the **content clause**.

Since in a language the copula may be zero and the marking of the dependent clause may be zero, it is possible for two of the three criterial features not to be overtly marked.[6]

The copular clause in a cleft consists minimally of the copula itself (with the possibility of a zero copula) and the constituent which is pragmatically marked as focus by the cleft construction as a whole. In languages that use expletive pronouns, such as *it*, in equational sentences, such a pronoun may also be required in the copular clause of the cleft, while optional adverbs may be present as well.

We represent the structure of the source construction in (2), which is not intended to represent a particular word order, either with regard to the internal structure of the two clauses or with regard to the order of the two clauses relative to one another:

(2)

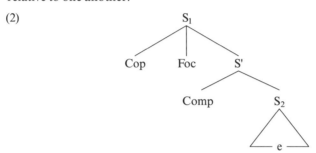

In (2), Cop represents the copula and Foc the focused constituent; the relativizer is in Comp. The relative order of Cop, Foc, and S' varies according to the language; the relative order of Comp and S_2 also varies, with Comp occurring before, after, or within S_2. We assume, however, that in a true cleft the copula and focus cannot be intercalated with S'.

The properties of clefts are exemplified in different ways in the two English clefts. In the *it*-cleft, (3a), the copular clause consists of the copula, *was*, the focused constituent, *the interrogation*, and the expletive pronoun *it*. The subordinate clause is marked with the complementizer *that* and has the empty position (marked with *e*) that characterizes this type of relative clause structure; here it is the subject that is left empty.

(3)   (a) it was the interrogation that frightened him most
       (b) what frightened him most was the interrogation

With respect to relative clauses, the formation used in the WH-cleft is currently restricted to headless relatives (compare **the interrogation what frightened him most* with grammatical *the interrogation which frightened him most*). The copular clause contains only the copula itself and the focused constituent.

Schachter (1973) may have been the first to note that the cleft in English marks focus, and Harries-Delisle (1978) suggested that this was universally true. While we assume that the marking of focus is at least one of the functions of the cleft universally, in the discussion below we retain another author's description of "emphasis." It is possible that focus is what was intended by that author, or that the construction has changed its function since reanalysis.

The arguments below for clefts relate to the function of the construction and to the following structural characteristics: (i) the case of the focused constituent; (ii) the presence of the copula; (iii) the presence of a relativizer; (iv) a special form of the verb used in relative clauses in some languages; and (v) lack of subject–verb agreement in S_2 when the subject is focused. Arguments of type (v) are based on the fact that in some languages empty subjects do not condition verb agreement, as discussed in more detail below. Clearly, arguments of types (ii), (iv), and (v) are based on the assumption that universally the subordinate clause of clefts has the structure of a relative, and all three depend upon drawing language-particular parallels between the structure of a relative clause and that of the subordinate clause in a cleft in that language.

7.2.2.2   *Breton*

Breton is a VSO language (Wojcik 1976; Anderson and Chung 1977; Anderson 1981; Timm 1989);[7] focused[8] constituents are fronted and marked with the particle *a*, for subjects and direct objects, or *e(z)*, used with most other constituents.[9] Examples (4)–(6) illustrate this for Modern Breton, and focused constituents are marked with boldface type:[10]

(4)   **me** a   zo karet
       I   that is loved
       "**I** am loved."   (Wojcik 1976: 275, n. 6)

(5)   **warc'hoaz** e   skrivo   ar paotr al lizher
       tomorrow that he.will.write boy   letter
       "**Tomorrow** the boy will write the letter."   (Wojcik 1976: 263)

(6)   **ar vugale** a   lenn levrioù
       the children that read books
       "**The children** read books."   (Borsley and Stephens 1989: 408)

The particle *a* was apparently originally a relative pronoun, a reflex of Indo-European **yo-s*, which, whatever its original use (disputed), functioned later as a relative clause marker (Lewis and Pedersen 1937: 243–4, but see also Thurneysen 1946: 323–4). Throughout the history of Breton, the particle *a* is used in relative clauses in which the subject or direct object has been relativized (Hemon 1975: 275, 286–7; Wojcik 1976: 275, n. 6). Examples (7) and (8) are from a late seventeenth-century manuscript:

(7)   dirac ur juge, a   guelou   scler
       before a judge that he.will.see clear
       "before a judge, who will see clearly"
       (*Christmas hymns in the Vannes dialect of Breton* 255, cited by Hemon 1975: 287)

(8)   en din a   clasquet
      the man that you.Pl.seek
      "the man that you seek"   (ibid., 1663)

Wojcik (1976: 275, n. 6) points out that the verb has a third person singular form in sentences in which the subject has been clefted, such as (6) above, because *a*, originally a relative pronoun, was formally third person. In sentences in which a constituent other than the subject has been clefted, such as (5), the subject was present in what was originally the subordinate clause, and the verb agrees with it.

Further confirmation of the cleft origin of this construction is found in the form of the verb "be." In the present indicative, there is a special form *so/zo* of the third person singular of "be," which originated in relative clauses as the root **es* of the copula, plus the **jo-s* relative pronoun (Lewis and Pedersen 1937: 243, 318). This special verb form is still used in relative clauses in which the subject is relativized; (9) is from Middle Breton (eleventh to mid-seventeenth century):

(9)   da-n   tan infernal a   so   cruel
      to-the fire infernal that is.REL cruel
      "to the infernal fire that is cruel"
                       (*Middle Breton Hours*, p. 7, cited by Hemon 1975:261)

Since *so/zo* marks the relative clause, *a* is sometimes omitted; (10) is from an eighteenth century manuscript:

(10)   da vn den so   ase
      to a   man is.REL there
      "to a man who is there"   (*Ar Varn Diwezhañ* 608, cited by Hemon 1975: 261)

In clefts, the clause that follows the copular clause has the structure of a relative. In Breton, if the clause following the focused constituent contains a copula, it will be in the special form used in relative clauses.[11]

(11)   **Jesus** a   so   quen truheus
      Jesus that is.REL so   merciful
      "**Jesus** is so merciful."
      (*Christmas hymns in the Vannes dialect of Breton*, 137, cited by Hemon 1975: 261)

(12)   **an boet** so   prest
      the food is.REL ready
      "**The food** is ready."
                 (*Le Grand Mystère de Jésus*, p. 7-b, cited by Hemon 1975:261)

This provides further evidence confirming the cleft origin of the focus construction.

Breton also has a focus cleft, illustrated in (13):

(13) **ar vugale** eo a   lenne al levrioù
      the children is that read the books
      "It is **the children** that read the books."   (Borsley and Stephens 1989: 419)

Example (13) differs from (6) above in having the copula, *eo* "is." Other Celtic languages also have a cleft or the focus construction derived from it. For example, Irish[12] has the cleft construction illustrated in (14a):

(14) (a) is   í   **an bhean** a   bhí tinn
           COP her the woman   that be sick
           "It's **the woman** who was sick."

      (b) bhí an bhean tinn
           be the woman sick
           "The woman was sick."   (Stenson 1981: 109)

It may be assumed that the antecedent of the Breton focus construction was a cleft of the type illustrated in Irish (14a) or in Breton (13).[13]

While the characteristics noted above show the cleft origin of the focus construction, other features show that it is no longer a cleft. First, the Breton focus construction lacks the copula that occurs in the cleft, (13). On the basis of (13) we may assume that the Breton cleft originally contained an overt copula.

A second reason for believing that the construction in (6) is no longer a cleft is that the construction shows signs of undergoing further change. For example, under certain circumstances the relativizer *a* can be omitted, as in (15):

(15) mé lavar
      "I say"   (Hemon 1975: 276)

We conclude that the focus construction bears these similarities to the cleft and to the relative clause because the Breton focus is derived historically from the cleft.

7.2.2.3   *Argumentation and explanation in diachronic syntax*
In section 7.2.2.2, three arguments are presented to show that what is presently a focus (or topicalization) construction was historically a cleft. These arguments are based on (a) other synchronic uses of a particle associated with the construction, together with comparative evidence about the use of that particle and its provenance, (b) facts about agreement in this construction, which is rather different from agreement elsewhere in the language, and (c) other synchronic uses of a special form of the copula. These facts must also be accounted for synchronically, and a number of analyses have been proposed. The argument based on agreement, (b) above, is discussed below as an example of a problem that plagues some arguments relating to a number of diachronic analyses.[14]

In a synchronic analysis one obviously does not account for anything by reference to the earlier structure of the language, and all characteristics must be accounted for through reference to synchronic generalizations. Borsley and Stephens (1989: 426) have argued effectively for rule (16) in Breton and have shown that it accounts for the synchronic facts of the language:

(16)   There is no agreement with WH-trace subjects in affirmative clauses.

For relative clauses, clefts, and focus constructions, they propose the following structures, where O is an empty operator (Borsley and Stephens 1989: 418, 419, 410):

(17)   Relative clause
[$_{NP}$ *ar   vugale* [$_S$ O$_i$ [$_S$ *a   lenne* t$_i$ *al   levrioù*]]]
            the children   that read   the books

(18)   Cleft (compare (13) above)
ar vugale eo [$_{S'}$ O$_i$ [$_S$ *a lenne* t$_i$ *al levrioù*]]

(19)   Focus (compare (6) above)
ar vugale$_i$ [$_S$ *a lenne* t$_i$ *al levrioù*]

Since the focused constituents in (4)–(6) above are considered WH-trace subjects, the question arises, why can we not simply assume that (16) has always applied in Breton? How can the evidence we have cited in favor of a cleft origin be taken as arguments for that origin, if (16) could have always applied? The fact that there is no agreement with empty subjects in relative clauses, clefts, and focus constructions can be attributed to synchronic structural similarities between these constructions, rather than to a shared origin.

The diachronic analysis proposed here explains why Breton (or pre-Breton) made the language-particular generalization stated in (16). The diachronic analysis proposed here, unlike rule (16) alone, explains why the focus construction is structurally similar to the cleft.[15] It explains the otherwise arbitrary synchronic fact in the sense that it relates one construction to another through a shared history.[16] Without this diachronic derivation the generalization (16) remains unexplained. In the rest of this section we explain further this structural similarity by relating this diachronic change to parallel changes from cleft to focus in other languages; in the remainder of the chapter we explain further the transition from cleft to focus by relating it to changes that are partially similar, but not entirely parallel, in a wide variety of other languages.

7.2.2.4 *East Cushitic*

In Somali and other East Cushitic languages, there are alternations in verb form which correspond to variable focus. Sometimes called the "extensive paradigm" and the "restricted paradigm," it has been pointed out that these are more appropriately labeled the "object focus conjugation" and the "subject focus conjugation," respectively. The Somali examples in (20)–(22) are from Antinucci and Publielli (1984: 19).

		Object Focus	*Subject Focus*

(20) (a) anigu muuska baan cunayaa   (b) aniga baa muuska cunaya
        I   banana FOC eat   I   FOC banana eat
        "I am eating the banana."

(21) (a) adigu muuska baad cunaysaa   (b) adiga baa muuska cunaya
        you banana FOC eat   you   FOC banana eat
        "You are eating the banana."

(22) (a) iyadu muuska bay cunaysaa   (b) iyada baa muuska cunaysa
        she banana FOC eat   she   FOC banana eat
        "She is eating the banana."

The particle *baa* marks focus on the nominal it follows; the form of the particle changes as it combines with the short form of the subject pronoun (*-n*, *-d*, *-y*). Observe that the (b) examples differ from the (a) examples also in the form of the subject pronoun and in the form of the verb.

Hetzron (1974) and others have shown that the sentence pattern in (20b)–(22b) is a fossilized cleft sentence of the type "It was she who was eating the banana." We argue that the sentence in (20a) originally had the structure in (23a), while that in (20b) had the structure in (23b):

(23)(a)

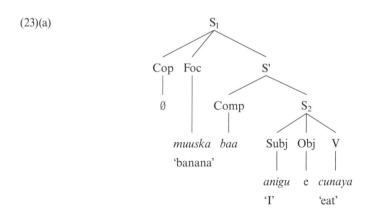

(23)(b)

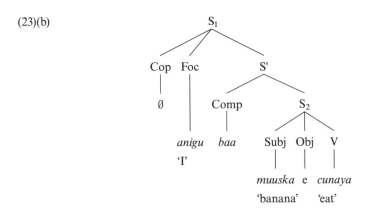

This analysis is supported by the following arguments. (i) The construction
has the function, marking focus, that is universally associated with the cleft
construction. The proposed analysis is consistent with facts about the use of
the subject and object focus constructions in relative clauses in two dialects of
Somali (Antinucci and Publielli 1984). (ii) The verb in the subject focus construction partly (i.e. in second person singular and in second and third persons plural) has default third person masculine agreement, rather than
agreeing with the subject. If the nominal that is presently subject of the sentence originated as the subject of a copular clause, the verb of the content
clause would not necessarily be expected to agree with it. The full paradigm of
the verb *ḍéh* "say," cited by Hetzron (1974: 276), illustrates the agreement facts
more clearly. (Agreement in the other persons is discussed below.)

(24)

		Object focus (extensive)	*Subject focus* (restrictive)
Sg.	1	idi	idí
	2	tidi	yidí
	3m.	yidi	yidí
	3f.	tidi	tidí
Pl.	1	nidi	nidí
	2	tidaahdèen	yidí
	3	yidaahdèen	yidí

(iii) Related to this is the fact that in (20a)–(22a), where the object was left
empty, the short form of the subject pronoun also occurred in the subordinate
clause. While not shown in the structure, this pronoun has the reflex *-n, -d, -y*
on *baa-*. However, in (20b)–(22b), where the subject was empty, no short form
of the subject pronoun was present; this has the reflex of a zero suffix on *baa-*.

Thus, in the cleft construction (20b)–(22b), empty subjects conditioned neither subject agreement nor the short form of the pronoun.

(iv) Sasse (1984: 113) has given an additional argument for this proposal based on the case of the subject nominal. He has shown that one case was used in Cushitic for predicate nominals (his "absolute case") and another for subjects (his "subject case"). The nominal that is presently the subject of the subject focus construction is not marked with the case otherwise used for subject, but rather with the case used for predicate nominals in equational sentences. This would be natural if (20b) is derived from (23b).

While the construction in (20)–(22) originated as a cleft, it does not have the structure of a cleft synchronically. Evidence of this comes from the fact that the elements of the sentence have been reordered, with the focused element occurring within the content clause, rather than outside of it. In addition, the paradigm in (24) shows that in some persons and numbers (namely first singular and plural, third feminine) the verb now agrees with the subject that in the original structure was empty. In other words, those persons and numbers that have the default third masculine forms (namely second singular and plural, third plural) are archaic, representing lack of agreement in (23b) above, while those persons and numbers that do have agreement are innovative, reflecting a reanalyzed monoclausal structure.[17]

7.2.2.5 *Japanese*

Work by Ōno (1964) and others suggests that the Japanese *Kakari-Musubi* construction with a "nominal" (also called "attributive") verb form likewise originated as a cleft construction used for focus.[18] Ōno has proposed that sentences like (25a) are derived historically from sentences like (25b):

(25)   (a)   teho no hi zo   kokoda ter=i- tar=u
              torch ASS fire EMPH brightly shine=I-PERF=URU
              "It is the torch fire that is brightly shining."   (Mannyoshu, 236)

        (b)   kokoda ter=i- tar=u   (ha) teho no hi zo
              brightly shine=I-PERF=URU HA torch ASS fire EMPH
              "What is brightly shining is the torch fire."
                              (Both sentences cited in Akiba 1978: 76)

Example (25a) illustrates the *Kakari-Musubi* construction, which consists of a focused constituent (here *teho no hi* "torch fire"), an emphatic particle (called a *Kakari* particle, here *zo*), and the rest of the clause, including the predicate. Ōno has proposed that the pattern illustrated by (25a) developed from (25b) by simple inversion of the subject, which was marked by a following *Kakari* particle, and the predicate. He has also suggested that the *Kakari* particles originated as forms of "be" or of a verb functioning as "be" (Kay 1985: 3).[19] Thus, as Akiba's glosses suggest, the original construction was a cleft, with "be" in final position, the focused constituent preceding it, and the subordinate clause preceding that.

Evidence to support biclausal analysis is the following. (i) In *Kakari-Musubi* constructions like (25a), the verb is in the "nominal" form used for relative clauses. This fact is explained by the proposal summarized above, since it is this clause that represents the subordinate clause portion of the cleft structure. The use of the "nominal" form of the verb would otherwise be unexplained since, when a verb is in clause-final position, as it is in (25a), it generally requires the "final" form rather than the "nominal" form. (ii) Some of the *Kakari* particles, such as *zo*, are identical to sentence-final particles. The unusual position of *Kakari* particles is explained by the hypothesis that these originated as forms of "be," since verbs are sentence final, together with Ōno's proposal that the (25a) pattern is formed by inversion of the (25b) pattern. The medial position of *zo* is otherwise unexplained, since outside the *Kakari-Musubi* construction it occurs only sentence-finally. (iii) According to Miyagawa (1984), in *Kakari-Musubi*, the direct object is always marked with the accusative particle *o* (Old Japanese *wo*). Under the cleft sentence proposal, this marking is explained, since in Old Japanese, marking of the direct object with the accusative particle *o* was rare in main clauses, but nearly always occurred in subordinate clauses (Miyagawa 1984).[20]

While the *Kakari-Musubi* in the oldest period corresponds to a cleft structure, later examples are not necessarily analyzable as clefts (Akiba 1978: 77). Some of the *Kakari* particles, such as *nan*, have essentially been lost (Sansom 1928: 266). In colloquial Modern Japanese, *zo* no longer requires the nominal form (Sansom 1928: 266); Miller (1967: 354) states that the construction had completely disappeared from the spoken language by Middle Japanese and was probably no longer productive as early as the Kamakura period (1086–1192). Thus, in the spoken language the structure is no longer a cleft, but a single clause with a focus particle.

7.2.3   Questions

Question words are generally in focus in content questions. It is therefore not surprising that in many languages it is possible to use a focus cleft in forming content questions, such as (26b), which may be compared with the unclefted (26a):

(26)   (a)   what frightened him?
         (b)   what was it that frightened him?

While both versions of (26) are perfectly natural questions in English, in some languages clefting becomes the preferred way of asking questions and may become a grammaticalized part of questioning. Such an instance of "idiomatic" use of clefted questions is found in French and Mingrelian.[21]

7.2.3.1   French

Old French used intonation together with inverted word order as a device for marking questions (M. Harris 1978: 31): Verb Subject . . . . In question inversion, the entire verb inverted with the entire subject; thus in Old French we find:

(27)   est morte m' amie?
        is   dead my friend
        "Is my friend dead?"   (*La Chastelaine de Vergi*; Foulet 1930: 233)

In content questions, the required order was Q-word Verb . . . , as in (28).

(28)   quant fust avenus   chis afaires?
        when was happened   this event
        "When had this event occurred?"
                            (Adam le Bossu, *Le Jeu de la feuillée*, 283; Foulet 1930: 233)

In the fifteenth century clefted questions became the preferred structure in content questions:

(29)   qui esse qui m' a   frappé?
        who be.it REL me has hit
        "Who is it who has hit me?" (i.e. "Who has hit me?")
                            (*Mystère du Vieux Testament*; Brunot and Bruneau 1933: 601)

Here, as in the clefts described in section 7.2.2, the copular clause consists of a question word and "be." The subordinate clause uses the ordinary relative clause strategies of the language, with the relative pronoun *qui*. The special word order of questions was maintained in the copular clause, where we find the order Q-word Verb . . . It is thought that at first this clefted question construction reinforced the question word (M. Harris 1978: 32). By the sixteenth century, French had developed the pattern in (30), where the pronoun *ce* "this, that, it" has been added:

(30)   pourquoi est ce que je me déconforte ainsi?
        why   be it REL I me discomfort so
        "Why is it that I am so discomforted?"
                            (Odet de Tournebu, cited by Brunot and Bruneau 1933: 351)

Again, the special question word order, Q-word Verb . . . , is maintained in the copular clause.

From the fifteenth or sixteenth century, the cleft construction was also used in yes/no questions.

(31)   est-ce que mon amie est morte?
        is it   that my friend is dead
        "Is it [the case] that my friend is dead?" "Is my friend dead?"

Again we can see that the cleft continues the special question word order, here as in (27) without a question word: Verb Subject . . .

The copular clause in the preferred yes/no question pattern in (31) has been reanalyzed as a sentence-initial question particle (M. Harris 1978: 32). That it functions as a particle is shown by the fact that the former verb can no longer occur in the full range of tense/aspect forms available for "be" in clefts, but occurs in the invariant form *est*. Once the copular clause was reanalyzed as a question particle, it ceased to be an independent clause. As a particle it is attached sentence-initially to a sentence which otherwise has the form of a simple declarative.

7.2.3.2   Mingrelian

In Mingrelian, a Kartvelian language, clefting has become a favored way of forming content questions; the cleft construction is not strictly obligatory in Mingrelian, though it is the usual way of forming content questions.

(32)   mu   re,   namusu   ortuk-i?
        what.NOM it.be which.DAT you.do.it-REL
        "What is it that you are doing?" (i.e. "What are you doing?")
                                        (Kipšiʒe 1914: 0141)

(33)   min   re,   ingars-ni?
        who.NOM it.be s/he.cry-REL
        "Who is it that is crying?" (i.e. "Who is crying?")

In both examples the interrogative pronoun and the verb "be" form the matrix copular clause. The second clause is structurally a subordinate clause, with the structure of an ordinary relative, including the use of the enclitic relative particle *-ni*. Clause-final *-ni* functions as an all-purpose subordinator (see Harris 1991b: 380–7). In (32) a relative pronoun, *namusu*, is used together with the subordinator *-ni/-i*, as can be done also in ordinary relative clauses (Abesaʒe 1965). In each example, *-ni* can be reduced to *-i*, and both forms are used today in this function.[22]

(34)   musenə re,   meurkə-i?
        why   it.be you.go-REL
        "Why is it that you are going?" (i.e. "Why are you going?")

The Mingrelian cleft has been reanalyzed, as can be seen in (35) and (36):

(35)   musu   re,   ortuk-i?
        what.DAT it.be you.do.it-REL
        "What is it that you are doing?" (i.e. "What are you doing?")
                                        (Kipšiʒe 1914: 0141)

(36)   musu   re,   čaruns   ni?
        what.DAT it.be s/he.write.it REL
        "What is it that s/he is writing?" (i.e. "What is s/he writing?")

The case of the focused constituent (the Q-word) provides evidence that the cleft of the type illustrated in (35) and (36) has been reanalyzed. In Mingrelian the copula in the present tense governs the nominative case for its subject and predicate nominal; in (32) the focused nominal is the subject (or predicate nominal) of the copula. However, in sentences (34) and (35), the focused constituent is not in the nominative, but in the case governed by the verb forms *ortuk* "you.do.it" and *čaruns* "s/he.write.it" for their objects. The fact that the lexical verb governs the case of the focused constituent supports the analysis of the structure in (35)–(36) as a single-clause construction.[23]

7.2.4   Topic

In some dialects of Laz, another Kartvelian language, we find cleft-like structures used to signal the topic, rather than the focus; this is illustrated in (37) from the Vic'-Arkab dialect.

(37)   mažura-pe-na   en,   va   uc'umess
       second-PL.NOM-COMP it.be NEG he.speak.to.them
       Lit.: "The others that are, he does not speak to [them]." "As for the
       others, he does not speak to them."   (Čikobava 1936b: 32, 19)

The peculiarity of the structure in (37), which we term an *anti-cleft*, is that, unlike focus clefts familiar from many languages, the subordinate clause, rather than the matrix, contains the copula and the topicalized element. Correspondingly, the empty position occurs in the matrix clause, rather than the subordinate. The structure we propose for this is given in (38):

(38)

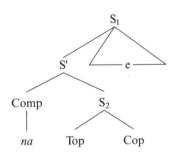

This structure is justified in more detail in Harris (1991c).

In other dialects, the anti-cleft structure in (38) has been reinterpreted in the form we see in (39)–(40), from the Xopian dialect:

(39)   ia   patišai-k-nay   badis   uc'veen
      that ruler-NAR-TOP old.man he.speak.him
      "As for that ruler, he apparently says to the old man . . ."

                                    (Asatiani 1974: 12, 4)

(40)   ia   k'ulani-muši-nay   patišais komeču
      that daughter-his-TOP ruler   he.give.her.to.him
      "As for his daughter, he gave her to the ruler."   (Asatiani 1974: 12, 35)

The anti-cleft construction has been reinterpreted as a single clause with the topic marked with the particle *nay*, the reflex of a contraction of *na*, the relative particle and all-purpose subordinator, and "be." This maintains the pragmatic function of the anti-cleft in (37) – indicating the topic. That reanalysis has occurred is shown by the fact that the topics in (39)–(40) are in the case governed by the tense–aspect and verb class of the content verb, not, in this dialect, by the copula. Similarly, in the Xopian dialect the topic triggers subject or object agreement when it occurs in the corresponding grammatical relation.

7.2.5   A universal characterization of cleft-to-highlighting
We use the term "cleft" now to include both the focus cleft and the topic-marking anti-cleft.

7.2.5.1   Universals of cleft-to-highlighting: stages
In sections 7.2.2–7.2.4 we have argued that monoclausal highlighting constructions often originate as biclausal structures – clefts or anti-clefts. As the biclausal structure is reanalyzed as monoclausal, its development falls naturally into three stages, outlined below (cf. section 4.4.3). Some languages do not make it to the third stage; a language may proceed quickly or slowly through the stages.

> *Stage I*: The structure has all of the superficial characteristics of a biclausal structure and none of the characteristics of a monoclausal one.
> *Stage II*: The structure gradually acquires some characteristics of a biclausal structure and retains some characteristics of a monoclausal one.
> *Stage III*: The structure has all of the characteristics of a monoclausal structure and no characteristics of a biclausal one.

Stage II is actualization; it may consist of one or many substages, depending on the characteristics that the particular language assigns to biclausal and monoclausal structures. During Stage II, there is typically a series of changes that have the effect of making the biclausal/monoclausal structure look more monoclausal. These may include (i) changing the case of the highlighted constituent (as in Mingrelian and Laz), (ii) changing the form of the highlighter to look less like the copula or relativizer (as in French), (iii) dropping the copula or relativizer altogether (as in Breton, where both may be dropped), (iv) ceasing to use a special verb form (as in Japanese), (v) (re)introducing agreement (as has been done partially in Somali), and (vi) reordering constituents (as in Somali). Synchronically, Stage II may be described by positing a biclausal underlying structure and a monoclausal surface structure, or by other devices within various theories. In Stage III, actualization has been completed.

7.2.5.2   Universals of cleft-to-highlighting: structure

Some discussions of the diachronic phenomena of the type dealt with here have focused on the development of the grammatical marker from another word, ignoring the fact that the source pattern is a construction consisting of two clauses, while the resulting pattern is a single-clause construction. Once we look at the syntactic change as a whole, three universals emerge clearly:

(41)   (a)   The two clauses of the cleft construction become a single clause in surface structure.
       (b)   The highlighted constituent is realized in the grammatical relation that the clefted constituent bore in the content clause in the input.
       (c)   A discourse marker (henceforth **highlighter**) is formed from some combination of (i) the copula, (ii) the relativizer, and (iii) the expletive pronoun.

The source construction, represented in (2) and (38), contains two clauses; the resulting pattern contains only one clause (see note 3 above). The grammatical relation of the clefted constituent is assumed by the highlighted constituent, but this does not mean that the highlighted constituent immediately takes on the encoding characteristics of the clefted constituent (see below, section 7.5). Since many languages make no use of expletive pronouns, and since either the copula or the relativizer may have a zero form, (41c) predicts the maximum constituents which may compose the highlighter.

Generalization (41) states our claim that in any language in which a highlighting construction is derived from a cleft construction, changes (41a–c) will occur.[24]

7.2.5.3   Language-particular aspects of cleft-to-highlighting

The changes in (41) follow reanalysis; the form taken by the actualization of this reanalysis is language-particular. As pointed out in section 7.2.2.4, in Somali the subject of the subject focus construction does not fully condition verb agreement and is not marked with the case otherwise used for subject, but rather with the case used for predicate nominals in equational sentences. Thus, little actualization has taken place. If further actualization takes place, it is likely that the subject, the highlighted constituent in the subject focus construction, would take on the case and agreement characteristics of other subjects. Precisely this has occurred in Mingrelian (section 7.2.3.2), where the highlighted constituent optionally bears the case marking appropriate for the grammatical relation of the clefted constituent.

The degree of cohesion (independent word, clitic, or affix) of the highlighter and its form after reanalysis are also language-particular. The form of the highlighter is determined by the constituents always present in the fixed expression that preceded the reanalysis; a language that does not use an expletive pronoun in its source cleft will not have a reflex of an expletive pronoun in its highlighter, and a language that has a zero relativizer will not have an overt reflex of a relativizer in its highlighter. The cohesion and form of the highlighter are often changed as part of the actualization; a highlighter often undergoes reduction. These changes are dependent upon language-specific conditions that are incompletely understood, including sentence stress and the degree of predictability of its constituent parts.

7.3   Quotation constructions

A simple sentence containing a quotative particle often develops from a complex sentence containing a matrix clause that includes an expression of saying.

7.3.1   Examples

In Old Georgian the quotative particle, *o*, was used to quote the words of another (third person). It was enclitic to the last word of a quotation, most frequently the verb; it often occurred with a complementizer, as in (42):

(42)   man macturman tkua, . . . vitarmed šemdgomad samisa dɣisa
       that deceiver   he.said   that   after   three   day

       aɣvdge-o
       I.arise-QUO

       "That deceiver said 'After three days I will arise.'" "That deceiver said that after three days he would arise."

                                       (Mt. 27: 63AB; cited by Ӡiӡiguri 1973: 195)

However, in the oldest texts, which are translations of the Gospels from Greek and Armenian originals, *o* is infrequent, either because of the usage of these originals or because the particle was infrequent in Georgian itself. In Middle Georgian, *o* became more frequent in texts (Ӡiӡiguri 1973: 195).

Two other quotative particles were introduced by the tenth or eleventh century.[25] One of the later additions, *metki*, is used just to quote the words of the speaker (first person). The second, *tko,* is less frequent because of its more restricted function; it is used just to quote the words which the hearer (second person) is advised to use on some future occasion. All three particles are used with or without a complementizer; if a complementizer is used, it comes between the clause expressing what is said and the (synchronic) verb of saying, as in (43), not between what is said and the particle:

(43) ara   vhk'itxe,   tu   romelsa kueq'anasa šina aris   metki
      NEG I.ask.it.to.him whether which   country   in   he.be QUO
      "I did not ask him which country he is in."
                        (*Amiran-darejaniani* II, 100, 1; cited in 3i3iguri 1973: 192)

(44) ase vtkvi, ca kuxs   da   mic'a ikceva-metki
      thus I.say.it sky it.thunder and earth it.tremble-QUO
      "I said, 'The sky thunders and the earth trembles'" or "I said that the sky thunders and the earth trembles."
                              (*Rusudaniani* 763, 4; cited in 3i3iguri 1973: 192)

(45) hk'adre,   iq'o-tko   aka ertisa c'amita
      you.SG.say.it.to.him he.was-QUO here one   moment
      "Say to him [respectfully], 'He was here for a moment.'"
                            (*Vepxis-t'q'aosani* 103, 4; cited in 3i3iguri 1973: 194)

The subordinate clause may precede or follow the matrix.

The particle *metki* is formed historically from the sequence *me vtkvi* (3i3iguri 1973: 446; Šani3e 1973: 610), where *me* is the pronoun "I" and *v-tkv-i* is the first person singular subject (*v-*) aorist indicative (*-i*) of "say": "I said (it)." The loss of *v* in both positions is consistent with a widespread, but apparently irregular, propensity of this consonant to weakening, deletion, and/or change. (For example, in forms of this verb, the labial stem consonant may show up as [u] or as [m] instead of [v/w].) The particle *tko,* is derived diachronically from a form *tkva* of the root *tkv* "say" (Vogt 1971: 217; Šani3e 1973: 610). The form *tkva* itself sometimes substitutes for *tko* in this function; *tkva* is the second person singular subject form of the optative: "may you say (it)." In addition to these reflexes, the verb *tkv* "say" continues as a fully conjugated verb.

On the basis of maintenance of a direct reflex of the subject (*me* "I") and the verb (*vtkvi* "I said") in the particle *metki*, we assume derivation from a complex structure in which *me vtkvi* "I said" is the matrix clause; this is referred to below as the clause of saying. We assume that which was said represented the complement of the clause of saying (see Partee 1973 and Munro 1982, on general syntactic properties of "say"). We assume that *tko* "(may) you say" derives from a similar complex structure.

The forms *metki* and *tko* have been reanalyzed and no longer represent a clause. This can be seen from two facts. First, when the reduced enclitic form, *metki,* based on an aorist, was first introduced in the literary language, it occurred most often, or entirely, with main verbs in the aorist. In the modern language, it no longer has a tense and is used freely with verbs in tenses other than the aorist, as in (46)–(47):

(46)   me vambob,   mivdivar-metki
        I   I.say.it.PRES I.go-QUO
        "I am saying, 'I am leaving.'"

(47)   me vit'q'vi,   c̀aval-metki
        I   I.say.it.FUT I.go.FUT-QUO
        "I will say, 'I will go.'"   (Ӡiӡiguri 1973: 446)

All three quotation particles are invariant, not distinguishing the verbal categories of Georgian – tense, mood, and aspect.[26] Second, the particle *metki* cannot stand alone as the verb in a simple sentence, as (48) shows.[27]

(48)   *(me) metki čemi saxeli
        I   QUO my   name

If *metki* were a verb, (48) could be expected to mean "I said (spoke) my name."

On this basis we conclude that after reanalysis the content clause and the quotative particle constitute a single clause. This single clause may be used with or without a synchronic clause of saying, but the reflex of the original biclausal quotation construction itself consists of only one clause. For example, in (46) the single-clause quotative construction is *mivdivar-metki*; it forms part of a new quotation construction that includes both clauses.[28]

7.3.2   A language-independent characterization of quotation-to-quotative
7.3.2.1   *The synchronic structure of quotation constructions*
We use the term **quotation construction** here to refer to a biclausal structure with "say" or a similar verb of speaking in the matrix clause.[29]

(49)   The quotation construction (a) consists of a matrix clause and a subordinate
        clause; (b) the matrix clause contains a verb "say."

The matrix clause, in a language with hypotactic quotation constructions, contains not only "say," but also a subject of that verb, though the subject may not be overtly expressed. The structure also optionally contains a complementizer and/or a pronoun referring to the complement. The structure of the quotation construction in a language using hypotaxis is represented in (50), which is not intended to include a representation of a particular word order, either with respect to clause-internal structure or with respect to the order of clauses:

(50)   [Subj *say* (*it*) [(*that*) S]]

English words are used in (50) to stand for both obligatory and optional elements of the structure: *it* represents the pronoun that occurs in some languages; *that* represents the complementizer that can be used with (direct or indirect) quotation.

7.3.2.2   *Universals of quotation-to-quotative*

The transition from the biclausal quotation to the monoclausal quotative construction takes place in the three stages identified in section 7.2.5.1, with the reflex structure gradually acquiring the characteristics of monoclausal structures in general.

Although both cleft-to-highlighting construction and quotation-to-quotative construction take place in the context of a biclausal structure, the changes that affect them differ in scope. In the former transition, the biclausal structure as a whole is reanalyzed, with constituents of both clauses combining to form the resulting clause. In the latter transition, only one clause is actually reanalyzed; the structure of the subordinate clause is unaffected.

We propose the following universals of the quotation-to-quotative transition in languages with hypotactic structure:

(51)   (a)   The two clauses of the hypotactic quotation construction become a single clause.
          (b)   No argument of the "say" clause becomes an argument of the output structure.
          (c)   A quotative particle is formed from some combination of the following: (i) the verb "say," (ii) its subject, (iii) the pronoun "it," and (iv) the complementizer.

All of the constituents of the "say" clause of the source construction form a single constituent, here a single word, in the reflex construction. Item (51c) specifies only the maximum constituents of the quotative particle, without making a specific claim about its form in any particular language. An example which clearly preserves the verb "say" itself is from Green Hmong:

(52)   nwg nug kuv (has) tas   koj nyob qhov-twg
          he   ask me (QUO) QUO you stay where
          "He asked me where you are staying."   (Li 1988: 3)

The verbal function of *tas* is shown in (53).

(53)   Tuam tas nwg nkeeg-nkeeg
          Tuam   he   very.tired
          "Tuam said that he was very tired."   (Li 1988: 1)

Rule (51) expresses our proposal that any language that develops a quotative from a quotation construction will undergo these changes. It embodies the view that the change involves a syntactic pattern which is changed into another syntactic pattern, not just a word that is changed into a quotative.

7.3.2.3   *Language-particular aspects of quotation-to-quotative*
Some aspects of actualization will be language-particular. Among the most frequent types of actualization are changes in the form or the degree of cohesion of the quotative particle. Changes to the form are dependent on factors which include sentence stress, degree of predictability, the degree to which the quotative may contrast with forms of the verb "say," and transparency of the quotative. In the two attested Georgian changes, different elements are included in the two resulting quotative particles as a result of different elements being included in the fixed expression that preceded reanalysis. The quotative *metki* is formed from two elements specified in (51c, i–ii), namely "say" and its subject; while *tko* does not include the subject.[30] Both underwent reduction after reanalysis. The third quotative particle, *o* "s/he said," formed before the historical period, also shows the effects of later reduction.[31]

7.4   Clause fusion

By **clause fusion** we mean a diachronic process which creates from a biclausal surface structure a monoclausal surface structure with an auxiliary and main verb. We suggest a two-part definition of clause fusion:

(54)   Clause fusion is a diachronic process in which
    (a) a biclausal surface structure becomes a monoclausal surface structure;
    (b) the verb of the matrix clause becomes an auxiliary, that of the
            subordinate clause becomes the main (lexical) verb.

The definition in (54) presupposes an understanding of the notion **auxiliary**. We begin our discussion of this notion with the characterization presented in Steele *et al.* (1981: 21), for that is frequently quoted: "Given a set of language-internal analyses, those constituents which may contain only a specified (i.e. fixed and small) set of elements, crucially containing elements marking tense and/or modality will be identified as nondistinct." We do not wish to limit our discussion to those languages in which it can be established that all such elements together form a constituent. On the other hand, we do not wish to include here affixal markers of tense and aspect; tense–aspect–modality (TAM) affixes often develop out of auxiliaries (in our sense), but this is typically a development that takes place subsequent to the one we focus on here. It is our intention to include instead those elements that are traditionally called auxiliaries, together with those invariant forms, often referred to as particles, that mark the tense, aspect, or mood of a main verb. We therefore identify auxiliaries with the following criteria:

(55)   Auxiliaries are
    (a)   independent words or clitics
    (b)   which form a closed set, and
    (c)   which mark tense and/or aspect and/or modality.

Georgian and English modal verbs are discussed in section 7.4.1, and an alternative view of English modals is proposed there. This is followed by brief descriptions of possessive perfects (section 7.4.2) and of progressives (section 7.4.3). In section 7.4.4 we discuss a previous proposal concerning the universals of this process. Our own specific proposal for the universals of fusion is included in section 7.5.

7.4.1   Modals
Changes concerning modals are one of the few areas in which previous treatments have focused attention on the change from a biclausal to a monoclausal strcture. We begin our discussion with a change in modals in historical times in Georgian (section 7.4.1.1) because this has an important bearing on the analysis of modals in English (section 7.4.1.2).

7.4.1.1   *Georgian*
In the historical period Georgian modal verbs have undergone changes that are to an extent parallel to those of English modals. We focus here on the one modal in which the change has gone farthest.

In Old Georgian the verb *hnebavs* "wants" could have a nominal object or a sentential object expressed in the subjunctive, in the aorist, or in any of several non-finite forms.[32]

Examples with the subjunctive are given in (56) and (57), though this construction only became common in a later period:

(56)   q'oveli romeli gindes   r~a giq'on   k'ac-ta. . .
      all   which you.want.it that they.do.it.you man-PL.OBL
      "everything which you want men to do to you"   (Mt. 7: 12 AB)

(Cf. King James: "Therefore all things whatsoever ye *would* that men should do to you. . ."; emphasis added.)

(57)   uk'uetu mindes, rayta dges   ege čemda moslvadmde
      if   I.want.it that he.stand he my   coming.until
      "if I wished that he stay until I come"   (John 21: 22 Ad.)

In the Old Georgian period the present was expressed with the forms *m-nebavs* "I want it," *g-nebavs* "you want it," *h-nebavs* "s/he wants it," and the imperfect (past) with the forms *minda* "I wanted it," *ginda* "you wanted it," *unda* "s/he wanted it." By the eleventh or twelfth century, the latter forms were used to express the present, as they are today, and a new imperfect was created: *mindoda, gindoda, undoda* (Sarǰvelaᴣe 1984: 412–13).[33] Thus, the present-day present-tense forms for "want" are so-called past-presents.

In both Old and Middle Georgian (from the twelfth century), then, the pattern in (58) occurred, among others:

(58)   [*mas_i*   *unda* [(*rayta*) Verb   S_{i,j} (DO) (IO). . .]][34]
        s/he.DAT want   COMP SUBJUNCTIVE

In Old Georgian the main verb, "want," of pattern (58) is imperfect, in Middle Georgian present; in both periods *unda* was part of a more complete verbal paradigm. As (56) and (57) above illustrate, it was not necessary at the oldest stages for the initial subject of *unda* (*mas* in (58)) to be coindexed (coreferential) with an argument of the verb of the subordinate clause; if it was coindexed, ordinarily the argument in the subordinate clause would not appear in surface structure.

The construction in (56) above establishes an important point about the syntax of the verb "want" as early as Old Georgian. In general in Georgian, question words and relative pronouns cannot be extracted from subordinate clauses; the three modal verbs are a systematic exception to this generalization in Modern Georgian (Harris 1981: 16–18). Example (56) shows that this exception was already established for *hnebavs* "want" by the eighth century. The establishment of this syntactic exception for modal verbs alone is one of the factors that made it possible for these three verbs to acquire other behavior that set them apart in the Georgian system.

The pattern in (58) was reanalyzed with two changes occurring: (i) the meaning changed from "want"; it now means either epistemic necessity or deontic obligation; (ii) the structure changed from biclausal to monoclausal, producing a pattern like (59):

(59)   [*mas*   *unda* Verb   (DO) (IO) . . .]
        s/he.DAT AUX   SUBJUNCTIVE

The change left the old construction intact, with the old meaning, with the old structure (permitting a Comp and a non-coreferential subject), and with the complete paradigmatic variation, as illustrated in part in (61a)–(63a) below. The new meaning occurs only with the single form *unda*. Thus in the modern language there is an invariant auxiliary *unda* "should, ought, must' beside a third person singular lexical verb form *unda* "s/he wants it," which still alternates paradigmatically with *minda* "I want it," *ginda* "you want it," and the plural forms. The auxiliary and the independent verb are illustrated below in (61)–(63).

After fusion to a monoclausal structure, actualization changed the government of the clausal syntax. In (59), after reanalysis, the initial subject is still expressed in the dative, the case governed by the syntax of the old verb "want."[35] This would seem to be inconsistent with the new monoclausal syntax, and this situation was changed.[36] The ordinary case pattern required with the subjunctive was extended to this construction; this would be the so-called narrative or nominative case, depending on the morphological class of the lexical verb.

(60) [*man/is*   *unda* Verb   (DO) (IO) . . .]
     s/he.NAR/NOM AUX SUBJUNCTIVE

The narrative and nominative cases are illustrated in the (b) sentences of (61)–(63), which have the new construction with reanalysis and extension; the dative case occurs in the (a) sentences, which have the construction directly inherited from Old Georgian:

(61)   (a) mas   unda   (rom) gaak'etos
           s/he.DAT s/he.want.it that   s/he.do.it.SBV
           "S/he wants to do it," or "S/he wants him/her to do it."

        (b) man   unda (*rom) gaak'etos
           s/he.NAR should
           "S/he should do it," "S/he must do it."

(62)   (a) minda   (rom) gavak'eto
           I.want.it that   I.do.it.SBV
           "I want to do it."

        (b) unda   (*rom) gavak'eto
           should
           "I should do it," "I must do it."

(63)   (a) mas   unda   (rom) c'avides
           s/he.DAT s/he.want.it that   s/he.go.SBV
           "S/he wants to go" or "S/he wants him/her to go."

        (b) is   unda (*rom) c'avides
           s/he.NOM should
           "S/he should go."

The (a) sentences consist of two clauses, with the sentential complement optionally marked by the all-purpose complementizer *rom*, and with the verb of the lower clause in the second subjunctive, as required by the "sequence of tense" rules. The (b) sentences are single clauses with the auxiliary *unda*[37] and the verb in the second subjunctive; use of the complementizer makes the sentences ungrammatical. Whether the subject is in the narrative or nominative case in the (b) sentences is determined by the main verb (*gaaketos* or *cavides*) according to the regular rules of the language.

There are a number of obvious parallels between the history of modals in English and the history of *unda* in Georgian. One similarity seems to provide a clue to understanding a problem with previous analyses of the English change, as discussed in the next section.

7.4.1.2   English

Lightfoot (1974; 1979a, ch. 2; 1991: 141–54) has proposed an analysis of English modals and a diachronic account of changes in the structure of clauses. This involves biclausal surface structures with modals (his "pre-modals") as main verbs in Old English, and monoclausal surface structures with modals as a special category in Modern English. (We use the term "modal" to encompass both their early verbal status and their later status as auxiliaries, distinguishing instead between **modal verbs** and **modal auxiliaries**.) Lightfoot proposes the structures (64) for modals in Old English, and (65) in Middle English, after the change from basic SOV to basic SVO order had occurred (1979a: 106–7):

(64)   (a) $NP_S [(NP_S) NP_O V]_O M$
        (b) $[NP_S NP_O V]_S M$
(65)   (a) $NP_S M [(NP_S) V NP_O]$
        (b) $[NP_S V NP_O] M$

In both (64) and (65), the (a) structures are Lightfoot's proposals for root modals, and the (b) structures represent the epistemic modals. Here parentheses indicate that the nominal does not appear on the surface.

Lightfoot (1979a: 101–9) has listed five changes in Middle English modals, which preceded the radical restructuring he describes as occurring in early Modern English. In Lightfoot (1991) these have been reduced to four by omitting (d); it is included here for completeness.

(66)   (a)   "The antecedents of the modern modals . . . lost the ability to take direct objects" (1979a: 101).
        (b)   The modals were so-called preterite-presents, past-tense forms that had been reinterpreted as presents. Verbs of this class lacked the *-s* ending of the present. Loss of all other verbs of this class left the modals as constituting "an identifiable class of verbs" (1979a: 103).
        (c)   There was a breakdown in the present/past relationship of *can/could*, *shall/should*, *will/would*, and *may/might*. The preterites *must* and *ought*

replaced the corresponding present-tense forms, taking on present meaning themselves.

(d)   After the change from SOV to SVO order in Early Middle English, special rules applied to prevent occurrence of the order SVOM, which is attested only rarely.

(e)   The use of the *to*-infinitive gradually replaced that of the bare infinitive during Middle English, but the modals never adopted this.

According to Lightfoot, the above were independent changes that had the combined effect of "making the premodals into a small and distinctive class" (1991: 148; see also 1979a: 109).

Lightfoot claims that reanalysis took place when all of the above changes were complete, and that reanalysis automatically set off another series of changes, which took place "together, within the same short period" (1979a: 110):

(67)   (a)   The modals lost the ability to occur as infinitives.
          (b)   The modals lost the -*ing* form.
          (c)   In most dialects a constraint against more than one modal per verb was introduced.
          (d)   The modals could no longer occur with *have* and an -*en* suffix (as *take* does in the expression *has taken*).
          (e)   The rule of Negative Placement was reformulated to treat modals differently from verbs.
          (f)   The rule of Subject-Verb Inversion was reformulated to treat modals as auxiliaries.
          (g)   A new set of "quasi-modals" – *be going to, have to, be able to* – was created that are true verbs but semantically equivalent to the modals.

                                                                    (1979a: 110–13)

Others have pointed out that the seven changes in (67) were in fact not so simultaneous, but occurred gradually. Further, the individual modals underwent both sets of changes ((66) and (67)) at different times. (On both points, see Warner 1982: 117–23; Roberts 1985; Goossens 1987; Nagle 1989: 48–9, 94ff.) Although Lightfoot mentions that a few individual verbs do not conform entirely to his timeframe (e.g. 1979a: 101, regarding *can*), his analysis depends upon uniformity among the several modals, and he makes no proposal for dealing with the time lag some verbs demonstrate. In 1991 (p. 142), Lightfoot admits, "This change may not have been as cataclysmic as I claimed in Lightfoot 1979[a]." Apart from the timing, we assume that Lightfoot's account is factually correct.

We propose a somewhat different analysis of these facts, based on (i) our understanding of the mechanisms of reanalysis and extension, (ii) the recognition that it is possible for a modal auxiliary to develop while a homophonous modal verb continues to exist, and (iii) the appreciation of the fact that the modals may not all have been reanalyzed at the same time and that, to an extent, actualization of the reanalyses also occurred at different times. Our view of reanalysis and extension is supported in detail in chapters 3–5. Evidence from Georgian to support the possibility of (ii) is given in section 7.4.1.1 above. In addition, we know that development of a modal auxiliary homophonous to a continuing modal verb can occur in English, since the Old English modal *agan* has not only the auxiliary reflex *ought*, but also the verbal reflexes *owe* and *own*, and the modal auxiliaries *need* and *dare* still coexist with homophonous verbs. The possibility of such a development specifically for English is further confirmed by the fact that beside the auxiliaries *be* and *have* are full verbs in the same forms. We do not provide specific arguments to support point (iii), but in several places we make note of differing timetables.

In our view, the reanalysis of the modals was brought about by the obsolescence of the subjunctive, already advanced in Old English, and by the general transition to periphrasis (see also Roberts 1985).

We suggest that in fact reanalysis of the modals as auxiliaries and of their structures as monoclausal occurred much earlier than Lightfoot proposes, at least by early Middle English. Wasow and Akmajian (in Steele *et al.* 1981: 288) and Warner (1982: 117–18) have likewise proposed an earlier date. Aitchison (1980: 141) points out that Lightfoot's own data even lead to an earlier date, if one approaches them without bias. Nagle (1989: 55–6) has raised the following objection to their analyses: "If the modals were reanalyzed as initial structure auxiliaries in OE, it is not clear why it would take hundreds of years for the ME changes to run their course. For example, why should initial structure auxiliaries continue to take direct objects for three centuries?" This seems to be a valid criticism if one does not recognize the possibility that the verb can continue to exist as a verb, even though one of its forms has been reanalyzed as an auxiliary, just as in contemporary Georgian. In Middle English it was not the modal auxiliaries that took direct objects, but the homophonous verbs.[38]

After reanalysis, modal verbs continued for a time to exist beside the innovative modal auxiliaries. The change which actually takes place primarily in early Modern English, the period to which Lightfoot ascribes reanalysis, is loss of the homophonous modal verbs, leaving the modal auxiliaries without parallel forms. Arguments to support our analysis are presented below, addressing each of the twelve characteristics cited in Lightfoot (1979a), though in a slightly different order.[39]

If reanalysis occurred by early Middle English times, given the view we have presented of reanalysis and actualization, it is not surprising that actualization, the twelve changes listed in (66) and (67), took place gradually, over an extended period of time, at different rates for different modals. The changes listed, with a few exceptions discussed below, were part of the actualization of the reanalysis. Like other reanalyses, this one left the surface patterns intact, but these patterns gradually changed in accordance with the new category of the modal and the new monoclausal structure.

The gradual inability of modals to occur with nominal direct objects (trait (66a)) reflects the gradual loss of the modal verbs (which occurred with direct objects), while the modal auxiliaries survived. It is to be expected that the auxiliaries would not themselves take direct objects.

Regarding the loss of other verbs in the preterite–present class (point (66b)) Lightfoot has written, "One can only assume that it was an accident that in this inflectional class only the pre-modals survived" (1979a: 103). Indeed, on his analysis, this can only be an accident. But if auxiliary variants of the modal verbs already existed, it was the entire class of preterite–present verbs that was lost, and it was no accident. This class was probably lost in part because it was highly irregular; its loss is thus in part independent of any changes in the modals. It is possible that its loss was accelerated by the fact that modal auxiliaries formed. It is likewise possible that the modal verbs survived somewhat longer than the other verbs of this class because they were reinforced by the existence of homophonous modal auxiliaries. Some of the modal verbs (as distinct from the modal auxiliaries) continued to exist for some time, as shown by the fact that *can* could take a noun direct object as late as 1659 (Lightfoot 1979a: 101).

To show why the breakdown of the present/past relationship of the modal auxiliaries (trait (66c)) was an expected consequence of the reanalysis of the modal verbs as auxiliaries, we must consider the way that auxiliaries, main verbs, and tense–aspect–mode (TAM) interact in languages generally. In most instances, TAM is marked only once in the verb complex; cross-linguistically it is unusual for TAM to be indicated redundantly in a monoclausal structure. In a verb complex that involves only one auxiliary, TAM may be indicated on the auxiliary, with the main verb in an invariant form (such as a participle), or TAM may be indicated on the main verb with the auxiliary in an invariant form (called a particle in some traditions), or TAM categories may be divided among these. In English the modal occurs in a verb complex with additional elements that carry the tense–aspect. Thus, in combinations such as *could have done*, *could be doing*, *could have been doing*, tense and aspect are marked by the other auxiliaries, *have* and *be*, while the modal carries the mood. A change to an invariant modal in English produces a verbal complex that corresponds to expectations, based on cross-linguistic evidence, that tense–aspect not be doubly marked. In English the breakdown of the present/past relationship in the modal auxiliaries was thus to be expected as part of the actualization of the new status as auxiliaries; in the homophonous modal verbs, the distinction would be expected to last longer.

Immediately after reanalysis, forms that formerly represented the past tense would have been used in past-tense environments, and those that formerly represented the present tense would have been used in present-tense environments. Even today, some past-tense environments require past tense forms.

(68)   I **could** jump a lot higher when I was a boy   (Goossens 1987: 115)
        *I **can** jump a lot higher when I was a boy

(69)   yesterday he **could** not do it
        *yesterday he **can** not do it

(70)   if I had known that you needed a pencil, I **might** have bought you one
        *if I had known that you needed a pencil, I **may** have bought you one

(71)   yesterday I promised that I **would** get it done by this morning
        *yesterday I promised that I **will** get it done by this morning

The patterns in (68)–(71) show that there is a persistence of the old surface pattern, even though *can, could, may, might, will,* and *would* are generally independent in Modern English. Reanalysis does not change the surface pattern, and actualization has still not completely effaced it. Persistence of the requirement for formerly past-tense forms in (68)–(71) is an effective demonstration of the gradual nature of actualization.

According to our analysis, modal auxiliaries were already auxiliaries at the time the new word order rules came into effect ((66d)). This means that the word order rules would automatically treat modal auxiliaries as auxiliaries, not as verbs. This in turn means that our analysis automatically predicts both that the modal auxiliary would precede the verb (as a harmonic of the new VO order) and that the modal and verb would be placed together between the S and O (section 8.5.1). It thus automatically accounts for the fact the word order SMVO would appear, and that other orders would be rare or non-occurring. Lightfoot's analysis, on the other hand, makes neither of these predictions and requires that "following the SOV-to-SVO base change some special mechanism would be needed to distinguish the epistemic pre-modals from other one-place predicates, avoiding the expected SVOM or *it* M [NP . . .]ₛ structures" (1979a: 108). Our analysis requires no such special rule.

Most modal auxiliaries never began to use *to* with the infinitive (trait (66e)) because they were no longer verbs. (Lightfoot [1979a: 108]: "It is not clear to me why the pre-modals consistently resisted the encroachment of *to*.") Verbs such as *try* have *to* (*she tried to leave*). If the modals had been reanalyzed by this period, as we have proposed, there would be no reason to identify them with verbs; they are treated instead like other auxiliaries (compare *is leaving* and *has left*).[40] Note that *ought* does take *to*, evidently because it was reanalyzed later than the other modals. The modal verbs homophonous with other modal auxiliaries were by that time obsolescent and therefore were unlikely to participate in changes.

Thus, of the five changes in (66) which Lightfoot considers "independent" (1979a: 109) and "accidental" (1991: 148), three (c–e) are on our analysis automatic consequences of the reanalysis of the modal verbs as modal auxiliaries. Trait (66,b), while not automatic, does not involve the accident described by Lightfoot.

Most of the changes listed in (67) are automatic consequences of the fact that modals were already auxiliaries, both on Lightfoot's analysis and on ours. Modals ceased to appear in infinitive constructions (characteristic (67a)), with *-ing* suffixes ((67b)), or in *have. . .-en* sequences ((67d)) because these are environments in which verbs occur, and the modal auxiliaries had already ceased to be verbs. It was the homophonous modal verbs that had been occurring in these environments in the intervening period, and they now died out.

It is likewise natural that the modals would have been treated as auxiliaries in the reformulation of Negative Placement ((67e)) and Subject–Verb Inversion ((67f)). Once the modals were reanalyzed as auxiliaries, the number of auxiliaries in the language was much larger (previously there were only *have* and *be*), and we can safely assume that the number of tokens of negative sentences having an auxiliary would be much greater than before reanalysis. This means that the pattern

(72)   Aux   Neg   Main Verb

would have occurred considerably more frequently than before, increasing its frequency relative to the pattern in (73):

(73)   Main Verb   Neg

With the increased frequency of (72) also being fed by the gradual increase in the use of *do*, it was reevaluated as the unmarked, then as the obligatory, pattern. The same considerations, *mutatis mutandis*, apply to the change in question formation.

Regarding the restriction imposed in most dialects against multiple modals ((67c)), this is not a consequence of reanalysis, on Lightfoot's analysis or on ours.[41] The continued existence of the construction with multiple modal auxiliaries in many dialects of the southern United States and in Scottish dialects shows that the multiple modal structure is compatible with the new category status.

It would be highly surprising if the language created the new "quasi-modals" ((67g)) at the very same time it was reanalyzing the old modals; it is far more likely that this part of the actualization, like the others, followed reanalysis with some lag.

According to Lightfoot's analysis, the five changes in (66) prepared for the reanalysis that came, indeed making it inevitable; yet it must have been a coincidence that these five changes took place. On our analysis it is no coincidence. Three of these are automatically predicted by our analysis; the other two are not automatic, but are steps taken to rid the grammar of the modal verbs homophonous with the new modal auxiliaries.

Regarding the possibility that the modals were already non-verbal at this period, Lightfoot has written "if we assume, as we must, that the pre-modals were still underlying verbs. . ." (1979a: 107), but he has given no reason to back up his "as we must." We conclude that (i) there is no reason to make the assumption Lightfoot makes, and (ii) the arguments we have provided show that reanalysis took place much earlier than Lightfoot assumes.

7.4.2   Possessive perfects

7.4.2.1   French

Latin made use of expressions involving a past passive participle with *tenēre* "hold," *habēre* "keep, hold," or other verbs meaning "hold, possess" to "represent something as *ready* or *kept* in a completed condition" (Hale and Buck 1966[1903]: 327).

(74)   ducēs comprehēnsōs tenētis
"You hold the leaders under arrest." (i.e. "arrested")
(Cicero, *The oration against Catiline* 3, 7, 16; Hale and Buck 1966[1903]: 327).

(75)   in eā   provinciā pecūniās magnās collocātās habent
in that province capital   great   invested   they.have
"They have great capital invested in that province."
(Cicero, cited by Vincent 1982: 82)

Linguists have long recognized that this was a biclausal structure. The possessor was the subject[42] of the matrix clause, and the possessed was the object. The subordinate clause included minimally (i) a subject, which could be distinct from (not coreferential to) the subject of the main clause, (ii) a deep structure direct object, which was necessarily coreferent with the direct object of the main clause, and (iii) a verb, realized as a passive participle. The subordinate clause formed a constituent with the direct object of the main clause. Passivization applied in the dependent clause, making the initial direct object the derived subject; it then deleted under identity with the direct object of the main clause.

Three aspects of this structure are important in our discussion: (i) the possibility of distinct subjects in the two clauses; (ii) agreement; and (iii) word order. In Latin examples such as (74)–(75) and in early French, the participle could be understood as having a subject distinct from (not coreferential to) the subject of the verb "hold, have." Brunot and Bruneau (1933: 473) illustrate this possibility in French with (76), where (a) *escrites* functions as an adjective, (b) its subject is not "the emperor," and (c) the verb *avoir* retains its basic meaning "have":

(76)   et   [chis empereres] avoit   letres seur lui   escrites qui . . .
         and this emperor   he-has letters on   him written which
         "and this emperor has letters written on him, which [say] . . ."
                                                        (Robert de Clari, p. 86, line 11)

The passage refers to a statue of the emperor with an inscription. Though it became less and less common to construe the past participle with a distinct subject, it remained a possibility throughout the Middle Ages (Brunot and Bruneau 1933: 473). The existence of two subjects, each with a verb, is accounted for by positing two clauses. In Old French the participle used with the verb *avoir* "have" could preserve its independence, filling the function of an adjective, while *avoir* retained its full meaning of possession (Brunot and Bruneau 1933: 472).

If the subordinate clause formed a constituent with the direct object of the main clause, as claimed, the participle (reflecting the verb of the dependent clause) should agree with the head noun, as other modifiers did in Latin and Old French. In general we find agreement of the participle in Latin; for example, in (75) *collocatas* "invested" agrees with the head noun *pecunias* "capital, wealth" in gender, case, and number. In French the matter is more complex, as is discussed further below.

By this time, SVO was a favorite word order in French, with SOV, VSO, and OVS also occurring (Foulet 1930:306). Of these, the second was found mainly in subordinate clauses (p. 316); while the last two, with subject–verb inversion, occurred when an adverb or the direct object was placed in clause-initial position (pp. 306–16). In (76) we see SVO order with *avoit*, the verb of the main clause, and the participle *escrites* following the noun that it modifies.

We conclude that the early biclausal construction had a structure like (77), where the word order is not necessarily intended to represent actual surface order in particular examples:

(77)   [Subject$_i$ *habēre* Object$_j$ [Subject$_{i,k}$ Verb Object$_j$]]
         (possessor) "have" (possessed)
                        Verb

The biclausal structure was reanalyzed, and the resulting structure is mono-clausal, as in (78):[43]

(78)   [Subject$_i$ *habēre* Object$_j$ Verb]
         Aux

The structure in (78) reflects the fact that *habēre* (French *avoir*) has become an auxiliary. It likewise reflects the fact that the meaning has changed; no longer is it "one possesses that which has been done," but "one has done it." The meaning change involves at least two structural changes: the category change from verb to auxiliary, and the elimination of the possibility of a distinct agent of the lexical verb.

Actualization of the reanalysis brought about additional changes in agreement, and word order. While participles agreed with their heads in Latin, the practice in French is not regular. Following Brunot and Bruneau (1933: 690–3), we may make these generalizations. In Old French the participle that followed its head agreed with it; the participle that preceded its head could agree or not. In the sixteenth century this general pattern was made a prescriptive rule, but with the pleasant twist that it was formulated as a clever rhyme incorporating examples. Additional conditions governing agreement are apparently arbitrary, not relating to structure at all. They depend on the position of the subject relative to the participle, whether the verb is a reflexive passive, etc. It is more important to observe that the general direction of change has been towards loss of agreement in the participle in construction with *avoir* (Brunot and Bruneau 1933: 693). The apparent arbitrariness of participial agreement in French is best understood as the result of a change from a structure where the participle modified the direct object, as argued above, and therefore agreed with it according to the general principles of the language, to a contemporary structure where the participle is (part of) the verb of a single clause and therefore should not – according to those general principles – agree with its direct object. The arbitrariness itself is due to the institutionalized conservative nature of French grammar: agreement reflects the archaic structure still held up as a norm under certain conditions; lack of agreement reflects the actual, viable structure in the spoken language. Thus, the rule imposing agreement is artificial (Brunot and Bruneau 1933: 693).

The position of the participle relative to *avoir* was likewise changed during actualization. While in Latin it was most common for these two to be separated, as in (78), in French it gradually became more common for them to occur together. In the modern language, the auxiliary *avoir* and the participle, used as the expression of the perfect, cannot be separated except by one of a small group of adverbs. Compare (79a) with *(79b), where the word order is that of (78):

(79)   (a)   J'ai écrit les lettres
               "I have written the letters."

        (b)   *j'ai les lettres écrit

While perfectly acceptable in Old French, this order is no longer possible in the perfect meaning. In French (and Italian) there is now a general correlation of inseparability of verb forms with monoclausal structure (Chamberlain 1982: 127–9; Strong 1983).

A final aspect of the actualization of the reanalysis is the extension of the "have" perfect to those intransitive verbs[44] that originally formed the perfect with "be" instead, itself another instance of a biclausal construction reanalyzed as monoclausal. In French (unlike more conservative Italian) most of the verbs that once occurred in the "be" perfect now take the "have" perfect, and in Canadian French the extension has gone even further (for details see Vincent 1982: 90–1 and sources cited there).

7.4.2.2   English

The origin of the English perfect is in many respects parallel to that in French. Old English had a possessive construction consisting of the possessor subject, "have," the possessed object, and a clause modifying the object, the verb of that clause expressed as a past passive participle:

(80)   gyt ge   habbaþ eowre heortan geblende?
        yet you have   your   hearts   blinded
        "Do you still have your hearts hardened?"
                        (*OE Gospels*, Mk. 8: 17, cited by Visser 1963–73, III, part 2: 2189)

Traugott (1972: 93–4) notes that in Old English these constructions had a possessive, rather than a perfect, meaning, as emphasized by the translations here. The participle was adjectival in form and had a stative sense. In the early forms of the construction, the adjectival nature of the participle shows up in the fact that it agrees with the head:

(81)   on eowrum geðylde ge   habbað eowre   sawla   soðlice
        on your.PL patience you.PL have   your.PL soul.PL.ACC truly

        gehealden-e
        protected.PTCPL-F.PL.ACC

        "In your patience you have your souls truly protected."
                        (Ælfric, *Saints' Lives* 360, 339; cited by Visser 1963–73, III, part 2: 2189)

In (81), the past participle *gehealden* "protected" marks by *-e* its agreement with the accusative plural of the feminine head noun, "soul." According to Traugott (1972: 94), the perfect had developed by the eighth century, though the possessive continued to exist side by side with it; she cites the pair in (82) as examples:

(82)   (a)   ða bec eallæ befullan geliornod hæfdon
               "(They) had completely learned those books."
                                         (King Alfred's *Pastoral Care*, 5.19)

        (b)   ða (he) þas boc hæfde geleornode
               "when (he) had those books learned"
               (King Alfred's version of Boethius' *De consolatione philosophiae*, 1.8)

In (82a), the construction has been reanalyzed as a perfect, and agreement does not appear; (82b) is a direct continuation of the old possessive, and agreement continues to appear on the participle (*geleornode*). We assume that the loss of agreement in the perfect, and not in the possessive, is part of the actualization of the reanalysis.

In some instances the subject of the subordinate clause was not coindexed with that of the matrix, and these eventually were reanalyzed as causatives, of the type in (83). (Example (83) is ambiguous between the causative and possessive readings.)

(83)   he hadde þare tweie castles bi-walled swiðe faste
        "He had there two castles walled very securely."
                       (Layamon (Otho) 18607, cited by Visser 1963–73, III, part 2: 2388)

In (83) the underlying subject of *bi-walled* is not *he*; someone else did the work for him. In Old English this was apparently not differentiated from the pattern where the underlying subject of the subordinate clause was coindexed with the subject of the matrix, as in (82). In particular, Visser (1963–73: III, part 2: 2190–2, 2387–8) notes that the order *have* Object Participle occurs in all types, as in the examples cited above. It was not until "after about Shakespeare's time" (1963–73: III, part 2: 2190) that the word order in the perfect changed to have the auxiliary and participle adjacent between subject and verb most of the time and in most dialects. But the possibility of S *have* O Participle order never completely disappeared in certain contexts (e.g. *I have him cornered*). This change to S *have* Participle O order, however incomplete, was part of the actualization.

A further part of the actualization of the reanalysis of the *have* perfect was the extension of this construction to transitives in which the object was not expressed, and eventually to intransitives.[45] The former occurs as early as late Old English; the latter begins in the Peterborough Chronicle, an. 1096, with *be* (Visser 1963–73, III, part 2: 2044, 2191):

(84)   he heafde gebeon on þes cynges   swicdom-e
          he had   been   on the king.GEN deception-DAT
          "He had been in on the deception of the king."

An older expression of the perfect with the intransitive made use of another auxiliary, *beo-*, *wes-*, or *weorþ-*, but, apart from a few relics, this construction was eventually completely replaced by the type in (80)–(84) (for more details, see Traugott 1973: 92–3).

In summary we note that in both French and English reanalysis took place even when the source construction tolerated an underlying subject of the subordinate clause not coindexed with the subject of the matrix; the basis of reanalysis (defined in chapter 4) was examples such as (82), with coindexed subjects. In both languages actualization included loss of participial agreement (only partial in French), innovation of word order requiring the auxiliary and participle to be adjacent (with some exceptions in English), and extension of the "have" perfect to those intransitives that did not originally take it (partial in French, some relics in English).

7.4.3   Present progressive: Avar

Avar, a language of the Daghestan (North East Caucasian) family, provides further clear evidence of actualization of reanalysis. The present progressive in Avar is similar to that in English in structure, in meaning, and in origin (see, for example, Traugott 1972: 90–1 on English).

In Avar the participle modifies nouns, as illustrated in (85):

(85)   (a)   emen   w-ec:ule-w   was
               father.ABSL   M-praising-M boy.ABSL
               "a father-praising boy," "a boy who praises his father"

     (b)   ebel   y-ec:ule-w   was
               mother.ABSL F-praising-M boy.ABSL
               "a mother-praising boy," "a boy who praises his mother"

     (c)   ču   b-ec:ule-w   was
               horse.ABSL   N-praising-M boy.ABSL
               "a horse-praising boy," "a boy who praises his horse"
                                    (Čikobava and Cercvaʒe 1962: 303)

The participle, like the verb in Avar, marks agreement by means of class markers, morphemes that indicate that a noun is a member of the masculine class (*w-*, glossed "M"), of the feminine class (*y-*, "F"), of the neuter class (*b-*, "N"), or of the plural (*r-*, "PL"), which is the same for all classes. In the participle, class prefixes indicate the class/number of the absolutive nominal – the subject of an intransitive, the direct object of a transitive. With the intransitive verb, not illustrated here, it is the subject of the participle that triggers the agreement prefix; with the transitive verb "praise," it is the direct object of the participle that conditions the agreement prefix, as seen in (85).

The only relative clause in Avar is formed with the participle, as in the examples above. In this construction, it is the syntactic head which conditions the agreement suffix. This can be seen in the contrasts in (86):

(86)   (a)   emen   w-ec:ule-w   was
                father.ABSL M-praising-M boy.ABSL
                "a father-praising boy," "a boy who praises his father"

         (b)   emen   w-ec:ule-y   yas
                father.ABSL M-praising-F girl.ABSL
                "a father-praising girl," "a girl who praises her father"

         (c)   emen   w-ec:ule-b   ł'imer
                father.ABSL M-praising-N child.ABSL
                "a father-praising child," "a child who praises his father"
                                      (Čikobava and Cercvaӡe 1962: 303)

The participle can occur in construction with the verb "be," illustrated in (87):

(87)   (a)   emen   čU   b-ec:ule-w   w-ugo
                father.ABSL horse.ABSL N-praising-M M-is
                "Father is one who praises the horse," " . . . the praiser of the horse."

         (b)   ebel   ret'el   b-uq'ule-y   y-ugo
                mother.ABSL clothing.ABSL N-sewing-F F-is
                "Mother is a sewer of clothing," " . . . one who sews clothes."

The source structure of these sentences is represented in (88):

(88)   [S_i [S_i (O) V] -*ugo*]
                  "be"

We suggest the following analyses of the source structures.[46] In the sentences in (87), "father" and "mother" are subjects of "be"; the participles and their objects are reduced sentential complements. The subjecthood of "father" and "mother" here is supported by (i) the fact that they are marked with the absolutive case, the case otherwise used for subjects of intransitive verbs, including "be," and (ii) the fact that "be" agrees with these nouns, as intransitive verbs do with their subjects. That the participle and its object form the predicate complement is supported by the fact that the suffix on the participle marks agreement with the subject of "be." The analysis of *čU b-ec:ule-w* "praiser of horse" and *ret'el b-uq'ule-y* "sewer of clothes" as reduced clauses is supported by (i) the fact that "horse" and "clothes" are in the absolutive case, the case otherwise used for the objects of transitive verbs like "praise" and "sew," and (ii) the fact that the prefix of the participle marks agreement with this nominal, in the way a transitive verb agrees with its direct object.

The status of these as subordinate clauses is also supported by the fact that the verb form is participial. In Avar, participles or other non-finite verb forms are generally used for subordinate clauses; for example, they constitute relative clauses in (85)–(86). However, participles can also be used, without auxiliaries, in complete main clauses in Avar (Ebeling 1966: 89–90); substitution for finite verbs is common among the Avaro-Andi languages (see Čikobava and Cercvaӡe 1962: 312; Gudava 1971: 133, n. 228).

The source construction (88) was reinterpreted as a single clause, as in (89), leaving the source construction still intact:

(89)   [S (O) V -*ugo*]
                "be"

As part of actualization several changes were made:

1   Ergative case marking has been extended to this construction, so that the subjects ("father," "mother") of the transitives in (90) below bear the ergative case.
2   Agreement with the absolutive has been extended to this construction, so that the prefix on the copula auxiliary is determined by the direct object in (90).
3   The agreement suffix on the participle is determined by the direct object in (90).

The transitivity of the verb complex (V + -*ugo*) now depends on the transitivity of V. The resulting structure is illustrated in (90):

(90)   (a)   ins:u-c:a   ču   b-ec:ule-b   b-ugo
                  father-ERG horse.ABSL N-praising-N N-is
                  "Father is praising the horse."

        (b)   ebel-aƚa   ret'el   b-uq'ule-b   b-ugo
                  mother-ERG clothing.ABSL N-sewing-N N-is
                  "Mother is sewing clothing."

(Examples (87) and (90) are from Čikobava and Cercvaӡe [1962: 328–30].)

In the sentences in (90), "be" is an auxiliary occurring with the main verb, which is in form a participle. The ergative-nominals are subjects of "is praising" and "is sewing," and the absolutive nominals are direct objects, as is usual for a transitive verb. Crucially, these sentences, in contrast to those in (87), are monoclausal.

This construction provides an example of formation of a periphrastic tense different from that discussed above and illustrates the same process of fusion in a language outside the Indo-European family.[47]

7.4.4   On universals of clause fusion

It is not claimed here that all constructions with an auxiliary that marks
TAM categories or all synthetic forms with an affix of identifiable auxiliary
origin developed out of biclausal constructions. On the contrary, we recognize that auxiliaries or the affixes derived from them may be extended to existing verb forms in monoclausal constructions (for examples, see Baramiʒe
1964).

Ramat (1987: 8–13) has outlined a four-stage universal process of
"auxiliarization":

I   *Full verbs*: At this stage the verbs that eventually become auxiliaries still
     "have their full semantic meaning" (p. 8).
II   *Predicative construction*: At this stage the verbs that eventually express the lex-
     ical verbal meaning of the clause may be omitted; the verbs that eventually
     become auxiliaries may be used without those that eventually express lexical
     meaning.
III *Periphrastic forms*: "We are dealing here with real (new) periphrastic perfect
     forms." At this stage the auxiliary "is really the marker for Tense, Mode, and
     Aspect, with no autonomous semantic meaning" (p. 10).
IV   *Agglutination*: In this stage the auxiliary is "reduced to a simple morphologi-
     cal sign, a prefix [or suffix] agglutinated to the main verb ('erosion' of the
     form)" (p. 11) or has cliticized.

Ramat does not define these stages, but provides examples and discussion;
we have extracted some portions of his description, hoping to do justice to the
meanings he intended, which are not always clear to us from the examples
alone.

Ramat's proposed universals are like most treatments of these phenomena
in individual languages in that they focus only on the verbal constituents, not
taking into consideration the context of the biclausal structures in which they
originate. Perhaps in part because of this exclusive focus on verbal constituents, Ramat's proposal is vague, not specifying the structures involved.[48] In
the general definition of fusion which we provide above in section 7.4, we take
the entire biclausal structure into consideration, making a specific proposal
concerning the fate of the two verbs. Notice that no statement is made, either
in Ramat's proposal or in our definition, concerning the argument structure
of the reflex clause; we provide this in section 7.5.1 below.

We find no evidence universally to support the existence of Ramat's Stage
II. Indeed, in many languages with quite old auxiliaries, languages well into
Stage III, the auxiliary can be used in constructions independently of a lexical
verb. His Stage IV, on the other hand, is indeed universal. We suggest, however, that it is not properly a part of the process of "auxiliarization," but is a
much more general process of reduction involved in all grammaticalization.

(This follows from our definition, but we believe that it also corresponds to the traditional meaning of auxiliary.) We make a specific proposal of universals governing fusion in section 7.5 below.

Concerning stages, we suggest that the general stages outlined in section 7.2.5.1 apply here too. As with other types of biclausal reduction, the gradual nature of actualization and the language-particular aspect it necessarily has do not lend themselves to detailed characterization in terms of stages.

7.5   Universal principles

The discussion above does not exhaust the set of processes that simplify biclausal structures. Nevertheless, we believe we can draw some generalizations from those processes included here.

7.5.1   A principle governing processes that simplify biclausal structures

In sections 7.2 and 7.3 above we proposed universal characterizations of individual changes, cleft-to-highlighting construction (accounting for both cleft-to-focus and cleft-to-topic) and quotation-to-quotative construction. In section 7.4 we have described a wider variety of phenomena, for they are governed by a single principle. Thus, possessive-to-perfective, being-to-progressive, volition-to-future, and the transition of constructions containing modal verbs to ones containing modal auxiliaries are accounted for by a single process below, with a single set of generalizations. We believe that this process also accounts for other transitions of a similar kind, discussion of which remains beyond the scope of this work.[49]

There is a regularity in the changes examined above that has not been noticed or has not been stated in the literature on diachronic syntax. When the two clauses are fused into one, the auxiliary (originally V of the matrix) governs those constituents that originate in the matrix clause, while the main verb (formerly the verb of the subordinate clause) determines the syntax of the reflex of its clause. Actualization (changes during Stage II), to the extent that it takes place in a given language, is in the direction of government of all constituents by the main verb, rather than by the auxiliary. When we say that a verb governs the syntax we mean that (a) it determines the number of arguments, the argument roles they fill, and the marking they bear, (b) it determines whether any lexically-conditioned obligatory synchronic rules are conditioned (for example, Inversion), (c) it determines whether the clause can undergo optional synchronic syntactic rules (for example, Antipassive), and (d) it determines any exceptional behavior (for example, Quirky Case, suppletion).

That each verb at first governs the syntax of the reflex of its clause follows from our definition of reanalysis. Reanalysis itself never changes the surface. As a result, immediately following reanalysis, the constituents that originated in the matrix clause will bear the case marking determined by the auxiliary. Word order, too, immediately following reanalysis will at first be according to the pre-reanalysis pattern. This often means that the main verb and auxiliary are separated; this can be seen in the French examples. There is generally some lag between reanalysis and actualization; but once in motion, actualization is likely to extend the regular rules of case marking, agreement, and word order to the reanalyzed structures.

Evidence to support our claim that after fusion the main verb governs the syntax of the clause comes from all examples where argument coding (case marking, agreement, and in some languages, word order) changes to that governed by the main verb, if in the language the same coding would not also be governed by the auxiliary. An example is the case marking of transitive subjects and the agreement pattern in the Avar examples referred to above. Another clear example is the Georgian modal structure, where the case marking in (61b) and (63b) is governed by the main verb; if the auxiliary governed it, it would be the pattern in (61a) and (63a) instead.

Arguments to support the claim that reanalysis occurs before actualization (including changes to the coding rules) were presented in chapter 4, but fusion provides additional evidence. In fusion, meaning is changed when reanalysis occurs. The meaning change precedes the coding changes in a language such as Georgian, and the meaning change precedes establishment of Aux-V (i.e. adjacent) order in French. English, however, probably provides the most evidence, for many other changes interacted with the newly fused clauses. The fact that the innovative SVO order treats the auxiliary and verb as a unit, placing them together between the S and O, and the fact that they are placed in the order that is harmonic with VO structure (see chapter 8) both show that the modals had already been reanalyzed as auxiliaries when SVO order was introduced. The loss of the modal infinitives, ceasing to occur with *-ing*, and ceasing to occur in *have . . .-en* structures are part of actualization of the reanalysis. Lightfoot dates the last occurring examples of each of these three structures in the sixteenth century (1979a: 110) and the introduction of SVO order to early Middle English (1979a: 106). (Middle English is dated from 1100 to 1500.) We may thus assume an actualization lag of at least 300 years in this instance. We find an even longer lag in the fact that traces of the former present/past distinction of modal verbs are still preserved in some environments, as shown in (68)–(71); here we must assume an actualization lag of at least 700 years.

It is not only changes which meet the definition of clause fusion (given in section 7.4) that show the regularity noted above in this section; the highlighting and quotative constructions have the same regularity. In the latter instances the regularity is hardly surprising; in most of these transitions it is only the main verb that has any verb-like qualities, and nothing other than the main verb is expected to govern the syntax of its clause. Yet notice that in Somali the nominal that is subject of the subject focus construction is not in the subject case and partly fails to condition subject agreement (see section 7.2.2.4). These facts, an example of the actualization lag, give the appearance that "be" of the old cleft still governs the syntax of the subject (in this construction), while other facts (including the partial subject agreement) show that the main verb actually governs it.

We assume that this regularity, found not only in the data discussed above, but in a variety of other changes in these and other languages, is a universal of diachronic syntax, which we state informally below:

> *The Heir-Apparent Principle*
> When the two clauses are made one by diachronic processes, the main verb governs the syntax of the reflex clause.

The Heir-Apparent Principle makes the claim that the main verb governs the syntax of its clause even though conservative rules at first make it appear that an auxiliary or the former copula governs constituents. This caveat makes it impossible to test the claim for some transitions in some languages, but this does not make the principle untestable. While reanalyses may at first resist actualization, making recent changes unsuitable as a testing ground for this proposal, later changes that affect the reanalyzed structure must treat it as governed by the main verb.

7.5.2   A universal that interacts with processes that simplify biclausal structures

Ramat is, of course, correct in writing that the process he calls "agglutination" applies in "auxiliarization," in his sense of that term (see section 7.4.4 above, Stage IV). It is well known that processes making independent words into clitics and affixes and phonologically altering their form interact diachronically with other processes that simplify biclausal structures, and indeed with a wide variety of other diachronic syntactic processes (for example, Meillet 1912; Heine and Reh 1984; Traugott and Heine 1991). The point we wish to make here is that this reduction is better viewed as an independent process or processes that apply to grammatical items generally, not just to auxiliaries resulting from clause fusion: for example, the same process may apply to postpositions, making them case markers, or to adverbs, making them verbal clitics then affixes. We suggest that this process is best viewed as one at the interface of syntax and phonology, one of the set of universal diachronic operations from which languages may draw. Reduction often follows fusion because it is at that stage that the conditions on its application are first met. The conditions on its application include that its target (the independent word to which it applies) not have a lexical meaning, but a grammatical function, such as marking tense, aspect, modality, location, direction, or other grammatical category.

A second principle that interacts with fusion, determining the linear placement of auxiliary and of main verb, is discussed in section 8.5.1.2. Like reduction, this word order principle applies generally and is not limited to auxiliary + main verb pairs.

7.5.3   Summary

In this chapter we have examined examples of the cleft-to-highlighter transition in diverse languages and by induction have derived the general principles governing this change. We have taken a similar approach to examples of the quotation-to-quotative transition in section 7.3, and in section 7.4 we have examined a wide variety of examples of fusion. In some ways the three processes studied here are very different from one another. In the cleft-to-highlighter transition and in the process we have termed fusion, arguments of the matrix clause join with arguments of the subordinate clause to form the argument structure of the reflex clause; in the quotation-to-quotative transition, on the other hand, no argument of the matrix clause survives as an argument. In the process of fusion, the matrix verb becomes an auxiliary; while in the other two processes, the verb, if it survives at all, becomes (part of) a particle. In spite of these important differences, there are general principles that apply to all of the changes considered here (section 7.5). We distinguish between principles governing diachronic processes that make biclausal structures monoclausal (section 7.5.1), on the one hand, and a principle that interacts with a wide variety of syntactic changes (section 7.5.2). The Heir-Apparent Principle can be tested against additional changes that took place long enough in the past to have provided time for actualization to affect the resulting structures.

8 *Word order*

8.1   Introduction

In the last two decades word order has perhaps received more attention than any other issue in diachronic syntax. Most of this work has looked at word order change from the point of view of word order universals, first discovered by Greenberg (1963) and further studied by many others since then. Diachronic studies inspired by Greenbergian universals have been widely criticized on grounds of methodology and are not widely accepted. We have tried to take a fresh approach to these issues. After a general introduction in the present section to the questions involved, we begin by examining the basis for the widespread assumption that the order of morphemes in a word and the order of words in a compound reflect, in some sense, the order of words in a clause (section 8.2). We show that while this is often true of bound morphemes, it is not always; in compounds there seems to be little basis at all for such an assumption. In section 8.3 we look at the types of word order change that result from reanalysis and show that through reanalysis it is possible for an order to be introduced that is *disharmonic* with the rest of the language. This offers a solution to the long-standing problem of how, if word order harmony is a preferred state, a language could begin to change from one harmony to another. In our examination of changes to harmony we include data from an attested change not previously brought to bear on this issue (section 8.5.2). This chapter is not, however, limited to word order change involving Greenbergian universals, but examines also a range of issues including origins of and resolutions of discontinuous constituency (section 8.5.1), origins of fixed word order (section 8.5.3), and causes of a variety of word order changes, including both those proposed by others (section 8.4) and ones we propose (sections 8.5.3 and 8.6).

Greenberg's pioneering 1963 study and subsequent work by Lehmann (especially 1973), Vennemann (especially 1973, 1974a), and others established the following "consistent" word order types:

(1)	OV	VO
	Po	Pr
	AN	NA
	GN	NG
	DetN	NDet
	RelN	NRel
	VAux	AuxV
	StAdj	AdjSt

where O is (direct) object, V verb, Po postposition, Pr preposition, A adjective, N noun, G genitive, Det determiner, Rel relative clause, Aux auxiliary, St standard of comparison, and Adj comparative adjective. For example, it is said that in a "consistent" OV language one finds postpositions, adjectives preceding nouns, genitives preceding nouns, etc. The list provided in (1) is typical, but some scholars would not include some of the lines included here, while others would add additional characteristics, such as NumN vs. NNum. Some proposals have preferred not to ignore the position of S (subject) as was done in (1), expressing the opinion that there do not exist consistent types for SVO, OSV, VOS, or OVS, only for SOV and VSO.[1]

In recent work with a far larger database, Dryer (1988, 1992) has challenged some of the correlations stated in (1), especially the correlation of AN/NA order with OV/VO order. The list in (2) is taken from a more complete list discussed in full in Dryer (1992: 108):

(2)	*Verb patterner*	*Object patterner*
	verb	object
	adposition	NP
	tense/aspect auxiliary verb	VP
	noun	genitive
	noun	relative clause
	adjective	standard of comparison
	verb	manner adverbial

Dryer (1992) proposes to account for the correlations in (2) through the Branching Direction Theory, stated in (3) (his (16)), or through the alternate version stated in (4) (his (19)):

(3)   *Branching Direction Theory* (revised version)
Verb patterners are nonphrasal categories or phrasal categories that are not fully recursive, and object patterners are fully recursive phrasal categories in the major constituent tree. That is, a pair of elements X and Y will employ the order XY significantly more often among VO languages than among OV languages if and only if X is not a fully recursive phrasal category in the major constituent tree and Y is a fully recursive phrasal category in the major constituent tree.[2]

(4)   *Branching Direction Theory* (alternate version)
        Verb patterners are heads and object patterners are fully recursive phrasal
        dependents. I.e., a pair of elements X and Y will employ the order XY signifi-
        cantly more often among VO languages than among OV languages if and
        only if X is a head and Y is a phrasal dependent of X.

Dryer points out that one difference between (3) and (4) is that (4) makes certain controversial assumptions regarding which constituent is head in a constituent.[3] We accept Dryer's (1992) as the most accurate approach to these
correlations to date, in spite of certain problems discussed by him (1992: 110–
15, 117–28). In the discussion in this chapter, we draw on the notions "head"
and "dependent" in the sense of (4), making the controversial assumptions
referred to.[4] If further work shows that this view is incorrect, the other version, (3), will account for the same facts without these assumptions.

  Neither the schema in (1) nor that in (2) entails that every language has these
correlations. Mallinson and Blake (1981: 379) estimate that about 40 percent of
languages are consistent for a set of six properties, which differs slightly from
that in (1).[5] From a synchronic point of view, these facts raise the following
question: why do languages with all of the properties in the first column or with
all of those in the second column exist in greater than chance quantities? Related to this are the diachronic questions: do languages with word order incon-
sistencies systematically become consistent over time, and if so, how and why?

  It was at first assumed that the synchronic consistency was to be explained
by a tendency to consistency and that one dyadic order could trigger analogical change in another dyadic order (Vennemann 1973, 1974a, 1974b, and elsewhere). This assumption was originally part of Vennemann's claim that word
order changes could only go in certain directions,[6] and his views were applied
by others to a typological method of reconstruction (Lehmann 1974); both
Vennemann's claim of unidirectionality and the typological method of reconstruction have been roundly rejected by other linguists (for example, Jeffers
1976a; Campbell and Mithun 1980; Mallinson and Blake 1981: 434–5). But the
question of whether analogical change alone can account for word order con-
sistencies is an issue distinct from unidirectionality and distinct from the typological method of reconstruction.

  Hawkins (1983: 133–56) proposed the Cross-Category Harmony Principle
(CCH) as an alternative to Vennemann's view that languages evolve towards
typological consistency. However, CCH is not intended to describe how languages change with regard to word order harmonies or to explain why they
change, but rather in part to make "a precise quantitative prediction to the
effect that the more a language type departs from the 'ideal' harmonic ordering, the fewer exemplifying languages there will be" (Hawkins 1983: 157).[7]

In our view, there are a number of problems with the typological approach to the study of word order change and word order reconstruction, discussed in greater detail in chapters 2 and 12; here we mention only those problems that are relevant to issues discussed in the present chapter.

It has been widely assumed among those who study word order typologically that the order of morphemes in a word reflects the order in which those morphemes occurred when they were independent words in phrases. While it is quite true that many morphemes are derived from independent words, there is a significant amount of research that challenges the view that the order of morphemes necessarily reflects an earlier order of words. Some of this research is summarized below in section 8.2.1. Those who approach the diachronic study of word order on the basis of typology have often reconstructed prior word order, or even identified basic concurrent word order, on the basis of the order of morphemes, a practice we consider unjustified.

Scholars taking a typological approach to the study of diachronic change in word order have often overlooked one order, XY, occurring in dyads when the opposite order, YX, was predominant; this point has been made by Friedrich (1975), regarding typologically based reconstructions of Proto-Indo-European word order. In at least one, rather extreme case, discussed further in section 8.2.2, the order is said to have been GN, even though the more complete studies indicate approximately equal occurrence of GN and NG, and at least some specialists have identified NG as *more* common. Often it has been assumed by those approaching the study of diachronic word order from typology that order of elements in one dyad is indicative of orders in other dyads. Watkins (1976: 315–16) has pointed out that when all of the daughters give a strong indication of both orders, both must be reconstructed to the proto-language, but typologists have often not followed this practice. Ignoring some frequently occurring orders distorts the analysis as a whole.

It is now known that some languages do become more consistent in word order over time, while others, such as Persian, stay inconsistent for long periods; some languages, such as Georgian, change from one mostly consistent type to another mostly consistent type. In this chapter, we, like earlier researchers, ask how and why changes in dyadic ordering and changes in type occur, but we do not make any of the typological assumptions discussed as problematic above in this section. In section 8.2 we ask whether independent words remain in the same position when they become bound morphemes or when they become part of a compound. In section 8.3 we ask whether words remain in the same position when they are reanalyzed as belonging to other categories. Three earlier proposals about the causes of word order change are examined in section 8.4. In section 8.5 we present a different approach to the causes of diachronic change in word order.

8.2 On the order of morphemes in words

8.2.1 Order of affixes and stems

In 1971 Talmy Givón proclaimed the provocative hypothesis that "Today's morphology is yesterday's syntax" (p. 413). Givón suggested that the earlier relative position of constituents could be reconstructed on the basis of the positions they occupy at a later time. In later work Givón used this principle as a key to his view of the earlier word order of numerous constructions (for example, Givón 1979: 238–46, 252–61). While we take up the implications of this issue for reconstruction in chapter 12, here we wish to consider the hypothesis that constituents cliticize and become affixes in the positions that they occupied as independent words.

Comrie (1980) points out that there are two distinct issues, stating these as hypotheses 1 and 2:

Hypothesis 1
The order of morphemes in a word reflects, in so far as those morphemes derive etymologically from separate words, the order of those separate words at the time they started being fused together into a single word.

Hypothesis 2
The order of morphemes in a word reflects, in so far as those morphemes derive etymologically from separate words, the basic word order of the language concerned at the time those separate words started being fused together into a single word. (Comrie 1980: 84)

Comrie presents a study of a series of attested changes in Mongolian languages. In Classical Mongolian, as in its contemporary daughter languages, the basic word order was SOV. In a permitted variant of this, an unstressed subject followed the verb. Examples from contemporary Khalkha illustrate the variation that existed also in Classical Mongolian:

(5)   (a)   bi   med-ne
           I   know-PRES
           "I know"

      (b)   med-ne   bi
           know-PRES   I
           "I know"   (Comrie 1980: 90)

Buryat and other daughters have subject agreement suffixes derived during the historical period from the variant in (5b). This order reflects the order in which the separate words stood at the time they cliticized, as in hypothesis 1, but not the basic order of the language. Thus, it shows that hypothesis 2 is incorrect.

There are other examples of the same type, some of them during the recorded period. For example, in Kartvelian languages, adverbs could precede or follow the verb with which they were associated; these orders are illustrated in (6) and (7) from Svan:

(6)   sga-ačad
       in=s/he.go   (*Svanskije teksty na laščhskom narečii*, cited by
                             Deeters 1930: 15 from A. Oniani's 1917, tale no. 7)
(7)   ačad sga
       s/he.go inside   (cited by Deeters 1930: 17 from the same source)

In the former position the adverbs were reinterpreted as preverbs (see the more complete description in the appendix to chapter 4; see also Deeters 1930: 16–17, 1969; Mart'irosovi 1960; Topuria 1967[1931]; Schmidt 1969, 1988), becoming markers of aspect and (with verbs of displacement motion) of direction.[8]

Steele (1977) shows that in Uto-Aztecan languages pronouns moved into second position as they cliticized, and this is probably of the same type as those changes discussed above, showing that a given change may be consonant with hypothesis 1, while showing that hypothesis 2 is incorrect. However, if Steele is correct that these pronouns moved only as they cliticized, or if it is found that elements in other languages move only as they cliticize, then hypothesis 1 is supported only in a trivial way. In the same article, Steele argued further that an additional clitic pronoun proclitic to the verb was derived by copying the first clitic pronoun. In this instance even hypothesis 1 is not supported.

As early as 1923–4 it was shown by Klingenheben that the noun class suffixes of Fula originated as prefixes. Anderson (1976 and 1992: 348–9) confirms that in Fula noun class prefixes were copied as suffixes and that in a later change the prefixes were deleted. This change, too, is evidence that hypothesis 1 is incorrect.

8.2.2   Order of elements in compounds

It has traditionally been assumed, especially in Indo-European studies, that the order of words in a compound reflects the order of words in phrases. This can be stated as hypothesis 3:

> *Hypothesis 3*
> In language L, the order of words in compounds that are coined at time t_i is the same as the order of words used in phrases at time t_i.

There is no doubt that many compounds in many languages do have the same order found in contemporaneous phrases. Lehmann (1969) presents numerous examples of parallel phrases and compounds with the same order in Vedic Sanskrit, such as (8a) and (8b):

(8) (a) yád ékena krátunā vidáṁse vásu
         "since with a single desire you obtain for yourself wealth"
                                                    (*Rigveda* 2.11.11)

     (b) vidád-vasu
         "gaining wealth"   (cited by Lehmann 1969: 13)

Assuming that (8a) represents the phrasal order at the time (8b) was coined, these and Lehmann's other examples support hypothesis 3. However, some Vedic compounds have an order different from that in the corresponding phrase. For example, the *Rigveda* has the phrase *pátir dán* "lord of the house" with two independent words, in which *dán* is the genitive (< *dans* < *dams* < *dems*) of "house"; beside this in the *Rigveda* is found the compound *dámpati* (< *daṃspati-*), in the same meaning, but with the constituents in the opposite order (Risch 1944–9: 12–13). Examples such as this last show that we cannot conclude on the basis of the kind of data Lehmann cites that hypothesis 3 is necessarily true for all examples.

In Modern English the productive pattern for compounds of verbs and their objects has the order OV. That the OV compound pattern is productive can be seen from the fact that not only older compounds, such as *wood-pecker* and *salt-shaker*, but also newer ones, such as *word-processor, food-processor, weed-eater, lawn-mower*, and *tape-recorder* have this pattern. Nor are OV compounds restricted to the OV-*er* pattern; recent compounds also occur in an OV-*ing* pattern, such as *fun-loving, heat-seeking (missile), letter-writing (campaign), earth-moving (equipment)*, in an OV pattern with no suffix, such as *face-guard, car-wash, self-serve, car-park* (British), and in OV patterns with miscellaneous suffixes, such as *garbage-disposal, life-insurance*.[9] In English the productive phrasal order, VO, is rare in compounds, though a few, such as *pick-pocket, scoff-law, seek-sorrow* (archaic), and *do-good-er*, do have this order.

This evidence from English shows clearly that it is not the case that verb + noun compounds directly and necessarily reflect the phrasal word order of the language at the time the given compound is coined. This clearly refutes hypothesis 3, but suggests another hypothesis, stated as hypothesis 4.

> *Hypothesis 4*
> In language L, the order of words in compounds that are coined at time t_i is the same as the order of words used in phrases at time t_{i-1}.

According to this hypothesis, compounds never reflect the word order used when the compound is formed, but only that of the word order system that preceded the current one. This seems to be consistent with the English facts, since the OV compounds can be related to the OV order generally attributed to Old English. However, hypothesis 4 is not consistent with the facts of Georgian word order and word order change.

Old Georgian had compounds in the order GN, where the reduced form, *-is*, of the genitive case marker is used (compare full form *-isa*). Examples are given in (9):

(9)   (a)   zetis-xili
             olive's-fruit, i.e. "olive"

       (b)   zetis-xe
             olive's-wood/tree, i.e. "olive wood, olive tree"

       (c)   xvalis(a)-dɣe
             tomorrow's-day, i.e. "tomorrow"

       (d)   xilis-mok'reba
             fruit's-gathering, i.e. "autumn"

       (e)   dɣesis dɣe
             today's-day, i.e. "today"

The large number of such compounds and the small number of compounds with the opposite order suggest that the GN pattern was productive.[10] Old Georgian clearly eschews GN order in phrases.[11] In historical times, Georgian has adopted GN order in phrases and retains GN order in compounds. For example, the compounds above are retained, and new compounds on the same pattern include those in (10):

(10)   (a)   sabč'o-ta   socialist'uri resp'ublik'-eb-is   k'avširi
             soviet-PL.GEN socialist   republic-PL-GEN union
             "Union of Soviet Socialist Republics"[12]

       (b)   ɣom-is-guli
             grits-GEN-heart
             "cake made of hominy grits"

       (c)   mč'ad-is-mč'adi (dialectal)
             cornbread-GEN-cornbread
             "cornbread"

The last two compounds are based on foodstuffs not available until the discovery of America; on this basis it is assumed that in Georgian these compounds could not have been formed until the last few centuries, by which time

Georgian had undergone profound word order change.[13] Obviously (10a) is a formation of the twentieth century.

Thus we have the following stages:

> Stage 1, Old Georgian: NG order in phrases, GN order in compounds;
> Stage 2, Modern Georgian: GN order in phrases, GN order in compounds.

Clearly the GN order in the productive pattern of compounds in contemporary Georgian is not the same as that of the phrasal order at time t_{i-1}, which would be the NG order of Old Georgian.

It would be possible to further revise the hypothesis as Hypothesis 5.

> *Hypothesis 5*
> In language L, the order of words in compounds that are coined at time t_i is the same as the order of words used in phrases at time t_i or at time t_{i-1}.

Compounds are usually composed of only two words, and where we are discussing the relative ordering of only two elements, the claim made in hypothesis 5 is vacuous. If, for example, we are discussing the order of two elements, G and N, and if at time t_i they are GN, then at time t_{i-1} they could only have been NG. The hypothesis that compounds involving genitives and nouns will have either the order GN or NG is vacuous.

A different possibility is stated as hypothesis 6.

> *Hypothesis 6*
> In language L, the order of words in compounds that are coined at time t_i is the same as the order of words used in phrases at some time before t_i.

It is possible that hypothesis 6 is correct, but it is an untestable hypothesis. There is no data that could, even hypothetically, disprove it. Even if hypothesis 6 could be shown to be true, it still could not serve as a tool of reconstruction, since we would not know how far back we were reconstructing, and could not relate a dyadic order reconstructed in this way to other features of the language.

In the discussion below we make the following additional points about word order in compounds: (i) generalizations about the order in compounds compared with historical order in phrases have not been based on diachronic studies of long-attested languages showing how patterns in compounds have been affected by word order change; (ii) the patterns in compounds in a given language can have other sources, and therefore these patterns do not necessarily reflect an earlier order; (iii) there may be other, language-internal reasons for a given pattern to be established in a language.

(i) Any statement of a diachronic generalization must be based in the first instance on attested change or on data reconstructed by independent, reliable methods, not merely on speculation. In order to establish a claim that word order in compounds reflects earlier word order in phrases, it is essential to undertake a study of several languages which have experienced word order change, to determine when and how the order in phrases changed and when and how the order in the corresponding compounds changed, and to correlate the results. For example, it is known that word order changed in the Italic languages in historical times. A study could correlate the predominantly OV and GN order of Latin phrases with the order of the same elements in compounds. Given that several Indo-European languages, some Turkic languages, Georgian (a Kartvelian language), Chinese, and some Semitic languages have attested changes in the relative order of object and verb, of genitive and noun, of adjective and noun, or of all three, it would be possible to obtain cross-linguistic data on this subject, even though this is still a relatively small number of languages. But this essential step has not been taken, at least not in the sources usually cited to authorize the view that the order in compounds reflects an earlier order or in other sources known to us.

Most earlier treatments have simply asserted that compounds reflect an earlier word order or have assumed this, citing still earlier sources as the basis for this assumption.[14] For example, Lehmann states: "Compounds have long been held to be reduced forms of sentences. Jacobi presented this point of view forcefully in his 1897 monograph; many other discussions derive compounds similarly (Richter 1898: 188; Frisk 1941)" (Lehmann 1974: 75). Jacobi (1897) does express forcefully the point of view that compounds preserve an earlier word order, but he does not present evidence to support this position, but rather assumes it. So strong is his assumption, that when he confronts Indo-European compounds with the order VO, coined at a time when he believes the phrasal order to have been OV, the only solution he can imagine is that there was a different phrasal order preceding these particular compounds:

> Warum nun bei den in Rede stehenden Composita eine abweichende Stellung? Ich könnte mir einen Grund für diese Verschiedenheit der Stellung denken: sie könnte nämlich durch das Bestreben veranlasst worden sein, den verbalen Bestandteil dem Worte, das als dessen Subjekt zu denken ist und von dem das Compositum selbst abhängt, möglichst nahe zu setzen, so dass also die gewöhnliche Stellung (obj.+verb.) bei denjenigen Composita galt, welche aus *attributiv* gebrauchten, vorgesetzten Nebensätzen, die umgekehrte (verb.+obj.) dagegen bei solchen, welche aus *appositionellen*, nachgesetzten Nebensätzen entstanden wären.   (Jacobi 1897: 55)

> Now why is there a divergent order in compounds in speech? I can think of one reason for this difference of order: namely, it could have been brought about through an effort to place the verbal constituent as close as possible to

the word which is to be thought of as its subject and on which the constituent itself is dependent, so that the ordinary order (obj.-verb) holds for those compounds that have developed out of attributively used, preposed subordinate clauses, while, on the other hand, the opposite [order] (verb-obj.) [holds] for ones which have developed out of appositional, postposed subordinate clauses.   [Our translation, ACH/LC]

In this passage Jacobi does not even consider the possibility that a VO compound might correspond to an OV phrasal sequence; yet we know that English OV compounds, such as *food-processor*, correspond to VO phrasal sequences, (*it*) *processes food*.

The other sources cited by Lehmann in the passage quoted likewise assume that order in compounds reflects order in phrases. In general the practice has been to cite others who make the same assumption, without ever questioning the basis of the assumption: for example, Bean (1983: 48) cites Lehmann (1975), Givón (1971), and Bradshaw (unpublished) as authorities that this traditional assumption is correct. Lehmann (1975) does not consider evidence directly relevant to this issue, but addresses the question of why Hittite has virtually no compounds and why English has no synthetic (OV, e.g. "honey-drinking") compounds. (As we note above, English actually has many recent OV compounds of this type, such as *crime-fighting* (*power*), a phrase used in an advertizement for a car alarm, circulated by Amoco Oil, April 1991.)

Givón (1971: 401) does, in fact, base his generalization on the kind of study discussed above. His entire discussion is the following:

> Germanic languages (as well as earlier Latin) used to have a genitive modifier *preceding* the head noun. Most of them have later on shifted the position of that modifier to *follow* the head noun. However, clear traces of the older syntax have survived, in set expressions as well as in noun-compounds which arose through use of the older pattern.   (1971: 401)

Examples follow this statement. While this is the right kind of evidence, Givón's report of the Germanic situation excludes some relevant data. We consider here the evidence for one kind of Germanic compound: the genitive + noun combination. The evidence for object + verb compounds is similar but not included because of length.

In the runic inscriptions, both GN and NG orders occur in phrases. One authority claims that GN predominates in the earlier inscriptions (McKnight 1897: 174), while another (Antonsen 1975: 24) counters that GN is more frequent for inanimate heads and NG for animates. Old Norse (Old Icelandic) likewise shows both GN and NG; examples follow, from Heusler (1932: 177, 179, 112).

(11)   NG
    (a) af   hende Hǫkon-ar
        from side Hakon-GEN
        "from Hakon's side"

    (b) son sinn
        son his
        "his son"

(12)   GN
    (a) afrek-s   verk
        heroicism-GEN work
        "work of heroicism"

    (b) þess kon-ar   sending
        this kind-GEN send.off
        "send off of this kind"

Heusler treats the NG order as unmarked.[15] In modern Norwegian, both NG and GN are still found in phrases under certain circumstances:

(13)   NG
    (a) en liten del av peng-ene
        a small part of coin-PL.DET
        "a small part of the money"

    (b) medlem av Storting-et
        member of Parliament-DET
        "a member of the Parliament"   (Marm and Sommerfelt 1967: 137)

(14)   GN
    (a) hans fine hund
        "his fine dog"

    (b) min kones nye hatt
        "my wife's new hat"

    (c) år-et-s mørke måned
        year-DET-GEN dark month
        "the dark month of the year"   (Marm and Sommerfelt 1967: 65–6)

In the runic inscriptions, compounds have predominantly GN order, though a few with the order NG are found (Hopper 1975: 62–3; Bean 1983: 48–9).

(15)   GN
    (a) owlþu-þewaz (A: 2)
        Wolþu-servant [a name]

    (b) skiþa-leubaz (*c.* 450) (proper noun) (A: 34)
        justice-lover   (Bean 1983: 48–9)

Modern Norwegian likewise has compounds with predominantly GN order:

(16)   (a)   dame-veske
              lady-bag
              "lady's bag"

        (b)   stol-rygg
              chair-back

        (c)   barn-e-sko
              child-Suffix-shoe
              "children's shoe"   (Marm and Sommerfelt 1967: 178)

In summary, we have the following situation:

> Runes (beginning 200 AD): GN and NG orders in phrases; GN order in compounds.
> Sagas (beginning eleventh–twelfth century): GN and NG orders in phrases; GN order in compounds.
> Modern Norwegian: GN and NG orders in phrases; GN order in compounds.

There may have been a change in the conditions under which the two phrasal orders occur. It is also possible that there has been a change in statistical distribution, but this has apparently not been very dramatic, and there has been no change in the range of possibilities available. Thus, with regard to North Germanic at least, it is therefore misleading to state, as Givón did, that early Germanic had GN order and now has NG.

Other early Germanic languages also have both NG and GN orders. Of Gothic, the oldest, Wright (1910: 184–5) makes no generalization concerning the order of genitives and nouns, but provides examples of both.

(17)   NG
        (a)   in Saraípta Seidōnáis
              "unto Sarepta (a city) of Sidon"

        (b)   sums mannē fram þis faúramaþleis synagōgeis
              "a certain man from (the house) of the ruler of the synagogue"

(18)   GN
        Tyrē jah Seidōnē land
        "the land of the Tyrians and Sidonians" (= Tyre and Sidon)

Wright gives only this single example of GN order, but quite a few of NG order. It must, however, be kept in mind that the translations of the Bible into Gothic (most of what exists in the language) follows the word order of the Greek text. Koppitz (1900: 435–6) separates those examples which are opposite to the Greek original or are without a corresponding original from those that

Table 8.1 *Comparison of genitive and head noun in various Old English sources*

	Proper names of persons		Common nouns for persons		Common nouns	
	GN	NG	GN	NG	GN	NG
Dialogues						
Books I + II H	100	36	146	34	321	233
Book I + II C	82	38	165	107	293	360
Book III	51	32	129	81	288	323
Book IV	33	15	110	77	278	411
Bede						
I	71	19	42	41	112	211
II	111	17	49	26	125	131
III	173	32	52	51	153	265
Boethius			83	37	187	200
Wulfstan			102	9	196	49
Aplllonius			40	4	59	18

Note: Evidently, the column we have labeled "common nouns" includes the numbers for "common nouns for persons." In introducing his table that gives the former category, Timmer writes "The general aspect of the place of the genitive with regard to its headword is presented by the total numbers of examples (excluding the genitives of proper names)" (1939: 51).
Source: Timmer 1939: 51, 52, 53

follow the order of the original; in the former group he gives about equal numbers of examples of NG and GN order. In addition, he notes (1900: 435) that NG and GN both occur in Gothic, implying that they are about equal, with the exception of the partitive genitive, which, he adds, generally follows the head.

In the earliest West Germanic sources both NG and GN are found, though some studies cite significantly lower numbers of NG (e.g. Hopper 1975: 62; Canale 1976). For example, Canale (1976) reports a preponderance of GN in all clause types in the Parker Manuscript (735–891) of the *Anglo-Saxon chronicle*, with GN being the sole order in some clause types. On the other hand, regarding King Alfred's *Pastoral care* (*c.* 900), Brown (1970: 40–1) reports that NG order is preferred under two circumstances: (i) if the phrase contains both an adjectival and a genitive modifier, and if the latter is not a possessive pronoun; and (ii) if the genitive modifier expresses the partitive, especially when the genitive itself is a noun. Timmer (1939) gives the relative numbers of preposed and postposed inflectional genitives in various prose sources shown in table 8.1.[16] Table 8.1 shows that in these Old English texts genitives of common and proper nouns for persons are statistically more likely to precede the head noun, while genitives of nouns that do not refer to persons are more likely to follow the head.

Thus, it is something of a distortion simply to say that Germanic had GN order in phrases, when the NG order in phrases is very strong in some of the oldest languages in all three branches of Germanic. We have seen that Heusler (1932: 177) states that NG is the general rule in Old Norse (see note 15), that Gothic is about evenly NG and GN when the influence of translation source is factored out, and that the most extensive study of Old English finds some preponderance of NG for common nouns. The comparative method requires that both GN and NG be reconstructed to Common Germanic (see Watkins 1976: 315–16). There is no clear basis for claiming that only GN existed at one time, and consequently the claim that the predominant GN pattern of compounds reflects the order in phrases is not supported by the data.

(ii) A pattern of compounding can be established through loan-translations (calques): for example, German *eisen-bahn* "railroad" (lit. "iron-way") and Greek *sidero-dromos* in the same meaning and order represent a calque, though the direction is not clear and other languages are also involved, though not relevant here (Bynon 1977: 234). What is important here is that in Modern Greek the order in phrases is GN (Aitchison 1979), whereas in this compound we have NG order.[17] English *pick-pocket* may have been influenced in a similar way by French *vide-poche* "pick-pocket" (literally "empty(V)-pocket"); as we have seen, its VO structure is unusual in English. (For additional examples see chapter 6.) Through loan-translation, a language can borrow a compound pattern; we have no reason to believe that languages in the past did not borrow, just as they do today. (And we must keep in mind that it is not possible to reconstruct the *original* language, which could be somehow "pure" and uncontaminated.) Generalizing from the pattern of a loan-translation, a language can produce a productive pattern that has a word order that has never existed in phrases in that language. Therefore, a given productive compound pattern does not necessarily reflect earlier word order.

(iii) In fact we have no reason to suppose that word order in compounds actually reflects independent word order in phrases at all, rather than a pattern established independently of phrasal word order. In some languages, at least, there is reason to believe that patterns in compounds are independent of order of individual words in phrases. In Old Georgian, the reversed order (GN) of compounds discussed above serves to mark these as compounds. Since Georgian has quite even word stress, stress alone may have been insufficient to distinguish a compound from a phrase. In Georgian, unlike English (compare *olive oil*), compounds consisting of noun stem forms Stem–Stem are interpreted as meaning Stem-and-Stem; for example *ded-mama* (mother-father) "parents," *col-kmari* (wife-husband) "couple." When one noun in a compound modifies the other, as in *zetis-xili*, the modifier must have the genitive marker, which may appear in the short form *-is* or reduced to *-i* (Šaniʒe 1973: 155). Since stress may be insufficient to distinguish compounds, and since the pattern Stem–Stem has another function, some other means was needed to distinguish the phrase from the compound. In Old Georgian, *zetis-xili* (olive's-fruit) "olive", the compound, differs from *xili zetisay* (fruit olive-GEN) "fruit of the olive", the corresponding phrase, primarily in order and use of the short form of the genitive suffix. We suggest that in some languages the pattern of compound formation serves to distinguish a compound from the corresponding phrase.

No one has yet presented evidence sufficient to indicate that the order of elements in a compound necessarily reflects the order of separate words in phrases at an earlier period or indeed to establish what relationship(s) there is (are) between the order of words in a phrase at any given time and the order in compounds. Until a systematic study is carried out along the lines suggested earlier in this subsection, no conclusion can be reached about this relationship. There is reason to believe that in at least some instances a compound pattern may represent a borrowed pattern, a word order more than one stage back, or a sequence created for the purpose of distinguishing compounds from their phrasal equivalents. On the basis of these considerations, we conclude that compounds do not necessarily reflect the phrasal word order of the immediately preceding period. Compounds are therefore not a reliable guide to reconstruction.

8.3   Construction reanalysis

Several authors have contributed to a growing view of the origin of word order harmonies, a view which elegantly explains how an existing word order can give rise to a harmonious order between other constituents (Greenberg 1963: 99; Givón 1971, 1974: 90ff.; Vennemann 1973: 31; Mallinson and Blake 1981: 373–448 *passim*; Heine and Reh 1984: 240–7; Aristar 1991). They suggest that in some languages the harmonies listed in (1) arise from the basic word order (OV or VO) through naturally occurring diachronic processes. They show that the VO harmonies may arise because VO is often reanalyzed as AdpN, while NG is often reanalyzed as AdpN, as VO, or as NA.[18] The OV harmonies arise because OV is often reanalyzed as NAdp, while GN is often reanalyzed as NAdp, OV, or as AN. We refer to this scenario below as the harmonies-through-reanalysis approach.

Until we have learned more about the nature of word order change in general, it is impossible to reconstruct word order with confidence (see chapter 12). Therefore, we rely here as much as possible upon attested changes as a source of information on universals of word order change. Data from several attested changes confirm that it is possible for word order harmonies to be established or renewed through developments of this kind. For example, Greenberg (1963: 99) pointed out that in English the prepositional order is renewed by the reanalysis of *in back of*, which has become virtually a preposition (as in *in back of the house*) and comes from an AdpNG structure, where *back* was the N and *of* NP the genitive. Andersen (1979) has shown that in Sanskrit, an SOV language, new post-positions have been derived from OV (NP-Gen–participle) sequences, renewing the postpositional harmony that already existed. In Sanskrit post-positions were derived from modified nouns, as in (19a), from verbs, as in (19b), and from other elements:

(19)   (a)   X (Gen) *santikā*
              of X   presence.ABL
              "from the presence of X" > "from X"

        (b)   X (Acc) *ādāya*
              take.ABSOLUTIVE
              "having taken X" > "with X"

Li and Thompson (1974a, 1974b) have shown that Ancient Chinese had some of the harmonies of SOV, although it showed SVO order; Ancient Chinese had AN, GN, RelN, and other properties in harmony with SOV but not included in (1). An important part of this change involved *bǎ*, originally a verb meaning "to take hold of"; in serial constructions it was reanalyzed as a marker of the object. In this way, the surface sequence

     S *bǎ* + O V . . .

remained; but, since *bǎ* was no longer a verb, the order could be reanalyzed as SOV. Thus, in historical times the order became (mostly) SOV, and additional harmonies were established.

These attested changes and others cited in the literature confirm the reality of harmony through reanalysis without doubt, showing specifically that:

(a)   certain constructions may develop out of certain others by reanalysis;
(b)   when this occurs the order of constituents in a phrase may reflect the order of the constituents in the construction from which it developed; and
(c)   in instances observed the order of the derived construction is harmonic with that of the source construction.

Bybee (1988) has gone on to claim that this is the only route to harmony:

> Both of these frequent diachronic developments [reanalysis of GN as NPo or
> of NG as PrN, and reanalysis of N Pr N as NG or of N Po N as GN] contri-
> bute heavily to the correlation of adpositional and genitive phrase orders. Yet
> in neither case do we find analogy in the form of rule simplification playing a
> role. One grammatical order is not established on analogy with or to harmo-
> nize with another order, rather a new grammatical construction develops in
> a language out of constructions that already exist and shows ordering consis-
> tent with the construction from which it developed.   (Bybee 1988: 354)

Thus Bybee proposes that the grammatical order of words (e.g. noun and
adposition) reflects an earlier order.[19] We state this as hypothesis 7, making the
assumption that she intended this to relate only to Greenbergian dyads.
(Aristar 1991 makes similar claims.)

> *Hypothesis 7*
> The order of words in dyads reflects, in so far as those morphemes derive ety-
> mologically from words of other categories, the order of those etymological
> precursors at the time they changed category.

In addition, Bybee, in the section quoted above, apparently rules out the possibility of establishing harmony in any other way. She seems to support hypothesis 8.

> *Hypothesis 8*
> Word order harmonies develop in a language out of constructions that
> already exist in that language and show ordering consistent with the con-
> structions from which they develop.

It is shown above that hypotheses 7 and 8 are true of some harmonies in some
languages; the question is whether they are true for all.

Among attested developments towards word order harmony, not all involve
category reanalyses of the kind proposed in the harmony-by-reanalysis view.
While it is clear that the changes discussed above involved this kind of change,
changes attested in a variety of Indo-European languages and in Georgian do
not support the view that this is the only way harmonic changes in dyadic
orders can come about. Sanskrit provides examples of ambipositions becoming fixed postpositions.[20] While these postpositions have developed out of
constructions that already existed, they do *not* show "ordering consistent with
the construction from which" they developed. It is not through construction
reanalysis that these ambipositions became postpositions, but through extension; that is, the order of existing postpositions was extended to these ambipositions. The latter process we refer to as harmony-by-extension.

German provides a good example of both harmony-by-reanalysis and harmony-by-extension. German, like English, permits both GN and NG orders:

(20)   des Königs   Schloß
              the king.GEN castle
              "the king's castle"   (Paul/Stolte 1949: 250)

(21)   die Hand des Menschen
              the hand the man.GEN
              "the hand of the man"   (Paul/Stolte 1949: 251)

Either order can provide a basis from which an adposition will develop through reanalysis; postpositions will develop from GN, and prepositions from NG. In fact, both changes have taken place in German. Givón (1971: 402) calls attention to the examples in (22) (our translations) of postpositions which have developed from the GN order:

(22)   (a)   des Vaters   wegen
                  the father.GEN reason
                  "because of the father"

           (b)   um   Himmels   willen
                  about Heaven.GEN sake
                  "for Heaven's sake"

           (c)   an   Vaters   statt
                  in/on father.GEN stead
                  "instead of father"

As Givón notes, the position of the postpositions *wegen*, *willen*, and *statt* result from their position in the original GN syntagm; this is a clear instance of harmony by reanalysis, as the postposition is harmonic with GN order. However, these three postpositions are not harmonic with the many prepositions in the language, including *um* and *an* in (22). The postpositions in (22) have become prepositions to varying extents. While *wegen* could be only a postposition in thirteenth-century German (Paul/Stolte 1949: 296), Givón (1971: 401) states that today (22a) is used "in more conservative German speech," and (23a) is more common now:

(23)   (a)   *wegen des Vaters* "because of the father"
           (b)   **um willen (des) Vaters* (but *um Vaters willen*) "for father's sake"
           (c)   *(an) statt Vaters* "instead of father"

Today *statt* rarely occurs as a postposition, but *willen* still cannot occur as a preposition.[21] The change of the postpositions *wegen* and *statt* into ambipositions is an example of harmony-by-extension; the rule placing other adpositions before heads was *extended* to these two (though not to *willen*). In their prenominal placement, these adpositions do not continue the order of the construction out of which they developed.

Aitchison (1979) traces partially attested changes from the SOV assumed for Proto-Indo-European through to the SVO of Modern Greek, showing that a number of individual changes were necessary to develop the VO order found in Greek today. There is nothing in her discussion to suggest reanalysis as a basis for these changes or to suggest that the various constituents in Modern Greek hold the position that they did in some other construction from which they developed. There is nothing in the word order changes from Latin into Western Romance (from SOV to mostly "consistent" SVO modern languages) to support the claim that new word orders must show "ordering consistent with the construction from which it developed." For example, there is no evidence that a GN construction was reanalyzed as AN in later stages of Latin;[22] adjectives simply began to occur after the noun instead of before it (for discussion see, for example, M. Harris 1978; Joseph 1989a, 1989b). In the large-scale word order change fully attested in Georgian (described in section 8.5.2), only one out of five affected dyads involved construction reanalysis.

On the basis of the examples cited above, we conclude that the order of words in dyads consisting of morphemes that are derived from words of other categories does not always reflect the order of those etymological precursors, and thus that hypothesis 7 cannot be maintained. That is, in changes where the order does at first reflect the order of the etymological precursors, that order may subsequently change by another mechanism. The order of such a dyad need not remain forever consistent with its earlier order, and hypothesis 8 must also be abandoned.

The harmony-by-reanalysis explanation alone (hypthotheses 7 and 8) would make it impossible for a language that is thoroughly harmonic ever to change its word order. For example if postpositions can only develop out of GN or OV order, both of which are harmonic with postpositions, it would be impossible for a language with NG and VO to develop *pre*positions and in this way change part of its word order type. It would be, *mutatis mutandis*, impossible for any thoroughly harmonic language to undergo word order change. In fact, however, construction reanalysis can introduce *disharmony*, instead of harmony, and this could provide the basis for extension to change the word order type of the language more completely. Andersen (1979: 28) has pointed out that in Old Indic modifiers preceded the noun, consistent with the OV typology of the language. Certain of these modifiers, such as *antarā* "in the inner part," were reanalyzed as prepositions.[23] In this way, a ModN construction, which was harmonic, became a preposition, which was disharmonic (and unlike other developments in the language, described above in this section). Thus, here we have disharmony by reanalysis. An additional example of disharmony by reanalysis is fully attested in Georgian (see Harris 1991e). During a period when several non-finite verb forms were reanalyzed as postpositions (e.g. *šesaxeb(i)* "about", *mixedvit* "according to") and when all existing ambipositions were becoming fixed postpositions (e.g. *c'ina(še)* "before", *šoris* "among"), one non-finite verb form, *miuxedavad*, was reanalyzed instead as a *pre*position. This is explained by the fact that *miuxedavad* "in spite of NP" is a learned word and usually occurred with a heavy NP. It is common in languages of all types for heavy NPs to be postposed (Hawkins 1983: 90–1). The participle *miuxedavad* "without having looked at" with its heavy NP postposed was reanalyzed as the preposition *miuxedavad* "in spite of" with its NP, disharmonic with the rest of the language.

We conclude then, that word order change can come about through reanalysis of one construction as another; harmonies can be initiated or renewed through reanalysis. Word order change can also be brought about by the drive towards harmony; harmonies can be initiated through extension and maintained by the force of the status quo. Word order change is not all driven by harmony; this was a mistake made early on in the study of word order typology. Nor is word order change all through reanalysis; this is a recent mistake. In some instances, development of a single harmonic adposition may involve both reanalysis and extension, as in the German instance cited above.

8.4   Three views of the causes of word order change

8.4.1   Wackernagel: cliticization

One hundred years ago in 1892 the Indo-Europeanist, Jacob Wackernagel, showed that in Proto-Indo-European unaccented words were placed in second position in the clause, that in Sanskrit the verb was accented in subordinate clauses but unaccented in main clauses, and that such rules must have applied also in Germanic. Thus, in Germanic, the finite auxiliary and certain other short and unemphatic verbs of the main clause would have been unaccented and would have been placed in second position; the verb of the subordinate clause would have been accented and placed in the basic verb position, clause-final. Later the verb-second construction was reanalyzed in such a way that it applied to all finite verbs. In this way verb-second position of main clauses in most Germanic languages and verb-final position of embedded clauses in many Germanic languages are generally accounted for; these positions are illustrated for Modern German in (24) and (25).

(24)   als   er aus dem   Zimmer **gehen wollte** . . .[24]
        when he out of.the room   to.go wanted
        "when he was about to go out of the room . . ."

(25)   durch die Felde **rannten** die Kinder
        "Through the fields ran the children."

Wackernagel's general argument has received much support from recent cross-linguistic studies in cliticization, confirming the importance, from the point of view of cliticization, of second position in the clause, and establishing the concept of second position in the phrase and perhaps even in the word (Kaisse 1985: ch. 4; Nevis and Joseph, 1992; Anderson 1984, 1993; and many other sources).

8.4.2   Vennemann: ambiguity

Vennemann (1973) suggests that a change to SVO order is motivated by a need to distinguish subject from object, and proposes that a language that loses its case marking must change to SVO order as an alternative means of distinguishing those essential grammatical relations. Vennemann particularly associates this with the change from SOV to SVO order in English.

It is quite true that a so-called fixed word order, that is, one assigned on the basis of grammatical relations (subject, direct object, indirect object, etc.), as in English, is capable of marking grammatical relations, while a language with so-called free word order, that is, order assigned according to other principles, such as pragmatic ones, cannot mark grammatical relations through word order. However, it is not clear that SVO is the only, or even the most efficient, fixed order for marking grammatical relations. It is certainly not the case that a language that loses its case marking must adopt SVO order. One example of a language that has recently lost case marking and which has most clauses in SOV order is the Artašen dialect of Laz. In Laz word order is relatively free, in the sense defined above, but the unmarked order is SOV (Holisky 1991). The marker of the dative case, -*s*, was lost as part of a general rule that deleted word-final *s*. The nominative case was already Ø, and the -*k* ending of the third grammatical case was also lost. (In Laz all noun stems must end in a vowel; formerly consonant-final stems, including those borrowed from Turkish, now end in -*i*, formerly the marker of the nominative case.) In this way the grammatical cases of the noun were all reduced to Ø. Pronouns were also reanalyzed in such a way that the form that was formerly nominative now serves all grammatical functions (Harris 1985: 385–9). Although there is no case marking of subject, direct object, and indirect object, texts recorded by Čikobava (1936b: 109–38) and by Dumézil and Esenç

(1972) have predominantly SOV order, as in the examples below.[25] In (26)–(28) the (a) sentences are from the Artašen dialect, and the (b) examples are from a dialect (Arhavi) with complete case marking:

(26)   (a) čyoyl-epe   hamu-ša ar čare   oziru-šeni idušunamtʼey
           villag(er)-PL it-ALL   one solution find-for   they.reflect.it

       (b) kyöyl-epe-k   hamu-še ar čare   oʒiru-šeni idušunamtʼes
           villag(er)-PL-NAR it-ABL   one solution.NOM find-for   they.reflect.it
           "The villagers thought (in order) to find a solution to it."

(27)   (a) ham dumani mzuɣa dvacʼonertʼey
           he fog   sea   they.think.it

       (b) ham dumani zuɣa   dacʼonetʼes
           he fog.NOM sea.NOM they.think.it
           "They thought the fog [was] the sea."

(28)   (a) šku ar didi mauna   dopʼatu   do ham mzuɣa ǰebumkvat
           we one big mahonne(boat) we.make.it and it   sea   we.float.it

       (b) čku ar didi maona   dopʼat   do ham zuɣa-s
           we one big mahonne.NOM we.make.it and it   sea-DAT

           gebumkvat
           we.float.it

           "Let us make a big mahonne and float it on the sea."
                    (Dumézil and Esenç 1972: 6 [3], [4], [6])

In (26a)–(28a), every noun and pronoun is in stem form (except *hamuša* "to it" in (26a)), whether it represents a subject, direct object, or other grammatical relation. The pronoun subject of (27) is in the form that serves as nominative singular in most dialects, even though other dialects would require the narrative case form in this instance; but both of the dialects represented here have made this form syncretic for three cases and two numbers. *šku/čku* is syncretic for three cases in all dialects and in the sister languages. Grammatical relations in Artašen are apparently encoded by position, not in the order SVO, but in the order SOXV, where X includes the predicate complement, *mzuɣa* "sea," in (27) and the locative, *mzuɣa* "[on the] sea" in (28). The fact that Artašen, which has lost case marking relatively recently, uses its preexisting SOV order to encode grammatical relations, rather than SVO, is one reason for rejecting the hypothesis that SOV order changes to SVO when case endings are lost.

   Sasse (1977: 94–6) describes another SOV language, Ostyak, that uses no case marking to disambiguate subject from object, as well as a VSO language, Bilaan, with the same trait (citing Steinitz 1950; Abrams 1961, 1970). According to Hyman (1975: 117), Ịjọ has SOV ordering and has never had case marking. Leinonen (1980: 149) points out that both Finnish and Russian have undergone a change from SOV to SVO, but that neither has truly ambiguous case marking. On the basis of these data, we conclude that ambiguity is neither a necessary nor a sufficient condition to trigger word order change to SVO.

8.4.3   Faarlund: information flow

There has been a recent spate of work on the syntax of word order in Germanic languages, including diachronic change.[26] Because this is a work on universals of diachronic syntax, we cannot discuss all of these, and we concentrate on Faarlund's (1990b) discussion. Faarlund describes the change from the SOV order found in Old Norse to the SVO order of Modern Norwegian, together with the origin of expletive topics and subjects.

Faarlund (1990b: 59–63) raises two objections to Wackernagel's explanation of the development of SVO order in Germanic languages. First, he points out that verb-second order, which Wackernagel's Law purports to account for, is not the same as VO order, which is found in some Germanic languages. However, it is generally assumed that Germanic verb-second was reanalyzed as SVO in languages such as English (for example, van Kemenade 1987), while this particular reanalysis was not made in languages such as German, which maintain verb-second order. Second, Faarlund observes that a language may be both verb-second and at the same time OV, since the "verb" referred to by the phrase "verb-second" is the auxiliary (Aux), while the "verb" referred to by the expression "OV" is the main verb (MV). This may be seen in the "bracketing" construction found in several Germanic languages and illustrated in (29) from Modern German:

(29)   sie wird ins   Kino   gehen
        she will in.the movie.theater go
        "She will go to the movies."

The change from the bracketing construction, with its S-Aux-O-MV order, to simple SVO order has been explained through Behaghel's First Law (Behaghel 1923–32, II), the observation that words that combine to form a constituent, including auxiliaries and main verbs, tend to occur together (see further section 8.5.1 below). In those languages that developed a simple SVO order from an earlier S-Aux-O-MV, Aux and MV tended to occur together, and S-Aux-MV-O (that is, SVO) was reanalyzed as the basic order. In languages such as German, which maintain the bracketing construction of (29), the tendency expressed in Behaghel's First Law was not fulfilled, and the reanalysis was not made.

Faarlund proposes to account for the innovative VO order of Norwegian in terms of information flow. In his view there is a universal tendency to begin a sentence with old information and end it with new: "The strategy of focusing an element by moving it to the right is based on a universal discourse- functional principle" (1990b: 58; see also pp. 23, 55). The notion of focus is defined pragmatically: "The focus of the sentence is that part of the sentence which carries new information, or which is least predictable from the context" (1990b: 55). He notes that in transitive sentences the object is generally the focus; combined with a sentence-final focus, this fact would explain the VO order of Norwegian. Notice, however, that if focus function, sentence-final focus position, and the frequent identification of focus with object are all valid universals, we would expect all languages to have SVO as their most common order; this, of course, is not what is found.

There is a substantial body of recent work on focus showing that there is, in fact, no universal focus position. It has been shown that in many languages focus occurs in immediately preverbal position; some examples are Hungarian (Kiss 1987 and elsewhere), Mayan languages (Aissen 1992), Korean and Armenian (Comrie 1988: 268–71), and Tsova-Tush (North East Caucasian, Holisky, in press). While there is considerable debate in the literature on its precise status, there is good reason to believe that sentence-initial position (which coincides with immediately preverbal position) is focus position in both Breton and Welsh (see chapter 7 of the present work; Dik 1980: 160–1). And in Aghem, an SVO Bantu language, focus position seems to be immediately postverbal (Watters 1979, cited by Rochemont 1986: 23ff.; also Abraham *et al.* 1986: 5 on postverbal focus generally). Preverbal focus, in particular, has been so well documented in recent work, that we must conclude that sentence-final position is not, in fact, a universal focus position.

Was clause-final position focus position in Old Norse? It is a well-documented universal that question words are in focus (Heine and Reh 1984: 147ff., 178; Abraham *et al.* 1986: 6; Rochemont 1986: 22; Kiss 1987: 52–3, 56 and *passim*; Huck and Na 1990: 57). Question words occur in sentence-initial position in Old Norse, just as in most Germanic languages (Heusler 1932: 169). It is entirely possible that question words in Old Norse had been grammaticalized to this position, rather than indicating a productive focus position. Certainly the sentence-initial position of question words alone does not establish that this was focus position in Old Norse. Nevertheless, since no specific evidence is presented to support the hypothesis that clause-final position is focus position in Old Norse, the position of question words is sufficient to throw doubt on the hypothesis that sentence-final position marked focus.

If it could be established that focus position in Norwegian is clause-final, would this explain the attested SOV to SVO change? If clause-final position became focus position in Norwegian, then this change might correlate with the change in basic word order, though it would still not be clear which change, if either, conditioned the other.

In sum, the SOV-to-SVO change in word order in Nordic may have correlated with a change in focus position, though we know of no specific evidence to support this. Because there is very good evidence that focus occurs in different positions in different languages, there is no universal focus position that could explain this or any other change in word order. In our view Faarlund's arguments against the explanations offered by Wackernagel's Law and Behaghel's First Law are unconvincing, for reasons given above and more extensively in Harris (1992b).

8.5   Towards an account of word order and word order change

We begin this section with a discussion of two operations (sections 8.5.1–8.5.2) affecting word order, not limited to word order typology. In section 8.5.3 we make some general observations regarding the fixing of word order. In section 8.5.4 we discuss the implications of these observations for synchronic syntax.

The discussion below differs from some other treatments of word order in that it does not assume that constituents are generated in a particular order and moved to other positions by the grammar. We assume rather that constituents are generated without reference to word order and are positioned by rules, usually on the basis of superficial syntax. This means that we treat constituent "movement" as a metaphor for occurrence in a position that differs from the basic position of that constituent.

8.5.1   Reordering head and dependent to adjacency
8.5.1.1   Examples of reordering to adjacency
Often constituents that are not adjacent are reordered to be adjacent; this is best seen in changes in which at an early period two words did not form a constituent at all and through reanalysis at a later period do. Numerous examples of this arise through clause fusion. In section 7.4.2.1 we described the reanalysis of a complex structure consisting of a "have" clause and a second, dependent clause in French. After reanalysis the resulting monoclausal construction had the structure

(30)   [$_S$ Subject$_i$ Aux Object$_j$ Verb]
         habēre

where the verb and auxiliary were separated by the object. Such structures often result from clause fusion, depending on the order of words and clauses in the input structures. Word order in Old French was not rigidly fixed (see Foulet 1930: 306-32), and the various constituents named in (30) could appear in other positions, with the Aux and V still separated. (For evidence that reanalysis had already occurred, see the discussion in chapter 7.) Gradually the Aux and V were placed in adjacent positions more often, and this was re-evaluated[27] as basic and fixed, with only a few adverbs permitted to intervene between them. The same force caused a parallel change in the "have" perfect in English (section 7.4.2.2), except that actualization of this reordering in English is incomplete; for some verbs the older order may be maintained, as in (31a), while the newer adjacent ordering in (31b) is also possible:

(31)   (a)   Sarah has the report finished
        (b)   Sarah has finished the report

Thus, while (31b) represents reordering to adjacency, the change is incomplete because of the continued existence of the pattern in (31a).

We assume that the present progressive in English also originated through clause fusion. The "be" + present participle construction is found in a wide variety of Indo-European languages, both ancient and modern (Mossé 1938). In English and in some others it has been reanalyzed as a periphrasis, with the participle losing its adjectival sense and the verb "be" losing its stative meaning. The construction must have been reanalyzed as monoclausal long before Old English times, for the present participle did not agree with the subject of the sentence (it had the invariant ending -*ende*).[28] Most examples, including (33) and (34) below, have objects in the case that the participial verb would govern if it were finite (generally accusative); however some, such as (32), have genitive objects:

(32)   his   **wæren** swiðe   **ehtende**
        him-GEN were   severely persecuting
        "They were severely persecuting him."
                (Ælfred, *Orosius* 88.21, cited in Visser 1963–73, III, part 2: 1930)

In Old English it was possible to separate the Aux and the non-finite verb form, as in (32) and (33)–(34).

(33)   mid þæm þeowum ic **eom** ealne þone hefon   **ymbhweorfende**
        with these servants I am   all   the   heaven encompassing
        "I am encompassing all the heaven with these servants."
                (Blickling Homilies (EETS) 71.3, cited in Mossé 1938: 79)

(34)   **wæs** þæt folc   þonan ut **sleande and hienende**
        was the people thence out striking and oppressing
        "He was driving out the people thence and oppressing them."
                (Ælfred, *Orosius* (EETS) 168.29, cited in Mossé 1938: 86)

While in (33) and (34) the object intervened between the Aux and V, this eventually became impossible, with only some adverbs permitted between them today, as in the translation of (32).

In the Kru languages a number of monoclausal Aux + V constructions have been fused from a biclausal structure (Marchese 1986: chs. 3 and 4). In these languages the Aux and V have begun to occur together in some instances, but they are not (yet?) fixed in adjacent positions.

In French, English, and the Kru languages, the following change in word order occurred:

(35)   S Aux O V > S Aux V O

In each language the content verb (V) moves to the position adjacent to the auxiliary, the head of the Aux + V construction.[29] Notice, however, that (35) records only the surface results of the change. In the grammar the rules placing constituents must have changed. After reanalysis of the verb of the main clause as an auxiliary, this auxiliary would have been in second position, and the content verb in final. Part of the actualization was a change in the ordering rules, now placing the verb complex, Aux + V, in second position.

In a number of languages adverbs are reanalyzed as an expression of a verbal category, such as tense; in many instances they are subsequently adjoined to the verb. For example, in Indo-European languages certain adverbs were reanalyzed as preverbs (Prev) that could express location or perfective aspect. For some types, even after reanalysis the V and Prev could occur together or could be separated, as in Sanskrit, (36):

(36)   prá   mā yuyujre
        forward me harnessed
        "They (have) harnessed me."   (*Rigveda* 10, 33, 1; cited in Schmidt 1969: 97)

While (36) was grammatical in Vedic, by the time of Classical Sanskrit this construction was impossible (Whitney 1971: 397).[30] In early Latin, (37a) is found; by Classical Latin it would have been (37b). (See note 33 below on Germanic.)

(37)   (a)   ab vōs sacrō, sub vōs plācō (Festus 190 b 2)
        (b)   obsecrō vōs, supplicō vōs
                        (both from Schmidt 1969: 97, citing Wackernagel)

These examples demonstrate a tendency of elements that are reanalyzed as a verbal category to occur adjacent to the verb. (See also Friedrich 1975: 34–9; Watkins 1976.)

Heine and Reh (1984: 29) observe that in Bari, an Eastern Nilotic language, an adverb *dé* "then, afterwards" in clause-initial position was reanalyzed (in our terms) as a marker of future tense. Eventually it began to occur in the pre-verbal position in which other tense markers occur:

(38) dé   nan kɔn . . .
      then I   do
      "I shall do . . . then"

(39) nan dé   kɔn . . .
      I   FUT do
      "I shall do . . ."   (from Heine and Reh 1984: 29, citing Spagnolo)

In Solomons Pidgin, the English adverb *by and by* was reanalyzed as a mar-ker of future or irrealis in forms such as *baebae, bae, baembae.* Originally it occurred in clause-initial position, as in (40) from Bislama:

(40) bae mi mi blok-im marid ya
      FUT   -TRANS
      "I will prevent this marriage."   (Keesing 1988: 184)

But in Solomons Pidgin this tense–aspect marker has begun to occur in the verb complex, as in (41);[31] in this example the "subject-referring pronoun" (SRP) is also part of the verbal complex and is coreferential to the noun sub-ject, here "the Japanese."

(41) Diapani baebae hem-i   kam   tudee, ia
      Japan   FUT   SRP(he) come today RHET
      "The Japanese are going to come today."   (Keesing 1988: 185)

Thus in Solomons Pidgin the tense marker has begun to occur adjacent to the verb.

We have looked at three examples in which an adverb is reanalyzed as a tense–aspect marker and in which the verb and marker come to occupy adja-cent positions. While the Indo-European example is not entirely clear because of different word orders found in the various daughters, in the other two instances the reanalyzed tense–aspect (T–A) marker moves to be adjacent to the verb in the position the verb previously occupied. In both, the word order change in (42) occurred:

(42)   T–A S V > S T–A V

Thus there was a change in the rules placing constituents. After the adverb had been reanalyzed as a tense–aspect marker, it at first continued in first position, and the verb in third. Corresponding to the change in order stated in (42) was a change of the rule placing the tense–aspect marker initial in the verb complex. Although all of our examples have the order shown in (42), we assume that the mirror-image of this also occurs, and that the subject in (42) could be replaced by any other constituent, as in (43):

(43)   T–A X V > X T–A V
        V X T–A > V T–A X

8.5.1.2   *Proposed universals of reordering to adjacency*

We can generalize the superficial effects of the two types of cases we have considered in this section as (44), where D represents a dependent, H a head, and the subscript indexes the dependency:[32]

(44)   (a) $X D_i Y H_i Z > X Y [D_i H_i] Z$
        (b) $X H_i Y D_i Z > X [H_i D_i] Y Z$

On the basis of the facts discussed above in section 8.2.1, it seems likely that the relative order of head and dependent can change at the same time they are reordered to adjacency, though we have little direct evidence of this in examples where reordering to adjacency occurs.[33] If this is possible, it would involve changes of the following types:

(45)   (a) $X D_i Y H_i Z > X Y [H_i D_i] Z$
        (b) $X H_i Y D_i Z > X [D_i H_i] Y Z$

The linear nature of the representations in (44) and (45) makes it impossible to state a single generalization, though that is easily stated in words, generalizing over (44a), (44b), (45a), and (45b). We hypothesize that in any language in which discontinuous constituents are reordered to be adjacent, the proposition in (46) will always hold.

(46)   Discontinuous constituents that are reordered to be adjacent occupy the position held by the grammatical head.

We are not suggesting that the change described here must apply when its input conditions are met; German is an obvious example of a language which has the input conditions for verb and preverb to be reordered to adjacency, yet which has not undergone this change.

It should be reiterated that in all of the examples in this subsection, the discontinuity arises through reanalysis of two words as a single constituent, in spite of the fact that they are separated by intervening material. The discontinuous constituents are gradually placed in adjacent positions, following (46), as part of the actualization.

8.5.1.3   *Reordering to non-adjacency*

While the specific changes described above in section 8.5.1.1 are found frequently among languages of the world, examples of separation of constituents, or creation of a discontinuous constituent construction, appear to be much less frequent, and it has not been clear that such reorderings occur at all. In some languages the history of the word order variants is not yet known well enough to determine whether discontinuous constituents were once continuous or whether they became discontinuous by reanalysis of non-constituents as constituents. For example, some of the Kru languages have some of the same discontinuities that English has, including Aux . . . V in (47), V . . . Prt in (48a), and N . . . Adpos in (49):

(47)   wǎ lā   mÓ dlá
       they PERF him kill
       "They have killed him."   (Koopman 1984: 28)

(48)   (a) Ò ɓIá sǎká kÒ
            s/he take rice PRT
            "S/he is taking rice."   (*ibid.*: 48)

       (b) à lā   sǎká kÒ   ɓIá
            we PERF rice PRT take
            "We have taken the rice."   (*ibid.*: 49)

(49)   táɓlĒᵢ kÉ m̄È [e]ᵢ kIÚ jI̋II̋Ò
       table FUT food on put.PASSIVE
       "The food will be put on the table."   (*ibid.*: 54)

The origins of these discontinuities cannot yet be determined.

Others may appear to be examples of reordering to non-adjacency, but really are similarly indeterminate. For example, in Modern English the verb + particle construction in (50a) alternates with the discontinuous constituent pattern in (50b):

(50)   (a) He used up the olive oil
       (b) He used the olive oil up

Visser (1963–73, I, 597–8) cites three patterns, which he schematizes as in (51), where *a* represents the adverb (later particle), *V* the verb, and *O* the object:[34]

(51)   (a) a V O (*or* O a V)
       (b) V a O
       (c) V O a

Since all three patterns are found in Old Saxon (Visser 1963–73, I: 598, n. 1), we must reconstruct the three to an earlier, pre-English stage. Some believe that (51a) represents the oldest pattern. Curme (1914) argues for this position not only on the basis of order in compounds, a basis of reconstruction we have argued against above, but also on the basis of stress. Kennedy (1920: 12–14) states that in older sources only the (51a) pattern is common, while the (51b) and (51c) patterns increase later, to the point that (51a) is lost for the verbs discussed here; this would be consistent with Curme's view. On the other hand, Hiltunen's (1983: 106) study of these patterns finds that the (a) order (fifty-six) is not much more frequent than the (b–c) order (forty-four combined for the (b) and (c) patterns) in main clauses in early Old English prose. Thus, there is very little evidence to support the view that one of the patterns in (51) is older than another, and thus that there was reordering to non-adjacency.

Our second example of the creation of discontinuous constituency is also from English; it is attested, and we can be certain of the order of development and the fact that discontinuous constituency is created. Allen (1980 [1977]) shows that in Old English preposition stranding occurred only in those relative clauses formed with the complementizer *þe* "that," never in Old English in relative clauses formed with the pronoun *se* (or *se þe*)(1977: ch. 3).[35] In relative clauses with a pronoun, the pronoun and preposition form a constituent; synchronically the rule of Pied Piping insured the placement of prepositions with their NPs when those NPs are placed in initial position. In those relatives formed with the complementizer *þe*, the complementizer served only to introduce and mark the relative clause; since it was not a pronoun in any sense, it did not form a constituent with the preposition. Because *þe* and the preposition did not form a constituent, Pied Piping did not apply to them, and Old English permitted the preposition to appear alone. While early sources have strictly preposition stranding with *þe* relatives and strictly Pied Piping with *se* (or *se þe*) relatives, around the twelfth century preposition stranding became possible in relatives formed with pronouns.[36] Further, preposition stranding came to occur optionally in any constructions in which an NP was placed in initial position for topicalization or focusing, including content questions, WH-relative pronouns, topicalization, and passivization.[37]

In spoken, but not written, contemporary Russian it is possible to separate a variety of constituents for emphasis (Leinonen 1980, citing Adamec 1966 and Lapteva 1976; examples in (52) from the same sources):

(52)   (a)   u Jurki ešče   interesnaja pojavilas' sposobnost'
               in Jurka another interesting appeared talent
               "In Jurka another interesting talent appeared."

        (b)   devočka emu staršaja pomogaet
               girl   him elder   helps
               "The older girl helps him."

The usual (but not only) AN order is maintained by the discontinuous constituents in (52a), but is reversed to N . . . A by those in (52b). The more neutral order for (52a) is (53a). Example (52b) might have more than one neutral order, depending on the context; one is given in (53b).

(53)   (a) u   Jurki   pojavilas' ešče   interesnaja sposobnost'
             in Jurka   appeared   another   interesting talent

        (b) staršaja devočka emu pomogaet
             elder   girl   him helps

Leinonen describes the permutation in this way: "The adjective is detached from its head noun and moved wherever necessary to produce an alternation of accented and unaccented units" (1980: 155). The importance of this observation becomes apparent below.

We suggest that constituents become discontinuous through processes such as (54), where ~ represents an alternation, and ⤳ is to be read "begins to alternate with" or "develops an alternation with":

(54)   (a) $X [H_i D_i] Y Z \rightsquigarrow X H_i Y D_i Z$
        (b) $X Y [D_i H_i] Z \rightsquigarrow X D_i Y H_i Z$

Process (54b) represents discontinuous constituents in Russian, of the type illustrated in (52a), where the dependent precedes the head. In preposition stranding, the head and dependent are not only separated, but also are reordered relative to one another, as in (55a):

(55)   (a) $X Y [H_i D_i] Z \rightsquigarrow X D_i Y H_i Z$
        (b) $X [D_i H_i] Y Z \rightsquigarrow X H_i Y D_i Z$

Process (55b) represents the discontinuous constituents of spoken Russian, of the type illustrated in (52b).

We note that in each of the examples examined, it is the head, not the dependent, which continues to occupy the basic position of the constituent. Here "basic position" refers to the position that would be occupied by the continuous constituent in neutral word order; if this does not apply, "basic position" is the position occupied by the head when there is no dependent in the example. For instance, it is the adposition, the head of an adpositional phrase, that remains in the position occupied by the phrase in neutral order. It is the auxiliary, the head according to the criteria adopted here, that occupies the position that a finite verb occupies in a clause where no auxiliary is used. It is the verb, the head of the particle + verb, that appears in basic verbal position if the constituent is broken up.

(56)   If a constituent appears in discontinuous positions, it is the head that occupies the basic position of that constituent.

Reordering to non-adjacency does not arise in the way reordering to adjacency does, but through optional synchronic separation of constituents, often for stylistic or rhythmic effects, as in modern spoken Russian.[38] Nor is the progression of the changes the same. In reordering to adjacency, over time more and more constraints are placed on the discontinuous pattern, and the continuous pattern becomes the norm, then the sole pattern. In reordering to non-adjacency, on the other hand, a single order has been expanded to an alternation of two orders, under the conditions specified. We know of no examples in which adjacency is replaced historically by a sole discontinuous order, and this is probably not a coincidence.[39]

8.5.2   Reordering head and dependent relative to one another

8.5.2.1   Examples of reordering

Reordering within dyads has been discussed a great deal in the literature, primarily on the basis of some attested examples in Indo-European languages and reconstructions of some language families of Africa. We briefly describe here an attested reordering of the same sort in a non-Indo-European language. The purpose of the example is to provide an attested basis for comparison in order to examine shared characteristics of the changes.

Old Georgian is attested from the fifth century. The relative order of object and verb in Old Georgian cannot be determined with certainty because nearly all of the earliest documents are translations, and the order of object, verb, and subject could be freely matched to that of the source; it is generally felt that even those texts that were not translations were indirectly influenced by Greek grammar. This reservation does not apply, however, within dyads, which were more fixed in position. Subject, object, and verb are excluded from the discussion below. The order within dyads in Old Georgian (attested from the fifth century) can be summarized as schema 1, below. Capital letters represent the unmarked order, lower case letters represent the marked order, and those in parentheses barely occur. Orders to the left of the slash (oblique) are those that are correlates of OV order, while those to the right are correlates of VO order. We have followed the list in (2), excerpted from Dryer (1992), except that we have added adjective/noun combinations to this, and we have omitted verb/manner adverbial combinations because we have been unable to get reliable data on this. Adp = adposition, N = noun, V = verb, Aux = auxiliary, G = genitive, A = adjective (see note 18), Rel = relative clause, St = standard of comparison.

1   *Order of constituents in Old Georgian*

    NAdp/adpn   VAux/auxv   gn/NG   an/NA   /NRel   /ASt

Example (57) illustrates the prepositional order and the NG order; (58) illustrates NA order:

(57)   romeli iq'o **zeda tav-sa**   **čemsa**
        which it.be on   head-DAT my
        "which was on my head"   (Genesis 40: 17; Imnaišvili 1957: 322)

(58)   sul-eb-i   igi arac'mida-y
        spirit-COL-NOM the unclean-NOM
        "the unclean spirit"   (Mk. 5:13AB)

Old Georgian had predominantly postpositions and auxiliaries following content verbs, but other dyadic ordering was predominantly (for each dyad) harmonious with VO ordering.

In Modern Georgian we find the order SOV; the order of other constituents is summarized below:

2   *Order of constituents in Modern Georgian*

    NAdp/(adpn)   VAux/auxv   GN/ng   AN/(na)   RelN/NRel   StA/ASt

Example (59) illustrates postpositional order and one kind of RelN order; (60) illustrates GN order.

(59)   **g. k'art'ozia-s**   **mier dadast'urebuli**   iseti magalit-eb-i
        G. K'art'ozia-GEN by   confirm.PTCPL such example-PL-NOM
        "such examples, which are confirmed by G. K'art'ozia"
                                     (Čxubianišvili 1972: 132)

(60)   šeni d-is   disert'acia
        your sister-GEN dissertation
        "your sister's dissertation"

In the modern language all dyads are either predominantly harmonic with OV (NAdp, VAux, GN, AN) or have no dominant order within the dyad (RelN/NRel, StA/ASt). The reordering of the remaining prepositions (except one), and of genitives, adjectives, and two types of relative clauses can be represented as (61) (see note 4 on determination of heads):

(61)   H D > D H

In these reorderings, nothing else occurred.[40] However, the StA construction is not merely a reordering of the ASt construction; it is not described by (61). This problem is discussed below in section 8.5.2.2.

In the transition from Latin to French, word order underwent an equally

Table 8.2 *Order of constituents in Latin*

12 Tables	OV/		gn/NG	AN/NA	RelN/nrel	
Plautus	OV/vo	/AdpN	gn/NG	AN/na	/NRel	
Caesar	OV/vo	/AdpN	/NG	AN/na	/NRel	/ASt
Tacitus	OV/vo		GN/ng	AN/na	reln/NRel	StA/ASt

sweeping change, predominantly in a direction opposite to that of Georgian. Table 8.2 is based on Friedrich (1975: 52–5); in this table, absence of a notation to one side of the slash does not mean that it absolutely does not occur, but that it does not occur in Friedrich's sample. Absence of any notation about adpositions in the Twelve Tables and in Tacitus indicates that Friedrich did not discuss them. Our representation of the dyads involving adjectives may be misleading; Friedrich's data show more AN in all four samples, but, except in some cases, the margin is small – 18/13, 16/14, 33/7, and 26/4, respectively. He mentions other evidence that supports AN for Plautus. The dyadic orders in table 8.2 may be compared with those below, representing Modern French:

3   *Order of constituents in Modern French*
       /VO   /AdpN   gn/NG   an/NA   /NRel   /ASt

Most specialists consider that there was at least a general shift from AN to NA and from OV to VO ordering, though there is disagreement about exactly when these changes took place (see Friedrich 1975: 52–8; M. Harris 1978: 58–9; J. Joseph 1989a). These changes may be represented as (62), stating simply that head–dependent order developed.

(62)   > H D

Additional changes affected adjectives and verbs, and the question of whether the reordering can be isolated from other changes, as in (62), is a complex one. What is important from our point of view is that none of the related changes in French appear to be universals of reordering within dyads. In addition, it is worth noting that if GN changed to NG, the change did not occur (entirely) through periphrasis, as is sometimes suggested. In fact, NG order predated periphrasis; in Latin, Friedrich finds NG predominating except in Tacitus. In Old French, under certain circumstances possessors could still follow possessed nouns with no preposition, as in (63) (Foulet 1930: 14–23):

(63)   fil   maistre Henri
          son master Henry
          "[the] son of master Henry"

                                                                        (Foulet 1930: 16)

At this period the Old French oblique case was syncretic for dative, genitive, and accusative; the periphrasis in (64), already present in some examples in Old French, later became obligatory:

(64)   la   grant route des   chevaus
         the grand way of.the horses   (Foulet 1930: 11)

Generalization (62) can represent a GN to NG change, to the extent that one took place.

In both Georgian and French, there were lexical and stylistic exceptions to these simple changes, and in a complete account these must be stated in addition to (61) and (62).

8.5.2.2 *Universals of reordering of head and dependent relative to one another*
Statement (61) makes a correct generalization about reordering in at least five dyads in Georgian, and (62) for at least two dyadic reorderings in Latin–French. Statements (61) and (62) relate the changes in individual dyads to each other and to the orderings in other dyads in the languages. That is, (62) states the insight that French developed relatively consistent ordering – consistent, that is, within all of the dyads shown in schema 3. Nevertheless, the combined formulae give inadequate accounts of changes in dyadic ordering. Generalizations (61) and (62) do not apply at all to certain kinds of changes. As noted in section 8.5.2.1, the Modern Georgian StA construction is not just a reordering of the old ASt construction, but a pristine creation; its creation is not described by (61) (see Harris 1991e on details of the word order change to StA). Similarly, the changes described in section 8.3 involve reanalysis, not superficial reordering; they are not described by (61) or (62).

We suggest that a single approach is needed to explain new dyadic ordering both of the simple type discussed in section 8.5.2.1 and the construction reanalysis discussed in section 8.3. Many languages tolerate non-harmonic systems for millenia, and it is clear that this situation can be stable. But the wholesale, purposeful reordering of almost every dyad, as seen in the Georgian changes discussed above, and to a lesser extent in French and many other languages, suggests that a change to a system with dyadic harmonies is a natural sort of change. Once we look beyond the ordered phrase structure rules of classic transformational grammar, and assume that word placement may be stated by more general rules, it is clear that the reason that dyadic harmony is preferred is that it requires a single word placement rule, where non-harmonic systems would require many. For example, all of the placement of dyads in (2), and consequently much of the unmarked word placement in Modern Georgian can be accomplished by rule (65).[41]

(65)   D H

Certain exceptions must be listed: for example, relative clauses formed with relative pronouns must follow their heads. In contrast, if we take this approach for an inconsistent language such as English, we must list whole dyads as exceptions. For example, if we state the rule (66), for English,

(66)   H D

we must list AN as an exception and GN as a restricted exception.

The reorderings in Georgian discussed in section 8.5.2.1 are **extensions** of the rule (65), which already existed for NAdp and for VAux, and the French reorderings discussed in that subsection are similarly extensions of (66), already used in AdpN and NRel. It is already known that extensions proceed by eliminating irregularity (see chapter 5) and that they simplify and regularize rules. Thus, it is no surprise that these simple reorderings eliminate irregularity from rules (65) and (66). However, again, this does not account for the construction reanalyses discussed in section 8.3.

If the reorderings in Georgian and in many Indo-European languages are extensions of an existing rule, and if cross-linguistically reordering takes this course, it is reasonable to ask what the origin of the rule is that is later extended (see Campbell and Mithun 1980). Put differently, if extension explains the development of harmonies, how can a new and different rule come to exist in a language? We have already seen the answer to this. Some examples discussed in section 8.3 illustrate the establishment of a *dis*harmonic order, not a harmonic one. While some of these disharmonies have already changed to become harmonic with the rest of the language, it would be possible instead for the new, disharmonic rule to be extended to some other part of the language. In this way, construction reanalysis of one of the types discussed in section 8.3 may provide the germ of the eventual development of an entirely new word order type.

We must conclude that construction reanalysis does have an important role to play in word order change, but construction reanalysis may introduce or otherwise lead to disharmony, rather than harmony. The universal word order harmonies are not to be explained by a special principle, but rather by the familiar process of extension. We have been prevented from seeing this simple fact by the now long-standing assumption that word order is the result of phrase structure rules, with each individual order independent of every other. Once this assumption is discarded, the order of one dyad can be seen as related to that of another.

8.5.3   On the fixing of word order

As discussed briefly in section 8.4.1, Wackernagel (1892), Delbrück (1878), Bernecker (1900), and others showed that in Proto-Indo-European unaccented words were placed in second position in main clauses. It is now known that placing an atonic element in second position is widespread outside the Indo-European family as well. Kaisse (1985: 81) states the following principle regarding this:[42]

(67)   All language[s] with S^1 clitics place those clitics in second position, after the first stressed constituent (or word) of the clause, regardless of the category of that constituent (or word).

Kaisse goes on to suggest that this is part of a more general principle of clitic placement, first stated in Zwicky 1977.

(68)   Clitics whose source is within a particular constituent move . . . to one of the margins of that constituent or to the head of that constituent (the N or the V).

Which elements are atonic varies considerably from one language to another, though not without limit. Zwicky (1977) points out further that any member of a closed class may become unaccented and is thus subject to cliticization, hence to second position placement.

Placement in second position is a prosodic rule, but it can become a syntactic rule. Second position placement, or indeed any synchronic prosodic placement rule, becomes syntactic, and word order may become fixed, when either of two changes occurs:

1   the prosodic condition that determines which elements would be placed according to (67) or (68) is reanalyzed as a category condition, or other syntactic condition; or
2   the prosodic definition of the position in which clitics occur is reanalyzed as a syntactic definition.

Examples are given below. A further possible cause of a fixing of order is that the element that occupies the prosodically conditioned position ceases to satisfy the prosodic condition but nevertheless continues to be placed there, but we know of no examples of this type.

German provides an example of change 1. In main clauses in Proto-Indo-European, auxiliaries and perhaps other short verbs were unaccented and were placed in Wackernagel's position, with other verb forms in the unmarked position for verbs, clause-final. Later, in Germanic the originally prosodic condition on placement in Wackernagel's position was reanalyzed as a syntactic condition, and all finite verbs (auxiliaries and other finite verbs) came to occur in second position, even though the finite verb forms other than auxiliaries were accented. As a result of this reanalysis, placement in second position was no longer conditioned prosodically, but on the basis of category (finite verb form). The second position order of verbs was fixed and syntactic.

South Slavic languages provide an example of change 2. In Serbo-Croatian the future, past or perfect, pluperfect, and future perfect tenses are all formed with auxiliaries. The auxiliaries were or became atonic, and were placed in second position. The position of the auxiliary is dependent upon the prosodic principle of placing unaccented words after the first accented word, as seen by the fact that in (69) the affirmative auxiliary, which is atonic, is in second position, while in (70) the negative auxiliary, which is tonic, is not in second position:

(69)   jâ   sam   mu   se   vèć   (bȉ-o)   prèdstavi-o
        I.NOM I.have him.DAT self.ACC already been-M.SG introduced-M.SG
        "I have already introduced myself to him."

(70)   jâ   mu   se   jȍš nî-sam   prèdstavi-o
        I.NOM him.DAT self.ACC yet neg-I.have introduced-M.SG
        "I have not introduced myself to him yet."   (de Bray 1980: 297)

As a strictly prosodic principle, second position placement of the atonic auxiliary sometimes interrupts a complex constituent, as in (71).

(71)   grešnik je   i   nevaljalac   bio od   svog prvog koraka[43]
        sinner he.has and good.for.nothing been from his first step
        "He has been a sinner and a good-for-nothing from his first step."
        (Bennett 1987: 272, quoting from the Serbian translation of Cankar's *Bela kri-*
        zantema, originally written in Slovene)

In (71), *grešnik i nevaljalac* "[a] sinner and [a] good-for-nothing" is a constituent, interrupted by the auxiliary *je*; other constituent types can also be interrupted (Bennett 1987: 273). Thus, in Serbo-Croatian, second position placement is a prosodic rule.

Bennett (1986, 1987) shows that Slovene, closely related to Serbo-Croatian, has innovated by placing unaccented words on a syntactic, rather than prosodic basis. As a consequence, in Slovene auxiliaries are generally placed to avoid interrupting a constituent, as in (72), the Slovene original from which (71) above was translated:[44]

(72)   grešnik in   maloprida   je   bil že   ob svojem
        sinner and   good.for.nothing he.has been already at his

        prvem koraku
        first step   (Bennett 1987: 271)

Here the auxiliary *je* follows the complex constituent "[a] sinner and [a] good-for-nothing," rather than interrupting it. Thus, in Slovene, auxiliaries are now placed on a syntactic basis, and this aspect of the order is fixed.[45]

The fixing of prosodic word order is not limited to second position. Heavy constituents are especially likely to occur in final position universally (Hawkins 1983: 98–9), and objects are more likely to be heavy because they often represent new information, which may need to be modified, making it heavy. For this reason, objects were often in final position in early English, and this position became fixed (Stockwell 1977; Faarlund 1990b: ch. 3). England (1991) shows that Proto-Mayan had basic VOS order and that objects were moved to final position if they were syntactically complex or if they satisfied another language-particular rule. In some Mayan languages, such as Mam, Tektiteko, and Awakateko, final position of the object was fixed, and today VSO is the basic order in those languages.

Just as prosodically defined positions can be reanalyzed as syntactically defined and can be fixed, pragmatically defined positions can also provide a basis for fixing of word order through reanalysis. Certain positions are favored by many languages for constituents with particular pragmatic roles. For example, clause-initial position is often reserved for topics, or less often clause-final position. Clause-initial position may alternatively be the position for the focused constituent in some languages, while preverbal position is used for this purpose in others (some examples are Hungarian – Kiss 1987; Korean and Armenian – Comrie 1988: 268–71; Mayan languages – Aissen 1992; and Tsova-Tush – Holisky, in press). While placement in a pragmatically determined position is a synchronic rule (or rules), the construction may be reanalyzed and syntactically fixed. Pragmatic order becomes syntactic and fixed when the following change takes place:

3   the pragmatic condition (role) that determines which elements would occur in the position specified is reanalyzed as a condition referring to a grammatical relation or other syntactic category.

An example of the fixing of topic position comes from English. It is widely accepted that in English SOV order was replaced by SVO order, and the latter became fixed. The change of word order and the fixing of word order are distinct processes, though probably related in this instance. SVO became a frequent order for main clauses in all Germanic languages because of Wackernagel's Law, described above in section 8.4.1, and because of the process of placing topics in clause-initial position, combined with an apparently universal preference for subject topics. At the same time the propensity to postpose heavy constituents worked to postpose objects, again on a synchronic basis. These changes together brought about the greater number of instances of SVO order but did not, in and of themselves, result in fixed order.

Fixed order in English was the result of a distinct change or changes, re-analysis of the *basis* on which this SVO order came about. Clause-initial position was earlier assigned on the basis of topicality and was only statistically correlated with the grammatical relation subject. The condition determining which constituent was placed in clause-initial position was subsequently re-analyzed as a condition determined by subjecthood.[46]

Comrie 1988 has argued that an earlier stage of Armenian placed focus in preverbal position and that in Modern East Armenian word order for this position has been fixed ("syntacticized"). It is known that universally question words and negatives occur in focus position, if the language has a specific focus position (Heine and Reh 1984: 178). In Modern East Armenian question words and negatives continue to occur in immediately preverbal position, as in (73):

(73)   (a)   Petros-n   inč'   e   utem?
               Peter-DEF   what   is   eating
               "What is Peter eating?"

        (b)   Petros-ə   č'-i   utum   xənjor-ə
               Peter-DEF   not-is   eating   apple-DEF
               "Peter is not eating the apple."   (Comrie 1988: 270)

However, other constituents when focused do not have to occur in immediately preverbal position. Evidence of this is that either sentence in (74) can answer the question "What did Peter eat?"

(74)   (a)   Petros-ə   mi   xənjor   kerav
               Peter-DEF   a   apple   ate

        (b)   Petros-ə   kerav   mi   xənjor
               Peter-DEF   ate   a   apple
               "Peter ate an apple."   (Comrie 1988: 269)

On this basis it is argued that the position that formerly functioned as focus position has been reanalyzed, such that only those constituents that regularly occurred there are now placed there obligatorily. No doubt a study of the millenium-and-a-half-long history of Armenian syntax would help to clarify this, if only to confirm that it is stable over a long period of time. Nevertheless, it is clear that reanalysis of a condition on a position, here the focus condition on preverbal position reanalyzed as a category position, can result in fixed order.

8.5.4   Implications for synchronic syntax

The facts of word order change raise an important problem for synchronic syntax and linguistic theory generally. A grammar that generates each constituent separately in a particular order, as by means of the phrase structure rules of classic transformation grammar, cannot easily and elegantly make the simple generalization behind a sweeping word order change such as that described above for Georgian. Because such a grammar states the order of each constituent independently of that of every other, and for specific categories, rather than for head and dependent generally, these facts are not easily related. A grammar that treats main verbs as heads cannot include VAux/ AuxV orders in the generalization stated in (46). In contrast to both, a grammar which generates elements without regard to order and places words by general rules, and which treats auxiliaries as heads can easily make both generalizations. For example, the first could be stated as (61), repeated here, though for the attested change in Georgian there would be a few exceptions on each side of the arrow:

(61)   H D $>$ D H

On the other hand, it is clear that for some languages, such as English, a rule such as (66) would require so many exceptions that it would fail to capture any generalization. It appears that some languages, such as English, order elements individually by specific categories, while others, such as Georgian, include broad generalizations, such as that stated in (65). Such facts suggest that theoretical syntax needs to take such differences into account, not only diachronically, but also synchronically.[47]

Although there are documented examples of reordering to non-adjacency, there are numerous observed examples of words that are reanalyzed as a constituent and are subsequently reordered to adjacency, and an account of the diachrony of word order would be incomplete without a statement of this observation. We state this as (75), which is, however, only a tendency and may, as we show in section 8.5.1.3, be reversed:[48]

(75)   *Constituency Principle*
        Words that form a constituent are placed in adjacent positions.

The common change of reordering to adjacency is a result of the force of (75), but examples such as English preposition stranding show that change can also override (75). The explanation for the Constituency Principle is probably ease of parsing (see, for example, Hawkins 1983); the explanation for the possibility of overriding it is not clear.

Both diachronic and synchronic facts reveal the need to recognize three types of rule of word placement, though some languages have no rules of one or another type:

(a)   *Relational word order rules* are rules that place constituents according to whether they are subject, direct object, verb, etc.

(b)   *Stylistic-prosodic rules* place constituents in certain positions, especially second and final, according to whether they are stressed, whether they are heavy, and other related criteria.

(c)   *Pragmatic rules* place focused or topicalized constituents in positions defined for that pragmatic role in a particular language.

An additional principle has been suggested in the literature, namely that subject precedes object, or more animate precedes less animate, or agent precedes patient. Tomlin (1986) has argued for this principle on a typological basis, as a way of accounting for the fact that VSO, SVO, and SOV are all more common among natural languages than any sequence in which O is ordered before S. Byrne and Davidson (1985) argue for this as a natural ordering on the basis of child language acquisition.

Actually, the facts stated above already entail a statistical preference for S-O ordering (VSO, SVO, or SOV) for the following reason. It is well known that subjects are the most common topics,[49] and that first position is the favored topic position. The object is statistically more likely to introduce new information; nominals are more likely to be described on first introduction, and description makes them heavy. Because they are often heavy, objects are more likely to be postposed. Both the likelihood of subject preposing and the likelihood of object postposing contribute to S-O being a common order. Because in languages with "free" word order S-O will occur more commonly, this positioning is more likely to be grammaticalized than is O-S order.

8.6   Summary: types of word order change and their causes

In the last few decades, work on word order change has concentrated exclusively on changes in the order of subject, object, and verb, and the orders of correlated dyads. Regarding these, we have suggested that word order harmony results from extension, a very common diachronic process that simplifies a grammar (section 8.5.2). The simple rules that result from extension, such as (65)–(66), are preferred from the point of view of ease of processing and ease of acquisition. Several researchers, notably Kuno (1974), Frazier (1985), and Hawkins (1990), have proposed that word order correlations are ultimately due to ease of processing. Kuno (1974) has shown that center embedding is difficult to process and that, for some dyads, unharmonious ordering results in center embedding: for example, in an SOV language with relative clauses following head nouns, relative clauses on either the subject or the object would be center-embedded; beyond one embedding this is very difficult to process. Hawkins (1990) has proposed a principle of Early Immediate Constituents, which has the effect that consistently left-branching or consistently right-branching trees are easier to process. We assume that it is considerations of this sort that are the ultimate explanation of changes towards word order harmony as well.

We have suggested that word order harmony in a language may be altered by construction reanalysis (section 8.3). That is, construction reanalysis may introduce into a language a dyadic order that is not harmonic with other dyads of the same type or with dyads of different types. When this occurs, the order of an existing dyad may be extended to the new dyadic order, making the new harmonic with the older; or the new dyadic order may be extended to an existing dyad. The latter may form the basis for a sweeping change in the order of dyads throughout the language, or it may apply to a single dyad.

A number of other types of word order change are also of interest. First, reanalysis often results in discontinuous constituents, and this is generally followed by a reordering to adjacency because of the Constituency Principle (sections 8.5.1.1–8.5.1.2). Reordering to non-adjacency may also occur, generally for prosodic or stylistic reasons (section 8.5.1.3). The fixing of word order is a distinct type of change concerning word order; specific causes of this are discussed in section 8.5.3, including reanalysis of the prosodic condition that determines which elements would be placed according to prosodic rules, reanalysis of the prosodic definition of the position in which clitics occur, and reanalysis of the pragmatic condition that determines which elements would be placed according to pragmatic rules. While the universal word order correlations pose a special challenge in the study of universal grammar, other aspects of word order are also of interest from a diachronic perspective.

9 *Alignment*

9.1 Introduction

In this chapter we treat changes in alignment and propose a universal which accounts for the strong limitations on possible alignment changes. In this work the term **alignment** is used to refer to the distribution of morphological markers or of syntactic or morphological characteristics; it is intended as a neutral way of referring to ergative, accusative, and other distributional patterns. The focus here is on the alignment of case marking. The alignment typology assumed is based on that established by Sapir (1917).[1] This includes the three types ergative, active(–inactive), and (nominative–)accusative, though Sapir did not use these names for them. Following Sapir, these may be represented as in table 9.1. We have added a further type in the same format, but the focus in this chapter is on the first three.[2] Table 9.1 represents the distributional definition of *ergative* alignment as a system having one marker, A ("absolutive case"), shared by the direct object and the subject of an intransitive, distinct from another marker, B ("ergative case"), used for the subject of a transitive. This may be illustrated from Andi, a language of the Daghestan (North East Caucasian) family, where the absolutive case has a zero marker.

(1)   voc:i   vuq'o
        brother.ABSL   came
        "The brother arrived."

(2)   voc:u-di   homoloyi   vuq'o[3]
        brother-Erg   comrade.Absl   brought
        "The brother brought his pal."   (Cercvaʒe 1965: 226)

(3)   imu-di   voc:i   vota
        father-Erg   brother.Absl   left
        "The father left the brother."   (Cercvaʒe 1965: 213)

In table 9.1 **active** is defined as an alignment in which one marker, A, is shared by the direct object and the subject of an inactive intransitive, while a second marker, B, is shared by the subject of an active intransitive and the

Table 9.1 *Some alignment types (after Sapir 1917)*

	Direct object	Subject of intransitive Inactive	Active	Subject of transitive
Ergative	A	A		B
Active	A	A	B	B
Accusative	A	B		B
Double oblique	A	B		A

subject of a transitive. Active verbs are generally volitional, under the control of the nominal that is subject; examples are "run," "chatter," "play," "dance." Inactive verbs may be (i) stative verbs, such as "exist" or "be sitting," (ii) changes of state, such as "become" or "wither," or (iii) dynamic non-volitional verbs, such as "close (intransitive)" or "flow." This case pattern is illustrated by Laz, a Kartvelian language, where a case (-*k*) traditionally called the "narrative" marks subjects of transitives (in (4)) and of active intransitives (in (5)), and another (-∅) occurs with direct objects (in (4)) and subjects of inactive intransitives (in (6)):

(4)   amu-k t'ufeɣi doxazyu
        he-NAR gun.∅ prepare
        "He prepared a gun."   (Asatiani 1974: 82)

(5)   joɣo-epe-k-ti   lales
        dog-PL-NAR-also bark
        "The dogs barked."   (Asatiani 1974: 44)

(6)   bee   dirdu
        child.∅ grow
        "The child grew."   (Asatiani 1974: 82)

Accusative alignment is found in systems where one marker, A ("accusative case"), marks just direct objects, while a second marker, B ("nominative case"), marks subjects of transitives and intransitives. This is illustrated by Russian, where the nominative case marks subjects, and the accusative marks direct objects:

(7)   on   pojmal ptičku
        he.NOM caught bird.ACC
        "He caught the little bird."

(8)   ptička   poletela
       bird.NOM   flew
       "The little bird flew off."

In the **double oblique** alignment, one case ("oblique") marks both the subject and the direct object of transitives, while the subject of intransitives is marked with a second case ("absolute"). This unusual alignment is illustrated from Rošani (of the Pamir branch of Indo-Iranian) and discussed further in section 9.4:

(9)   duf   xawrič-ēn um   kitōb x̄ēyt
       these.OBL boy-PL   that.OBL book read(PAST)
       "These boys read (past tense) that book."

(10)   dāδ   xawrič-ēn-an tar Xaraγ sat
       these.ABS boy-PL-3RD to Xorog go(PAST)
       "These boys went to Xorog."   (Payne 1980: 155)

It is well known that a language may have mixed alignment; for example, Laz has active nominal case marking and accusative verb agreement (Harris 1985: 52–5, 278–9), Choctaw has accusative case marking and active verb agreement (see Davies 1986). In this sense, the grammar seems to be able to treat the alignment of case and verb agreement distinctly, though there is some tendency for them to harmonize (Harris 1985: ch. 16). The alignment of one rule may likewise shift independently of the alignment of another, or both may change together. In this chapter, alignment shifts are approached as individual phenomena, affecting individual rules or small groups of rules, rather than as changes affecting an entire language.

Several types of "split" alignment have been found, and it has been noted that each is identified with a specific distribution: for example, some languages exhibit a split based on tense or aspect, where ergative case marking (or its reflex) is used with one aspect and accusative case marking with another. Dixon (1979: 95) states:

(11)   If a split is conditioned by tense or aspect, the ergative marking is *always* found either in past tense or in perfect aspect.

A second type of split involves the nature of the NP; this NP Hierarchy (Silverstein 1976) is here stated after Garrett (1990), for reference in the discussion in section 9.2.2 below.

NP Hierarchy

| bound morphemes | > | 1st and 2nd person pronouns | > | 3rd person pronouns or demonstratives | > | human nouns | > | animate nouns | > | inanimate nouns |

Regarding the NP Hierarchy, it has been noted that accusative alignment is associated with the left of the hierarchy, and ergative alignment with the right. Thus, if a given category of substantive on the hierarchy makes a morphological distinction between ergative and absolutive, then every substantive to its right does so also; and if a given type of substantive on the hierarchy makes a morphological distinction between nominative and accusative, then every substantive to its left does so also.

A third type of split in alignment involves a distinction between main and subordinate clauses, such that one alignment type is found in main clauses in a language, and another alignment type in subordinate clauses. Here, however, there is no universal distribution. In Sierra Popoluca, a Zoquean language, agreement is ergative in main clauses of most types and accusative in embedded clauses of most types (Marlett 1986: 362–5; see Austin 1981a for an example from Australia). On the other hand, some Cariban languages, such as Carib of Surinam and Carijona (Gildea 1992) have accusative verb agreement and word order in main clauses and ergative verb agreement and word order in subordinate clauses.

It may be noted that active and other types of alignment have been incompletely integrated into the study of universals such as those stated in (11) and the NP Hierarchy 1. In spite of some particular studies regarding other alignments in specific languages, most studies have concentrated on the accusative and ergative types, and these are consequently better understood.

In section 9.2, we examine the origins of these alignment splits and the universals of origins of alignment change. In section 9.4 we look at a universal governing change in alignment.

9.2   Origins of alignment change

9.2.1   Reanalysis of passives
The most dramatic examples of alignment change take place through reanalysis. Probably the best-documented change of this type is the reanalysis of perfective passives as involving ergative alignmnent. Iranian languages provide an example of passive-to-ergative (or accusative-to-ergative) reanalysis (see Allen 1950; Matthews 1952; Anderson 1977, 1988; Payne 1979; Pirejko 1979; Bynon 1980; Bubenik 1989b). In Old Persian inscriptions, the inherited Indo-European case alignment was still intact, with all subjects assigned the nominative case and all direct objects the accusative. This is illustrated in (12).

(12)   (a)   adam -šam   xšāyaθiya āham
               I.NOM-them.GEN king.NOM I.be
               "I was king of them."   (Darius the Great, *Behistan*, I, 14)

(b) adam   kāram   Pārsam   frāišayam
I.NOM army.ACC Persian.ACC I.send
"I sent forth a Persian army."   (*ibid.*, III, 1-2)

In the same inscriptions are examples of the perfect passive participle used predicatively in the past tense, as in (13):

(13)   avaθā-šam   hamaranam   kartam
then-them.GEN battle.NOM.NEUT.SG do.PERF.PTCPL.NEUT.SG
"Then the battle was fought by them."   (*ibid.*, II, 69)

(Examples (12) and (13) cited by Payne 1979: 436–7.) In (13) and other examples, the participle agrees in gender and number with the subject derived by passivization. The agent is in the genitive, in this example expressed as a clitic pronoun. In this example, "battle" is the underlying direct object and surface subject, while -*šam* "them" is the underlying subject and surface oblique. In glossing (12)–(13) we have followed Payne (1979), but it should be noted that the case marking is not particularly clear. Case marking in the pronouns is clear; this can be seen from the example of the first person.[4] The nominative, as in (12a, b) was *adam*, whereas the first person singular genitive, as seen in (37) below, was *manā*. The similarity of the case markers may have been one of the causes of the reanalysis.

The perfect passive participle construction, exemplified by *kar-ta-m* in (13), was later reanalyzed, and this brought about the following changes in the grammar. (i) A new rule of case marking is introduced for the past-tense system only (case alignment has been reanalyzed as ergative). We might say that the reflex of the Indo-European nominative case is nominative–absolutive (absolutive in past tenses, nominative in others), while the reflex of the genitive is genitive–ergative (functioning as an ergative to mark transitive subjects in the past, and as a genitive in other contexts). (In addition, the genitive and accusative have fused, producing a genitive–ergative–accusative case.) (ii) A new rule of agreement is introduced for the past-tense system, for while verbs in the present tense continue to agree with their subjects, those in the past now agree with their absolutive arguments.[5]

This change is best understood if the nature of the verb is also taken into account. The Proto-Indo-European deverbal adjective in *-*to* naturally had passive interpretation with transitive verbs, but active with intransitives (e.g. *$b^h\bar{r}$-to-* "carried" [*$*b^h$er-* "carry"] vs. *mř-to-* "dead" [*mer-* "die"]). This form was reanalyzed as a perfective participle, part of the verb system, between Old and Middle Indic and Iranian (*-*to-* > -*ta-*), e.g. copula + *bhř-ta-* "has been carried," but copula + *mř-ta-* "has died" – the copula was often null. Throughout Middle Indic and Iranian, the transitive forms with passive participles were reinterpreted as active verbs, that is forms equivalent to (14a) were reanalyzed as (14b):

(14) (a) serpent-NOM.SG Indra-INST.SG kill-PARTICIPLE-NOM.SG
           "The serpent has been killed by Indra."

      (b) serpent-ABS.SG Indra-ERG.SG kill-PERF-NOM.SG
           "Indra has killed the serpent."

The correlation of perfective aspect and ergativity is a natural outcome of the passive meaning associated with the deverbal adjectives which are frequently reinterpreted as past participles, where those of transitive verbs have passive associations, and where passive is a common source of reanalysis to ergativity (Garrett 1990: 263–4).[6]

9.2.2   Reanalysis of antipassive (object demotion)

In some languages that had ergative case marking, an ancient object demotion construction has been reinterpreted, providing a second source of aspectual splits in alignment. This antipassive-to-accusative (ergative-to-accusative) reanalysis has taken place in Kartvelian languages.[7] The reflex of the ancient ergative marking is illustrated from Modern Georgian in (15) and (16):

(15) tamar   didi   mepe   iqʼo
      Tamar.ABSL great monarch.ABSL was
      "Tamar was a great monarch."

(16) deda-m   pʼerang-i garecxa
      mother-ERG shirt-ABSL washed
      "Mother washed the shirt."

In (15)–(16), the case names are those that are historically appropriate, though not usually used in the description of these languages. The object demotion construction was associated with the imperfective aspect;[8] it is illustrated in (17):

(17) deda   pʼerang-s recxavs
      mother.ABLS shirt-DAT washes
      "Mother is washing the shirt."

In (17), "shirt" functioned as an indirect object, bearing the indirect object case (dative) and originally conditioning indirect object agreement, no longer used. When the direct object, here *pʼerang-* "shirt," was demoted to indirect object, the verb became intransitive, and the subject was put into the case productively used for subjects of intransitives, here called the absolutive. When

an intransitive, such as (15), was put into the imperfective, only the form of the
verb changed; compare (18) with (15):

(18)   tamar   didi   mepe   aris
        Tamar.ABSL   great monarch.ABSL is
        "Tamar is a great monarch."

The constructions of the imperfective, (17)–(18), were reanalyzed as accusative alignment, with subjects in each marked with the "absolutive" and objects
with the dative. It should be noted that both the ergative alignment and the
aspectual nature of the split have undergone further changes in the modern
language. The reanalysis of the object demotion construction and other
changes associated with it are more completely described in Harris (1985: 151–
267).

Anderson (1988: 340–9) has pointed out that the correlation stated above in
(11) and long noted by linguists is in fact the secondary effect of changes such
as the passive-to-ergative reanalysis and the antipassive-to-accusative reanalysis. Perfectives are a frequent source for passives, and reanalysis of a passive
is a well-documented source for ergative alignment.[9] The object demotion
construction is associated with imperfective aspect or incomplete effect on
the object in a number of languages (see, for example, Comrie 1978: 362), and it
in turn is a well-documented source of accusative alignment. In each
instance, the reanalyzed surface pattern continues for some time to be associated with this aspect. Generalization (11) is not in fact an accurate universal
synchronically. The ergative alignment in the Kartvelian languages evolved
further to active alignment, and both the imperfective and the perfective paradigms also underwent change. The result is that in the modern languages
neither alignment can be associated exclusively with either aspect. While (11)
is not universally valid from a synchronic point of view, the kernel of truth it
still contains is due to the independent associations of passive with perfectiv-
ity and object demotion with imperfectivity.

9.2.3   Reanalysis of nominalizations
Gildea (1992) has shown that Proto-Cariban had nominative–accusative
agreement and no case marking of subjects or objects. Word order, like agreement, treated subjects of transitives and intransitives alike. In nominalizations, on the other hand, subjects of intransitives and direct objects were
treated alike; both were marked as possessors of the nominalization (i.e. genitives) by preposed word order. Subjects of transitive nominalizations contrasted with these in being marked with a special affix and in following the
nominalization in unmarked order. The structure of these nominalizations is

illustrated in (19), from one of the modern languages, Tiriyo (examples cited by Gildea 1992: 128, 129):

(19) y-itö-∅   se-pa   wai
      1-go-NMLZR want-NEG   1.be
      "I don't want to go." (lit. "I am not wanting my going.")

(20) . . . mahak-uya y-eri-∅-k
      mosquito-DAT 1-bite-NMLZR-INST
      " . . . (because of) my being bitten by mosquitos"

Here the subject of the intransitive in (19) and the object of the transitive in (20), both first person singular, condition the agreement prefix *y-* on the nominalization. The subject of the transitive in (20) is marked with the dative *-uya*. Because this groups together direct objects and subjects of intransitives and treats subjects of transitives distinctly, this pattern is ergative. When the absolutive nominal (subject of intransitive or direct object) is an independent substantive, no agreement shows up in the verb form; this is illustrated from Carib of Surinam (examples cited by Gildea 1992: 126):

(21) pandi:ia ∅-wotïxto-xpo   ipookoro
      flag   3-descend-PFCT.NMLZR following.it
      "It has been followed by the lowering of the flag." (Lit. "The flag's descending followed it.")

(22) ayaura   ∅-eta-xpo   ke   ï-'wa eero sukuusa
      your.words 3-hear-PFCT.NMLZR INST 1-by this I.know
      "Because your words have been heard by me, I know this."

This nominalization pattern, typical of Cariban languages, has direct objects ("your words" in (22)) and subjects of intransitives ("flag" in (21)) preceding the nominal, just as possessors of concrete objects do. Subjects of transitives (*ï-'wa* "by me" in (22)), on the other hand, are marked with a postposition, here - *'wa*, and follow the nominalization.

Gildea shows that in some languages of the family, a biclausal structure consisting of a nominalized complement of a finite copula in the matrix clause was reanalyzed as a monoclausal structure; this main clause structure continues the ergative agreement pattern of the nominalizations (examples from Pemóng cited by Gildea 1992: 188):

(23) i-tö-'pä
      3-go-PAST
      "He went."

(24) i-kä'pa-'pä-i-ya
      3-smear-PAST-3-ERG
      "He smeared him."

As in nominalizations, agreement affixes do not cooccur with independent substantives; this is illustrated in (25)–(26) from Makushi (examples cited in Gildea 1992: 196, 197):

(25)   to'   Ø-erepamî-'pî Ø-wanî-'pî
        3.PRO.PL Ø-arrive-PAST Ø-be-PAST
        "They had not arrived (before)."

(26)   paapa-ya   yei   Ø-ya'tî-pîtî-Ø
        father-ERG tree Ø-cut-ITER-UNIV
        "Father cuts the tree (repeatedly)."

As in nominalizations (21)–(22), in these finite main clauses, absolutives condition prefixal agreement in (23)–(24), but independent substantives in an absolutive relation in (25)–(26) have no agreement. In (24) the ergative nominal is marked in the verb form, while in (26) it is an independent substantive. The identification of main clauses in (25)–(26) with nominalizations is supported by a variety of evidence, including especially cognate morphology. Thus, Gildea (1992) has shown that ergative agreement in Cariban languages has its origin in the reanalysis of biclausal constructions consisting of a matrix verb and its nominalized complement.[10]

The Cariban languages provide additional counterexamples to (11) as a synchronic universal (Gildea 1992: 255–8). The variety of ergative/accusative splits in these languages further emphasizes the need to understand the origins in order to make sense of the synchronic distribution.

9.2.4   Reanalysis of instrumentals

Garrett (1990) has argued that in Anatolian and in the Gorokan subgroup of the Eastern Highlands family of Papua New Guinea ergative case marking originated through the reanalysis of null subject transitives with instrumentals. Example (27) illustrates the basis for reanalysis in Anatolian:

(27)   n=at   witen-anza   parkunuzi
        PTCL=3.SG.ACC water-ABL.SG pure.CAUS.PRES.3.SG
        "S/he purifies it with water."

As Garrett shows, the ablative with this type of neuter expressed the instrument, and it was this instrumental that was reanalyzed as an ergative, as in (27'), found in Hittite and other Anatolian languages:

(27')   n=at   witen-anza   parkunuzi
        PTCL=3.SG.ABS water-ERG.SG pure.CAUS.PRES.3.SG
        "Water purifies it."

Some problems with this analysis remain to be worked out.[11] Nevertheless, reanalysis of an instrumental in a null subject transitive appears to be a likely way for ergative alignment to gain a small foothold in a language. Garrett has shown that, if this analysis is correct, it would explain the diachronic origins of one part of the NP Hierarchy (p. 242). In particular, since only neuter nominals bore the special ergative case in Anatolian languages, this innovation would show how ergative case marking can enter the hierarchy on the right.

9.2.5 Reanalysis of topic copy pronouns

Proto-Daghestan (North East Caucasian) was a language with ergative case marking, and this is preserved in most of the daughter languages, including Tabassaran. But Tabassaran differs from other languages of the Daghestan family in having innovated a system of agreement with nominative–accusative alignment. In Pre-Tabassaran it became possible to encliticize to the verb a pronoun copy of a topic nominal. Subjects, both transitive (ergative case) and intransitive (absolutive case), are the most frequent topics, and hence they were copied most frequently onto the verb.[12] Eventually this copying became obligatory for subjects. This stage is preserved in the southern dialect of Tabassaran:

(28)   uzu   gak'wler   urgura-**za**
         I.ERG firewood.ABSL burn-I.ERG
         "I burn firewood."   (Magometov 1965: 201)

(29)   uzu   urgura-**zu**
         I.ABSL burn-I.ABSL
         "I burn, am on fire."   (Magometov 1965: 201)

The different forms of the endings in (28)–(29) preserve the ancient distinction between ergative (*za*) and absolutive (*zu*) forms of the pronoun "I." While this distinction is lost in the independent pronouns themselves in Tabassaran (*uzu* is synchronically both absolutive and ergative), it is preserved in the closest sister languages.[13] A non-subject topic may still be copied, occurring after the obligatory subject marking, as in (30).

(30)   uzu   uwu   bisura-**za-wu**
         I.ERG you.SG.ABSL catch-I.ERG-you.SG.ABSL
         "As for you, I catch you."   (Magometov 1965: 202)

In the northern dialect this agreement system has become entirely nominative–accusative,[14] having lost the distinction between the two types of verbal subject markers.

(31)   izu   bisnu-**za** ӡaq'a
         I.ERG catch-I bird.ABSL
         "I caught a bird."   (Magometov 1965: 198)

(32)   izu   t'irxnu-**za**
        I.ABSL fly-I
        "I flew."   (Magometov 1965: 197)

Thus, in the northern dialect of Tabassaran, agreement with nominative–accusative alignment has developed through the following steps: (i) pronominal copies of topics cliticized to verbs, preserving the case of the topic itself; (ii) with absolutive and ergative subjects most often the topics, topic copies were reanalyzed as obligatory markers of subject agreement, still preserving the ergative or absolutive case of the subject; (iii) the distinction between ergative and absolutive verbal subject markers was lost, and suffixal agreement in the northern dialect has nominative–accusative alignment.

If reanalysis of instrumentals accounts for the inception of ergativity at the right end of the NP Hierarchy, it says nothing about the inception of accusativity at the left end. The reanalysis of pronominal copies of topics in Tabassaran demonstrates one way that accusativity can be introduced into bound morphemes.

9.2.6   Reanalysis of other constructions

All of the changes described in sections 9.2.1–9.2.5 involve accusative and ergative alignment; as far as we are aware, the only active system whose origin has been identified is that in Kartvelian languages (Šaniʒe 1973: 472ff.; Nozaʒe 1974; Harris 1985: ch. 14). More subtle changes in active alignment systems have been described by Mithun (1991). The ergative-to-active transition is unlike others discussed here in that there is good evidence that it involved reanalysis of more than one construction. Among those reanalyzed were incorporations, such as that in (33), cognate object constructions, as in (34), and constructions with body part objects, as in (35):

(33)   da   c'q'aloba-q'o   mat   zeda
        and pity-make.3.SG   them   on
        "and he took pity on them"   (Mk. 6: 34Ad.)

(34)   nu uk'ue(y)   marxva-y   imarxet   čem tvis
        whether   fasting-ABSL fast.2.PL me for
        "whether you fasted (a fast) for me"   (Zak. 7: 5)

(35)   aɣixil-n-a   tual-ni   zecad
        look.up-PL-3.SG eye-PL.ABSL heaven.ADV
        "He looked up toward heaven."   (Lk. 9: 16)

These constructions have in common that they are formally transitive, but also have properties of intransitives (for details see Harris 1985: 333–42). Their transitivity led to their taking ergative case subjects, even after they were reanalyzed as simple intransitives. However, even these multiple sources do not fully explain the transition from ergative to active alignment in Kartvelian languages, since not all of the verbs that presently take the etymological ergative case appeared in one of the constructions in (33)–(35) or in the other contributing constructions. It is clear that after reanalysis of these constructions, the use of the ergative subject was extended to other verbs of the same general syntactic class, and the mechanism of extension is an important element in this alignment change (Harris 1985: 344–5).[15]

9.2.7   Alignment change through extension and borrowing

Some alignment changes have been effected through extension of an existing system. Dixon (1977) cites extension as the mechanism in a change in D^{y}irbal pronouns. More extensive changes have taken place in case alignment in the Pamir languages (Payne 1980), in some other Indo-Iranian languages (Bubenik 1989a: 208, 1989b), and in several Kartvelian languages and dialects (Harris 1985: 371–89). Some of these are discussed below in sections 9.4.2 and 9.4.3. It has often been suggested that an alignment type can be borrowed, and the existence of linguistic areas containing languages of different families with the same or similar alignment (e.g. India, the Caucasus) is *prima facie* evidence to support this. Nevertheless, most alignment change in contact also has an internal mechanism (see Heath 1978).

9.2.8   Does alignment originate in discourse?

Du Bois (1985, 1987) has studied the structure of clauses in discourse in Sacapultec, a Mayan language with ergative agreement. He found that in Sacapultec discourse most clauses contain only one full noun phrase, with zero noun phrases also very common. In transitive and intransitive clauses alike, the full NP that commonly occurs is the absolutive; ergative full noun phrases are very infrequent.[16] Du Bois refers to the strong tendency for absolutive full noun phrases to occur but not ergative full noun phrases as the "preferred argument structure" (PAS).[17] The PAS, he says, is "itself founded on characteristic patterns of *preferred information flow* in Sacapultec narratives" (1985: 349). This is manifested in the mention of new material (as opposed to old/given) as the subject of intransitives, as the direct object of transitives, and in various oblique roles, but not in the agent of a transitive.[18]

Du Bois claims further that the morphological ergativity in Sacapultec results from the PAS, the preferred information flow, and a principle of economy, representing absolutive agreement with a zero morpheme. He goes on to argue that grammatical relations in languages in general are shaped by "forces arising out of discourse" and consequently suggests that this is involved in the explanation of the rise of ergativity, of changes which result in ergative alignment within languages.

There is, however, no convincing evidence that there is any causal relationship between the ergative alignment and the discourse phenomena. If there does exist such a causal relationship, it may be in the other direction. That is, it is equally likely that ergative alignment may cause speakers of a language to structure clauses in discourse with a higher frequency of the absolutive. Du Bois does not propose a specific mechanism for the origin of the ergative marker in the verb, and thus his hypothesis, if correct, would be at best an incomplete picture of the origin of the ergative alignment in Sacapultec and in ergative languages generally.

There are, in addition, a number of practical problems with Du Bois' account of the discourse origins of ergativity. The actual paths known to have been taken in the development of ergativity in a number of languages are inconsistent with the expectations of Du Bois' thesis. To show this, we first repeat some of Du Bois' claims and then show why they are inconsistent with known historical developments. His PAS contains the following (S = subject of intransitive, O = direct object of transitive, A = agent/subject of transitive):

1	one lexical argument constraint (generally only one full NP is permitted per clause);
2	non-lexical A constraint (A is generally not filled with full lexical NPs);
3	one new argument constraint (only one new information/ first mention may be introduced per clause);
4	given A constraint (A's almost always represent only old/given information, not new/first mention) (Du Bois 1987: 829);
5	the factor of topic continuity links S with A more than with O (p. 842) (also, human referents are most topical and overwhelmingly occur in the roles S and A, but not O; S/A represents the preferred position for human mentions [p. 841]);
6	there is a conflict between the ergativity-oriented discourse patterning (packaging of information flow – constraints 1-4 above) and the pressures of topic continuity (constraint 5).[19]

We turn now to the example of one known origin of ergativity and how it relates to Du Bois' account. As we saw in section 9.2.1, one of the best-understood pathways whereby languages can acquire ergative alignment is the development from passive to ergative.[20] In Du Bois' terms, before the change we have the passive structure in (36a) (the order here of constituents is irrelevant):

(36)   (a)   S(logical O) V oblique-A (e.g. Mary was.hit by Jane)

By Du Bois' reckoning, the S of intransitives can be either old/given information or new information/first mention (p. 830), but in any case it would most likely be the topic. The oblique NPs pattern with S and O (and hence contrast with A as subject of transitives) "in several key dimensions" (p. 832); like S, they can introduce new information or refer to old/given information (p. 826). The change of such passive structures to ergative alignment is as in (36b):

(36)   (b)   O V ergative-A

(where O = former S of passive (36a), and ergative marker = former oblique marker of (36a), e.g. Mary[A B S] hit by-Jane[E R G]). In (36b) ergatively marked A has become a new argument of the core clause. However, this violates several of the expectations of Du Bois' hypothesis. First, the new A (from former oblique) is now the subject of the transitive verb and hence, by Du Bois' account, is expected to be non-lexical (constraint 2 above), though by Du Bois' count, S and oblique are roughly even as percentages of lexical mentions (S at 32.8, oblique at 31.1, contrasting with A at only 3.4; p. 837). The move from an expected lexical NP in obliques to the expected non-lexical A in the shift from passive to ergative goes against the grain of Du Bois' account. Second, the new ergative A (from former oblique) is expected to convey only old/given information (constraint 4 above), although the obliques in this regard pattern with S/O and can freely introduce new mentions/new information (p. 832). This change of oblique (potentially introducing new information) to A (prohibited almost totally from introducing new information), too, is contrary to what Du Bois' account would lead us to expect. The spirit of the first constraint above is blatantly violated by this change. From a construction (e.g. (36a)) with only one core clause NP argument, S (which can be new information and lexical), the shift to ergativity introduces two NP arguments to the verb (where the former oblique was very frequently lexical). The switch from only one NP (which guarantees constraint 1 with its single lexical NP) to the ergative structure with two possible NPs, both in their original roles easily exhibiting lexical NPs, is clearly not a direction of change predicted by Du Bois' account. Finally, given that topic continuity marking mostly goes along S/A lines, while obliques tend to pattern with S/O in several ways (as indicated above, constraint 5), again the expectation would be not for an oblique (with its S/O associations) to become an A (with its basic incompatibility with O).

In short, in all these ways, the fairly frequent shift from passive to ergative does not conform to what Du Bois' account would lead us to expect. Similar problems are found with the development of ergativity through reanalysis of instrumentals, the pathway described in section 9.2.4.

Du Bois' framework provides (as he mentions in a footnote on p. 845) no account of the most frequent kind of split ergativity, that of ergative alignment in past or perfective tense–aspect environments, but nominative–accusative alignment with non-past or imperfectives. We find this to be a serious short-coming. There is a straightforward account of the frequent typological asso-ciation of perfective aspect and ergativity which does not rely on discourse patterning (see sections 9.2.1–9.2.2).

Finally, the known history of Mayan languages points to an unpleasant cir-cularity in Du Bois' picture. As is now well demonstrated (Norman and Campbell 1978; England 1989, 1991), Proto-Mayan had VOS basic word order, with VSO for marked objects, that is, objects occurring under the three condi-tions: (a) complex objects (when the object of a transitive contained a relative clause or consisted of coordinately conjoined NPs, all or part of that object underwent right-dislocation to facilitate processing); (b) animacy (when both the subject and object of a transitive were equal on the animacy hierarchy, both human or both animate for example, the order was VSO; when the subject of a transitive was higher than the object on the animacy hierarchy, then the order was VOS); and (c) definiteness (VOS occurs when the subject of a transitive is definite and the object indefinite; VSO occurs when both the subject and the object of a transitive are definite). K'ichean (Quichean) languages (the Mayan subgroup of which Sacapultec is a member) have a constraint against basic VOS order under one condition; they require VSO when the object is definite and the subject of the transitive is indefinite. Some K'ichean languages are con-strained further, permitting no indefinite subjects of transitives, regardless of the definiteness of the object. As England points out, K'ichean has, in effect, grammaticalized Du Bois' PAS by making the constraint against indefinite subjects of transitives, which prohibits VOS orders with indefinite (= new) sub-jects, part of the syntax and not just sensitive to pragmatics and discourse structure. However, if the syntax of Sacapultec, as a K'ichean language, prohi-bits the very structures Du Bois' perferred argument structure is intended to select against, then we must ask, is there any basis for postulating the PAS? While it is possible that the syntactic rule came into existence as a reflex of the pragmatic, discourse-based PAS, it is also possible that the PAS is an artifact of the analysis, that it follows directly from the nature of Sacapultec syntax. That is, given that there is a syntactic constraint in the language to the effect that subjects of transitives must be definite and hence represent old/given information, we must ask whether there really is an ergative bias in discourse structure, as Du Bois claims, or whether what he perceives to be such is but a direct reflection of this syntax. For Du Bois' arguments to be persuasive, they would have to be made on the basis of other languages which do not have built-in syntactic features which make the results he considered PAS inevitable.

In summary, the discourse-based account which Du Bois offers does not account for known changes in ergative alignment. While portions of it may be headed in the right direction it does not form the basis of an adequate account. Much more work needs to be done on the structure of discourse in languages with rules of ergative, active, and other alignment types. Work done to date (see notes 12 and 18) is limited to ergative or accusative alignment. Some studies, such as Du Bois', are careful and complete, but concentrate on a single language, which may have idiosyncratic features. Others are merely impressionistic. Existing studies reach contradictory conclusions. We know of no study that provides data from a sufficiently diverse cross-linguistic sample to reach any conclusions about the interaction of alignment with discourse.

9.3 Consistency in alignment

Some languages demonstrate relative consistency of alignment type, while others are inconsistent in this regard. Although alignment may be relevant to some other syntactic and morphological rules, in this discussion we limit our attention to case marking and agreement, rules where the alignment can be easily discerned. The issue is whether, in languages with inconsistent alignment, the alignment of one rule in a language changes to be consistent with the alignment of another rule in that language.

A number of the languages in which case marking has undergone change in alignment have no agreement and therefore offer no evidence relevant to the issue of consistency.

Some changes in alignment by reanalysis involved changes in the alignment of both case marking and agreement. This is true, for example, in the reanalysis in the Indo-Iranian languages, where both agreement and case marking took on ergative alignment through a single reinterpretation (see Payne 1980: 151–2, and section 9.2.1 above). Example (37) illustrates the once passive construction, which was reanalyzed as ergative:

(37) ima   tya   manā   kartam
      this.NOM.NEUT.SG what.NOM.NEUT.SG me.GEN done.NOM.NEUT.SG

      Parθavaiy
      Parthia.LOC

      "This is what was done by me in Parthia."
                    (Darius the Great, *Behistan*, III, 10, cited by Payne 1980: 151)

Before reanalysis, the derived subject of the passive conditioned agreement; after reanalysis, this nominal – now direct object at all levels – continued to condition agreement. As a result, agreement took on ergative alignment. This,

Table 9.2 *Case-marking changes in the Pamir subgroup (after Payne 1980: 152)*

	Transitive past			Transitive present			Intransitive past	
Old Iranian	S	O	V	S	O	V	S	V
(ergative)	[obl]	[abs]	[active]	[abs]	[obl]	[active]	[abs]	[active]
Pamir	S	O	V	S	O	V	S	V
(double oblique)	[obl]	[obl]	[active]	[abs]	[obl]	[active]	[abs]	[active]

then, is not change towards consistency, in the sense intended above; the case and agreement changed together, rather than one changing to be consistent with the other.

While the changes mentioned above provide no evidence relative to the issue addressed here, the question can be studied in changes that took place in the Pamir subgroup of Iranian languages. The changes described in the preceding paragraph resulted in a system which Payne (1980) represents as in the first line of table 9.2. After the creation of the ergative system, the Pamir subgroup further changed the system. In Old Iranian, as in other Indo-Iranian languages, ergative case marking and agreement were used in the past tense, while the inherited accusative case marking and agreement occurred in other tenses. The case Payne labels "absolute" is the reflex of the nominative case, while the "oblique" is a syncretic form of the inherited genitive and accusative. In Pamir, the rule that formerly assigned the oblique case to the object in the non-past was extended to assign that case to the object in the past as well.[21]

The agreement system in the past also changed in Pamir, but not by the same mechanism. Agreement in the non-past is the direct reflex of the inherited system; conditioned by the subject, it is marked by means of verbal suffixes. Agreement in the intransitive past is also with the subject; this set of agreement markers is derived from present forms of the cliticized copula. Transitive past verb forms also agree with subjects; these markers are reanalyzed forms of the genitive pronoun and are enclitic to a constituent that precedes the verb.[22] Although these three sets of agreement markers each has a different source, they are very similar. Agreement in the past tenses is not (yet) of a canonical type, since the markers themselves are different; nevertheless they all mark agreement with the subject, and thus may be considered to have (non-canonical) accusative alignment.

Can these changes be considered harmonic? The changes did not establish

Table 9.3 *Case-marking in Orošori (after Payne 1980: 167)*

	Transitive past			Transitive present			Intransitive past	
Orošori	S	O	V	S	O	V	S	V
(accusative)	[abs]	[obl]	[active]	[abs]	[obl]	[active]	[abs]	[active]

harmony within the past tenses, since case marking is of the double oblique type, while agreement is accusative. On the other hand, the changes in agreement in the past tenses did establish a kind of harmony with agreement and case marking in the non-past.

Some Pamir languages have made additional changes. Orošori, for example, has extended the case-marking system of the present tense to the past and has melded the two sets of past-tense agreement markers to make a single system (still not identical to that of the present tense). The case marking is indicated in table 9.3, parallel to table 9.2. Thus, case marking and agreement in both sets of tenses have the same alignment.

The Pamir languages provide evidence of a pull towards intra-rule harmony, but not towards inter-rule harmony. That is, agreement in the past changes to be like that in the present, and case marking in the past changes to be like that in the present; and there is no evidence of any pull towards harmony between case marking and agreement in the past tenses. When case and agreement change to the Pamir stage, they go in opposite directions: case marking in the past changes from ergative to double oblique; agreement changes from ergative to accusative. This does not give the appearance of change that arises because of consistency, but the evidence is difficult to interpret because of the separate issue of consistency between subsystems (present and past).

In the Kartvelian languages several changes in the alignment of case marking have taken place, but agreement has not developed alignment harmony with case marking. The case changes took place before first attestation, 1,500 years ago for Georgian, and no change in alignment of agreement has occurred in the attested period. These languages, like the Pamir languages, provide evidence that the pull towards consistency between subsystems (here the so-called Series I and Series II) is stronger than that between rules (case marking and agreement), though it is not clear that this is universal.

It is known that changes away from consistency can occur (see section 9.2.5 for an example).[23] Although the data are somewhat difficult to interpret, there

Table 9.4 *Hypothetical example of alignment change*

	Direct object	Subject of intransitive		Subject of transitive
		Inactive	Active	
Before change:				
Active	A	A	B	B
After change:				
Accusative	A	*B*	B	B

is no firm evidence that alignment changes in order to be consistent with the alignment of another rule.[24]

9.4   A universal of alignment change

9.4.1   The Complementarity Principle

Examining a number of changes in alignment, we find that shifts of some sorts occur, while others do not. Scanning the distributional definitions in table 9.1, we see that a shift in the marking of a single grammatical relation would result in change of type. For example, if the marking of the subject of an inactive intransitive in a system with active alignment shifted from marker A to marker B, this would constitute a change from the active type to the accusative type, as shown in table 9.4, following Sapir's format. The system after the change, marked "Accusative," is equivalent to the accusative system in table 9.1. While the simplest changes are of this sort, involving the marking of a single grammatical relation, in more complex changes the marking of more than one grammatical relation may be altered. In this chapter we refer to the grammatical relations whose marking changed as the **recipient relations**; in the hypothetical example of table 9.1, the subject of the inactive intransitive (which changed in marking) is the recipient relation. **Donor relations** is the term used here to refer to the grammatical relations which before the change already bore the marking that was adopted by the recipient relation; in the example above, the donor relations are the subject of the active intransitive and subject of the transitive.

It is noteworthy that these changes always involve donor grammatical relations that are, in an intuitive sense, closely related to those of the recipient grammatical relations. In the hypothetical example mentioned above, the two grammatical relations involved are of just this sort: the recipient, the subject of the inactive intransitive, seems related to the donor relations, the subjects of transitive and active intransitive verbs. One feels that, by virtue of all being subjects, these relations are related. In order to give more substance to this intuitive notion of relatedness, we must state this universal constraint explicitly.

In many common linguistic changes, there are similarities between the grammatical categories or functions that shift. In the particular case of alignment, it seems to be possible to make a precise statement of the nature of this similarity.

When we look at a number of case studies, we find that the donor and recipient grammatical relations may be the "same" in one of three ways in a change of alignment:[25] (i) they may be instances of the same grammatical relation under different linguistically characterizable circumstances; (ii) they may be different relations that are subsumed by a more inclusive relation, as in the example above, where the donor and recipients together constitute the relation, **subject**; (iii) they may be different grammatical relations borne by the same nominals at different syntactic levels. Since in each of these three instances the donor and recipient combine to form a whole, we will refer to the relationship between them as one of **complementarity**.

The observed universal may be stated informally as the Complementarity Principle.[26]

> *The Complementarity Principle*
> If in grammatical structures of language L, at time t_i, nominals N_x bear a grammatical relation R_j coded by marker C, and nominals N_y bear a grammatical relation R_k which is coded by D, where $C \neq D$ and D does not contain C, and if at time t_{i+1} in L nominals N_x and N_y are marked with marker C, then at time t_i, R_j and R_k are complementary with respect to N_y,
>
> where two relations, R_j and R_k, are complementary (stand in a relationship of complementarity) with respect to N_y if and only if (i) $R_j = R_k$, or (ii) R_j and R_k together constitute a superordinate relation, or (iii) nominals N_y bear both R_j and R_k, at different syntactic levels.

A marker D is said to **contain** a marker C if D consists of the phonological material of marker C plus additional material. This occurs commonly when a postposition takes a particular case; for example, if C is the genitive case and D is a postposition that takes the genitive, then the Complementarity Principle does not necessarily rule out any instance of D being replaced by C. Note that if C is a zero marker, then D necessarily contains C. Thus, it is possible for a postposition or case marker to be eroded or deleted, changing the system of case marking without violating the Complementarity Principle.[27]

The notion **grammatical relation** is here intended to include subject, direct object, and indirect object, or some specific subordinate or superordinate relation of one of these. This notion is further explored in section 9.4.3.1.

In the terms used above, R_j is the **donor relation**, while R_k is the **recipient relation**. According to the claim made here, an alignment change can occur only if the donor and recipient nominals are related in one of the three ways specified. Each of these three is examined in some detail below and examples are discussed; in the sections below, these three are referred to respectively as "conditions (i), (ii), and (iii)" on the Complementarity Principle.

The Complementarity Principle does not predict that change will occur. Nevertheless it has predictive value, in the sense that it specifies conditions which must obtain in order for change to occur. Thus, the Complementarity Principle is a statement of necessary conditions.

In this section we use the following terminology. A grammatical relation is **coded by** a marker C if C is the case or set of agreement markers **regularly** associated with that grammatical relation and serving to indicate it. While a grammatical relation is said to be coded by a marker, a nominal is said to be **marked with** it. In the statement of the Complementarity Principle, condition (i) can be true if the language has a split, according to which a given grammatical relation is coded by one marker under one set of linguistically specifiable circumstances and by another marker under another set of circumstances.

In the description of the notion of complementarity, we have left an important detail unspecified. It was not stated whether the two grammatical relations that are in a relationship of complementarity must be the only constituents of a more inclusive grammatical relation or whether they might be only two among several such constituents. These two ways of understanding complementarity correspond to a stronger and a weaker hypothesis concerning the universals of alignment change. We will here assume the position that the stronger hypothesis is correct, while bearing in mind that future research may show that only the weaker version holds.

This hypothesis states that, by virtue of condition (ii) (inclusion), it is possible, for example (as in table 9.4), for the subject of inactive intransitives to be the recipient of a marker from a donor that includes both the subject of transitives and the subject of active intransitives. Similarly, it would be possible for an indirect object to be a donor to a direct object recipient. The hypothesis similarly predicts that it is *not possible*, by virtue of inclusion (but see also section 9.4.3.1), for a subject (or any particular kind of subject) to be the donor of a marker to an indirect object recipient or vice versa. The stronger form of the hypothesis states that a donor/recipient relationship is impossible between the subject of transitives and the subject of inactive intransitives, but the weaker form would permit a change involving these grammatical relations.

The Complementarity Principle is discussed here in terms of case marking, but it applies equally to agreement. Within case marking, it constrains not only changes that affect case alignment, but also smaller changes in case marking, such as those discussed in section 9.4.5, and changes that leave the alignment intact.[28]

The statement that the donor grammatical relation and the recipient grammatical relation together constitute a grammatical relation is intended to apply to the grammatical relations in a general sense, but not necessarily to every nominal bearing such a grammatical relation. It is a commonplace of historical linguistics that changes leave **residue**. The fact that a handful of words may fail to undergo a phonological change for some particular reason does not mean that it is not valid to make a generalization that such a change occurred; syntactic changes may also have such residual exceptions.[29] However, this does not make the claims untestable. The issue addressed here is not whether all of the items in a category (here nominals bearing certain grammatical relations) were affected, but rather whether the two grammatical relations involved (the donor and recipient) were in a relationship of complementarity. In section 9.4.5 are discussed some specific changes where the nominals affected constitute a systematic subset of the recipients permitted by the Complementarity Principle.

9.4.2   The Complementarity Principle and extension in a syntactic split

9.4.2.1   Condition (i) on complementarity

As discussed briefly in section 9.2.7, one of the mechanisms which plays an important role in alignment changes is extension. By this mechanism, the functional scope of a particular case or agreement marker is enlarged. In extension, a case or agreement marker is assigned to more grammatical relations at a later stage than at an earlier stage.

The simplest case of complementarity, condition (i) above, occurs when the two grammatical relations under discussion are the same. In some languages the *same* grammatical relations may be marked with *different* cases under certain linguistically specifiable conditions. These conditions include the three types of alignment split described in section 9.1, splits originally conditioned by tense or aspect, the nature of the NP, or the main vs. subordinate status of the clause. It is clear that when any one of these situations occurs, a case-marking rule may be extended from one linguistic environment to another.

The Complementarity Principle makes specific predictions about the sorts of changes that could take place involving more than one such system of encoding. Let us consider a hypothetical situation that is not intended to correspond to any of the real situations named above or discussed below. Suppose

Table 9.5 *Hypothetical example, with two environments*

	Direct object	Subject of intransitive	Subject of transitive
Environment₁	A	A	B
Environment₂	C	D	D

that there are, in this language, two syntactically specifiable environments; these are labeled "environment₁" and "environment₂" in table 9.5. The two environments might be different tenses or aspects or a contrast of main to subordinate clause, as described in the preceding paragraph. It is *not* intended that these include the sort of phonological environment that might condition allomorphy. The capital letters represent cases, as in previous tables. The Complementarity Principle makes specific predictions about which alignment changes are possible in such a language and which are not possible. In considering what the specific predictions are, we must first clarify which grammatical relations are in a relationship of complementarity. According to the statements made in section 9.2, we consider two grammatical relations to stand in a relationship of complementarity if they are instances of the same grammatical relation under different syntactically characterizable circumstances. That is, in table 9.5, the direct object in environment₁ is in a relationship of complementarity to the direct object in environment₂. The subject of the intransitive in environment₁ is in a relationship of complementarity to the subject of the intransitive in environment₂, but not to the subject of the transitive in environment₂. Similarly, the subject of the transitive in environment₁ is complementary to the subject of the transitive in environment₂.

Thus, the Complementarity Principle predicts that in the hypothetical language described in table 9.5 the following alignment changes could take place under condition (i): (i) the direct object in environment₁ comes to be marked with case C; (ii) the subject of the intransitive in environment₁ comes to be marked with case D; (iii) the subject of the transitive in environment₁ comes to be marked with case D; (iv) the direct object in environment₂ comes to be marked with case A; (v) the subject of the intransitive in environment₂ comes to be marked with case A; (vi) the subject of the transitive in environment₂ comes to be marked with case B.

The Complementarity Principle rules out the following alignment changes in table 9.5: (i) the direct object in environment₁ comes to be marked with case D; (ii) the subject of the intransitive in environment₁ comes to be marked with

Table 9.6 *Alignment of case reconstructed in Proto-Pamir (following Payne 1980)*

	Direct object	Subject of intransitive	Subject of transitive
Present	OBL	ABS	ABS
Past	ABS	ABS	OBL

case C; (iii) the subject of the transitive in environment$_1$ comes to be marked with case C; (iv) the direct object in environment$_2$ comes to be marked with case B; (v) the subject of the intransitive in environment$_2$ comes to be marked with case B; (vi) the subject of the transitive in environment$_2$ comes to be marked with case A.[30]

In table 9.5, cases or agreement markers used in different environments are labeled with distinct letters. It is possible, however, that some of these may be the same; for example, A may be the same as C, or B may be the same as C, and in either instance there would be fewer exclusions. Since the Complementarity Principle refers only to diachronic innovations, it does not rule out the possibility that non-complementary relations be marked synchronically with the same form. For example, exclusion (v) does not rule out the possibility that B and D be the same synchronically.

9.4.2.2   Indo-Iranian examples

In part because the changes are actually attested, the Indo-Iranian languages are among the most discussed and best-understood examples of change in alignment. The discussion here is based on some of the languages of the Pamir subgroup of Iranian, and the facts are drawn from Payne (1980). Out of the relatively simple accusative case system of Old Iranian, most of the Iranian languages developed a complex system, where case markers are used in different patterns with different verbal categories. For the Pamir languages, Payne refers to the case that is a reflex of the Old Iranian nominative as the "absolute," and to that which continues the accusative as the "oblique";[31] we have used "absolute" and "oblique" to include the cases of which these are reflexes and have represented distribution of cases in a table following the format used above. Table 9.6 shows the alignment of Proto-Pamir.[32] In the daughter language Rošani, the modern case system is as indicated in table 9.7. In this and subsequent examples of case systems in modern languages, the cases of recipient nominals are italicized to make easier comparison with an earlier stage of the language. The change from the system of table 9.6 to that of table

Table 9.7 *Alignment of case in Rošani Pamir (following Payne 1980)*

	Direct object	Subject of intransitive	Subject of transitive
Present	OBL	ABS	ABS
Past	OBL	ABS	OBL

9.7 illustrates one of the shifts sanctioned under the Complementarity Principle. Under the influence of the case system used in the present, the direct object in Rošani came to be marked with the oblique, producing the pattern Payne refers to as "double oblique" (1980: 152, 155). This illustrates the extension of the marker of the direct object in one environment (present) to nominals bearing the same grammatical relation in another environment (past), one of the changes sanctioned by the Complementarity Principle under condition (i).

Orošori, with the case marking summarized in table 9.8, illustrates additional alignment changes. The changes from the system of table 9.6 to that of table 9.8 include the shift described above for Rošani. In addition, in Orošori the preposition *az* "from" has developed into a marker, *a-*, of the direct object. It is used with both the present and the past tense (Payne 1980: 167; see also page 161 on a related, but optional, development in Rošani). Under the influence of the present, Orošori has also replaced the oblique case for the subject of transitives in the past by the absolutive case. The resultant systems of Orošori are identical, and the two lines of table 9.8 could be combined into one.

Although the several changes in the Pamir languages provide examples of the kinds of shifts sanctioned by the Complementarity Principle, the fact that there are only two cases involved means that it is not really clear that these are examples of condition (i). We turn now to a group of languages in which the greater number of cases makes it clear that we are indeed dealing with condition (i).

9.4.2.3   *Kartvelian examples*

As already noted, in several Kartvelian languages, nominals bearing the *same* grammatical relations are marked with *different* cases according to the tense–aspect category of the verb of the clauses of which the nominals are constituents. The conditioning circumstances can be fully described in terms of sets of verbal paradigms, with one set traditionally called Series I, the other Series II.

Table 9.8 *Alignment of case in Orošori Pamir (following Payne 1980)*

	Direct object	Subject of intransitive	Subject of transitive
Present	(a)-OBL	ABS	ABS
Past	(a)-OBL	ABS	ABS

Table 9.9 *Alignment of case reconstructed in Common-Georgian-Zan*

	Direct object	Subject of intransitive Class 2	Class 3	Subject of transitive
Series I	DAT	NOM		NOM
Series II	NOM	NOM	NAR	NAR

As discussed in section 5.2.2, Laz, a member of the Zan branch of Kartvelian, derives its case marking from the Common-Georgian-Zan pattern represented in table 9.9 (see Boeder 1979; Harris 1985). The traditional names of the cases of these languages are maintained here, even though the names do not correspond closely to the actual functions. NOM represents the case usually called nominative, NAR the so-called narrative or ergative case, and DAT the dative case. The verbs characterized generally as inactive or active are also called Class 2 or Class 3, respectively, and are identified on a morphological basis. Table 9.9 is equivalent to table 9.10, with which subsequent charts can be more easily compared. The extension made by Laz had the result of bringing the two series under a unified single system of case marking, as shown in table 9.11. An intermediate stage attested in the Maxo dialect of Laz shows that the marking assigned to direct objects in Series I must have changed first (Harris 1985: 380–5). Since the direct object of Series I is in a relationship of complementarity to the direct object of Series II, the Complementarity Principle sanctions the latter being a donor to the former. Later, the narrative case was extended to Series I, coding the same relations in that Series as it had previously in Series II. Since the subject of the transitive of Series I is in a relationship of complementarity to that of Series II, and since the subject of the active intransitive of Series I is complementary to that of Series II, the Complementarity Principle sanctions both changes.

Table 9.10 *Alignment of case reconstructed in Common-Georgian-Zan*

	Direct object	Subject of intransitive Class 2	Class 3	Subject of transitive
Series I	DAT	NOM	NOM	NOM
Series II	NOM	NOM	NAR	NAR

Table 9.11 *Alignment of case in Laz*

	Direct object	Subject of intransitive Class 2	Class 3	Subject of transitive
Series I	NOM	NOM	NAR	NAR
Series II	NOM	NOM	NAR	NAR

Lower Ačarian, a dialect of Georgian, has undergone changes similar to those undergone by Laz, as well as to other changes undergone by Mingrelian, discussed below in section 9.4.3.3. Lower Ačarian further exemplifies the applicability of the Complementarity Principle; however, because it is less well documented, it is not discussed further here (but see Harris 1985: 376–80, 382–3).

9.4.3   The Complementarity Principle and simple extension

9.4.3.1   Condition (ii) on complementarity

Extensions may take place within a single system of case marking (or agreement) or within a language that has, before the change, more than one system of case marking (or agreement) in use in different linguistic environments. An extension that applies within a single system is here termed simple extension, and it is this type that provides examples of condition (ii) on complementarity. Condition (ii) itself is here also referred to as inclusion.

Examples of applicability of condition (ii) are the following. The two relations, direct object and indirect object, are in a relationship of complementarity because together they constitute the relation, object. The two relations, direct object and subject of an intransitive, together constitute the (secondary) grammatical relation, absolutive, and are thus in a relationship of complementarity. The two relations, subject of a transitive and subject of an intransitive, are in a relationship of complementarity because they constitute the relation, subject. The two relations, subject of an inactive intransitive and subject of an active intransitive, constitute the inclusive relation, subject of an intransitive, and thus they are in a relationship of complementarity. Other relations do not together constitute a superordinate relation; for example, subjects of transitives and direct objects do not constitute a recognized relation, nor do subjects of transitives and subjects of inactive intransitives (to the exclusion of subjects of active intransitives).

What is the principled basis for considering that some grammatical relations constitute a superordinate relation in universal grammar, while others do not? A superordinate grammatical relation, in the sense used above, is here considered to exist in universal grammar if cross-linguistic work in synchronic syntax has shown that relation to be recognized in a variety of ways by the syntax of numerous diverse languages. That is, if in diverse languages two (or more) grammatical relations pattern in significantly the same way, they may be considered to constitute a superordinate relation. For example, subjects of active intransitives and subjects of inactive intransitives, which are distinguished in languages with case marking of active alignment, pattern in the same way with respect to agreement in the Mayan languages, with respect to both agreement and case marking in many languages of the Daghestan family, with respect to agreement in languages of the North West Caucasian family, with respect to case marking in Eskimo, and with respect to either case or agreement or both in most indigenous languages of Australia. Subject of intransitive is therefore recognized here as a superordinate relation consisting of subject of inactive intransitive and subject of active intransitive. The notion subject plays a role in the syntax of many languages, including ones of the Finno-Ugric, Indo-European, and Semitic families. It is therefore here considered a superordinate relation in the sense defined above.

The Complementarity Principle predicts that either of the members of the complementary relationships listed above could be the donor, while the other could be its recipient: for example, the direct object could be the donor, and the indirect object the recipient, or vice versa. Similarly, the subject of transitives could be the donor, the subject of intransitives the recipient, with the marker of the former being extended to the latter; the reverse could also occur.

Condition (ii) on the Complementarity Principle rules out the possibility of certain other changes occurring: for example, the subject of a transitive could not by virtue of inclusion be the donor for a direct object recipient. Similarly, the marker of an indirect object could not be extended to a subject. These and

Table 9.12 *Reconstructed and actual case alignment in Wappo (after Li and Thompson 1976: 454–5 and Li, Thompson, and Sawyer 1977: 98–9)*

	Direct object	Subject of intransitive	Subject of transitive
Pre-Wappo	Ø	Ø	-i
Wappo	Ø	-i	-i

other changes ruled out through (i) or (ii) could, however, take place through reanalysis, via (iii).

9.4.3.2   Wappo
Li and Thompson (1976: 454–5) and Li, Thompson, and Sawyer (1977: 98–9) propose that the ancestor of Wappo may have had ergative case marking, with the ergative marker, -i, being extended to all subjects. While the authors agree that the evidence in the instance of Wappo is not substantial, a change of this sort seems plausible and not different in kind from better-documented shifts. We can summarize the change the authors propose in a chart modeled on Sapir's, as in table 9.12. The extension that these authors propose is from the donor grammatical relation, subject of a transitive, to the recipient, subject of an intransitive. The donor and recipient are in a relationship of complementarity by virtue of constituting the more inclusive relation, subject.

9.4.3.3   Mingrelian
A further example is provided by the change which took place in case marking in Mingrelian, the other member of the Zan branch of Kartvelian. The case marking reconstructed for this branch of the Kartvelian family is represented in table 9.10 above. In Mingrelian, series I was left intact, remaining as it was in Common-Georgian-Zan, table 9.10. In Series II, however, the narrative case was extended to subjects of Class 2 verbs, resulting in a system in which all subjects (in this series) are marked with the same case. It is clear that this is an accusative system according to the definition given in table 9.1. Case marking found in Mingrelian today may be presented as in table 9.13. Table 9.14 is equivalent to the simpler table 9.13. Although Mingrelian, both before and after the change, was a language with two distinct systems of marking cases, the change occurred within one, in the sense that the donor and recipient were clearly both in Series II. For that reason this change is discussed here as an example of simple extension. Nevertheless, it is clear that

Table 9.13 *Alignment of case in Mingrelian*

	Direct object	Subject of intransitive Class 2	Class 3	Subject of transitive
Series I	DAT	NOM	NOM	NOM
Series II	NOM	NAR	NAR	NAR

Table 9.14 *Alignment of case in Mingrelian*

	Direct object	Subject of intransitive	Subject of transitive
Series I	DAT	NOM	NOM
Series II	NOM	NAR	NAR

Series I provided a weak analogue for Series II, inasmuch as in Series I before and after the change and in Series II after the change, all subjects were marked with a single case (though different for the two series).

Before the change, the so-called narrative case marked the subjects of transitive verbs and of active intransitive (Class 3) verbs, as it does today in the other Kartvelian languages. After the change in Mingrelian, this marking was found also for the subjects of inactive intransitive (Class 2) verbs. Since these three subject relations constitute the more inclusive relation, subject, they stand in a relationship of complementarity by virtue of inclusion, even by the stronger of the conditions stated above. It is clear, then, that the Complementarity Principle sanctions the change described here.

9.4.4   The Complementarity Principle and syntactic levels
9.4.4.1   Condition (iii) on the Complementarity Principle
When we consider instances that involve more than one syntactic level, it is especially important to consider what is meant by a grammatical relation being coded by a marker, C. In a language like Latin, the grammatical relation, subject, is coded by the nominative case; the grammatical relation, direct object, is not coded by the nominative case. However, a nominal that bears the relation, direct object, may be marked with the nominative case if it is also the subject of a passive. This distinction between a given grammatical

relation being coded by a marker C and certain nominals that bear that grammatical relation at one level and another grammatical relation at another syntactic level being marked with C is crucial to our understanding of realignment involving more than one syntactic level (see also section 9.4.1).

9.4.4.2   Lardil

Klokeid (1978) describes a change in the alignment of cases in Lardil, a Pama-Nyungan language of Australia. Pre-Lardil, like most of the other Pama-Nyungan languages, had ergative case marking. It developed an object demotion construction, in which the underlying transitive direct object was realized as a surface indirect object under certain circumstances. The underlying direct object that underwent this productive synchronic rule was marked, as other surface indirect objects were, with the dative case. When the direct object underwent this synchronic rule, the resulting clause was intransitive. Its subject was marked, like the subjects of other intransitives, with the absolutive case. Several related languages, including Nyamal and Yukulta, retain a similar construction synchronically. In Lardil, however, the construction was reanalyzed, so that now the marking assigned to transitive direct objects is that originally used only for indirect objects. The names of cases used in table 9.15 do not reflect their current usage, but rather their origin; consequently these are not the names usually used in the synchronic description of Lardil. If one disregards the case name, "absolutive," and looks at the distribution in the abstract, as in table 9.1, it is clear that the current alignment is accusative (i.e. the "absolutive" of table 9.15 is now really a nominative, while the "dative" includes accusative in its functions). Thus, Lardil provides an example of a change from ergative to accusative alignment.[33]

In the change from Stage 1 to Stage 2 the markings of two grammatical relations – the subject of the transitive and the direct object of the transitive – were altered. In the first, the underlying subject of a transitive that was at the same time the subject of a derived intransitive was reanalyzed as simply the subject of a transitive (at all levels). Before the reanalysis, subjects of intransitives (as well as direct objects) had been marked with the absolutive case; it was by virtue of being the subject of intransitive object demotion constructions that the underlying subject of a transitive could be marked with this case. Let us consider how the Complementarity Principle applies to this shift. Before the change (time t_i) certain nominals (N_x) bore the absolutive relation (subject of intransitive + direct object, R_j), coded by the absolutive case (C); certain other nominals (N_y) bore the ergative relation (subject of transitive, R_k) and were not coded by the absolutive, but by the ergative (D). After the change (time t_{i+1}), both sets of nominals were coded by the absolutive. This

Table 9.15 *Change in case alignment in Lardil*

Stage 1 (Direct construction)			
	Direct object	Subject of intransitive	Subject of transitive
	ABSL	ABSL	ERG

Stage 1 (Object demotion construction)			
Underlying:	Direct object	Subject of intransitive	Subject of transitive
Surface:	Indirect object	Subject of intransitive	Subject of intransitive
	DAT	ABSL	ABSL

Stage 2 (Obligatory pattern)			
	Direct object	Subject of intransitive	Subject of transitive
	DAT	ABSL	ABSL

was possible because before the change the nominals that bore the ergative relation (N_y) (in underlying structure) also bore the relation, subject of an intransitive, (in surface structure) through the application of Object Demotion. Thus, nominals N_y bore both R_j and R_k at different syntactic levels.

The absolutive relation is the donor relation, since it was marked with the absolutive case before the change. The subject of the transitive is the recipient relation, since it was not marked with the absolutive case before the change, but was after. The donor and recipient relations are in a relationship of complementarity by virtue of being borne by one set of nominals at different syntactic levels.

In the other part of this change from Stage 1 to Stage 2, the underlying direct object that was at the same time the derived indirect object was reanalyzed as simply the direct object (at all levels). Before the reanalysis, certain nominals (N_x) bore the indirect object relation (R_j), encoded by the dative, /-intha/. A second group of nominals (N_y) bore the relation, direct object (R_k), which was not encoded by the dative, but by the absolutive. After the change, in Lardil both groups of nominals are coded by the dative case. This was possible because the second set of nominals, N_y, bore two grammatical relations: direct object in underlying structure and indirect object in surface structure. Thus before the change, N_y bore the same grammatical relation, indirect object, as N_x bears.

In this change, the indirect object is the donor relation, while the direct object is the recipient relation. The donor and recipient are in a relationship of complementarity by virtue of one set of nominals bearing both relations at different syntactic levels.

9.4.4.3 Kartvelian, Series I

Common Kartvelian, the reconstructed proto-language of the small Kartvelian, or South Caucasian, family, underwent a change similar to that in Lardil; this Kartvelian change was described in section 9.2.2. In Kartvelian languages the Complementarity Principle is satisfied in the same way as in Lardil, except that all relations involved in the change are limited to Series I.

9.4.4.4 Kartvelian, Series II

Subsequent to the change described in section 9.4.4.3, Series II changed in some of the Kartvelian languages. Relics of the situation before the change are best preserved in Old Georgian and Svan, and they point to several kinds of reanalysis, as mentioned in section 9.2.6. One of these instances of reanalysis is described here in the context of the Complementarity Principle.

In the incorporated object construction, the underlying direct object did not bear the grammatical relation, direct object, in surface structure. Lacking a surface direct object, the resulting verb form with incorporated object was intransitive, but it retained the narrative case, which also marked the subject with the corresponding verb and object when the latter failed to incorporate. Thus, for example, the incorporated form, *cq̇aloba-q̇o* "take pity (on)," required the same subject case as the unincorporated *q̇o cq̇aloba-y*, in the same meaning. In the reanalysis, the underlyingly transitive, surface intransitive verb was reanalyzed as simply intransitive (at all levels), and its form was changed slightly to indicate this. This can be represented schematically by means of table 9.16, which again uses the traditional case names.

In this instance, it is the subject of the transitive that was marked with the case in question, the narrative, before the change, and it is thus the donor. The recipient in this change is the subject of a small set of intransitive verbs. This set cannot be identified by general criteria, but must be listed, and the subject of verbs of this set do not constitute an identifiable grammatical relation. However, the reanalysis did not take place in isolation; a number of related changes also occurred.

Let us consider how the Complementarity Principle applies to this re-

Table 9.16   *Change in object incorporation in Pre-Georgian*

Stage 1 (Series II, Direct construction)

	Direct object	Subject of intransitive	Subject of transitive
	NOM	NOM	NAR

Stage 1 (Series II, Incorporated object construction)

Underlying:	Direct object	Subject of transitive
Surface:	(other)	Subject of intransitive
	(stem form)	NAR

Stage 2 (Series II, Obligatory pattern)

	Direct object	Subject of intransitive	Subject of transitive
	NOM	NOM/NAR	NAR

analysis. At an early stage (time t_i) in pre-Georgian, a set of nominals (N_x) were subjects of transitive verbs, a grammatical relation marked with the narrative case (in Series II). Nominals N_y were subjects of incorporated object constructions; these were transitive in underlying structure and intransitive in surface structure (Harris 1985: 333–6). The nominals N_y bore the grammatical relation, subject of an intransitive, a relation that was not originally marked by the narrative case. At a subsequent stage (t_{i+1}), both N_x and N_y were marked by the narrative case. This change was possible because the nominals N_y (subject of incorporated object constructions) bore two relations at once: underlying structure subject of a transitive, and surface structure subject of an intransitive. Thus, the change schematized in table 9.16, like other changes it combined with (Harris 1985: 330–42), is sanctioned by the Complementarity Principle.

9.4.5   The putative problem of the partial recipient
In some instances, only a specific portion of the nominals bearing the recipient relation is affected, although the Complementarity Principle would permit all nominals bearing this relation to be affected. This is referred to here as

the "partial recipient," and it may at first be perceived as a problem. In this section we first examine some actual changes of this sort and then, in section 9.4.5.2., discuss this as a problem for the Complementarity Principle. In some languages, such as Spanish, it is semantic properties of the nominals bearing the recipient relation that determine the scope of the change; in other languages, such as Hua, it is the subclass of the verb that delimits the change; in others, such as Rembarrnga, it is properties of the clause that determine the case marking of a nominal.

9.4.5.1   *Examples of partial recipients*

In Spanish the marker of the indirect object, the preposition *a*, was extended to marking just those direct objects that are both referentially specific and human (or perceived as having human characteristics).[34] The grammatical relations, direct object and indirect object, are in a relationship of complementarity by inclusion (condition (ii)); an extension of the indirect object marker to the whole direct object would thus be sanctioned by the Complementarity Principle. However, it was not the whole direct object that was affected, only a proper subset.[35]

In Hua (a Papuan language of New Guinea), reanalysis has led to the optional use of ergative case markers with the subjects of some intransitives, including ones that appear to be active, such as *fina-hu* "fight" (from the noun *fina* "fight"), and ones that appear to be inactive, such as *kmoru-hu* "be yellow" (from the noun *kmoru* "yellow flower") (Haiman 1980: 117–20; see also note 15 in the present chapter). Since transitive subjects, the nominals generally marked by the ergative case, and intransitive subjects are in a relationship of complementarity by inclusion, this change is sanctioned by the Complementarity Principle. Note, however, that it is only some of the active intransitives and some of the inactive intransitives that may optionally take ergative subjects. In Hua, the ergative is also permitted with vocative subjects of imperatives and with subjects of auxiliary + main verb complexes (Haiman 1980: 361–2). Garrett (1990: 281, n. 29) argues that this is a secondary development. Note that, while not all subjects in Hua have been affected, it is only subjects that are affected and not, for example, direct objects.

In Rembarrnga (Australia) subjects of intransitive verbs may be marked with the ergative suffix under certain circumstances; for example, if a verb has an indirect object, or if the verb usually takes an indirect object, its subject may be in the ergative case (McKay 1975: 276–7; see also 1975: 255). We assume that the two uses of the ergative are historically related. Regardless of the direction of the change, the donor and recipient are in a relationship of complementarity by inclusion. If the ergative case spread from the subject of transitives to this subset of subjects of intransitives, then this is an additional example of a partial recipient.[36]

9.4.5.2   *Partial recipients as a problem for the Complementarity Principle*

In this discussion we use the Spanish change described above in section 9.4.5.1 as our example. The Spanish change does not violate the Complementarity Principle, for that statement requires only that there exist a relationship of complementarity between the donor grammatical relation (R_j, here the indirect object) and the grammatical relation of the recipient (R_k, here direct object). It is not stated that the affected nominals must include all those bearing the recipient grammatical relation. This is not a "trick" of wording, but is entirely consistent with the spirit of the proposal. It is true in the Spanish example that inanimate direct objects are, according to the Complementarity Principle, eligible to receive personal *a*, yet do not in fact get marked with it. Note, however, that in other languages considered above, some changes were sanctioned but did not actually occur. For example, in the first change we considered, from table 9.6 to table 9.7, other nominals were eligible to have new marking, but these changes did not actually apply in Rošani. The subject of the transitive in the past could have come to be marked with the absolute, as happened in Orošori, but this did not occur in Rošani. Alternatively, the cases used with the past could have been extended to the present; these changes are sanctioned but did not occur. More generally, the Complementarity Principle is not intended to predict change – or its scope – but to state the limits on possible change. Neither the Spanish example nor the other examples in section 9.4.5.1 nor the Finnish example in section 9.4.6.2 violates the Complementarity Principle in letter or in spirit.

9.4.6   Interaction with the Unaccusative Hypothesis

9.4.6.1   *Condition (iii) and the Unaccusative Hypothesis*

The notion of complementarity draws on the insights of recent work in syntax, and some of this work must be briefly reviewed here. The recognition that there exists a syntactic relationship between direct objects and the subjects of certain intransitive verbs has been discussed by a number of linguists. It has been shown that in some languages the nominals bearing these grammatical relations share a variety of syntactic properties (Perlmutter 1978). In two fundamentally different syntactic frameworks, Relational Grammar and Government and Binding, this set of syntactic properties is accounted for in essentially the same way: the subjects of intransitive verbs of this type, termed unaccusatives, are underlyingly direct objects (Perlmutter 1978; Burzio 1986; cf. Pullum 1988). While Perlmutter first made this observation as a way of

Table 9.17   *Change in case alignment in Finnic (after Itkonen 1979)*

	Direct object	Subject of intransitive		Agentive	Subject of transitive
		Non-agentive			
		Existential	Non-existential		
Early Proto-Finnic	ACC/PART	NOM	NOM	NOM	NOM
Late Proto-Finnic	ACC/PART	PART	NOM	NOM	NOM

accounting for selection of auxiliaries in Italian, it has been shown to play a role in a variety of phenomena in unrelated languages. This supports the view that the *relationship* is universal, even though it may not be manifested by all languages. It should be noted that the Unaccusative Hypothesis, as this is sometimes known, is not necessarily correlated with case marking; indeed, in Italian, where it was first observed, there is no correlation with case marking.

If we accept the insights of the cross-linguistic, cross-framework research on the Unaccusative Hypothesis, we identify an additional relationship of complementarity. With respect to nominals that bear the underlying relation, direct object, and the surface relation, subject of an intransitive, these two grammatical relations are complementary by condition (iii).

9.4.6.2   *An example involving the Unaccusative Hypothesis: Finnish*
Itkonen (1979) describes a change in the marking of subjects of certain intransitive verbs in Finnic. In affirmative sentences in early Proto-Finnic, the direct object could normally be marked with either the partitive case or the accusative case.[37] At this stage subjects were marked with the nominative. Observing the relationship between the direct objects of certain transitive sentences and the subjects of the corresponding intransitives (1979: 91–3), Itkonen suggests that it was in these intransitives that the partitive case subject first developed. Later, he notes, the use of the partitive case was extended to the so-called existential verbs. By changing the labels to reflect Itkonen's presentation, we can represent these Finnic changes with a chart similar to those used elsewhere in this chapter. Itkonen uses the terms "agentive" and "non-agentive" (rather than "active" and "inactive") to describe the two sorts of intransitive, and his terms are used in table 9.17. We must make an additional division among the non-agentive intransitives to represent the facts Itkonen presents.

Table 9.17 does not represent the intermediate stage suggested by Itkonen, in which the subjects of existentials were not (yet) marked with the partitive, though the subjects of certain non-agentive intransitives with corresponding transitives were so marked. The system described for late Proto-Finnic is similar to that found in Modern Finnish (Itkonen 1979: 90). In the modern language we find the contrasts with intransitive verbs as in (38a), the only construction originally available, and (38b) the newer one with partitive subject:

(38)   (a) lapse-t   leikki-vät   piha-lla
            child-PL.NOM play-3RD.PL.PRES yard-On
            "The children are playing in the yard."

        (b) laps-i-a   leikki-i   piha-lla
            child-PL-PART play-3RD.SG.PRES yard-On
            "(Some) children are playing in the yard."

There are restrictions on the possibility of partitive subjects appearing (see Hakulinen and Karlsson 1979: 166–7). (i) The subject NP cannot be referential (but must be non-specific, or indefinite, and refer to a portion of a mass or of an unrestricted group). Thus contrast (39b) with its definite, specific subject appearing in the nominative and (39a) with partitive subject for the indefinite, non-specific, non-refential NP:

(39)   (a) maljako-ssa   on   kukk-i-a
            vase-In   is.3RD.SG.PRES flower-PL-PART
            "Some flowers are in the vase." (= "There are flowers in the vase.")

        (b) kuka-t   o-vat   maljako-ssa
            flower-NOM.PL are-3RD.PL vase-In
            "The flowers are in the vase."

(ii) The verb does not agree with the partitive subject (but rather appears in the third person singular), and cannot take a direct object. Thus number agreement is as in (38a) and (38b) above; plural partitive subjects do not govern plural agreement on the verb; thus (40) is ungrammatical:

(40)   *laps-i-a   **leikki-vät**   piha-lla
        child-PL-PART play-3RD.PL yard-On

Similarly, sentences with partitive subjects normally permit no direct object, so that (41b) is ungrammatical; compare the following:

(41)   (a) jotku-t   tutkija-t   syö-vät   lounas-ta
            some-NOM.PL investigator-NOM.PL eat-3RD.PL lunch-PART.SG

            kello 12-lta
            clock 12-From

            "Some researchers eat lunch at 12 o'clock."

(b) *joitaku-i-ta   tutkijo-i-ta   syö   lounas-ta
some-PL-PART investigator-PL-PART eat.3RD.SG lunch-PART.SG

kello 12-lta
clock 12-From

(iii) The pragmatic function of the predicate also determines whether a partitive subject is possible (this factor does not concern our arguments here; for details, see Hakulinen and Karlsson 1979: 167–9).

It is clear that the donor relation in the change described above is the direct object; it is this relation that is marked by the partitive case (among others) before the change.[38] In the shift in question, the recipients of the partitive case marking are the subjects of certain non-agentive intransitive verbs. (The putative problem of the partial recipient is discussed above in section 9.4.5.) According to the Unaccusative Hypothesis, surface subjects of inactive intransitives of this sort (sometimes referred to as "unaccusatives") may be derived from underlying structure direct objects. It is through the fact that a nominal may bear both of these relations at different syntactic levels that the grammatical relations satisfy condition (iii) of the Complementarity Principle. Thus, a change of the sort described above for Finnish is sanctioned by the Complementarity Principle, under a condition that is independently needed to account for changes discussed in section 9.4.4 and others like them.

Of considerable interest for our purposes is the fact that the partitive subject construction is beginning to be extended to subjects of transitive sentences, but only under very restricted conditions, namely only when the sentence is not indexical, that is, when it is interpretable without reference to things present in the speech situation. Thus contrast (42a), with no specific reference, and (42b) where the demonstrative pronoun makes it indexical:

(42)   (a)   yhä enemmän amerkkalais-i-a   käyttää
            ever more   American-PL-PART use.3RD.SG

            äänioikeu-tta-an
            right.to.vote-PART.SG-3RD.POSS

            "More and more Americans are using their right to vote."

    (b)   *yhä enemmän nä-i-tä   amerkkalais-i-a   käyttää
            ever more   these-PL-PART American-PL-PART use.3RD.SG

            äänioikeu-tta-an
            right.to.vote-PART.SG-3RD.POSS

            "More and more Americans are using their right to vote."

Some other examples of the extension of the partitive subject to constructions with transitive verbs and direct objects are:

(43) vuosittain korkeakouluissa antaa   tuntiopetus-ta use-i-ta
      yearly   high.schools.in give.3RD.SG lesson-PART.SG several-PL-PART

      tuhans-i-a   henkilö-i-tä
      thousand-PL-PART person-PL-PART

      "Several thousands of persons give lessons yearly in the high
      schools."

(44) venäjä-ä   luke-e   hyvin vähän suomalais-i-a
      Russian-PART.SG read-3RD.SG.PRES very few   Finn-PL-PART
      "Very few Finns study Russian."[39]

This provides a clear example of an extension in two stages, each sanctioned
by the Complementarity Principle, and each with a partial recipient. In the
first change, the partitive is extended from direct objects to subjects of
"unaccusatives" (condition (iii)); in the second, it was extended from these
subjects to subjects of transitives (condition (ii) on the Complementarity
Principle).

9.4.6.3 The putative problem of the extended accusative

Anderson (1977: 353ff.) and Dixon (1979: 78) have suggested that certain
changes in alignment are possible because the nominals involved (the donor
and recipient in our terms) have something important in common. Using
terms somewhat different from those of the present work, both authors state
that it is natural for the case that marks the subject of transitives to be
extended to subjects of intransitives on the basis of both being subjects.
Although the statements of both authors are limited in the first instance to
this specific donor and recipient, in spirit their statements are much the same
as the more general Complementarity Principle. However, both go on to rule
out specifically the possibility of the marker of a direct object being extended
to subjects of intransitives, exactly the kind of change that we have seen took
place in Finnish. As shown above, the Complementarity Principle, taken in
conjunction with the Unaccusative Hypothesis, predicts that changes of this
sort are possible, as long as the recipient is limited in the first instance to subjects of inactive intransitives. According to the Complementarity Principle, it
would also be possible for a subsequent change to extend the marker of the
direct object and subject of inactive intransitives to mark also subjects of
active intransitives.

  Plank (1985: 294–5) argues against the positions of Anderson (1977) and
Dixon (1979) on three grounds. First, their statements are crucially dependent
on the syntactic relations, subject and object; Plank states that certain aspects
of these notions are controversial. Second, Plank interprets the existence of

examples like Finnish, described above, as evidence against the principle that the donor and recipient must have something in common syntactically (i.e. must be analogically related). Plank's third objection to Anderson's approach is not relevant to the proposal made in the present work, for we have not adopted the framework Plank criticized. Let us consider his first two objections in turn.

Plank considers the grammatical relations, subject and object, to be controversial and takes a "paradigmatic–identificational" approach to identifying (or defining) accusative, ergative, and active. Plank's approach is similar to Sapir's (1917) followed in the present work, except that it relies instead on the notions agent and patient. But surely these notions cannot be considered uncontroversial, and some of the problems associated with them are well known. For example, the subjects of the verbs "bear (of pain)" and "undergo" are not agents according to the usual understanding of that term; yet in many languages they have the case marking assigned to agents of other transitive verbs. Subjects of "see," "hear," and other similar verbs are not agentive (compare "look," "listen"); yet many languages mark them as agents of transitive verbs. While some consider the subjects of the following sentences to be agentive, their status is not uncontroversial: *the wind opened the door, the key opened the door, the earthquake broke my dishes.* Many discussions of alignment use "agent" ("A") only for agents of transitive verbs, not for agents of agentive intransitives, such as "sing," "bellow," "shout," "dance," "jump" are in many languages. Nor are the subjects of all verbs that fall syntactically into the category of so-called active intransitives actually agentive.[40] Thus, while Plank may be right in considering the grammatical relations to be controversial notions, agent and patient are no less so. The very fact that known changes in alignment, as shown above, can be stated in terms of subject and object – and evidently not without them – confirms the importance of these notions in any treatment of alignment.

Plank's second point of objection is based upon the existence of examples like the Finnish one described above. He writes

> In light of the findings in [a section of the article], Anderson's considerations must at least be relativised. By the same logic one would have to conclude that (some or. . .all) intransitive core actants and transitive patients must have something in common syntactically so as to invite extensions of the accusative from transitive patients to (some or all) intransitive actants – if not generally, then at least in the languages where such extensions of the accusative occurred.

Exactly such a conclusion had already been reached, not on the basis of diachronic considerations, but on the basis of synchronic analyses of a number of widely divergent languages (see Pullum 1988). Plank seems to regard this conclusion as self-evidently impossible. However, it should be considered that the insights of the Unaccusative Hypothesis have been developed within at least two very different syntactic frameworks; it is not an artifact of a single approach or the invention of theoreticians on the fringe of linguistics. As shown here, it has explanatory value, not only synchronically, as originally envisioned, but also diachronically.

We have claimed above that alignment change operates systematically, strictly constrained by an explicit set of relationships between donor and recipient. The alternative which Plank (1985) appears to espouse is that change in alignment operates without constraint, there being no limits on the kinds of relationships (or lack thereof) that may exist between donor and recipient. If one accepts that position, it is then encumbent upon that linguist to explain why many kinds of alignment change do not occur and why these happen to be the same as those disallowed by the Complementarity Principle.

9.4.7 Conclusion

The constraint proposed here has antecedents in the works cited above, but is not stated there in a general form. The Complementarity Principle is an explicit statement of a constraint on change in alignment and other changes in coding by case marking or agreement. It makes generalizations based on well understood changes in alignment and draws on syntactic relations (subject, direct object, indirect object) which have been recognized for generations and whose validity for many languages has been demonstrated. It is true that the Complementarity Principle has nothing to say about constraints on changes from instrumental or other non-relations, such as those discussed in section 9.2.4. However, it makes the correct statement for a wide variety of additional changes known to us but not discussed here, including alignment changes in Mayan languages, Indic and Dardic languages, and in Daghestan languages. In some instances these are not discussed here because some of the details regarding them are not yet fully known; nevertheless, even without all details it is clear that the Complementarity Principle states the limits on known instances of change covered by it. The fact that these changes are not random, but rather can be generalized, strongly suggests that they are not accidental gaps, but correlate with universals of change.

10 *On the development of complex constructions*

10.1   The problem

In chapter 7 we discussed a number of processes by which clauses are fused, resulting in change from a more complex to a less complex structure. Given that languages do continue to have complex structures, change cannot be uniformly in the direction of simplification. We examine here the questions of how and why complex structures are renewed.[1]

It is extremely common in natural languages for relative pronouns to be formally identical to or derived from Q-words in the same language. This raises a second question to be addressed in this chapter: what is the relationship between these two kinds of pronouns? While they may be somewhat less common, there are numerous other dependent clause types that bear a similarity to questions of one kind or another. This, in turn, raises the question of what relation dependent clauses (or certain types of dependent clauses) bear to questions.

In section 10.2 we outline the traditional view that hypotaxis develops out of parataxis and discuss several interpretations of it; in section 10.3 we develop a simple alternative hypothesis. Section 10.4 provides a treatment of the relationship of questions to subordinate clauses, and in section 10.5 we propose an analysis of the origins of complex constructions.

10.2   The traditional view: hypotaxis from parataxis

Traditionally it has been suggested that hypotaxis develops out of parataxis, but this view has also been questioned. In this section we examine first some of the different conceptions of how hypotaxis develops out of parataxis, and we then look closely at the assumptions and arguments on which this view is based. The view that hypotaxis develops out of parataxis is referred to here as the Parataxis Hypothesis.

Examination of different conceptions of the Parataxis Hypothesis revolves, to a large extent, around differing interpretations of the words that state the slogan. First, the claim that hypotaxis **develops** from parataxis has often been made with reference to the first appearance of hypotaxis in a language, not to its repeated renewal. We use the term **origin** here strictly to refer to the first appearance of a construction in a language; **renewal** refers to the continuing process of replacing or otherwise revising existing construction types. Because we believe that understanding attested and well-understood recent changes will help us to gain a better grasp of the processes in the origins of complex structures, we examine first and foremost the various processes by which complex structures are renewed. Most of the changes we discuss here are attested. Only in section 10.6 do we turn to the issue of the ultimate, first origins of subordination.

In the context of the Parataxis Hypothesis, the term **hypotaxis** seems usually to include only finite dependent clauses, not reduced (non-finite) clauses. In keeping with more recent views, we include both types, but distinguish between them. The term **parataxis** has been used to mean either asyndetic joining, or loose (imprecise) joining, or both at the same time. Asyndetic joining is simply joining without a conjunction (other than intonation or punctuation); it is thus usually easily determined whether two clauses are joined asyndetically. However, determining how loosely or tightly two clauses are joined requires either some rather slippery judgments or assumptions about structural equivalents of looseness or tightness. For example, it is sometimes assumed that a clause that is (or alternatively, that can be) surrounded by material from another is more tightly joined to that clause than is one which entirely precedes or follows another. Another view is that two clauses are more tightly joined if one has some grammatical marking of a relation to the other, often in the form of a pronoun, gap, or grammatically determined tense or mood. A further interpretation of parataxis in the context of subordinate clauses that resemble questions is that hypotactic structure is preceded by structures joined only in discourse, as two sentences. When they write that hypotaxis developed out of parataxis, some authors seem to have in mind conjunctionless joining, others loose joining, and still others discourse. Thus, even if, for the time being, we limit our inquiry to renewal, in approaching the question of whether hypotaxis develops out of parataxis we encounter the problem that different linguists have in mind different ideas of parataxis, and that at least some of them are vague.

What reasons are there to suppose that parataxis, rather than some other structure, provides the source or prototype for hypotaxis? We know of two types of arguments. One, relating to the ultimate origins of hypotaxis, is based on the claim that parataxis is more common in the early stage of a written language than is embedding; this is discussed in section 10.5.1. Another type of argument is based on the origin of the subordinator. Since subordinators in many languages originate as markers of questions – either yes/no or content questions – it is sometimes assumed that the subordinate clauses they mark must have originated as actual questions. Many languages have subordinators that originated as demonstrative pronouns, and some investigators see this as evidence that those pronouns were "pointing to" a loosely adjoined clause. Notice that it is by no means necessary to assume that the structure in which a particular innovative grammatical element is found developed out of the structure in which that grammatical element originated. It is logically possible that one *word* simply developed from another, with little reference to context. It is also possible that structural marking that developed in one context was later *extended* to another. While the issue of whether the sources of markers logically imply the sources of structures is an empirical one, we shall refer here to the *assumption* that they do as the Marker/Structure Fallacy.

An example of the Marker/Structure Fallacy in recent work comes from Hewitt (1987: 141–2, 260–1), where it is assumed without further evidence that a subordinate clause with marking otherwise found in questions in Georgian must have developed from an "independent interrogative clause":[2]

> The basic alternative-question-forming role of the words *tu ara* surely requires us to hypothesise an earlier (albeit Implicational hypotactic) structure . . . which, to my mind, quite logically and naturally further pre-supposes an original, *fully* paratactic sequence . . . How else is one to account for the presence here of words that basically mark an alternative question?
>
> (1987: 261)

In section 10.4 we return to the question posed in this quotation. For the time being we note only that there are at least two other logical possibilities, as noted in the preceding paragraph.

The Parataxis Hypothesis is not supported by evidence from attested instances of the rise of the use of subordinators. A case in point is English, though evidence from this language has been used many times to support the Parataxis Hypothesis. Prior to the use in English of relative pronouns based on question pronouns, the language made use of demonstratives and the particle ðe to form relative clauses. If relative clauses that make use of relative pronouns that derive from Q-words developed from independent questions, that is paratactic constructions containing actual questions, we would expect to find these questions in attested forms of English during this change. But there is no evidence that questions were involved in this change; rather, the facts suggest that the Q-words began to replace the demonstratives and particles found in the existing relative clause structure (Allen 1980 [1977]: ch. 5). Example (1) is among the earliest occurrences of the wh-relative, and it provides no hint of an actual question (that is, a request for information).[3]

(1) ðis waes swiðe gedeorfsum gear her on lande ðurh   gyld   ðe
     this was   very grievous   year here in land through money that

     se cyng nan for his dohter   gyfte & ðurh   ungewaedera **for**
     the king took for his daughter's dowry and through unweather   for

     hwan eorðwestmas wurdon swiðe amyrde
     which harvests   became very spoiled

     "This was a very grievous year in the land because of the money
     which the king took for his daughter's dowry and because of the bad
     weather, on account of which the crops were badly spoiled."
             (Peterborough Chronicle 1111.23, quoted in Allen 1980[1977]: 198)

Note here in particular the parallel structure of the ðe-relative and the wh-relative and the fact that they modify conjoined nouns. The fact that actual question sequences are not attested in the encroachment of the wh-relative on the ðe-relative and the parallel use of these two types in examples like (1) lead to the clear conclusion that the innovative relative clause type developed out of the older kind, not out of actual paratactic questions. The source of the subordinator (Q-word) does not imply the source of the construction into which it is introduced.

Additional attested examples come from the development of the colloquial German relative clause formation strategy using *wo* "where" (Ramat 1982: 285), and the somewhat similar use of *ia* (from English *here*) to bracket relative clauses in Tok Pisin (Sankoff and Brown 1976). In each language the structure containing the invariant relativizing particle (which developed from the place adverb) developed out of an existing relative clause structure. The innovative structures are illustrated in the (a) sentences below and their apparent source structures in (b).

(2) (a) der Mann, den wo   ich gestern   gesehen habe
          the man   that where I   yesterday seen   have
          "the man that I have seen yesterday"

     (b) der Mann, den ich gestern   gesehen habe
          the man   that I   yesterday seen   have
          "the man that I have seen yesterday"   (Ramat 1982: 285)

(3) (a) disfela liklik boi **ia** [tupela kisim em ikam **ia**] em, em, ilaik igo huk
          "This little boy, [**that** the two of them had brought], was going to go fishing."

(b)   some place [me go] man he no good
      "Some places [I went] the people were bad."

(Sankoff and Brown 1976: 632, 661)

While most languages have parataxis, we have no direct evidence of it developing into hypotaxis.

Perhaps the biggest problem with the Parataxis Hypothesis is that, by itself, it really explains very little. Even if parataxis does develop into hypotaxis, in and of itself this does not tell us how hypotaxis, true subordination, developed. (We are speaking now of parataxis as loose joining, not as conjunctionless subordination.) Whatever kind of theory of syntax we adopt, and whatever the exact relations we see between clauses, the beginning of subordination is not explained merely through parataxis. For example, (4a) gives one view of the relationship between clauses in parataxis, while (4b) gives one simplified view of the structure of hypotaxis:

(4)   (a)

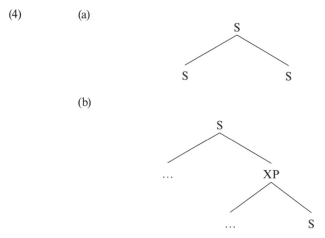

           (b)

Thus, whether the Parataxis Hypothesis is accepted or rejected, we must explain how subordination changes over time. This hypothesis, which has dominated diachronic discussions of complex clauses, explains little.

10.3   A hypothesis of the development of complex constructions

We suggest a simple hypothesis: Developments relating to complex constructions can be accounted for through the mechanisms already described in relation to simplex constructions and through sentence structures known to exist. This seems straightforward and even obvious until we return, in section 10.4, to the issue of subordination marked with devices that otherwise mark questions. In section 10.3.1–10.3.4 we show how some of the simple, well-documented changes in subordination arise through the mechanisms of reanalysis and extension. In section 10.4 we examine the relationship between questions, subordination, and the devices that mark both. We suggest that in explaining complex structures it is not necessary to go beyond the boundary of the sentence (to discourse) or to cite structures in which subordinate clauses have vague relationships to matrix clauses.

10.3.1   Reanalysis of constituent structure (and of word category)

In earliest German, the demonstrative pronoun with deictic force was used in pointing out the subordinate clause. The demonstrative pronoun, at least originally, was a constituent of the matrix clause, and the subordinate clause was its complement. The nominative-accusative singular of the neuter demonstrative pronoun, *das* (here *thaʒ*), was used "to point" to subordinate clauses:

(5)   joh gizalta   in   sâr   thaʒ, thiu sâlida untar in
       and told.PRET.3.SG them immediately that the luck   among them

       uuas
       was

       "and he told them immediately that good fortune was among them"
                                        (Otfrid, cited in Paul/Stolte 1949: 376)

In (5), *thaʒ* is a constituent of the matrix clause; it is generally considered that *das* became a complementizer when it was reinterpreted, even in Old High German, as a constituent of the subordinate clause, as shown by divisions made in verse. The complementizer began to be written *dass* (*daß*) to distinguish it visually from the demonstrative pronoun *das*. After it had been reinterpreted, *daß* began to cooccur with a matrix clause demonstrative, as in (6), or with a neuter personal pronoun (Paul/Stolte 1949: 376–7):

(6)   das glaube ich wohl, daß du dies gern möchtest
       that believe I   truly that you this want
       "I really believe it, that you like this."

Example (6) thus provides clear evidence of the reanalysis. The innovation of structures containing *daß* involved the reanalysis of (7a) as (7b), together with reanalysis of the demonstrative pronoun in structure (7a) as a complementizer, shown in structure (7b):

(7)   (a)   (b)

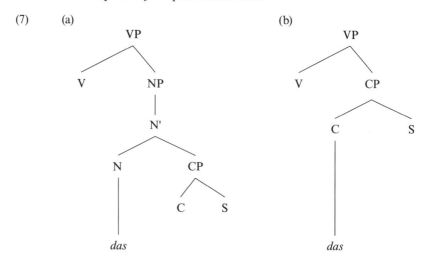

In this instance the new spelling, *daß*, was introduced in recognition of the functional reanalysis.[4]

Another example of reanalysis of constituency is the Old English expression *ðe hwile ðe* "the while that", with the alternate forms *þa hwila þe, þa hwile þa, a hwilæ ðæ, ðe hwile ðæt*, etc., from which the Modern English subordinator *while* is derived. The first *ðe* (*þa, a*) here is the determiner, *hwile* the accusative case form of the noun "while," and the second *ðe* the relativizer (Pasicki 1983). The NP, consisting of a noun head and a relative clause, was reanalyzed as an adverbial clause, with the noun head reanalyzed as the subjunction, *while*. Note that both the determiner and the older complementizer were lost as a result of this reanalysis; this contrasts with the reanalysis described in the next paragraph.

In French the expression *par ce que* originally consisted of the preposition *par* "by," the pronoun *ce* "this, that," and the general complementizer *que*. When introduced, *par ce* was a constituent of the matrix clause, and *que* the complementizer. Later the whole prepositional phrase, including the embedded clause, was reinterpreted as an adverbial clause, with *par ce que* reanalyzed with a complementizer with the meaning "because" (Schlieben-Lange 1989).

Reanalysis involving reduction of two levels of structure to one is discussed in more detail in chapter 7, including reanalysis of a biclausal quotation to a monoclausal quotative. The quotative is itself a kind of complementizer, marking subordination with matrix verbs of speaking. As discussed in the next section, extension of this function also occurs.

Reanalysis of constituency is an important type of change undergone by subordinate clauses and usually also involves reanalysis of the word category of the word that ends up as complementizer.[5]

10.3.2   Extension of subjunctions and conjunctions from other clause types

It comes as no surprise that many complementizers come from markers of some other kind of subordinate clause. An example of this is the further development of German *daß* "that" described in the preceding section. Although originally used only with sentential subjects and objects, as indicated by its nominative–accusative form, once *daß* was reinterpreted as a complementizer it could mark clauses in other functions.

English *that* has a history similar to German *daß*. *That* comes from the neuter demonstrative pronoun. In Old English *þæt* was used to introduce indirect statements, clauses of extent and purpose, and occasionally as a relative marker in certain types of headed relative clauses. In the thirteenth century *þat* began to be used in free relatives with a WH-pronoun. About the same time it began to be used to introduce complements of prepositions (such as *before*) and adverbs (such as *now*). It began to occur with the subjunctions *hwile* "while," *þēah* (*þohh*) "although," *þa* (*þo*, later *hwan*) "when," *gif* "if," and others. In some of these constructions *þat* replaced an earlier marker, *þe* or *swa*. About the fourteenth century, *þat* began to occur in complementizer position in any kind of subordinate clause (Allen 1980 [1977]: 239–59).[6]

Another example of substitution of an existing subordinator in existing types of subordinate clauses is traced through early and late Biblical Hebrew to Mishnaic Hebrew in Givón (1974). He shows that in early Biblical Hebrew the subordinator *ʔašer* was used only in relative clauses; verb complements were formed differently. Reduced to the form *še*, this subordinator was extended to adverbial clauses and eventually to verb complements.[7]

In a number of languages complementizers derived from a verb of saying have been extended from restricted types of clauses to additional types of subordinate clauses (see, for example, Larkin 1972; Steever 1987b). Lord (1976) offers examples from Ewe, a Kwa language. The verb "say" in (8) is reinterpreted as a subordinator, probably first with complement clauses, as in (9), and later with other clause types, as in (10):[8]

(8)   me-be   me-wɔ-e
        I-say   I-do-it
        "I said, 'I did it'" or "I said that I did it."   (Lord 1976: 179)

(9)   me-gblɔ bé   mewɔe
        I-say   that I-do-it
        "I said, 'I did it'" or "I said that I did it."   (Lord 1976: 179)

(10)   me-dí bé máple   awua ḍewó
          I-want that I-sʙv-buy dress some
          "I want to buy some dresses."   (Lord 1976: 180)

A clear example involving extension from a coordinating, rather than subordinating, conjunction is found in Mingrelian. The marker *da*, which forms conditional clauses, comes from the coordinating conjunction "and"; it always
occurs in clause-final position, as do several others in the language.

(11)   skua   koʔundu-a **da**, gverdo ɣureli iʔuapudu-a
          child.ɴᴏᴍ have-ǫᴜᴏᴛ if half   dead be-ǫᴜᴏᴛ
          "If he had a child, he would be half dead."   (Xubua 1937: 21, 6)

Such clauses usually precede the main clause, but may follow or be
embedded within the matrix. *Da* is of the same form as the coordinating conjunction "and" in the proto-language and in related Georgian, while in
Mingrelian "and" has the form *do*. The latter can also be used as a subordinator, in the sense "as soon as" (Abesaʒe 1965: 251–2):

(12)   baɣanak mučʼot ginirtu viti cʼanero **do**
          child   such   become ten year   and
          "As soon as the child turned ten, . . ."   (Xubua 1937: 1, 9)

(Examples (11) and (12) are cited by Abesaʒe 1965.)
   For certain Gorokan languages, Haiman (1987) reconstructs a coordinating conjunction as a crucial part of the unusual "medial" verb morphology
that characterizes these, as well as other Papuan languages. The medial verb
morphology is used with all verbs in clauses before the last; some of the
clauses in which medial morphology occurs are coordinated, some subordinated (Haiman 1987: 360). Coordinated medials are illustrated below from
Hua, one of the members of this subgroup. (The morpheme glossed "Medial"
varies according to the person and number of the subject of the following
verb.)

(13)   fumo doro-na   vie
          pork he.ate-ᴍᴇᴅɪᴀʟ he.went
          "He ate the pork and went."   (Haiman 1980: 393)

(14)   fumo dmisiga-da   ugue
          pork he.give.ꜰᴜᴛᴜʀᴇ-ᴍᴇᴅɪᴀʟ I.go
          "He will give me pork and I will go."   (Haiman 1980: 396)

Haiman reconstructs the coordinating conjunction as *KV*, that is, consisting
of a velar stop unspecified for voicing and a vowel of indeterminate quality,
showing that among the coordinating conjunctions used today in languages

of the subgroup are *-ge, -oge, -gate, -ki ~ -ke, -Ki,* and points out other parallels at greater remove within the family.

We have seen in sections 10.3.1–10.3.2 that a variety of subordinators are derived from structural sources reflecting the structure out of which the subordinate clause developed. At the same time we recognize that subordinators easily extend from one type of subordinate clause to another; for this reason, the etymology of the subjunction does not always reveal the structure out of which the recipient clause developed.

10.3.3   Extension of case marker or adposition

While the examples surveyed in section 10.3.2 involved extension of a subordinator to use as a subordinator in a different type or subtype of subordinate clause, those discussed here exemplify a case marker or adposition that is extended for the first time to use as a subjunction. In recent work Genetti (1986, on languages of the Bodic branch of Tibeto-Burman) and Thurgood 1986a (on languages of the Lolo-Burmese) have shown that case postpositions can be extended to finite clauses (see also sources on Australian, Papuan, and Chibchan languages, cited in Genetti 1991). Using historical documents and contemporary data, Genetti (1991) shows that in Newari this change took place in stages, with postpositions first extended to nominalized verb forms, which had overt nominalizing suffixes only optionally; later the postpositions were reanalyzed as subordinating morphemes. The nominalized stage of the change is documented in Classical Newari texts, dating from the fourteenth to the nineteenth century.

Laz, a language of the Kartvelian (South Caucasian) family, has innovated use of genitive and allative cases and several postpositions with finite verb forms.[9] Examples (15) and (16) illustrate a clause marked with *-ši,* the genitive case; and (17) and (18) a clause marked with the postposition *-k'ule* "after," which governs the genitive:

(15)   guin-c'k'ed-u-ši   mendra   nimt'et'es
       around-look-3.SG-GEN   far.away   flee.3.PL
       "While he was looking around, they were running far away."
       (K'art'ozia 1968: 159, 45)

(16)   me-xt-u-ši,   didii   k'ardala   gelobut'u
       there-go-3.SG-GEN   big   pot   hang
       "When he arrived, a big pot was hanging . . ."   (K'art'ozia 1968: 154, 25)

(17)   geide   ek'i-c'k'ed-es-š-k'ule
       behind   behind-look-3.PL-GEN-after
       "after they looked behind"   (Čikobava 1936b: 40, 19; cited in Jikia 1967: 371)

(18)   v-imt'i-š-k'ule,   eššeɣi mižoleen
        1.sɢ-flee-ɢᴇɴ-after donkey fell
        "After I ran away, the donkey evidently fell."   (Asatiani 1974: 2, 27)

In each example the genitive (with or without the postposition) is affixed to a
fully inflected finite verb form: for example, *vimt'i* "I fled, ran away" in (18)
consists of the first person subject marker *v-*, the so-called character vowel *-i-*,
the verb root *-mt'-*, and the aorist marker *-i*.

The Laz innovation of using case markers and postpositions was relatively
simple. The language already had postpositional phrases, such as that in (19),
where the postposition is enclitic to an entire NP *ar tuta-* "one month":

(19)   . . .ar tuta-š-k'ule   konočku xčini   k'ulaniša
        one   month-ɢᴇɴ-after he.sent old.woman girl.to
        "After a month he sent an old woman to the girl."   (Asatiani 1974: 47, 13)

Evidence that the direction of development is from postposition to subordinator (rather than the reverse) is the fact that genitive case is reconstructed to
Common Kartvelian (Mačavariani 1970; Harris 1985: 74), the allative case is
reconstructed to a somewhat later stage (Topuria 1937; Gigineišvili and
Sarǰvelaʒe 1978; Harris 1985: 251–2), while some of the postpositions can also
be reconstructed to an earlier stage (Čikobava 1936a: 65–6). Neither the cases
nor the postpositions can be reconstructed in the subordinator function,
showing that the language-particular development in Laz was in the direction
of postposition to subordinator. In addition, the use of the genitive case marker *-š* with the postposition *-k'ule* "after" in its subordinator function, and the
use of the ablative case marker *-še* with the postposition *-ni* "because" in its
subordinator function are best explained as deriving from the original use of
these as postpositions.[10]

It is not clear that the change in Laz involved an intermediate stage in
which the postposition occurred with a nominalized form of the finite verb,
though such a stage cannot be ruled out. Example (20) provides possible evidence for such a stage:

(20)   na   bigzalit-u-pe-ši   lazut'i hini dok'orobey
        ᴄᴏᴍᴘ we.go-u-ᴘʟ-ɢᴇɴ corn   they they.collect
        "They collected the corn of the we-wents (i.e. those of us who went)."
                        (K'art'ozia 1970: 1, 8; cited by Holisky 1991: 409)

In (20) the genitive case marker, *-ši*, is attached to the fully inflected verb, *big-
zalit* "we went." Plurality (of the subject, "we") is indicated in the verb form by
the suffix *-t*, but the suffix *-pe* also occurs; it is a pluralizer of nouns and does
not ordinarily occur on verbs. The use of the noun pluralizer with a finite verb
form does not offer evidence beyond the use of the genitive case with the same

form, but the unidentified suffix *-u* might. The function of this morpheme is not known (Holisky 1991: 410), but it is possible that it is the same as the formant of the masdar, a verbal noun (Čikobava 1936a: 174–6). If this is correct, it may be evidence of an intermediate stage in this development in Laz, evidence that the postpositions were first extended to finite verb forms that had been nominalized, while the marker of nominalization was later lost.

Alternatively it may be that *k'ule* "after" (together with the genitive case, which it governs) was first extended from nouns, as in (19) and structure (21a), to subordinate clauses, as in (17)–(18) and structure (21b). A later change, which may or may not have taken place in Laz, would involve reinterpreting *-š-k'ule* as a complementizer, occupying the Comp position in (21b) (omitting case).[11]

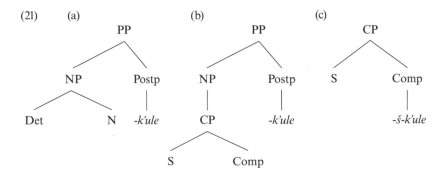

In each instance, the case marker or adposition is extended from nouns to subordinate clauses.

10.3.4   Extension of Q-structure into existing subordinate clause structures

In sections 10.3.1–10.3.3 we have argued that the familiar mechanisms of reanalysis and extension from well-understood constructions are responsible for a variety of changes in the structure and marking of subordinate clauses. We suggest here that extension from questions is likewise responsible for the development of question-like structures in subordinate clauses. In section 10.4 we develop this argument and explain the basis for such an extension.

10.4   The relation between questions and subordinate clauses

In this section we establish that a relation exists between the marking of questions and the marking of subordination, we explore the nature of that relation, and show that extension can fully account for changes of this type. In section 10.4.1.1 we survey the devices used for marking questions in the languages of the world, and in section 10.4.1.2 we show that each of these devices is used by some language to mark subordination. Section 10.4.2 is devoted to showing that both questions and dependent clauses are non-assertions and that it is this relationship that is the basis for extension of markers from the former to the latter.

10.4.1   Inventory of devices

10.4.1.1   In questions

Universally, simple yes/no questions may be marked by means of (a) a question particle, (b) special word order, (c) special intonation, (d) the A-not-A structure, (e) tag questions, or some combination of these.[12]

A question particle, -*o*, is used in Mingrelian to form yes/no questions.

(22)   (a)   cxen-(i)   kimeči   skua-s
                horse-NOM you.give.it.him   child-DAT
                "You gave a horse to (your) child."

        (b)   cxen-(i)   kimeči-o   skua-s?
                horse-NOM you.give.it.him-QUES child-DAT
                "Did you give a horse to (your) child?"

Special word order, in particular the inversion of the ordinary subject–verb order, is familiar from English:

(23)   (a)   you are dreaming
        (b)   are you dreaming?

Intonation alone is the principal way of marking yes/no questions in Georgian, where questions stress is shifted to the last syllable of the last word in the clause, this vowel is lengthened, and pitch is raised markedly. Long vowels are not part of the ordinary phonetic inventory of Georgian:

(24)   (a)   mcxeta-ši c'avida
                Mcxeta-in s/he.go
                "S/he went to Mcxeta."

        (b)   mcxeta-ši c'avidá:?
                "Did s/he go to Mcxeta?"   (Harris 1984a: 68–9)

Of course in many languages, including English, intonation alone is sufficient to form a question, as in (25):

(25)   that's the best you can do?

The A-not-A structure has been described as a marker of yes/no questions in Mandarin (Li and Thompson 1984: 52–4, and other works by these authors).

Example (26a) is an affirmative statement, (26b) its negative counterpart, and (26c) the corresponding yes/no question:

(26)   (a) tā   zài jiā
            3.SG at home
            "S/he is at home."

        (b) tā   bu   zài jiā
            3.SG NEG at home
            "S/he is not at home."

        (c) tā   zài jiā   bu   zài jiā
            3.SG at home NEG at home
            "Is s/he at home?"   (Li and Thompson 1984: 52–4)

A similar construction is found in Turkish, where the A-not-A is combined with a question particle:

(27)   kadın tarla-ya git-ti-mi   git-me-di-mi?
        woman field-DAT go-PAST-Q go-NEG-PAST-Q
        "Did the woman go to the field (or didn't she go)?"

Here an affirmative verb form, *git-ti-mi*, and its negative counterpart, *git-me-di-mi*, are juxtaposed. The Turkish construction apparently differs from the Mandarin not only in that the former uses a question particle, but also in that the question is fully grammatical (and is a question) even without the "-not-A" portion of the construction.

    Tag questions are a further device widely used for forming questions; (28) provides an example from English:

(28)   he has left, hasn't he?

The expression *or not* functions in a way similar to tags in many languages, though its structure suggests that it may be derived from an A-not-A structure. We refer to this as an alternative tag. The example below is from Modern Georgian:

(29)   mova   vano, tu ara?
        s/he.come Vano or NEG
        "Will Vano come, or not?"

While *tu ara* is a tag in (29), the same expression may occur clause-internally:

(30)   mova   tu ara   vano?
        s/he.come or NEG Vano
        "Will Vano come (or not)?"

One further device for forming yes/no questions is known to us: in American Sign Language, yes/no questions are marked by raising of the eyebrows.

Content questions are formed with Q-words (interrogative pronouns or adverbs), with or without one of the devices listed above for yes/no questions; example (31) provides an illustration from Udi:

(31)   ma-n   finax   buγabe
        where-2.SG wine.DAT   get.AOR
        "Where did you get wine?"

10.4.1.2 In subordinate clauses

Each of the six devices listed above for forming yes/no and content questions may be used to mark subordinate clauses.

The question particle *-o* in Mingrelian can also form clauses with the meaning "when, as soon as" (Abesaʒe 1965):

(32)   boši-k   ešelə do gioǯinu-o, kičinu ʒyab-i
        boy-NAR   go and look-QUES   know girl-NOM
        "As soon as the boy went up and looked, he recognized the girl."
                                                        (Xubua 1937: 34, 24)

Special word order (subject–verb inversion) occasionally marks conditional clauses in English:

(33)   were I the organizer, I would have done things differently

This is more common in German, and has existed since Old High German times:

(34)   gîst du mir dîn swester, sô   will   ich ëʒ tuon
        give you me your sister   then   intend I   it do
        "If you give me your sister [to marry], then I will want to do it."
                                                    (Nibelungen, Paul/Stolte 389)

(35)   treten im selben Wort zwei *l* auf, so   wird das erste zu *r* dissimiliert
        step   in same   word two *l* on   then   will the first to *r* dissimilate
        "If two *l*'s appear in the same word, then the first will dissimilate to *r*."
                                (from a manuscript, published in English translation as Fähnrich 1991)

(36)   sind mehrere koordinierte Subjekte vorhanden, so   steht   das Verbum
        are several conjoined   subjects present   then stands   the verb

        normalerweise im   Plural . . .
        normally   in.the plural

        "If several conjoined subjects are present, then the verb normally is in the plural."
                                                            (Jensen 1959: 141)

The unmarked word order in (35) would be *zwei l treten* . . . "two *l*'s occur" and in (36) *mehrere koordinierte Subjekte sind* . . . "several conjoined subjects are . . ." Subject–verb inversion here serves to mark the clause as a conditional.

In two Georgian dialects, Gurian and Ačarian, special intonation, together with an all-purpose complementizer, marks some types of subordinate clause:

(37)   (a) Gurian
              ʒaɣl-i   rom   deinaxavs axla q'urdgé:l-s
              dog-NOM COMP spot.3.SG now hare-DAT
              "now when the dog spots the hare"

         (b) Ačarian
              ikit   om   gexvá:l, aɣma om   šexedav   da q'ana om
              there COMP go.2.SG up   COMP look.2.SG and field COMP

              aí:
              be.3.SG

              "when you go over there, when you look up and there is a field"
                                    (both examples, Lomtatiʒe 1946: 338)

Like the intonation used for marking yes/no questions, this type involves shifting stress to the final vowel of the clause and lengthening of this vowel (Lomtatiʒe 1946).[13]

The A-not-A structure of Turkish questions is also used to form temporal clauses with the meaning "as soon as."[14]

(38)   kadın   tarla-ya   gid-er   git-me-z
         woman field-DAT go-AORIST go-NEG-AORIST
         "as soon as the woman went to the field"

The affirmative, *gid-er*, and its negative counterpart, *git-me-z*, are juxtaposed, as in (27) above. The latter form contains the negative marker, *me*, and *z*, the form of the aorist marker that must be used with a negative.

Alternative tags can also mark subordination; the question device illustrated in (29)–(30) is used to mark a temporal clause meaning "as soon as" in the Georgian examples (39) and (40):

(39)   c'avida tu ara   kali   q'ana-ši
         s/he.go or NEG woman field-in
         "as soon as the woman went into the field"   (Jikia 1967: 377)

(40)   k'abas švils gavucmend tu ara, imas davban
         dress child clean   or NEG her bathe
         "At the moment I finish cleaning the dress for the child, I'll bathe her."
                                                        (Holisky 1981: 135)

One way of expressing a conditional in American Sign Language is to use the marker of yes/no questions: for example, the first clause in "If it rains tomorrow, I will stay home" may contain the "if" sign; but an alternative is to raise the eyebrows while signing "it will rain tomorrow."[15]

Q-words or forms derived from Q-words function as relative pronouns in many languages.

(41)   a professor whom the students all love

Q-words or forms derived from them also mark some kinds of adverbial clauses and verb complements. In the Georgian example (42), *ray-ta-mca* "that" is derived from *ray* "what?," a Q-word:

(42)   da   ara unda,   raytamca icna   vin
        and not he.want that   he.know someone
        "and he did not want that anyone know"   (Mark 9:30Ad.)

We have surveyed a wide variety of question strategies and have shown that each of them may be used to mark subordination of at least one type. Why should this be so?

10.4.2   Towards an explanation
In this section we argue that questions and dependent clauses share certain logical properties, and that this makes extension from one to the other possible.

10.4.2.1   Non-assertions
We begin by considering one aspect of the semantics of subordinate clauses: With certain exceptions detailed below, a subordinate clause does not express a speaker **assertion**. As a characterization of speaker assertion, we adopt Searle's, "An assertion is a (very special kind of) commitment to the truth of a proposition" (1970[1969]: 29). Sentence (43), for example, commits the speaker to the truth of the proposition expressed by it:

(43)   it's rainy and grey here in Paris

While subordinate clauses are usually considered not to be assertions, Hooper and Thompson have argued that the notion of assertion should be expanded "to cover [certain] structures that are not traditionally considered assertions" (1973: 473). They achieve this expansion in part by rejecting the usual view that assertions include only speaker assertions (1973: 475) and in part by developing the notion of an uncommitted assertion (1973: 477).[16] In the present context we are interested in drawing on both versions of the notion but distinguish the traditional notion of speaker assertion from their broader version.

Hooper and Thompson surveyed subordinate clauses and suggested that some types express assertions, some express logical presuppositions, and some neither.[17] Among the criteria they use for identifying assertions are (i) that they "can be negated [and] questioned by the usual application of the processes of negation and interrogation" (1973: 473), (ii) that the complement clause may be preposed (1973: 470, 477, 478, 480), (iii) that a tag question may be formed from the complement (1973: 471, 477) and (iv) that root transformations may apply in them (see Green 1976: note 7). Green (1976), Ogle (1981), and others have shown that the fourth criterion does not consistently identify assertions, and that criterion is not discussed further here.

One methodological problem must be discussed at the outset. Part of our objective is to distinguish speaker assertions from other phenomena, including both (speaker) presuppositions and non-speaker (i.e. indirect) assertions. When the speaker is also the subject of the matrix verb (i.e. when the subject is first person singular) and the present tense is used, it is more difficult to distinguish a speaker assertion from an indirect assertion. From this point of view it is unfortunate that many of Hooper and Thompson's examples have *I* subjects with present tense, but their objectives were entirely different from ours. In the discussion below, we point out differences between sentences with *I* subjects and those with other subjects.

Hooper and Thompson begin with *that* complements, listing five types of predicates taking such complements.

(44)   (a)   Mary claimed that her sister is a spy
        (b)   Mary thinks that her sister is a spy
        (c)   Mary doubts that her sister is a spy
        (d)   Mary regrets that her sister is a spy
        (e)   Mary realized that her sister is a spy

(45)   Mary's sister is a spy

Their Class A includes verbs of speaking: *say, report, exclaim, assert, claim, vow, be true, be certain, be sure, be obvious.* They claim that sentences with matrix verbs of this class have two readings: on one reading the complements do not express (main) assertions, for example, (44a) reports that Mary asserted the proposition in (45), but the speaker of (44a) does not commit himself to the truth of this proposition and thus does not assert it; on the other reading sentences with matrix verbs of this class express indirect assertions, "not necessarily speaker assertions" (1973: 473). Hooper and Thompson refer to the matrix verb on this reading as "parenthetical"; the reason for this is made clearer by considering example (46) (their (55)):

(46)   it's just started to rain, he said

Hooper and Thompson claim that the verbs of Class B (*suppose, believe, think, expect, guess, imagine, it seems, it happens, it appears*) likewise have two possible meanings – one literal, and one parenthetical. On the latter reading, the complement is an assertion, and "the speaker is indicating that he is not fully committed to the truth of the assertion" (1973: 477). Notice that this statement is inconsistent with Searle's characterization of assertion, according to which a statement is not an assertion without this commitment. On their view, sentences (47a) and (47b) (their (80) and (84)) make the same assertion (47c) (their (82)) makes, and the matrix verb serves only parenthetically to qualify the assertion, making it an uncommitted assertion:

(47)   (a) I guess to read so many comic books is a waste of time
        (b) to read so many comic books is a waste of time, I guess
        (c) to read so many comic books is a waste of time

Notice, however, that some sentences containing a matrix verb from this class, such as our (48), lack the parenthetic reading.[18] Finally, observe that to the extent that an assertion is expressed, it is again an indirect assertion, not a speaker assertion. To see this, compare (47a) with (48):

(48)   Jim guessed (that) to read so many comic books was a waste of time

Sentence (48) does not commit its speaker (who is someone other than Jim) to the truth of the proposition in (47c), and so is not a speaker assertion. Hooper and Thompson, however, argue explicitly that (47a–b) express speaker assertions, not indirect assertions: "the speaker is indicating that he is not fully committed to the truth of the assertion." Then, on the basis of sentences like (49), they argue, "Given that the function of the tag question is to ask for confirmation about the truth of an assertion made by the speaker, it follows that the complements in [(49) and a similar example] are speaker assertions" (1973: 477).

(49)   I guess it's a waste of time to read so many comic books, isn't it?

As Hooper and Thompson point out (1973:471), tags may be formed from complements only where the subject of the matrix clause is the same as the speaker (i.e. is first person singular). When we try to form a tag from the complement clause of a sentence in which the subject is not the speaker of the example, the result is ungrammatical.

(50)   *Jim guessed (that) to read so many comic books was a waste of time, wasn't it(?)
        *Jim guessed (that) to read so many comic books is a waste of time, isn't it(?)

We can see that in the context of the weaker notion of uncommitted assertion it is true that a tag question is used to ask for confirmation about the truth of an assertion made by the speaker, and it is for this reason that tags can be formed from the complement only when the speaker is the subject of the matrix clause, as in (49). A tag cannot be formed from the complement of (48) and other examples where the subject of the matrix is not first person singular precisely because the complement is then not a speaker assertion, in their sense. Thus, the ungrammaticality of (50) in fact shows that the complement in (48) is not a speaker assertion.

Hooper and Thompson (1973: 478) show that verbs of Class C (*be (un)likely, be (im)possible, be (im)probable, doubt, deny*) neither assert nor presuppose the propositions expressed by their complements.

It is well known that the complements of the factive verbs in Class D (*resent, regret, be sorry, be surprised, bother, be odd, be strange, be interesting*) presuppose, not assert, the proposition in their complements (Kiparsky and Kiparsky 1970).

Class E consists of Karttunen's (1971) semifactives: *realize, learn, find out, discover, know, see, recognize*. Hooper and Thompson's analysis of these is similar to that of the verbs of Classes A and B.

Hooper and Thompson argue that reduced complement clauses, such as in (51) (adapted from their (155)) are never assertions:

(51)   it bothers me for the mayor to smoke that big cigar

Similarly, noun complements, as in (52) (their (169)) are neither asserted nor presupposed (1973: 485):

(52)   the claim that the math department was folding was denied by Professor Cantor

Turning now to relative clauses, Hooper and Thompson (1973: 486–91) show that we must distinguish among several types. Non-restrictive relatives assert the proposition which they express;[19] example (53a), adapted from their (198), is a non-restrictive relative and demonstrates the speaker's commitment to the truth of the proposition (53b), as well as to that of (53c):

(53)   (a)   this car, which I only rarely drove, is in excellent condition
        (b)   I only rarely drove this car
        (c)   this car is in excellent condition

Restrictive relative clauses with definite head nouns are presupposed (and thus not asserted); (54a) (their (190)) illustrates such a relative and presupposes (54b):

(54)   (a)   the man who's wearing a party hat is my uncle
        (b)   a man is wearing a party hat

They go on to state that restrictive relative clauses with indefinite head nouns are not presupposed (see also Huck and Na 1990: 60–1 on both types of heads); (55a) (their (218)) asserts (55b), as well as (55c):

(55)   (a) I know a girl who speaks Basque
        (b) a girl speaks Basque
        (c) I know a girl

But Ogle (1981: 137) points out that it is not always true of restrictive relatives with indefinite heads that they are assertions; (56) (his (86)) illustrates this:

(56)   I am looking for a girl who speaks Basque

On its non-specific reading, (56) does not assert (55b). We must conclude that certain restrictive relative clauses are assertions, while others are not.

Lastly we look at assertions in adverbial clauses. Utterances containing time adverbials presuppose the proposition stated by the subordinate clause (Keenan 1971):

(57)   (a) by the time Bill arrived, Ann had already caught a fish
        (b) Ann caught a fish before Bill arrived
        (c) as soon as Bill arrived, Ann caught a fish
        (d) Bill arrived

In utterances (57a–c), the proposition in (57d) is presupposed; what is asserted is that Ann caught a fish and the timeframe in which she did so. Utterances containing manner adverbials seem also to presuppose the propositions that the subordinate clauses express.[20]

(58)   (a) the secretary saved this letter (just) as you saved the memo yesterday
        (b) the secretary saved this letter the way you saved the memo yesterday
        (c) you saved the memo yesterday

Some types of adverbial clause, on the other hand, make no such presupposition. The utterances in (59a)–(60a) do not imply the propositions in the (b) sentences, a precondition for their being presuppositions (see note 20):

(59)   (a) NASA sent up the Hubble Telescope in order that it take high quality photos
        (b) the Hubble Telescope takes high quality photos

(60)   (a) if you (had) won the lottery, the yard would be swarming with reporters
        (b) you won the lottery

The propositions in (59b)–(60b) are neither presupposed nor asserted by the utterances (59a) and (60a).

Hooper and Thompson (1973: 492–4) show that *because* clauses and (*al*)*though* clauses may or may not be asserted. On their ordinary readings the utterances of (61) and (62) do not assert the propositions expressed by the *because* and *although* clauses:

(61)   Sam is going out for dinner because his wife is cooking Japanese food

(62)   Mildred loves her husband although he seldom brings her flowers

However, (63) and (64) on their ordinary readings do assert the propositions expressed in the *because* and *although* clauses:[21]

(63)   Sam is going out for dinner, because I just talked to his wife

(64)   Mildred loves her husband, although Sarah told me he's unfaithful

Preposing the adverbial clause rules out the assertion reading for the *because* clause, but not for the *although* clause:

(65)   because I just talked to his wife, Sam is going out to dinner

(66)   although Sarah told me he's unfaithful, Mildred loves her husband

Unlike its unpreposed counterpart, (63), (65) can only be interpreted as asserting the causal relation between the two clauses. Example (66), however, does not assert the concession relation between its two clauses.[22]

We summarize this section by providing a partial typology of subordinate clauses according to expression of assertion (see table 10.1). Some clause types appear in more than one of the categories, for reasons discussed above.

Thus, although the frequent claim that subordinate clauses do not express speaker assertions in the sense defined above is generally true, there are systematic exceptions to this generalization, as specified in the typology above. The semantics of subordinate clauses has been explored here only with respect to English; and some types of subordinate clause in English have been omitted. Other languages may have different exceptions to the generalization that subordinate clauses do not express assertions. However, although it is impossible to prove it at this time, we remain confident that it will be found that in all languages a significant proportion of subordinate clauses are non-assertions.

Yes/no questions are like subordinate clauses in not expressing an assertion. Sentence (67a), for example, does not commit the speaker to the truth (or falsity) of the proposition in (67b):

(67)   (a)   is Fred building a dog house?
        (b)   Fred is building a dog house

In marking an utterance as a question, each of the devices inventoried in section 10.4.1 is marking it as a non-assertion. We hypothesize that it is this non-assertion marking that is extended to the function of marking (certain) subordinate clauses. If this is correct, then we might expect that in a language

Table 10.1 *Typology of subordinate clauses, by assertion type*

	Example number
Speaker assertions	
Non-restrictive relative clauses	(53)
Restrictive relatives with indefinite heads (certain examples)	(55)
Postposed *because* clauses with comma intonation	(63)
Although clauses (one of two readings)	(64), (66)
Indirect (non-speaker) assertions	
Complements of Class A verbs (parenthetic reading)	(44a), (46)
Complements of Class E verbs (parenthetic reading)	(44e)
Uncommitted indirect assertions	
Complements of Class B verbs (parenthetic reading)	(44b), (48)
Non-assertions	
Complements of Class A verbs (literal reading)	(44a)
Complements of Class B verbs (literal reading)	(44b), (48)
Complements of Class C verbs	(44c)
Complements of Class D verbs	(44d)
Reduced complement clauses	(51)
Noun complements	(52)
Restrictive relatives with definite heads	(54)
Restrictive relatives with indefinite heads (certain examples)	(56)
Time adverbials	(57)
Manner adverbials	(58)
Purpose adverbials	(59)
Conditionals	(60)
Preposed *because* clauses, *because* clauses without comma intonation	(65)
Although clauses (one of two readings)	(64), (66)

a specific question-marking device would always be extended to marking those subordinate clauses that are non-assertions in that language, before it is extended to marking those subordinate clauses that are assertions.[23] Furthermore, it seems likely that a yes/no question marker that was extended to marking subordinate clauses that are non-assertions would next be extended to marking indirect assertions before being extended to marking speaker assertions. These predictions are borne out by the examples we know of, but in order to be validated they should be tested on a wide variety of languages, especially ones in which a yes/no question marker has extended as an all-purpose subordinator. A related hypothesis regarding content questions is proposed below.

10.4.2.2   Other semantic factors

In a study of the relations between the logical properties of content questions, relative clauses, and clefts, which draws on logical representations of questions, proposed in Keenan and Hull (1973a: 444) and of relative clauses in Keenan (1972: 425–6, 433–46), Keenan and Hull 1973b state:

> Our logical representations enable us to see a number of logical similarities between these three constructions. First, all three have a condition given by a sentence S that they impose in some way on the noun phrase separated off from it. Further, they all presuppose that some member of the world satisfies this condition, and are concerned with the member or members which actually *do* satisfy the condition.   (1973b: 350)

Among the questions and relatives they consider are (68) and (69):

(68)   which student did Mary invite?

(69)   the student who Mary invited

In these sentences the noun phrase that is "separated off" is *student* (in (68)) and *the student* (in (69)), or (*student, x*). In each example the condition is given by the "restricting sentence," *Mary invited x*. In addition, each sentence presupposes that Mary invited someone.[24] This type of question and this type of relative are like each other and differ from most other sentence types (except clefts) in these respects.

Notice the important way that Keenan and Hull's sentences differ from those below, which Keenan and Hull (in the three papers cited above) do not discuss:

(70)   who did Mary invite?

(71)   whoever Mary invited

Example (71) is a headless relative, which might occur in a sentence like *whoever Mary invited will arrive late* or *I'll dance with whoever Mary invited*. Examples (70) and (71), like (68) and (69), have the restricting sentence *Mary invited x* and presuppose (with the caveat stated above) that Mary invited someone. In (68) and (69) it is presupposed that Mary invited a student, while in (70)–(71) it is only presupposed that Mary invited someone (human). Clearly there are additional differences between (68)–(69), on the one hand, and (70)–(71), on the other; but for our purposes it is only important that all four clause types presuppose that Mary invited someone and contain a variable, which represents the index in the "restricting sentence."

We hypothesize that because both kinds of content questions (that in (68) and that in (70)) are non-assertions, their marking (namely the Q-word) can be directly extended to all non-assertion types of subordinate clause (see table

10.1). This accounts for the use of Q-words in complement clauses and adverbial clauses, such as the one illustrated in (42). We further suggest that, because of the affinity of content questions and relative clauses stated above, Q-words are especially appropriate for use in relatives.

10.4.2.3   Additional non-assertions

Questions are not the only main-clause type that does not make an assertion; imperatives and expressions of wishes, desires, and counterfactuals are likewise non-assertions. If we are going to explain the use of the question–subordination devices surveyed in section 10.4.1 in part by appealing to the notion assertion, then we must ask why markers of other non-assertion utterance types are not used to mark subordination. In part the answer is "they are."

Bickerton (1981: 31–3) argues that Hawaiian Creole English complementizer *go* derives from the imperative marker *go* of Hawaiian Pidgin English. Imperatives that are equivalent to subjunctives are used in subordination in Pipil (Campbell 1985). Muysken (1977: 69ff.) argues that the Quechua third person imperative or exhortative is used in Ecuadorian Quechua as a subordinator. We assume that imperatives would be used more frequently to form dependent clauses if they did not have other properties that are incompatible with dependent clauses. First, in some languages imperatives do not have a full range of person–number forms; often they are limited to the second person. Presumably it would be inconvenient to have dependent clauses that could only have second person subjects. Second, in many languages imperatives are undermarked; that is, they bear little or no specific marking. For example, in Swahili the imperative lacks the tense prefix that characterizes most verb forms, as well as the special ending that characterizes the subjunctive; it may consist of a bare verb stem, such as *soma* "read" (second person singular subject, no object agreement; Perrott 1957: 46–7). Such a lack of marking seems to be inadequate to indicate subordination. While imperatives are not universally undermarked, this may be part of the explanation of their apparent infrequency as subordinators.

In many languages wishes, desires, and counterfactuals in matrix clauses are marked with a special mood, often subjunctive; in these same languages this mood may be used, often together with other markers, in subordination. Sentence (72) is an example of a subjunctive in a main clause; in (73) the subjunctive is said to indicate subordination (Paul/Stolte 1949: 353).[25]

(72)   bei besserer Ernährung hätte   er länger gelebt
       with better nourishment had.SBV he longer lived
       "With better nourishment he would have lived longer."
                               (Paul/Stolte 1949: 346, 4)

(73)   ihm scheint, ich sei   böse
        him seems   I   were.sbv angry
        "To him it seems that I am angry."   (Paul/Stolte 1949: 353, 3)

In this way another marker of non-assertion is extended to a subordinate clause.

In many languages quotative particles function to mark indirect assertions.[26] From this function, the quotative can extend to the marking of other kinds of non-speaker assertion (or speaker non-assertion). Example (74) shows the Georgian third person quotative enclitic *-o* marking the complement of the verb "think," and in (75) "think" is only implied. Sentence (76) illustrates the Japanese quotative *to* with the matrix verb "know." (Here we are focusing on the extension of the quotative to a more general complementizer; on the origin of the quotatives themselves, see section 7.3 and Sansom 1928, Akiba 1978: 92–6.)

(74)   glexi. . .midis da pikrobs, ra   miq'o   im beberma, raze
        peasant go and think   what he.did.me that old.nar   why

        damɣup'a-o
        s/he.ruin.me-quot

        "The peasant goes and thinks: what did that old man do to me, why
        did he ruin me?"
                                                    (Čikobava *et al.* 1950–64, VII: 124)

(75)   sazedao   kcevis   pormeb-ši -en-. . .element'i ise xširad
        superessive version-gen forms-in -en- element so frequently

        gvevlineba, [rom titkos   igi-a   mac'armoebeli-o]
        it.comes.us that as.though it-it.be formant-quot

        "We encounter the element *-en-* so frequently in forms of superessive
        version that [we think] as though it is the formant" or ". . .that it is as
        though it were the formant."   (Topuria 1967: 172)

(76)   nagori na-ku moy-u **to** sir-i-se-ba
        trace not-ku burn-u quot know-I-past-a-ds
        "Had (I) known that (it) would burn without (leaving) any trace
        behind, . . ."   (*Taketori Monogatari*, 44, quoted in Akiba 1978: 90)

In this way, this device that marked non-speaker assertions is extended to mark other non-assertions.

In summary we note again that devices that mark questions and certain other non-assertions are frequently extended to the marking of subordinate clauses, which are also non-assertions.

10.4.3   Conclusion

We suggest that the appearance that subordination represents dialogue is a secondary effect of the fact that certain devices that mark subordination do indeed originate in questions and are then extended to subordination. Our account makes it unnecessary to rely on the vague structures proposed for parataxis (with the relationship of the subordinate clause to the matrix not specified). Under our analysis there is no need to go beyond the syntax to the structure of discourse to explain syntactic change. Our analysis does not assume mechanisms that have not been clarified or explored, as does the claim that an independent question becomes a dependent clause. Such mechanisms have not been specified, and no evidence to support them has been adduced. In fact, there is no need to do so. As we have shown, developments in complex structures can be accounted for through the mechanisms known to apply in simplex sentences.

10.5   On the ultimate origins of complex constructions

In this section we examine the view that subordinate clauses have originated in relatively recent times (section 10.5.1) and develop our own hypothesis about how hypotaxis originated, regardless of when that took place.

10.5.1   Origins of subordination in recent history

The view that hypotaxis appears later in the development of language is based in part on the assumption that hypotaxis is a sophisticated, highly developed construction, often coupled with an assumption that parataxis is primitive. The assumption that hypotaxis is highly developed is, in turn, based in part upon the distribution of hypotaxis in languages of the world and in part upon the common belief that parataxis is more common in spoken language, while hypotaxis is more characteristic of writing.

The distribution of hypotaxis is sometimes simplified to the claim that written languages have hypotaxis and unwritten languages lack it.[27] This could possibly be true only of finite subordinate clauses, for most or all languages – written or unwritten – have non-finite subordination (reduced clauses). Most unwritten languages, too, have finite subordinate clauses, but rigid supporters of the Parataxis Hypothesis explain this through borrowing or through community literacy in another language. Yet if claims of borrowing are accepted without specific evidence, the attribution of hypotaxis to borrowing is often impossible to refute, even theoretically (see chapter 6). In addition, claims that parataxis is primitive cannot be supported, for parataxis occurs even in English and other languages spoken in the most sophisticated of societies.[28]

The view that finite subordinate clauses are more common in writing than in speech has now been documented (Chafe 1982),[29] but it is not clear that it is correct to equate frequency in spoken language with primitiveness, and frequency in writing with sophistication. It is clear that hypotaxis is well suited to written language, for it provides a means for packing a great deal of information into a few words and has the potential of making the relationships among ideas specific. Complex hypotaxis is less appropriate in spoken language, since it places a greater burden on memory and processing ability. Because non-finite clauses typically lack some verb categories (such as tense and aspect) some arguments (often the subject), and subjunctions that could specify the relation between the subordinate clause and the matrix, they are typically somewhat less precise. It is obvious that written language developed after spoken. But none of these considerations rules out the possibility that devices that are especially effective and necessary in written language, in this case hypotaxis, preexisted writing.

A second phenomenon that has been used as a basis for the claim that fully subordinate finite clauses developed late in English (i.e. only in the historical period) is that subordinate clauses (or their predecessors, depending upon one's analysis) typically followed main clauses, rather than being surrounded by elements of the matrix clause (O'Neil 1977).[30] It is not clear, however, that this is not a matter of stylistic preference, a shifting of heavy material to the right to avoid breaking up the flow of the matrix clause. It may also be related to the greater flexibility of word order in Old English, since that would permit heads to be final in their own clauses to resolve possible ambiguities. In any case, no independent evidence has been presented to show that clauses that follow (or precede) main clauses are any less subordinated than are those that are surrounded by constituents of the main clause.

Third, it may be argued that relative pronouns or other subordinators become increasingly independent of their sources throughout the early history of certain languages. In Classical Latin Q-words and relatives were only slightly differentiated, but in the early history of French and other Romance languages they became increasingly different. As a result of separate changes in these two types of pronouns in French, (a) the relative distinguishes subject/object/disjunctive/genitive, while the interrogative distinguishes only nominative/oblique, (b) the relative distinguishes specific from non-specific, while the interrogative does not, and (c) only the interrogative distinguishes direct from indirect discourse (M. Harris 1978: 205–12).[31] This set of changes, of course, took place after relative clauses were already established in Latin by a relatively long tradition; it cannot be assumed that such changes occur only soon after the introduction of a structure.

A final reason offered by some for believing hypotaxis to be a late development is that in some language families or subgroups there are no reconstructible subjunctions or relative pronouns, though often the various subordinators in different languages in the group have parallel sources: for example, no specific relative marking can be reconstructed for the Germanic languages (O'Neil 1977: 208; Ebert 1978: 22; Ramat 1982: 284). It should be added that in some families there are likewise no reconstructible subordinate structures.

In our view it has not been established that hypotaxis appears late in the development of a language. We find no compelling argument to distinguish the changes in subordinate clauses that are undergone early in the literary history of a language from changes undergone as existing constructions are renewed.[32]

10.5.2   A possible mechanism

Whether or not one believes that hypotaxis is a recent development in the history of language, one can contemplate its origins without reference to time. Those who see hypotaxis as a recent development typically point to parataxis as its origin. But if we reconstructed parataxis as the origin of hypotaxis, we would be assuming a change of a kind which, as argued above, is not attested in the history of language.[33] We accept instead the Uniformitarian Principle, that the processes which operated in prehistoric times are the same ones that operate in historic times. In addition, as is the case with regard to changes in historic times, the Parataxis Hypothesis does not explain how paratactic structures became complex structures with subordination. Another way to put this is that, given a rule of grammar (77), the Parataxis Hypothesis does nothing to explain how the complement first comes to be expanded as a complementizer phrase.

(77) $X^1 \rightarrow X$ (Complement)

We suggest a different view, that no special mechanism is needed for the first introduction of subordination. Non-finite verb forms – deverbal nouns and adjectives – have an inherent dual nature, which can lead naturally to dual analysis. As nouns or adjectives, non-finite verb forms can function as members of these categories in a sentence; that is, they may be generated in a tree as instances of N or Adj. Since they are formed on verbal bases, they are open to an interpretation as a verb. In many languages a clause frequently consists of only a verb, and it is natural for a verb, even without specified arguments, to be open to analysis as a clause.[34]

This dual nature of non-finite verb forms has long been recognized by proposing for them a sentential initial structure and a simple (N or Adj) final structure. It was shown as long ago as 1970 (Chomsky 1970) that at least certain types of non-finite verb form do not have a complex (sentential) initial structure. We are proposing not that all non-finite verb forms have complex initial structures, but that, being at once substantival and (de)verbal, they have the potential for being diachronically *reanalyzed* as having a complex initial structure. This, we suggest, is true whether or not a non-finite form of a particular type has a complex initial structure from a synchronic point of view. This is a potential that substantives like *table* and *yellow* do not have.[35]

Although this is a general proposal, it is perhaps best understood in terms of a real change in a specific language. It is believed that Proto-Lezgian did not possess finite relative clauses (Alekseev 1985), since the modern languages generally lack them, as do sister languages in subgroups of North East Caucasian language family.[36] At least one Lezgian language, Udi, has developed relative clauses in recent times, and it is this very typical sort of development that we use as our example here.[37] The sentence in (78) contains a past participle of a type inherited from Proto-Lezgian.

(78)   azak'e xinär-ax gölöšp-i
        I.saw   girl-DAT dance-PTCPL
        "I saw the girl who danced" or "I saw the dancing girl."

We assume that *xinär-ax gölöšpi* has a simple structure like that in (79):

(79)

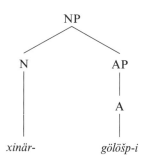

The structure in (79), while itself simple, was open to reanalysis; the modifier *gölöšp-i* "danced," derived from the verb *gölöšp-* "dance," could be analyzed as a finite verb. Udi, like many other languages, permits clauses consisting at surface structure of just a finite verb form, such as *gölöš-ne-p-i* "s/he had danced." This means that the AP of (79) could be reinterpreted as an S. As soon as it is reanalyzed as an S, all of the possibilities of expanding any other (main-clause) S were opened up. The finite relative clause that developed in this way is illustrated in (80), and its structure represented as (81):

(80)   azaǩe xinär-ax mat'in-te gölöš-ne-p-i
        I.saw girl-DAT who-REL dance$_1$-3.SG-dance$_2$-PERF
        "I saw the girl who had danced."

(81)

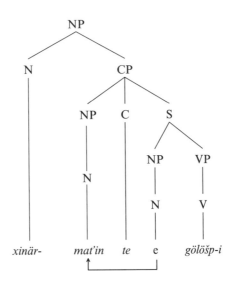

Notice that we are not proposing that finite subordinate clauses developed out of non-finite clauses directly or in a concrete way; we are suggesting that the dual nature of non-finite clauses makes it possible for them to be (re)analyzed as clauses and that this fact makes it possible to develop full finite subordinate clauses instantly, using the rules of clause and phrase construction already possessed. Finite subordinate clauses are recognized as more complete than non-finite ones in that they may all possess all arguments possible for a given verb and may express all of the verb categories available for other finite verbs, such as tense, voice, and aspect (see, for example, C. Lehmann 1988). We are not suggesting that finite subordinate clauses developed by adding these categories to non-finite proto-clauses, but that they can develop instantaneously by applying in an embedded S' all of the rules that are already available for simple clauses.[38]

Thus, we suggest that the dual nature of non-finite verb forms, together with strategies for constructing a simple sentence provide a means for the introduction of hypotaxis. We believe that no special mechanism is needed to explain this development. Any language that has non-finite verb forms has the potential for introducing a finite subordinate clause.[39] This is one manifestation of the productivity of language.

As a consequence of our hypothesis about the origin of subordination and our discussion of the logical nature of subordinate clauses, we further hypothesize that languages introducing subordination for the first time derive their subordinators primarily from one or both of two kinds of sources: (a) cases and prepositions, such as those discussed in section 10.3.3; (b) markers of non-assertions, such as those discussed and illustrated in section 10.4.

10.6   Conclusion

In this chapter we have examined the Parataxis Hypothesis and discussed several problems with it. We have pointed out that even if the Parataxis Hypothesis is correct, it does little to illuminate the kinds of changes languages undergo involving complex structures. In section 10.3 we developed a simple hypothesis that developments in complex structures can be accounted for through the mechanisms already discussed in this work in connection with simplex structures. In section 10.4 we examined the nature of the relation between the structures of questions and of subordinate clauses and suggested that markers of the former are extended to structures containing the latter.

We have emphasized that the origin of the structure of a particular type of subordinate clause and the origin of the subordinator that marks it (if any) is not necessarily the same. In many instances, discussed especially in section 10.3.1, subordinators do indicate the structural origin of a particular clause type. In others, however, the etymology of the subordinator does not reveal the structural origin of the clause type because the subjunction was extended from a different type of clause; for example, markers of relative clauses have become all-purpose subordinators in a number of languages. It is this possibility that marking of subordination can be extended from one type of structure to another that explains the Marker/Structure Fallacy, discussed briefly in section 10.2.

11 *The nature of syntactic change and the issue of causation*

11.1   Introduction

In the preceding chapters we have laid out a framework for the study of diachronic syntax. We have examined the nature of syntactic change in detail from the point of view of specific mechanisms (chapters 4–6) and from the point of view of certain recurrent types (chapters 7–10). In this chapter we take up questions relating to syntactic change as a whole. Earlier in this book, in chapter 1, we only briefly introduced the topic of the explanation of change and associated notions of prediction and causation, touching upon them briefly in later chapters in connection with specific changes. We have not yet drawn these points together to provide a general statement on explanation, causation, and prediction. Moreover, two important aspects of the nature of syntactic change have thus far been left unexamined, namely regularity and directionality. Our goal in this chapter is to consider these matters that bear importantly on the overall nature of syntactic change. Throughout, our discussion is informed by the investigations of individual changes reported in earlier parts of this work, as well as by our separate and collaborative investigations into a diverse array of languages.

If one is able to deduce universals of syntactic change, in the way we have proposed in the preceding chapters, it is clear that progress is being made towards understanding change. However, it might be argued that a full understanding is reached only with the ability to identify the causes of particular changes, to explain those changes, and to predict them. But the identification of causes, like the whole matter of the explanation of linguistic change, is often hotly contested. In section 11.2 we attempt to cut through some of the misunderstanding and misconceptions to show how the approach we have developed can contribute to explaining syntactic change.

While most historical linguists accept that sound change is regular, many have expressed the opinion that syntactic change has no analogue to the regularity of phonological changes.[1] This is generally held to be due to the fact that the set of phonemes (the inventory or set of phonological elements) is finite, but is learned in context within individual lexical items; however, languages do not have finite sets of sentences, and sentences are not learned in the way sounds are, embedded in lexical items. Thus, a sound is learned conventionally in combinations with other sounds, which together are associated with meanings to constitute the different morphemes which happen to contain the particular sound. The sound, a "type," has multiple "tokens" as it recurs in the morphemes that contain it. It has been claimed that syntactic patterns or rules are different; they are not acquired embedded in some broader conventional context (as the sounds are acquired in the context of the words which contain them) – individual sentences are not learned, but are generated by the rules of grammar. It is said that the rule is the "type" and has but a single "token," the rule itself, learned without phonological substance, hence without broader associations of the kind that make it possible to view phonological change as regular.

In section 11.3 below we argue that many kinds of syntactic change are indeed regular. The structure of our argument is essentially the same as that used by the Neogrammarians to argue that sound change is regular.

Historical linguists accept that certain sound changes typically occur in only one direction; for example, while a change of voiceless stops to voiced intervocalically is a typical change, voiced to voiceless in this position is unexpected. However, some argue that syntactic change does not exhibit comparable directionality in this sense. Understanding this natural directionality is a part of understanding sound change, and, as discussed in chapter 12, the directionality provides a practical tool in reconstruction. In section 11.4 we argue against several specific proposals that particular syntactic changes are truly unidirectional. Nevertheless, we point out that the prospects for understanding the direction of many kinds of grammatical changes seem much brighter than they once did, and progress on implicational universals and typological interconnections is helping to establish directionality for certain specific grammatical changes.

Although related to each other only loosely, the three issues of explanation, regularity, and directionality each must be informed by a broad study of many changes in a wide range of languages. Our findings in these areas are discussed below.

11.2   Explanation, causation, and prediction

A crucial ingredient for explanation is an understanding of the causes which bring about linguistic change, and for our interests, specifically those involved in syntactic change.

11.2.1   Causation

In the literature on linguistic change one often reads that there are *internal* and *external* causes, or explanations, for changes. The internal causes are based on the limitations and potentials of human speech production and perception – that is, they are determined for the most part by the physical realities of human biology. *Internal* causes include (i) **physical** explanations involving the physiology of human speech organs[2] and (ii) **psychological** or **cognitive** explanations involving the perception, processing, and learning of language.[3] The psychological factors have played the more important role in discussions of diachronic syntax. *External* causes involve factors that are largely outside of language *per se* (outside the human organism); they include, for example, expressive uses of language, positive and negative social evaluations (prestige, stigma), the effects of literacy, prescriptive grammar, and educational policies, political decree, language planning, and language contact. (For discussion and several examples, mostly phonological and morphological, see Campbell and Ringen 1981; Ohala 1981, 1989; Jahr 1989; for processing explanations of word order changes, see Hawkins 1983, 1991; Campbell, Bubenik, and Saxon 1988; for syntactic examples involving external factors, see chapter 6.)

A wide variety of specific causes have now been identified, and it is known that these interact in complex ways, sometimes overlapping, sometimes competing with one another, complicating the task of trying to understand change. Among the causes we have already discussed are contact, ambiguity, and analogy (all in section 3.3.3; see also section 4.3.1, and chapter 6), as well as ease of processing and stylistic causes (section 8.6), and rule harmony (section 9.3).

At least one category of causes requires further discussion. It is now well known that change in one part of a language, one component of the grammar, can have consequences for other parts of the grammar. In the process of grammaticalization syntactic or morphological changes often lead to phonological changes. An example is the once main verb *will* (meaning "want") changing to an auxiliary (meaning "future") and then undergoing phonological reduction, as in *I'll go* (see Heine and Reh 1984: 63–6 for additional examples). Also, while it has been claimed that it is not possible for phonetic change to lead to morphosyntactic change,[4] in fact this does occur. Klokeid (1978) has shown that phonological change which resulted in loss or reduction of the ergative case marker in Lardil triggered reanalysis of an antipassive construction, resulting in a change from ergative to accusative alignment. (The syntactic change is further described in section 9.4.4.2.) In the Artašen dialect of Laz, a general deletion or reduction of the dative case-marker (a feature partly shared with sister dialects and languages) appears to have conditioned loss of the case marking system (Harris 1985:385-9). In Pre-Georgian, reduction or loss of the narrative (ergative) case marker (*-n*), led to its replacement by the narrative case form of the postposed article (*man*), later itself reduced to *-ma* by the same phonetic process that triggered the morphological change (Harris 1985: 75–9, summarizing the views of a number of scholars cited there). Several such examples are presented in this book, such as section 4.3.3, where the new tense system of Cakchiquel (Mayan) is seen to be largely dependent upon phonetic modifications which changed the form of the old aspect markers to the extent that they were reanalyzed. Similarly, section 4.4.1 describes a change in Finnish participles, which was caused by the phonological change of *-m* > *-n*.

Some have cited the notions of "targets," "conspiracy," or "drift" as possible causes of change in syntax, as well as in other parts of the grammar.[5] In many instances at least, these are reanalysis with complex actualization, often involving lexical extension (see chapter 5). The change in the system of English modals is an example of a set of changes that may be viewed in this way (see section 7.4.1.2). Thus, we see these notions, not as causes of change, but as characterizations of the way in which syntactic change often proceeds.

It is now clear that most changes have more than one cause. One of the more interesting aspects of multiple causation is that internal and external causes often interact: for example, a feature that seems to be contact-induced may also have an internal motivation. In Tabassaran, the shift from gender-class agreement to person agreement is an example of a rule that appears to have been in part triggered by contact with Indo-European and Turkic languages. Yet the innovative agreement system was not borrowed outright from one of the neighboring languages, and an account that did not take into consideration the internal development of clitic copies of topic pronouns and subsequent reanalysis of these as agreement would be incomplete (Harris, in press a; for other examples, see Campbell 1975, 1977, 1990a; Campbell and Ringen 1981).

11.2.2 Prevention, compensation, and neglect

In our view, the causal factors which determine changes may interact in complex ways. The overall outcome of the changes is usually (though not always) in the direction of maintaining or achieving the language's functional needs (of which we speak loosely here, but which will become clearer in the course of the discussion). These functional needs may be served in some cases by preventing or deflecting certain changes in order to avoid detrimental effects on the grammar, or by permitting such disruptive changes and then following them by subsequent compensatory changes which rectify the situation.[6] In this regard we differ from Kiparsky, Lightfoot, and Paul (see section 2.2.6.1) when they assert "languages do not practice prophylaxis, only therapy." We argue that language change may involve both. The examples that follow support our point.

1 *Prevention (prophylaxis)*. In a well-known example of a morphologically conditioned sound change in Estonian (see Kettunen 1962: 106–7; Kiparsky 1965: 1.28; Anttila 1972: 79–80; Campbell and Ringen 1981) final *n* was lost, except that in Northern Estonian the change was morphologically conditioned so that the -*n* of "first person singular" in verb forms was not lost. This change was blocked in Northern Estonian to prevent loss of important morphological distinctions, since without the final -*n*, "first person singular" and "second person imperative" (and some other) verb forms would not have been distinct. Thus, this is a case of "prevention" ("prophylaxis") of the sort whose existence is denied by the slogan cited above. The basis of this claim is seen in the following comparison of relevant Northern and Southern Estonian verb forms:

(1)   N. Estonian   S. Estonian
        *kanna**n***   *kanna*   **kanna-n*   "I carry"
        kanna   *kanna?*   **kanna-?*   "carry!"

Loss of both *?* and *n* in Northern Estonian would have left the first person singular and second person singular imperative forms indistinct, therefore loss of final *n* was prevented in the first person singular forms. In Southern Estonian, where the *?* was not lost, the forms remained distinct and final *n* could be freely lost in first person singular forms as well. The needs of functional distinction in the case of Northern Estonian prevented the change where the first person singular would have lost the form necessary to signal its function and to maintain important morphological differences, but it was not prevented in Southern Estonian, where the meaning difference could still be signaled.[7] It should be noted, however, that this does not mean that loss under similar circumstances will always be prevented when the phonological loss would entail loss of morphological distinctions. In some instances, loss of morphological distinctions is permitted (see below).

2 *Compensation (therapeutic change)*. For a case of therapeutic change after the deleterious effects of an earlier but associated change, we can look once again at the Estonian loss of final *n*. Formerly, the accusative singular was also signaled by -*n*, but this *n* was lost, thereby damaging the ability of the

grammar to signal this morphological category with its importance for the syntax of the language – a primary marker of direct objects. Estonian in this case compensated after the damaging change by utilizing consonant gradation (with other phonological differences) and particles to signal the accusative case, formerly signaled by *-n*. For example, the nominative singular *kant* (< **kanta*) "heel [NOM SG]" is distinguished from the accusative singular *kanna* (< **kanna-n*) "heel [ACC SG]" in this way. The phonological difference between the two compensated for the lost accusative singular *-n* in forms such as these which had undergone apocope (in the nominative singular) and consonant gradation (*nt* > *nn* in closed syllables, in this case formerly closed by the final *-n* of the accusative ending). In other nouns, however, such as *kala* "fish" which did not fit the structural description for consonant gradation or apocope and consequently underwent neither change, there simply was no phonological difference to compensate for the lost accusative ending (*kala* (< **kala*) "nominative singular," *kala* (< **kala-n*) "accusative singular"). In such instances, partial compensation for the lost accusative ending was achieved through the use of the particle *ära* "up," as in *sõõn kala ära* "I eat the fish (up)."

Lapp illustrates a different kind of compensation after the same disruptive change. Lapp, too, lost final *-n*, independently of Estonian, but this change also affected certain grammatical cases, such as genitive singular (formerly *-n*, lost in this change). Lapp, like other Balto-Finnic languages, had consonant gradation in closed syllables, and as in Estonian, the difference in gradated and non-gradated stems could take over the function of signaling the genitive vs. nominative cases, respectively, in many words and thus compensate for the lost genitive *-n*. Lapp, however, underwent a subsequent change of further therapy in which consonant gradation was extended to include those consonants that formerly had not undergone it. (Originally it was limited to stops.) Thus, for example, today we have the following situation, illustrated here in (2) with the change from Proto-Lapp to Southern Lapp (Korhonen 1981: 148; Lehtiranta 1989: 60):

(2)   *guolle*   < **kōlē*   "fish" (nominative singular)
        guole   < **kōlē-n* "fish's" (genitive singular)

3 *Another example of compensation.* In Estonian and Votic (and formerly in Old Finnish), the partitive case marks pronoun objects, where one would expect the accusative. The reason for this has to do with the change of **-m* to *-n* that took place in Late Proto-Balto-Finnic.[8] Formerly distinct pronouns, e.g. **minu-m* I-ACC.SG ("me") and **minu-n* I-GEN.SG ("my"), were left homophonous after the change, both *minu-n*. The partitive case already func-

tioned to signal objects in many instances, such as partial (not totally affected) objects and objects of negative verbs. Given the surface ambiguity of *minu-n*, either "genitive" or "accusative," the partitive took the place in these three languages (Estonian, Votic, and Old Finnish) of the accusative in pronouns to signal all object functions, including pronouns which were both partially and totally affected objects, in order to prevent confusion of the direct object with the genitive case. In this way, the accusative, identical in shape with the genitive, was lost for pronouns in these languages.

Old Finnish, on the other hand, has examples of pronominal objects both in the partitive case (e.g. *minu-a*) and in the ambiguous genitive-like accusative (e.g. *minu-n*). However, in time Finnish rectified the disruption and stabilized the situation with an alternative solution; namely, it generalized the "accusative plural" ending *-t* to signal the "accusative singular" of pronouns. Thus today Finnish pronouns bear the following endings, as illustrated for "I":

(3)   *minä*   Nominative
       minu-t   Accusative (cf. *miehe-t* [man-ACC.PL] "men")
       minu-a   Partitive
       minu-n   Genitive

In Zyrian, Votyak, and Ostyak (more distant, non-Balto-Finnic sister languages), corresponding pronouns are in the (original) accusative case with *-m*. In seeking an explanation for the deviation of these Balto-Finnic languages (Estonian, Votic, and Finnish) from the original Finno-Ugric (and pre-Balto-Finnic) pattern, we soon turn up the ambiguous surface forms and discover the shifts that took place in order to remedy the situation and create an unambiguous pronominal object form. (See Hakulinen 1968; Ikola 1968; Laanest 1982.)

4 *Neglect.* An example from German illustrates a grammatical change in which neither prophylaxis nor direct therapy was exercised, and portions of the grammar were just lost as a result. The treatment of objects in German grammar has changed due to reanalyses, showing the consequences for syntax of phonological (and morphological) change (Ebert 1978: 51–2). Old and Middle High German marked some objects as partitives by means of the genitive case; this construction is illustrated in (4) from the Middle High German period:

(4)   ich will im   mîn-es   brôt-es   geben
       I   want to.him my-GEN   bread-GEN to.give
       "I want to give him some of my bread."
                                    (Hartmann von Aue, cited by Ebert 1978: 52)

In Middle High German times the construction in (4) started to lose ground and in Modern German the few survivals are seen as relics only. The reduction of these constructions is attributed to the changes in inflectional endings and to the loss of the partitive meaning of the genitive object in contrast to the accusative object, which was more common. Due to phonological merger, the former -*es* "genitive" and -*ez* "nominative/accusative" of neuter adjectives were no longer distinguishable in many instances. The old -*es* ("genitive") was re-analyzed as "accusative" in examples like (4), and the use of accusative case was extended to pronouns (e.g. *das* "this"). The outcome was that the partitive object construction was simply given up in German as a result of the phonological merger which left the genitive and accusative undifferentiated in so many forms – neither prevention nor compensation occurred to rescue it.

We argue, then, that languages may practice prevention or therapy, or they may fail to undergo either.

11.2.3   Prediction

A major portion of the debate about explanation of linguistic change has revolved around the issue of prediction. It is sometimes objected that prediction is necessary for explanation but that prediction of linguistic change is not possible, and therefore all theories addressing language change are inadequate (for discussion see Lass 1980, 1987; Aitchison 1987; Eaton and Koopman 1987; Toon 1987; Davis 1990).[9] For example, from this point of view, it might be objected (as Lass 1987: 252 does explicitly) that appeal to such things in the examples above as morphological conditioning (prevention/prophylaxis), compensating changes to fix up the grammar after deleterious changes (therapy), or reanalysis of a syntactic construction in the face of surface ambiguity cannot predict when such changes will take place, what exact form they may take, or when they may fail to occur even though the appropriate condition may have been present.

In response to this, we make the following points in the discussion below:

1   Various sorts of syntactic changes do permit certain predictions, though others do not.
2   It is more constructive to provide a partial explanation, combined with further study, than to give up.
3   Prediction is not necessary for valid explanation.

It is important to distinguish what is impossible to predict (e.g. that a change will occur, which change will occur, when a change will occur) from what is possible to predict (e.g. the nature of the changes that do occur, the conditions under which they occur, what changes cannot occur). To illustrate this point, let us consider the example of a rabbit fleeing a pursuing dog (from Wright 1976). Given certain circumstances, we may be able to predict that the rabbit will flee, but we may not be able to predict the escape route the rabbit will attempt to follow. Nevertheless, in spite of this inability to predict, we may still be able to determine in an objective manner that the rabbit indeed will flee from the dog, and that the paths the rabbit follows are indeed appropriate for the goal of attempting to escape the dog. In the case where change in form puts tension on function (as in the morphologically conditioned changes discussed above), there may be a variety of alternative means for resolving the conflict. For example, the following are all alternatives that might be selected: morphological conditioning to block the harmful effects of the change (as in example 1 in section 11.2.2), compensation by subsequent changes to rectify the harmful effects of the unblocked change through extension of consonant gradation in Lapp, or through the use of particles in combination with consonant gradation in Estonian (as in example 2 in section 11.2.2). We may be able to predict under given conditions that a language will attempt to change to avoid the detrimental effects of the change, but not to predict which of the alternatives for attaining that goal it will actually follow. We may be able to identify objectively when such a state of affairs comes to obtain in a language in order to predict change (as in the analogy above, to predict when the rabbit will flee the dog) and to determine objectively when a given change would contribute to remedying the situation (when the rabbit chooses an appropriate escape route).

This is all that the legitimacy and testability of such explanations for syntactic change require. In this sense the issue of scientific testability and legitimacy of such explanations seems to be separable from the fact that such explanations may not render precise mechanistic predictions. That is, there are different kinds or degrees of prediction: weak prediction (something is likely to happen), strong prediction (something will happen, though when and where is unclear), and absolute prediction (something will happen at a specifiable time and place) (Aitchison 1987: 12).

Multiple causation has thus far been one deterrent to prediction. Nevertheless, given that it is known that linguistic changes often have multiple causes and that more than one of these causal factors may operate simultaneously on particular linguistic forms in particular linguistic changes,[10] we have absolutely no choice, if we ever hope to understand – to explain – linguistic change, but to investigate the multiple causes and how they jointly operate in some cases and compete in others to determine the give and take among causal factors and the interaction of chance and necessity in linguistic change. As Faarlund (1990b: 41) points out:

whatever cause we are able to establish, that cause never seems to be a sufficient condition for the event. We can always find languages where the change
does not seem to have taken place . . . It is even hard to determine whether
any given cause can be said to be a necessary condition for a change . . . A
linguistic change is an event that takes place within an extremely complex system, and any causality within complex systems such as languages or living
organisms or societies must involve a great number of causes that are interre-
lated in complex ways.

Because we do not yet understand fully the complex interactions of the causal
factors, we cannot predict all outcomes. The internal causal factors we have
mentioned rely on the limitations and potentials of human speech production
and perception, physical explanations of change stemming from the physiology of human speech organs, and cognitive explanations involving the perception, processing, or learning of language. These internal explanations are
largely responsible for the nature and regular, universal aspects of language.
But, it should be noticed that even well-defined mechanistic causal factors can
compete in their interactions in ways which make prediction difficult and, at
least for the present, impossible. Consider another analogy, an instance of an
automobile smashed against a tree, where the following conditions obtain: it is
dark and foggy (poor visibility), the road is narrow and covered with ice
(poor driving conditions), the driver is intoxicated and suffers from several
physical disabilities (driver impaired), and the car was in very poor operating
condition (worn tires, bad brakes, loose steering), the driver was exceeding the
speed limit and not watching the road at the time of the accident (poor judg-
ment), and finally, the tree happened to be situated at just the spot where the
vehicle left the roadway (chance circumstance). In such a situation, how could
we determine a unique cause (or even joint interaction of causes) of the accident with sufficient precision to allow us to predict the crash? Linguistic
changes are often akin to this crash in that competing or overlapping causal
factors may be at play, but precise prediction of whether a change will take
place (will the car in fact crash?) or when and how a change (a crash) will be
realized is not possible.

   Lass (1987) opposes all "functionalist" explanations, prophylactic or therapeutic, claiming "both are absurd" and that "all functionalist arguments can
ultimately be reduced to instances of the fallacy of affirming the consequent"
(Lass 1987: 252; see also 1980: 79). That is, he rejects *post hoc* explanations (Lass
1980: 32, 69–70), objecting to what he perceives as the lack of predictability of
linguistic change. However, at this stage of our understanding, it would be
foolish to turn our backs on any potential causal factor, such as morphological conditioning or avoidance of homophony or reanalysis to avoid ambiguity

or to resolve multiple analyses (as discussed in the examples above), and thus cut off inquiry before the fuller picture is understood. We take the position that if we tentatively accept explanations that appear to be reasonable, such as those mentioned in section 11.2.1, and further study the correlation between actual change and apparent cause, we are likely to learn more about syntactic change than we would if we just gave up, as Lass proposes. It is only upon further extensive investigation of the interaction of these overlapping and competing factors that we will come to understand linguistic change more fully.

Even if causal mechanistic (internal) explanations were more readily available for linguistic change, that would not necessarily invalidate other sorts of explanations. "There are many kinds of explanation, and not even the physical sciences are limited to only explanation of the strongest type – the covering law variety" (Toon 1987: 276). Consider an analogy (from Wright 1976: 44). To answer the question, "why did the window break?" with "because John slammed it" is a completely adequate answer/explanation, even if shock waves and crystal structure may lie further behind the breaking. There are contexts in which an answer of "because of a certain causal factor x," or, "because it achieved a certain goal/result" is adequate and appropriate, even if there are more mechanistic things one could say. For example, consider the constraint, "no language will assume a form in violation of such formal principles as are postulated to be universal in human languages" (Weinreich, Labov, and Herzog 1968: 100). That languages avoid changes which would violate universals is an adequate explanation in certain contexts even if we discover the aspects of human physiology and cognition (mechanistic, internal factors) which explain universals, why certain features are found universally in the world's languages. The existence of the underlying mechanistic (internal) explanation of universals at some level does not invalidate explanations such as "because languages avoid violating universals" at some other level. Even if we may ultimately come to understand more fully the aspects of human cognition which underlie reanalysis, at another level reanalysis remains a valid explanation for the syntactic changes it deals with.

In this way, the mechanisms we propose as basic to our approach – reanalysis, extension, and borrowing – are adequate explanations of change. The interaction of reanalysis and extension explains why, in the course of change, a language has characteristics of two different constructions in one: extension typically affects one aspect of the reanalyzed structure before another, producing a mixture of surface characteristics of both the inherited and the innovative constructions. The same characteristic of extension – applying first to one aspect of a complex structure, then to another – provides part of the explanation of the gradual nature of syntactic change. The view we propose of reanalysis provides an explanation of the origins of certain kinds of gradual changes (see especially sections 8.3, 8.6, 9.2 and 5.4). We have characterized kinds of changes that occur (for example, sections 7.2.5.2, 7.3.2.2, 7.4.4, 8.5.1.2, 8.5.2.2 and 9.2), stated constraints on their occurrence (for example, sections 7.5 and 9.4), and elucidated the nature of transitions that do take place (for example, sections 11.3, 11.4). All of this is a valid part of explanation.

However, absolute prediction of change is not, as sometimes suggested, an appropriate goal for diachronic syntax, or indeed for any retrospective science. Evolution by natural selection is recognized as scientifically legitimate explanation in spite of the fact that it does not predict the evolutionary changes it is almost universally acknowledged to explain. Predicting that any particular evolutionary change will occur at any particular time is not an important goal of the study of biological evolution. The well-known color change in the peppered moth provides a good example. During the industrial revolution, this white moth became highly visible in its soot-blackened environment and was easily picked off by predators. Those moths with the mutant gene for blackness, however, were significantly less visible and survived in greater numbers, passing on their life-saving gene to their progeny. In this way, the peppered moth changed from a white moth to a black moth. The mechanisms involved – including random mutation, coding of the message in the DNA, and natural selection – are well understood. Even once the mechanisms involved were understood, this change and others could not be fully predicted because of the random nature of mutation and because the change that would occur in the environment was not known in advance.[11] Although change in language does not operate in the same way as biological evolution, it is likewise affected by the presence in some instances of similarly random innovations[12] and by a social environment which changes in ways that are at present mostly unpredictable. For both reasons, our goal is an understanding of the mechanisms of change, rather than the prediction of change. We believe that it is appropriate that our primary objective be to understand the mechanisms and characteristics of language change, just as well as mutation, the structure of DNA, and natural selection, for example, are understood.

11.3   Regularity

The issues of directionality and regularity of syntactic change are often brought up in discussions of explanation, in particular of prediction, in diachronic syntax. These two matters, however, are much more specific than those aspects of explanation, prediction, and causation discussed in section 11.2, and we take these up in this section and the next.

11.3.1.   Regularity of synchronic parallels

The assumption that sound change is regular is a cornerstone of the comparative method. In formulating the regularity hypothesis, the Neogrammarians were influenced by regular phonological processes observed in the description of living German dialects, which they took to be the result of sound changes (Osthoff and Brugman 1878: ix). (See Weinreich, Labov, and Herzog 1968: 115–16.) Regularity of this sort can be observed also in synchronic syntactic descriptions. **Regular** is here understood to mean not "exceptionless," but "rule-governed and non-random."

We suggest that a regular difference between two living dialects or between two stages of a language provides evidence for the regularity of syntactic change. For example, in one subdialect of Svan, subject case marking differs regularly from that in other (sub)dialects. Specifically, in the Nak'ra-Laxamula subdialect it is all and only the subjects of Class 3 verbs in Series II forms that may differ in case marking from those of other dialects. The difference consists of the possibility of marking these nominals with just the nominative case (as an optional alternative to the narrative case required by other dialects), not with any other case. Regularity, as used here, does not entail that a single variant is permitted, but that which variants are permitted is a rule-governed phenomenon.

(5)   (a)   mare   ädšwep'inal
             man.NOM   he.whistle.II

       (b)   mare-m   ädšwep'inale
             man.NAR   he.whistle.II
             "The man whistled."

(6)   (a)   čäž   ädkinal däb-isga
             horse.NOM it.run.II field-in

       (b)   čäž-d   ädkinale däb-isga
             horse-NAR it.run.II field-in
             "The horse ran in the field."

In other dialects, only the pattern of the (b) examples is grammatical, while in Nak'ra-Laxamula both (a) and (b) patterns are acceptable.[13] Variation in subject case marking in Nak'ra-Laxamula occurs only under the following conditions: (i) the finite verb that governs the clause is in one of the tense–aspect categories grouped under the traditional name of "Series II"; (ii) the verb belongs to morphological Class 3; (iii) the so-called "nominative" case is used with the verb form lacking the suffix -*e*; the so-called "narrative" case is used with the verb form having the suffix -*e*. Regular differences of this sort give us a basis for postulating that change in case marking is likewise regular.

Since (5)–(6) are merely illustrative of a more general pattern (see Harris 1985: 120–3 for additional examples), we must acknowledge that syntactic patterns change in a rule-governed way. Otherwise, there would be no explanation for the regularity of such differences among dialects.

For another example, dialects of Laz (see section 5.2.2) likewise exhibit a regular, rule-governed difference in the use of cases marking subjects under certain conditions.

Thus, change can be shown to be regular in syntax in a way similar to that which Osthoff and Brugman (1878) originally used to show it to be regular in phonology. Because syntactic differences from one dialect to another are synchronically regular, we are compelled to infer that syntactic change, too, is regular, not haphazard.

11.3.2 Constructions embedded in broader syntactic patterns

In section 5.3.2, we discussed the fact that in Standard Finnish, verbs of obligation take genitive subjects (with fully affected direct objects, if present, in the nominative case), as in (7):

(7)   minu-n täyty-y   sanoa se
         I-GEN   must-3RD.PRES   to.say it.NOM
         "I have to say it."

In Western Finnish dialects, however, these verbs of obligation have shifted to the pattern of non-obligation verbs, no longer taking genitive subjects (and nominative objects, where appropriate), but rather nominative subjects, with which the verb agrees (and accusative objects when fully affected[14]), as shown in (8):

(8)   (mä)   täydy-n tehdä   (sä)   pidä-t   mennä
         (I.NOM) must-I to.do   (you.NOM) must-You to.go
         "I must do (it)."   "You must go."   (see Saukkonen 1984: 184)

The Western Finnish grammatical change is regular in the sense of phonological regularity in that it did not randomly affect only one or a few of the obligation forms, but rather it regularly affected every occurrence of the pattern, shifting from former genitive marking for subjects to the nominative case with verb agreement in each of the verbs and compound constructions involving obligation, and with all persons ("I," "you," "he/she/it," etc.). Here it is the recurrence of the same grammatical notion in the multiple forms of a particular grammatical pattern that renders it possible for the change to be considered regular. Our argument here is that changes in patterned syntactic phenomena can be seen as regular, since they recur in a broader context of interconnected patterns.

In syntax, the specific pattern is the "type," and any sentence created using that pattern is the "token." In this way the "type" has multiple "tokens" in the numerous sentences created that make use of it. If, in sound change, regularity means that the same sound ("type") under equivalent conditions changes in the same way in its various occurrences ("tokens") in different morphemes, then in syntactic change regularity means that the same pattern under equivalent conditions changes in the same way in its various manifestations in the *context* of the whole pattern. We find this view of regularity especially compelling with regard to phenomena governed by lexical items, for those lexical items strictly limit the pattern(s) available and changes in these limits can more easily be observed. For example, in the Finnish example above in this subsection, the matrix verb strictly governs the cases of the subject and object, and the regularity of the change from genitive-case subject (and nominative-case object, where present) to nominative subject (and accusative object, where relevant) can be clearly observed. In the Svan example in section 11.3.1, the case of the subject is also determined by the specific verb, as well as the tense–aspect category of the verb. The "type" in each of these examples is limited by the restrictions on the specific patterns in particular languages.

11.3.3   Explanation of exceptions in a regular change
Although syntactic change is regular in the sense defined above, it is not exceptionless: for example, there is at least one exception to the regular correspondence described above in Svan.[15] Exceptions and variation, which together we might consider as **residue**, result from several phenomena.

1   As discussed in section 4.3, in syntax it is not necessary that all of the sentence patterns in a given construction constitute the basis for reanalysis.

As a consequence, there may be a gap between reanalysis and actualization. For example, in the Finnish example discussed by Timberlake (1977) and in chapter 4, it was only those participles that occurred with singular noun accusative/genitives that formed the basis for reanalysis; pronouns and plural nouns showed no ambiguity and were not immediately affected by reanalysis. This meant that until they were further changed, they required case marking that was exceptional for subjects of participles.

2   In all language change there are two conflicting forces: the new general pattern is a force towards change; the conventional form is a force towards the status quo. While the former is stronger in most contexts and generally wins

out, the latter is strong in the syntax governed by frequently occurring words or expressions, in kinship terms and sacred terms, and in fixed expressions.

As a consequence, frequently occurring words or expressions, kinship terms, and sacred terms may fail to undergo regular phonological and morphological change, and the syntactic patterns they govern may fail to undergo syntactic change, leaving them as exceptions. An example of the syntax of the frequently occurring verbs "come," "go" as an exception is discussed in Harris (1985: 111–15, 116–18).

The syntax governed by certain kinship terms is an exception to an attested change of word order in Georgian. In Old Georgian, possessors regularly followed possessed nouns, as in (9):

(9)   (a)   saidumlo-y igi   sasupevel-isa   mis   ɣmrt-isa-ysa-y
           secret-NOM DET kingdom-GEN DET God-GEN-GEN-NOM
           "the secret of the kingdom of God"   (Mk. 4: 11 Ad.)

      (b)   moc̣ape-ni   mis-ni
           disciples-NOM.PL his-NOM.PL
           "his disciples"   (Mk. 5: 31)

      (c)   mama-sa   šen-sa
           father-DAT your-DAT
           "your father"   (Mt 6: 6 Ad.)[16]

In Modern Georgian, on the other hand, possessors precede the possessed in unmarked order:

(10) (a)   čemi saidumlo
           my   secret.NOM
           "my secret"

      (b)   masc̣avlebl-is moc̣ape-eb-i
           teacher-GEN pupil-PL-NOM
           "the teacher's pupils"

      (c)   misi ṭanisamosi
           his   clothing
           "his clothing"

A few kinship terms retained the old order.

(11) mama-čemi
      father-my
      "my father"

Example (11) may be compared with *mama-šeni* "your (Sg) father," *mama-misi* "his/her father," *mama-čveni* "our father," *mama-tkveni* "your (Pl) father."[18]

In addition to the linguistic environments listed above in point 2, it is known that expressives often have exceptional syntax (Diffloth 1972; Harris 1985: 354–9; Joseph 1983), just as they are often exceptional in other respects (Campbell 1980: 22–3; Emeneau 1980: 1–18, 250–93). Because the diachronic syntax of expressives has been little studied, it is not yet known whether they are like the other environments named above in being ones in which change (at least at first) fails to take hold, or whether they are rather environments in which changes apply which do not affect the rest of the grammar, or whether both of these may be true. There is evidence that suggests that expressives form a coherent subsystem which is partially independent, with its own rules of phonology, morphology, and syntax, which only partly overlap with those of the rest of the grammar (references cited above).

Aside from the reasons for genuine exceptions, cited above, there are phenomena which make syntactic change appear less regular than it is. Perhaps the most important of these is synchronic variation. Many speakers control both a standard and a non-standard dialect, or a general norm and a local norm. Where these conflict in their treatment of a given phenomenon, a speaker may use either form, producing variation. In extension there is nearly always a period during which the old and the new norms exist side by side. Literary languages often prolong an extension, as the written standard may curb the regularization of exceptions.

We conclude that syntactic change is regular in the sense that it is rule-governed, not random. While it is regular, it is not exceptionless, for the reasons specified above.

11.4   Directionality

11.4.1   Methods

An understanding of the nature of syntactic change includes a knowledge of individual changes or types of changes that can proceed in only one direction. Changes that are not reversible, that is, cannot occur in the reverse order, are often called unidirectional.

The methods of establishing universal directionality of a particular change are similar to those that establish other universals. It is not possible to *prove* that a phenomenon is universal; one can only prove that it is widespread in well-attested instances in diverse language families. It is only possible to *disprove* universals; that is, while negative evidence can show a hypothesized universal to be incorrect, no amount of evidence can show it definitely to be correct. Additional evidence can, of course, add support. It is important to remember that near-universals (in all areas) are also important; they are relevant both for understanding the nature of change and for reconstruction.

Attested changes have a special importance for establishing universal directions of change, but well-supported reconstructed instances can also provide important evidence.

We may consider a universal to be established when the community of scholars concurs that the supporting evidence is *sufficient* and that any negative evidence that may have been proposed is invalid. For this reason it is important for scholars to review and evaluate proposed universals.

In section 11.4.2 we discuss several proposals of unidirectionality and suggest that they are based on insufficient evidence. In section 11.4.3 we discuss other proposals, which we believe stand up to close scrutiny.

11.4.2   Some failed proposals and partial truths

11.4.2.1   Active-to-ergative-to-accusative

Klimov (1973) proposes a typology of language structures that would include the following types: ergative, active, nominative [–accusative], multiclass, and neutral. The last two are not treated in detail in his work. (Klimov's "nominative" is more often called "nominative–accusative" or just "accusative" in the West; in this type all subjects are marked with the nominative case.) Although the first three include the morphological encoding of alignment that define these types in other typologies (see chapter 9), they also include other language properties. For example, for Klimov the active type by definition requires not only the distribution of cases or agreement markers usually understood under this rubric, but also a lexicon that is organized according to a principle of dividing both nouns and verbs into animate vs. inanimate categories (see also Klimov 1977). Thus, Klimov proposes establishing a typology that includes the whole language, not just alignment. One of the problems in his definition of these types is that it is not clear how languages are to be categorized when they are characterized by one or a few of the properties that define a particular type, but not by all of them. Because his typology is based on many characteristics of languages, it is, in principle, not directly comparable to the alignment typologies that are better known in the West (Sapir 1917; Fillmore 1968: 54; Comrie 1978; Dixon 1979; Plank 1985: 269–70). Nevertheless, from a practical point of view, the categories to which Klimov assigns individual languages are usually based primarily on the alignment of case marking and/or agreement. For this reason, the discrepancy between the types to which individual languages are assigned by Klimov and the types to which they would be assigned by other scholars is not too great.

Diachronically, Klimov hypothesizes unidirectional development among these types, as indicated schema 1:

1   *Klimov's hypothesized unidirectional change of language type*
      ACTIVE > ERGATIVE > NOMINATIVE

According to Klimov's proposal, active languages may become ergative, and ergative languages may become nominative. Active languages may also skip the ergative "stage" and become nominative directly. But according to Klimov's claims, change cannot proceed in the opposite direction. He rules out nominative- to-ergative, ergative-to-active, and nominative-to-active changes.

The Indo-Iranian branch of Indo-European is the only language (sub)family that provides evidence of attested change of language type in Klimov's sense, and Klimov's proposal is inconsistent with some of the changes that have occurred in this group. In the historical period, several languages of the Indo-Iranian group underwent a change from nominative to ergative case marking and agreement in the past-tense system (Anderson 1977; Payne 1979; Bynon 1980; Bubenik 1989a, 1989b). Several languages of the Iranian branch have undergone or seem to be undergoing a loss of this ergative system, returning to a nominative structure in those domains that were previously ergative (Payne 1980). Klimov disputes the relevance of the nominative-to-ergative shift in Indo-Iranian on the grounds that it developed through contact with other languages with a partially similar system and on the grounds that the ergative structure has remained limited to the past-tense system. Nevertheless, he assigns Georgian to the ergative type, even though it similarly has – on his analysis – ergative case marking in only one system. Thus, because Klimov provides no consistent way to determine the type of a particular language, he simply discounts the evidence of attested change where it does not fit his preconceptions.

One of the families on which Klimov rests his overall hypothesis is the Kartvelian family, which he claims is undergoing an ergative-to-nominative shift. On his analysis, case marking in the so-called Series II system is ergative. This analysis has been disputed on the grounds that synchronically the alignment of cases does not in fact involve ergativity, but follows exactly that which defines the active type (Harris 1981: ch. 16). For example, active intransitives, such as (12) take subjects in the so-called narrative (or ergative) case, while inactive intransitives, such as (13) take subjects in the so-called nominative case:

(12)   bavš-ma   icoca
         child-NAR   crawl.II
         "The child crawled."

(13)   bavšv-i   darča
        child-NOM stay.II
        "The child stayed."

Nevertheless, it is quite true that Georgian does not have some of the other characteristics which, in Klimov's system, define the active type, such as a grammaticalized distinction between animate and inanimate nouns. On Klimov's analysis, sentence (12) provides evidence that Georgian is becoming nominative (1973: 50); although, as pointed out by Comrie (1976: 259), he elsewhere claims that an example with exactly the same structure provides evidence that Georgian was formerly active (1973: 189). In fact, there is good evidence that the pattern of (12) is relatively new and that formerly such sentences had subjects in the so-called nominative case (Šaniʒe 1973: 483–4). But this means that in this system the marking of subjects of active intransitives was like the marking of subjects of inactive intransitives, such as (13), and like that of direct objects; hence it was ergative. In Harris (1985: 107–47) it is argued in greater detail that case marking in this system in the Kartvelian languages was once truly ergative and that case marking has undergone subsequent change, becoming active. The Kartvelian languages have undergone several other changes in case marking that take the direction claimed in Klimov's schema,[18] but the change described above stands as a second counterexample to his proposal.

    Some other examples that might support Klimov's proposal are not agreed upon by specialists or are not clearly documented: for example, differing views on the direction of alignment change in Polynesian are presented in Chung (1978) and Clark (1981).

    It must be concluded that the evidence available does not support the hypothesis sketched above; indeed much the strongest evidence opposes Klimov's view.[19]

11.4.2.2 Relative clause types

Maxwell (1982) has suggested that changes in relativization strategies are unidirectional, allowing for change in only a single direction. He identifies four principal relativization strategies; his definitions are given in (14) (from Maxwell 1982: 137):

(14)   GAP-S: the relativized NP (NP rel) has no reflex in surface structure.
        PRO-S: the NP rel is reflected by an anaphoric pronoun in surface structure.
        REL-S: the NP rel is reflected by a casecoding relative pronoun in surface
           structure.
        NR-S: the NP rel is reflected by a full NP in surface structure.

Examples of those that are considered in our discussion are given below.

Maxwell proposes unidirectional developments involving only three of these: the "non-reduction" (NR-S) type may give rise to the "relative pronoun" type, which may in turn be replaced by the "postnominal gap" type. He represents these possibilities schematically as in schema 2 (Maxwell 1982:150).[20]

2   *Maxwell's hypothesized unidirectional change of relative clause type*
     NR-S > REL-S > Postnom GAP-S

Consideration below of additional examples establishes that change from one relativization strategy to another is not unidirectional. In particular, it is shown in the following subsection that the change of a relative pronoun strategy (REL-S) to a non-reduction strategy (NR-S) is attested in Georgian; consequently the first arrow in schema 2 should point in both directions. It is likewise shown that there are reasons to consider the second change to be bidirectional also.

There are several problems with testing the claim embodied in Maxwell's schema 2; among these are (a) that some innovative strategies have multiple sources, (b) that some types do not fit well within this typology, and (c) that some substantive changes do not constitute an example of change in type according to the typology. For example, (a) Georgian developed a prenominal gap strategy at a relatively late stage in its history; already in place were a relative pronoun strategy (REL-S), a participial relative, a postnominal gap strategy (GAP-S), and a prenominal non-reduction strategy (NR-S). While the first two probably did not directly influence the development of the prenominal gap type, it is likely that the last two did. How is this change to be typed?

(b) The North East Caucasian languages provide an example of a type that does not fit well within this typology. Although many traditional grammarians do not consider participles (and other non-finite forms) to be relative clauses, the trend more recently is to consider these to be relatives (e.g. Lehmann 1984; Keenan 1985). Technically, we must put the participial relatives of the North East Caucasian into the category of the prenominal gap, but this obscures an important distinction between finite and non-finite prenominal gap relatives.

(c) As an example of an important change in relativization strategy that does not change type on this hierarchy, we cite Japanese. As discussed by Lehmann (1984: 293), Japanese originally used a nominalized relative clause type, where the subordination and clause type were indicated by a suffix *-uru* on the verb. Due to reinterpretation of the verbal morphology, this became a finite form, left without a subordinator. Throughout the change, however, the Japanese relative has belonged to the prenominal gap type, according to the typology above.

Georgian examples of REL-S → NR-S

In section 4.2.4, we described an attested change in Georgian, during which the relative pronoun (in the REL-S strategy) was reanalyzed as a relative particle, used first in a NR-S, and later in a variety of other structures. An example of the REL-S strategy of Old Georgian is given in (15), and the NR-S derived from it is illustrated in (16):

(15)   miugo   iuda romel-man misca   igi
           he.respond.it Judas which-NAR he.give.him him
           "Judas, who betrayed him, replied."   (Mt. 26: 25 AB)

(16)   minda, betaniaši   rom k'olmeurnobaa, is vnaxo
           I.want.it Betania-in that collective-is   it I.see.it
           "I want to see the collective-farm that is in Betania."

(Example (16) cited by Hans Vogt 1971: 51.) It is clear that the non-reduction strategy, not occurring in the older language, developed out of the relative pronoun structure, and this establishes that in Maxwell's schema of directionality the first arrow must point in both directions, indicating that NR-S can become REL-S (his example) or vice versa.

Partial counterexamples regarding the second arrow in Maxwell's schema

Maxwell cites French as a potential counterexample to the unidirectionality of REL-S > Postnom GAP-S, though the change from GAP-S to REL-S there applied only to nouns that were neuter in Latin (1982: 145–6). Maxwell states of these that they are "only a transitional phenomenon in the overall trend toward GAP-S" (1982: 145).

As described in section 10.5.2, in Udi, an inherited participial relative has been supplemented with a REL-S. The inherited construction is illustrated in (17), and the innovative one in (18):

(17)   zu   yaq'ab-al-a   kaɣəz-ax aq'a
           I.ERG send-FUT.PTCPL   letter-DAT take
           "Take the letter that I am to send."

(18)   e-q'un-sa   ail-ux   mat'-ɣon-te
           come-3.PL-PRES child-NOM.PL which-ERG.PL-REL

           dava-q'un-sak-e
           quarrel$_1$-3.PL-quarrel$_2$-AOR

           "The children who quarreled are coming."

The participle in Udi usually precedes its head, as in (17); the relative clause with a relative pronoun, here *mano-te* "which," follows the head (see also Harris 1992a).

An additional example of a language which had GAP-S that developed into REL-S is Finnish. Originally Finno-Ugric had only preposed participles, which agreed in case with the head noun. Finnish created a new postnominal relative using relative pronouns fashioned from the joining of two other pronouns, *jo-* and *-ka*. As in the instance of Udi, this innovative construction is often attributed to the influence of other languages.

Neither of these examples is a clear-cut counterexample to the change in the first arrow. First, each structure that we have identified as a GAP-S is a participle. While the participle does not fit into any of the other categories, it is not clear that the claim embodied in Maxwell's schema was meant to apply to participles. In addition, schema 2 specifies "Postnom GAP-S," while the two examples we have given are Prenom GAP-S. We have introduced these examples, not for the purpose of proving schema 2 to be wrong, but to add to our general understanding of directionality in the sphere of relative clauses. On the other hand, the attested Georgian change, juxtaposed with the changes Maxwell adduces, clearly shows that at least some changes of relative clause type are not unidirectional. We suggest that it is unlikely that true unidirectionality will be found between any two general types of relative clauses. If true unidirectionality is discovered in relative clause types, it is more likely to relate to the direction of change via a particular pathway or in a specific syntactic context.

11.4.2.3   Word order
The unidirectional hypothesis expressed in schema 3 was proposed by Givón 1979, and has been much discussed in the literature:

3   *Givón's hypothesized unidirectional change of word order type*
     SOV > VSO > SVO

As discussed in section 8.1, Vennemann (1973, 1974a, and 1974b) has proposed other restrictions on changes in word order type, without claiming that they are strictly unidirectional. Data pertinent to both claims are presented in chapter 8. Because both claims have been so much discussed and so clearly rejected (for example, Mallinson and Blake 1981: 434–5; Hawkins 1983), it seems sufficient here to mention these as another example of change that is not unidirectional.

11.4.2.4   Grammaticalization
One version of grammaticalization holds that the process of grammaticalization proceeds in one direction only, from independent word to clitic to affix,

from lexical item to grammatical item (see Campbell 1991 for discussion).[21] While it is generally agreed that grammaticalization involves both a reduction in phonetic form and a "bleaching" of meaning, we use only the form in schema 4 to symbolize both aspects of the process:

4   *Unidirectional change in grammaticalization hypothesized by some*
       UNBOUND WORD > ENCLITIC > INFLECTIONAL AFFIX >
       DERIVATIONAL AFFIX

While there is little doubt that this schema accurately symbolizes the observed general direction of change, there are examples that proceed in the opposite direction. The several examples cited below show that the arrows in the schema should point in two directions.[22]

Several examples of the reversal of grammaticalization have been discussed in work by Nevis (1984, 1985); one is repeated here. In Estonian in historical times, word-final vowels were lost through apocope; e.g *keltä* "from whom?" > *kelt*, *päällä* "on (top of)" > *pääll.* Where vowels were protected by an enclitic, such as *-pä* "Emphatic" or *-s* "Question," apocope applied to the final vowel (if any) of the enclitic, but not to that of the base; e.g. *päällä-pä* > *päällä-p, keltä-s* (later *peallep* and *keltes* through vowel changes). Apocope produced alternations between frequently occurring consonant-final forms and infrequently occurring combinations of the non-apocopated form with an enclitic; e.g *kelt/ keltes, pääll/päällep*. Given the frequency and salience of the apocopated bases, these forms with attached clitics were ripe for reinterpretation. The forms were reanalyzed as having a final -VC clitic. Because vowel harmony had been lost, there was now no evidence that the base and the clitics were a single phonological word. The new clitics, *es* and *ep*, were further reanalyzed as independent words and were subsequently shifted to sentence-initial position. This example shows that the first arrow in schema 4 must be bidirectional.[23]

An example from English shows that the process represented by the second arrow in this schema must also be reversible; that is, affixes can become clitics. Janda (1980) has observed that the English case marker that was eventually generalized for the genitive as *-'s* was an affix as far back as Proto-Germanic, as shown by the fact that it attached to individual words, including nouns and their modifiers. In historical times, however, this ending has degrammaticalized, becoming a clitic. Its clitic status is shown by the fact that it now attaches to phrases, such as *the king of England's hat, a friend of the family's house.*[24]

The third arrow in schema 4 can also be reversed. In most Germanic languages the neuter nouns that had ended in derivational *-os/-es* in Proto-Indo-European fell together with the neuter *a*-stems; this is an example of

Table 11.1 *Declension of neuter -os/-es nouns in Old, Middle, and New High German.*

	OHG	MHG	NHG
Singular			
Nominative, accusative	lamb	lamp	lamm
Genitive	lambes	lambes	lamm(e)s
Dative	lambe	lambe	lamm(e)
Plural			
Nominative, accusative	lembir	lember	lämmer
Genitive	lembiro	lember(e)	lämmer
Dative	lembirum	lember(e)n	lämmern

Source: Wright (1907: 190)

paradigm leveling.[25] In Old High German this also occurred, and these nouns were declined in the singular according to the *a-* (strong) declension, though in the plural they retained their inherited stem-forming suffix, *-ir.* Occurring during the Old High German period only in the plural, the formant *-ir* was reanalyzed as a marker of the plural, an inflectional morpheme. The sample declension in table 11.1. follows Wright (1907: 190). Only a handful of nouns belonged to this declension at the oldest stage, but even in Old High German times about twenty additional neuter nouns began to make use of the reanalyzed plural ending, *-ir*, later *-er.* Among the nouns that take on this new paradigm, Wright (1907: 190) cites *ei* "egg," *buch* "book," and *haus* "house." This reanalysis is an example of an affix changing from a stem formant (derivational affix) to an inflectional affix, though this is the opposite of the more common direction of change.[26]

It must be noted that there are hundreds of known examples of grammaticalization that proceed in the direction indicated in schema 4 and relatively few that reverse this direction. Thus, unlike the proposals discussed in sections 11.4.2.1 and 11.4.2.3, there is a strong tendency for grammaticalization to proceed in one direction, though it is not strictly unidirectional. Nevertheless, no reasonable theory can ignore data just because they are inconvenient; an adequate theory must account for infrequent phenomena, not merely for the most common patterns.

11.4.2.5   *The importance of explicit hypotheses*
It is only by advancing specific, testable hypotheses of the sort embodied by the four schemas above that linguists will make progress in understanding the

nature of language. When specific hypotheses of this sort are stated in the literature, linguists with access to previously unavailable data can test reasonable theories against known facts. Although we believe that there are convincing counterexamples to the first three hypotheses considered which show them to be mistaken, as a community of scholars, we have also learned by having these hypotheses "on the table." The counterexamples to the grammaticalization hypothesis show that it cannot be maintained in its strong form, but confirm that it is true as a tendency of language change.

11.4.3   Apparently reliable instances of directionality

While the progression from independent word to clitic, then to inflectional and derivational affix, as schematized in schema 4, is not entirely unidirectional, it is possible that when we examine other claims of this sort we may find some specific types of changes that are unidirectional. In the subsections below we discuss examples of proposals that seem promising as real instances of unidirectional change. The second of these is a specific example of grammaticalization and is thus a subtype of the progression discussed in section 11.4.2.4.

11.4.3.1   *Locatives, genitives, and partitives*

The partitive construction generally develops from a locative in the meaning "from" or from a genitive, as schematized in schema 5:

5   *Hypothesized unidirectional change to partitive*

In Lithuanian a partitive use has developed out of the inherited Indo-European genitive, which may itself have come from a locative expression. Example (19), with a partitive genitive object and an accusative (whole) shows that this is indeed a partitive, rather than simply a verb that governs genitive objects. A partitive object in (20a) likewise contrasts with a whole in (20b):

(19)   pàdavė vandeñs   ir   kė̃dę
          gave   water.GEN.SG and chair.ACC.SG
          "(He) gave (him) some water and a chair."

(20)   (a)   prirìñko úogų,
                gathered berries.GEN.PL
                "(He) gathered (some) berries."

(b) pririñko krĕpšị   úogụ
     gathered bag.ACC.SG berries.GEN.PL
     "(He) gathered (a) bag (full) of berries."
                    (Schmalstieg 1988: 166–9, citing examples from Grenda)

A partial[27] was also expressed by a genitive in Latin, when the noun was dependent upon another noun, of quantity (e.g "most **of the water**"). The Latin genitive in general was replaced in French by an analytic expression with the preposition *de* "from, of." In the partial, too, this preposition was used. At first an indefinite sense of the partitive (e.g "[some] beer") was expressed without a determiner (e.g. *burent cervoise* "they drank beer") and contrasted with the definite sense of the partitive (e.g "[some] of **the** water"), which was expressed with *de* + the definite article and the noun (e.g. *je bois de l'eau* "I drink [some] of the water"). Later the contrast between these was lost. *De* fused with the definite article (*de* + masculine *le* becoming *du, de* + feminine *la* becoming *de la*, and *de* + plural *les* becoming *des*) and came to be used in definite or indefinite contexts (e.g. *j'ai bu du vin* "I drank some of the wine" or "I drank some wine") (M. Harris 1978: 77–9). Thus, the so-called partitive article of French is from the definite article plus the genitive, with the genitive *de* itself from an older locative expression.

Balto-Finnic developed a partitive case from the inherited Uralic ablative case *-ta*. The ablative "from" meaning which was original to this case can be seen in its use in languages of other branches of the Uralic family, and it is preserved as relics in certain expressions, such as those in (21), and in the cases *-stA* "from within" and *-ltA* "from without," composed historically from the combination of the locatives *-s* and *-l*, and the old ablative *-tA*, where A = *a* or *ä*, depending on vowel harmony.

(21)   (a) mies on suur-ta   suku-a
             man is big-PART family-PART
             "The man is from an important family."

        (b) kärsiä   nälkä-ä
             to.suffer hunger-PART
             "to suffer from hunger"

The use of the partitive in the expression of the partial object is exemplified by (22):

(22)   juo-n   puhdas-ta vet-tä
        drink-I pure-PART water-PART
        "I drink (some) pure water."

Further details are given in Campbell (1990a: 65–8) and sources cited there.

The development of a partitive out of the expression of a partial through a genitive or through a locative (in roughly the meaning "from") is a well- documented directional change, also known, for example, in Russian and Old German. It is a good candidate for a unidirectional change, to which we know no counterexamples.

11.4.3.2 Demonstratives, definite articles, markers of case or of gender-class

Greenberg (1978) proposes that a common path of change is that outlined in schema 6; while Greenberg does not seem to intend that this represents unidirectional change, we discuss it as a hypothesis to that effect.[28]

6   *Hypothesized unidirectional change in determiners and noun marking*

$$\text{DEM PRONOUN} > \text{DEFINITE ARTICLE} > \begin{cases} \text{CASE MARKER} \\ \text{GENDER-CLASS} \\ \text{MARKER} \end{cases}$$

The changes summarized here are the development of a demonstrative pronoun into a definite article, which may in turn become either a case marker or a marker of gender-class. These changes may have the effect of creating new, pristine case or gender-class markers or may renew an existing set of markers. Greenberg shows that some of the sequence we represent in schema 6 has taken place in a wide variety of languages, including Aramaic, with attested changes, and a number of Niger-Congo languages.

M. Harris (1980a, 1980b) has pointed out that Romance languages provide support for the direction represented in schema 6 and has emphasized that it is generally the remote member of a two- or three-way deictic opposition that provides the source for the definite article. Classical Latin made no consistent marking of definiteness, but in Vulgar Latin definiteness increasingly came to be marked, using the demonstrative *ille* "that," the remote member of a three-way opposition of deixis. *Ille* is the source of the definite articles in the Romance languages. Posner argues, further, that the article *le, la, les*, of Modern French has lost much of its force as a definite article (i.e. does not always indicate specificity) and that it primarily functions to mark gender and number (1966: 181).

The Scandinavian languages developed a definite article from the demonstrative **eno-* "this, that," Old Norse *-enn, -et, -en* (Noreen 1923: 316–17; Prokosch 1939: 273–4). In Gothic, the weak demonstrative (from the stem **to-*), *sa* (masculine, nominative), *ðata* (neuter, nominative), *sō* (feminine, nominative) "this, that," came to be used as a definite article (Prokosch 1939: 267). In the West Germanic languages the article developed further. For example, in Old English this stem opposed "this"; "that," with the forms *sē, se* (masculine, nominative), *ðæt* (neuter, nominative), *sēo* (feminine, nominative), served both as the remote demonstrative and as the definite article. A single uninflected form, *þē*, came to be used for all cases and genders in early Middle English (Wright and Wright 1928: 167), and the demonstrative and article were distinguished by 1200 in some dialects (Wright and Wright 1928: 168). The same stem, **to-*, is the basis of the Greek definite article, *'o, to, 'ē* (Prokosch 1939: 267). Classical Armenian has an enclitic definite article that maintains a three-way deictic opposition (proximate *-s*, contingent *-d*, remote *-n*)(Jensen 1959: 81–2), but by Modern Armenian only the remote member, *-n/ə*, remains, but in the function of definite article.[29]

Evidence to support the sequence in schema 6 is not limited to Indo-European languages. Greenberg presents numerous examples from African languages to support this line of change, especially with regard to the markers of gender classes. Šaniʒe (1957) and Čikobava (1939) establish that the same sequence is responsible for attested case endings in Kartvelian languages, and Harris (1985: 75–86) shows that relics of the Old Georgian definite article occur in exactly the positions Greenberg's hypothesis predicts for them.

Thus it is well established that the changes represented in schema 6 can and frequently do proceed in the direction indicated. We are not aware of examples of change in the opposite direction, and this is a likely candidate for a unidirectional sequence of changes.[30]

11.4.4 Conclusions

The proposals for unidirectional changes discussed above differ from one another in important ways. On the one hand, Klimov's schema 1 involves whole language types and is non-renewable. That is, in his proposal, it is suggested that a language improves, evolves in a single direction, never to return again. Although the word "primitive" may be avoided, it is certainly implied that some languages have come a lot further from their beginnings than others. Neither Givón's proposal nor Maxwell's (sections 11.4.2.2–11.4.2.3) seems to be intended in this way, yet each involves a major typological change, and all of the attested examples that can be mustered offer only a relatively restricted database. Hence, these proposals are inherently speculative. On the other hand, the grammaticalization proposal (section 11.4.2.4) and the two proposals discussed in section 11.4.3 concern renewable resources; they might also be termed "cyclic" or "spiraling" changes. The proposal that grammaticalization is a unidirectional process hypothesizes that free-standing words become further and further grammaticalized as indicated in schema 4; but researchers in this area acknowledge that more and more words are created, and some of these in turn become more and more grammaticalized. Thus these processes occur cyclically, creating clitics out of words, and affixes out of clitics. What emerges as important from this comparison is that *there is little or no evidence to support hypotheses that languages – or their syntax – are evolving in a single direction through non-renewable changes*. There is considerably more evidence to support the unidirectionality of certain renewable changes.

Each hypothesized example of unidirectionality to which we have shown clear counterexamples (section 11.4.2.1–11.4.2.4) involves a context-free change, without reference to the mechanism and pathway or to syntactic or semantic conditions in the starting point. Sound change, since it is well understood, provides a valuable reference point. Most, though not all, accepted unidirectional sound changes are context-sensitive: for example, the voicing of voiceless stops is unidirectional in *intervocalic context*.[31] It appears that a proposal of unidirectionality of a syntactic change is more likely to prove to be true if it is stated narrowly, with reference to context or to mechanism or pathway, than if it is stated generally, as those in sections 11.4.2.1–11.4.2.4 were. For example, while Klimov's claims, in schema 1, do not stand up to scrutiny, there are other generalizations regarding alignment that appear to be true. It appears to be predictable that reanalysis of a passive structure in a language with accusative rules will result in some ergative rules, while reanalysis of an object demotion construction in a language with ergative rules will result in some accusative rules (see chapter 9). Section 11.4.3 provides other examples of generalizations that are relatively specific and narrow in their claims, relating not to languages as a whole, syntax as a whole, or even to large categories of changes, but rather to specific shifts. Like a context-sensitive change, these hold promise of proving to be unidirectional.

12 *Reconstruction of syntax*

12.1   Introduction

Although comparative and internal reconstruction have a long and honorable history in linguistics, application of these techniques to syntax has frequently been criticized as unworkable and as fundamentally different from phonological and morphological reconstruction. For example, Jeffers (1976b: 5) contends that: "A straightforward transfer of the principles of the comparative method to the reconstruction of syntax seems totally inappropriate." Similar opinions concerning the assumed non-feasibility of syntactic reconstruction abound. While no one would suggest that the techniques of comparative reconstruction can be applied in syntax *exactly* as in phonology, we argue here that it is nevertheless both possible and appropriate to use the methods of comparative and internal reconstruction to reconstruct syntax. Although there are clear limitations on the effectiveness of these techniques, they are applicable to a wide variety of problems in diachronic syntax. In section 12.2 we discuss how correspondences (or equations) can be established in syntax. Although most of the discussion in the literature has focused on reconstruction, the comparative method relies upon correspondences which establish that change has taken place. We show in section 12.3 how the established techniques of the comparative method can be applied to reconstruct syntax. Section 12.4 deals with obstacles – real and imagined – to the establishment of correspondences or to actual syntactic reconstruction.

The comparative method operates in two steps. First, as described further in section 12.2, correspondences are established. We may say, for example, that **a** of language A corresponds to **b** of language B. The second step is the actual reconstruction, which consists of determining the source from which both **a** and **b** descended. In our schematic example, there are three obvious hypotheses to be considered: (i) that **a** represents the original form, which remains unchanged in A, and that it became **b** in language B; (ii) that **b** reflects unchanged the older form, which became **a** in language A; (iii) that both **a**

Table 12.1 *OS d*: OHG *t* (examples from Krahe 1966: 107)

Old Saxon	Old High German	
dura	**t**ura	"door"
lē**d**ian	lei**t**en	"lead"
wal**d**an	wal**t**an	"govern"
bi**dd**ian	bi**tt**en	"request"

and **b** derive historically from a third form, **c**. In reconstructing, the linguist compares these hypotheses, at least implicitly. Methods for doing so are discussed further in section 12.3 and section 12.4. Internal reconstruction differs only in stating correspondences from within a single language (usually from related paradigms or variant forms); we do not discuss internal reconstruction separately from comparative reconstruction.

12.2   Correspondences: preliminaries for syntactic reconstruction

In this section we first discuss briefly the use of correspondences in diachronic phonology, then show that the same approach can be taken in syntax, *mutatis mutandis*. We provide several concrete examples of correspondences in syntax. Criticisms that have been advanced with respect to this approach are analyzed, and it is shown that they do not constitute major obstacles.

12.2.1   Correspondences in phonology

In phonology, the comparative method relies on sound correspondences, that is, "cognate sounds," sounds which are related to one another in cognate words by virtue of descent from a common ancestral pronunciation reflected in the corresponding sounds of the related languages. For example, Old Saxon (OS) *d* corresponds to Old High German (OHG) *t*, stated in the correspondence set in (1):

(1)   OS *d*: OHG *t*

Such correspondence sets, sometimes called "equations," are an abstract statement of a pattern of correspondence attested in numerous cognates. In this example, some of the concrete data on which this correspondence is based are listed in table 12.1. Table 12.1 presents some cognate sets – in a sense the "same" lexical items in the two languages. From these concrete data the correspondence set of (1) can be abstracted.

12.2.2   Why not in syntax?

The question is, why should this way of establishing correspondences not also be possible in syntax? As discussed in section 11.3, a frequently expressed opinion is that the application of the comparative method to syntax is severely limited because syntactic change has no analogue to the regularity of phonological changes (see Norman and Campbell 1978; Campbell and Mithun 1980). Jeffers (1976b: 4) states it this way:

> In syntax, only patterns can be compared, and patterns, in general, do not "evolve" the way sounds do. There is no series of one to one correspondences between the syntactic patterns of a language and the syntactic patterns of that language at some earlier point in its history, as there are between the sounds of a language between any two stages in its history. A straightforward transfer of the principles of the comparative method to the reconstruction of syntax seems totally inappropriate . . . The history of syntactic systems is a history of pattern replacement and reanalysis. In phonological reconstruction, when sounds do not reflect the continuous tradition which results from the operation of sound changes . . . CM [the comparative method] collapses.

Jeffers (1976b: 6) adds that: "In the comparison of morphological and syntactic systems . . . there exists no correspondence which is not a correspondence of identity." Winter (1984: 616) affirms a similar view:

> Reconstructional comparative linguistics as practiced in the fields of phonology and morphology . . . is a discipline concerned with both substance and form (with substance taking precedence), while comparative syntax à la Lehmann is limited to a comparison of form. Or, to use a different terminology, comparative phonology and morphology are interested in tokens and, through them, in types, whereas the domain of comparative syntax as practiced in recent years is exclusively that of types.

Winter (1984: 622–3) goes on to say:

> Reconstructional comparative linguistics is concerned with what is "inherited" . . . acquired through a learning process . . . For sentences . . . acquisition by learning is most unusual . . . Sentences are formed, not learned; morphemes and simple lexemes are learned, not formed . . . Syntax deals almost exclusively with entities not learned, but constructed – or generated.

(See also Ivanov 1965 [quoted in Birnbaum 1977: 33]; Jeffers 1976a; Jucquois 1976: 243–4; Lightfoot 1979a: 9; Campbell and Mithun 1980.)

A consequence of the observations above and a problem noted for syntactic reconstruction is the perceived absence of correspondence in syntax. Thus, while the comparative method relies in part on correspondences like (1), the use of this technique in syntax has been criticized and termed "incoherent" (Lightfoot 1979a: 8). Lightfoot adds that "there is no clear basis for saying that a certain sentence of Old English 'corresponds' to some sentence of Middle English, and there is no reason to claim that a surface structure is mapped by a historical rule into another form occurring in a later stage of the language" (1979a: 8).

12.2.3   Correspondences in syntax
In this section we show that it is indeed possible to establish syntactic correspondences – between successive stages of a single language, among related languages, or among dialects.

12.2.3.1   Patterns in syntax
Many doubt the applicability of the comparative method to syntax because they believe syntactic change lacks the regularity found in sound change. In the previous chapter we showed that syntactic change is indeed regular, in the sense that it is rule-governed, non-random. We showed this in a way similar to that in which the Neogrammarians established the regularity of sound change, by demonstrating that differences between dialects are regular and predictable. We showed that at least certain parts of syntax do have multiple "tokens" of a single "type"; although syntactic "tokens" are not memorized in the context of words, as phonological "tokens" are, they are often embedded in the context of a strictly limited syntactic pattern, which is the "type." While it may be true that this kind of regularity cannot be shown to exist for all parts of the syntax, the fact that it does exist in some allows us to establish syntactic correspondences (at least in those parts of the syntax), and this provides a basis for syntactic reconstruction. In this way, the prerequisite of regularity of change can be met in syntax.

It is, of course, true that languages do not have finite inventories of sentences; however, the consequence of this is not that the study of diachronic syntax cannot be successful, but that individual *sentences* cannot be tracked over time or reconstructed in the sense that words can. It could never be claimed that a particular sentence was replaced by another, except for formulaic utterances. Nor could it be claimed that a reconstructed sentence ever actually occurred. Establishing change in syntactic *patterns*, however, does not depend on there being a finite set of sentences.

As observed above, the establishment of a correspondence shows that change has taken place and is a preliminary step in reconstruction. Let us consider just how a correspondence might be made in syntax. In the examples below, there are simple sentences in Mingrelian, the (a) examples, which *correspond to* sentences in Laz, the (b) examples:

(2)   (a)   zaza   oškviduans   nodar-s
            Zaza.NOM   he.drown.him Nodar-DAT
            "Zaza drowns Nodar."

      (b)   zaza-k   oškvidaps   nodari
            Zaza.NAR   he.drown.him Nodar.NOM
            "Zaza drowns Nodar."

(3)   (a)   ate k'oč-i   ǰgiro ibirs
            this man-NOM well he.sing
            "This man sings well."

      (b)   aya k'oči-k   k'ai ibirs
            this man-NAR well he.sing
            "This man sings well."

(4)   (a)   k'oč-i   γuru
            man-NOM   he.die
            "The man dies."

      (b)   k'oči   γurun
            man.NOM   he.die
            "The man dies."   (Harris 1985: 52–3, 56)

In these closely related languages,[1] the paired Mingrelian (2a)–(4a) and Laz (2b)–(4b) examples are in an intuitively clear sense (see section 12.2.3.2 below) cognate sentences, the "same" sentence in the two languages. Yet the case-marking patterns used in the Mingrelian examples are entirely different from those used in Laz; the Laz case pattern produces ungrammatical sentences in Mingrelian and vice versa. In these examples, Mingrelian uses the nominative case for subjects and the dative for objects, while Laz uses the so-called narrative case for subjects and the nominative for direct objects in (2b)–(3b) and the nominative case for subject in (4b).[2] These marking patterns are completely regular in each language (see Harris 1985: ch. 3 for details). These and other examples establish that in syntax it is indeed possible to state correspondences that are not "correspondences of identity."

Given a set of corresponding sentences (e.g. (2a)–(4a)/(2b)–(4b) and others like them), we can reach by induction the generalization in table 12.2, which sets out the distribution patterns of cases illustrated in (2)–(4). Classes 1, 2, and 3 are identified on a morphological basis (Harris 1985: 54–5, 57). Table 12.2, like (1) above, is an abstraction based upon concrete data, in this instance, examples (2)–(4) and many others like them. Table 12.2 is itself an equation, a statement of the correspondence of one syntactic pattern to another.

The pattern set out above for Mingrelian is sometimes called "nominative/ accusative" or just "accusative," while that displayed for Laz has been termed

Table 12.2 *Distribution of cases in Series I*

	Subject of Class 1 *Example (2)*	Subject of Class 3 *Example (3)*	Subject of Class 2 *Example (4)*	Direct object *Example (2)*
Mingrelian	NOM	NOM	NOM	DAT
Standard Laz	NAR	NAR	NOM	NOM

"active" (see chapter 9 for definitions). Using this terminology, we can state the equation for this environment as:

(5)   Mingrelian   Laz
        Accusative : Active

In syntax, no particular way of stating such correspondences has been agreed upon.

12.2.3.2 Safeguards

Could it be objected that there are insufficient safeguards on the comparability of (2a)–(4a) to (2b)–(4b)? Although syntax has nothing quite like the duality of patterning (double articulation) in phonology, it is possible to state that (2a) is equivalent to (2b) on the following grounds. (i) The verbs are entirely cognate. The relevance of this is that in these languages various case patterns are associated in part with specific verbs. (ii) The tense–aspect and verb class are the same within each pair. This is important because the tense–aspect and class partly determine the case pattern in these languages. (iii) The individual verbal morphemes, such as agreement markers, are cognate. (iv) The meaning is the same within each pair. (v) Cases occur regularly in the context of other cases and in the context of particular verb morphology. That is, just as sounds occur in the context where they are associated with other sounds in a word, particular cases in Kartvelian languages occur with particular morphological patterns (see Harris 1985: esp. ch. 3). (vi) The examples given in (2)–(4) are representative of all regular verbs in each language.[3] There is no basis on which it might be argued that the sentences do *not* correspond. In fact, in this problem in the Kartvelian languages, it is not necessary for condition (i) to be fulfilled. Other conditions are more than sufficient safeguards that the sentences correspond. The patterns under investigation, involving case marking of nominals, are determined by the tense–aspect category (so-called series) and the class of the verb and by the grammatical

relations borne by the nominals. Because our goal is to establish correspondence patterns, not corresponding sentences, it is not necessary that the lexical material in the example sentences be cognate. The conditions that are
adequate to insure comparability will vary from language to language. While
it is essential to insure that the sentences compared correspond in the relevant respects, the conditions that make this possible need not be the same in
syntax as in phonology.

12.2.3.3   Sources of correspondences

As noted above, Lightfoot has objected that "there is no clear basis for saying
that a certain sentence of Old English 'corresponds' to some sentence of
Middle English" (1979a:8). This may be true in comparing Old English with
Middle English, but let us examine carefully the general implied assertion
that one cannot claim that a certain sentence of one stage of a language corresponds to a particular sentence of a later stage.

When there are responses to identical or essentially identical stimuli in
two stages of a language, we may be justified in saying that those responses
correspond. This occurs any time a single version of a text is translated at
two stages of a language, or into two languages that can be independently
shown to be relatively closely related. It was and is, of course, common to
translate the Bible and certain other religious texts into many languages.
When sources of this type are used it is clear that examples must be chosen
with care, but it is possible to find sentences and their later equivalents that
use many cognate lexical items and ones that differ syntactically only (or
chiefly) in the single phenomenon being investigated. For example, in a study
of case marking one would look for examples where other factors, such as
word order, did not differ in the "corresponding" sentences from different
periods.

Lockwood (1968: 245–6) uses correspondences of this sort in a description
of the "natural affinity between an interrogative and a relative clause." By comparing translations of the Gospels into two languages that are independently
known to be related, and by selecting examples that contain cognates, he
establishes a correspondence in syntactic patterns.

(6)   (a)   Old High German (Monsee Matthew)
                 inu   ni   lârut   ir   hwaȝ   David
                 INTERJ   NEG   read.2PL.PRET   you.PL   what.ACC   David

                 teta
                 do.3SG.PRET

(b) Old English (West Saxon Gospels)
ne   rædde ge   þæt hwæt David dyde
NEG read   you.PL that what David did

"Have ye not read what David did?" (both (a) and (b))

The specific examples support a correspondence (not specifically stated by Lockwood) that has the interrogative pronoun used to introduce a headless relative clause.

While translations offer a fruitful source of cognate sentences, it is absolutely essential that the linguist exercise great care in dealing with some translations in order to overcome the many well-known and serious philological problems they can bring, including distortions of native word order and grammatical constructions, purposeful attempts at archaic and stylistically very elevated genres, and sheer textual errors, among others. Nevertheless, when such problems receive careful attention, they can usually be controlled and thus very often correspondences from translations prove very valuable for reconstruction.

Specific sentences in language L_1 may be said to correspond to their *translation* into language L_2, if the languages are closely related, if a relatively close translation is used, and if the proper precautions are taken, as outlined above. This source has been used to advantage by Bennett (1986, 1987), who cites examples from Cankar's *Bela krizantema*, originally written in Slovene, and corresponding examples from its translation into closely related Serbian:

(7)   (a) Slovene
          moj prijatelj Peter Košenina je velik junak
          my friend   P.   K.   is big   hero
          "My friend Peter Košenina is a big hero."

       (b) Serbian
          moj prijatelj Peter Košenina veliki je junak
          (same meaning as (7a))   (Bennett 1987: 271, 272)

In his study of word order, especially regarding the order of clitics, Bennett chooses examples consisting mainly of words that are cognate, examples that differ chiefly in terms of the order of words in "second" position.

The fact that the Serbian translation of *Bela krizantema* was made by someone other than the linguist analyzing the data lends Bennett's examples particular credence. However, translations made by a native speaker linguist or by a native speaker for use by a linguist need not be ruled out, as long as appropriate care is taken to state clearly options that are grammatical. For example, if in the study above, Serbian can optionally use the word order of Slovene, that obviously needs to be indicated and taken into account.

While Bennett uses the translation from L_1 to L_2 where L_1 and L_2 are closely related languages, the same technique can be used where L_1 is an early stage and L_2 a later stage of the same language. In many cultures educated people can read fluently in an earlier stage of their own language and can supply exact, yet linguistically naive, modern correspondences of ancient sentences. Again, it is clear that care must be taken to use examples that are representative and to analyze the full text to determine the range of variation possible.

Where correspondences involving dialects or closely related contemporary languages are needed, responses to identical stimuli are relatively easy to obtain. The examples in (2)–(4) and numerous others like them were obtained by presenting examples from Georgian, relatively close to both Mingrelian and Laz, to speakers bilingual in Mingrelian and Georgian, on the one hand, and to speakers bilingual in Laz and Georgian, on the other. Similar correspondences can be obtained by presenting examples from one dialect to a speaker of another, asking the latter to "translate" into his or her own dialect. Using this method, Dumézil and Esenç (1972) provide seven short texts in the Artašen (Ardeşen) dialect of Laz consisting entirely of sentences that have correspondences given in two other dialects, Arkabe (Arhavi) and Xopa (Hopa). The corresponding sentences below illustrate two significant syntactic differences between the Artašen and Arkabe dialects:

(8)   (a) Artašen
"xoja, hašo p'eya mušeni ikuy?" t'k'vey
Hodja thus   why   he.do they.say
"'Why is the Hodja behaving thus?' they said."

(b) Arkabe
"xoja-k   hašo p'eya mušen ikoms?" ya   tkves
Hodja-NAR thus   why   he.do   QUOT they.say
"'Why is the Hodja behaving thus?' they said."
(Dumézil and Esenç 1972: 35–6 (examples 3, 3))

When numerous other corresponding pairs like (8) are consulted, the following generalizations emerge: (i) Artašen systematically lacks any marking of the narrative case (as well as of other grammatical cases) found in other dialects; and (ii) Artašen systematically lacks the quotative particle, *ya*, used in other dialects.

Another dialect example comes from Finnish. While the so-called passive of Standard Finnish allows no expression of the agent, in American Finnish it is possible to express one, especially if it is an institution, as in (9):

(9)   (a)   Standard Finnish passive
             häne-t   hauda-ttin   (*kirko-sta)
             he-ACC bury-PAST.PASS (*church-from)
             "He was buried (*by the church)."

      (b)   American Finnish passive
             häne-t   hauda-ttin   kirko-sta
             he-ACC bury-PAST.PASS church-From
             "He was buried by the church."   (Campbell 1988: 89–90)

The correspondence could be stated as (10).

(10) *Correspondence: Finnish "Passive"*
      Standard Finnish   American Finnish
      object-ACC verb-*ttiin* : object-ACC verb-*ttiin* (agent-BY),

where BY represents one of the cases -*stA* "from (within)" or -*ltA* "from
(without)."

All of these sources must, of course, be used judiciously. For example, use
of the slavish translations of the Bible into Gothic may be tempered by philological work such as Koppitz (1900), which helps to distinguish the characteristics of Gothic from those of the Greek original by separating those
examples which are opposite to the Greek or are without a corresponding original from those that follow the order of the original.

Examples such as those adduced by Lockwood, Bennett, Dumézil and
Esenç, and Campbell, as well as ones discussed earlier in this chapter, show
that the notion of correspondence in syntax is not "incoherent." Large sets of
such pairs of examples provide the basis for determining abstract patterns of
correspondence, which can be stated as in table 12.2, in (5), (10), or in other
ways. Sets of such pairs likewise provide evidence that sentence patterns do
indeed evolve, even if not in the way that sounds do.

12.2.4   Conclusion

We conclude that, contrary to some claims, it is possible to establish correspondences in syntax. In part as a result of this, it is also possible to establish
with certainty that syntactic change has taken place, although some changes
may remain indeterminate. In the next section we argue that it is likewise possible to reconstruct syntactic changes.

12.3   Reconstructing

12.3.1   Introduction

Our purposes in this section are to present aspects of the comparative
method that can be successfully applied to syntax, to describe positive aids to

syntactic reconstruction, and to argue that syntactic reconstruction can be successful and productive. Ultimately, this section serves to illustrate how apsects of the framework we have developed for analysis of syntactic change can be applied to the solving of practical historical problems.

12.3.2   Relics

Relics, or archaisms, are held by many scholars to be perhaps the single most useful source of evidence for syntactic reconstruction. Hock (1985: 33) asserts this strongly: "The traditional approach with its emphasis on aberrant, archaic patterns can be applied without circularity and . . . it yields more satisfactory results than an approach which focuses on the synchronically most regular patterns." This is Meillet's (1954 [1925]: 27, 1922 [1964]: 46) famous dictum that we reconstruct on exceptions, not on rules (Watkins 1976: 312). While there is probably little dispute in general about the value of true relics or archaism for reconstruction, in practice there is the problem of how they are to be identified and how one can be certain that a relic is at stake rather than some peculiar innovation.

Relics have two essential properties: (i) they are *exceptions* in an otherwise regular system; and (ii) they are *archaic*. As exceptions, they have somehow been bypassed or exempted by the otherwise regular processes of change. In a synchronic description, relics, like other exceptions, may not fit into otherwise valid generalizations. While exceptions could be innovative, only those exceptions that can be identified as archaic qualify for consideration in reconstruction.

Some ways to determine relics that are sometimes suggested in the literature are the following. *An archaism normally recedes over a period of time, whereas an innovation spreads.* Thus for reconstruction, the safer archaisms are those which are synchronically felt to be old-fashioned and in observable history their use is seen to be decreasing (Hock 1985: 55). Also, "the more widespread a particular complex form turns out to be among related languages without contact in time and space, the stronger the argument for 'inheritance' becomes" (Winter 1984: 623).

Relics often occur in the most commonly used expressions of a language (Meillet 1922[1964]: 31–2). Evidently frequent use can reinforce specific patterns in such a way that general rules are not always applied. Since this is as true in syntax as in phonology and morphology, an effective heuristic for locating syntactic relics would involve examining the syntax of clauses and phrases governed by lexical items with more readily identifiable morphological irregularities.

Relics are likely to be preserved in proverbs and proverb-like sayings (Watkins

1976: 317). Other types of language that tend to preserve relic forms best include legal documents and traditional literary forms, such as epic poetry, popular ballads, and, to a lesser extent, folk narratives (see Hock 1985: 54). As discussed in section 11.3.3, kinship terms and sacred expressions also often preserve archaic exceptions (see Meillet 1922[1964]: 28).

It has been traditional to treat compounds as fixed expressions that preserve relics of an earlier word order. Lightfoot (1979a:160) rightfully criticizes an inappropriate application of this technique where English compounds such as *coathanger* were taken as evidence of the former OV structure of English, while old forms suggesting VO were simply ignored, e.g. *breakfast* (first attested in 1413). In section 8.2.2, we drew on comparative data to show, among other things, that (i) generalizations about the order in compounds compared with historical order in phrases have not been based on diachronic studies of long-attested languages showing how patterns in compounds have been affected by word order change, and (ii) the patterns in compounds in a given language do not necessarily reflect an earlier order. Therefore, compounds are not, as previously supposed, in the category of syntactic relics and cannot be relied upon in reconstruction. The lesson we draw from this case is not that it is wrong to use relics, but that it may frequently be difficult and that one needs compelling evidence of the "oldness" of assumed archaic forms before basing syntactic reconstructions on them.

Archaism is not intended to form the basis for reconstruction; this is the role of the correspondence, discussed in section 12.2. Rather, the relic is one tool in the historical syntactician's arsenal that can be used to determine which of two or more patterns in a differential correspondence is the oldest. Relics are best combined with data concerning the direction of change in a historical period, and this combination is most effective when used with additional types of data, discussed in section 12.3.3 and in subsections of section 12.4.

Examples given in the subsections below illustrate some of the types of relics named above and, at the same time, the way those relics can be used in reconstruction.

12.3.2.1   Romance relics of the internal structure of the noun phrase
In early Latin, adjectives and nouns occurred in the order AN; during the Latin period this gradually changed, and in all Romance languages the unmarked order is now NA. In both Classical Latin and the contemporary languages, the order AN continues to occur with some of the most frequently occurring adjectives (M. Harris 1978: 58–9).[4] If we had no attestation of Latin and wished to reconstruct the order of adjectives and nouns in Pre-Romance,

we would set up a table of correspondences based on unmarked order; but at the same time we would note exceptional, marked orders. (As in chapter 8, we use capital letters to indicate the unmarked order, lower case to indicate marked order.)

Word order correspondences involving adjective and noun in some Romance languages.

French	Italian	Spanish	Portuguese	Rumanian
an/NA	an/NA	an/NA	an/NA	an/NA

By itself, the facts summarized in these columns, including the relic word order, would not be sufficient to reconstruct *AN as the unmarked order in Pre-Romance. However, there are dialects, such as Eastern French and Sursilvan Rhetian, which prefer AN order (Posner 1966: 177). Reconstructions must fully take these dialects into account. If we also had access to some historical data, such as Old French, which would provide evidence of the recession of AN order over time and the corresponding expansion of NA order, we would be able to reconstruct AN order to the Pre-Romance stage.[5] This partially hypothetical example is intended to illustrate both the limits of relic data alone, and the way in which it can successfully be used in combination with other data (in this instance recession and expansion) to reconstruct with confidence.

12.3.2.2   *Finnish relics of participial subjects*
Proto-Balto-Finnic had participial constructions in which the logical subjects of the participles were originally arguments of the main verb, but were reinterpreted in Finnish as genitive subject arguments of the participle, due to the homophony of accusative and genitive singular case endings (see section 4.4.1). Finnish relics preserve evidence of the former state in, for example, folk poems. One example is:

(11)   kuul-tihin   kala-t   kute-va-n,
        hear-PAST.PASS fish-ACC.PL spawn-PRES.PARTICIPLE-SUF

        lohe-n-pursto-t   loiskutta-va-n
        salmon-GEN-tail-ACC.PL splash-PRES.PARTICIPLE-SUF

        "The fish were heard spawning, salmon-tails splashing."

                                                        (see Campbell 1990a)

In Modern Standard Finnish, instead of the accusative plural of "fish" and "salmon-tails," we would have the genitive plural, as in (12):

(12) kuul-tiin   kalo-j-en   kute-va-n,
      hear-PAST.PASS fish-GEN.PL spawn-PRES.PARTICIPLE-SUF

      lohe-n-pursto-j-en   loiskutta-va-n
      salmon-GEN-tail-GEN.PL splash-PRES.PARTICIPLE-SUF

Thus this poem contains a relic, in (11), of the former construction. This is supportive of the reconstruction already securely established on the basis of comparative evidence from cognate languages, but without other supporting evidence it would be insufficient for reconstruction.

12.3.2.3 Kartvelian relics of the internal structure of the noun phrase

In the Zan languages, genitives usually precede head nouns (Čikobava 1936a:68; Lomtaӡe 1954: 227). This unmarked GN order is illustrated in (13) from Mingrelian and (14) from Laz:[6]

(13) (a) komortes ost'at'-ep-iš   ʔude-ša
           they.come artisan-PL-GEN house-ALL
           "They came to the artisans' house."   (Lomtaӡe 1954: 208)

      (b) etiš   otaxu-š   kǝla
           his.GEN room-GEN key-NOM
           "the key of (to) his room"   (Lomtaӡe 1954: 209)

(14) (a) baba-ši   ǰuma   ǰumadi   ren
           father-GEN brother-NOM uncle-NOM he.be
           "A father's brother is an uncle."   (Lomtaӡe 1954: 209)

      (b) č'ubri-ši   picai   en
           chestnut-GEN board-NOM it.be
           "It is a chestnut board," "It is a board of chestnut."
                                                          (Lomtaӡe 1954: 209)

In Old Georgian the usual order is NG, as exemplified in (15) (examples cited in Pätsch 1971):

(15) (a) nac'il-i   suet'-isa-y   cxovel-isa-y
           piece-NOM column-GEN-NOM living-GEN-NOM
           "a piece of a living column"

      (b) mdinare-ni   sisxl-isa-ni
           river-PL.NOM blood-GEN-PL.NOM
           "rivers of blood"

The evidence from Old Georgian, attested since the fifth century, bears a greater burden in comparative reconstruction because of its relative age. Nevertheless, a reconstruction based only on the correspondences below would be unsatisfactory:

Unmarked word order in noun phrases

Old Georgian	NG
Zan	
Mingrelian	GN
Laz	GN

We are fortunate, therefore, that Zan preserves the order noun–genitive as a relic in a restricted set of expressions. The examples in (16) are Laz; parallel expressions are found in Mingrelian (Lomtaʒe 1954: 209):[7]

(16)　　(a)　baba　čkimi
　　　　　　　father　my
　　　　　　　"my father"

　　　　(b)　j̃uma　čkimi
　　　　　　　brother　my
　　　　　　　"my brother"

In this instance, we have independent evidence that these expressions are fossils of an earlier word order. While Old Georgian used the order NG, in Modern Georgian the norm is GN. Modern Georgian preserves expressions parallel to those in Zan:

(17)　　mama-čemi
　　　　father-my
　　　　"my father"

In Georgian we have attestation that (17) preserves an older structure. It is well known that kinship terms of this sort are likely to be linguistic relics (see section 11.3.3; Meillet 1922[1964]: 28). From this it follows that the forms in (16) are most likely relics of the order NG in Zan as well.[8] On the basis of the relic status of (16) in Zan and the relatively greater age of the order NG in Georgian, this order can be reconstructed to Common-Georgian-Zan.

12.3.3　Morphology

Morphology is concrete and phonologically endowed and for this reason is widely regarded as lending itself to reconstruction. In those languages with a rich morphology, there is typically a close relationship between the morphology and the syntax. To the extent that the morphology can be reconstructed by the comparative method, many aspects of a proto-syntax will become clear. That is, the normal techniques of lexical reconstruction, based on the sequence of recurring sound correspondences in cognate words, can be used to reconstruct polymorphemic words. Morphological analysis of these reconstructed proto-words provides the morphology free, as it were, so long as the

Table 12.3 *Balto-Finnic morphological comparisons (based on Laanest 1982: 250–71)*

	Finnish	Votic	Estonian	PBF
1SG IND	luen	lugẹn	loen	*luɣe-n
1IND PAST	luin	lud'in	lugesin	*luɣ-i-n
1IND PERF	olen	ẹlẹn	olen	*ole-n
	lukenut	lukẹnnu	lugenud	luke-nut
PRES PASS	luetaan	lukẹassa	loetakse	*luɣe-tta-k-sen
PAST PASS	luettiin	lugẹtti:	loeti	*luɣe-ttiin
1ST INF	lukea	lukẹa	lugeda	*luke-taX
3RD INF	lukemaan	lukẹma:	lugema	*luke-ma-han
PRES PTCPL	lukeva	lukẹva	lugev	*luke-vaX
PAST PTCPL	lukenut	lukẹnnu	lugenud	*luke-nut
PRES PASS PTCPL	luettava	lugẹttava	loetav	*luɣe-tta-vaX
PAST PASS PTCPL	luettu	lugẹttu	loetud	*luɣe-ttu

cognate morphemes have not undergone substantial functional or positional shifts. In the history of Indo-European studies, this kind of morphological reconstruction was often taken to be the major part of "comparative grammar," where the reconstruction of morphological (and grammatical) paradigms attracted the most attention (see Allen 1953; Jeffers 1976b: 3–4; Jucquois 1976: 233–4; Birnbaum 1977: 25–30; for some typical examples, see Brugmann 1904; Watkins 1969; Krahe 1972; see also chapter 2).

The following example illustrates the application of morphological reconstruction to syntactic domains in Proto-Balto-Finnic. The data, presented in table 12.3, involve syntactically important aspects of verb morphology, illustrated with the verb "to read" (IND = indicative, INF = infinitive, PTCPL = participle, PASS = passive, PERF = perfect, PRES = present; BF = Balto-Finnic, PBF = Proto-Balto-Finnic).

The reconstruction of this morphology follows directly from the lexical reconstruction by the comparative method, given well-established sound changes (e.g. vowel apocope, vowel syncope, and loss of final -n in Estonian, Livonian, and Votic [with compensatory lengthening in the latter], loss of intervocalic t, seen here in Finnish and Votic). (Note that ɣ in the reconstructions represents the gradated variant of *k in closed syllables.) While the sound changes are complex, they are well documented and well understood. The only real complications stem from: (a) the Finnish present passive, which has changed to look more like the first infinitive (which is marked with -ta in many verb classes); also in the present passive, Votic ss < ks, and the last a of both Finnish and Votic is from the assimilation of e to the preceding a; and (b)

Estonian first person indicative past, *lugesin*, where the marker of the past originally was *-i*, but was lost by apocope in third person forms (marked only by ∅) where the *i* was word-final; because a large class of verbs with a *t* in the root changed this to *s* before the *i*, including the *i* of past tense (cf. Finnish *vastata* "to answer," *vastas-i* "he answered"), in compensation for the lost *-i* (former past-tense marker), the *s* of these verbs was extended to others which had formerly had no *t* in the root, to signal past tense. (Since first person ends in *-n*, the *i* of past tense is protected from apocope, and hence the Estonian form *luge-si-n* [read-PAST-I], with the new past in *-si-*.)

The phonological shape of these words can be reconstructed through regular lexical reconstruction, based on sound changes and phonological correspondences, but this does not guarantee an understanding of the function of the various affixes that are reconstructed in this way. In this instance, each form in each of the three languages has the function (meaning) listed for it in the left-most column. Because the functions in each language are identical, in this instance reconstruction of the function of each morpheme is straightforward. The lexical reconstruction of the forms and the determination of the original function (meaning) of each together constitute morphological reconstruction.

This morphological reconstruction provides a firm foundation for understanding the historical syntax; for example, from these forms and their reconstructed functions it is clear that Proto-Balto-Finnic had a passive construction and had both indicative and passive participles (both with present and perfect versions) – markers of subordinate clauses (complex sentences). Morphological reconstruction via the comparative method thus can provide considerable syntactic information about the proto-language.[9]

12.4   Obstacles and purported obstacles

Establishment of correspondences and syntactic reconstruction are understandably made difficult by the factors that complicate reconstruction by the comparative method in general, including reanalysis and extension, borrowing, accidental similarity, and parallel (independent) developments which accord with typological considerations and linguistic universals. In this section we examine the claimed obstacles to syntactic reconstruction via the comparative method, and assess the potentials for circumventing the troubles they occasion. Many assert that syntactic change lacks a direct analogue to the *regularity* of sound change, which provides a basis for reconstruction. Many researchers affirm that syntactic change lacks the *directionality* that is so useful in phonological reconstruction (see section 11.4; cf. Miranda 1976;

Campbell and Mithun 1980; Harris 1985; Hock 1985; Lightfoot 1979a). In addition, it has been claimed (e.g. Lightfoot 1979a, 1981a; Warner 1983) that syntactic reconstruction is not possible in principle, since grammars are created anew by each subsequent generation; that is, there is no *continuity* between the grammars of different generations. Other purported obstacles to syntactic reconstruction include the difficulty of recovering prior states after reanalysis and/or extension, misuse of typology, and complications occasioned by borrowing.[10] We discussed the purported lack of regularity in sections 11.3 and 12.2.3.1; we consider each of the others in turn below.

We argue here that some of the purported obstacles to syntactic reconstruction are spurious or overstated. In other instances, however, we agree that a genuine obstacle exists, and we discuss ways of overcoming or circumventing it. Our major goal is to show that syntactic reconstruction can be successful through judicious application of the comparative method. We illustrate the difficulties and the proposed solutions to these problems with comparative grammatical material from a variety of languages, but with emphasis on Finno-Ugric, especially the Balto-Finnic branch, since the changes have been studied extensively and the evidence is generally very well understood and uncontroversial.

12.4.1 Directionality

The predictable direction of many sound changes is helpful to phonological reconstruction: for example, the change of *p* to *b* between vowels is natural and recurs independently in many languages, while the reverse possible change ($b > p$/V__V) is highly unlikely. Knowing this helps in reconstruction. In a case where one language, let us call it L_1, has V*p*V and a related language, L_2 has corresponding V*b*V, all else being equal, the known directionality of this change requires us to postulate **p* for the proto-language, with the change to *b* intervocalically in L_2. Lightfoot (1979a: 10) has taken a dim view of the value of implicational universals in establishing directionality for syntactic change (see also Jeffers 1976b; Winter 1984); Campbell and Mithun (1980) were optimistic, but noted that not many such universals had yet been established (see also Dressler 1971). Miranda (1976: 14) made the same point about the value of directionality for syntactic reconstruction, alluding to cases where the general direction of grammatical change is known – changes of postpositions to case suffixes, of modal auxiliary verbs to modal suffixes, and of passive constructions to ergativity, where the opposite direction is not found.

In section 11.4 we argued that there is no evidence to support the view that languages progress unidirectionally along a one-time course of development from less to more complex, or from one whole-language type to another. On the other hand, there is a genuine tendency, albeit with exceptions, for independent words to become clitics, which may in turn become affixes. We argued that today, the prospects for understanding the direction of some specific kinds of grammatical changes seem much brighter than they once did; this information is useful for syntactic reconstruction.

As an example of the use of directionality in grammatical reconstruction we cite the development of the partitive case in Balto-Finnic. In section 11.4.3.1, we showed that constructions for signaling objects which are only partially affected by the action of the verb develop from locatives (with the meaning of roughly "from") or from genitival constructions ("of"). There we discussed this development of the partitive in French, in Lithuanian, and in other languages. It is assumed that this development is unidirectional, from genitive or locative to partitive use. In the discussion below, we first consider the historical development of the Balto-Finnic partitive case, then apply it to the issue of directionality in syntactic reconstruction.

Most Uralic languages have no special case for partially affected objects. Originally, the *-m "accusative singular" indicated that the object was animate or specific, while inanimate and/or non-specific objects were in the nominative case, that is, they had Ø case marking. This is still the case in some Uralic languages outside the Balto-Finnic group. With plural objects there was no such distinction, and both nominative plural and accusative plural were signaled by *-t, as they are still today in Finnish and some other Balto-Finnic languages. The partitive object case is an innovation in Balto-Finnic and its close relatives from a former ablative case ending. In Mordvin, closely related to Balto-Finnic, there is a small number of verbs (e.g. "eat," "drink") which employ the ablative case for partially affected objects, as in Moksha Mordvin:

(18)   aru   vet'-ta   sima-n
        pure water-ABLATIVE drink-I
        "I drink pure water."

Compare Finnish:

(18')   juo-n puhdas-ta vet-tä
        drink-I pure-PART water-PART

Erza Mordvin:

(19)   veŕgiześ veŕgiz-de   a   suski
        wolf.NOM wolf-ABLATIVE NEG bite
        "A wolf does not bite (any) wolf."   (Laanest 1982: 298)

This shows the beginnings in the Volga-Balto-Finnic period of the development of the syntactically and functionally complicated partitive case, from the

Table 12.4 *Reconstruction of Finno-Ugric object cases.*

Finnic	Lapp	Mordvin	Others	PFU
*-ta PART	*-j-de: PL-ACC < *-j-ta PL-PART *	*-ta ABL/PART	*-ta ABL	*-ta ABL
*-m ACC.SG	*-m ACC.SG	*-m ACC	*-m SPEC.ACC	*-m SPEC.ACC

Note: See Korhonen (1981: 214–15) on the development of the plural accusative from the plural partitive in Lapp.

ablative case to one that expresses a partial object. The Mordvin ablative can be used as a "restricting" object case, for example where "to eat of/from bread" develops the meaning "eat some (of the) bread," from which the grammatical function of the partitive case developed, used at first only with certain irresultative acts: "to seek," "to ask for," "to follow," "to hope for," "to long for," etc.[11]

The forms of the Proto-Finno-Ugric (PFU) ablative and accusative singular are straightforwardly reconstructed as summarized in table 12.4. Given the syntactic distribution of partitive and ablative cases in the Finno-Ugric languages and the knowledge that partitive cases typically develop from restricting case markings (e.g. ablatives), but not vice versa, we can reconstruct for Finno-Ugric the syntax of these cases as illustrated in table 12.4 (PART = partitive, ACC = accusative, SPEC = specified, ABL = ablative, LOC = locative).[12] In Finnic new ablatives, *-stA "from within" and *-ltA "from without," are formed by compounding the locatives *-s and *-l with the old ablative *-ta.

The first step in this reconstruction is to state the syntactic correspondence, which may be simplified to:

*-ta PART : *-ta ABL

The known universal directionality (ABL >PART) of the change provides part of the means by which we determine that ablative was the original syntactic function of this case form. Thus, this example shows how directionality of change can provide a basis for reconstruction. In this particular example relics (see note 11) confirm the correctness of this conclusion.

12.4.2   Typology, implicational universals, and reconstruction of word order

Early work in historical linguistics based on Greenberg's (1963) study of word order universals attempted reconstructions of word order of proto-languages (see section 8.1 for a summary of current understanding of these universals).

The best-known and most extensive such reconstruction was Lehmann's (1974). His method assumes that the existence in a language of a feature that correlates with one word order type, while the language as a whole exibits another word order, is indicative of an earlier stage. For example, if a language L_1 possesses postpositions, which correlate with the SOV order type, while L_1 generally has VOS order, this method assumes that the existence of postpositions in L_1 makes it possible to reconstruct SOV order for an earlier stage of the language. This method has been widely criticized (see Campbell and Mithun 1980; Hawkins 1983; Comrie 1989[1981]: 210–25; see chapter 8); on the whole, this use of word order typology in reconstruction has been so thoroughly rejected that it may be thought of as an obstacle to reconstruction. Yet some more restricted parts of word order typology, if judiciously used, may provide an aid to reconstruction.

In effect, only SOV languages can naturally have the order RelN (Relative Clause–Head, that is, preposed relative clauses). That is, VO languages tend to have NRel in harmony with their typical Head–Dependent orders within the NP. SOV languages may have RelN in accord with the tendency towards Dependent–Head orders. Nevertheless, the Heaviness Serialization Principle (HSP) is also involved, so that heavier constituents tend to be placed to the right of their heads to avoid the perceptual difficulty of processing the roles of nominal arguments (Hawkins 1983: 90). Therefore, only some SOV languages naturally contain RelN, in harmony with their preferred Dependent–Head orders, while many others conform to the HSP with relative clauses shifted after their head nouns.[13] (See Dryer 1992: 86–7 for a detailed demonstration of this point, based on a sample of 625 languages.) Only in an SOV language could RelN arise naturally, and even here it may naturally shift to NRel by the HSP.

Balto-Finnic (together with Lapp, for the most part) has the basic word order SVO, while the rest of the Uralic languages have SOV order:

(20)   Balto-Finnic, Lapp   Other Uralic
                     SVO : SOV

Finnish, to take one example, exhibits the word order patterns:

S–V–O
Adjective–Noun
Genitive–Noun
Noun–Postposition
Auxiliary–Main Verb
Adverb–Adjective
Relative Clause–Head/Head–Relative Clause (RelN/NRel)
Adjective–Marker–Standard/Standard+Part–Adjective (AMS/SMA)[14]

Comparing Finno-Ugric languages, we find that the SOV languages have preposed relative clauses (though a few have also developed postposed relatives under foreign influence). Moreover, as in many SOV languages, these preposed relative clauses do not contain finite verb forms, but rather are made of nominalized or participial constructions which bear case markings, and these relatives contain no relative pronouns (see Keenan 1985; Comrie 1989[1981]). While Balto-Finnic also has postposed relative clauses (consistent with its SVO order and with the HSP), the presence of its preposed relative clauses strongly suggests former SOV structure, since only in SOV languages is RelN order natural. These two relative clause orders are illustrated in the following Finnish examples:

RelN

(21) huomasin kova-lla ääne-llä puhu-va-n   miehe-n
      noticed.I hard-By voice-By speak-PRES.PTCPL-ACC man-ACC
      "I noticed the man who speaks with a loud voice."

(22) näin joke-en   aja-nee-n   miehe-n
      saw.I river-Into drive-PAST.PTCPL-ACC man-ACC
      "I saw the man who drove/has driven into the river."

NRel

(21') huomasin miehe-n   joka   puhu-u   kova-lla ääne-llä
       noticed.I man-ACC REL.NOM speak-3RD.PRES hard-By voice-By
       (same meaning as (21))

(22') näin miehe-n   joka   ajoi   joke-en
       saw.I man-ACC REL.NOM drove river-Into
       "I saw the man who drove into the river."

Second, the order Standard–Marker–Adjective (SMA) in constructions of comparison is very much like preposed relative clauses, essentially occurring only in SOV languages, while Adjective–Marker–Standard order (AMS) is most common in other word order types (Comrie 1989[1981]: 91, 98). The fact that Balto-Finnic has both, but would not have acquired SMA without an SOV background, argues for its former SOV status. Some examples from Finnish are:

SMA

(23) hän   on sinu-a   nopea-mpi
      he.NOM is you-PART fast-Er
      "He is faster than you (are)."

(24) hän   juokse-e   sinu-a   hitaa-mmi-n
      he.NOM run-3RD.PRES you-PART slow-Er-ADV
      "He runs slower than you (do)."

AMS

(23')   hän   on nopea-mpi kuin sinä
         he.NOM is fast-Er   than you.NOM
         (same meaning as (23))

(24')   hän juokse-e hitaa-mmi-n kuin sinä
         he.NOM run-3RD.PRES slow-Er-ADV than you.NOM
         (same meaning as (24))

Finally, while postpositions are sometimes found in other word orders, their existence in Finnish is consistent with a reconstructed SOV order in the proto-language.

Given these restrictions that RelN and SMA can cooccur with SVO order, but that they do not develop in non-SOV orders, it seems clear that the reconstruction of SOV with RelN, SMA, and Postpositions is on safe ground. For syntactic reconstruction, we consider the correspondences given in (25):

(25)   *Balto-Finnic*   *Others*
        NRel/RelN   RelN
        SMA/AMS   SMA
        Postpositions   Postpositions
        SVO   SOV

The change away from RelN and SMA in Balto-Finnic, the non-SOV languages of the family, has given Balto-Finnic the dual orders, and the firm typology cited above involving these changes supports the reconstruction of SOV with RelN and SMA in the proto-language.

The use made of typology here differs from early uses of typology in word order reconstruction in two essential respects. First, synchronic data were first used to set up a correspondence of patterns, (20); this essentially limits the task of reconstruction to determining which of these is the older and explaining how the change came about.[15] Second, the analysis is centered on one strong argument, which is based on the very tight correlation of preposed non-finite relative clauses with SOV order. In essence, relative clauses of this type are found only in languages that either have SOV order or for which there is some independent reason to suppose that they once had SOV order. In this instance that independent reason is that the sister languages have SOV order. Because of these restrictions on the way typology is used in this example, the reconstruction is secure.

Misuse of typology in reconstruction in the past has not been limited to word order. For example, Gamkrelidze and Ivanov (1984) reconstruct active distribution of case markers (see chapter 9 for definition) in Proto-Indo-European without reference to distribution of cases in the daughter languages, but instead on the basis of an opposition of animate to inanimate nouns. This reasoning is based on the typology proposed by Klimov (1973).[16] Others have reconstructed the alignment of case marking on the basis of alignment of agreement marking, even though it is known that the tendency to establish alignment harmony is only slight, if indeed it exists at all.[17] All of these reconstructions have in common the problem that the basis for reconstruction is a putative typological correlation which, if it exists at all, is too weak to form the basis for a secure reconstruction.

12.4.3   The effects of analogy

Analogical changes in grammar have been considered particularly devastating to attempts at syntactic reconstruction. As Lightfoot (1979a: 164) puts it:

> Syntactic change is in large measure analogical, based on a re-analysis or "regrammatization" of old surface structure patterns, levelling former distinctions or creating new ones. That is, existing strings are given a new structural analysis, which eventually supplants the former analysis, presumably by some kind of analogical function . . . Such analogical processes will cause as much interference for the usual methods of reconstruction as they do in phonology and other areas of grammar; *but in syntax such changes are the normal type and therefore the methods will be particularly limited.* (our emphasis)

(See also Jeffers 1976b: 4.)

Again, it is possible to admit the serious effects of analogy in syntactic change and still remain optimistic about reconstruction. Analogical change may obscure phonological correspondences, making reconstruction of phonology more difficult, but weight of the conforming daughter languages often supersedes these effects, allowing for successful phonological reconstruction. For example, in the cognate set given in (26):

(26) | English | German | Gothic | Old Norse | |
      | *adder* | *natter* | *naðr-* | *naðra* | "adder" |

English is clearly deviant, and the testimony of the other languages would lead us to postulate an initial **n-* in the proto-language, while seeking an explanation for the English deviation. Knowing the article pattern in English of *a #C-*, *an #V-*, we would postulate a reanalysis of *a #nadder* as *an #adder* virtually on the strength of the correspondences in this cognate set alone. However, in addition there is abundant confirming evidence in English of this sort of reanalysis in other instances, for example in changes attested in documents (as is the case with "adder"), and in parallel forms, e.g. *napkin/apron*, etc. The effects of the analogical change are not devastating to reconstruction in this phonological example, and it is the application of the comparative method which helps determine that such a change has in fact taken place.

Analogical change or reanalysis is also recoverable in the same way in syntactic reconstruction in many instances. For a stimulating example of the reconstruction of aspects of Indo-European sentence structure, recovering the effects of a series of boundary reanalyses, surface reinterpretations, and levelings in Old Irish, through comparison with Hittite, Vedic Sanskrit, etc., see Watkins (1963, 1964). We use changes in the negative imperfect and perfect constructions in Finnish to illustrate the way the effects of reanalysis can be analyzed.

Balto-Finnic and Lapp have a complex perfect with a copular auxiliary verb; the other languages use Ø-copula where possible (see below). Thus where formerly Balto-Finnic would have had Ø-copula for example as in (27), an overt copula was adopted and now the form is (28) (based on Finnish forms):

(27)   koivu vihreä
        birch green
        "The birch is green."

(28)   koivu on vihreä
        birch is green

When the copula was added to forms like (27), it also extended automatically to the perfect. That is, formerly the form was as for example in (29); after the adoption of the copula it was as in (30):

(29)   koivu kaatu-nut
        birch fall-PAST.PARTICIPLE
        "The birch has fallen." (literally "birch fallen")

(30)   koivu on kaatu-nut
        birch is fall-PAST.PARTICIPLE

This development, however, complicated the negative paradigm, which in Uralic was based on negative verbs. Before the adoption of the copula, forms like those illustrated in table 12.5 were employed. After the introduction of the copula, the negative perfect came also to be formed with the copula, as in (31), for example:

(31)   isä   ei   ole   tul-lut
        father NEG.he COPULA come-PAST.PTCPL
        "Father has not come."

Example (31) corresponds to the positive (32), containing the copula, *on*:

(32)   isä   on tullut
        "Father has come."

Table 12.5 *Reconstructed pre-copular Balto-Finnic verb tenses and aspects*

	Positive	Negative
Present	*minä tule-n* I come-I "I come"	*minä en tule* I NEG.I come "I don't come/am not coming"
	isä tule-e father come-he.PRES "father comes"	*isä ei tule* father NEG. come "father doesn't come/isn't coming"
Preterite	*minä tul-i-n* I come-PAST-I "I came"	*minä esin tule* I NEG.PAST.I come "I didn't come"
	isä tul-i father come-PAST "father came"	*isä esi tule* father NEG.PAST come "father didn't come"
Perfect	*minä tul-lut* I come-PAST.PTCPL "I have come"	*minä en tul-lut* I NEG.I come-PAST.PTCPL "I have not come"
	isä tul-lut father come-PAST.PTCPL "father has come"	*isä ei tul-lut* father NEG come-PAST.PTCPL "father hasn't come"

This leaves the former copulaless negative perfect (*isä ei tullut*) in competition with the original negative preterites (past), such as *isä esi tule*, as the new negative preterite; this is seen in table 12.6. The competition between the two negative preterites was sorted out; some Balto-Finnic-Lapp languages (Finnish, Estonian dialects, Norway Lapp, Southern Lapp, etc.) eliminated the past negative verb constructions (those with *esi, esin*) entirely, leaving the copulaless *minä en tullut* form as the only negative preterite; others (e.g. Livonian, some Estonian dialects [Kodavaere], Swedish Lapp) eliminated these former copulaless perfect forms, retaining the past negative verbs (the *minä esin tule* forms) for the preterite negatives.

In order to reconstruct this history, we begin with a correspondence such as that in (33):

(33)   *minä en tullut* "I didn't come" : *minä esin tule* "I didn't come"

Reanalysis of the form on the left of the equation in (33) as a preterite obscured the history of the construction. However, when we consider the corresponding forms in Finno-Ugric languages outside the Balto-Finnic group,

Table 12.6 *Reconstructed post-copular Balto-Finnic competition for negative preterite marking*

	Positive	Negative
Preterite	*minä tul-i-n* I come-PAST-I "I came"	*minä esin tule* I NEG.PAST.I come "I didn't come"
	isä tul-i father come-PAST "father came"	*isä esi tule* father NEG.PAST come "father didn't come"
		or
		minä en tul-lut I NEG.I come-PAST.PTCPL "I didn't come"
		isä ei tul-lut father NEG.PAST come-PAST.PTCPL "father didn't come"
Perfect	*minä ole-n tul-lut* I be-I come-PAST.PTCPL "I have come"	*minä en ole tul-lut* I NEG.I be come-PAST.PTCPL "I have not come"
	isä on tul-lut father is come-PAST.PTCPL "father has come"	*isä ei ole tul-lut* father NEG is come-PAST.PTCPL "father hasn't come"

the reanalysis of the former copulaless negative perfect (*ei tullut*) to the negative preterite is clear, as seen in (34):

(34)   (a) Kodavere Estonian (Balto-Finnic)
        ma esin aṅṅà "I didn't give"
        sa esiD aṅṅà "you didn't give"
        ta es aṅṅà "he didn't give"

        (b) Livonian (Balto-Finnic)
        ma iz ùɔ "I wasn't"
        sa ist ùɔ "you weren't"
        ta iz ùɔ "he wasn't"

        (c) Erza Mordvin (Volga group)
        eźiń pala(k) "I didn't kiss"
        eźit́ pala(k) "you didn't kiss"
        eś pala(k) "he/she didn't kiss"

(d)   Cheremis (Volga group)
      śəm   bit
      NEG.PAST.I tie
      "I didn't tie"

(e)   Zyrian (Permic group)
      eg   mun
      NEG.PAST.I go
      "I didn't go"   (Korhonen 1981: 305–6; Laanest 1982: 244)

The examples in (34) from beyond the Balto-Finnic branch (34c–e), each containing a negative verb conjugated for person plus a personless main-verb stem, are structurally cognate to the structure on the right of the equation in (33), both sides of which represent Balto-Finnic. Because the structure beyond Balto-Finnic is cognate to the structure to the right of the correspondence in (33), it seems clear that this structure must be reconstructed. Given this clear situation, the Finnish negative preterite with a verb form corresponding to the past participle which is used with the perfect in other instances is odd and these data call for an explanation. With the knowledge of the later addition of copulas to the complex tenses, it is not hard to understand the shift in the negative paradigm, and in the negative preterite form in particular. Thus, while Finnish has undergone rather wide-reaching reanalyses in these constructions, reconstruction is not greatly hampered, since the other languages provide abundant evidence to establish the original pattern and to indicate that Finnish has departed from it.

12.4.4   Discontinuity of grammar acquisition

Lightfoot (1980:37) has objected that syntactic reconstruction cannot be done because of the lack of continuity from one generation to the next:

> Grammars are not transmitted historically, but must be created afresh by each new language learner. Each child hypothesizes or "abduces" a grammar; this enterprise is quite independent of what his parents hypothesized . . . one generation earlier . . . If this is correct, one can deduce very little about the form of a proto-grammar merely through an examination of the formal properties of the daughter grammars.   (Lightfoot 1980: 37)

The objection stated here might be correct if we sought to reconstruct proto-grammars, but most historical linguists are more interested in reconstructing syntactic patterns than the grammars that account for them. For example, in section 12.3.2.3, when we reconstructed the pattern NG (the order Noun–Genitive) in Common Kartvelian, we said nothing about the grammar(s) that accounted for this order. Obviously, this order could be accounted for by (a) a grammar that generates the order directly, (b) a grammar containing a rule that generates the order GN, together with a rule that reverses this order, (c) a grammar containing a rule that generates NYG (where Y represents some other constituent), and a rule that deletes Y, or by many other grammars.

Note that if Lightfoot's objection were valid, it would presumably apply equally to that portion of the grammar that handles phonology. This would equally mean that phonological reconstruction were impossible.

If Lightfoot is right, there may be discontinuities between grammars without discontinuities between syntactic patterns. Historical linguists have traditionally been primarily interested in discontinuities in the data, in the syntactic patterns. It is the application of the comparative method that can identify when such discontinuities have taken place and what the patterns underlying them were. Once the patterns have been reconstructed, one might be in a position to begin to consider what form the grammar of speakers at that stage must have had in order to produce these patterns.

12.4.5 Borrowing

It is to be presumed that grammatical borrowing may complicate reconstruction of syntax just as it does the reconstruction of phonology, morphology, and the lexicon. It should follow that the same techniques for dealing with complications occasioned by borrowing in these areas should also be helpful in syntactic reconstruction (see also Birnbaum 1977, 1984). For example, at the lexical level we find cognates across the Finno-Ugric languages reflecting *ema* "mother," but Finnish *äiti* "mother" clearly does not fit this set. Its very lack of fit leads us to suspect possible borrowing, and seeking a source, we find it in Germanic (cf. Old High German *eidi* "mother").

Syntactic deviations in some daughter language from an otherwise common pattern shared by the other daughters of a family may similarly suggest possible borrowing and urge us to investigate further for possible sources. To take one example, Western Finnish has changed the pattern with verbs of obligation from original subjects in the genitive case, as in (35), to conjugated verbs with nominative subjects and verbs in agreement, as in (36) (see sections 5.3.2 and 11.3.2):

(35)   minu-n täyty-y   mennä
        I-GEN must-3RD.PRES to.go
        "I have to go."

(36)   mä   täydy-n mennä
        I.NOM must-I   to.go
        "I have to go."

Scholars of Finnish have generally attributed this change to Swedish influence (see Saukkonen 1984: 184); Swedish has been strong in western Finland, and many other examples of the impact of Swedish on local Finnish exist. When this borrowed Western Finnish pattern (with nominative subjects) is compared with that of the many other Finnish dialects, which have the genitive-subjects pattern, it is clear that Western Finnish does not fit in the correspondence set, as seen in the examples in (37):

(37)   (a)   Western Finnish
            mä   pidä-n mennä
            I.NOM must-I to.go
            "I must go."

       (b)   Standard Finnish (SF)
            minu-n pitä-ä   mennä
            I-GEN must-3RD.SG to.go

       (c)   Eurajoki
            se-n   täyty ols semmosta ku sano-ttin
            it-GEN must be that.kind as say-PAST.PASSIVE
            "It has to be some such thing as was said."

    (cf. SF: se-n täyty-y olla(s) semmoista kuin sano-ttiin)

       (d)   Vermland
            niij-en   ois   pitän-nä   lahata   oamuśe-lla
            these-PL.GEN would must-PAST.PTCPL to.slaughter morning-On
            "They should have (were supposed to) slaughter(ed) in the morning."

    (cf. SF: nii-den   olisi   pitä-nyt   lahdata aamu-lla
           these-PL.GEN would must-PAST.PTCPL slaughter morning-On)

       (e)   Pieksämäki
            häe-m   pit   ruvetal lapikkaan-tekko-o'
            he-GEN.SG must.PAST start   leather.boot-deed-Into
            "He had to (was supposed to) begin the leather-boot making."

    (cf. SF: häne-n   pit-i ruveta(l) lapikkaan-teko-on
           he-GEN.SG must-PAST . . .)

       (f)   Parikkala
            miu-m pittää marja-t   poimiiv vasemma-la käi-lä
            I-GEN must berry-ACC.PL pick   left-With   hand-With
            "I have to pick the berries with my left hand."

    (cf. SF: minu-n pitää marja-t   poimia(v) vasemma-lla käde-llä
           I-GEN must berry-PL-ACC pick . . .)

       (g)   Inkeri (Koprina)
            sulhaśe-n   pit' antaa kolme ruplaa pojil   viinarahaa
            bridegroom-GEN had to.give three rubles boys.to wine.money

"The bridegroom had (was supposed) to give three rubles to the boys to buy liquor."

(cf. SF: sulhase-n   piti antaa kolme ruplaa pojille viinarahaa
bridegroom-GEN had.to . . .)

(examples from Virtaranta and Soutkari 1964)

These dialects extend from Sweden (Vermland) to the former Soviet Union (Inkeri). From the fact that all dialects except Western Finnish have genitive subjects in this construction, it appears that the genitive subject pattern is to be reconstructed for Finnish, and that Western Finnish has departed from the original state of affairs. Swedish influence is an important factor in the explanation for the change. Given the weight of the correspondences in the sister dialects, the natural tendency to change from marked genitive subjects to unmarked nominative subjects, and the known influence of Swedish on Western Finnish, the borrowing or contact-induced change presents no great obstacle to reconstruction in this case.[18] It should be noticed that the success of the reconstruction in this case does not rest on whether or not it is possible to show these constructions conclusively to have been borrowed in Balto-Finnic. The reconstruction is secure, based on the sheer weight of the distribution of corresponding structures through the other subgroups of the family and on the directionality of change that can be brought to bear on explaining some of these innovations.

12.5   Conclusions

There are many obstacles to successful syntactic reconstruction and their impact should not be underestimated. Nevertheless, prospects for successful syntactic reconstruction are brighter than many have thought them to be. Establishing more grammatical implicational universals increases our knowledge of possible directions of syntactic change and, hence, has the potential to improve our ability to reconstruct. In certain implicational universals we have an analogue to the directionality of sound change. Regularity of syntactic change can be found when phenomena are embedded in more encompassing patterns. Morphological reconstruction can carry us along the road towards the proto-grammar. The difficulties produced by analogical change (restructuring) and borrowing for syntactic reconstruction are probably not different in kind from their effects on phonological, morphological, and lexical reconstruction. Relics provide specific, concrete evidence of an earlier state of affairs.

Another way of assessing the prospects for syntactic reconstruction in general is to evaluate the practical results, the success of the method when applied to the actual reconstruction of the syntax of particular language

Table 12.7   *Bloomfield's reconstruction of Proto-Central-Algonquian*

	Fox	Ojibwa	Plains Cree	Menomini	PCA
1	hk	k	sk	čk	*čk
2	k	k	sk	sk	*k
3	hk	hk	sk	hk	*xk
4	hk	hk	hk	hk	*hk
5	k	k	hk	hk	*çk

families. This has been done for many aspects of the syntax of Finno-Ugric (Janhunen 1982; Campbell 1990a), Kartvelian (Harris 1985), Mayan (Norman and Campbell 1978; Kaufman 1989; Robertson 1992), Uto-Aztecan (Jacobs 1975; Langacker 1977a), and Germanic, Polynesian, Tibeto-Burman, and other languages. From these cases we must judge that the reconstruction of many aspects of syntax appears to be plausible.

The lessons of the past tell us that all techniques and aids to reconstruction must be used judiciously; most are liable to misuse. Clearly a reconstruction is always on firmer footing if it is based on considerations of various kinds, rather than a single type of argument. In complex instances, the fact that a single solution accounts for all of the morphology, all of the syntactic distributions, distribution among the daughter languages, via a plausible change can provide assurance of the reliability of the solution. Nevertheless some will remain skeptical.

In phonological reconstruction, the accuracy of our methods is reconfirmed in cases where unattested things reconstructed via the comparative method have later been vindicated when additional documentation or attestations from information not known at the time of the reconstruction have provided support for the reconstruction. Perhaps Bloomfield's reconstruction of *çk in Proto-Central-Algonquian is the best-known case of this.

Bloomfield's (1925, 1928) famous proof of the applicability of the comparative method in unwritten ("exotic") languages was based on the correspondence sets and reconstructions for Central Algonquian, which he extracted from linguistic descriptions, represented in table 12.7. He postulated the reconstruction of *çk for set 5 as distinct from the others on the basis of scant evidence, but under the assumption that sound change is regular and the difference in this correspondence set (though exhibiting only sounds that occur in different combinations in the other sets) could not plausibly be explained in any other way. Later, his decision to reconstruct something different for this set was confirmed when Swampy Cree was discovered to contain the correspondence *htk* for set 5, distinct in Swampy Cree from the reflexes of the other four reconstructions.[19]

The 1920s saw another dramatic confirmation of the methods of reconstruction, this time in the sphere of grammar, drawing on phonology, morphology, and syntax alike. It was known that Old Georgian used prefixes (and suffixes) to mark the person (first, second, or third) of subjects and of dative objects, and it was known that the markers of second person subjects were identical to those of third person dative objects, each with the base form *x-*. Each of these prefixes had the variants *s-* and *h-* before certain consonants, in phonological environments that were defined in the same way for the two markers; and each had the realization Ø before a vowel. In a paper dated 1922–3, Ak'ak'i Šaniʒe reconstructed **x-* for second person subjects and for third person dative objects before vowels in pre-Georgian. He did so on the basis of five relics. One was the very common form *x-ar* "you (SG) are," which contrasted with *v-ar* "I am" and *ar-s* "s/he is," where *v-* and *-s* could be independently identified as markers of first and third person subjects, respectively. This was the only verb form that retained **x-* as a second person subject marker before a vowel. One of the relics of the **x-* as third person dative object marker before a vowel adduced by Šaniʒe was the noun *xertvisi* "peninsula, island," which Šaniʒe showed to be derived from the verb *ertvis* "it joins (to) it," by adding the nominative case ending *-i* and the otherwise mysterious prefix *x-*. The verb is used as in (38).

(38)   mt'k'var-s axalkalak-is   c'q'al-i   ertvis
        Kura-DAT Axalkalaki-GEN water-NOM it.joins.it
        "The Axalkalaki stream joins (flows into) the Kura."   (Šaniʒe 1957: 274)

Šaniʒe argues that at least three villages in Georgia were named *Xertvisi* because they were located at the point where two rivers flow together, that this is the source of the new meaning "peninsula" (later also "island"), and that this noun retains the **x-* marker of the third person dative object, while that marker was lost in verb forms. In this way he combines the phonological and morphological data with the syntactic distribution to reconstruct **x-* before vowels. Within a year of the publication of this article in Tbilisi, word reached Šaniʒe where he was studying in Russia that palimpsest texts discovered in Oxford had been found to contain exact equivalents of the reconstructed *x-*. These texts, now known as *xanmet'i* "[containing] too many *x*'s," confirm the particular grammatical reconstruction. Like the example cited above, Šaniʒe's reconstruction, with its subsequent material realization, confirms our belief in the correctness of the comparative method, when used with care and applied judiciously.

Appendix

This appendix provides statements of the relationship within some of the families from which many examples are cited.

Finno-Ugric

I

  I.1

    I.1.i Early Balto-Finnic group (i.e. Lapp + Late Balto-Finnic)

    a Late Balto-Finnic (i.e. Balto-Finnic minus Lapp)

      Finnish, Estonian, Karelian, Veps, Votic, Livonian

    b Lapp

    I.1.ii Volga group

      Mordvin

      Cheremis (or Mari)

  I.2 Permic group

    Zyrian (or Komi)

    Votyak (or Udmurt)

II

  II.1 Ob-Ugric group

    Ostyak (or Khany)

    Vogul (or Mansi)

  II.2 Hungarian

Kartvelian

I

  I.1 Georgian

  I.2 Zan group

    I.2.i Mingrelian

    I.2.ii Laz

II Svan

Mayan

I Huastecan

  Huastec

  Chicomuceltec

II Mayan core

  II.1 Yucatecan

    II.1.i Yucatec, Lacandon

II.1.ii Mopan, Itza (Itzá)
II.2 Cholan-Tzeltalan (Greater Tzeltalan, Greater Tzotzilan):
  II.2.i Cholan
    a Chol (Cho'l), Chontal
    b Ch'orti' (Chortí), Choltí
  II.2.ii Tzeltalan (Tzotzilan)
    Tzeltal, Tzotzil
II.3 Q'anjob'alan-Chujean (Greater Q'anjob'alan)
  II.3.i Q'anjob'alan
    a Q'anjob'al (Kanjobal), Akateko (Acatec), Jakalteko (Jacaltec)
    b Motocintlec (with Tuzantec)
  II.3.ii Chujean
    Chuj, Tojolabal
II.4 K'ichean-Mamean (Eastern Mayan)
  II.4.i K'ichean (Quichean)
    a Q'eqchi' (Kekchí)
    b Uspantec (Uspanteko)
    c Poqomchi' (Pokomchí), Poqomam (Pokomam)
    d Core K'ichean
      K'iche' (Quiché)
      Kaqchikel (Cakchiquel), Tz'utujil (Tzutujil)
      Sacapultec (Sakapulteko)
      Sipacapa (Sipakapense, Sipacapeño)
  II.4.ii Mamean
    a Teco (Tektiteko), Mam
    b Awakateko (Aguacatec), Ixil

North East Caucasian
I Nax
  Čečen
  Inguš
  Batsbi (Tsova-Tush)
II Daghestan
  II.1 Avar-Andi-Cez
    II.1.i Avar
    II.1.ii Andian
      Andi, Botlix, Godoberi, K'arat'a, Č'amalal, T'indi, Bagvalal, Axvax
    II.1.iii Cezian
      Cez, Hinux, Xvarši, K'ap'uč', Hunzib
  II.2 Lak-Dargva
    Lak
    Dargva
  II.3 Lezgian
    II.3.i West Lezgian
      Lezgi, Tabassaran, Aɣul
    II.3.ii C'axur, Rutul
    II.3.iii Šah-daɣ
      Budux, Xinaluɣ, K'ryc'
    II.3.iv Udi
    II.3.v Arči

Uto-Aztecan
I   Northern Uto-Aztecan
  I.1   Numic (Plateau Shoshoni)
    I.1.i Western
       Paviotso-Bannock-Snake (= Northern Paiute)
       Mono (= Monachi)
    I.1.ii Central
       Shoshoni-Goshiute-Panamint
       Comanche
    I.1.iii Southern
       Southern Paiute
       Ute-Chemehuevi
       Kawaiisu
  I.2 Tübatulabal
  I.3 Takic (Southern Californian Shoshoni)
       Serran: Serrano, Kitanemuk
       Cahuilla, Cupeño
       Luiseño-Juaneño
       Gabrielino-Fernandeño
  I.4 Hopi
II Southern Uto-Aztecan
  II.1 Pimic (Tepiman)
       Pima-Papago (Upper Piman)
       Pima Bajo (Lower Piman) (Névome)
       Northern Tepehuan, Southern Tepehuan
       Tepecano
  II.2 Taracahitic
    II.2.i Tarahumaran
       Tarahumara
       Guaríjío (Varihio)
    II.2.ii Tubar
    II.2.iii Cahitan (Yaqui-Mayo-Cahita)
    II.2.iv Opatan
       Ópata
       Eudeve (Heve, Dohema)
  II.3 Corachol-Aztecan
    II.3.i Cora-Huichol
       Cora
       Huichol
    II.3.ii Nahuan/Aztecan (Nahua, Nahuatlan)
      a Pochutec
      b Core Nahua
         Pipil
         Nahuatl (Aztec, Mexicano; several dialects)

Notes

1 Introduction

1 As Lightfoot, perhaps the best-known and most vocal advocate of such an approach, puts it, "one will investigate the predictions for historical change which stem from principles of grammar" (Lightfoot 1981a: 238), where it is clear that this refers to formal theory of syntax.

2 As Allen (1980[1977]: 11) put it: "The one thing which all students of diachronic syntax agree on is that we know very little about the subject, and that the investigation into particular changes is necessary before a real theory of diachronic syntax can be formulated."

3 A theory of syntactic change may prove to be part of a larger theory of language change or even part of a general theory of language. We cannot, however, begin by assuming, for example, that the class of possible syntactic changes is derivable from the class of possible changes in phonology, or from the class of possible synchronic grammars. Each of these must be investigated separately and the results compared.

4 **Alignment**, as used here, refers to the distribution of case, agreement, or other markers with respect to their indexing of various combinations of grammatical relations. The alignments most frequently found are here called **accusative** (also known as "nominative–accusative"), **ergative** (or "ergative–absolutive"), and **active** (or "active–inactive"). These notions are defined in chapter 9, which deals with the diachrony of alignment.

5 Here Lightfoot (1979a: 124) states, "The second assumption is that these therapeutic re-analyses take place only when necessary and not randomly." It may appear from this sentence alone that the claim "only when necessary" applies to only one kind of change, namely "therapeutic re-analyses." However, for Lightfoot this is an epithet which applies to a wide variety of syntactic change.

6 The term "intersystemic" is borrowed from Russian Formalism, especially Tynjanov; its meaning there, however, is restricted to the last discussed in the text.

7 Lightfoot has suggested that it is not always possible to *identify* change even in attested languages.

8 Or, where such borrowings as exist are for the most part clear, well documented, and not controversial.

9 In this context it is interesting to note that in the same year, 1979, in which Lightfoot introduced the Ebeling Principle in criticism of what he perceived as imprecision in the articles of the Li 1977 book, his own *Principles of diachronic syntax* was published, whose centerpiece is the Transparency Principle, a principle

which has never been stated other than informally, and was later described by Lightfoot as "a rather imprecise, intuitive idea about limits on a child's ability to abduce complex grammars" (1981b: 358).

10 It eliminates the "severe limitations on the number of languages wherein one can work on diachronic syntax" (Lightfoot 1979a: 7).

11 Heine and Reh (1984: 72, 75) argue that certain analyses are less than entirely convincing because they depend crucially upon what is only reconstructed, not "actual language evidence." Yet many of their own analyses of diachronic processes rely *implicitly* on internal or comparative reconstructions; that is, when they juxtapose two constructions from a single language, for example, they are implicitly reconstructing one of these as predating the other. Through this judicious use of implied reconstruction they have contributed many valuable examples to the literature.

12 American Sign Language and other complete manual languages are in a similar position. We cannot assume that their development will entirely conform to that of spoken languages, but must investigate whether that is the case.

13 We have no objection to clear evidence from creole languages, but we would insist on careful documentation of changes without the acrimonious or politically motivated assumptions which often pervade/motivate discussions in which creole language change is discussed. We share many of these social concerns, but wish the evidence to speak for itself with regard to language change, and not to be filtered through a non-linguistic agenda which may inaccurately reflect aspects of the actual changes.

2 The history of historical syntax: major themes

1 In keeping with practice from Miklosich (1868–79, vol. I) and before, and consistent with many formal theories of syntax since 1957, we make no effort to eliminate morphology (i.e. morphosyntax) from our discussion.

2 For example, in 1977, Cynthia Allen could declare: "Because we have relatively few studies of syntactic change, we know little about what kinds of change to expect in syntax, . . . nevertheless, there has been a certain amount of speculation on the way syntax changes" (Allen 1980 [1977]: 4–5). And Langacker could urge that: "We should work to enlarge the pool of well-grounded and accessible empirical data available for discussions of syntactic change; to translate informal and intuitive notions of the nature and causes of change into explicit proposals that can be scrutinized for their adequacy" (Langacker 1977a: 100). We agree with both Allen and Langacker that the database should be enlarged, but we find the poverty that they seem to suggest in both theory and data illusory, more in the eye of the contemporary beholder than in the actual historical facts.

3 When the Sanskrit linguistic tradition (see Pāṇini's description, dating from the fifth century BC) came to be studied by Europeans, it also influenced Western linguistics deeply. Attention was given especially to its notion of the origin and development of language from primitive roots which came to be combined to produce grammar and morphology.

4 Adam Smith's (1761) *Dissertation on the origin of languages* distinguished "uncompounded" (simple, primitive, older, original, later to be called "analytic") and "compounded" (more modern, later called "synthetic") structural types of

languages, both the result of historical evolution. His "uncompounded" type was flexional (with declensions and conjugations), reflected by morphology (paradigmatic structure), and was "purer"; the "compounded" type was characterized by periphrasis (his "composition," i.e. "syntax"), and was "less pure" (i.e. mixed) (Coseriu 1977a: 119). Smith's typology, like later ones, was endowed with both cognitive and historical attributes. Thus, flexion (uncompounded) was connected with more concrete ideas, composition with greater abstraction. Periphrasis (composition) was said to be introduced in large part by foreign speakers of the languages. Smith explained the development of fixed word order as the result of a reduction in the case system, which in turn was due to language mixture.

5   The long-standing debate concerning the priority of nouns vs. verbs and the discussion of the origin of grammatical categories in general stemmed from Aristotle's reductionism, interpreted as a historical claim (see section 2.2.1.1). See also section 2.2.1.2.

6   In view of obvious past excesses, perhaps grammaticalizationists would do well to recall the marked similarities that exist between these former views and their current ones. This should seem to demand greater rigor and substance from current researchers.

    One example of a grammaticalization claim (perhaps not shared by all grammaticalizationists) is that changes in structure always affect syntactic relations before the morphology that encodes them, with the result that morphology reflects a previous syntactic situation – hence Givón's (1971) slogan, "yesterday's syntax is today's morphology." There are, however, clear counterexamples to this claim (see Anderson 1980; Comrie 1980; Givón 1984; see especially our chapter 8).

7   John Ries (1880) claimed that originally the verb was at the end of all clauses in Old German, but gradual differentiation between main and subordinate clauses left the verb in second position in main clauses. Karl Tomanetz (1879) and Oskar Erdmann (1886), to the contrary, proposed that second position was original, that the shift of verb to final position in subordinate clauses was a late development (Scaglione 1981: 110). Somewhat later, Clemens Biener (1922a, 1922b, 1926) called on the importance of German school grammar as an explanation for the same phenomenon. However, Wackernagel (1892) (see section 2.2) successfully demonstrated that Proto-Indo-European's original final verb (SOV) shifted to second position rather early as a result of accent (Scaglione 1981: 109, 111).

    Meanwhile, Otto Jespersen (1894: 361) argued that fixed (rigid) word order (SVO) was the cause, and not the result, of the loss of cases, on the grounds that fixed order represents progress over the more primitive inflectional stage. Elise Richter (1903), on the other hand, argued that in the Romance languages the loss of cases caused fixed word order to be established and was not the result of earlier fixed order (Scaglione 1972: 357, 1981: 117). Jespersen's order of events is supported in recent work (M. Harris 1978, 1984; Plank 1980).

8   In a more relative sense, however, this claim does appear to have value. That is, in general, subordinate clauses do contain fewer morphosyntactic contrasts than main clauses, suggesting that on the whole fewer changes would begin in subordinate clauses, since main clauses would normally also already have most of the essential morphosyntactic trappings of the subordinates, plus additional things

not found in lower clauses. With respect to the second claim, the foreground–background distinction (while somewhat imprecise) plays an important role. Subordinate clauses and irrealis tense–aspect–modal categories tend to correlate in discourse with "backgrounded" material (see Givón 1984: 288). This being the case, it is not so surprising that the Estonian "indirect" (an irrealis form) should have developed in subordinate clauses.

Lightfoot (1981a: 228, 1988a, 1991) also sees change as limited for the most part to main clauses and certain accessible parts of subordinate clauses, including INFL, where the Estonian new finite verbal morphology would reside. However, his is not a functional discourse-based explanation, but rather he relates it to constraints on child language acquisition, claiming that children are degree-∅ learners (∅-depth learners), meaning that for parameter setting only the matrix clause (plus bits at the beginning of embedded clauses) matters; see below.

9 It might legitimately be objected, however, that Meillet's example of the value of child language acquisition in explanations of grammatical change is misleading. Given that the "compound past" is the most common, least marked past tense in spoken German (with the "simple past" restricted to special contexts, more marked in its status, rarer in its occurrence), one might assume that the discovering of a frequent compound past in the speech of children reflects merely their successful learning of the German norms, with no particular implications for how children's language acquisition may be involved in grammatical change. That is, to make his case successfully, Meillet would need to show evidence that German children's language acquisition led them to different forms (or to a different frequency of usage of alternate forms) from that of former grammars.

10 Perhaps an analogy from outside of linguistics may help clarify the presentation of reanalysis. Grammatical reanalysis is equivalent to the principle of "preadaptation" in biology, that is, "functional change in structural continuity," which resolves some issues in biological evolution (Gould 1977: 110): "In short, the principle of preadaptation simply asserts that a structure can change its function radically without altering its form as much. We can bridge the limbo of intermediate stages by arguing for a retention of old functions while new ones are developing" (Gould 1977: 108). A biological example which illustrates change which is like linguistic reanalysis is that of the development (evolution) of the "fish" found in the freshwater mussel *Lampsilis*. This "fish" is an extension of the mantle, the "skin" that encloses the soft parts of clams, which is shaped and colored like a fish, with a flaring tail at one end and an eye-spot at the other. The mussel's larvae need a free ride upon fish during their early growth; the *Lampsilis'* fake fish functions to attract real fish; when they approach, the *Lampsilis* discharges larvae, some of which are swallowed by these real fish and thus find their free ride. The "preadaptation," better called "reanalysis," leading to the *Lampsilis'* "fish" decoy came about as follows. Flapping of the mantle skin evolved either to aerate the larvae within the mussel or to keep them suspended in the water after their release; that is, the flapping provided other advantages (functions), so that the fortuitous resemblance of the flaps to fish might be a preadaptation, that is, might have led to a shift (reinterpretation, reanalysis) of this inherited structure's primary function (of aerating or suspending larvae) to its new function (attracting fish for the larvae's free ride) (Gould 1977: 104–9).

11 Humboldt (1836 [1988]: 81–2), in his notion of language evolution, seems to have recognized the infinitive example as what we today would call reanalysis, but attributes to it a different direction of change. Thus, he says:

> The same occurs [where in this instance Sanskrit uncharacteristically remained less developed than Greek] with *infinitive*, which has furthermore been drawn over to the noun, with a total misconception of its verbal nature. For all that one may justly prefer Sanscrit, it has to be admitted that in this respect it lags behind the later language . . . It allows one form to take the place of another . . . the blame for this may sometimes fall upon the sound-form, which, once accustomed to certain formations, leads the mind to pull even concepts that require new kinds of formation into this its formative path.

12 Another example is Paul's explanation (Paul 1920 [1898]: 147) of how the old optative/potential/subjunctive has been reinterpreted in German as a marker of indirect speech and the grammar has been restructured accordingly.

13 Not everyone, however, was favorably disposed towards borrowing explanations. Wilhelm von Humboldt, though inclined to accept the existence of language mixing and the influence of contact, held that "structure cannot be borrowed" or "is not borrowed easily" (Hoenigswald 1986: 176). Sapir (1921: 203) was of the same opinion; in the chapter "How languages influence each other" in his influential book *Language*, he asserted, "Nowhere do we find any but superficial morphological interinfluencings." This view has had considerable consequences in shaping opinion, especially in America. Strong doubts about grammatical borrowing are still found, such as: "Borrowing is generally regarded as a weak tool for explanation. This certainly holds for borrowing at the sentence level, since . . . no convincing example has ever been presented" (Gerritsen 1984: 118). (See also Paul 1920 [1898]: 399; Lightfoot 1981b: 357.)

14 The outlooks of Coseriu, Andersen, and Anttila have also been influential in some studies of grammatical change. They are similar to one another since they share a common point of view and they do not align themselves directly with generative grammar. While they have not been concerned particularly with diachronic syntax *per se* (and for that reason are not treated fully in this chapter), dealing more with linguistic change in general, they have each been the inspiration for certain works which do deal primarily with syntactic change.

   Raimo Anttila's (1972 [1989], 1976) slogan, "one meaning, one form," is intended as a general principle of linguistic change, thought to operate at a fairly abstract level and fairly generally in language. (Similar views are also attributed to von Humboldt and others.) Anttila sees it as a driving force behind analogy. His basic idea is that linguistic changes tend to be in the direction of eliminating instances where a single form has two (or more) meanings/functions or where two (or more) forms have the same meaning/function, resulting in a one-to-one relationship between form and function. For example, Anttila (1972 [1989]: 103) explains the loss of infinitive in Greek in this way. Formerly Greek had:

   (i)   thélō graphein "I want to write"
   (ii) thélei graphein "he wants to write"

Later, Greek underwent the sound change in which final *n* was lost, leaving the shape of the infinitive ending the same as that of the third person singular (both in *-ei*):

(i') thélō graphei "I want to write"
(ii') thélei graphei "he wants to write"

The single form in (ii'), *graphei*, with two possible interpretations ("third person singular" or "infinitive") was reinterpreted, based on the tendency to develop "one meaning–one form" relationships, as "he wants (that) he write," and was then later extended to other persons, for instance:

(iii) thélō graphō "I want that I write"

In this way, infinitives were eliminated, replaced by constructions with finite verbs, and the single form, *-ei*, came to have a single meaning. (For greater detail, see Joseph 1983.)

Anttila's view is useful and important; however, it is perhaps best seen as a cause of change, but as such it operates at such a general level that it is not possible to tell when it will apply or will fail to have effect. More specific mechanisms are necessary to get a firmer handle on how such a causal factor may be implemented, and reanalysis in the Greek example just cited ultimately provides the greater resolution researchers require in order to explain the more particular aspects of specific syntactic changes, such as this one (see chapter 4).

Henning Andersen's (1973) notion of "abduction" has been extremely influential in discussions of linguistic change in general, including syntactic change. Abduction is also a cornerstone of Anttila's approach and plays a role also in Lightfoot (1979a). Abduction is defined as hypothetical inference, where the rules and results are given and the case is inferred – that is, a reasoned guess. Children abduce their grammars from the output of other grammars. In this regard, Andersen's abduction and generative grammar's emphasis on language acquisition coincide. Again, as was the case with Anttila's slogan, "abduction" in the explanation of syntactic changes operates at a very abstract level, and particular cases of syntactic change, which may well involve abduction, also lend themselves to satisfying explanations via principles and mechanisms that rest comfortably beneath abduction at a more concrete level: for example, a great many of the syntactic changes which have been treated in terms of abduction actually rely on reanalysis and/or extension as the more immediate means of explanation (see Timberlake 1974, 1977; see also Andersen 1980, 1989). (For more discussion of explanation at different levels, see chapter 11.)

Coseriu's outlook on linguistic change (see Coseriu 1978 [1957], 1985) has received a considerable following, particularly among European linguists; his views have influenced many, including both Anttila and especially Andersen (see Timberlake 1974, 1977; Ebert 1978; Lenerz 1984; Anttila 1985; and many others). Again, Coseriu's approach, like Anttila's and Andersen's, deals with linguistic change in general and at a rather abstract level, though it has been applied by others also to syntactic change.

Briefly, Coseriu claims that language is a system (or perhaps better said, a set of patterns), where not all potential patterns permitted by the rules are utilized in actual speech, but where change is mostly new utilizations of formerly unused but permitted patterns. This deployment of formerly unused potentials is constrained socially. Coseriu's "norms" refer to what speakers actually do use. Change for Coseriu is primarily in these norms; that is, it is change in the socially permitted use of formerly unused portions of the system/patterns. Thus, linguistic change in this view is a matter of specific historical events. Coseriu's slogan is that "change does not exist" (see Coseriu 1985); this means, apparently, that Coseriu sees change not as in the language's rules, but rather as in the social acceptance of things already licensed by the system (i.e. change in the norms, the extension to things permitted by the patterns which result in new norms). Coseriu also applies this view to instances which others would call reanalysis, this apparently playing a key role in his view of how the language system and the language type, not merely the norms, might also change (though this in general is imprecisely described within his approach). For example, he mentions the case of reanalysis where:

> certain speakers of French interpreted the /z/ of the *liaison* as a plural prefix; hence forms as *zieux* [‹ *les ieux* "the eyes"], *quatre-z-officiers* [‹ *quatre des officiers* "four of the officers" (?)] . . . Objectively one can surely say that there is a "change" in such cases. But the speakers behave even in the case of a reinterpretation [reanalysis] as if they were not changing the language, for they are convinced that their interpretation is correct, that is, that the corresponding procedures are already "given" in the language.
>
> (Coseriu 1985: 62)

And he concludes: "More thorough investigations would show, I think, that language norm changes almost exclusively through the application of the system, the system in turn changes largely through the application of language type and partly through reinterpretation, and language type changes almost exclusively through reinterpretation" (Coseriu 1985: 63).

Some questions for Coseriu's general approach include such things as, (1) How do shifts in the structural type or in the system of the grammar come about, and where do they come from? (2) How are recurrent changes which are the same in form but take place independently in language after language to be explained? (3) Is there room for generalization concerning linguistic change beyond the individual historical events/changes?

In brief, central to the Coseriu-Andersen view of language change is the asymmetrical relationship between norms (actual usage) and system (productive rules) – for example, unproductive patterns defined in the norms may be curtailed and superseded by the productive patterns of the system (Andersen 1989: 19). For Andersen, since grammar acquisition is based on abduction, divergent interpretations of the same usage are possible (an essential ingredient of reanalysis as we define it, see chapter 4). Different speakers are capable of producing usage which conforms to the same norms in spite of differences in their internal grammatical systems.

In short, all three, Coseriu, Andersen, and Anttila, provide useful insights, but their approaches operate at a level too abstract to form a very compelling basis for explaining syntactic change, and Coseriu provides no useful means for dealing with change in a language's overall type or basic structure, or for generalizing about syntactic change in general.

15 This "hypothetical" case, based on Klima's (1964) more extensive and realistic treatment, ignores the real picture in English, complicated by various sociolinguistic
and stylistic factors which condition patterned variation in English grammar.

16 We believe that a bottom–up approach holds greater potential; for us, it is the
well-grounded syntactic changes which inform the theory. Lightfoot (1979a: 10)
asserts that "many of the difficulties [in the study of diachronic syntax] . . . stem
from a lack of an adequate theory of possible (synchronic) syntactic descriptions."
He contends:

> Thus given the looseness of the theories being used, current work re-
> veals no more about possible syntactic changes than did the work of the
> Neogrammarians and their contemporaries. Work in this area will
> make significant progress when conducted within the context of a re-
> strictive theory of grammar. A restrictive theory will make predictions
> about possible historical changes; investigation of actual changes will
> have consequences for the restrictions imposed by theory.
>
> (Lightfoot 1979a: 15)

We respond in the following way to this oft-repeated claim that the current lack
of an adequate synchronic theory of syntax is crippling for successful work in
diachronic syntax. Such a lack is unfortunate, but it is hardly the case that in
the absence of a definitive formal theory we cannot talk about grammatical
changes in the languages we study. With both traditional grammar and the modern theories there is enough clear terminology and common concepts for us to
be able to talk reasonably well about how grammars work, how their pieces fit
together, and how they change. Lack of complete success at framing an adequate formal theory of language in no way means that we cannot investigate
grammatical changes within languages or describe and compare aspects of
grammars for the purposes of postulating earlier stages in clear, respectable,
and replicable ways. The current attention to linguistic typology is a case in
point; it reveals much about the interaction of grammatical elements without the
benefits of a formal theory. Moreover, as we come to understand what can and
cannot change, how and why things change, and what the limitations on syntactic change are, we contribute significantly to an understanding of human language in general, to universal grammar, and hence to the general formal theory
itself.

17 In Lightfoot's words: "a child is tempted to entertain or 'abduce' a novel and simpler analysis which produces the same or almost the same output as the analysis
or 'grammar' of his models . . . Thus language acquisition is seen as a major locus
of historical innovation" (Lightfoot 1979a: 375); and: "The availability of this kind
of indeterminacy or multiple analysis permits abductive innovations" (Lightfoot
1979a: 351).

18 Lightfoot (1981b: 362), in response to his critics, seems to concede this point and
yet curiously argues that it is really not a problem for his approach:

> If syntactic change can be autonomous, i.e. if a change can affect only the
> phrase structure rules of the syntactic component, it is hard to see why
> this should deprive the approach of any explanatory force. Needless to say

> (I hope), the fact that there is a separate set of syntactic rules does not entail that considerations of meaning or use play no role when people speak or when languages change, as Romaine [1981] seems to imagine.

Nevertheless, this defense seems just as crippling as the actual criticism. This is even clearer in Lightfoot's (1981b: 363) defense against Romaine's (1981) criticism of "differential failure," that some dialects undergo a particular change at a given point, while others do not (see examples in chapter 4). Lightfoot's reply confirms the fallaciousness of the autonomy thesis. He responds that since children of different dialect areas have different trigger experiences, their grammars can differ and different changes can occur: "A certain change may affect one speech community for stylistic or social reasons (i.e. for reasons having little or nothing to do with U[niversal] G[rammar] . . .) spreading later or perhaps never to other communities" (Lightfoot 1981b: 363). This more considered opinion is given more attention in his later publications (see Lightfoot 1988a, 1988b, 1991). However, this clearly concedes that syntax is not autonomous, at least as far as syntactic change is concerned.

19 A recurrent criticism of Lightfoot's work, which we do not go into here, is that several of the changes he deals with are not described accurately and that the time he attributes to various changes in many of them (as clusters of changes, relatively simultaneous, and thus, in his view, the result of some wholesale reanalysis triggered by the TP) is inaccurate. (See our section 7.4.1.2.)

Both Breivik (1989) and Faarlund (1989, 1990a) make a very important point – what might be called Faarlund's slogan – that "today's syntax may be the product of yesterday's discourse pragmatics" (Faarlund 1989: 71). They present compelling demonstrations that the view is misguided which claims that syntactic change is confined to autonomous syntax, and they demonstrate that discourse pragmatics must be accorded a role in the explanation of grammatical change.

20 Specifically the six are:

> the new verb–complement order at D-structure [essentially the change to VO word order] . . ., the ability of the infinitival *to* marker to transmit case-marking and head-government properties of a governing verb [basically changes which allowed NPs formerly not so employed to become the subject of passive] . . ., the loss of the inherent D-structure oblique case [change in the impersonal verbs from *him* [Dat] *like pears* [Nom] to *he likes pears* and changes in W H-movement] . . ., the emergence of a reanalysis operation [in Lightfoot's analysis verb and preposition, e.g. *slept* + *in* are reanalyzed as a complex head in movement with preposition stranding, as in *this bed was slept in*] . . ., the recategorization of the premodal verbs, and the loss of the ability of verbs to move to a governing INFL position [rise of the modals and do].   (Lightfoot 1991: 166–7).

21 For a closer parallel to Lightfoot's English *like* example, cf. Spanish, where (a) and (b) are both fully grammatical:

(i)   (a) si te   gusta, pasa adelante
           if you. DAT like   pass forward
           "If you like (it), come forward."

(b) si gusta-s, pasa adelante
   if like-you pass forward
   "If you like/want to, come forward."

22 Of course, it is possible that some universals have both biological and functional motivations – they are not necessarily mutually exclusive. One might even imagine that original discourse-motivated universal patterns may have evolved until they became part of a biological endowment. Moreover, it is, of course, absolutely clear that the needs of discourse and the limitations on discourse processing are mediated in some fashion by the mental abilities of speakers.

3 Overview of a theory of syntactic change

1 As pointed out in chapter 2, there are different outlooks on the nature of universals. In generative approaches, all universals are taken to be part of the human biological endowment, hard-wired in the brain of the child language learner and therefore very important in regulating syntactic change. However, functionalist orientations (involving typology, discourse analysis, and "grammaticalization") see universals as not necessarily genetically controlled and exhibited in child language acquisition, but rather as the result of language fulfilling its discourse and communication functions. This raises the question, must all linguistic universals be innately available to the child language learner, part of the biological endowment hard-wired in the infant's brain, or do some universals stem from the function of language independently of the speaker's genetic mental make-up? (See Givón 1984, 1990a; Heine and Reh 1984; Campbell, Bubenik, and Saxon 1988; Hopper 1991; Traugott and Heine 1991.)

2 This definition is based on that given in Langacker (1977a: 58); we have also been much influenced by the discussion of reanalysis provided in Timberlake (1977).

3 The justification for treating word order as part of the surface manifestation is discussed in chapter 8.

4 It should be pointed out in this context that while very often the borrowed pattern will be an exact duplication in the borrowing language of the pattern in the donor language, this is by no means necessary. As pointed out in chapter 6, some borrowed constructions show up in the borrowing language in a form not exactly identical to that of the donor language: for example, borrowed constructions often lack certain constraints which obtained in the donor language.

5 The structural-compatibility requirement for grammatical borrowing (discussed in chapter 6), which has been proposed by many, would essentially impose constraints on syntactic borrowing that would make it impossible to change both underlying and surface structures at the same time. Since there are many counterexamples to this claim, however, this view of how structural borrowing may be constrained is simply inaccurate. We can acknowledge that the incorporation of borrowed structures into a language is probably facilitated in some way when the borrowed phenomenon is structurally compatible with the grammar of the borrowing language; however, this in no way rules out structurally less compatible borrowings.

6 Contrast (1) with (i):

(i)   söin omena-n
              ate.I apple-ACC.SG
              "I ate the (whole) apple."

Finnish has relics of the partitive's former "ablative" functions. These relics of *-ta* "ablative" are found in some pronouns and postpositions (note *t* is lost intervocalically after a short unstressed vowel, giving the allomorphs -ta and -a, -tä and -ä):

(ii)   sii-**tä** talo-sta [it-From house-From] "from that house"
             talo-n taka-**a** [house-GEN back-From] "from behind the house"
             isä-n luo-**ta** [father-GEN presence-From] "from father's presence"

This former ablative sense is also preserved in certain sayings, such as:

(iii)   (a)   mies on suur-ta   suku-a
                 man is big-PART family-PART
                 "The man is from an important family."

         (b)   veitsi on teräs-tä
                 knife is steel-PART
                 "The knife is (made) out of steel."

(For details, see Hakulinen 1968: 437; Laanest 1982: 299; Campbell 1990a.)

7 There are, of course, additional patterns such as *coffee color(ed)*, *smoke-color(ed)*, and *the color of coffee, the color of blood*.

8 In chapter 8 we discuss a set of four principles of word order placement, which have a status different from that of constraints. We suggest that these are basic principles, which languages exploit to different extents.

9 The establishment of these operations would begin to address the tasks defined by Vincent (1980: 64):

> Future research, I would suggest, need[s] to concern itself with the properties associated with [various changes]. Two major prerequisites seem to be: . . .
>
> (a) to establish inventories of possible grammaticalization chains, perhaps in the context of a universal theory of semantic and morphosyntactic features;
> (b) to establish inventories of possible construction types – e.g. passive, comparative, conditional, etc. – and their various realizations in the languages of the world.

10 Nevertheless, it may help the reader to have a few examples of what we refer to as operations. We list below a few of the sorts of operations which have been identified in the literature or by us. This list imparts a good sense of what is intended by the notion of operation, and illustrates how operations work. Not all the examples listed here are clearly defined; some overlap with others, some are interconnected, and some are on the right track but incomplete.

Adjectives < nouns of physical qualities (shape, texture, color, taste, smell) (Givón 1984: 53).
Adjectives < past participles (see Campbell 1987).
Adpositions < adverbs (Watkins 1964; Schmidt 1969).
Adpositions < nouns (Givón 1971, section 3; Thurgood 1977: 687ff.; Heine and Reh 1984: 101, 189).
Adverbs < lexical words (noun, verb, adjective) (Thurgood 1977: 689; Heine and Reh 1984: 85, 269, 277).
Agreement markers < auxiliaries (Haas 1977; Harris 1985: 295, 322, 400).
Agreement markers < "give" (Steever 1981: 60).
Agreement markers < other verbal morphology (Chafe 1977).

11 King (1969: 106–19) argues for a view of change, particularly phonological change, that involves "abrupt implementation [in the individual; language change is grammar change] and gradual spread [in the community]" (p.119).

12 Lightfoot (1991: chapter 7) has recently restated the problem of accounting for the gradual nature of change, which he now acknowledges to exist.

13 Kroch (1989a) is a partial exception to this; he accepts the position of Ellegård that *do*-support originated as causative *do*. However, little attention is given to how this interacts with the implementation that he documents carefully.

4 Reanalysis

1 Reanalysis has been treated under such varied other names as misassignment of constituent structure (Parker 1976), reinterpretation, rebracketing, relabeling, and restructuring. For a variety of examples and discussion, see such representatives as Allen 1980 (1977), Anttila 1972, Bennett 1979, Butler 1977, Bynon 1980, Chung 1977, Chung and Seiter 1980, Craig and Hale 1988, Dixon 1981, Ebert 1976, 1978, Fujii 1985, M. Harris 1984, Heine and Reh 1984, Hinton 1980, Langacker 1977a, Lightfoot 1979a, Lord 1976, Payne 1980, Platzak 1983, Saltarelli 1980, Timberlake 1977, Traugott 1972, Warner 1983, etc. For useful historical antecedents, see chapter 2.

2 Part of a speaker's knowledge of a language is the knowledge of which forms or constructions are the norm and which are odd or unusually expressive; a speaker knows which alternative syntactic patterns can be used for special effect. Certainly these aspects of language change, and that means that speakers' knowledge changes; we refer to these changes as changes in markedness. A simple example of a change in markedness is found in the change in order of noun and modifier in Russian. Comparing Old Russian with the modern colloquial language, Berneker (1900: 32–3) notes that both possible orders occur at both stages, but that in Old Russian the order NA (noun-modifier) is unmarked and AN is marked, while in modern colloquial speech the reverse is true. Modern linguistic theory has given little attention to the relation between a speaker's knowledge of markedness and how this is to be accounted for formally. This is a question that requires additional study, from both diachronic and synchronic perspectives.

3 Our discussion here follows closely that of Ebert (1978), and the examples cited

are from his work. Lightfoot (1991: 83) also sees structures with *for . . . to* as reflecting a reanalysis "whereby *for* came to be construed as a preposition in Comp governing the lexical subject," although he treats this in connection with the overall development of infinitives and complementizers, discussing their formal analysis in the theory he supports (see also Lightfoot 1979a: 186–99).

4 As in the English example above, this is confirmed by the fact that the reanalyzed constituent can be fronted, as in the following:

> [um Wasser zu holen] [ging er aus]
> for water to fetch went he out
> "He went out (for) to fetch water."

5 The development of relative clauses in Germanic languages presents another example of constituency reanalysis. Probably the asyndetic (markerless, juxtaposed) type is the oldest in Germanic, as in Old High German:

> (i)   in droume sie in   zelitun then weg sie   faren scoltun
>   in dreams they him told   the   road they travel should
>   "In dreams they told him the road (which) they should travel."
> (Otfrid; cited in Ebert 1978: 22)

In West Germanic in prehistoric times a relative pronoun developed out of the demonstrative pronoun (our discussion follows Ebert 1978: 21–3). This started in cases with an asyndetic type relative clause as complement of a demonstrative pronoun in the main clause. For example, in the Old High German sentence (ii), *demo* "to the (one)" is the dative object of *antwurta* "answered" and clearly distinguishable from *imo* the dative object of *sprach* "spoke":

> (ii)   [antwurta demo]   [za imo   sprach]
>   answered DEM.DAT to him.DAT spoke
>   "He answered the one who spoke to him."

However, the reanalysis of the constituent structure was possible in cases where the main clause and the relative clause required the same case, as in:

> (iii) [tho liefen sar . . . thie]   [nan minnotun meist]
>   there ran   instantly they. NOM.PL him loved   most
>   "There they ran instantly who loved him most."   (Otfrid)

This permitted the possibility of interpreting the demonstrative, which properly belonged to the main clause, as a member of the relative clause: [NP . . . Demonstrative] [Relative clause] > [NP . . .] [Demonstrative Relative clause] (Ebert 1978: 23).

6 In the articles cited, Li and Thompson do not use the term reanalysis, but the change they describe is consistent with the definition given here.

7 Pipil underwent a different sort of reanalysis involving *nemi* which stops short of cliticization. In Pipil *nemi* is still an independent word, but has been grammaticalized as copula (especially meaning "to be located somewhere") and as the auxiliary in progressives, for example:

(i)   i-na: n   wan i-te: ku   ne: tik arkuh nemi-t
        his-mother and his-father there in   arch   are-PL
        "His mother and father are there in the arch."

(ii)   ki-tantia   nemi
        it-sharpen PROGRESSIVE
        "She is sharpening it."   (Campbell 1985: 111, 137)

8 Langacker (1977a: 80) provides a wealth of useful examples of reanalysis from Uto-Aztecan languages, and Heine and Reh (1984) furnish others from African languages. Many of these examples involve morphology more than syntax.

   Perhaps the simplest sort of reanalysis is that which is so restricted that it reanalyzes a local syntactic pattern as a lexical item, as is the case with English *daring-do, derring do*, the result of a reanalysis well documented in the *OED* (p. 233), based on a misreading of a passage in Chaucer's *Troylus*, where he speaks of "those who (their deeds of) daring do," where "daring do" was misinterpreted and reanalyzed as a noun *derring-do* with the assumed meaning of "desperate courage."

   Other such examples are easy to find. Ebert (1978: 14) calls these "isolation" and points out several, e.g. English *maybe* from *may be*, French *peut-être* "perhaps" from *peut être que* "it could be that," German *nur* "only, just" from *ne weiz ich wer* "I don't know who," and South German *gel, gelt* "isn't that so?, don't you think so?, eh?" from *gelte* "it may be valid, it may hold true."

9 Schulze (1982: 148) has suggested that the fossilized *b* may have functioned as the plural marker of Classes I and II, since in several Daghestan languages the singular of Class III has this function as well.

10 A more complete description of this change is provided in Harris (in press b).

11 Lightfoot (1979a, 1981b, 1988a) has claimed numerous times that opacity is prerequisite to reanalysis.

12 The analysis summarized here does not apply to numerals below five, which were adjectives in Old Russian (Babby 1987: 100–1). Babby provides evidence that this reanalysis has been actualized (see section 4.4 below) in oblique cases, but not in the nominative and accusative.

13 It has been proposed in the literature that "the single constraint on syntactic change is the continuity of surface configurations" (Muysken 1977: 169, more generally pp. 166–9 and sources cited there). This proposed constraint cannot be maintained in this form in the face of examples such as the Russian one discussed by Babby (1987); here the reanalysis, which Babby clearly establishes on the basis of a number of phenomena in the modern language, seems to defy the surface structure.

14 Description based on M. Harris (1978: 25), Möhren (1980), and Winters (1987).

15 A further change has taken place here in the colloquial language, with *pas* being reanalyzed as the *only* obligatory component of negation.

16 Heine and Reh (1984: 66) suggest that "Morphosyntactic processes may trigger phonetic processes, but not vice versa." The examples discussed or cited in this section seem to show that their proposal is incorrect.

17 Stein (1988, 1990) argues that reanalysis of *do* periphrasis in English was set off by desire to avoid certain consonant clusters. This requires further scrutiny.

18 It may be helpful to present what the example would be in modern orthography,

since this change is discussed also in other places in this book, with modern examples; thus:

> Old Finnish orthography: seurakunna-n hen lupasi pysyueise-n ole-ua-n;
> Modern Finnish orthography: seurakunna-n hän lupasi pysyväise-n ole-va-n.

19 We are grateful to Graham Thurgood for calling to our attention this example and its relevance.

20 The French question particle *ti* provides a similar example. Because [t] was originally part of the marker that signaled third person subjects in the forms of (12), it could not have been extended into other persons until it had been reanalyzed, in *ti*, as having some other function, namely the marking of questions.

21 To say that *kè* has been reanalyzed as "and" is really a shorthand way of saying that the serial verb structure with the verb *kè* "be with" has been reanalyzed as the coordination of two NPs by means of the coordinator *kè* "and."

22 Reanalysis of the internal structure of NPs containing quantifiers in Russian (see section 4.3.1) provides a similar example. The regular case-marking pattern that corresponds to the innovative structure, having the quantified noun as head, has been extended to oblique cases, as shown by (i) and (ii):

(i)   s   pjat'ju   butylkami   (*butylok)
         with five.INST bottles.INST (bottle.GEN)
         "with five bottles"

(ii)   k   pjati   butylkam   (*butylok)
         to five.DAT bottles.DAT (bottles.GEN)
         "towards five bottles"   (Babby 1987: 105)

This regular case marking has not, however, been extended to NPs in the nominative or accusative case, as shown in (iii):

(iii)   pjat'   butylok   razbilos'
         five.NOM bottles.GEN broke
         "Five bottles broke."   (Babby 1987: 107)

When the NP is nominative or accusative, as in (iii), the case marking used is that appropriate for the structural analysis of Old Russian. Babby (1987) shows, however, that nominative and accusative NPs containing quantifiers have also been reanalyzed, such that the quantified noun is the head. That the case marking in (iii) does not yet reflect that fact is further evidence that reanalysis and actualization are independent processes.

23 We do not provide a rigorous definition of actualization because this seems unnecessary. What does seem necessary to a better understanding of diachronic syntax is the distinction between a reanalysis (a change in underlying structure) and the subsequent ways in which the grammar accommodates this reanalysis. On the other hand, determining whether some particular subsequent change was part of the actualization of a particular reanalysis is not the central issue. The series of changes affecting Spanish reflexives provides an example. After certain reflexives were reanalyzed as *se*-passives, agent phrases were extended to the

innovative passive from the older analytic passive, where they already occurred. While this is clearly part of the actualization, it is less clear whether the subsequent reanalysis of some *se*-passives as impersonals should also be considered part of the actualization of the first reanalysis. The second reanalysis could be viewed as dependent on the first, and in some sense part of its actualization, but this does not seem to be an important issue. For this reason, we leave open the question of the boundaries of actualization.

24 This extension may have been aided by a pattern with pronominal subjects of various non-finite verb forms signaled by these pronominal possessive suffixes, found already in several other constructions, as in:

(i)   ostin   lipu-n   matkusta-a-kse-ni   sinne
         bought.I ticket-ACC travel-IST.INF-TRANSL-l.PER.POSS there
         "In order to travel there, I bought a ticket."

(ii)   matkusta-essa-ni   sinne näin hirve-n
         travel-INESSIVE-l.PER.POSS there saw.I moose-ACC.SG
         "While I was travelling there, I saw a moose."

25 Actualization of a number of reanalyses in the Kartvelian languages are discussed in detail in Harris 1985: reanalysis of Series III, pp. 288–95; reanalysis of Series II case marking, pp. 342–50; reanalysis of Series I, pp. 363–70.

26 It could be argued that there are actually three reflexes, with the additional example,

         Sarah has the report finished.

This example is discussed further in section 8.5.1.1.

27 Heine and Reh (1984: 57–9) discuss the existence of two reflexes from a single input under the rubric "functional split," but their discussion is limited to splits involving grammaticalization.

28 Many scholars who have written on the so-called impersonal verbs of English have commented that many of the constructions are not impersonal at all (van der Gaaf 1904: 1; Fisher and van der Leek 1983: 347; Lightfoot 1991: 128). In English these verbs have also been called "psych" verbs, but the label we use, "inversion" verbs, is from a different tradition and has been used in recent work to describe verbs of this type in many languages (see Harris 1984b).

29 Specifically, Harris (1973 and 1980), with reference to an analysis in universal grammar in Harris 1984b, proposes that in underlying structure the experiencer is subject and the theme direct object, while in surface structure the theme is subject and the experiencer object. One of the arguments presented in Harris 1973 (and referred to specifically by Butler [1977: 162–3]) is based on the ability to control deletion of coordinate subjects such as (i).

(i)   Arthur **loked** on the swerd, and **lyked** it passynge wel; whether **lyketh** yow better, said Merlyn, the swerd or the scaubard? Me **lyketh** better the swerd, sayd Arthur.
                            (Malory, *Morte Darthur*, cited in Jespersen 1894: 220–1)

The verb *loked* never takes the inversion construction, while *lyked* never occurs without it in Malory, except in this and a similar example (Jespersen *ibid*.). This same fact is discussed by Lightfoot (1979a: 234–5) as an argument that these datives are subjects in Middle English. According to Allen (1986: 390), the same construction is "not at all unusual in OE" (but see also van der Gaaf 1904: 33–6). It is this property which Harris (1973) interprets as one argument that the experiencer of *lyked* is subject underlyingly. (Similar examples are plentiful in Middle English and are cited in van der Gaaf [1904: 33–6, 72] and in Visser [1963-73: 31].) Allen (1986), working in a different framework, interprets the same fact as evidence that the dative experiencer is the (only) subject. Harris (1973) interpreted the fact that the inversion verb in Old English agrees with the nominative theme and not with the dative as evidence that the nominative is *surface* subject. Allen says of this fact, "It is clear that postposed nominative cause [our theme] NPs with *lician* could trigger subject–verb agreement, but such agreement does not prove that the cause NP was the subject" (1986: 395). She cites transitional (late Old English and Middle English) examples lacking agreement as evidence that the nominative theme is not subject, but does not mention the problem that the dative experiencer, which she analyses as subject, does *not* condition agreement.

Harris' (1973) second argument that the experiencer is underlying subject is based on the so-called objective with infinitive construction (Zeitlin 1908; Fischer 1989). In this construction the subject of the complement S appears in the accusative case on the surface; in the construction, only subjects and experiencers are marked with the accusative. This is illustrated for the experiencer in (ii).

(ii)   ye **me**   cause so to smerte
              me.ACC
         "You cause me to ache so."
                          (Chaucer, *Troylus and Cryseide*, cited in van der Gaaf 1904: 33)

Additional examples are cited in van der Gaaf (1904: 32–3).

Lightfoot (1991: 158) introduces a description of the analysis in Harris 1973 and 1980 as follows: "Harris' (1980) concern for gradualness led her to analyze Old English sentences . . ." (One may well wonder how a concern for gradualness would lead to this analysis.) In fact, of course, it was the syntactic facts cited above in this note and universals of inversion (see Harris 1984b; Perlmutter 1984), not any concern about gradualness, that led to the analysis. He writes further, "Harris offered no evidence for this analysis . . ." (1991: 158). It is true that, due to the constraints of length, the 1980 article only refers (1980: 165) to arguments presented in the earlier (1973) paper and to other arguments for this analysis in universal grammar, including both Harris 1984b and Perlmutter 1984. While it is regrettable that the evidence could not be presented in all of the articles, citing an analysis made in previous works as a basis for further analysis is hardly the same as offering "no evidence."

30 This is supported by the fact that in Old English some, but not all, verbs did have both patterns (48) and (49), that during Middle English times most verbs lost the pattern in (48) and acquired or retained the pattern in (49), and that no verb that had only pattern (49) in early Middle English later acquired inversion, pattern (48). Van der Gaaf (1904: 12–13) makes it clear that some verbs added the inversion pattern, (48), in early Middle English through a radical change of meaning (e.g. OE *dremen* "to make a joyful sound" came to mean "dream" and, like *mætan*, the verb

which expressed the meaning "dream" in OE, began to use pattern (48)), through new formation from existing stems, or through borrowing a verb which already used the inversion pattern.

31 Allen (1986) raises specific objections to treating this as reanalysis: (a) ambiguity is not present in most examples in Old English (1986: 378–9); (b) these constructions most often did not occur in OVS order, which might then be reinterpreted as SVO (1986: 379); and (c) different verbs undergo the change at different times (1986: 380–1). The view of reanalysis developed in the present work is entirely consistent with these facts, which we do not challenge. Regarding (a), we have shown in section 4.3.1 (and Timberlake 1977 had already pointed out) that ambiguity, or the possibility of multiple analyses, need exist only in a minority of examples. In our view, this is not a criterion for reanalysis, and we have given instances (section 4.2.4) where only a very small number of tokens of the construction had the possibility of dual analysis. Regarding (b), we believe that word order in Old English was not fixed (see chapter 8) and that therefore it played a limited role in coding relations. That is, the language learner could not depend even upon the first NP always being subject. Concerning point (c), this is exactly what is expected in the actualization of this sort of reanalysis (see section 5.3.3). We show in 5.3.3 generally (as well as chapters 7-10 *passim*) that many changes, but especially those that are of the types that are synchronically lexically conditioned, undergo actualization at different rates for different lexical items.

32 Fischer and van der Leek (1983: 347) cite one example which they gloss with dative experiencer and accusative theme (their "cause"). Allen (1986: 388), however, has pointed out that in this example the case of the theme is syncretic, that it could equally well be a nominative, and that agreement here does not disambiguate the example. She writes, "Note that none of the three comprehensive studies of 'impersonal' verbs in OE (Van der Gaaf 1904; Wahlén 1925; Elmer 1981) make any mention of a construction with a dative experiencer and an accusative cause" (Allen 1986: 388). Indeed, we might add that van der Gaaf, in citing (52) (our number) and one other similar example, refers to this as a "blending" of his type A and type D (our inversion, (48), and direct, (49)) constructions (1904: 68). Butler (1977: 159–61) has adduced four other examples of this sort, with the earliest from the *Ancren Riwle* (c. 1225). Concerning these, he comments, "The double object construction is then not one normally found with impersonal verbs" and suggests further that perhaps "these sentences argue that as early as the *Ancren Riwle* reanalysis of surface structures was beginning to take place in spite of dative/accusative case marking and verbs marked third person singular" (Butler 1977: 160–1). We conclude that the accusative theme was not part of the original inversion construction and that it occurred only occasionally during the transitional period and resulted from the two analyses.

33 Two other examples of extension of a case first to only one NP in a sentence are found in Harris (1985: 374–7).

34 Specifically, Butler's (1977) examples parallel to (50) date from the period 1378–1571, while his examples parallel to (51) date from 1378-1450; therefore, variation in agreement existed at least during the period 1378–1450. Ellegård's (1953: 166) figures (cited by Kroch 1989a: 135) for variation in *do*-support show variation beginning in the period 1400–25 and continuing until at least 1700. Therefore, during the period

1400-50, speakers had to account at the very least for variation in case marking with inversion verbs, variation in agreement with the same verbs, and variation in *do*-support. Accordingly, Lightfoot's proposal would, in fact, require eight grammars to account just for this variation.

35 Lightfoot (1979a: 232–3), not at that time proposing a diglossic account, can and does account for these facts.

36 Van der Gaaf (1904: 4) suggests that *behofian* "behoove" was similarly used "personally" in Scottish English before returning in that dialect to its earlier inversion construction. We consider modern *it seems to me* the same construction as *hit semit me* in (54), with *to me* a reflex of the Old English dative.

37 A further example of a change that appears to have been reversed is the loss of Negative–Verb word order in fifteenth- to sixteenth-century English, as described by van Kemenade (1987: 186).

38 In the earliest period of Northern Estonian literature (sixteenth and seventeenth centuries), the postpositions *kas, kaes, kaas, kaass, kahs* appeared (cognate with Finnish *kanssa*), which governed the genitive case (as in Finnish). These forms were in use until the late seventeenth century. In Estonian literature, the forms ending in a vowel (*kaa, ka*; also *kah*) appeared somewhat later.

39 A similar process is discussed by Dahl (1985: 11) under the label "conventionalization of implicatures," illustrated with development of additional interpretations of tense–aspect–mood categories in English.

40 This Finnish change is paralleled rather closely by the kindred development of English passive constructions (as presented by Parker 1976). In Old English adjectives agreed in gender, number, and case with the nouns they modified, as in:

(i)   hie wordon gebrohte
       "They were (in the state of being) brought."

The -e on *gebrohte* signals that it is an adjective agreeing with the subject *hie* ([*hie*.Subj [*wordon*.Verb *gebrohte*.Adj]vp]. In some sentences, the structural description could be subject to misinterpretation, for example those with strong Masc.Nom.Sg Adjectives, which happened to end in zero, such as:

(ii)   he wæs besett
       "He was (in the state of being) surrounded."

This could be analyzed as V-Adj as above, or misinterpreted as [*he*.Subj [*wæs*.Aux *besett*.V]vp], with *wæs* interpreted as an auxiliary, rather than as the main verb (i.e. copula), and *besett* as the main verb rather than the Adjective complement of the copula (as in the earlier analysis). The ambiguity survives in Modern English, as seen in:

(iii) the dress was torn (and dirty) (torn = A D J)
(iv)   the dress was torn (by someone) (torn = V E R B).

41 The term "reanalysis" is used with other meanings in some works, especially in certain studies of grammaticalization, notably in Heine and Reh (1984). For example, in our view reanalysis may apply in lexical and grammatical morphemes just as in phrases or clauses (cf. Heine and Reh 1984: 95); that is, we view the processes that fit our definition as being of a single type, regardless of the level of the constituents

affected. As pointed out above, our definition and discussion draw on those of Langacker (1977a) and Timberlake (1977) and follow, we believe, the sense of "reanalysis" most frequent in the literature.

42 In fact, in the grammaticalization literature, one frequently sees discussion to the effect that such coexistence is the normal and expected state of affairs.

43 It cannot be shown with certainty that the set of prefixal preverbs originated as adverbs, but it is generally assumed that their origin was parallel to that of the adverb/proclitics (see, for example, Schmidt 1969).

44 While Saniʒe cites *c̆arsuli* in this context, it really is no longer a verb. It is historically the past passive participle of the verb *c̆ar = svlay*, but has been reanalyzed as a distinct lexical item, not synchronically derived. This is not true of the other three forms in this column.

45 The usage of the members of the last pair overlap a great deal; some meanings of *ganaxleba* are marked "literary" in the *Academy Dictionary* (Čikobava *et al.* 1950–64, II: 1973).

46 Perhaps *gan-* here meant "from" in the sense of "**from** the old to the new," and in that case the preverb might be viewed as relevant to the meaning of the verb. The real point here is that the meaning of the preverb is equally relevant or irrelevant to both verbs.

47 The modern meanings of *ganaxleba* and *gaaxleba* are more difficult to distinguish; the former may continue the meaning "dedicate," used especially of a temple or church, as in the title of Psalm 29 (30), though it no longer has precisely this meaning.

5 Extension

1 Many reconcile this matter by suggesting that the needs of speech production tend to make language simpler or shorter by fusing things together and eroding them phonologically, while the needs of speech perception tend to create analytic structures which are easier to process. The constant interaction of these two insures that grammars will not exhibit only changes favorable to the one and not the other of these needs (see Langacker 1977a; Birnbaum 1984).

2 The discussion here follows that of Campbell (1991), which can be consulted for greater detail.

3 In Estonian, the reported speech form also functions to mark the evidential or "non-commitment." Comrie (1981: 125) calls these forms "inferential."

4 Cross-linguistically it is not at all unusual for participles to be reanalyzed as finite verb forms, though not necessarily taking the route described above: for example, in several Slavic languages this has occurred, as well as (apparently independently) in several North East Caucasian languages, including Bagvalal (Gudava 1971), an Avaro-Andi-Dido language, and Udi, a member of the Lezgian group.

5 This statement of the rules relies on final grammatical relations in all instances.

6 In fact, in Laz the case-marking system discussed here was extended to all TAM categories, including evidentials; this change may have been later and for this reason is omitted from the main discussion (see Harris 1985: 297–8).

7 Nevertheless, lexical exceptions to extensions do develop; see section 5.3.3 and chapters 11 and 12.

8 A question for future research is whether more than one condition may be removed at a time. At present our data are unclear about this.

9 Finnish first and second person singular pronouns have two nominative variants, the longer, more formal *minä* "I," *sinä* "you," and the shorter and more colloquial *mä* "I" and *sä* "you."

10 These changes are well documented historically (see Sorsakivi 1982; Mielikäinen 1984, Saukkonen 1984).

11 The verbs that were regularized were *pyrkiä tehdä* "strive to do" (SF *pyrkiä tekemää*), influenced presumably by such verbs as SF *yrittää tehdä* "try to do," and *ruveta tehdä* "start to do" (SF *ruveta tekemään*), based on other verbs such as SF *alkaa tehdä* "to begin to do." It is believed that it was the semantic similarity between a regular (first infinitive) and an irregular verb (third infinitive of verbs which are no longer motion verbs) that led these two verbs to be regularized first.

12 Wang's proposal poses a challenge to the Neogrammarian view, according to which sound change is exceptionless, gradual, and phonetically conditioned. The lexical diffusion view of sound change is highly controversial and is rejected by many historical linguists. Some others have adopted the view that there are (at least) two polar types of sound change – the Neogrammarian type and the lexical diffusion type – with some specific changes following one route and others another (see, Labov 1981, especially page 296ff.; also Hoenigswald 1978). Lexical diffusion in syntax, on the other hand, does not challenge the Neogrammarian hypothesis of the exceptionlessness of sound change, since it was not intended to cover syntactic change.

13 Notice, however, that the lexical diffusion of a syntactic change that we document here neither depends on the notion of lexical diffusion of sound change nor offers any additional argument for it.

14 Other aspects of complementation that Warner mentions as being lexically governed by the matrix verb include *þæt*-deletion (1982: 171) and the infinitive clause (1982: 142, 146).

15 It should be pointed out that Saltarelli's (1980) "syntactic diffusion" seems to mean syntactic change that proceeds gradually, or in increments or stages. This is not what we mean.

16 Ard (1975) deals specifically with the development of complement types in English and argues that raising-to-object in these complement types appears to have developed by spread through the lexicon. Ard (1975: 28) shows that verbal complements using infinitives, participles, and gerunds have increased, not only in percentage of occurrence within texts, but also by expansion through the lexicon as more and more verbs have come to be used with these complements. He proposes certain principles which describe how lexical diffusion in syntactic change might operate. One is his Principle of Synonymy, which holds that synonymous lexical items tend to have the same syntactic privileges of occurrence. That is, they tend to occur in the same underlying structural configurations and be subject to the same transformations. His Principle of Polysemy maintains that there is a tendency for a lexical item to be used in a syntactic construction in P2 (P = priviledges of occurrence) but not in P1 with S1 (S = sense). These principles in effect claim that different senses of a polysemous item tend to have different syntactic properties under the Principle of Synonymy, but the Principle of Polysemy (which is imprecisely stated)

seems to intend that there is a tendency for a single lexical item to have a single set of privileges of occurrence to cover both S1 and S2, and all its senses. Ard (1975: 75) says that this tendency is weak and rarely leads to P1 and P2 becoming equivalent. We might wonder, if indeed it is that weak, is it not just wrong, or if not wrong, then just unrevealing? At stake is the role of the form wanting a uniform syntactic treatment versus the possibility for distinct meanings to seek uniform syntactic treatment with other items of their semantic class(es). These notions may prove useful, but they need clearer exposition. They appear to be included in our notion of extension.

17 Lakoff (1968) makes the interesting claim that change in complementation from Latin to Spanish takes place not in the transformational rules, but in the redundancy rules. Below we treat prerequisites as part of the rules of grammar, but do so with no intention of either challenging or supporting Lakoff's claim. For the point we are making, it is simply irrelevant where the listing of governing verbs takes place, and the format (for it is no more than that) we have adopted here is more convenient for making our point.

18 While ultimately the category of infinitive was lost in Greek, this is not relevant for this example. As Joseph (1983: 49–74) shows, the gradual retreat of the infinitive had its origins in late Classical Greek. In the New Testament early Christian writings, for the most part the infinitives and finite verbs alternate, though only the infinitive was still required in a small number of environments. By late Hellenistic times the infinitive was a dying category, though "systematic traces of its use can be found in Greek up through approximately the 16th century" (Joseph 1983: 57). "During the early Byzantine period, the infinitive continued to figure in the grammar of Greek, though it lost more ground to its various replacements" (Joseph 1983: 57). Even in Modern Greek the infinitive remains (a) in the perfect tense which continues the late Medieval Greek perfect with *ŋkho*: plus infinitive; (b) with "a handful of isolated lexical items and a few fixed phrases which have either survived or been artificially revived by borrowing from the learned language" (Joseph 1983: 69); and (c) in some dialects which have kept the infinitive to a greater extent than the standard language has. That is, clearly the loss of the infinitive in Greek was not an all-or-nothing sort of change, but exhibits the attributes of lexical diffusion and gradual change over a long period of time.

19 Fischer and van der Leek (1983, 1987) do not directly address the issue of variation in agreement of the kind we have discussed and its intersection with case variation.

20 Elizabeth Traugott has pointed out to us that, in spite of van der Gaaf's statement to the contrary, there are a few cases of *lician* in Old English with experiencers in the nominative case. She notes, however, that they are in the glosses and may reflect Latin influence. However, even if this represents an inherited pattern, it does not affect the point we intend to make here, namely that there was variation in the time at which individual verbs began to occur with nominative case experiencers.

21 The verbs listed by Anderson (1980) and Anderson and Williams (1935: 128), as well as verbs listed as taking genitive objects in the other early Germanic dialects (Old Icelandic, Heusler 1932: 113; Gothic, Krause 1953: 130; Old High German, Paul 1949: 262–3) appear to have in common that they are atelic, as are inversion verbs.

On the analysis outlined in section 4.4.3.2 and in sources cited in note 29 there, the theme is the underlying direct object. Thus, it could be marked genitive by the same rule that marks genitive objects of non-inversion verbs.

22 The entry for *hreowan* "rue, grieve" is incomplete, as shown by examples above; it is here simplified for purposes of comparison. Parentheses here indicate optionality.

23 See Faarlund (1990b: 17–18) for the term "missed opportunities" and for this line of reasoning in diachronic syntax. Ogura (1986: 25–33) provides a brief comparison of Old English "impersonals" of all types with those of the ancient sister languages. Neither she nor the standard handbooks mention for the sister languages the alternative nominative experiencer construction found with some inversion verbs in Old English. If this pattern is indeed missing in the sister languages, its absence there would provide confirmation that the absence of the same construction with verbs like *lician* is not accidental in Old English.

24 We take lexical entries such as (33) to be simple variants of the prerequisite line of a rule, such as (24c); the lexical conditioning of a rule can thus be indicated either way.

25 Steever (1987b) provides an example of extension of a prerequisite.

26 Sentences (41) and (42b) are apparently from a single speaker; (42a) is evidently from a different speaker of the same dialect, though the labeling of this text is not entirely unambiguous. The data from Maxo are discussed in greater detail and with additional examples in Harris (1985: 374–5). Exceptions discussed on pages 118–19 of the same work offer further substantiation, but these facts are open to more than one interpretation. The extension as a whole is discussed in greater detail in Harris (1985: 371–85).

27 The source of *do* is a matter of dispute; several views are summarized in Garrett (1992). For our present purpose that source is not relevant.

6 Language contact and syntactic borrowing

1 In some instances it may not be easy to determine whether something is a borrowing in our sense or a change of another sort stimulated by language contact, and in principle it is possible for both borrowing and other mechanisms jointly to motivate certain changes. For example, word order changes are very frequently seen in language contact situations, and are said to be borrowed. While it may be possible for a language to import the word order of another, resulting in syntactic changes, it is more typical for such word order changes to have language contact as their catalyst, realizing the change through some other mechanism, such as through some reanalysis or the extension of some existing but minor pattern. The distinction between borrowing and language contact is necessary for expository purposes and for explaining just how changes come about. However, an exact determination of whether something is a borrowing or some other kind of change due to contact is not crucial to the present discussion of most cases, and in this chapter and elsewhere we discuss many aspects of borrowing and contact-induced changes without always attempting to make an exact distinction.

2 See, however, Allen (1980 [1977]), Campbell (1987), Campbell, Bubenik, and Saxon (1988), Ebert (1978), Johannisson (1960), Maher (1985), Platzak (1983, 1985), Thomason and Kaufman (1988).

Some claims concerning grammatical borrowing have been discussed generally but not in terms of any particular theoretical framework by Aitchison (1981: 120–1), Brody (1987), Campbell, Bubenik, and Saxon (1988), Moravcsik (1978), and Thomason and Kaufman (1988).

3 Allen illustrates this by reference to the following examples, which she treats in her book:

> The changes which we have attributed to French influence were not changes which brought about radically new constructions to English. *More* and *less* were always used to compare nouns, as in *more men*, so extending this construction to adjectives was not too difficult. English always had a Question Movement rule, so extending Question Movement to infinitival phrases was not too drastic. (1980: 380–1)

These changes may be contact-induced extensions, rather than syntactic borrowings in our sense.

4 It is, of course, conceivable that a language might undergo a reanalysis of such a relational noun to a preposition independently, without it being the result of language contact, and, indeed, this is a reanalysis regardless of whether language contact was its catalyst. However, given its fit with other changes known to be induced by Spanish contact, such as the borrowing of Spanish prepositions, and the absence of any similar change from any of the great number of other varieties of Nahua (closely related languages and dialects) which exhibit less influence from Spanish, the inference that Spanish contact was instrumental here seems not unreasonable. For details, see Campbell (1987).

5 Lightfoot (1981b) suggested a restriction similar to Weinreich's claim (above), which is also closely related to the "structural-compatibility" requirement, though he goes further in claiming severe restrictions on borrowing or contact as a possible cause of innovated or lost constructions. He reluctantly admits the possibility of borrowing or contact-induced syntactic change, but claims: "Where a productive new construction type appears, or where certain kinds of expressions or structures drop out of the language, it will be hard to attribute this to foreign borrowing or stylistic novelty; rather, a change in grammar [i.e. theory-motivated, internal] is likely to be involved" (Lightfoot 1981b: 357). This in effect, while not clearly explicated, amounts to a claim (or at least a belief) that borrowing and contact will not lead to the introduction of productive new construction types nor loss of old ones from a language – that is, that the effects of syntactic borrowing and language contact are minor and rather severely limited. This is clearly not the case, as seen in examples presented in this chapter and in Nadkarni (1975) and Campbell, Bubenik, and Saxon (1988). Even the examples Lightfoot himself refers to disprove his claim.

6 In addition to those already discussed, Heath (1978: 105–8) proposed several structural strictures on borrowability. He doubts several of Weinreich's (1953) constraints on borrowing and the explanatory value of a hierarchy of borrowable categories. With respect to morphology, Heath prefers to focus on phonological, semantic, and other features which favor or impede direct borrowing in Arnhem Land. Favoring factors include syllabicity, sharpness of boundaries, unifunctionality, categorial clarity, and analogical freedom. By and large these reflect the ease a borrower might have in identifying morphemes of a foreign language. Syllabicity means a bound morpheme is pronounceable as a syllable in and of itself, not, say, a single

consonant. Sharpness of boundary means that a morpheme is easily distinguished and segmented from others with which it may appear. Unifunctionality means the borrowed morpheme has a single function rather than several which might make it more difficult to identify. Categorial clarity means that a morpheme can be labeled without the need to examine the broader syntactic environment. By analogical freedom and subordination Heath refers to morphemes which lack analogical pressure from other morpheme classes.

While on the whole these constraints seem reasonable to us, we do not discuss them in depth here because they relate mostly to the shape and identifiability of borrowed morphology rather than to the grammar these may represent in the receiving language.

7 Perhaps related to this in some way is Maher's (1985) claim for enclave languages that they tend gradually to lose inflectional morphology, sometimes with just loss of redundancy, sometimes also entailing loss of real distinctions such as gender, honorifics, etc.

8 Maher (1985) makes rather astounding claims for changes in what she calls the "enclave language" phenomenon – several of these overlap (at least in part) the universal claims already considered in this chapter. She defines "the enclave speech community" as a special case of language contact involving a multilingual community in which native speakers of one language are surrounded and/or dominated by speakers of a different language in a defined political or geographic area, and the surrounded or dominated language is a minority of the polity and the community exists within a single polity or on the borders between two polities. That is, enclaves in this sense generally emerge through major demographic shifts, dislocations (colonies, immigrants), or as relic communities which have been surrounded by speakers of another language. She claims (Maher 1985: 115–16) that enclave speech communities gradually develop the following characteristics:

1 Reduced number of allomorphs when compared to non-enclave versions of the same language; more invariable forms; increased paradigmatic regularity; reduced syntagmatic redundancy.
2 Replacement of synthetic by analytic or periphrastic constructions; increased form/meaning transparency.
3 Gradual loss of inflectional morphology; sometimes with just loss of redundancy, sometimes also entailing loss of real distinctions such as gender, honorifics, etc.
4 Less flexibility in word order.
5 Greater reliance on aspect than on tense morphology in the verbal system.

These claims are difficult to evaluate because her sample of linguistic enclaves includes a very high percentage of creoles and dying languages. Since creolization and language death (see Campbell and Muntzel 1989) are claimed to have characteristic changes and patterns of development of their own, some reflected in her claims, it is difficult to assess whether a stable multilingual enclave community (of which many examples exist in America, Europe, and South Asia) would tend to exhibit the same tendencies. Her theory is that these are reflexes of incomplete language learning, which may well be true, but may not be an accurate characterization of language acquisition in all enclave situations, particularly those with stable, viable enclave languages.

9 The introduction to chapter 8 provides a general discussion of word order principles which may prove useful to the reader.

10 While for the purposes of discussion in this chapter we consider word order patterns in the same way as others (especially Greenberg 1963 and Hawkins 1983), we hasten to point out that we believe there to be serious difficulties with this approach to dealing with word order. We believe that word order patterns typically reflect discourse needs. Even the definitions of "subject" and "object" and even "verb" are disputed. In actual texts, it is rare for two overt NPs in the role of subject and object to cooccur in the same sentence; that is, in some sense sentences with both a full NP subject and object are themselves marked patterns in normal discourse. Moreover, the now demonstrated OVS and OSV language types have not been integrated into Hawkins' discussion of word order patterns and universals.

For our purposes, we need not be too troubled by these serious problems, since on the one hand it is easy to criticize claims made by this sort of word order study on their own criteria, and on the other hand our main point has to do with the development of certain patterns due to borrowing, for which on the whole no greater refinement of word order is necessary for a successful discussion.

11 Others have also proposed some word order universals which involve borrowing. James Tai (1976) argued that SOV word order does not arise through internal developments, but only from contact with SOV languages; he cited cases of Chinese (claimed to have SOV varieties due to Altaic influence) and Munda (due to Dravidian impact). Faarlund (1990a: 84) also reports that "all known instances of a change from VO to OV are due to contact with OV languages." Indeed, many cases which involve change to SOV order have been argued to be due to language contact: for example, Ethiopian Semitic languages with SOV from Cushitic contact; Akkadian (Semitic) SOV from Sumerian contact; Yaqui (Southern Uto-Aztecan) SOV (changed from VSO) presumably due to contact with neighboring so-called Hokan and Northern Uto-Aztecan languages, which are SOV; Chichimeco Jonaz (Otomanguean), with SOV from neighboring so-called Hokan languages (see Campbell, Bubenik, and Saxon 1988 for details).

Tai's and Faarlund's hypothesis that SOV arises in a language only due to contact with other SOV languages is interesting, but clearly overstated. There is evidence of cases of languages having changed to SOV with no known language contact motivating the change. If new SOV languages arose only from contact with older SOV languages, then where did the prior SOV languages come from; and if they too are assumed to be due to contact with SOV languauges, then how did the very first SOV language come about? A more modest claim, which can be sustainable and which is worthy of more attention, is that a very common path for the development of SOV basic word order is through language contact. The question of what other paths may contribute to the rise of SOV orders, however, deserves careful consideration.

12 The discussion in this section relies heavily on Campbell, Bubenik and Saxon (1988). For other aspects of word order change, see chapter 8.

13 Type 17 is not represented strongly in Hawkins' sample; six of its ten languages (Iraqw, Akkadian, Neo-Aramaic, Younger Avestan, Tajik, and Persian)

show evidence that significant parts of their word order patterns are the results of borrowing within their respective *Sprachbünde* (linguistic convergence areas); we do not know the historical facts concerning the other four (Gunwinggu, Khamti, Bandem, and Tunen). The SOV order of Akkadian is unexpected, given that it is the oldest documented Semitic language. However, the order is generally ascribed to Sumerian influence (with type 21 word order: SOV/Postp/NG/NA).

14 Campbell, Bubenik, and Saxon (1988: 211–12) also show that although Papago is not a type 7 language (the only example in Hawkins' sample), Copainalá Zoque is a type 7 language. Thus examples of type 7 exist, but Copainalá Zoque owes its VOS order to Mayan contact (as do Xinca and Pipil, both with VOS). That is, type 7, like types 18, 19, and 20, appears to exist only in cases of borrowing or language contact.

15 For other similar proposed explanations for the harmonies, see Kuno (1974) and Frazier (1985), and discussion in Dryer (1992).

16 Dryer (1992, which appeared after the writing of this book was essentially complete) argues for an empirically more adequate alternative to the Head-Dependency (Head-Modifier) orientation of Hawkins and others; Dryer presents evidence that it is the direction of branching which determines word order harmonies, that is, that phrasal (branching) categories tend to precede nonphrasal (non-branching) categories in OV languages and vice versa in VO languages. A very similar approach is urged by Hawkins (1990), and in both views language processing is seen as being facilitated by the consistent ordering of branching categories with respect to non-branching ones (in Dryer's view) or of Early Immediate Constituent identification (in Hawkins' view). Both of these alternative views comply with our claims here, that consistent, harmonic word order arrangements facilitate language processing.

17 Given the existence of previously unrecognized word order types, it is necessary to revise several of Hawkins' (1983) proposed universals of word order; see Campbell, Bubenik, and Saxon (1988) for details. Thus, for example, Tigre, the sole representative of type 18 (see above), not in Hawkins' expanded sample, contains the configurations SOV/Prep/NG/AN due to Cushitic influence. Nevertheless, given that at least one real language exemplifies this type, albeit due to borrowing, we must revise Hawkins' universal I:

$$SOV > (AN > GN)$$

It is no longer an absolute universal, but now merely statistical, Tigre being an exception. While the basic word order of German and Dutch are disputed, later Hawkins (1985: 580) was inclined to consider them to be exceptions to universal I as well. At issue is whether German and Dutch are basically SOV and GN or NG. If accepted, these would merely be additional cases of non-conforming languages against the majority of languages which conform to the universal.

It is also interesting to point out that Asia Minor Greek, while having acquired abundant Turkish features, including GN, RelN, the Turkish comparative construction, agglutinative inflections, and even vowel harmony in some dialects, has retained VSO/SVO unaffected (Dawkins 1916: 200). This configuration constitutes an exception to Hawkins' universal XIII:

Prep ⊃ (–SOV ⊃ NRel)

That is, in prepositional non-SOV languages, the relative clause is postposed after its head. Asia Minor Greek is prepositional, VSO/SVO (i.e. non-SOV), but has RelN order. Since this exception is the result of language contact, it should not be treated as seriously as it would be if it had developed internally; the universal, nevertheless, must now be considered statistical rather than absolute.

18 We thank Jacklin Kornfilt for the Turkish information.

19 While some varieties of American Finnish have been studied from the point of view of language death, the borrowed structures considered here cannot be attributed to language obsolescence. These examples are from Finnish American newspapers written by fully fluent, essentially native speakers of the language. (See Campbell 1980 for details.)

20 The discussion of this example follows Campbell (1987); see also Campbell (1985).

21 It may be important to point out that contact is not the only causal factor in some of the changes considered (e.g. the Laz example, some of the Pipil cases, the case of Balto-Finnic "modus obliquus," as discussed elsewhere in this volume), and parallel internal causes can often be found. That is, it is important also to stress the potential for multiple causation (see Appel and Muysken 1987: 162; Campbell 1988). While we may, in many of the cases presented here, be reasonably certain that language contact was a principal causal factor, this may not always be the only element bringing about the changes. Other concomitant factors contribute to some changes; we mention two cases from Pipil.

One such factor is naturalness. Some changes are so natural that languages easily undergo them independently, and instances of the change are found repeatedly in the world's languages. An example is the "third person pural" for impersonal verb forms of Pipil, which replaced an earlier passive construction (see Campbell 1987 for details). This is so common in languages generally (Heine and Reh 1984) that Pipil could have acquired it independently. Nevertheless, given its presence also in Spanish and given Spanish's strong influence in other areas of Pipil grammar, it seems reasonable to suppose that both Spanish influence and the natural tendency for easy innovation of such constructions converged, multiply causing this particular Pipil change, promoting this impersonal construction to the demise of others. Pipil's periphrastic future (see above) may be another example.

The other factor that may work together with foreign influence to multiply cause syntactic change is grammatical "gaps" (see above). Some structural phenomena are highly valuable as communicative resources in a language, and any language which lacks them may be said to have a "gap" in its grammar. Clearly, such languages find it easy to acquire the missing but valuable grammatical resources (see K. Hale 1971; Karttunen 1976; Hill and Hill 1981; Campbell and Mithun 1980). This is very likely what happened in the case of, for example, Pipil complex sentences. Formerly the language had very limited and perceptually none-too-salient resources of coordination and subordination (e.g. Ø [juxtaposition] for coordinate clauses, *i-wan* [relational noun] "with" for coordination of nominals, and *ne* for many kinds of subordinate clauses, relatives included). While this state of affairs did not represent a complete "gap" or lack of any means for indicating these kinds of complex sentences, it clearly was not as efficient as a grammar with overt conjunctions, different for the varied kinds of clauses involved. Thus, it is probable that the changes in Pipil (through the borrowing of Spanish conjunctions and the reshaping of certain relational nouns to function as conjunctions) were motivated in part by the fact that such "grammatical gaps" are very susceptible to change and in part by contact with Spanish. So, probably the changes in Pipil complex sentences involved multiple causation, both Spanish influence and the tendency for "gaps" to get filled.

7 Processes that simplify biclausal structures

1 As **particles** we include independent grammatical words, clitics, and affixes.
2 For example, we do not include here topic markers derived from definite articles (see Heine and Reh 1984: 64–5), question markers derived from indicators of colloquial speech (see Campbell 1991), question markers derived from third person agreement and the third person pronoun (see M. Harris 1978: 33), or topic markers derived from conditionals. We are grateful to John Whitman for drawing our attention to conditionals as a possible source for topic markers in Japanese and Mongolian.
3 It is correct to formulate this in terms of two clauses, rather than "at least two clauses," since, although a given sentence with a cleft may contain more than two clauses, the cleft construction itself consists of only two.
4 Constituents other than NPs can be clefted, as in the examples below:

> where I went yesterday was to the art museum
> it was over there that I saw a red-winged hawk

5 See Keenan and Comrie (1977) on these constraints in relative clauses in a variety of languages; see Larsen and Norman (1979) for similar constraints in relatives and in clefts in some Mayan languages.
6 Harries-Delisle (1978) takes a different approach to providing a universally valid definition of clefts. Omitting her references to focus and presupposition, topics that are taken up below, we may paraphrase her three features that characterize clefts as follows: (a) cleft sentences are equational sentences, which contain a copula; (b) cleft sentences have as their subject a neutral head noun, such as *the one, the man*, etc.; (c) in a cleft sentence, the neutral head noun is more closely defined by a relative clause. Having listed these features (1978: 422–3), she argues that one, two, or even all three of the characteristics that define a cleft may be absent in a given language. It should be noted, however, that what her data actually show is that overt marking of these may be absent, not the feature itself: for example, her data do not suggest that the relative clause (or a subordinate clause with the structure of a relative) may be absent, only that it may lack overt marking as a relative. We have not made use of Harries-Delisle's approach because it specifically excludes the possibility of the kind of cleft described below for Laz.
7 This is the traditional view, based on surface order, as well as the view of a number of contemporary researchers. However, the assumptions of certain other frameworks force one to consider SVO the deep structure order; see Stump (1984), Borsley and Stephens (1989), and other works cited there.

8 Dik (1980: 160–1) refers to the cognate construction in Welsh as focus, commenting that it can also be used for topics. Many sources refer to both the Welsh and the Breton constructions as topicalization (or give it no name), and some traditional grammars typically simply note that the construction is used when (certain) constituents are fronted (e.g. Hemon 1975). Anderson (1981) is the only source we are aware of that provides a rationale for describing it as topic vs. focus (with the partial exception of Dik, regarding its Welsh counterpart), and he makes the following statement: "Apparently both topicalization and focus . . . are conflated in this construction, which (roughly) divides the content of the clause into old information and comment, but in which the initial element may constitute either of these, depending on other factors not examined here" (Anderson 1981: 28–9).

We refer to the construction as focus here on the basis of the structure of the cleft; that is, the cleft from which the highlighting construction derives historically is structurally of the focus cleft type, rather than the topic anti-cleft type (see below on the latter).

9 See Wojcik (1976: 275–6, n. 8), Hemon (1975: 275, n. 1), and Anderson (1981) for more precise statements of the conditions that determine which particle is used.

10 Negative clauses have a different structure, and we will be concerned here only with affirmative clauses of the type in (4–6).

11 There are exceptions to this generalization, though apparently less often when a subject is topicalized.

12 Welsh is more closely related to Breton, but from the data available it is not clear whether the cognate Welsh construction remains a cleft or has been reanalyzed. For data, see Dik (1980: 160–1) and sources cited there. Cornish is also more closely related, but relevant data are not available. See McCloskey (1979) on the Irish cleft.

13 The two clefts differ in word order. Since VSO is known to have been the order of Proto-Celtic, we assume that the Irish cleft is closer to the original in word order and that the Breton cleft has been reworked by extending focus fronting even to the focus cleft construction. However, the original order of words in the cleft is not crucial to our analysis.

14 We are grateful to Wayne Harbert for calling this problem to our attention.

15 Within the Celtic group, the cleft construction was common to Insular Celtic (Le Roux 1957: 469). On the basis of the data from Breton, Welsh, and Irish cited or mentioned above, we assume tentatively that derivation of a focus construction from a cleft was an innovation shared by at least these languages. This assumption is by no means crucial to any conclusion reached here.

16 See chapter 10 for explanations of other relations among clause types.

17 The structure proposed for focus in recent work (for example, Rochemont 1986; Kiss 1987), while highly insightful for the languages discussed there, presents certain problems when applied to some other languages, including Somali. The only aspect of the focus highlighting that is essential to our purposes is that it is monoclausal.

18 The discussion which follows is based on English descriptions (Akiba 1978: 76–7; Kay 1985) of work in Japanese by Susumu Ōno.

19 Kay's paper argues against Ōno's analysis, but we find her arguments unconvincing. She looks for a simple increase in the number of *Kakari* particles in medial position, relative to those in final position, over a space of about one hundred years.

Several aspects of her approach throw doubt on her conclusions, including her interpretation of the low numbers and her failure to propose an alternative explanation of the development of this construction.

20 Akiba (1978: 105–14) provides a different analysis of the occurrence of *wo*.

21 In addition to these two languages, described below, a number of African languages are said to favor a similar clefting for formation of yes/no questions. Akiba (1978: 77–9) has argued that question formation in Japanese originated in a way similar to that observed in French.

22 This *-i* (< *-ni*) is probably cognate with the question particle, *-i*, of the closely related sister language, Laz. That is, the Laz question particle is probably also derived from a focus cleft construction with a subordinate clause marked with the clause-final particle *-ni*, which reduced to *-i*. The Mingrelian question particle, *-o*, and its cognates in the other sister languages probably originated from the same sort of structure, where the verb *oren* "it is" and its cognates in the other languages were reduced to the vowel.

23 The cleft in Mingrelian is further described in Harris (in press c).

24 Our description of the cleft-to-highlighting reanalysis is complemented by the observation that certain aspects of structure remain unchanged. The following elements do not change in reanalysis, but it is possible that in the actualization of the reanalysis some languages do change these: the position of the highlighter relative to highlighted constituent, the position of the highlighter and highlighted constituent relative to the rest of the clause, the pragmatic function of the construction, the grammatical relations of constituents of the content clause.

25 Ertelišvili (1963: 184) cites examples from *Marxvata sak'itxebi*, which is dated to this period; Abulaӡe (1973: 229b) cites contemporary examples for *metki*.

26 The fact that these particles preserve in a limited way the category of person should not mislead the reader into thinking that this makes them verbs. Note that the demonstrative pronouns *es, igi, is* also show person, meaning "near the speaker (first person)," "near the hearer (second person)," and "near the other (third person)," respectively, as observed in the standard grammars; yet no one would suggest that this fact indicates that these pronouns are verbs. Neither are the quotative particles verbs in the modern language.

27 Ӡiӡiguri (1973: 446) reports that there is a dialect, K'axian, where the form *metki* can still stand alone today as a main verb in the meaning "I said." Clearly, in this dialect the change is incomplete, and the statements made above do not apply to it.

28 Structures of this general type are the sources of quotative particles in a number of Indic and Dravidian languages (Steever 1987a, 1987b), and this source is reconstructed for a number of Tibeto-Burman languages (Saxena 1988; of Akha, Lolo Burmese, Thurgood 1986b), Japanese (Akiba 1978: 92–6), several Uto-Aztecan languages (Munro 1978), and Hmong (Li 1988).

29 Although we have no examples of serial verbs developing into quotatives, it is likely that they can do so. It seems entirely possible to have the verb "say" contained instead in the subordinate clause (e.g. "which she said"), but we know of no examples of this. We characterize the source construction in terms that are applicable only to a hypotactic construction with a matrix verb of saying, but we recognize that this could require broadening.

30 It is probable that the subject, *me* "I," was used with *vtkvi* "I say" for emphasis; this

is the usual reason that independent subject pronouns are used in Georgian (Harris 1981: 32–8). The function of *tkva* (> *tko*) is quite different (see above), and it is perhaps not surprising that no emphatic pronoun was used with this construction.

31 Among the aspects of sentence structure which are not affected by reanalysis, but which may be changed later are the relative positions of the various constituents of the quotative particle, the position of this particle relative to the quoted material, and the function of the construction. Regarding the second point, we may note in passing that in the source construction in Georgian, the "say" clause either precedes or follows the subordinate clause, but it was only the latter position that was grammaticalized in each instance.

32 In the Adiši manuscript, one of the oldest available, we find the second subjunctive at Mark 6: 25, the aorist at Mark 10: 43, the masdar at Mark 8: 35, the infinitive (so-called masdar in the adverbial case) at Matthew 5: 40, and an infinitive of secondary importance (so-called masdar in the genitive case) at Matthew 2: 18. Each of these is confirmed by other examples.

33 All of these verbs are inversion verbs; that is, synchronically their initial subjects are demoted to indirect objects and are marked with the dative case in all TAM categories.

34 V-initial seems to be the most common order in this construction.

35 If a direct object were present, it would have been marked with the so-called nominative case, regardless of which verb governed it; thus the syntactic pattern would have been ambiguous with regard to this nominal. If an indirect object were present, it could have been marked with one of several cases at this period and thus might also be somewhat ambiguous.

36 This statement is not intended to imply that this extension was inevitable; in the periphrastic perfect in Modern Georgian exactly the same "inconsistency" persists thus far unchanged.

37 Georgian grammarians consider *unda* a particle on the grounds that its form does not vary for grammatical categories such as person, number, and tense (Šaniʒe 1973: 616; Kiziria 1982: 113); see discussion of definition of auxiliary, above in the text. *Unda* cannot be viewed as an adverb because of certain restrictions on positions. First, in general, the negative *ar* is required to occur immediately before the finite verb; *unda* may – indeed, if it occurs, must – intervene between *ar* and the finite verb:

(i)   man ar   unda   gaak'etos
         s/he NEG should s/he.do.it.SBV
         "He should not do it."
(ii)   *man unda ar gaak'etos
(iii)   *man unda gaak'etos ar
(iv)   *ar man unda gaak'etos

However, adverbs, like other words, cannot intervene between *ar* "Neg" and the finite verb:

(v)   *man ar   čkara gaak'etos
        s/he NEG fast   s/he.do.it.SBV
        "May he not do it fast."

(vi)   man čkara ar gaak'etos
(vii)   man ar gaak'etos čkara

Q-words, too, must occur immediately before the finite verb (Harris 1981: 14). *Unda,* if present, can only occur between the Q-word and the finite verb:

(viii)   is   sad   unda   c'avides?
         s/he where should s/he.go.s b v
         "Where should she go?"
(ix)   *is unda sad c'avides?
(x)   *is sad c'avides unda?

An adverb cannot occur in the position occupied by *unda*:

(xi)   *is   sad   čkara   c'avides?
         s/he where fast   s/he.go.s b v
         "Where would she go fast?"
(xii)   is čkara sad c'avides?
(xiii)   is sad c'avides čkara?

In both respects, *unda* occupies the position of a finite verb, even though it is no longer finite in these examples.

38 The fact that other Germanic languages have also undergone changes (66, a–c, e) suggests that reanalysis may have occurred much earlier. This is especially true if these are automatic consequences of reanalysis, as we suggest below. As might be expected, these changes have not proceeded at the same rate in all languages. For example, "can" still may take the name of a language as a direct object in German (*kannst du Deutsch?* "Do you know German?") and Norwegian (*kan De norsk?* "Do you speak Norwegian?"). We are grateful to Mark Hale for bringing this implication of the analysis to our attention.

39 For simplicity we assume that the modal verbs took noun direct objects, and that those modals that occurred in biclausal structures were reanalyzed.

40 Lightfoot does not note that one modal did acquire *to*: *ought to*. This combination occurs even in double modal constructions, such as *you ought to could buy that at the grocery store.* We assume that *ought* acquired *to* because it was reanalyzed later, possibly much later, than the other modals. Independent support for this view is the fact that its cognate modal verb survives into Modern English: *owe, own*.

41 Roberts suggests that the loss of the double modal construction is indeed a consequence of the reanalysis: "Aux does not iterate, so double-modal sequences do not appear" (1985: 53). Thus his analysis cannot account for those dialects in the southern United States in which modal auxiliaries have all of the other characteristics discussed here and *do* occur in double modal constructions.

42 Vincent characterizes this as a locative subject (1982: 79).

43 It is not clear whether this involved two distinct changes or only one. If two changes took place, the first would have kept the biclausal structure, but made it obligatory to have the subject of the subordinate clause coindexed with that of the matrix (eliminating the k possibility in (77)); the second would have reanalyzed this as a monoclausal structure. The view that separate changes were involved here is consistent with the fact that a non-coindexed subject died out gradually. However,

there is no reason in principle that the reanalysis could not have changed both features at once.

44 This is the class of verbs Perlmutter (1983) calls "unaccusative," and Burzio (1986, using the term in a sense other than its traditional one) "ergative"; syntactically the verbs are characterized by an underlying direct object and no underlying subject.

45 We are using the terms "transitive" and "intransitive" rather loosely here, for we do not know whether this was the real distinction, or whether, as in Romance languages, it was somewhat different; "transitive" vs. "intransitive" is the traditional differentiation, and the details are not important for present purposes.

46 These seem to be the analyses that Čikobava and Cercvaӡe (1962: 328–30) have in mind, which they term respectively a "complex predicate" and a "periphrastic form."

47 While examples can be found in many languages, some particularly interesting and complex ones come from Cariban languages, where changes in word order and alignment are also involved (Gildea 1992). In Burmese an interesting kind of evidence for reconstructing the main verb is provided by creaky tone, which acts as a "tracer"; see Thurgood (1977).

48 Some treatments of this process in individual languages have avoided this problem; an example is Vincent (1982). See Munro (1984) and Dik (1987) for other generalizations on processes discussed in this chapter.

49 For example, it appears that possessive-to-future, possessive-to-progressive, location-to-progressive, go-to-future, among others, are governed by the principles proposed below. In addition, it appears that certain other periphrastic expressions are formed in the same way, but all of these cannot be dealt with here.

8 Word order

1 Dryer (1992), drawing on a much larger database than most previous studies, shows that a dichotomy of OV vs. VO is supported. That is, SVO languages have most of the characteristics of V-initial languages.

2 The notions "fully recursive" and "major constituent" as used here are explained in Dryer (1992), but the details of how these statements are formulated are not essential to our discussion.

3 What is deemed controversial here depends upon the theory one adopts; perhaps most controversial is the assumption that an auxiliary is the head of the VP.

4 This assumption leaves the determination of the head unsettled in those dyads where there is no correlation with verb–object order. In those situations we use the following criterion:

The head is that element which bears more detailed inflection.

5 On percentages of languages that are harmonic see also Hawkins (1983: 134).

6 Specifically, Vennemann (1973) permitted only the following changes, where FWO is free word order:

$$\begin{array}{ccc} \text{VSO} & \rightarrow & \text{FWO} \\ \updownarrow & \nearrow & \downarrow \\ \text{SVO} & \leftarrow & \text{SOV} \end{array}$$

7 The CCH could be applied to predict, within limits, the order in which dyads will change their word order, but the diachronic predictions are just as inaccurate as the synchronic ones. To take but one example, his universal XVI (1983: 80) predicts diachronically that if postpositions are established, GN order must be established before NumN, but this is not true diachronically or synchronically in Old Georgian (see Harris 1991e).

8 According to Schmidt (1969), the same is true of Indo-European; he cites examples from Ancient Greek and Vedic Sanskrit in which the preverb follows the verb. However, these examples are open to the interpretation that the "adverb" does not so much follow the verb as it precedes a noun, having already been reinterpreted as an adposition.

9 Some of these data suggest that the order OV may be used in certain compounds in some languages, such as English because of the dominance of AN order in phrases. This explanation seems plausible for *heat-conductor, garbage-disposal, life-insurance*, which may be viewed as kinds of conductor, disposal, and insurance. It does not work at all for *car-wash*, which cannot be compared with other kinds of *washes*; in American English, at least, other machines that wash things are *washers*, e.g. *dish-washer, clothes-washer*, whereas washes are liquids used for washing, such as *eye-wash*. AN order can likewise not be invoked successfully to explain the *heat-seeking* type, since *heat* cannot plausibly be seen as modifying a nominal *seeking*.

10 A less frequent pattern in compounds is NG, as in *dia-saxl-isa* "housewife" (< *deda-saxl-isa* [mother-house-GEN]); though less frequent, this is likewise attested from the earliest time. Compounds in this pattern, including this particular word, are still found, but have always been infrequent.

11 NG is the unmarked order in Old Georgian, and GN is found less frequently than other modifier–head orders. GN order occurs relatively frequently in Old Georgian only when the head is a non-finite verb form and the genitive is its argument, usually object (Harris 1991e). A study of word order in the Adiši manuscript of Matthew 1–8 uncovered the following distributions, where the number of tokens was counted for phrasal order, but the number of different compounds for compound order:

	NG	*GN*	*Total*
Phrasal order	287	12	299
Compound order	0	10	10

If non-finite verb forms are excluded from both counts, the numbers are

Phrasal order	262	2	264
Compound order	0	3	3

12 Note that while the Georgian has GN order, the Russian has NG order,

> sojuz   sovetskix   socialističeskix   respublik
> union soviet   socialist   republic.PL.GEN
> "Union of Soviet Socialist Republics"

showing that the Georgian order is not due to calquing.

13 In addition, Abulaʒe 1973, the comprehensive dictionary of Old Georgian, does not list either item.

14 An example of such an assertion is quoted in chapter 2 from Behaghel (1878: 283).

15 Bean states that "Heusler notes that the nominal genitive follows its head unless the genitive plus noun combine to form a unitary concept" (Bean 1983: 50). This is not exactly what Heusler says:

> Der das Substantiv bestimmende *Genitiv* pflegt nachzustehn. Beim Gen. *partit.* ist dies alte . . . Regel. Man beachte das Nachstehn der *Eigennamen* . . . *Voraus* gehen die Genitive der Beschaffenheit und des Maßes . . . ferner solche, die mit dem andern Hauptwort zu einheitlichem Begriff und Kolon verschmelzen   (Heusler 1932: 177)

> The *genitive* modifying a substantive tends to follow it . . . With the *partitive* genitive this is the old norm. One notices the postposing of *personal names* . . . Genitives of quality and of mass go *before* . . . as do those which fuse with the other head word to a unitary concept and colon [metrical unit].   [Our translation, ACH/LC; emphasis in the original]

Thus Heusler actually states that in phrases both GN and NG orders are found.

16 Bede's *Ecclesiastical history* dates from 731, Wulfstan from between 1002 and 1023.

17 This does not mean that loan-translations of compounds always retain the word order of the original; they do not. For example, French, also with the order NG in phrases, does not put up with GN in this compound, and instead calques "railroad" as *chemin de fer* literally "way of iron."

18 According to Dryer (1992), the relative order of noun and adjective does not correlate (positively or negatively) with the order of verb and object, as has been widely believed. As Dryer also points out (1988: 197) this is probably due to the fact that their grammatical properties vary from language to language, such that they are not a homogeneous category (cf. Dryer 1992: 118–22). In particular, while in many languages nouns are heads of a phrase containing adjective + noun, in some languages adjective-like modifiers are grammatically verbs or nouns and may be grammatically the head of their phrase, with the modified noun being grammatically the object of the verb. It is also possible that some languages interpret Dryer's Branching Direction Theory (alternate version), quoted here as (4), without the notion "fully recursive" (see Dryer 1992), with the result that all phrasal dependents, including adjectives, exhibit the characteristic of being dependents, while other languages interpret the generalization with the notion "fully recursive," in this way excluding adjectives. As Dryer (1988: 196) also notes, there is evidence of a different kind that adjectives, at least in some languages, are verb patterners, contrary to his findings. This is the fact that the relative order of adjectives and nouns is affected as part of a large-scale change of word order within dyads in a number of attested changes, two of which are discussed in this section. If the adjective is not a verb patterner in these languages, then we must consider it a coincidence that its order relative to the noun changed as part of a general change involving heads and dependents.

19 From the wording ("One grammatical order is not established . . ."), it is not clear whether Bybee intends this as a general (universal) statement or only as a descrip-

tion of the examples she discusses. We interpret her statement in the former sense; in any case, this provides an opportunity to clarify this issue.

20 For examples from Sanskrit, see Andersen (1979: 26–8) and sources cited there.

21 Grammars often refer to *willen* (or to the combination *um . . . willen*) as a preposition, but this is simply to avoid the more accurate, but linguistic, designation "postposition" (or "circumposition").

22 In Heine and Reh (1984: 242) it is suggested briefly that such a mechanism is one way by which an AN harmony may develop; while that may be true, it does not seem to happen in that way in every instance.

23 Andersen, of course, was not the first to notice such prepositions; he cites Delbrück (1888) and Bloch (1934 [1965]). According to Andersen, the same observation led Lehmann and Ratanajoti (1975) to conclude that later stages of Old Indic were in transition from postpositional to prepositional (and hence SOV to SVO). Andersen (1979: 30) further points out that Lehmann and Ratanajoti's analysis is not consistent with the fact that early Middle Indic has a consistent OV typology.

24 Modern German examples in this section are from Corbett (1948: 251–3) or were suggested by examples given there.

25 Other glossed examples from these sources can be found in Harris (1985: 385–8).

26 See Platzack (1985) for a summary of work to that date, and since then Weerman (1989); Haider and Prinzhorn (1986); Hellan and Koch Christensen (1986); Faarlund (1990b: ch. 3); Lightfoot (1991: ch. 3).

27 By *reevaluate*, we mean reanalyze with respect to markedness.

28 In Old Icelandic the participle occasionally agrees, as in the example below.

> þeir   eru unnend-r guð -i
> they.NOM are loving-PL God-DAT
> "They love God."
>
> (*Gammel norsk Homiliebog* 178.6, cited by Mossé 1938: 72)

29 Stockwell (1977) and Marchese (1986: 218–67) treat this as "exbraciation," movement of other constituents out of the "brace" created by the Aux and V, rather than movement of the V to be adjacent to the Aux.

30 Whitney (1971: 398) points out that "three or four instances" have been discovered of the preverb separated from the verb stem in Classical Sanskrit; he suggests that these are still adverbs. In chapter 4 we observed several other examples of a word or construction being reanalyzed and continuing to coexist with its unreanalyzed variant.

31 Keesing (1988: 185, 186) points out that in Solomons Pidgin it is still possible to have the future-irrealis marker in clause-initial position. He attributes this to fronting for emphasis, but it would seem possible that it may function as an adverb in clause-initial position, or that its repositioning to adjacency is simply incomplete.

32 As noted above, we assume that all of the verb patterners of (2) are heads. In constructions that have no word order correlations, we apply the criterion stated in note 4. Thus, we assume that tense-aspect markers of the types discussed in Sanskrit, Latin, Bari, and Solomons Pidgin are dependents of content verb heads, because it is the content verb that bears inflection (see also Dryer 1992: 95, 98–9). A

theory that assumes instead that the content verb is head and the auxiliary its dependent must restate our generalization (46) as follows:

> Discontinuous constituents that are reordered to be adjacent occupy the position held by the grammatical head, except that auxiliaries and verbs are reordered to occupy the position held by the auxiliary.

33 Data adduced in Allen (1977) suggest that it is possible to reorder constituents relative to one another while reordering to adjacency, at least as an optional and temporary variant. Assuming that reanalysis of modals in English produced the order SMOV in main clauses and SOVM in embedded clauses (see chapter 7), the development of SMVO order in main clauses is to be expected because of (44b). The orders SMOV and SMVO in embedded clauses are to be expected by extension of main clause order (respectively old and new) into embedded clauses. Allen shows that in addition to those, SOMV and SVMO occur in embedded clauses. The former is the result of (66), applied to the original order of embedded clauses; the latter is the result of (45b) applied to the extension of main clause order into embedded clauses.

34 This discussion does not include the inherited Germanic inseparable prefix. In the reflexes of the verbs of the latter type, the prefix remains inseparable; these include verbs such as *forgive, forget, outgrow, overdraw*, and *upset* (Kennedy 1920).

35 In Allen's terms, preposition stranding occurred only when the relativized NP was deleted in place. It never occurred when the relative pronoun was moved; in those instances Pied Piping was obligatory (1980 [1977]: 91–3).

36 The twelfth century is the date of Allen's earliest examples; it is, of course, quite likely that the change appeared slightly earlier in the spoken language.

37 In Allen's terms, these four constructions all involve movement; she observes that stranding seems to have appeared in relatives with relative pronouns slightly earlier than in the other three constructions named here (see Allen 1980 [1977]: 226–31).

38 Constraints on non-adjacency of verb and particle in English with reference to whether the object is a noun or pronoun, shown in the sentences below, suggest that rhythmic effects may have once played a role in this rule as well:

(i)   (a)   they put up my friend
         (b)   they put my friend up
(ii)   (a)   *they put up him
         (b)   they put him up

39 In a grammar with PS rules that generate ordered strings, the difference between reordering to adjacency and reordering to non-adjacency can be described in the following way: in reordering to adjacency, two elements that are in non-adjacent positions in deep structure and are reanalyzed as a single constituent tend to come, diachronically, to occupy adjacent positions, conforming to (46). In reordering to non-adjacency, two elements of a constituent, in adjacent positions in deep structure, may come, synchronically, to occupy non-adjacent positions, conforming to (56). These statements are based on the assumption that after actualization of the reanalysis is underway, head and dependent are necessarily continuous constituents in deep structure. Note that the truth behind Behaghel's First Law, the obser-

vation that elements of a constituent tend, over time, to come together, is that this is so at deep structure, not at surface structure. In surface structure a constituent may, in fact, become discontinuous.

40 In the NG order, double case marking was used, but not in the GN order:

> NG
> ʒe-man   kʼac-isa-man
> son-NAR   man-GEN-NAR
> "son of man"
>
> GN
> kʼac-is(a)   ʒe-man
> man-GEN   son-NAR
> "man's son"

The double case marking occurred because in Old Georgian the case markers were phrasal affixes (clitics), assigned to both the head and the last element of the NP. When the head was the last constituent of the NP, only one marker was assigned, which occurred anytime a noun was used without modifiers. In GN order, the head and the last element of the NP were likewise the same, and only one marker was assigned. Therefore, even though the transition from NG to GN order appears to involve the loss of double case marking, its disappearance is automatically accounted for by rules already in the language.

41 Here "unmarked" order excludes ordering conditioned by pragmatic, stylistic, and prosodic factors, as discussed in section 8.5.4.

42 Kaisse's footnote is omitted from the quotation in (67); together it and the broader text make it clear that the statement quoted here applies generally to sentential clitics, such as ones in COMP, topics, or non-lexical subjects. For further clarification, see Kaisse (1985: 75–89).

43 The transliteration used by Bennett in this example and those that follow differs from the system used by de Bray in examples (69) and (70) quoted above; these differences do not affect understanding of the syntax.

44 Bennett (1987) and others have shown that Serbo-Croatian has begun to undergo the same change that Slovene has completed; the sentences cited here from Serbo-Croatian represent the older situation (Bennett 1987: 272–4). Bennett shows that the change in Slovene (and Serbo-Croatian) is more complex than represented here, for the auxiliaries that formerly could only be enclitic now may occur as proclitics after a pause. In addition, the change may be due in part to German influence on Slovene (Bennett 1987).

45 This change also provides another example of non-adjacent constituents being reordered to adjacency, since in innovative Slovene first position constituents are no longer split. Although the evidence is less clear, it appears from the facts presented in Bennett (1986: 15–17) that the auxiliary and main verb are also being drawn together in Slovene. Bennett's comparison of a Slovene text and its Serbo-Croatian translation yielded sixty-two examples in which Slovene auxiliary + main verb were adjacent while they were separated in the Serbo-Croatian translation. It also yielded twenty examples in which the opposite situation obtained, but many of these are the result of other obligatory constraints. On the basis of this and other

data presented there, one may say that on the whole Slovenian is significantly more likely to place the auxiliary and main verb together than is Serbo-Croatian. If this is correct, it provides another example of the process discussed in section 8.5.1.

46 England (1991) shows that Ch'orti', the only Mayan language which today has SVO as the basic order, reanalyzed the topic/focus condition in the Proto-Mayan order,

TOPIC FOCUS [VOS] REORDERED O

as applying instead to subjects. Givón (1976, 1977) shows that the position occupied by a shifted topic was reanalyzed as subject position in Biblical Hebrew.

47 Dryer (1988: 196) suggests that there may be languages that are head-ordering and others that are not.

48 In a grammar with PS rules that generate ordered constituents, this need not be stated as a tendency only:

(75')   *Constituency Principle*
         Words that form a constituent are placed in adjacent positions in deep structure.

However, this is an artefact of the analysis, inasmuch as we construct the rules to generate the words that form a constituent in adjacent positions precisely because we analyze them as a constituent. Thus, (75') is implicitly recognized through phrase structure rules that generate deep structure constituents together.

49 See further discussion in section 9.2.5.

9 Alignment

1 We consider the definitions given in Fillmore (1968: 54) and Plank (1985: 269–270) to be essentially similar to those provided by Sapir and represented in table 9.1. Differences between Plank's approach and that taken here are briefly discussed in section 9.4.6.3.

2 Because it does not figure in the examples discussed in this work, tripartite alignment (see, for example, Comrie 1978: 332), has been omitted from table 9.1. So-called neutral alignment, where all subjects and direct objects are treated alike, is omitted here because it is not clear that it should be considered an alignment type at all. Accordingly, the statements made in this chapter are not intended to include changes involving a system of "neutral alignment."

3 In Andi, [c:] is described as an intensive alveolar affricate, [q'] as a uvular ejective. We are grateful to Rieks Smeets for discussion.

4 According to Bynon (1980: 154), by Middle Persian "the case system rested entirely on the pronouns; for, while in nouns the formal opposition had become lost, at least certain pronouns still inflected for case."

5 A change of a parallel type is posited for Polynesian, but Polynesian does not preserve an aspectual split (Hohepa 1969; Chung 1978; Chung and Seiter 1980).

6 Trask (1979) and Estival and Myhill (1988) claim that all ergative alignment originates as a reanalysis of passives. This is clearly wrong, as shown by the origins of ergativity discussed in sections 9.2.3 and 9.2.4 below.

7 A similar change in Lardil, a Pama-Nyungan language of Australia, is discussed in section 9.4.4.2 (Klokeid 1978).

8 Object demotion may be compared with English sentences such as *she read in the book* (cf. *she read the book*) or *he worked at the puzzle* (cf. *he worked the puzzle*).

9 Anderson (1988, like Anderson 1977) recognizes two distinct origins of the ergative, but others have argued that this is incorrect (e.g. Bynon 1980: 152–3) or have ignored this distinction (e.g. Payne 1979). For our purposes it is immaterial whether these two are essentially the same or not.

10 Reanalysis of non-finite verb forms under similar circumstances in other languages could potentially be the basis for a number of different kinds of changes, since these forms themselves do not use a single alignment in all languages. Comrie (1978: 377–8) has proposed nominalizations as the basis for two distinct developments in Mayan languages. In Chol there is an alignment split of the type discussed elsewhere in this section. Comrie suggests that the innovative nominative–accusative system here arises from nominalizations, but there is no specific evidence to support this hypothesis. He proposes that nominalizations are independently the source for nominative–accusative alignment in subordinate clauses in Jacaltec. In this instance, however, there is no clear evidence that these nominalizations have been reanalyzed as finite subordinate clauses. In spite of the lack of evidence to support these proposed changes in Mayan languages, it is clear that nominalizations are potentially a source of a variety of changes in alignment type, as shown by Gildea (1992), described in this section in the text.

11 For example, the question of why instrumentals would have been associated only with subjects of transitive, and not of intransitive, clauses requires further study. Garrett (1990: 265) argues that "a similar reanalysis cannot occur in clauses with intransitive predicates because thematic instruments are rare or absent altogether in the subject position of intransitive clauses" and gives as an example the English sentences *John walks with a cane* and **a cane walks*. While intransitive pairs of this sort do not exist, he argues, transitive pairs such as *John opened the door with the key* and *the key opened the door* do exist. According to Garrett, it is the asymmetry of these pairs that leads to only instruments of the second sort, instruments in transitives, being reanalyzed as ergatives. However, in English pairs of the first sort, instruments in intransitives are plentiful. For example *John writes with a pen* beside *this pen writes well, John cuts with a dull knife* beside *this dull knife cuts poorly*. It might be argued in these instances that the verbs selected are transitive in some sense, even though they occur in clauses without direct objects. It is difficult to find verbs in English that cannot take a direct object; even *walk*, the verb Garrett uses, does so. However, there are some that are somewhat awkward with a direct object, and at least some of these permit an instrument: for example, *John squawked with a broken whistle, the broken whistle squawked; John signaled with a light, the light signaled* (*in the darkness*). Whether or not thematic instruments can occur as subjects of intransitives in English, it is not clear whether or not they can occur in this role in Anatolian and other languages. However, it is unlikely that a complete ban of such intransitives is necessary in order for the instrument to be reanalyzed as associated with transitives. We have shown in chapter 4 that in many instances only a subset of occurring sentences forms the basis of reanalysis, and it is possible that transitive clauses with instruments need only be more frequent or more salient than comparable intransitives in order to be reinterpreted as ergatives.

12 Mallinson and Blake (1981: 103–14) marshal evidence that absolutives are more

highly topical in languages with ergatively aligned phenomena, but others disagree. For example, Du Bois (1985: 351; also 1987: 842) notes that agents and hence transitive subjects are frequently topics in Sacapultec; Plank (in press: 2.2.3) states that an ACT_t (the active argument of a transitive verb) is "the topicworthier argument especially if verbs are imperfective or progressive and the INACT_t is less than fully affected." Modini (1989) claims that, at least historically, patients, and therefore presumably absolutives, are topics in "ergative languages."

13   Since it is sometimes thought that first and second person pronouns never show an ergative–absolutive distinction, the data to support this reconstructed distinction are presented here.

Comparison of pronouns in Lezgian and Aɣul with verbal suffixes of the southern dialect of Tabassaran

	Lezgian Pronouns	Aɣul Pronouns	Tabassaran Suffixes
ABSOLUTIVE			
1st person SG	zun	zun	zu
2nd person SG	wun	wun	wu
1st person PL	čun	čin (EXCL)	
		x̌in/šin (INCL)	x̌u
2nd person PL	k'yun	čun/kün/č°un	č°u
ERGATIVE			
1st person SG	za	za-š/zun	za
2nd person SG	na	wa-š/wun	wa
1st person PL	čna	če-š/čin (EXCL)	ča
		x̌e-š/x̌in	
		/šin (INCL)	
2nd person PL	k'yune	čwe-š/čun/kün	č°a
		/č°un	

Source: Andɣulaʒe (1968: 117); Magometov (1970: 101–2; 1965: 198–9).

14   We have simplified this account by omitting discussion of the inherited system of agreement, which uses prefixes to mark gender-class and number agreement with the absolutive nominal. A more complete account is found in Harris (in press a).

15   Some other languages with ergative case marking have also reanalyzed incorporated constructions or noun + verb compounds. In these instances the verb of the source construction is transitive (at least in underlying structure) and takes an ergative case subject; these are reanalyzed as intransitive verbs, still taking an ergative case subject. For example, in Hua (Papuan language of the Eastern Highlands of New Guinea), the verb *hu* "do" combines with a wide variety of adjectives and nouns, such as *ausi* "flame" to form a compound, *ausihu* "blaze." Such compounds may take the ergative case, which is optional with transitive verbs, but is disallowed with intransitives other than these derived ones (Haiman 1980: 117–20). In Udi (Daghestan family of the Caucasus) there are several verbs that combine with nouns or adjectives to form compounds of all types, including transitive, active intransitive, and inactive intransitive. Those of the second type are similar to those

cited from Hua, in that they use a transitive verb, for example *pesun* "say," and an ergative case subject. An example is (i):

(i)   xinär-en geläš-ne-p-e
        girl-ERG dance-3.SG-AUX(say)-AOR
        "The girl danced."

This compound and at least some of those similar to it may take an absolutive subject instead of ergative. Other classes of verbs in Udi require an ergative (transitives) or absolutive (intransitives) consistently, permitting no such options (Harris 1991d).

Bandjalang (Australia) is a language which shows evidence of reanalysis of cognate object constructions, similar to those in Old Georgian illustrated in (34) (Austin 1982: 38–9).

16 Sacapultec, like other Mayan languages, does not mark NPs for case; "absolutive" here refers instead to the verbal agreement marker this NP would condition.

17 "'Preferred argument structure' is that grammatical structuring of arguments which is statistically 'preferred' in clause tokens in discourse" (Du Bois 1985: 349).

18 Estival and Myhill (1988), who do not cite Du Bois 1985 or 1987, reach the opposite conclusion in their examination of the relationship between passive and ergative. They claim that in English, passives are more likely to occur when the agent of a transitive represents new information and when the patient represents old information and that in languages with ergative rules, subjects of transitives are more likely to represent new information and objects old (1988: 456–8).

19 Du Bois explains alignment splits based on the NP Hierarchy as the result of the competition between information flow and topic continuity; see pages 845, 850.

20 There is no evidence, however, that this is the path by which Mayan languages became ergative, and hence no evidence to support this as the source of ergativity in Du Bois' examples from Sacapultec. Mayan languages typically contain two distinct passives as well as their ergative alignment.

21 That this is extension is implied by Payne's statement that this occurred "under the influence of the present tense" (1980: 152) and also by Bubenik (1989a: 208).

22 This description of Pamir verb agreement is based on Payne (1980) but omits language-particular details. The intention in the present work is only to consider the issue of alignment consistency. The system described here is preserved, with differences of details that are not mentioned here, in Rošani and Bartangi.

23 Another change away from consistency in alignment type has occurred in Udi, as summarized in the following chart. These changes took place independently of those in Tabassaran, a related language.

	Direct object	Subject of intransitive		Subject of transitive
		Inactive	Active	
Case marking				
Proto-Lezgian	ABSL	ABSL	ABSL	ERG
Udi	ABSL/*DAT*	ABSL	ABSL/*ERG*	ERG
Agreement				
Proto-Lezgian	Class prefix	Class prefix	Class prefix	Ø
Udi	Ø	Person suffix	Person suffix	Person suffix

In Proto-Lezgian, case marking and agreement both had ergative alignment. The modern agreement in Udi is with subjects (thus of accusative alignment). Case changes have taken place independently of agreement, and do not harmonize with it (see Harris 1991d, in press a). The mechanisms of these changes are as yet incompletely understood.

24 Plank (to appear: 4.4) states,

> If different alignments obtain for the syntactic behavior of arguments of the morphological encoding of their relations, the latter will be adjusted to the former but not vice versa; or if constructions differing in alignment also differ in their expressive potential, perhaps owing to the loss of a morphological contrast in one of them, the more expressive will succeed.

Plank did not present the data these claims are based upon, and we have found no support for them.

25 The term "grammatical relation" is used in this work to refer to any one of the following notions, some of which are superordinate to others: subject, direct object, indirect object, object (= direct object + indirect object), ergative (= subject of transitive), absolutive (= subject of intransitive + direct object of transitive), subject of inactive intransitive, subject of active intransitive, subject of intransitive (= subject of inactive intransitive + subject of active intransitive). This is discussed further in section 9.4.3.1.

26 At the time we first used this term (in Harris 1990a, the published version of a talk given in 1987), we were unaware of the use of the same term in a very different way in Stump (1984), to refer to a proposed constraint in Breton. Since the two terms refer to such entirely different concepts, and since Stump (1989) has retracted his principle, we see no harm in using the term as we used it in the earlier publication.

27 An apparent example of this occurs in the Indo-Aryan language Lahndā, where the ergative postposition may be dropped, leaving the oblique case. At an earlier stage, Lahndā evidently had the following distribution:

	Direct object	Subject of intransitive	Subject of transitive
"Non-ergative tenses"	Oblique	Direct	Direct
"Ergative tenses"	Direct	Direct	Oblique (+Ergative)

Today the situation is considerably more complex (Bubenik 1989a), apparently because of additional changes in the marking of direct objects.

28 An example of a case change that leaves the alignment intact is given in Stump (1983). According to Stump's data, following several other changes in case marking, Vernacular Hindōstānī made the change indicated in our chart below:

	Direct object	Subject of intransitive	Subject of transitive
Middle Indic			
Non-participial tenses	Obl	Nom	Nom
Participial tense	Nom	Erg	Erg
Vernacular Hindōstānī			
Non-participial tenses	Obl	Nom	Nom
Participial tense	*Obl*	Erg	Erg

(The case names used here have etymological value.) The change of the marking of the direct object in the participial tense from nominative to oblique did not make any change in the alignment of case marking in this tense; nevertheless this change, like changes in alignment, is governed by the Complementarity Principle as stated.

29 This principle is discussed in Harris (1985: 21–6, 108–19, 344–7) and elsewhere.

30 In these statements "case A (B, C, or D)" is understood to mean the case as it was before the alignment change. In other words, these statements refer only to syntactic change; they do not rule out the possibility of two cases merging by morphological or phonological change, as the nominative and accusative of Old English nouns merged to a single form. For example, exclusion (vi) does not rule out the possibility that cases D and A merge morphologically or phonologically, with all instances of both realized in a single manner. Similarly, the statements are not intended to rule out examples where a case has previously extended to additional nominals; for example, exclusion (vi) is not intended to rule out the possibility that case A has previously been extended to the subject of transitives in environment₁, but only the extension of A *directly from the system depicted in table 9.5.*

31 This is further explained in Payne (1980: especially section 1.2).

32 The alignment of Proto-Pamir is reconstructed by Payne, though the same system is attested for other Iranian languages (see Payne 1980: 152).

33 Dench (1982) proposes a similar analysis of an independent change in the Ngayarda languages of Australia.

34 See, for example, M. Harris (1978: 19) on this change. There are certain contexts in which *a* can be used with a direct object that does not satisfy the conditions stated here.

35 In connection with this Spanish example, one may think also of the spread of the genitive just to animate masculine direct objects in Russian. However, this is a morphological change, not a syntactic one: the form derived from the genitive occurs in all functions where the accusative occurs (for example, as the object of certain prepositions), not just in the marking of direct objects.

   A real parallel to the Spanish example is found in Marathi. Rosen and Wali (1989) show that the dative suffix *-laa* marks all indirect objects, animate direct objects, and animate subjects of passives. The first two are complementary by condition (ii) and are parallel to Spanish; the second and third are complementary by condition (iii).

36 Austin (1982) describes six Australian languages, each with a small set of verbs that are, in one way or another, outside the more general case-marking patterns of the

language. In each language, the two sets of nominals are in a relationship of complementarity. If it is assumed that the uses of the case at issue are related historically, and if the direction of change is from more general to less general, then these are additional examples of partial recipients. There are many additional examples of partial recipients.

37 The conditions governing the use of the partitive and the accusative are described in Itkonen (1979: 90). The nominative marks direct objects when the subject is genitive or when there is no overt subject, as in the imperative; the use of the nominative for the object is not discussed further here.

38 This use of the partitive case itself is not original, but according to Itkonen (1979: 90) the partitive was already established in this function by early Proto-Finnic (see also chapter 12).

39 This change extending the partitive subject to transitive sentences with direct objects has also taken place in Veps under similar circumstances, as seen in:

(i)   endẹ   kika-t   pidel-ī-bad   moŕźm-ī-d'
        before bonnet-PL.PART wear-PAST-3RD.PL bride-PL-PART
        "Earlier, young married women wore bonnets."

(See Hakulinen 1968: 415; especially Hakulinen and Karlsson 1979: 166–70; and Laanest 1982: 296.)

40 Some of these problems are discussed in Dixon (1979: 103ff.), Harris (1982: 301–3), and Rosen (1984).

10 On the development of complex constructions

1 We are grateful to an anonymous reviewer of our grant application for helping us to focus our inquiry on this issue.

2 The words *tu ara* mean "or not" and may be used in an alternative question, such as (i), or in certain types of subordinate clause:

(i)   midixar, tu ara?
        you-go   or not
        "Are you going or not?"

Hewitt (1987: 209–11) proposes a similar, but more completely worked out, analysis of the development of relative clauses in Georgian. In both instances it is not altogether clear whether renewal or ultimate origin is intended.

3 It might be argued that the question that preceded the hypotactic structure was a rhetorical question, instead of an actual request for information. But a rhetorical question is a way to introduce information, a request for information that is filled by the speaker/writer, rather than by the interlocutor. This is clearly not the function served by the clause containing the interrogative/relative pronoun in example (1).

4 Extension following this reanalysis is described in the next section. A related innovation in German was the introduction into relative clauses of definite articles, themselves derived from the demonstrative *das*, as well as from the corresponding masculine and feminine forms.

5 Another example of reanalysis of subordinate clause structure with change of constituency is reanalysis of Georgian *romel* "which" as a complementizer, with

reduction to *rom* "that," as described in chapter 4. It also involved reanalysis of the relative pronoun *romel* as a relative particle; that is, in its new function its form was invariant. It also underwent the changes described for other languages in section 10.3.2, being extended from relative clauses to virtually all subordinate clause types.

Mithun (1988) gives a variety of sources of coordinating conjunctions, most of them presumably derived through reanalysis.

6 Sankoff and Brown (1976) suggest that a deictic pronoun in Tok Pisin was extended to marking relative clauses via a somewhat different pathway. Additional discussion of the use of deictic pronouns in relative clauses may be found in Ertelišvili (1963: ch. 4).

7 A further example of the extension of a complementizer is Georgian *rom* "that." In Old Georgian (fifth century) declinable *romeli* "which" functioned as both a Q-word and a relative pronoun. While *romeli* remains in both functions, a clipped undeclinable version developed, first *rome*, then *rom*, often pronounced today as *ro*. It has been extended to prenominal relatives (as well as occurring in the original postnominal variety), to new types of relative clause, to noun clauses, and to most types of adverbial clause (Harris, in press b). For other examples see Disterheft (1980: 183) and sources cited there on Indo-Iranian languages, Thurneyson (1946: 316ff.) on Old Irish, and Friedrich (1960: 163ff.) on Hittite.

8 Other languages that have extended quotatives to certain other subordinating functions include Georgian, where the construction in (i) makes use of the quotative *-o*.

(i)   . . . t'arieli mixvda, revolvers iɣebs-o
         Tariel   realized revolver he.takes-QUO
         " . . . Tariel realized that he was taking out a revolver."
                                                       (Čikobava *et al.* 1950–64, III: 778)

See also ʒiʒiguri (1973: 167–8) and Hewitt (1987: 113–15, 116, 219–21) on Georgian; Hewitt (1987: 41, 120–1, 215) on Abxaz. According to Akiba (1978: 89–92), Japanese *to* is a quotative particle; her examples 3.66–3.68 show it used as a complementizer with verbs other than those of speaking.

9 This use of *-š-k'ule* and of the genitive case is believed to be borrowed from Turkish; of course, that does not change the fact that case markers and postpositions that originated as markers of noun phrase functions have been extended to mark subordination. In the comparable Turkish constructions, postpositions are used with non-finite forms, while in Laz a variety of non-finite forms are eschewed in favor of finite forms; see section 6.5.1.

10 Holisky (1991: 419–20) lists the following postpositions that can be used as subordinators in Laz: *-k'ele* "towards," *-steri* "like; as soon as," *-šaki(s)* "until, up to; until, as long as," *-šeni* "for; since," *-(u)k'ule* "after, afterwards; after, when," *yerine, yeis* "in place of, instead of; in the place where." Examples with some of these are given (1991: 460–1). She notes that it is thought that not only the genitive and allative, but also the dative serve as a subordinator (1991: 460). Just as *-še-ni* consists (at least etymologically) of the marker of the ablative plus the postposition *-ni*, *-ša-ki(s)* is probably allative plus *-kis* (and both are identified in this way by Čikobava 1936a: 65–6); it is possible that *-steri* also incorporates the dative marker *-s*.

11 In Laz, various kinds of complementizers may occur clause-initially, clause-finally,

or in "floating position" between the first constituent and the verb (Harris 1989); here we have simply placed Comp in the position *-š-k'ule* actually occupies.

12 We are not considering *do*-support a device for forming questions in English, not because it is used with other devices, but because it is not used in all questions, such as those in (i), and because it *is* used in non-questions, such as (ii):

(i)   is that all?
        have you done your homework?
        can you speak Swahili?
(ii)   I didn't get there in time
        I did get there in time (emphatic or contrastive)

13 Lomtatiʒe does not mention in connection with this intonation the rise in pitch that characterizes questions. According to Nižaraʒe (1975: 66–7), long vowels are also formed in Ačarian when two like short vowels fall together, but this does not account for vowel length in (37b). Nižaraʒe (1975: 162) describes stress and lengthening in Ačarian questions as falling on the penultimate syllable, rather than on the final, as in other dialects.

14 We are grateful to Jaklin Kornfilt for examples (27) and (38) and for discussing this phenomenon with us.

15 We are grateful to Annie Lloyd for providing information about American Sign Language.

16 Hooper and Thompson (1973: 477) do not use the term **uncommitted assertion**, but write of certain examples that "the speaker is indicating that he is not fully committed to the truth of the assertion." It is sentences of this type that we term uncommitted assertions. Compare the "hedged assertion" of Lakoff (1984).

17 We assume here the definition of presupposition offered by Keenan (1971), which Hooper and Thompson also accept. See note 20 below.

18 While it is not our goal to provide a complete semantic characterization of subordinate sentence types, it appears that three factors contribute to a parenthetic reading: (i) complement preposing; (ii) absence of complementizer *that*; and (iii) first person singular subject and present tense.

19 Hooper and Thompson (1973: 486–8) present arguments that we and others have found convincing opposing the view that non-restrictive relatives presuppose, as developed in Keenan (1971: 45–6).

20 The clauses in (57), like those in (58), meet Keenan's (1971: 45) two-part definition of presupposition:

> A sentence S is said to be a logical consequence of a set of sentences S* just in case S is true in every world (that is, under all the conditions) in which all the sentences of S* are true. In such a case we also say that S follows logically from S*, and that S* logically implies S.
>
> A sentence S logically presupposes a sentence S' just in case S logically implies S' and the negation of S, ~S, also logically implies S'.

21 An assertion *because* clause ordinarily seems to require comma intonation, while this intonation is optional with the non-assertion *because* clause. This partial distinction is not made for the *although* clause.

22 Lehmann (1988: 194) suggests that assertion readings for *because* clauses are possible only when the main clause is affirmative indicative, but we do not agree with this assessment. In his example (23b), repeated as (i), the *because* clause can be an assertion, even though the matrix clause is interrogative; the meaning is then something like "Did you steal the caviar(?), I ask because I know that you were hungry."

(i)   did you steal the caviar [,] because you were hungry?

Contrary to his claim, the *because* clause may be assertive even when the matrix clause is negated, as illustrated in (ii):

(ii)   you didn't steal the caviar [,] *because* I was with you the whole time

23 That a question device can be extended at all to assertions follows as a consequence of the fact, discussed above, that a subordinator can be extended from one type of subordinate clause to another type.
24 Keenan and Hull (1973b: 350) say in what follows the passage quoted above that the question, (68), and the cleft, not illustrated here, presuppose that Mary invited someone, while the relative clause, (69), "only refers when Mary invited someone." See section 10.4.2.1 above and note 20.
25 It is difficult to justify a claim that subjunctive actually marks subordination, since a subjunctive occurs in a main clause in (72) and since the subordinate clause in (i) below (similar to (73)) contains no subjunctive.

(i)   mir scheint, er ist   böse
       me seems   he is.INDIC angry
       "To me it seems that he is angry."   (Paul/Stolte 1949: 353)

Nevertheless, through the frequency of its correlation with subordination, the subjunctive may help to alert the hearer/reader that a given clause may be embedded.
26 First person quotatives would be a systematic exception, marking speaker assertions.
27 In some instances this is put in the more general context of differences between literate and oral societies; see, for example, Ong (1982: 36–8).
28 A recent example of parataxis can be heard in a commercial for Dial soap airing on American television from 1991–3, in which the announcer declares

(i)   you got kids? you got germs!

The intonation after the word *kids* is neither that of a declarative nor that of a question, but suggests instead that these two clauses constitute a single sentence. The content reaffirms this, since the former appears to be conditional to the latter.
29 Actually, the study reported in Chafe (1982) compares formal written language with informal spoken languages, and we therefore cannot be certain of whether the higher percentage of hypotaxis he finds characterizes written language, formal language, or only the intersection of the two. He promises a more complete comparison in later work.
30 O'Neil does not use the term *parataxis*, but rather *clause adjunction*; he makes it clear that he views the relative clause at the earliest period of English as immediately dominated by the matrix clause, not by NP. That is, it is subordinate, not paratactic, but not subordinate to NP.

31 M. Harris does not suggest that this is a basis for supposing that relatives are a late development.

32 Lehmann (1980: 116) makes also the important point that it is not reasonable to assume a primitive stage when human beings knew only simple clauses.

33 The same point is made by Lightfoot in a footnote (1979a: 30).

34 If there exist languages without non-finite verb forms, such forms can be derived through derivational processes, which exist in every known natural language.

35 Of course, it has been proposed that adjectives like *yellow* have a sentential source synchronically, at least when they are used attributively. Regarding *table*, if you take into consideration the fact that you can verb any noun in English, then in English any noun, which is potentially a verb, has the potential to be reanalyzed as a clause. In many other languages this would not be true.

36 See the appendix on language families for the relationships of Udi to other languages in the North East Caucasian family.

37 There is circumstantial evidence that this development of finite relative clauses was influenced by Azeri, Armenian, and/or Georgian, each of them a language unrelated to Udi with which Udi has been in contact for long periods of time. If this is correct, it does not change the fact that the change in Udi required an internal mechanism, which we explore here. It is difficult or impossible to find any change in any language where the possibility of the influence of another language can be categorically excluded.

38 This does not deny the existence of main-clause phenomena, but assumes that there are inherent properties of clauses that block the application of certain rules, rather than that a language develops a set of constraints that block application of those rules.

39 Of course, this does not imply that such structures could occur with any predicate, but rather only with those predicates that are capable of taking abstract arguments in the relevant function.

11 The nature of syntactic change and the issue of causation

1 The issues of the regularity and directionality of syntactic change have most often been discussed in the context of reconstruction (see Jeffers 1976b: 4; Miranda 1976: 14; Norman and Campbell 1978; Lightfoot 1979a: 10; Campbell and Mithun 1980; Winter 1984: 619). In this chapter we discuss regularity and directionality simply as aspects of the nature of syntactic change, and in chapter 12 we relate both issues to reconstruction.

2 These play no direct role in syntactic change, but are extremely important in the explanation of sound change: for example, the typical change which voices stops between vowels is in some senses explained by reference to the limitations of human muscle control, which tends to maintain the vibration of the vocal cords (inherent in vowels) across the intervening consonant.

3 To continue the parallel with examples from phonological change, the frequent change in which nasalized vowels are lowered is explained by the fact that under nasalization vowel height tends to be perceived as lower. Thus [ɛ̃] tends to be perceived as [æ̃], for example.

4 Heine and Reh (1984: 66) suggest that "Morphosyntactic processes may trigger

phonetic processes, but not vice versa." The examples we adduce show that that proposal is incorrect.

5 Malkiel (1981) clarified a number of different meanings of "drift," as well as the notions "slope" and "slant." The meaning we are referring to here is parallel developments within a single language.

6 While some might object to the teleological sound of this description, there is, in fact, no serious problem with this metaphoric mode of description. Most of the instances so described can be recast in non-teleological terms, and the explanatory value is secure in any case (see Campbell and Ringen 1981).

7 Another famous example is that of Classical Greek, which lost s between vowels ($s > \emptyset$ / V_V) except in certain future and aorist forms, where loss of s by regular sound change would have obliterated the form of the future; its loss was prevented, and as a result the future and present remain distinct. However the s of the future was freely lost in verbs ending in a nasal or a liquid, where the future/present distinction could be signaled formally by the e of these future stems. The difference between the two sorts of verbs is seen in:

> *lu-ō* "I loosen"   *stel-le* "I send"
> *lū-s-ō* "I will loosen"   *stele-ō* "I will send"

The needs of the "meaning" pole in this case prevented the change where the future would have lost the form necessary to signal its function, but it was not prevented elsewhere, where the meaning difference could still be signalled.

8 A statement of affiliations helps in understanding this example; see the appendix on language families.

9 Much of the following discussion of prediction follows that of Campbell and Ringen (1981).

10 Even Lass (1980: 103) gives lip service to the fact that "a single event may not have a single cause, but rather a set of causes," but here he is reporting Mayr (1968) on biology, and this recognition plays no significant part in Lass' overall negative argument about prediction. Rather, he finds that "in more complex systems (e.g. ecological interactions) the success rate of prediction is much lower, and interesting patterns of indeterminacy arise" (Lass 1980: 105), and "at the low end of the gradient, prediction of evolutionary outcomes is virtually impossible" (p. 105).

11 Recently this change has begun to be reversed by change in the environment. Strong environmental laws have had the effect of reducing the soot and permitting the lichen on which the moths lived to return (*Discover* 11: 20). In this instance the ongoing evolutionary change now nearing completion could more nearly have been predicted because (i) it could be assumed that whiteness remained in the gene pool, and (ii) the environmental change was planned and controlled.

12 We intend to limit the epithet "random" to what we term **exploratory expressions** in chapter 3; we do not mean to suggest here that all syntactic change is random.

13 In other dialects the morphology may differ, especially that of the verb forms.

14 In Finnish the partitive case is used with partially affected objects, and this partitive is employed in both dialects discussed here.

15 A verb, "s/he sledded," may have either subject case in the Nak'ra-Laxamula subdialect (*ädčarxal(e)*), only the narrative in the Upper Bal dialect (*läičirxāle*), but – exceptionally – only the nominative in the Lašx dialect (*edčīrxān*). The last-named

form is a relic of the original ergative case marking; the variation in Nak'ra-Laxamula represents a transitional stage; and the Upper Bal form represents the change in case marking undergone by all Svan (sub)dialects other than Nak'ra-Laxamula. (The difference between the *äd/ed-* forms and the *lä-* form is due to the verb root governing different preverbs in the different dialects.)

16 Compare the A and B versions, which have the same word order but add a postposition: *mam-isa šen-isa mimart* "father-GEN your-GEN towards." Different cases and/or different pronouns occur in other examples but show the same word order: *mama-y igi šeni* (Mt. 6: 6 Ad.) "father-NOM the.NOM your.NOM," *mama-y šeni* (Mt. 6: 6 AB) "father-NOM your.NOM," *mama-o čven-o* (Mt. 6: 9 Ad.AB) "father-VOC, our-VOC."

17 While the possessor has become enclitic, the fact that all three persons and both numbers of the possessor pronoun occur with the lexical items *mama* "father," *deda* "mother," etc. show that these lexical items are exceptions to the ordinary word order, not lexicalized compounds. If these were lexical compounds, we would expect instead to find only certain arbitrary combinations, rather than the full system of possibilities.

18 This remark applies to his typology of alignment only; the changes in alignment have not been accompanied by the other changes in language structure that would confirm his general hypothesis.

19 A more complete discussion of Klimov's theory of directional change in language types can be found in Comrie (1976) and in Harris (1985: 415–20).

20 Although we treat Maxwell's schema as a "claim" of unidirectionality, it is not quite true to say that he *claims* that change within types of relativization strategies is unidirectional; he rather *assumes* it. Having made this assumption, he sets out to find out what develops into what (among other aims): for example, on page 149 he states, apparently without reference to particular languages, "the NR-S is the forerunner of the REL-S" and on page 151, "the NR-S tends to recede and be replaced by the REL-S, and this in turn tends to recede and be replaced by postnom GAP-S." With this caveat, we continue to interpret this as a strong claim about language change, for by testing such claims against known examples, we can deepen our understanding of language.

21 Such a claim is made only for Latin by Janson (1979: 115–19) and more generally by Vincent (1980: 58), "Lexical items may be grammaticalized, but grammatical items [d]o not become lexicalized." These citations are only suggestive, however, for the claim is widespread.

22 Joseph and Janda (1988) provide a discussion and examples both of "demorphologization" into syntax and of "demorphologization" into phonology. They propose an explanation of the greater tendency towards morphologization (from both syntax and phonology) in terms of the centrality of morphology in the grammar.

23 Other examples of changes reported in the literature that appear to reverse the first arrow in schema 4 include decliticization of the subject pronoun in the history of English, as argued by Kroch, Myhill, and Pintzuk (1982: especially pp. 287 and 289ff.; see van Kemenade 1987, especially ch. 4 on clitic status of pronouns in Old English) and decliticization of a number of "connective" particles in the history of Japanese (Matsumoto 1988). Jeffers and Zwicky (1980) summarize the history of

much-discussed Indo-European clitics that separated from their hosts to serve as the basis for accented pronouns. Several examples discussed in section 8.5.1.3 ("Reordering to non-adjacency") are other possible examples of decliticization, though in some cases the status of a morpheme as a clitic cannot be satisfactorily established. A related example is the change in which certain Spanish particles form the basis for new verbs; in Central American dialects, for example, *dentro* "inside" became the root of *dentrar* "to insert," while more generally in Spanish *sobre* "over, on, above" became *sobrar* "to be extra, leftover."

24 Another example of an affix becoming what appears to be a clitic is Slavic decoupling of the conditional auxiliary from its inflectional affixes in certain rare examples (Abel 1975: 6–7).

25 Old English was an exception, retaining the stem formant: NOM, ACC *lemb* "lamb," GEN *lombur*, DAT *lombur* (Krahe and Meid 1969: 43–4).

26 Another example of this type is adduced by Alekseev (1985: 41–3, 1987), where it is argued that the formant of the oblique stem (a derivational morpheme) is reanalyzed as the marker of the ergative case (an inflectional morpheme) in Rutul, Kryts, Budux, and Udi.

27 In this discussion, **partial** refers to the meaning, as in English *some of the water*; **partitive** refers to a grammatical expression usually employed for partially affected objects.

28 It appears, rather, that Greenberg intends to claim that this is the single ordinary source of gender class markers and of case markers, though he acknowledges instances where these seem to have other sources (1978: 74).

29 We are grateful to John Greppin for help with the Armenian facts and interpretation.

30 Since some languages mark direct objects only when they are definite or only when they are specific, leaving them unmarked when they are indefinite (viz. non-specific), it seems possible that under extraordinary circumstances, the accusative case marker might be reanalyzed as a definite article, then be generalized. If this occurred, it would be an example of reversing the direction of schema 6. We know of no example of this occurring.

31 The change of [s] to [h] is an example of a unidirectional change that is not necessarily context-sensitive.

12 Reconstruction of syntax

1 By some accounts these are not distinct languages at all, but dialects of one language. See discussion in Harris (1991a: 10–11).

2 These grammatical relations are established on the basis of shared syntactic properties; see Harris (1985, 1991b) and Holisky (1991).

3 A small number of exceptions to these patterns are described in Harris (1985: 116–19).

4 This is not intended to imply that all of the contemporary Romance languages apply the same criteria to the NA/AN variation; differences among the languages in this respect are summarized in M. Harris (1978: 59). For a summary of other views on the timing of this change see our section 8.5.2.1 and sources cited there.

5 This example is based on the further assumption that the historical data are too

close in time to the contemporary to permit the changes NA > AN > NA as a practical possibility.

6 While GN is the unmarked order in Zan, the order noun–genitive is possible, as illustrated in the Mingrelian example (i) (Čikobava 1936a: 67–72; Lomtaȝe 1954):

(i)   uc'u   vezir muši-s
        he.say vizier his.GEN-DAT
        "He said to his vizier . . ."   (Lomtaȝe 1954: 209)

7 The expressions in (16) are not compounds, as shown by the fact that all other persons and numbers of the possessive pronoun may be substituted here (Čikobava 1936a: 68, Lomtaȝe 1954: 227).

8 The possibility that the expressions in (16) are simply calques of Georgian (17) is much reduced by the fact that in Georgian, *ȝma* "brother" is not used in this construction as its cognate is in Zan (16b) (Čikobava 1936a: 68).

9 We do well also to recognize the limits of the usefulness of morphological reconstruction applied to syntactic reconstruction. In Harris (1985: ch. 4) it is shown that reconstruction of the morphology of case marking in the Kartvelian languages contributes little to an understanding of the syntactic distribution of those cases.

10 We do not take up here certain issues sometimes presumed to be serious obstacles to syntactic reconstruction (some of which have been addressed in other portions of this book). For example, some cite limitations on available data (e.g. lack of earlier attested stages or gaps in the corpus of available texts for dead languages) as a serious problem (e.g. Lightfoot 1979a: 5–7). The quality of the available information is an important consideration in all historical enterprises, and has no special status in historical syntax; one does the best one can with the extant material. In the many instances where one compares the grammars of living languages, serious gaps in the data should not be a serious problem, since they could be filled in with additional investigation. The same comment holds for the lament about the lack of native speaker intuitions for dead languages; one has to work with what is available. With living languages, one can be on firmer ground; with texts one has to employ careful philological techniques. (See chapter 1, note 16.)

11 Finnish has relics of the partitive's former ablative functions. The modern "separation" cases are -*stA* "from within" and -*ltA* "from without," the result of fusion of the old ablative *-*ta* and locatives *-*s* and *-*l*. However, relics of *-*ta* "ablative" are found in some pronouns and postpositions, even in combination with nouns and adjectives which bear the new separation cases. For example (note *t is lost intervocalically after a short unstressed vowel, giving the allomorphs -*ta* and -*a*, -*tä* and -*ä*):

(i)   *sii*-**tä** talo-sta [it-From house-From] "from that house"
        talo-n taka-**a** [house-GEN back-From] "from behind the house"
        isä-n luo-**ta** [father-GEN presence-From] "from father's presence"

This former ablative value is also seen in certain sayings, such as

(ii)   (a) mies on suur-ta   suku-a
              man is big-PART family-PART
              "The man is from an important family."

       (b) veitsi on teräs-tä
             knife is steel-PART
             "The knife is (made) out of steel."

       (c) mi-tä   mieh-i-ä   te ole-tte?
             what-PART man-PL-PART you are-you
             "What kind of men are you?"

       (d) kärsiä   nälkä-ä
             to.suffer hunger-PART
             "to suffer from hunger"

       (e) ontua jalka-a
             to.limp foot-PART
             "to limp due to one's foot"(Hakulinen 1968: 437; Laanest 1982: 299)

Another relic is seen in the Finnish comparative construction, which employs the partitive case as a holdover from a former ablative sense:

(iii)   Jussi   on sinu-a   vanhe-mpi
       Jussi.NOM is you-PART old-COMPARISON
       "Jussi is older than you (are)."

12 It has sometimes been thought that the Balto-Finnic partitive may be due to foreign influence. Whether the partitive is the result of an independent innovation or areal convergence, it clearly does not represent the Proto-Uralic pattern and consequently the reconstruction is not affected one way or the other by what may have caused this innovative departure from the pattern of the proto-language. See Korhonen (1981: 214–15) on the development of the plural accusative from the plural partitive in Lapp.

13 Dryer (1992) argues that it is not the Head–Dependent (Head–Modifier) relationship which accounts for word order harmonies, but rather that what is important is the direction of branching. That is, he argues, phrasal (branching) categories tend to precede non-phrasal (non-branching) categories in OV languages and vice versa in VO languages. We accept Dryer's arguments as probably quite sound, but do not recast the discussion here in his terms, since for the categories we examine the Head–Dependent view and Dryer's branching approach coincide in their prediction of word order dyads.

14 It is often assumed that SVO languages show much greater variation across these patterns than do, for example, SOV or VSO languages; however, Dryer (1992) argues persuasively that this is not so. Either way, these data can prove useful in reconstruction.

15 Of course, one cannot *a priori* rule out the less likely possibility that some third word order was original, with both changing. However, with only two possibilities for most of the correlate orderings (e.g. either RelN or NRel), a third possible word order will not often be a problem.

16 See section 11.4.2.1 on Klimov's proposals; see Harris (1990b) on Gamkrelidze and
Ivanov's reconstructions of Proto-Indo-European and of Common Kartvelian on
the basis of Klimov's proposals.

17 See section 9.3 for a study of the question of alignment harmony. See Harris (1985:
17–18) for specific arguments against basing reconstruction of alignment of one
rule on the alignment of another.

18 While Finnish scholars agree in attributing the change to Swedish influence, it is
not difficult to imagine that the weight of the nominative subject pattern of the non-
obligation verbs has also exerted pressure for these to conform to the larger class,
as well: for example, Estonian and Votic also have "personal" verbs (with nomina-
tive-subjects) in this case, normally attributed to Germanic influence. In any event,
for the purposes of reconstruction it is ultimately of no real consequence whether
the Western Finnish (and the Estonian and Votic) personal pattern (with nominative subjects) is borrowed or due to internal reanalysis, since in either case these are
seen to deviate from the pattern of the other cognate dialects (and languages,
where earlier states are attested in documents), leading us to base our reconstruction on the clear, widespread correspondence, not on the one deviation from it
which otherwise has very plausible explanations for how and why it changed.

19 Based on this, Bloomfield (1928: 100) concluded: "As an assumption, however, the
postulate [of sound-change without exception] yields, as a matter of mere routine,
predictions which otherwise would be impossible. In other words, the statement
that *phonemes change* (sound-changes have no exceptions) is a tested hypothesis: in
so far as one may speak of such a thing, it is a proved truth."

References

Aarsleff, Hans. 1974. The tradition of Condillac: the problem of the origin of language in the eighteenth century and the debate in the Berlin Academy before Herder. In Dell Hymes (ed.), *Studies in the history of linguistics: traditions and paradigms*, 93–156. Bloomington: Indiana University Press.

1982. *From Locke to Saussure: essays on the study of language and intellectual history.* Minneapolis: University of Minnesota Press.

1988. Introduction. In Wilhelm von Humboldt, *On language: the diversity of human language-structure and its influence on the mental development of mankind*, trans. Peter Heath, vii–lxv. Cambridge University Press.

Abailard, Pierre (Peter Abelard). 1970 [*c*.1130]. *Dialectica*, ed. L. M. de Rijk, 2nd edn. (Philosophical Texts and Studies, 1.) Assen, Holland: Van Gorcum.

Abel, V.P. 1975. The transposition of pronominal and verbal enclitics in the Štokavic dialect of Serbo-Croat. *The Slavonic and East European Review* 53:130.1–16.

Abesaʒe, Nia. 1965. Hip'ot'aksis c'evr-k'avširebi da k'avširebi megrulši. [Subordinating conjunctions in Mingrelian.] *Tbilisis Saxelmc'ipo Universit'et'is Šromebi* 114.229–57.

Abraham, Werner, Laci Marácz, Sjaak de Meij, and Wim Scherpenisse. 1986. Introduction. In Werner Abraham and Sjaak de Meij (eds.), *Topic, focus and configurationality*, 1–13. Amsterdam: John Benjamins.

Abrams, Norm. 1961. Word base classes in Bilaan. *Lingua* 10.391–402.

1970. Bilaan morphology. *Papers in Philippine Linguistics*, 3 (Pacific Linguistics, Series A, Occasional Papers, no. 24). Canberra). 1–62.

Abulaʒe, Ilia. 1973. *Ʒveli kartuli enis leksik'oni.* [Dictionary of the Old Georgian language.] Tbilisi: Mecniereba.

Adamec, Přžemysl. 1966. Porjadok slov v sovremennom russkom jazyke. *Rozpravy československé akademie věd, Rada společenských věd*, 76, no. 15.

Adelung, Johann Christoph. 1781. *Deutsche Sprachlehre; zum Gebrauche der Schulen in den Königlich-Preussischen Landen, mit allergnädigsten Privilegien.* Berlin: C. F. Voss.

1782a. Beweis der fortschreiten den Cultur des menschlichen Geistes aus der Vergleichung der älteren Sprachen mit den neueren. *Magasin für die deutsche Sprache*, vol. 1. Leipzig.

1782b. *Umständliches Lehregebäude der Deutschen Sprache: zur Erklärung der Deutschen Sprachlehre für Schulen.* 2 vols. Leipzig: Johan Gottlob Immanuel Breitkopf. (Facsimile edn., 1971. Hildesheim: G. Olms.)

1806–17. *Mithridates, oder allgemeine Sprachenkunde mit dem Vater Unser als Sprachprobe in bei nahe fünfhundert Sprachen und Mundarten.* 4 vols. Berlin: Voss.

Aissen, Judith L. 1992. Topic and focus in Mayan. *Language* 68.43–80.

Aitchison, Jean. 1979. The order of word order change. *Transactions of the Philological Society*, 43–65.

1980. Review of David Lightfoot, *Principles of diachronic syntax*. *Linguistics* 18.137–46.

1981. *Language change: progress or decay?* London: Fortuna.

1983. On the roots of language. *Language and Communication* 3.83–97.

1987. The language lifegame: prediction, explanation and linguistic change. In Willem Koopman, Frederike van der Leek, Olga Fischer, and Roger Eaton (eds.), *Explanation and linguistic change*, 11–32. Amsterdam: John Benjamins.

Akiba, Katsue. 1978. A historical study of Old Japanese syntax. UCLA dissertation.

Alekseev, M.E. 1985. *Voprosy sravnitel'no-istoričeskoj grammatiki lezginskix jazykov: morfologija, sintaksis*. Moscow: Nauka.

Allan, W. Scott. 1987. Lightfoot noch einmal. *Diachronica* 4.123–57.

Allen, Cynthia Louise. 1974. Old English modals. In Jane Grimshaw (ed.), *Papers in the history and structure of English*, 89–100. Amherst: University of Massachusetts.

1980 [1977]. Topics in diachronic English syntax. University of Massachusetts dissertation, 1977. (Published 1980. New York: Garland.)

1986. Reconsidering the history of *like*. *Journal of Linguistics* 22.375–409.

Allen, W.S. 1950. A study in the analysis of Hindi sentence structure. *Acta Linguistica* 6.68–86.

1953. Relationship in comparative linguistics. *Transactions of the Philological Society*, 52–109.

Alvar, Manuel and Bernard Pottier. 1987. *Morfología histórica del español*. Madrid: Gredos.

Andersen, Henning. 1973. Abductive and deductive change. *Language* 49.765–93.

1974. Towards a typology of change: bifurcating changes and binary relations. In J.M. Anderson and C. Jones (eds.), *Historical linguistics: proceedings of the first International Conference on Historical Linguistics*, vol. II: *Theory and description in phonology*, 17–60. Amsterdam: North Holland.

1980. Morphological change: toward a typology. In Jacek Fisiak (ed.), *Historical morphology*, 1–50. The Hague: Mouton.

1989. Understanding linguistic innovations. In Leiv Egil Breivik and Ernst Håkon Jahr (eds.), *Language change: contributions to the study of its causes*, 5–27. Berlin: Mouton de Gruyter.

Andersen, Paul Kent. 1979. Word order typology and prepositions in Old Indic. In Bela Brogyanyi (ed.), *Studies in diachronic, synchronic, and typological linguistics: festschrift for Oswald Szemerényi on the occasion of his 65th birthday*, part I, 23–34. Amsterdam: John Benjamins.

Anderson, John M. 1986. A note on Old English impersonals. *Journal of Linguistics* 22.167–77.

Anderson, Marjorie and Blanche Colton Williams. 1935. *Old English handbook*. Boston: Houghton Mifflin.

Anderson, Stephen R. 1976. On the description of consonant gradation in Fula. *Studies in African Linguistics* 7.93–136.

1977. On the mechanisms by which languages become ergative. In Charles N. Li (ed.), *Mechanisms of syntactic change*, 317–63. Austin: University of Texas Press.

1980. On the development of morphology from syntax. In Jacek Fisiak (ed.), *Historical morphology*, 51–70. The Hague: Mouton.

1981. Topicalization in Breton. *Proceedings of the Berkeley Linguistic Society* 7.27–39.

1988. Morphological change. In Frederick J. Newmeyer (ed.), *Linguistics: the Cambridge survey*, vol. I, 324–62. Cambridge University Press.

1992. *A-morphous morphology.* Cambridge University Press.

1993. Wackernagel's revenge: clitics, morphology, and the syntax of second position. *Language* 69.68–98.

Anderson Stephen R., and Sandra Chung. 1977. On grammatical relations and clause structure in verb–initial languages. In Peter Cole and Jerrold M. Sadock (eds.), *Grammatical relations* (Syntax and Semanatics 8), 1–25. New York: Academic Press.

Andɣulaʒe, N. 1968. *Kʼlasovani da pʼirovani uɣvlilebis istʼoriis zogi sakʼitxi iberiul–kʼavkʼasiur enebši.* [Some questions of the history of class and person conjugation in the Ibero-Caucasian languages.] Tbilisi: Mecniereba.

Andresen, Julie Tetel. 1990. *Linguistics in America 1769–1924: a critical history.* London: Routledge.

Andrews, J. Richard. 1975. *Introduction to Classical Nahuatl.* Austin: University of Texas Press.

Anonymous. 1720 [1692]. Cakchiquel grammar. (Ed. and publ. Daniel G. Brinton. 1884. A grammar of the Cakchiquel language of Guatemala. *Proceedings of the American Philosophical Society* 21.345–412.)

Antinucci, Francesco and Annarita Publielli. 1984. Relative clause construction in Somali: a comparison between the Northern and Coastal dialects. In James Bynon (ed.), *Current progress in Afro-Asiatic linguistics: papers of the third Hamito-Semitic Congress*, 17–31. Amsterdam: John Benjamins.

Antonsen, Elmer H. 1975. *A concise grammar of the older Runic inscriptions.* Tübingen: Niemeyer.

Anttila, Raimo. 1972. *An introduction to historical and comparative linguistics.* New York: Macmillan. (2nd edn. 1989. Amsterdam: John Benjamins.)

1976. *Analogy.* The Hague: Mouton.

1985. Dynamics in morphology. *Acta Linguistica Academiae Hungaricae* 35.3–20.

Appel, René and Pieter Muysken. 1987. *Language contact and bilingualism.* London: Edward Arnold.

Ard, William Josh. 1975. Raisings and word order in diachronic syntax. UCLA dissertation.

Arens, Hans. 1969. *Sprachwissenschaft: der Gang ihrer Entwicklung von der Antike bis zur Gegenwart*, 2nd edn. (1st edn. 1955.) Freiburg, Munich: Karl Alber.

Aristar, Anthony Rodrigues. 1991. On diachronic sources and synchronic pattern: an investigation into the origin of linguistic universals. *Language* 67.1–33.

Ariste, Paul. 1968. *A grammar of the Votic language.* (Uralic and Altaic Series, 68.) Bloomington: Indiana University Press.

Arnauld, Antoine and Claude Lancelot. 1660. *Grammaire générale et raisonée de Port Royal.* Paris: Pierre le Petit. (English translation: 1975. *General and rational grammar: the Port-Royal grammar*, ed. and trans. Jacques Rieux and Bernard E. Rolling. [Janua Linguarum, Series Minor, 208.] The Hague: Mouton.)

Asatiani, Irine. 1974. *Čanuri (lazuri) t'ekst'ebi.* [Laz texts.] Tbilisi: Mecniereba.

Auroux, Sylvain. 1990. Representation and the place of linguistic change before comparative grammar. In Tullio de Mauro and Lia Formigari (eds.), *Leibniz, Humboldt, and the origins of comparativism,* 213–38. Amsterdam: John Benjamins.

Austin, Peter. 1981a. Case marking and clausal binding: evidence from Dhalandji. *Chicago Linguistic Society* 17.1–7.

1981b. Switch–reference in Australia. *Language* 57.309–34.

1982. Transitivity and cognate objects in Australian languages. In Paul J. Hopper and Sandra A. Thompson (eds.), *Studies in transitivity,* 37–47. New York: Academic Press.

Babby, Leonard H. 1987. Case, prequantifiers, and discontinuous agreement in Russian. *Natural Language and Linguistic Theory* 5.91–138.

Baker, C.L. 1979. Syntactic theory and the projection problem. *Linguistic Inquiry* 10.533–81.

Baramiʒe, L. 1964. Zogierti t'ip'is mešvel-zmnian pormata časaxva da ganvitareba kartulši. [On the origin and development of certain types of auxiliary verb constructions in Georgian.] *Ʒveli kartuli enis k'atedris šromebi* 9, 95–150.

Bauer, Heinrich. 1833. *Vollständige Grammatik der neuhochdeutschen Sprache.* Berlin: G. Reimer. (Repr. 1967. Berlin: Walter de Gruyter.)

Bean, Marian C. 1983. *The development of word order patterns in relation to theories of word order change.* London: Croom Helm.

Beauzée, Nicolas. 1756. Langue. In Denis Diderot and Jean le Rond d'Alembert (eds.), *Encyclopédie ou dictionnaire raisonné des sciences, des arts et des métiers.* Paris. (New edn. 1961, introduction and annotations by Maurice Piron. Bruges: De Tempel; New Facsimile edn.: 1967. Stuttgart: Frommann.)

1767. *Grammaire générale ou exposition raisonnée des éléments nécessaires du langage pour servir de fondement à l'étude de toutes les langages.* 2 vols. Paris: J. Barbou. (Facsimile edn., introduction by B.E. Bartlett. 1974. [2 vols.] Stuttgart: Frommann.)

Bednarczuk, Leszek. 1980. Origin of Indo–European parataxis. In Paolo Ramat, Onofrio Carruba, Anna Giacalone Ramat, and Giorgio Graffi (eds.), *Linguistic reconstruction and IE syntax,* 145–54. Amsterdam: John Benjamins.

Behaghel, Otto. 1878. Die neuhochdeutschen Zwillingswörter. *Germania: Vierteljahrsschrift für deutsche Alterthumskunde* 23.11: 257–92.

1892. Zur deutschen Wortstellung. *Zeitschrift für die deutschen Unterricht* 6.265–7.

1909. Beziehungen zwischen Umfang und Reihenfolge von Satzgliedern. *Indogermanische Forschungen* 25.110–42.

1923–32. *Deutsche Syntax: eine geschichtliche Darstellung.* 4 vols. Heidelberg: Carl Winters Unversitätsbuchhandlung. [See especially vol. IV, 1932, *Siebtes Buch: die Wortstellung.*]

Beller, Richard and Patricia Beller. 1979. Huasteca Nahuatl. In Ronald W. Langacker (ed.), *Studies in Uto-Aztecan grammar,* vol. II: *Modern Aztec grammatical sketches,* 199–306. Arlington: Summer Institute of Linguistics and the University of Texas at Arlington.

Benfey, Theodor. 1860. Ein Abschnitt aus meiner Vorlesung über vergleichende Grammatik der indogermanischen Sprachen. *Zeitschrift für vergleichende Sprachforschung* 9.81–132.

Bennett, David C. 1986. Toward an explanation of word-order differences between Slovene and Serbo-Croat. The Slavonic and East European Review 64.1–24.

1987. Word–order change in progress: the case of Slovene and Serbo-Croat and its relevance for Germanic. *Journal of Linguistics* 23.269–87.

Bennett, Paul A. 1979. Observations on the transparency principle. *Linguistics* 17.843–61.

Benveniste, Emile. 1968. Mutations of linguistic categories. In Winfred Lehmann and Yakov Malkiel (eds.), *Directions for historical linguistics,* 83–94. Austin: University of Texas Press.

Bernecker, E. 1900. *Die Wortfolge in den slavischen Sprachen.* Berlin: Behr.

Bibliander (Buchmann), Theodor. 1548. *De ratione communi omnium linguarum et literarum commentarius.* Zurich: C. Froschauer.

Bickerton, Derek. 1981. *Roots of language.* Ann Arbor: Karoma

Biener, Clemens. 1922a. Zur Methode der Untersuchungen über deutsche Wortstellung. *Zeitschrift für deutsches Altertum und deutsche Literatur* 59.127–44.

1922b. Wie ist die neuhochdeutsche Regel über die Stellung des Verbums entstanden? *Zeitschrift für deutsches Altertum und deutsche Literatur* 59.165–79.

1926. Die Stellung des Verbums im Deutschen. *Zeitschrift für deutsches Altertum und deutsche Literatur* 63.225–56.

Birnbaum, Henrik. 1977. *Linguistic reconstruction: its potentials and limitations in new perspective. (Journal of Indo-European Studies,* Monograph 2.) Washington, DC: Institute for the Study of Man.

1984. Notes on syntactic change: cooccurrence vs. substitution, stability vs. permeability. In Jacek Fisiak (ed.), *Historical syntax,* 25–46. Berlin: Mouton.

Blake, Robert P. 1974. *The Old Georgian version of the Gospel of Mark.* (Patrologia Orientalis, 20, fascicle 3.) (1st edn., 1928.) Turnhout: Editions Brepols.

1976. *The Old Georgian version of the Gospel of Matthew.* (Patrologia Orientalis, 24, fascicle 1.) (1st edn., 1933.) Turnhout: Editions Brepols.

Blake, Robert P. and Maurice Brière. 1950. *The Old Georgian version of the Gospel of John.* (Patrologia Orientalis 26, fascicle 4.)

Bleichsteiner, Robert. 1919. *Kaukasische Forschungen: Georgische und mingrelische Texte.* Vienna: Verlag des Forschungsinstitutes für Osten und Orient.

Bloch, Jules. 1934. *L'Indo–aryen du Veda aux temps modernes.* Paris: Adrien-Maisonneuve. (English edn.: *Indo-Aryan: from the Vedas to modern times,* 1965, trans. Alfred Master. Paris: Librairie d'Amérique et d'Orient, Adrien-Maisonneuve.)

Bloomfield, Leonard. 1925. On the sound system of Central Algonquian. *Language* 1.130–56.

1928. A note on sound-change. *Language* 4.99–100.

Boas, Franz. 1930. Spanish elements in Modern Nahuatl. In John D. Fitz-Gerald and Pauline Taylor (eds.), *Todd memorial volume,* vol. I, 85–99. New York: Columbia University Press.

Boeder, Winfred. 1979. Ergative syntax and morphology in language change: the South Caucasian languages. In Frans Plank (ed.) *Ergativity: towards a theory of grammatical relations,* 435–80. New York: Academic Press.

Bopp, Franz. 1816. *Über das Conjugationssystem der Sanskritsprache in Vergleichung mit jenem der griechischen, lateinischen, persischen und germanischen Sprache, nebst*

Episoden des Ramajan und Mahabharat in genauen, metrischen Übersetzungen aus dem Originaltexte und einigen Abschnitten aus den Vedas. Frankfurt-on-Main: Andreäische Buchhandlung. (Repr. 1974. [Amsterdam Classics in Linguistics, 15.] Amsterdam: John Benjamins.)

1833–52. *Vergleichende Grammatik des Sanskrit, Zend, Armenischen, Griechischen, Lateinischen, Litauischen, Altslavischen, Gothischen und Deutschen.* 6 vols. Berlin: Ferdinand Dümmler.

1845–53[1833]. *Comparative grammar of the Sanscrit, Zend, Greek, Latin, Lithuanian, Gothic, German, and Slavonic languages.* (Translation of Bopp 1833 by Lieutenant Eastwick.) London: Madden and Malcolm.

Borsley, Robert D. and Janig Stephens. 1989. Agreement and the position of subjects in Breton. *Natural Language and Linguistic Theory* 7.407–27.

Borst, Arno. 1959. *Der Turmbau von Babel.* Stuttgart: Hiersemann.

Bradshaw, D. 1976. A compound solution. UCLA thesis. (Cited by Bean 1983.)

Breckenridge, Janet and Auli Hakulinen. 1976. Cycle and after. In Sanford B. Steever, Carol A. Walker, and Salikoko S. Mufwene (eds.), *Papers from the Parasession on Diachronic Syntax*, 50–68. Chicago Linguistic Socity.

Breivik, Leiv Egil. 1989. On the causes of syntactic change in English. In Leiv Egil Breivik and Ernst Håkon Jahr (eds.), *Language change: contributions to the study of its causes*, 29–70. Berlin: Mouton de Gruyter.

Breva–Claramonte, Manuel. 1983. *Sanctius' theory of language: a contribution to the history of Renaissance linguistics.* (Studies in the History of Linguistics, 27.) Amsterdam: John Benjamins.

Brink, Lars and Jørn Lund. 1975. *Dansk Regsmal.* Copenhagen: Gyldendal.

1979. Social factors in the sound changes of modern Danish. In Wolfgang Dressler and Wolfgang Meid (eds.), *Proceedings of the 12th International Congress of Linguists*, 196–203. Innsbruck: Institut für Sprachwissenschaft.

Brockway, Earl. 1979. North Puebla Nahuatl. In Ronald W. Langacker (ed.), *Studies in Uto–Aztecan grammar*, vol. II: *Modern Aztec grammatical sketches*, 141–98. Arlington: Summer Institute of Linguistics and the University of Texas at Arlington.

Brody, Jill. 1987. Particles borrowed from Spanish as discourse markers in Mayan languages. *Anthropological Linguistics* 29:4.507–21.

Brown, William H., Jr. 1970. *A syntax of King Alfred's "Pastoral Care."* The Hague: Mouton.

Brugman[n], Karl. 1878. Zur Geschichte der Personalendungen. *Morphologisiche Untersuchungen* 1.133–86.

1904. *Kurze vergleichende Grammatik der indogermanischen Sprachen.* Strasburg: Karl J. Trübner.

1925. *Die Syntax des einfachen Satzes im Indogermanischen.* Berlin and Leipzig: Walter de Gruyter.

Brunot, F. and C. Bruneau. 1933. *Précis de grammaire historique de la langue française, entièrement refondu.* Paris: Masson.

Bubenik, Vit. 1989a. An interpretation of split ergativity in Indo-Iranian languages. *Diachronica* 6.181–212.

1989b. On the origins and elimination of ergativity in Indo-Aryan languages. *Canadian Journal of Linguistics* 34.377–98.

Bursill-Hall, G. L. 1974. Toward a history of linguistics in the middle ages, 1100–1450. In Dell Hymes (ed.), *Studies in the history of linguistics: traditions and paradigms*, 77–92. Bloomington: Indiana University Press.

Burzio, Luigi. 1986. *Italian syntax: a government–binding approach*. Dordrecht: Reidel.

Butler, Milton Chadwick. 1977. Reanalysis of object as subject in Middle English impersonal constructions. *Glossa* 11.155–70.

Bybee, Joan L. 1988. The diachronic dimension in explanation. In John A. Hawkins (ed.), *Explaining language universals*, 350–79. Oxford: Basil Blackwell.

Bybee, Joan L. and William Pagliuca. 1984. Cross-linguistic comparison and the development of grammatical meaning. In Jacek Fisiak (ed.), *Historical semantics and historical word formation*, 59–83. Berlin: Mouton de Gruyter.

1987. The evolution of future meaning. In Anna G. Ramat and G. Bernini (eds.), *Papers from the seventh International Conference on Historical Linguistics*, 109–22. Amsterdam: John Benjamins.

Bybee, Joan L., William Pagliuca, and Revere D. Perkins. 1990. On the asymmetries in the affixation of grammatical material. In William Croft, Keith Denning, and Suzanne Kemmer (eds.), *Studies in typology and diachrony: papers presented to Joseph H. Greenberg on his 75th birthday*, 1–42. Amsterdam: John Benjamins.

1991. Back to the future. In Elizabeth Closs Traugott and Bernd Heine (eds.), *Approaches to grammaticalization*, vol. II: *Focus on types of grammatical markers*, 17–58. Amsterdam: John Benjamins.

Bynon, Theodora. 1977. *Historical linguistics*. Cambridge University Press.

1980. From passive to active in Kurdish via the ergative construction. In Elizabeth Closs Traugott, Rebecca LaBrum and Susan Shepherd (eds.), *Papers from the fourth International Conference on Historical Linguistics,* 151–63. Amsterdam: John Benjamins.

1986. August Schleicher: Indo-Europeanist and general linguist. In Theodora Bynon and F.R. Palmer (eds.), *Studies in the history of Western linguistics, in honour of R. H. Robins*, 129–49. Cambridge University Press.

Byrne, Brian and Elizabeth Davidson. 1985. On putting the horse before the cart: exploring conceptual bases of word order via acquisition of a miniature artificial language. *Journal of Memory and Language* 24.377–89.

Campbell, Lyle. 1975. Constraints on sound change. In K.-H. Dahlstedt (ed.), *The Nordic languages and modern linguistics*, vol II, 388–406. Stockholm: Almqvist and Wiksell International.

1977. *Quichean linguistic prehistory.* (California Publications in Linguistics, 81.) Berkeley: University of California Press.

1980. Towards new perspectives on American Finnish. In H. Paunonen and M. Suojanen (eds.), *Central problems in bilingualism*, 43–54. Vol. III, part 4 of Osmo Ikola (ed.), *Congressus Quintus Internationalis Fenno-Ugristarum*. Turku: Suomen Kielen Seura.

1985. *The Pipil language of El Salvador*. Berlin: Mouton de Gruyter.

1986. Theories of syntactic change and Finnish historical syntax. *Journal of the Atlantic Provinces Linguistic Association* 8.72–93.

1987. Syntactic change in Pipil. *International Journal of American Linguistics* 53.253–80.

1988. Syntactic change in Finnish dialects. In Jacek Fisiak (ed.), *Historical dialectology*,

85–110. Berlin: Mouton de Gruyter.

1990a. Syntactic reconstruction and Finno-Ugric. In Henning Anderson and Konrad Koerner (eds.), *Historical linguistics 1987: papers from the eighth International Conference on Historical Linguistics*, 51–94. Amsterdam: John Benjamins.

1990b. Philological studies and Mayan languages. In J. Fisiak (ed.), *Historical linguistics and philology*, 87–105. Berlin: Mouton de Gruyter.

1991. Some grammaticalization changes in Estonian and their implications. In Elizabeth C. Traugott and Bernd Heine (eds.), *Approaches to grammaticalization*, vol. I: *Focus on theoretical and methodological issues*, 285–99. Amsterdam: John Benjamins.

in press a. Historical syntax in historical perspective. In Joachim Jacobs, Arnim von Stechow, Wolfgang Sternefeld, and Theo Vennemann (eds.), *An international handbook of contemporary research, syntax handbook* (Handbücher zur Sprach- und Kommunikations- wissenschaft). Berlin: Walter de Gruyter.

in press b. On proposed universals of grammatical borrowing. In Robert Jeffers (ed.), *Selected papers of the ninth International Conference on Historical Linguistics*, Amsterdam: John Benjamins.

in press c. Areal issues in grammar and typology. In Keith Brown and Nigel Vincent (eds.), *Encyclopedia of language and linguistics*, London: Pergamon Press.

Campbell, Lyle and Marianne Mithun. 1980. Syntactic reconstruction: priorities and pitfalls. *Folia Linguistica Historica* 1:1.19–40.

Campbell, Lyle and Martha Muntzel. 1989. The structural consequences of language death. In Nancy Dorian (ed.), *Investigating obsolescence: studies in language death*, (Studies in the Social and Cultural Foundations of Language, 7), 181–96. Cambridge University Press.

Campbell, Lyle and Jon Ringen. 1981. Teleology and the explanation of sound change. In Wolfgang U. Dressler, Oskar E. Pfeiffer, and John R. Rennison (eds.), *Phonologica 1980*, 57–68. Innsbruck: Innsbrucker Beiträge zur Sprach- wissenschaft.

Campbell, Lyle, Vit Bubenik, and Leslie Saxon. 1988. Word order universals: refine- ments and clarifications. *Canadian Journal of Linguistics* 33.209–30.

Campbell, Lyle, Terrence Kaufman, and Thomas Smith-Stark. 1986. Mesoamerica as a linguistic area. *Language* 62.530–70.

Canale, Michael. 1976. Implicational hierarchies of word order relationships. In William M. Christie Jr. (ed.), *Current progress in historical linguistics: proceedings of the second International Conference on Historical Linguistics*, 39–69. Amsterdam: North Holland.

Carranza Romero, Francisco. 1986. Asimilación de morfemas españoles en el que- chua. In Benjamin F. Elson (ed.), *Language in global perspective: papers in honor of the 50th anniversary of the Summer Institute of Linguistics, 1935–1985*, 417–20. Dallas: Summer Institute of Linguistics.

Castelvetro, Lodovico. 1572. *Corretione d'alcune cose del dialogo delle lingue di Benedetto Varcchi, et una giunta al primo libro delle prose di M. Pietro Bembo dove si ragiona della vulgar lingua*. Basle: P. Perna.

Cercvaʒe, Ilia. 1965. *Andiuri ena*. [The Andi language.] Tbilisi: Mecniereba.

Chafe, Wallace L. 1976. Givenness, contrastiveness, definiteness, subjects, topics, and point of view. In Charles N. Li (ed.), *Subject and topic*, 25–55. New York: Academic Press.

1977. The evolution of third person verb agreement in the Iroquoian languages. In Charles N. Li, (ed.), *Mechanisms of syntactic change*, 493–524. Austin: University of Texas Press.

1982. Integration and involvement in speaking, writing, and oral literature. In Deborah Tannen (ed.), *Spoken and written language: exploring orality and literacy*, 35–53. Norwood, NJ: Ablex.

Chakravarti, Prabhatchandra. 1933. *The linguistic speculations of the Hindus*, University of Calcutta Press.

Chamberlain, Jeffrey Thomas. 1982. A study concerning the Latin origins of French causatives. University of Illinois dissertation.

Chomsky, Noam. 1970. Remarks on nominalization. In Roderick A. Jacobs and Peter S. Rosenbaum (eds.), *English transformational grammar*, 184–221. Waltham, MA: Ginn.

1981. *Lectures on government and binding*. Dordrecht: Foris.

Christy, T. Craig. 1980. Uniformitarianism in nineteenth-century linguistics: implications for a reassessment of the neogrammarian sound-law doctrine. In Konrad Koerner (ed.), *Progress in linguistic historiography*, 249–56. (Studies in the History of Linguistics, 20.) Amsterdam: John Benjamins.

1983. *Uniformitarianism in linguistics*. Amsterdam: John Benjamins.

1987. Steinthal and the development of linguistic science: the convergence of psychology and linguistics. In Hans Aarsleff, Louis G. Kelly and Hans–Josef Niederehe (eds.), *Papers in the history of linguistics: proceedings of the third International Conference on the History of the Language Sciences*, 491–9. (Studies in the History of Language Sciences, 38.) Amsterdam: John Benjamins.

Chung, Sandra. 1977. On the gradual nature of syntactic change. In Charles N. Li (ed.), *Mechanisms of syntactic change*, 3–55. Austin: University of Texas Press.

1978. *Case marking and grammatical relations in Polynesian*. Austin: University of Texas Press.

Chung, Sandra and William J. Seiter. 1980. The history of raising and relativization in Polynesian. *Language* 56.622–38.

Čikobava, Arnold. 1936a. *Čanuris gramat'ik'uli analizi*. [A grammatical analysis of Laz.] 1936b. *Čanuri t'ekst'ebi*, vol.II: *Vic'ur-Arkabuli k'ilok'avi*. [Laz texts, vol.II: The Vic-Arkab sub-dialect.] The two titles bound together. T'pilisi: Mecnierebata Ak'ademiis Sakartvelos Pilialis Gamocema.

1939. Motxrobiti brunvis genezisisatvis kartvelur enebši. [On the origin of the narrative case in the Kartvelian languages.] *Tbilisis Saxelmc'ipo Universit'et'is Šromebi* 10.167–83.

Čikobava, Arnold and Ilia Cercvaʒe. 1962. *Xunʒuri ena*. Tbilisi: Universit'et'i.

Čikobava, Arnold, G. Axvlediani, Sim. Pačnaʒe, Vikt'. K'up'raʒe, Tamar Lomouri, V. Topuria, G. C'ereteli (eds.) 1950–64. *Kartuli enis ganmart'ebiti leksik'oni (KEGL)*. [Explanatory dictionary of the Georgian language (=*Academy Dictionary*).] Tbilisi: Ak'ademia.

Clark, Ross. 1981. Review of Sandra Chung, *Case marking and grammatical relations in Polynesian*. *Language* 57.198–205.

Claudi, Ulrike and Bernd Heine. 1986. On the metaphorical base of grammar. *Studies in Language* 10.297–335.

Colebrooke, Henry Thomas. 1805. *A grammar of the Sanscrit language.* Calcutta: Honorable Company's Press.

Collinge, N.E. 1960. Some reflexions on comparative historical syntax. *Archivum Linguisticum* 12.79–101.

1985. *The laws of Indo-European.* Amsterdam: John Benjamins.

Comenius [Komenský], J.A. 1657. *Opera didactica omnia. Variis hucusque occasionibus scripta, diversisque locis edita: nunc autem non tantùm in unum ut simul sint, collecta, sed & ultimô conatu in Systema unum mechanicè constructum, redacta.* Amsterdam.

Comrie, Bernard. 1976. Review of G.A. Klimov, *Očerk obščej teorii èrgativnosti. Lingua* 39.252–60.

1978. Ergativity. In Winfred P. Lehmann (ed.), *Syntactic typology: studies in the phenomenology of language.* Austin: University of Texas.

1980. Morphology and word order reconstruction: problems and prospects. In Jacek Fisiak (ed.), *Historical morphology,* 83–96. The Hague: Mouton.

1988. Topics, grammaticalized topics, and subjects. In Shelley Axmaker, Annie Jaisser, and Helen Singmaster (eds.), *General Session and Parasession on Grammaticalization,* 265–79. Berkeley Linguistics Society.

1989 [1981]. *Language universals and linguistic typology.* University of Chicago Press. (1st edn., 1981; 2nd revised edn., 1989.)

Condillac, Etienne Bonnot de, l'abbé. 1746. *Essai sur l'origine des connoissances humaines, ouvrage oú l'on réduit à un seul principe tout ce qui concerne l'entendement humain.* Amsterdam: Pierre Mortier. (2nd edn., 1798. Paris: C. Houel.) (English translation 1756: Thomas Nugent, *An essay on the origin of human knowledge.* London: J. Nourse; facsimile edition with introduction by Robert G. Weyant 1971. Gainsville, FL: Scholars' Facsimiles and Reprints.)

Corbett, J.A. 1948. *Essentials of modern German grammar.* London: Harrap.

Cordemoy, Geraud de. 1668. *Discours physique de la parole.* Paris: F. Lambert. (New edition by Pierre Claire and François Girbal, 1968. Paris: Presses Universitaires de France.) (Edition of 1677 version by H.E. Brekle, 1970, Stuttgart: Bad Cannstatt.)

Coseriu, Eugenio. 1977a. Adam Smith y los comienzos de la tipología lingüística. In *Tradición y novedad en la ciencia del lenguaje,* 117–30. Madrid: Gredos. (Originally in 1968 *Wortbilbung, Syntax und Morphologie: Festshcrift Hans Marchand,* 46–54. The Hague.)

1977b. Sobre la tipología lingüística de Wilhem von Humboldt. In *Tradición y novedad en la ciencia del lenguaje,* 142–84. Madrid: Gredos. (Originally in 1972 *Beiträge zur vergleichenden Literaturgeschichte, Festschrift Kurt Wais,* 235–66. Tübingen.)

1978 [1957]. *Sincronía, diacronía e historia.* (1st edn. 1957; 3rd edn. 1978.) Madrid: Gredos. (German translation: 1974. *Synchronie, Diachronie und Typologie: das Problem des Sprachwandels.* Munich: Wilhelm Fink.)

1985. Linguistic change does not exist. *Linguistica Nuova ed Antica,* 51–63.

Coteanu, I. 1957. *A propos des langues mixtes (sur l'istro-roumain).* Bucharest: Mélanges linguistiques.

Covington, Michael A. 1986. Grammatical theory in the Middle Ages. In Theodora Bynon and F. R. Palmer (eds.), *Studies in the history of Western linguistics, in honour of R. H. Robins,* 23–42. Cambridge University Press.

Craig, Colette and Kenneth L. Hale. 1988. Relational preverbs in some languages of the Americas. *Language* 64.312–44.

Curme, George O. 1914. The development of verbal compounds in Germanic. *Beiträge zur Geschichte der deutschen Sprache und Literatur* 39.320–61.

Curtius, Georg. 1867. *Zur Chronologie der indogermanischen Sprachforschung.* Leipzig: S. Hirzel.

1870. Zur Geschichte der griechischen zusammengezogenen Verbalformen. *Studien zur griechischen und lateinischen Grammatik* 3.377–401.

1871. Zur Erklärung der Personalendungen. *Studien zur griechischen und lateinischen Grammatik* 4.211–30.

Čxubianišvili, D. 1972. *Inpinit'ivis sak'itxisatvis ʒvel kartulši.* [On the question of the infinitive in Old Georgian.] Tbilisi: Mecniereba.

Dahl, Östen. 1985. *Tense and aspect systems.* New York: Blackwell.

Dai, John Xiang-Ling. 1990. Historical morphologization of syntactic words: evidence from Chinese derived verbs. *Diachronica* 7.9–46.

Dante, Alighieri. *c.* 1305. *De vulgari eloquentia.* (English trans. 1981. *Dante in hell: the "De vulgari eloquentia,"* introduction, translation, and commentary by Warman Welliver. Ravenna: Longo Editore.)

Davies, Anna Morpurgo. 1986. Karl Brugmann and late nineteenth-century linguistics. In Theodora Bynon and F.R. Palmer (eds.), *Studies in the history of Western linguistics, in honour of R.H. Robins,* 150–71. Cambridge University Press.

Davies, William D. 1986. *Choctaw verb agreement and universal grammar.* Dordrecht: Reidel.

Davis, Gary W. 1990. On the causes of language change (review article). *Diachronica* 7.251–68.

Dawkins, R. M. 1916. *Modern Greek in Asia Minor: a study of the dialects of Silli, Cappadocia, and Phárasa, with grammar, texts, translations and glossary.* Cambridge University Press.

de Bray, R.G.A. 1980. *Guide to the South Slavonic languages.* Columbus, OH: Slavica.

Deeters, Gerhard. 1930. *Das kharlwelische Verbum.* Leipzig: Markert and Petters.

DeLancey, Scott. 1985. The analysis–synthesis–lexis cycle in Tibeto-Burman: a case study in motivated change. In John Haiman (ed.), *Iconicity in syntax* (Typological studies in language, 6), 367–89. Amsterdam: John Benjamins.

1990. The origins of verb serialization in modern Tibetan. *Studies in Language* 15.1–23.

Delbrück, Berthold. 1878. *Die altindische Wortfolge aus dem Çatapathabrâ mana.* (Syntaktische Forschungen, 3.) Halle an der Saale: Buchhandlung des Waisenhauses.

1888. *Altindische Syntax.* (Syntaktische Forschungen, 5.) Halle an der Saale: Buchhandlung des Waisenhauses. (Repr. 1968. Darmstadt: Wissenschaftliche Buchgesellschaft.)

1893. *Einleitung in das Sprachstudium: ein Beitrag zur Geschichte und Methodik der vergleichenden Sprachforschung* (1st edn. 1880; 3rd edn. 1893; 6th edn. 1919). Leipzig: Breitkopf and Härtel.

1893–1900. *Vergleichende Syntax der Indogermanischen Sprachen.* (Part 3, Karl Brugmann and Berthold Delbrück. 1900. *Grundriss der vergleichenden Grammatik der indogermanischen Sprachen.*) Strassburg: Karl J. Trübner.

1901. *Grundfragen der Sprachforschung: mit Rücksicht auf W. Wundts*

Sprachpsychologie erördert. Strassburg: Karl J. Trübner.

Dench, Alan. 1982. The development of an accusative case marking pattern in the Ngayarda languages of Western Australia. *Australian Journal of Linguistics* 2.43–59.

Deroy, Louis. 1956. *L'Emprunt linguistique.* Paris: Les Belles Lettres.

Diakonoff, Igor M. 1965. *Semito-Hamitic.* Moscow: Nauka.

di Cesare, Donatella. 1990. The philosophical and anthropological place of Wilhelm von Humboldt's linguistic typology: linguistic comparison as a means to compare the different processes of human thought. In Tullio de Mauro and Lia Formigari (eds.), *Leibniz, Humboldt, and the origins of comparativism*, 157–80. Amsterdam: John Benjamins.

Diderichsen, Paul. 1974. The foundation of comparative linguistics: revolution or continuation? In Dell Hymes (ed.), *Studies in the history of linguistics: traditions and paradigms*, 277–306. Bloomington: Indiana University Press.

Diffloth, Gerard. 1972. Notes on expressive meaning. *Chicago Linguistic Society* 8.440–7.

Dik, Simon C. 1980. *Studies in functional grammar.* New York: Academic Press.

1987. Copula auxiliarization: how and why? In Martin Harris and Paolo Ramat (eds.), *Historical development of auxiliaries*, 53–84. Berlin: Mouton de Gruyter.

Disterheft, Dorothy. 1980. *The syntactic development of the infinitive in IE.* Columbus, OH: Slavica.

1984. Irish complementation: a case study in two types of syntactic change. In Jacek Fisiak (ed.), *Historical syntax*, 89–106. Berlin: Mouton.

Dixon, Robert M.W. 1977. The syntactic development of Australian languages. In Charles N. Li (ed.), *Mechanisms of syntactic change*, 365–415. Austin: University of Texas Press.

1979. Ergativity. *Language* 55.59–128.

1981. Grammatical reanalysis: an example of linguistic change from Warrgamay (North Queensland). *Australian Journal of Linguistics* 1. 91–112.

Dondua, K'arp'ez. 1967. Mimartebiti nacvalsaxelisa da misamarti sit'q'vis urtiertobisatvis ʒvel kartulši. [On the relationship between the relative pronoun and the head noun in Old Georgian.] In Al. Г˘lont'i (ed.) *Řčeuli našromebi* I, 20–9. Tbilisi: Mecniereba.

Dressler, Wolfgang. 1971. Über die Rekonstruktion der indogermanischen Syntax. *Zeitschrift für vergleichende Sprachforschung* 85.5–22.

Dryer, Matthew S. 1988. Object–verb order and adjective–noun order: dispelling a myth. *Lingua* 74. 185–217.

1992. The Greenbergian word order correlations. *Language* 68.81–138.

Du Bois, John. 1985. Competing motivations. In John Haiman (ed.), *Iconicity in syntax*, 343–65. Amsterdam: John Benjamins.

1987. The discourse source of ergativity. *Language* 63.815–55.

Dumézil, G., and T. Esenç. 1972. Textes en laze d'Ardeşen. *Bedi Kartlisa* 29–30.32–41.

Duponceau, Pierre–Etienne [Peter Stephen]. 1819 [1816]. Report to the corresponding secretary to the Committee, of his progress in the investigation committed to him of the general character and forms of the languages of the American Indians. II. A correspondence between the Rev. John Heckewelder, of Bethlehem, and Peter S. Duponceau, Esq., corresponding secretary of the Historical and Literary Committee of the American Philosophical Society, respecting the languages of the American Indians. *Transactions of the Historical and Literary Committee of the American Philosophical Society, held at Philadelphia, for promoting useful knowledge* 1.xvll–xlvi.351–465.

Eaton, Roger and Willem Koopman. 1987. Introduction. Willem Koopman, Frederike van der Leek, Olga Fischer, and Roger Eaton (eds.), *Explanation and linguistic change*, 1–10. Amsterdam: John Benjamins.

Ebeling, C.L. 1966. The grammar of Literary Avar (a review article). *Studia Caucasica* 2.58–100.

Ebert, Robert Peter. 1976. Introduction. In Sanford B. Steever, Carol A. Walker, and Salikoko S. Mufwene (eds.), *Papers from the Parasession on Diachronic Syntax*, vii–xviii. Chicago: Chicago Linguistic Society.

1978. *Historische Syntax des Deutschen*. Stuttgart: Sammlung Metzler.

Ellegård, Alvar. 1953. *The auxiliary "do": the establishment and regulation of its use in English*. (Gothenburg Studies in English.) Stockholm: Almqvist and Wiksell.

Elmer, Willy. 1981. *Diachronic grammar: the history of Old and Middle English subjectless constructions*. Tübingen: Max Niemeyer.

Emeneau, Murray B. 1980. *Language and linguistic area, essays by Murray B. Emeneau*, selected and introduced by Anwar S. Dil. Stanford University Press.

England, Nora C. 1989. Comparing Mam (Mayan) clause structures: subordinate versus main clauses. *International Journal of American Linguistics* 55.283–308.

1991. Changes in basic word order in Mayan languages. *International Journal of American Linguistics* 57.446–86.

Erdmann, Oskar Theodor. 1886. *Grundzüge der deutschen Syntax nach ihrer geschichtlichen Entwicklung*. Stuttgard: J. G. Gotta.

Ertelišvili, P. 1963. *Rtuli c'inadadebis ist'oriisatvis kartulši*, vol. I: *Hip'ot'aksis sak'itxebi*. [On the history of complex sentences in Georgian, vol. I: Questions of subordination.] Tbilisi: Universit'et'i.

Estival, Dominique and John Myhill. 1988. Formal and functional aspects of the development from passive to ergative systems. In Masayoshi Shibatani (ed.), *Passive and voice*, 441–91. Philadelphia: John Benjamins.

Faarlund, Jan Terje. 1989. Pragmatics and syntactic change. In Leiv Egil Breivik and Ernst Håkon Jahr (eds.), *Language change: contributions to the study of its causes*, 71–99. Berlin: Mouton de Gruyter.

1990a. Syntactic and pragmatic principles as arguments in the interpretation of runic inscriptions. In Jacek Fisiak (ed.), *Historical linguistics and philology*, 165–86. Berlin: Mouton de Gruyter.

1990b. *Syntactic change: toward a theory of historical syntax*. Berlin: Mouton de Gruyter.

Fähnrich, Heinz. 1991. Old Georgian. In Alice C. Harris (ed.), *The indigenous languages of the Caucasus*, vol. I: *The Kartvelian languages*, 129–217. Delmar, NY: Caravan Press.

Ferguson, Charles A. 1959. Diglossia. *Word* 15.325–40. (Repr. 1972. In Pier Paolo Gigliolo (ed.), *Language and social context*, 232–51. Harmondsworth, England: Penguin.)

1976. The Ethiopian language area. In M. L. Bender, J. D. Bowen, R. L. Cooper, and C. A. Ferguson (eds.), *Language in Ethiopia*, 63–76. Oxford University Press.

Fick, August. 1881. *Gelehrte Anzeigen*. Munich.

Fillmore, Charles J. 1968. A case for case. In Emmon Bach and Robert Harms (eds.), *Universals in linguistic theory*, 1–88. New York: Holt, Rinehart and Winston.

Fischer, Olga. 1989. The origin and spread of the accusative and infinitive construction in English. *Folia Linguistica Historica* 8.143–217.

Fischer, Olga C.M. and Frederike C. van der Leek. 1981. Optional vs. radical reanalysis: mechanisms of syntactic change; review of David Lightfoot, *Principles of diachronic syntax*. *Lingua* 55.301–50.

1983. The demise of the Old English impersonal construction. *Journal of Linguistics* 19.337–68.

1987. A "case" for the Old English impersonal. In Willem Koopman, Frederike van der Leek, Olga Fischer, and Roger Eaton (eds.), *Explanation and linguistic change*, 79–120. Amsterdam: John Benjamins.

Fisiak, Jacek (ed.). 1984. *Historical syntax*. Berlin: Mouton.

Foulet, Alfred Lucien. 1930. *Petite syntaxe de l'ancien français*. 3rd edn. Paris: Librairie Ancienne Honoré Champion.

Frazier, Lyn. 1985. Syntactic complexity. In David R. Dowty, Lauri Karttunen, and Arnold M. Zwicky (eds.), *Natural language parsing: psychological, computational, and theoretical perspectives*, 129–89. Cambridge University Press.

Friedrich, Johannes. 1960. *Hethitisches Keilschrift-Lesebuch*. Heidelberg: C. Winter.

Friedrich, Paul. 1975. *Proto-Indo-European syntax*. (*Journal of Indo-European Studies*, Monograph 1.) Butte: Montana College of Mineral Science and Technology.

Frisk, Hjalmar. 1941 [1966]. Über den Gebrauch des Privativpräfixes im indogermanischen Adjektiv. *Göteborgs Högskolas Årsskrift* 47.1–47. (Reprinted in Hjalmar Frisk (ed.), *Kleine Schriften*, 183–229. [Studia Graeca et Latina Gothoburgensia, 21.] Stockholm: Almqvist and Wiksell.)

Fujii, Noriko. 1985. A diachronic study of grammatical subject in Japanese. University of Michigan dissertation.

Fulda, Friedrich Carl. 1777–8. *Grundregeln der Teutschen Sprache. Der Teutsche Sprachforscher, allen Liebhabern ihrer Muttersprache zur Prüfung vorgelegt*, vol. II. Stuttgart: J. Metzler.

Gabelentz, Georg von der. 1891. *Die Sprachwissenschaft: ihre Aufgaben, Methoden und bisherigen Ergebnisse*. Leipzig: Weigel.

Gair, James W. 1980. Adaptation and naturalization in a linguistic area: Sinhala focused sentences. *Berkeley Linguistics Society* 6.29–43.

Gamkrelidze, T.V. and Vjač. Ivanov. 1984. *Indoevropejskij jazyk i indoevropejcy*. Tbilisi: Universiteta.

Garibay K., Angel María. 1961. *Llave del náhuatl: colección de trozos clásicos, con gramática y vocabulario, para utilidad de los principiantes*. 2nd edn. Mexico: Porrua.

Garrett, Andrew. 1990. The origin of NP split ergativity. *Language* 66.261–96.

1992. The origin of *do*-support. Ms., University of Texas, Austin.

Genetti, Carol. 1986. The development of subordinators from postpositions in Bodic languages. *Berkeley Linguistics Society* 12.387–400.

1991. From postposition to subordinator in Newari. In Elizabeth Closs Traugott and Bernd Heine (eds.), *Approaches to grammaticalization*, vol. II: *Focus on types of grammatical markers*, 227–55. Amsterdam: John Benjamins.

Gerritsen, Marinel. 1984. Divergent word order developments in Germanic languages: a description and a tentative explanation. In Jacek Fisiak (ed.), *Historical syntax*,

107–36. Berlin: Mouton.

Gigineišvili, Bakar and Zurab Sarǰvelaʒe. 1978. Nanatesaobitari mimartulebitisa da nanatesaobitari danišnulebitis adgili ʒveli kartulisa da kartveluri enebis brunvata sist'emaši. [The place of the degenitive directional and of the degenitive designative in the system of cases of Old Georgian and the Kartvelian languages.] *Mravaltavi* 6.123–36.

Gildea, Spike Lawrence Owen. 1992. Comparative Cariban morphosyntax: on the genesis of ergativity in independent clauses. University of Oregon dissertation.

Girard, Abbé Gabriel. 1747. *Les Vrais Principes de la langue françoise: ou la parole réduite en méthode, conformément aux loix de l'usage: en seize discours.* 2 vols. Paris: Le Breton. (New edn. with introduction by Pierre Swiggers. 1982. Geneva: Droz.)

Givón, Talmy. 1971. Historical syntax and synchronic morphology: an archaeologist's field trip. *Chicago Linguistic Society* 7.394–415.

1974. Verb complements and relative clauses: a diachronic case study in Biblical Hebrew. *Afroasiatic Linguistics* 1: 4.1–22.

1975. Serial verbs and syntactic change: Niger-Congo. In Charles N. Li (ed.), *Word order and word order change*, 47–112. Austin: University of Texas Press.

1976. Topic, pronoun, and grammatical agreement. In Charles N. Li (ed.), *Subject and topic*, 149–88. New York: Academic Press.

1977. The drift from VSO to SVO in Biblical Hebrew: the pragmatics of tense–aspect. Charles N. Li (ed.), *Mechanisms of syntactic change*, 181–254. Austin: University of Texas Press.

1979. *On understanding grammar.* New York: Academic Press.

1981. The development of the numeral "one" as an indefinite marker. *Folia Linguistica Historica* 2.35–53.

1984. *Syntax: a functional-typological introduction*, vol. I. Amsterdam: John Benjamins.

1990a. *Syntax: a functional-typological introduction*, vol. II. Amsterdam: John Benjamins.

1990b Isomorphism in the grammatical code: cognitive and biological considerations. *Studies in Language* 15.85–114.

1991. Serial verbs and the mental reality of "event": grammatical vs. cognitive packaging. In Elizabeth Closs Traugott and Bernd Heine (eds.), *Approaches to grammaticalization*, vol. I: *Focus on theoretical and methodological issues*, 81–127. Amsterdam: John Benjamins.

Goddard, Ives. 1988. Stylistic dialects in Fox linguistic change. In Jacek Fisiak (ed.), *Historical dialectology: regional and social*, 193–209. Berlin: Mouton de Gruyter.

Gołąb, Zbigniew. 1959. The influence of Turkish upon the Macedonian Slavonic dialects. *Folia Orientalia* 1.26–45.

Goossens, Louis. 1987. The auxiliarization of the English modals: a functional grammar view. In Martin Harris and Paolo Ramat (eds.), *Historical development of auxiliaries*, 111–43. Berlin: Mouton de Gruyter.

Gould, Stephen Jay. 1977. *Ever since Darwin: reflexions in natural history.* New York: W.W. Norton.

1987. *Time's arrow, time's cycle: myth and metaphor in the discovery of geological time.* Cambridge, MA: Harvard University Press.

Green, Georgia M. 1976. Main clause phenomena in subordinate clauses. *Language*

52.382–397.

Greenberg, Joseph H. 1963. Some universals of grammar with particular reference to the order of meaningful elements. In J. H. Greenberg (ed.), *Universals of language*, 73–113. Cambridge, MA: MIT Press.

1973. The typological method. In Thomas Sebeok (ed.), *Current trends in linguistics*, vol. XI: *Diachronic, areal and typological linguistics*, volume eds. Henry M. Hoenigswald and Robert E. Longacre, 149–93. The Hague: Mouton.

1975. Research on language universals. *Annual Review of Anthropology* 4.75–94.

1978. How does a language acquire gender markers? In J. H. Greenberg, C.A. Ferguson, and Edith A. Moravcsik (eds.), *Universals of human language*, vol. II, 47–82. Stanford University Press.

1980. Circumfixes and typological change. In Elizabeth Closs Traugott, Rebecca LaBrum, and Susan Shepherd (eds.), *Papers from the fourth International Conference on Historical Linguistics*, 233–41. Amsterdam: John Benjamins.

Gudava, Togo. 1971. *Bagvaluri ena*. [The Bagvalal language.] Tbilisi: Mecniereba.

Gumperz, John and Robert Wilson. 1971. Convergence and creolization: a case from the Indo-Aryan/Dravidian border in India. In Dell Hymes (ed.), *Pidginization and creolization of languages*, 151–67. Cambridge University Press.

Gyarmathi, Sámuel. 1794. *Okoskodva tanító magyar nyelvmester* [Hungarian grammar taught rationally], 2 vols. Cluj and Sibiu: Hochmeister.

1799. *Affinitas linguae Hungaricae cum linguis Fennicae originis grammatice demonstrata*. Göttingen: Joann. Christan Dieterich. (Photolithic reproduction of 2nd edn. 1968, ed. Thomas A. Sebeok. [Ural and Altaic Series, 95.] Bloomington: Indiana University Press; The Hague: Mouton.) (English trans. 1983. *Grammatical proof of the affinity of the Hungarian language with languages of Fennic origin*, trans., annotated, and introduced by Victor E. Hanzeli. [Amsterdam Classics in Linguistics, 15.] Amsterdam: John Benjamins.)

Haas, Mary R. 1977. From auxiliary verb phrase to inflectional suffix. In Charles N. Li (ed.), *Mechanisms of syntactic change*, 525–37. Austin: University of Texas Press.

Haider, Hubert and Martin Prinzhorn (eds.) 1986. *Verb second phenomena in Germanic languages*. Dordrecht: Foris.

Haiman, John. 1977. Reinterpretation. *Language* 53.312–28.

1980. *Hua: a Papuan language of the Eastern Highlands of New Guinea*. Amsterdam: John Benjamins.

1987. On some origins of medial verb morphology in Papuan languages. *Studies in Language* 11.347–64.

Hakulinen, Auli and Fred Karlsson. 1979. *Nykysuomen lauseoppia*. [Modern Finnish syntax.] Helsinki: Suomalaisen Kirjallisuuden Seura.

Hakulinen, Auli and Pentti Leino. 1987. Finnish participial construction from a discourse point of view. *Ural-Altaische Jahrbücher* 59.35–43.

Hakulinen, Lauri. 1968. *Suomen kielen rakenne ja kehitys*. [The structure and development of the Finnish language.] 3rd edn. Helsinki: Ottava.

Hale, Kenneth. 1971. Gaps in grammar and culture. In Dale Kinkade, Kenneth Hale, and Oswald Werner (eds.), *Linguistics and anthropology in honor of C. F. Voegelin*, 295–315. Lisse, Belgium: Petter de Ridder.

Hale, Mark. 1991. Synchronic and diachronic aspects of noun incorporation and related constructions in the Nuclear Micronesian languages. Ms., Harvard University.

Hale, William Gardner and Carl Darling Buck. 1966 [1903]. *A Latin grammar.* University: University of Alabama Press.

Halhed, Nathaniel Brassey. 1778. *A grammar of the Bengal language.* Calcutta. [Facsimile edn. 1980. Calcutta: Ananda.]

Halle, Morris. 1961. On the role of simplicity in linguistic descriptions. In *Structure of language and its mathematical aspects* (Proceedings of Symposia in Applied Mathematics, 12), 89–94. Providence: American Mathematical Society.

1962. Phonology in generative grammar. *Word* 18.54–72. (Repr. 1964. In Jerry A. Fodor and Jerrold J. Katz (eds.), *The structure of language: readings in the philosophy of language*, 334–54. Englewood Cliffs, NJ: Prentice Hall.)

1964. On the bases of phonology. In Jerry A. Fodor and Jerrold J. Katz (eds.), *The structure of language: readings in the philosophy of language*, 324–33. Englewood Cliffs, NJ: Prentice Hall.

Hanzeli, Victor E. 1983. Gyarmathi and his *Affinitas.* In *Grammatical proof of the affinity of the Hungarian language with languages of Fennic origin*, trans., annotated, and introduced by Victor E. Hanzeli, (Amsterdam Classics in Linguistics, 1800–1925, vol. 15.), xi–lv. Amsterdam: John Benjamins.

Harries-Delisle, Helga. 1978. Contrastive emphasis and cleft sentences. In Joseph H. Greenberg, Charles A. Ferguson, and Edith A. Moravcsik (eds.), *Universals of human language*, vol. IV, 419–86. Stanford University Press.

Harris, Alice C. 1973. Psychological predicates in Middle English. Paper delivered at the Linguistic Society of America, Annual Meeting.

1980. On the loss of a rule of syntax. In Elizabeth Closs Traugott, Rebecca LaBrum, and Susan Shepherd (eds.), *Papers from the fourth International Conference on Historical Linguistics*, 165–71. Amsterdam: John Benjamins.

1981. *Georgian syntax: a study in relational grammar.* Cambridge University Press.

1982. Georgian and the Unaccusative Hypothesis, *Language* 58.290–306.

1984a. Georgian. In William S. Chisholm, Louis T. Milic, and John A.C. Greppin (eds.), *Interrogativity*, 63–112. Amsterdam: John Benjamins.

1984b. Inversion as a rule of universal grammar: Georgian evidence. In David M. Perlmutter and Carol G. Rosen, *Studies in relational grammar*, vol. II, 259–91. University of Chicago Press.

1985. *Diachronic syntax: the Kartvelian case.* (Syntax and Semantics, 18.) New York: Academic Press.

1989. On hypotaxis in Laz, *Čelicdeuli* 15.87–103.

1990a. Alignment typology and diachronic change. In Winfred P. Lehmann (ed.), *Language typology 1987: systematic balance in language*, 67–90. Amsterdam: John Benjamins.

1990b. Kartvelian Contacts with Indo-European. In Thomas Markey and John A.C. Greppin (eds.), *When worlds collide: the Indo-Europeans and the Pre-Indo-Europeans*, 67–100. Ann Arbor: Karoma Press.

(ed.) 1991a. *The indigenous languages of the Caucasus*, vol. I: *The Kartvelian languages.* Delmar, NY: Caravan Press.

1991b. Mingrelian. In Alice C. Harris (ed.), *The indigenous languages of the Caucasus*, vol. I: *The Kartvelian languages*, 313–94. Delmar, NY: Caravan Press.

1991c. Anti-clefts and one origin of topic markers. Ms., Vanderbilt University.

1991d. Contact and internal mechanisms of syntactic change. Ms., Vanderbilt

University.

1991e. On explanation of word order harmonies. Ms.,Vanderbilt University.

1992a. Changes in relativization strategies: Georgian and language universals. In Catherine Paris (ed.), *Actes du colloque Caucase,* 391–403. Paris: Peeters.

1992b. Review of Jan Terje Faarlund, *Syntactic change: toward a theory of historical syntax. Diachronica* 9: 2.287–96.

in press a. Ergative-to-accusative shift in agreement: Tabassaran. In Howard I. Aronson (ed.), *Linguistic Studies in the Non-Slavic Languages of the Commonwealth of Independent States and the Baltic Republics,* Chicago Linguistic Society.

in press b. On the history of relative clauses in Georgian. In Howard I. Aronson (ed.), *Non-Slavic Languages of the USSR: Papers from the fourth Conference,* (Folia Slavica). Columbus, OH: Slavica.

in press c. Toward a universal definition of clefts: problematic clefts in Mingrelian and Laz. In *Meore saertošoriso kartvelologiuri simp'oziumis masalebi.* [Proceedings of the Second International Symposium in Kartvelian Studies.] Tbilisi: Universit'et'i.

Harris, Martin B. 1978. *The evolution of French syntax: a comparative approach.* London: Longman.

1980a. The marking of definiteness: a diachronic perspective. In Elizabeth C. Traugott, Rebecca LaBrum, and Susan Shepherd (eds.), *Papers from the fourth International Conference on Historical Linguistics,* 75–86. Amsterdam: John Benjamins.

1980b. The marking of definiteness in Romance. In Jacek Fisiak (ed.), *Historical morphology,* 141–56. Berlin: Mouton.

1984. On the strengths and weaknesses of a typological approach to historical syntax. In Jacek Fisiak (ed.), *Historical syntax,* 183–98. Berlin: Mouton.

Harris, Martin and Paolo Ramat (eds.) 1987. *Historical development of auxiliaries.* Berlin: Mouton de Gruyter.

Harris, Roy. 1980. *The language makers.* Ithaca: Cornell University Press.

Haugen, Einar. 1950. The analysis of linguistic borrowing. *Language* 26.210–31.

1954. Review of Uriel Weinreich, *Languages in contact. Language* 30.380–8.

1956. *Bilingualism in the Americas: a bibliography and research guide.* (Publication of the American Dialect Society, 26.) University: University of Alabama Press.

Hawkins, John A. 1983. *Word order universals.* New York: Academic Press.

1985. Complementary methods in Universal Grammar: reply to Coopmans. *Language* 61.569–88.

1990. Seeking motives for change in typological variation. In William Croft, Keith Denning, and Suzanne Kemmer (eds.), *Studies in typology and diachrony for Joseph H. Greenberg,* 95–128. (Typological Studies in Language, 20.) Amsterdam: John Benjamins.

1991. A parsing theory of word order universals. *Linguistic Inquiry* 21.223–61.

Heath, Jeffrey. 1978. *Linguistic diffusion in Arnhem Land.* (Australian Aboriginal Studies Research and Regional Studies, 13.) Canberra: Australian Institute of Aboriginal Studies.

Heine, Bernd and Ulrike Claudi. 1986. *On the rise of grammatical categories: some examples from Maa.* Berlin: Dietrich Reimer.

Heine, Bernd and Mechtild Reh. 1982. *Patterns of grammaticalization in African lan-*

guages (Arbeiten des Kölner Universalienprojekts, 47). University of Cologne, Institute of Linguistics.

1984. *Grammaticalization and reanalysis in African languages.* Hamburg: Helmut Buske.

Heine, Bernd, Ulrike Claudi, and Friederike Hünnemeyer. 1991. *Grammaticalization: a conceptual framework.* Chicago: University of Chicago Press.

Hellan, L. and K. Kock Christensen (eds.). 1986. *Topics in Scandinavian syntax.* Dordrecht: Reidel.

Hemon, Roparz. 1975. *A historical morphology and syntax of Breton.* Dublin Institute for Advanced Studies.

Herder, Johann Gottfried. 1772. *Abhandlung über den Ursprung der Sprache.* Berlin: C. F. Voss. (New edn. 1966. Stuttgart: Philipp Reclam.)

Hermann, Edward. 1895. Gab es im Indogermanischen Nebensätze? *Zeitschrift für vergleichende Sprachwissenschaft* 33.481–534.

Herring, Susan C. 1988. Aspect as a discourse category in Tamil. In Shelley Axmaker, Annie Jaisser, and Helen Singmaster (eds.), *General Session and Parasession on Grammaticalization*, 280–92. Berkeley Linguistics Society.

Hervás y Panduro, Lorenzo. 1784. *Catalogo delle lingue conosciute e notizia della loro affinità ed diversità.* Cesena: Biasini.

1800–5. *Catálogo de las lenguas de las naciones conocidas y numeracion, division, y clases de estas segun la diversidad de sus idiomas y dialectos.* 6 vols. Madrid: Ranz. (Facsimile edition. 1979. Ed. and introduced by Agustín Hevia Ballina. Madrid: Linotipias Monserrat.)

Hetzron, Robert. 1972. *Ethiopian Semitic.* Manchester University Press.

1974. An archaism in the Cushitic verbal conjugation. IV [i.e. *Quarto*] *Congresso internazionale di studi etiopici*, vol. II: *Sezione linguistica*, 275–81. Rome: Accademia Nazionale dei Lincei.

1980. On word order and morpheme order. In Gunter Brettschneider and Christian Lehmann (eds.), *Wege zur Universalien Forschung: Sprachwissenschaftliche Beiträge zum 60. Geburtstag von Hansjakob Seiler*, 175–9. Tübingen: Gunter Narr.

Heusler, Andreas. 1932. *Altisländisches Elementarbuch.* Heidelberg: Carl Winter.

Hewitt, Brian George. 1987. *The typology of subordination in Georgian and Abxaz.* Berlin: Mouton de Gruyter.

Hill, Jane H. and Kenneth C. Hill. 1981. Variation in relative clause construction in modern Nahuatl. In Frances Karttunen (ed.), *Nahuatl Studies in Memory of Fernando Horcasitas* (Texas Linguistic Forum, 18), 89–103. Austin: Department of Linguistics, University of Texas.

1986. *Speaking Mexicano: dynamics of syncretic language in central Mexico.* Tucson: University of Arizona Press.

Hiltunen, Risto. 1983. *The decline of the prefixes and the beginnings of the English phrasal verb: the evidence from some Old and Early Middle English texts.* Turku: Turun Yliopisto.

Hinton, Leanne. 1980. When sounds go wild: phonological change and syntactic reanalysis in Havasupai. *Language* 56. 320–44.

Hirt, Hermann. 1934–7. *Indogermanische Grammatik: Syntax.* Parts VI–VII. Heidelberg: Carl Winter.

Hock, Hans Henrich. 1985. Yes, Virginia, syntactic reconstruction is possible. *Studies in the Linguistic Sciences* 15.49–60. (University of Illinois.)

1986. *Principles of historical linguistics.* Berlin: Mouton de Gruyter.

Hoenigswald, Henry M. 1963. Are there universals of linguistic change? In Joseph H. Greenberg (ed.), *Universals of language*, 23–41. Cambridge, MA: MIT Press.

1974. Fallacies in the history of linguistics: notes on the appraisal of the nineteenth century. In Dell Hymes (ed.), *Studies in the history of linguistics: traditions and paradigms*, 346–58. Bloomington: Indiana University Press.

1978. The *Annus Mirabilis* 1876 and posterity. *Transactions of the Philological Society*, 17–35.

1986. Nineteenth-century linguistics on itself. In Theodora Bynon and F.R. Palmer (eds.), *Studies in the history of Western linguistics, in honour of R.H. Robins*, 172–88. Cambridge University Press.

1990. Descent, perfection and the comparative method since Leibniz. In Tullio de Mauro and Lia Formigari (eds.), *Leibniz, Humboldt, and the origins of comparativism*, 119–32. Amsterdam: John Benjamins.

Hohepa, Patrick W. 1969. The accusative-to-ergative drift in Polynesian languages. *Journal of the Polynesian Society* 78.295–329.

Holisky, Dee Ann. 1981. Aspect theory and Georgian aspect. In Phillip J. Tedeschi and Annie Zaenen (eds.), *Tense and Aspect* (Syntax and Semantics 14), 127-44. New York: Academic Press.

1991. Laz. In Alice C. Harris (ed.), *The indigenous languages of the Caucasus*, vol. I: *The Kartvelian languages*, 395–472. Delmar, NY: Caravan Press.

Holisky, Dee Ann and Rusudan Gagua. In press. Tsova-Tush (Batsbi). In Rieks Smeets (ed.), *The indigenous languages of the Caucasus*, vol. IV: *North East Caucasian languages*, 147–212. Delmar, NY: Caravan Press.

Hook, Peter Edwin. 1988. Paradigmaticization: a case study from South Asia. In Shelley Axmaker, Annie Jaisser, and Helen Singmaster (eds.), *General Session and Parasession on Grammaticalization*, 293–303. Berkeley Linguistics Society.

Hooper, Joan B. and Sandra A. Thompson. 1973. On the applicability of root transformations. *Linguistic Inquiry* 4.465–97.

Hopper, Paul J. 1975. *The syntax of the simple sentence in Proto-Germanic.* The Hague: Mouton.

1987. Emergent grammar. *Berkeley Linguistics Society* 13.139–57.

1991. On some principles of grammaticalization. In Elizabeth Closs Traugott and Bernd Heine (eds.), *Approaches to grammaticalization*, vol. I: *Focus on theoretical and methodological issues*, 17–35. Amsterdam: John Benjamins.

Hopper, Paul J. and Sandra A. Thompson. 1984. The discourse basis for lexical categories in universal grammar. *Language* 60.703–52.

Huck, Geoffrey J., and Younghee Na. 1990. Extraposition and focus. *Language* 66.51–77.

Humboldt, (Friedrich) Wilhelm (Christian Karl Ferdinand) von. 1822. Ueber das Entstehen der grammatischen Formen, und ihren Einfluss auf die Ideenentwicklung. *Abhandlungen der königlichen Akademie der Wissenschaften zu Berlin*, 401–30. (Repr. 1963. In *Wilhelm von Humboldt, Werke in fünf Bänden*, ed. Andreas Flitner and Klaus Giel, vol. III, 31–63. Stuttgart: J.G. Cotta.)

1836. *Ueber die Verschiedenheit des menschlichen Sprachbaues und ihren Einfluss auf die geistige Entwicklung des Menschengeschlechtes.* Berlin: Königliche Akademie der Wissenschaften. (Repr. 1963. In *Wilhelm von Humboldt, Werke in fünf Bänden*,

ed. Andreas Flitner and Klaus Giel, vol. III, 368–756. Stuttgart: J.G. Cotta.)
(English translation: 1988. *On language: the diversity of human language-structure
and its influence on the mental development of mankind*, trans. Peter Heath.
Cambridge University Press.)

Hyman, Larry. 1975. On the change from SOV to SVO: evidence from Niger-Congo. In
Charles N. li (ed.), *Word order and word order change*, 113–47. Austin: University of
Texas Press.

Ibrahim, Muhammad H. 1987. A medieval Arab theory of language acquisition. In
Hans Aarsleff, Louis G. Kelly, and Hans-Josef Niederehe (eds.), *Papers in the history of linguistics: proceedings of the third International Conference on the History of
the Language Sciences* (Studies in the History of Language Sciences, 38), 95–105.
Amsterdam: John Benjamins.

Ikola, Osmo. 1953.Viron ja Liivin modus obliquuksen historiaa. [On the history of the
oblique mode of Estonian and Livonian.] *Suomi* 106: 4. 1–64. Helsinki: Suomalaisen Kirjallisuuden Seura.

1959. Eräistä suomen syntaktisista siirtymistä. [On some Finnish syntactic changes.]
Suomen Kielen Seuran Vuosikirja 1.39–60. (Helsinki.)

1968. Zum Objekt in den ostseefinnischen Sprachen. In Paavo Ravila (ed.),
*Congressus secundus Internationalis Fenno-Ugristarum, Helsingiae habitus 23–28.
VIII. 1965*, Part I: *Acta linguistica*, 188–95. Helsinki: Societas Fenno–Ugrica
(Suomalais-Ugrilainen Seuran).

Imnaišvili, I. 1957. *Saxelta bruneba da brunvata punkciebi ჳvel kartulši.* [The declension
of nouns and the function of cases in Old Georgian.] Tbilisi: Universitet'i.

Itkonen, Erkki. 1966. *Kieli ja sen tutkimus.* [Language and its study.] Helsinki: Werner
Söderström.

Itkonen, Terho. 1979. Subject and object marking in Finnish: an inverted ergative system and an "ideal" ergative sub-system. In Frans Plank (ed.), *Ergativity: towards a
theory of grammatical relations*, 79–102. New York: Academic Press.

Ivanov, V. V. 1965. *Obščeindoevropejskaja, praslavjanskaja i analtolijskaja jazykovye sist-
emy (sravnitel'no-tipologičeskie očerki)*. Moscow: Nauka.

Jacobi, Hermann. 1897. *Compositum und Nebensatz: Studien über die indogermanische
Sprachentwicklung.* Bonn: Friedrich Cohen.

Jacobs, Roderick A. 1975. *Syntactic change: a Cupan (Uto-Aztecan) case study.* Berkeley:
University of California Press.

Jacobsen, Thorkild. 1974. Very ancient linguistics: Babylonian grammatical texts. In
Dell Hymes (ed.), *Studies in the history of linguistics: traditions and paradigms*, 41–
62. Bloomington: Indiana University Press.

Jacobsen, William H., Jr. 1980. Inclusive/exclusive: a diffused pronominal category in
Native Western North America. In Jody Kreiman and Almerindo E. Ojeda (eds.),
Papers from the Parasession on Pronouns and Anaphora, 204–27. Chicago
Linguistic Society.

1983. Typological and genetic notes on switch–reference in North American Indian
languages. In John Haiman and Pamela Munro (eds.), *Switch reference and universal grammar* (Typological Studies in Language, 2), 151–83. Amsterdam: John
Benjamins.

Jahr, Ernst Håkon. 1989. Language planning and language change. In Leiv Egil
Breivik and Ernst Håkon Jahr (eds.), *Language change: contributions to the study of*

its causes, 99–113. Berlin: Mouton de Gruyter.

Jakobson, Roman. 1938. Sur la théorie des affinités phonologiques des langues. In *Actes du quatrième Congrès International de Linguistes*, 48–59. Copenhagen: Einar Munksgaard. (Repr. as appendix to N. Troubetzkoy. 1949. *Principes de phonologie*, 351–65. Paris; repr. 1962 in *Selected writings of Roman Jakobson*, vol. I, 234–46. The Hague: Mouton; trans. into English and repr. 1972. In Allan R. Keiler (ed.), *A reader in historical and comparative linguistics*, 241–52. New York: Holt Reinhart and Winston.)

Janda, Richard. 1981. A case of liberation from morphology into syntax: the fate of the English genitive-marker -(*e*)*s*. In Brenda B. Johns and David R. Strong (eds.), *Syntactic change*, (Natural Language Studies 25), 59–114. University of Michigan Press.

Janhunen, Juha. 1982. On the structure of Proto-Uralic. *Finno-Ugrische Forschungen* 44.23–42.

Jankowsky, Kurt R. 1972. *The Neogrammarians: a re-evaluation of their place in the development of linguistic science.* The Hague: Mouton.

Janson, Tore. 1979. *Mechanisms of language change in Latin*. Stockholm: Almqvist and Wiksell International.

Jeffers, Robert J. 1976a. Review of Winfred P. Lehmann, *Proto-Indo-European syntax*. *Language* 52.982–8.

1976b. Syntactic change and syntactic reconstruction. In William M. Christie, Jr. (ed.), *Current progress in historical linguistics: proceedings of the second International Conference on Historical Linguistics*, 1–15. Amsterdam: North Holland.

Jeffers, Robert J. and Arnold M. Zwicky. 1980. The evolution of clitics. In Elizabeth Closs Traugott, Rebecca LaBrum, and Susan Shepherd (eds.), *Papers from the fourth International Conference on Historical Linguistics*, 221–32. Amsterdam: John Benjamins.

Jeiranišvili, Evgeni. 1956. Gramat'ik'uli k'lasis gakvavebuli nišnebi udur zmnebsa da nazmnar saxelebši. [Petrified markers of grammatical class in Udi verbs and deverbal nouns.] *Iberiul-K'avk'asiuri Enatmecniereba* 8.341–67.

Jensen, Hans. 1959. *Altarmenische Grammatik*. Heidelberg: C. Winter.

Jespersen, Otto. 1894. *Progress in language, with special reference to English*. London: S. Sonnenschein.

Jikia, Sergi. 1967. Turkul-lazuri enobrivi urtiertobidan: 2. Turkuli sint'aksuri k'alk'ebi lazurši. [On the Turkish-Laz linguistic relationship: 2. Syntactic calques of Turkish in Laz.] In *Orioni: Ak'ak'i Šaniʒes*, 367–77. Tbilisi: Universit'et'i.

Johannisson, Ture. 1960. Eine syntaktische Entlehnung im Schwedischen. In *Indogermanica: Festschrift für Wolfgang Krause*, 38–43. Heidelberg: Carl Winter Universitätsverlag.

Jolly, Julius. 1873. *Die Geschichte des Infinitivs im Indogermanischen*. Munich: Theodor Ackermann.

Joseph, Brian Daniel. 1983. *The synchrony and diachrony of the Balkan infinitive: a study in areal, general, and historical linguistics*. Cambridge University Press.

1987. A fresh look at the Balkan *Sprachbund*: some observations on H. W. Schaller's *Die Balkansprachen*. *Mediterranean Language Review* 3.105–13.

Joseph, Brian D. and Richard D. Janda. 1988. The how and why of diachronic morphologization and demorphologization. In Michael Hammond and Michael Noonan (eds.), *Theoretical morphology: approaches in modern linguistics*, 193–210. San Diego: Academic Press.

Joseph, John E. 1989a. Inflection and periphrastic structures in Romance. In Carl Kirschner and Janet Decesaris (eds.), *Studies in Romance linguistics*, 195–208. Amsterdam: John Benjamins.

1989b. Typology, diachrony, and explanatory order. *Diachronica* 6.55–74.

Jucquois, Guy. 1976. *La Reconstruction linguistique: application à l'indo-européen*. 2nd edn. Louvain: Editions Peeters.

Kaisse, Ellen M. 1985. *Connected speech: the interaction of syntax and phonology*. Orlando: Academic Press.

Kaldani, M. 1964. K'itxviti, gansazɣvrebiti da gaȝlierebiti nac'ilak'ebi svanurši. [Interrogative, definite, and emphatic particles in Svan.] *Iberiul–k'avk'asiuri enatmecniereba* 14.227–34.

Kany, Charles E. 1951. *American–Spanish syntax*. University of Chicago Press.

K'art'ozia, Guram. 1968. Masala lazuri zep'irsit'q'vierebisatvis. [Material on Laz traditional oral literature.] In *Kartuli lit'erat'uris sak'itxebi*, 132–78. Tbilisi: Mecniereba.

1970. Lazuri t'ekst'ebi (Atinuri k'ilok'avis nimušebi). [Laz texts (Examples of the Atinian dialect).] *Macne* 4.213–32.

Karttunen, Frances. 1976. Uto–Aztecan and Spanish-type dependent clauses in Nahuatl. In S.B. Steever, C.A. Walker, and S.S. Mufwene (eds.), *Papers from the Parasession on Diachronic Syntax*, 150–8. Chicago Linguistic Society.

Karttunen, Lauri. 1971. Implicative verbs. *Language* 47.340–58.

Kaufman, Terrence. 1989. Mayan comparative studies. Unpublished ms., University of Pittsburgh.

Kay, Karen. 1985. Syntactic correlation and Old Japanese morphology. Paper delivered at the Linguistic Society of America, Annual Meeting.

Keenan, Edward L. 1971. Two kinds of presupposition in natural language. In Charles J. Fillmore and D. Terence Langendoen (eds.), *Studies in linguistic semantics*, 45–52. New York: Holt, Rinehart and Winston.

1972. On semantically based grammar. *Linguistic Inquiry* 3.413–61.

1985. Relative clauses. In Timothy Shopen (ed.), *Language typology and syntactic description*, vol. II: *Complex constructions*, 141–70. Cambridge University Press.

Keenan, Edward L. and Bernard Comrie. 1977. Noun phrase accessibility and universal grammar. *Linguistic Inquiry* 8.63–99.

Keenan, Edward L. and Robert D. Hull. 1973a. The logical presuppositions of questions and answers. In János S. Petöfi and Dorothea Franck (ed.), *Präsuppositionen in Philosophie und Linguistik*, 441–66. Frankfurt-on-Main: Athenäum.

1973b. The logical syntax of direct and indirect questions. In Claudia Corum, T. Cedric Smith-Stark, and Ann Weiser (eds.), *You take the high node and I'll take the low node*, 348–71. Chicago Linguistic Society.

Keesing, Roger M. 1988. *Melanesian Pidgin and the Oceanic substrate*. Stanford University Press.

Kemenade, Ans van. 1987. *Syntactic case and morphological case in the history of English*. Dordrecht: Foris.

Kennedy, Arthur Garfield. 1920. *The Modern English verb–adverb combination*. Stanford University Publications, *Language and Literature*, vol. 1, no. 1.

Kettunen, Lauri. 1930. *Suomen murteet II: murrealueet*. (Suomalaisen Kirjallisuuden

Seura, Toimituksia 188.) Helsinki: Suomalaisen Kirjallisuuden Seura.

1962. *Eestin kielen äännehistoria.* [The historical phonology of the Estonian Language.] (Suomalaisen Kirjallisuuden Seura, Toimituksia 156.) Helsinki: Suomalaisen Kirjallisuuden Seura.

King, Robert D. 1969. *Historical linguistics and generative grammar.* Englewood Cliffs, NJ: Prentice Hall.

Kiparsky, Paul. 1965. Phonological change. MIT dissertation.

1968. Tense and mood in Indo-European syntax. *Foundations of Language* 4.30–57.

1971. Historical linguistics. In W.O. Dingwall (ed.), *A survey of linguistic science*, 576–649. College Park: Linguistics Program, University of Maryland.

1974a. From paleogrammarians to Neogrammarians. In Dell Hymes (ed.), *Studies in the history of linguistics: traditions and paradigms*, 331–45. Bloomington: Indiana University Press.

1974b. On the evaluation measure. In A. Bruck, R. Fox and M. LaGaly (eds.), *Papers from the Parasession on Natural Phonology*, 328–37. Chicago Linguistic Society.

1982. *Explanation in phonology* (Publications in Language Science, 4). Dordrecht: Foris.

Kiparsky, Paul and Carol Kiparsky. 1970. Fact. In Manfred Bierwisch and Karl Erich Heidolph (eds.), *Progress in linguistics*, 143–73. The Hague: Mouton.

Kipšiʒe, I. 1914. *Grammatika mingrel'skogo (iverskago) jazyka.* St. Petersburg: Akademija Nauk.

Kiss, Katalin E. 1987. *Configurationality in Hungarian.* Dordrecht: D. Reidel.

K'iziria, Ant'on. 1982. *Mart'ivi c'inadadebis šedgeniloba kartvelur enebši.* [On the structure of the simple sentence in the Kartvelian languages.] Tbilisi: Mecniereba.

Klima, Edward S. 1964. Relatedness between grammatical systems. *Language* 40.1–20.

1965. Studies in diachronic transformational syntax. Harvard University dissertation.

1969. Relatedness between grammatical systems. David A. Reibel and Sanford A. Schane (eds.), *Modern studies in English*, 227–46. Englewood Cliffs, NJ: Prentice Hall.

Klimov, G.A. 1973. *Očerk obščej teorii èrgativnosti.* Moscow: Nauka.

1977. *Tipologija jazykov aktivnogo stroja.* Moscow: Nauka.

Klokeid, Terry J. 1978. Nominal inflection in Pamanyungan: a case study in relational grammar. In Werner Abraham (ed.), *Valence, semantic case, and grammatical relations*, 577–615. Amsterdam: John Benjamins.

Koerner, E. Konrad. 1978. *Toward a historiography of linguistics: selected essays.* (Studies in the history of linguistics, 19.) Amsterdam: John Benjamins.

1983. Editor's foreword. In *Linguistics and evolutionary theory: three essays by August Schleicher, Ernst Haeckel, and Wilhelm Bleek*, ed. Konrad Koerner, ix–xvi. Amsterdam: John Benjamins.

Koopman, Hilda. 1984. *The syntax of verbs: from verb movement rules in the Kru languages to universal grammar.* Dordrecht: Foris.

Koppitz, A. 1900. Gotische Wortstellung. *Zeitschrift für deutsche Philologie* 32.433–63.

Korhonen, Mikko. 1981. *Johdatus lapin kielen historiaan.* [Introduction to the history of the Lapp language.] Helsinki: Suomalaisen Kirjallisuuden Seura.

Krahe, Hans. 1966. *Germanische Sprachwissenschaft*, vol. I: *Einleitung und Lautlehre.* 6th edn. Berlin: de Gruyter.

1972. *Grundzüge der vergleichenden Syntax der indogermanischen Sprachen.* (Innsbruck: Institut für vergleichende Sprachwissenschaft der Universität Innsbruck.

Krahe, Hans and Wolfgang Meid. 1969. *Germanische Sprachwissenschaft.* 7th edn. (Sammlung Göschen, nos. 238, 780, 1218.) Berlin: de Gruyter.

Kraus, Christian Jakob. 1787. Rezension des Allgemeinen vergleichenden Wörterbuches von Pallas. *Allgemeine Literatur-Zeitung* nos. 235–7. (Repr. In Arens 1969: 136–45.)

Krause, Wolfgang. 1953. *Handbuch des Gotischen.* Munich: C.H. Beck'sche Verlagbuchhandlung.

Kroch, Anthony S. 1989a. Function and grammar in the history of English: periphrastic *do.* In Ralph W. Fasold and Deborah Schiffrin, *Language change and variation,* 133-72. Amsterdam: John Benjamins.

1989b. Reflexes of grammar in patterns of language change. *Language Variation and Change* 1.199–244.

Kroch, A., J. Myhill, and S. Pintzuk. 1982. Understanding *do. Chicago Linguistic Society* 18.282–94.

Kroeber, Paul. 1988. Discourse and functional factors in the development of Southern Interior Salish ergative case marking. In Shelley Axmaker, Annie Jaisser, and Helen Singmaster (eds.), *General Session and Parasession on Grammaticalization,* 114–23. Berkeley Linguistics Society.

Kuno, Susumu. 1974. The position of relative clauses and conjunctions. *Linguistic Inquiry* 5. 117–36.

Kuryłowicz, J. 1964. *The inflectional categories of Indo-European.* Heidelberg: Winter.

1965. Zur Vorgeschichte des germanischen Verbalsystems. In *Beiträge zur Sprachwissenschaft, Volkskunde und Literaturforschung: Wolfgang Steinitz zum 60. Gerburtstag,* 242–7. Berlin: Akademie-Verlag.

Laanest, Arvo. 1982. *Einführung in die ostseefinnischen Sprachen.* Hamburg: Helmut Buske.

Labov, William. 1963. The social motivation of a sound change. *Word* 19.273–309.

1981. Resolving the Neogrammarian controversy. *Language* 57.267–308.

1982. Building on empirical foundations. In Winfred P. Lehmann and Yakov Malkiel (eds.), *Perspectives on historical linguistics,* 17–92. Amsterdam: John Benjamins.

Lakoff, George. 1984. Performative subordinate clauses. *Berkeley Linguistics Society* 10.472–80.

Lakoff, Robin. 1968. *Abstract syntax and Latin complementation.* Cambridge, MA: MIT Press.

Lamy, Bernard. 1675. *La Rhétorique ou l'art de parler.* Paris: A. Pralard.

Langacker, Ronald W. 1977a. Syntactic reanalysis. In Charles N. Li (ed.), *Mechanisms of syntactic change,* 59–139. Austin: University of Texas Press.

1977b. *An overview of Uto-Aztecan grammar.* (Studies in Uto-Aztecan grammar, 1.) Arlington: Summer Institute of Linguistics, University of Texas at Arlington Press.

Lapteva, O.A. 1976. *Russkij razgovornyj sintaksis.* Moscow: Nauka.

Larkin, Don. 1972. "Enru" and "enpatu" as complement markers in Tamil. In S. Agesthialingom and S.V. Shanmugam (eds.), *Third seminar on Dravidian linguistics,* 37–73. Annamalainagar, Tamilnadu, India: Annamalai University, Department of Linguistics.

Larsen, Thomas W. and William M. Norman. 1979. Correlates of ergativity in Mayan grammar. In Frans Plank (ed.) *Ergativity: towards a theory of grammatical relations*, 347–70. New York: Academic Press.

Lasnik, Howard. 1981. Restricting the theory of transformations. In Norbert Hornstein and David W. Lightfoot (eds.), *Explanation in linguistics*, 152–73. London: Longman.

Lass, Roger. 1980. *On explaining language change*. Cambridge University Press.

 1987. Language, speakers, history and drift. In Willem Koopman, Frederike van der Leek, Olga Fischer, and Roger Eaton (eds.), *Explanation and linguistic change*, 151–76. Amsterdam: John Benjamins.

Law, Vivien. 1990. Language and its students: the history of linguistics. In N.E. Collinge (ed.), *An encyclopaedia of language*, 784–842. London: Routledge.

Lehiste, Ilse. 1988. *Lectures on language contact*. Cambridge, MA: MIT Press.

Lehmann, Christian. 1982. *Thoughts on grammaticalization: a programmatic sketch.* (Arbeiten des Kölner Universalien-Projekt 48.) Cologne: Institut für Sprachwissenschaft der Universität.

 1984. *Der Relativsatz*. Tübingen: Gunter Narr.

 1986. Grammaticalization and linguistic typology. *General Linguistics* 26.3–22.

 1988. Towards a typology of clause linkage. In John Haiman and Sandra A. Thompson (eds.), *Clause combining in grammar and discourse*, 181–225. Amsterdam: John Benjamins.

Lehmann, Winfred P. 1969. Proto-Indo-European compounds in relation to other Proto-Indo-European syntactic patterns. *Acta Linguistica Hafniensia* 12.1–20.

 1973. A structural principle of language and its implications. *Language* 49.47–66.

 1974. *Proto-Indo-European syntax*. Austin: University of Texas Press.

 1975. A discussion of compound and word order. In Charles N. Li. (ed.), *Word order and word order change*, 151–62. Austin: University of Texas Press.

 1980. The reconstruction of non-simple sentences in PIE. In Paolo Ramat (ed.), *Linguistic reconstruction and Indo-European syntax* (Current Issues in Linguistic Theory, 19), 113–44. Amsterdam: John Benjamins.

Lehmann, W. P. and Undirapola Ratanajoti. 1975. Typological syntactical characteristics of the *Śatapathabrāhmana*. *Journal of Indo-European Studies* 3.147–59.

Lehtiranta, Juhani. 1989. *Yhteissaamelainen sanasto*. [Common Saame (Lapp) dictionary.] Helsinki: Suomalais–Ugrilainen Seura.

Leinonen, Marja. 1980. A close look at natural serialization. *Nordic Journal of Linguistics* 3.147–59.

Le Laboureur, Louis. 1669. *Les Avantages de la langue françoise sur la langue latine*. Paris: G. de Luyne.

Lenerz, Jürgen. 1984. *Syntaktischer Wandel und Grammatiktheorie: eine Untersuchung an Beispielen aus der Sprachgeschichte des Deutschen*. Tübingen: Niemeyer.

Leopold, Joan. 1984. Duponceau, Humboldt et Pott: la place structurale des concepts de "polysynthèse" et d' "incorporation." In Sylvain Auroux and Franciso Queixalos (eds.), *Hommage à Bernard Pottier: pour une histoire de la linguistique amérindienne en France*, (*Amérindia, revue d'ethnolinguistique amérindienne*, numéro spécial, 6), 65–105.

Le Roux, Pierre. 1957. *Le Verbe breton*. Rennes: Librairie J. Plihon.

Leslau, Wolf. 1945. The influence of Cushitic on the Semitic languages of Ethiopia: a problem of substratum. *Word* 1.59–82.

1952. The influence of Sidamo on the Ethiopic languages of Gurage. *Language* 28.63–81.

Lewis, Henry and Holger Pedersen. 1937. *A concise comparative Celtic grammar.* Göttingen: Vandenhoeck and Ruprecht.

Li, Charles N. (ed.) 1975. *Word order and word order change.* Austin: University of Texas Press.

(ed.) 1977. *Mechanisms of syntactic change.* Austin: University of Texas Press.

1983. Languages in contact in western China. *Papers in East Asian languages* 1.31–51.

1988. Grammaticization in Hmong: verbs of saying. Ms., University of California, Santa Barbara.

Li, Charles N. and Sandra A. Thompson. 1974a. An explanation of word order change. *Foundations of Language* 12.201–14.

1974b. Historical change of word order: a case study of Chinese and its implications. In J.M. Anderson and C. Jones (eds.), *Historical linguistics: proceedings of the first International Conference on Historical Linguistics,* vol. I: *Syntax, morphology, internal and comparative reconstruction,* 199–217. Amsterdam: North Holland.

1976. Strategies for signaling grammatical relations in Wappo. *Chicago Linguistic Society* 12.450–8.

1984. Mandarin. In William S. Chisholm, Jr., Louis T. Milic, and John A.C. Greppin (eds.), *Interrogativity,* 47–61. Amsterdam: John Benjamins.

Li, Charles N., Sandra A. Thompson, and Jesse O. Sawyer. 1977. Subject and word order in Wappo. *International Journal of American Linguistics* 43.85–100.

Lightfoot, David W. 1974. The diachronic analysis of English modals. In J. M. Anderson and C. Jones, (eds.), *Historical linguistics: proceedings of the first International Conference on Historical Linguistics,* vol. I: *Syntax, morphology, internal and comparative reconstruction,* 219–49. Amsterdam: North Holland.

1979a. *Principles of diachronic syntax.* Cambridge University Press.

1979b. Review article of Charles N. Li (ed.), *Mechanisms of syntactic change. Language* 55.381–95.

1980. On reconstructing a proto-syntax. In Paolo Ramat (ed.), *Linguistic reconstruction and Indo-European syntax: proceedings of the Colloquium of the "Indogermanische Gesellschaft"* (Amsterdam Studies in the Theory and History of Linguistic Science, series 4, vol. 19), 27–45. Amsterdam: John Benjamins. (Revised version = Lightfoot 1983.)

1981a. Explaining syntactic change. In Norbert Hornstein and David Lightfoot (eds.), *Explanation in linguistics,* 209–40. London: Longman.

1981b. A reply to some critics. *Lingua* 55.351–68.

1981c. The history of NP movement. In Teun Hoekstra, Harry van der Hulst, and Michael Moortgat (eds.), *Lexical grammar,* 255–84. (Publications in Language Sciences, 3), Dordrecht: Foris.

1983. On reconstructing a proto-syntax. In Irmengard Rauch and Gerald F. Carr (eds.), *Language change,* 128–42. Bloomington: Indiana University Press.

1988a. Syntactic change. In Frederick J. Newmeyer, *Linguistics: the Cambridge survey,* vol. I: *Linguistic theory: foundations,* 303–23. Cambridge University Press.

1988b. Creoles, triggers, and universal grammar. In Caroline Duncan-Rose and

Theo Vennemann (eds.), *On language: rhetorica, phonologica, syntactica: a festschrift for Robert P. Stockwell from his friends and colleagues*, 97–105. London: Routledge.

1991. *How to set parameters: arguments from language change.* Cambridge, MA: MIT Press.

Little, Greta D. 1974. Syntactic evidence of language contact: Cushitic influence in Amharic. In Roger W. Shuy and Charles-James N. Bailey (eds.), *Towards tomorrow's linguistics*, 267–75. Washington, DC: Georgetown University Press.

Locke, John. 1690. *Essay concerning human understanding.* London: Basset.

Lockwood, W. B. 1968. *Historical German syntax.* Oxford University Press.

Lomtatiʒe, Ketevan. 1946. Damok'idebuli c'inadadebis erti tavisebureba zog kartul dialekt'ši. [One peculiarity of dependent clauses in certain Georgian dialects.] *Iberiul-k'avk'asiuri enatmecniereba* 1.337–44.

Lomtaʒe, E. 1954. Msazɣvrel–sazɣvrulis urtiertoba megrulši. [The modifier–modified relationship in Mingrelian.] *Iberiul-k'avk'asiuri enatmecniereba* 6.207–42.

Lord, Carol. 1973. Serial verbs in transition. *Studies in African Linguistics* 4.269–96.

1976. Evidence for syntactic reanalysis: from verb to complementizer in Kwa. In Sanford B. Steever, Carol A. Walker, and Salikoko S. Mufwene (eds.), *Papers from the Parasession on Diachronic Syntax*, 179–91. Chicago Linguistic Society.

Ludolf, Hiob. 1702. *Dissertatio de harmonia linguae aethiopicae cum ceteris orientalibus.* Frankfurt-on-Main: Johannis David Zunner and Nicolas Wilhem Helvig.

Lyell, Charles. 1830[–1833]. *Principles of geology, being an attempt to explain the former changes of the earth's surface by reference to causes now in operation.* London: John Murray.

Mačavariani, Givi. 1970. The system of Ancient Kartvelian nominal flection as compared to those of the Mountain Caucasian and Indo-European languages. In L. Dezsö and P. Hajdu (eds.), *Theoretical problems of typology and the Northern Eurasian languages*, 165–9. Amsterdam: B.R. Grüner.

Magometov, A.A. 1965. *Tabasaranskij jazyk.* Tbilisi: Mecniereba.

1970. *Agul'skij jazyk.* Tbilisi: Mecniereba.

Maher, Julianne. 1985. Contact linguistics: the language enclave phenomenon. New York University dissertation.

Maher, J. Peter. 1983. Introduction. In Konrad Koerner (ed.), *Linguistic and evolutionary theory: three essays by August Schleicher, Ernst Haeckel, and Wilhelm Bleek*, xvii–xxxii. Amsterdam: John Benjamins.

Malkiel, Yakov. 1981. Drift, slope, and slant. *Language* 57.535–70.

Mallinson, Graham and Barry J. Blake. 1981. *Language typology: cross-linguistic studies in syntax.* (North-Holland Linguistic Series, 46.) Amsterdam: North-Holland.

Marchese, Lynell. 1986. *Tense/aspect and the development of auxiliaries in Kru languages.* Arlington: SIL.

Marlett, Stephen A. 1986. Syntactic levels and multiattachment in Sierra Popoluca. *International Journal of American Linguistics* 52.359–87.

Marm, Ingvald and Alf Sommerfelt. 1967. *Teach yourself Norwegian.* New York: David McKay.

Mart'irosovi, A. 1960. Zmnisartisa da tandebulis sint'aksuri urtiertobisatvis. [On the syntactic relationship of adverbs and adpositions.] *Iberiul-k'avk'asiuri enatmecniereba* 12.231–8.

Masica, Colin P. 1976. *Defining a linguistic area: South Asia.* University of Chicago Press.

Matisoff, James A. 1976. Lahu causative constructions: case hierarchies and the morphology/syntax cycle in a Tibeto-Burman perspective. In Masayoshi Shibatani (ed.), *The grammar of causative constructions,* (Syntax and semantics, 6), 413–42. New York: Academic Press.

Matsumoto, Yo. 1988. From bound grammatical markers to free discourse markers: history of some Japanese connectives. In Shelley Axmaker, Annie Jaisser, and Helen Singmaster (eds.), *General session and parasession on Grammaticalization,* 340–51. Berkeley Linguistics Society.

Matthews, W.K. 1952. The ergative construction in Indo-Aryan. *Lingua* 3.391–406.

Maxwell, Dan. 1979. Strategies of relativization and NP accessibility. *Language* 55.352–72.

    1982. Implications of NP accessibility for diachronic syntax. *Folia Linguistica Historica* 3: 2.135–52.

Mayr, E. 1968. Cause and effect in biology. In Ernst Waddington (ed.), *Towards a theoretical biology,* vol. I: *Prolegomena,* 42–54. Edinburgh University Press.

Mazzocco, Angelo. 1987. Dante's notion of the *vulgare illustre*: a reappraisal. In Hans Aarsleff, Louis G. Kelly, and Hans-Josef Niederehe (eds.), *Papers in the history of linguistics: proceedings of the third International Conference on the History of the Language Sciences* (Studies in the History of Language Sciences, 38), 129–42. Amsterdam: John Benjamins.

McCloskey, James. 1979. *Transformational syntax and model theoretic semantics: a case study in Modern Irish.* Dordrecht: Reidel.

McConvell, Patrick. 1981. How Lardil became accusative. *Lingua* 55.141–79.

McKay, Graham Richard. 1975. Rembarnga: a language of Central Arnhem Land. Australian National University dissertation.

McKnight, George H. 1897. The primitive Teutonic order of words. *Journal of Germanic Philology* 1.136–219.

Meillet, Antoine. 1909. Sur la disparition des formes simples du prétérit. *Germanisch-romanische Monatsschrift* 1. (Repr. 1951. In *Linguistique historique et linguistique générale,* 149–58. Paris: C. Klincksieck.)

    1912. L'évolution des formes grammaticales. *Scientia* 12/26 (Milan). (Repr. 1951. In *Linguistique historique et linguistique générale,* 130–48. Paris: C. Klincksieck.)

    1916. *Caractères généraux des langues germaniques.* Paris: C. Klincksieck. (English trans. 1970. *General characteristics of the Germanic languages.* Coral Gables, FL: University of Miami Press.)

    1914. Le problème de la parenté des langues. *Scientia* 15/35. (Repr. 1921 In *Linguistique historique et linguistique générale,* 76-101. Paris: Champion.)

    1922. *Introduction à l'étude comparative des langues indo-européennes.* (8th edn. 1937.) Paris: Hachette. (Repr. 1964. [Alabama Linguistic and Philology Series, 3.] University: University of Alabama Press.)

    1951 [1921]. *Linguistique historique et linguistique générale.* Paris: C. Klincksieck. (Repr. 1982. Geneva: Slatkin; Paris: Champion.)

    1954 [1925]. *La Méthode comparative en linguistique historique.* Paris: Champion. (Reissued 1966.)

Metcalf, George J. 1974. The Indo-European hypothesis in the sixteenth and seventeenth centuries. In Dell Hymes (ed.), *Studies in the history of linguistics: traditions and paradigms*, 233–57. Bloomington: Indiana University Press.

Mielikäinen, Aila. 1984. Nykypuhesuomen alueellista taustaa. [On the regional background of Modern Spoken Finnish.] In Heikki Pounonen and Päivi Rintala (eds.) *Nykysuomen rakenne ja kehitys*, vol. II: *Näkökulmia kielen muuttumiseen*, 187-208. [The structure and development of Modern Finnish, vol. II: View points on language variation and change.] (Tieto Lipas 95.) Helsinki: Suomalaisen Kirjallisuuden Seura.

Miklosich, Franz, Ritter von. 1868–79. *Vergleichende Grammatik der slavischen Sprachen.* Vienna: Braumüller. (2nd edn. 1926. Heidelberg: Winter.)

Miller, Roy Andrew. 1967. *The Japanese language*. University of Chicago Press.

Miranda, Rocky V. 1976. Comments on Jeffers. In William M. Chiristie, Jr. (ed.), *Current progress in historical linguistics: proceedings of the second International Conference on Historical Linguistics*, 12–14. Amsterdam: North-Holland.

Mithun, Marianne. 1980. A functional approach to syntactic reconstruction. In Elizabeth Closs Traugott, R. LaBrum, and S. Shepherd (eds.), *Papers from the fourth International Conference on Historical Linguistics*, 87–96. Amsterdam: John Benjamins.

1988. Lexical categories and the evolution of number marking. In Michael Hammond and Michael Noonan (eds.), *Theoretical morphology*, 211–34. New York: Academic Press.

1991. Active/agentive case marking and its motivations. *Language.* 67.510–46.

Miyagawa, Shigera. 1984. Case theory and the accusative case in Old Japanese. Paper delivered at the Linguistic Society of America, Annual Meeting.

Modini, Paul. 1989. Ergative, passive and the other devices of functional perspective. *Folia Linguistica Historica* 8.351–63.

Möhren, Frankwalt. 1980. *Le Renforcement affectif de la négation par l'expression d'une valeur minimale en ancien français.* Tübingen: Max Niemeyer.

Mondloch, James L. 1978. Disambiguating subjects and objects in Quiché. *Journal of Mayan Linguistics* 1.3–19.

Moore, Terence and Christine Carling. 1982. *Understanding language*. London: Macmillan.

Moravcsik, Edith. 1978. Language contact. In Joseph H. Greenberg, Charles A. Ferguson, and Edith A. Moravcsik (eds.), *Universals of human language*, vol. I: 93–123. Stanford University Press.

Mossé, Fernand. 1938. La périphrase verbale *être* + participe présent en ancien germanique. L'Université de Paris dissertation. Also in *Histoire de la forme périphrastique "être" + participe présent en germanique*. Paris: Klincksieck, 1938.

Müller, Max. 1865. *Lectures on the science of language: first and second series*. 5th edn. New York: Charles Scribner.

Munro, Pamela. 1978. Chemehuevi "say" and the Uto-Aztecan quotative pattern. In Donald Tuohy, *Selected papers from the fourteenth Great Basin Anthropological Conference*, 149–71. Socorro, NM: Ballena Press.

1982. On the transitivity of "say" verbs. In Paul J. Hopper and Sandra A. Thompson (eds.), *Studies in transitivity* (Syntax and Semantics, 15), 301–18. New York: Academic Press.

1984. Auxiliaries and auxiliarization in Western Muskogean. In Jacek Fisiak (ed.),

Historical syntax, 333–62. The Hague: Mouton.

Muysken, Pieter. 1977. *Syntactic developments in the verb phrase of Ecuadorian Quechua*. (Studies in Generative Grammar, 2.) Lisse: Peter de Ridder Press (Dordrecht, Holland: Foris).

1981. Halfway between Quechua and Spanish: the case for relexification. In Arnold Highfield and Albert Valdman (eds.), *Historicity and variation in Creole studies*, 52–78. Ann Arbor: Karoma.

Nadkarni, M. 1975. Bilingualism and syntactic change in Konkani. *Language* 51.672–83.

Nagle, Stephen J. 1989. *Inferential change and syntactic modality in English*. Frankfurt-on-Main: Peter Lang.

Naro, Anthony J. 1981. The social and structural dimensions of a syntactic change. *Language* 57.63–99.

Naro, Anthony J. and Miriam Lemle. 1976. Syntactic diffusion. In Sanford B. Steever, Carol A. Walker, and Salikoko S. Mufwene (eds.), *Papers from the Parasession on Diachronic Syntax*, 221–40. Chicago Linguistic Society.

Nevis, Joel A. 1984. A non-endoclitic in Estonian. *Lingua* 64.209–24.

1985. Language-external evidence for clitics as words: Lappish particle clitics. *Chicago Linguistic Society* 21.289–305.

Nevis, Joel A., and Brian D. Joseph. 1992. Wackernagel affixes: evidence from Balto-Slavic. Ms., Ohio State University.

Nižaraʒe, Šota. 1975. *Ačaruli dialekt'i: ponet'ik'a, gramat'ik'a, leksik'a*. [The Ačarian dialect: phonetics, grammar, lexicon.] Batumi: Sabčota Ačara.

Noreen, Adolph. 1923. *Altisländische und altnorwegische Grammatik*. 4th edn. Halle: Max Niemeyer.

Norman, William M. and Lyle Campbell. 1978. Toward a Proto-Mayan syntax: a comparative perspective on grammar. In Nora C. England (ed.), *Papers in Mayan linguistics*, 136–56. Columbia: Department of Anthropology, University of Missouri.

Nozaʒe, L. 1974. Medioakt'iv zmnata c'armoebis zogi sak'itxi kartulši. [Some questions of the formation of medioactive verbs in Georgian.] *Iberiul-k'ark'asiur enatmecniereba* 19.25–51.

Ogle, Richard. 1981. Redefining the scope of root transformations. *Linguistics* 19.119–46.

Ogura, Michiko. 1986. *Old English "impersonal" verbs and expressions*. (Anglistica 24). Copenhagen: Rosenkilde and Bagger.

Ogura, Mieko. 1993. The development of periphrastic *do* in English: a case of lexical diffusion in syntax. *Diachronica* 10.51–85.

Ohala, John. 1981. The listener as a source of sound change. In C.S. Masek, R.A. Hendrick, and M.F. Miller (eds.), *Papers from the Parasession on Language and Behavior*, 178–203. Chicago Linguistic Society.

1989. Sound change is drawn from a pool of synchronic variation. In Leiv Egil Breivik and Ernst Håkon Jahr (eds.), *Language change: contributions to the study of its causes*, 173–98. Berlin: Mouton de Gruyter.

Oinas, Felix. 1961. *The development of some postpositional cases in Balto-Finnic languages*. (Suomalais-Ugrilaisen Seuran Toimituksia, 123.) Helsinki: Suomalais-Ugrilaisen Seura..

O'Neil, Wayne. 1977. Clause adjunction in Old English. *General Linguistics* 17.199–211.

Ong, Walter. 1982. *Orality and literacy*. London: Methuen.

Ōno, S. 1964. [What is the origin of Kakari-Musubi?] [*Kashaku to Kanshō*], October. Cited by Akiba 1978.

Osthoff, Hermann and Karl Brugmann. 1878. *Morphologische Untersuchungen auf dem Gebiete der indogermanischen Sprachen*. Leipzig: S. Hirzel.

Oswalt, Robert L. 1976. Switch reference in Maiduan: an areal and typological contribution. *International Journal of American Linguistics* 42.297–304.

Owens, Jonathan. 1988. *The foundations of grammar: in introduction to medieval Arabic grammatical theory*. (Studies in the History of the Language Sciences, 45.) Amsterdam: John Benjamins.

Pallas, Peter Simon. 1786–89. *Linguarum totius orbis vocabularia comparativa*. 2 vols. St. Petersburg: Schnorr.

Parker, Frank. 1976. Language change and the passive voice. *Language* 52.449–60.

Partee, Barbara Hall. 1973. The syntax and semantics of quotation. In Stephen R. Anderson and Paul Kiparsky (eds.), *A festschrift for Morris Halle*, 410–18. New York: Holt, Rinehart and Winston.

Pasicki, Adam. 1983. *While*-clauses in Old and Early Middle English. *Folia Linguistica Historica* 4.287–303.

Pätsch, Gertrud. 1971. Zur Entwicklung der attributiven Wortfolge im Georgischen. *Bedi Kartlisa* 28.253–61.

Paul, Hermann. 1920 [1898]. *Prinzipien der Sprachgeschichte*. 5th edn. (1st edn. 1880; 1970 printing.) Tübingen: Max Niemeyer.

(selected by Heinz Stolte). 1949. *Kurze deutsche Grammatik*. Halle: Max Niemeyer.

Payne, John R. 1979. Transitivity and intransitivity in the Iranian languages of the USSR. In Paul R. Clyne, William F. Hanks, and Carol L. Hofbauer (eds.), *The elements: papers from the Conference on Non-Slavic Languages of the USSR*, 436–47. Chicago Linguistic Society.

1980. The decay of ergativity in Pamir languages. *Lingua* 51.147–86.

Pedersen, Holger. 1962 [1931]. *The discovery of language: linguistic science in the nineteenth century*. Bloomington: Indiana University Press.

Penny, Ralph. 1991. *A history of the Spanish language*. Cambridge University Press.

Percival, W. Keith. 1986a. The reception of Hebrew in sixteenth-century Europe: the impact of the Cabbala. In Antonio Quilis and Hans-J. Niederehe (eds.), *The history of linguistics in Spain*, (Studies in the History of the Language Sciences, 34), 21–38. Amsterdam: John Benjamins.

1986b. Renaissance linguistics: the old and the new. In Theodora Bynon and F.R. Palmer (eds.), *Studies in the history of Western linguistics, in honour of R. H. Robins*, 56–68. Cambridge University Press.

Perlmutter, David M. 1978. Impersonal passives and the Unaccusative Hypothesis. *Berkeley Linguistics Society* 4.157–89.

1983. Personal vs. impersonal constructions. *Natural Language and Linguistic Theory* 1.141–200.

1984. Working 1s and inversion in Italian, Japanese, and Quechua. In David M. Perlmutter and Carol G. Rosen (eds.), *Studies in Relational Grammar*, vol. II, 292–330. University of Chicago Press.

Perrot, Daisy V. 1957. *Teach yourself Swahili*. New York: David McKay.

Pinborg, Jan. 1982. Speculative grammar. In Norman Kretzmann, Anthony Kenny, and Jan Pinborg (eds.), *The Cambridge history of later medieval philosophy from the rediscovery of Aristotle to the disintegration of scholasticism, 1100–1600*, 254–69. Cambridge University Press.

Pirejko, L. A. 1979. On the genesis of the ergative construction in Indo-Iranian. In Frans Plank (ed.), *Ergativity: towards a theory of grammatical relations*, 481–8. New York: Academic Press.

Plank, Frans 1980. Encoding grammatical relations: acceptable and unacceptable non-distinctness. In Jacek Fisiak (ed.), *Historical morphology*, 289–326. Berlin: Mouton.

　　1985. The extended accusative/restricted nominative in perspective. In Frans Plank (ed.), *Relational typology*, 269–311. Berlin: Mouton.

　　in press. Syntactic change: ergativity. In Joachim Jacobs, Arnim v. Stechow, Wolfgang Sternefeld, and Theo Vennemann (eds.), *Syntax: an international handbook of contemporary research*. Berlin: de Gruyter.

Platzack, Christer. 1983. Three syntactic changes in the grammar of written Swedish about 1700. In Erik Andersson, Mirja Saari, and Peter Slotte (eds.), *Struktur och variation: Festskrift till Bengt Loman*, 43–63. Turku: Åbo Academy Press.

　　1985. Syntaktiska förändringar i Svenskan under 1600-talet. In Sture Allén, Jonas Löfström, Bo Ralph, Lars-Gunnar Andersson, and Kerstin Nordenström (eds.), *Svenskans Beskrivning*, 15.401–17, Göteborg Universitet.

Posner, Rebecca. 1966. *The Romance languages: a linguistic introduction*. Garden City, NY: Anchor Books.

　　1985. Diachronic syntax – free relatives in Romance. *Journal of Linguistics* 21.181–9.

Pray, Bruce. 1980. Evidence of grammatical convergence in Dakhini Urdu and Telegu. *Berkeley Linguistics Society* 6.90–9.

Prokosch, Eduard. 1939. *A comparative Germanic grammar*. Philadelphia: Linguistic Society of America and University of Pennsylvania Press.

Pullum, Geoffrey K. 1988. Topic . . . comment: citation etiquette beyond thunderdome. *Natural Language and Linguistic Theory*, 6.579–88.

Ramat, Anna Giacalone. 1982. Explorations on syntactic change (relative clause formation strategies). In Anders Ahlqvist (ed.), *Papers from the fifth International Conference on Historical Linguistics*, 283–92. Amsterdam: John Benjamins.

Ramat, Paolo. 1987. Introductory paper. In Martin Harris and Paolo Ramat (eds.), *Historical development of auxiliaries* (Trends in Linguistics: Studies and Monographs 35), 3–19. Berlin: Mouton de Gruyter.

Raun, Alo and Anrus Saareste. 1965. *Introduction to Estonian linguistics*. (Ural-Alatische Bibliothek.) Wiesbaden: Otto Harrassowitz.

Rédei, Károly. 1970. Russische Einflüsse in der permjakischen Syntax: über Interferenzerscheinungen beim Verb. In Wolfgang Schlachter (ed.), *Symposion über Syntax der uralischen Sprachen*, 154–64. Abhandlungen der Akademie der Wissenschaften in Göttingen. (Philologisch–Historische Klasse, Dritte Folge, 76.) Göttingen: Vandenhoeck and Ruprecht.

Richter, Elise. 1903. *Zur Entwicklung der romanischen Wortstellung aus der lateinischen*. Halle: Niemeyer.

Richter, Oswald. 1898. Die unechten Nominalkomposita des Altindischen und Altiranischen. *Indogermanische Forschungen* 9.1–62, 183–252.

Ries, John. 1880. *Die Stellung von Subject und Prädicatsverbum im Hêliand: ein Beitrag zur germanischen Wortstellungslehre.* Strasburg: Karl J. Trübner.

Risch, Ernst. 1944–9. Griechische Determinativ-Komposita. *Indogermanische Forschung* 59.1–61, 245–94.

Rivarol, Antoine de. 1784. *Discours sur l'universalité de la langue française.* (Repr. 1966. Paris: Pierre Belfond.)

Roberts, Ian G. 1985. Agreement parameters and the development of English modal auxiliaries. *Natural Language and Linguistic Theory* 3.21–58.

Robertson, John S. 1992. *The history of tense/aspect/mood/voice in the Mayan verbal complex.* Austin: University of Texas Press.

Robins, Robert H. 1990. Leibniz and Wilhelm von Humboldt and the history of comparative linguistics. In Tullio de Mauro and Lia Formigari (eds.), *Leibniz, Humboldt, and the origins of comparativism,* 85–102. Amsterdam: John Benjamins.

Rochemont, Michael S. 1986. *Focus in generative grammar.* Amsterdam: John Benjamins.

Romaine, Suzanne. 1981. The transparency principle: what it is and why it doesn't work. *Lingua* 55.277–300.

Rosen, Carol G. 1984. The interface between semantic roles and initial grammatical relations. In David M. Perlmutter and Carol G. Rosen (eds.), *Studies in relational grammar,* vol. II, 38–77. University of Chicago.

Rosen, Carol and Kashi Wali. 1989. Twin passives, inversion, and multistratalism in Marathi. *Natural Language and Linguistic Theory* 7.1–50.

Rosiello, Luigi. 1987. Turgot's "étymologie" and modern linguistics. In Dino Buzzetti and Maurizio Ferriani (eds.), *Speculative grammar, universal grammar and philosophical analysis of language,* 75–84. Amsterdam: John Benjamins.

Rousseau, Jean. 1980. Flexion et racine: trois étapes de leur constitution: J.C. Adelung, F. Schlegel, F. Bopp. In Konrad Koerner (ed.), *Progress in linguistic historiography,* (Studies in the History of Linguistics, 20), 235–47. Amsterdam: John Benjamins.

Sahlman–Karlsson, Siiri. 1976. *Specimens of American Finnish: a field study of linguistic behavior.* (Acta Universitatis Upsaliensis, Studia Uralica et Altaica Upsaliensia, 11.) Stockholm: Almqvist and Wiksell International.

Sajnovics, Joannis [János]. 1770. *Demonstratio idioma Ungarorum et Lapponum idem esse.* (1st edn. 1770. Copenhagen: Typis Collegi Societatis Iesu; 2nd edn. 1770. Trnava (Tyrnau), Hungary.) (Photolithic reproduction of 2nd edn. 1968, ed. by Thomas A. Sebeok. [Ural and Altaic Series, 91.] Bloomington: Indiana University Press; The Hague: Mouton.) (German trans. 1972, by M. Ehlers. Wiesbaden: Harassowitz.)

Saltarelli, Mario. 1980. Syntactic diffusion. In Elizabeth Closs Traugott, R. LaBrum, and S. Shepherd (eds.), *Papers from the fourth International Conference on Historical Linguistics,* 183–91. Amsterdam: John Benjamins.

Samuels, M.L. 1987. The status of the functional approach. In Willem Koopman, Frederike van der Leek, Olga Fischer, and Roger Eaton (eds.), *Explanation and linguistic change,* 239–50. Amsterdam: John Benjamins.

Sanctius (Brocensis), Franciscus [Francisco Sánchez (de las Brozas)]. 1585/1587. *Minerva seu de causis linguae latinae.* Salamanca: Ioannes and Andreas Renaut.

Sandfeld, Kristian. 1930. *Linguistique balkanique: problèmes et résultats.* (Collection Linguistique, Publication par la Société de Linguistique de Paris, 31.) Paris: Champion.

Šaniʒe, Akʼakʼi. 1922–3. Naštebi mesame pʼiris obiektʼuri pʼrepiksis xmarebisa xmovnebis cʼin kartul zmnebši. [Traces of the use of the third person object prefix before vowels in the Georgian verb.] *Tʼpilisis Universitʼetʼis Moambe* 2: 262–81. (Repr. 1957. In *Kartuli enis stʼruktʼurisa da istʼoriis sakʼitxebi*, 267–81. Tbilisi: Universitʼetʼi.)

1957. Umlautʼi svanurši. [Umlaut in Svan.] In *Kartuli enis stʼruktʼurisa da istʼoriis sakʼitxebi*, 323–76. Tbilisi: Universitʼetʼi.

1973. *Kartuli enis gramatʼikʼis sapuʒvlebi.* [Fundamentals of the grammar of the Georgian language.] 2nd edn. Tbilisi: Universitʼetʼi.

Sankoff, Gillian and Penelope Brown. 1976. On the origins of syntax in discourse: a case study of Tok Pisin relatives. *Language* 52.631–66.

Sankoff, Gillian and Suzanne Laberge. 1973. On the acquisition of native speakers by a language. *Kivung* 6.32–47.

Sansom, George. 1928. *An historical grammar of Japanese.* Oxford: Clarendon Press.

Sapir, Edward. 1917. Review of C.C. Uhlenbeck, *Het passieve karakter van het verbum transitivum of van het verbum actionis in talen van Noord-Amerika. International Journal of American Linguistics* 1.82–6.

1921. *Language.* New York: Harcourt, Brace and World.

Sarjvelaʒe, Zurab. 1984. *Kartuli salitʼeratʼuro enis istʼoriis šesavali.* [Introduction to the history of the Georgian literary language.] Tbilisi: Ganatleba.

Sasse, Hans-Jürgen. 1977. Gedanken über Wortstellungsveränderung. *Papiere zur Linguistik* 13/14.82–142.

1984. Case in Cushitic, Semitic, and Berber. In James Bynon (ed.), *Current progress in Afro-Asiatic linguistics: papers of the third Hamito-Semitic Congress*, 111–26. Amsterdam: John Benjamins.

Saukkonen, Pauli. 1984. Infinitiivirakenteidemme historiaa. [On the history of our infinitive constructions.] In Heikki Paunonen and Päivi Rintala (eds.), *Nykysuomen rakenne ja kehitys*, vol. II: *Näkökulmia kielen vaiteluun ja muuttumiseen* [The structure and development of Modern Finnish, vol. II: View points on language variation and change], (Tieto Lipas 95), 176–86 Helsinki: Suomalaisen Kirjallisuuden Seura.

Saussure, Ferdinand de. 1949. *Cours de linguistique générale.* Paris: Payot.

Saxena, Anju. 1988. On syntactic convergence: the case of the verb "say" in Tibeto-Burman. In Shelley Axmaker, Annie Jaisser, and Helen Singmaster (eds.), *General session and parasession on Grammaticalization*, 375–88. Berkeley Linguistics Society.

Sayce, Archibald H. 1880. *Introduction to the science of languages.* London: C. K. Paul.

Scaglione, Aldo. 1972. *The classical theory of composition: from its origins to the present, a historical survey.* Chapel Hill: University of North Carolina Press.

1981. *The theory of German word order from the Renaissance to the present.* Minneapolis: University of Minnesota Press.

Scaliger, Joseph Justus. 1610. Diatriba de Europaeorum linguis, 119–22; Diatriba de varia literarum aliquot pro nuntiatione, 127–32. In *Opuscula varia antehac non edita.* Paris.

Scaliger, Julius Caesar. 1540. *De causis linguae latinae.* Lyons: S. Gryphius.

Schachter, Paul. 1973. Focus and relativization. *Language* 49.19–46.

Schaller, Helmut Wilhelm. 1975. *Die Balkansprachen: eine Einführung in die Balkanphilologie.* Heidelberg: Carl Winter Universitätsverlag.

Scherer, Wilhelm. 1868. *Zur Geschichte der deutschen Sprache*. Berlin: Weidmann.

Schlegel, August Wilhem von. 1820. *Indische Bibliotek*. Bonn: E. Weber.

Schlegel, (Karl Wilhelm) Friedrich von. 1808. *Ueber die Sprache und Weisheit der Indier*. Heidelberg: Mohr und Zimmer. (Repr. 1977. [Amsterdam Classics in Linguistics, 1.] Introduction by Sebastiano Timpanaro, translation by Peter Maher. Amsterdam: John Benjamins.)

Schleicher, August. 1848. *Zur vergleichenden Sprachengeschichte*. Bonn: H.B. König.

1861–2. *Compendium der vergleichenden Grammatik der indo-germanischen Sprachen: Kurzer abriss einer Laut- und Formenlehre der indogermanischen Ursprache*. (3rd edn., 1871.) Weimar: Hermann Böhlau.

1983 [1863]. The Darwinian theory and the science of language. In Konrad Koerner (ed.), *Linguistics and evolutionary theory: three essays by August Schleicher, Ernst Haeckel, and Wilhelm Bleek*, 1–70. Amsterdam: John Benjamins.

1983 [1865]. On the significance for the natural history of man. In Konrad Koerner (ed.), *Linguistics and evolutionary theory: three essays by August Schleicher, Ernst Haeckel, and Wilhelm Bleek*, 73–82. Amsterdam: John Benjamins.

1869. *Die deutsche Sprache*. 2nd edn. Stuttgart: Cotta.

Schlieben-Lange, Brigitte. 1989. The history of subordinative conjunctions from Old French to modern French. Unpublished paper presented at the ninth International Conference on Historical Linguistics, Rutgers University.

Schmalstieg, William R. 1988. *A Lithuanian historical syntax*. Columbus, OH: Slavica.

Schmidt, Karl Horst. 1969. Zur Tmesis in den Kartvelsprachen und ihren typologischen Parallelen in indogermanischen Sprachen. In *Giorgi Axvledians*, 96–105. Tbilisi: Universit'et'i.

1988. Zur Verbalkomposition in den Kartvelsprachen. *C'elic'deuli* 15.82–5.

Schottelius, Justus Georgius (Schottel, Justus Georg). 1663. *Ausführliche Arbeit von der teutschen Haubt-Sprache*. Brunswick: C.F. Zilliger. (Facsimile edn. 1967. 2 vols. Tübingen: Max Niemeyer.)

Schuchardt, Hugo. 1919–20. *Sprachursprung*. Sitzungsberichte, l'Académie de Berlin. (Repr. 1922. *Hugo Schuchardt-Brevier: ein vademecum der allgemeinen Sprachwissenschaft*, ed. Leo Spitzer. Halle: Max Niemeyer.)

Schulze, Wolfgang. 1982. *Die Sprache der Uden in Nord-Azerbajdžan*. Wiesbaden: Otto Harrassowitz.

Schulze-Fürhoff, Wolfgang. 1992. How can class markers petrify? Towards a functional diachrony of morphological subsystems in the East Caucasian languages. In Howard I. Aronson (ed.), *The non-Slavic languages of the USSR*, 189–233. Chicago Linguistic Society.

Searle, John R. 1970 [1969]. *Speech acts*. Cambridge University Press.

Shafeev, D.A. 1964. *A short grammatical outline of Pashto*. The Hague: Mouton.

Sherry, Richard. 1550. *Treatise of schemes and tropes*. London: John Day.

Silverstein, Michael. 1974. Dialectal developments in Chinookan tense–aspect systems: an areal-historical analysis. *International Journal of American Linguistics*, Memoir 29.

1976. Hierarchy of features and ergativity. In R.M.W. Dixon (ed.), *Grammatical categories in Australian languages*, 112–71. Canberra: Australian Institute of Aboriginal Studies.

Sischo, William R. 1979. Michoacán Nahual. In Ronald W. Langacker (ed.), *Studies in*

Uto-Aztecan grammar, vol. II: *Modern Aztec grammatical sketches*, 307–80. Arlington: Summer Institute of Linguistics and the University of Texas at Arlington.

Smith, Adam. 1761. *Dissertation on the origin of languages, or considerations &c. added to the theory of moral sentiments*. 3rd edition. London: A. Millar, A. Kinkaid, and J. Bell. (New edn. 1970. [Tübinger Beiträge zur Linguistik.] Tübingen: Gunter Narr.) (Translated and published in French in 1784 as a supplement to Beauzée's article "*Langue*," 2nd edn. of *Encyclopédie*.)

Smith, Neil V. 1981. Consistency, markedness and language change: on the notion "consistent language." *Journal of Linguistics* 17.39–54.

Smith, Norval S.H., Ian E. Robertson, and Kay Williamson. 1987. The Ijo element in Berdice Dutch. *Language in Society* 16.49–90.

Sommerfelt, Alf. 1960a. External versus internal factors in the development of language. *Norsk Tidsskrift for Sprogvidenskap* 19.296–315.

1960b. Mixed languages versus remodelled languages. *Norsk Tidsskrift for Sprogvidenskap* 19.316–26.

Sorsakivi, Merja. 1982. Infinitiivijärjestelmän muutoksia lasten kielessä. [Infinitive structure changes in children's language.] *Virittäjä* 86.377–91.

Sridhar, S.N. 1978. Linguistic convergence: Indo-Aryanization of Dravidian languages. *Studies in the Linguistic Sciences* 8.197–215.

Staal, J.F. 1974. The origin and development of linguistics in India. In Dell Hymes (ed.), *Studies in the history of linguistics: traditions and paradigms*, 63–74. Bloomington: Indiana University Press.

Stankiewicz, Edward. 1974. The dithyramb to the verb in eighteenth and nineteenth century linguistics. In Dell Hymes (ed.), *Studies in the history of linguistics: traditions and paradigms*, 157–90. Bloomington: Indiana University Press.

Steele, Susan. 1975. On some factors that affect and effect word order. In Charles N. Li (ed.), *Word order and word order change*, 197–268. Austin: University of Texas Press.

1977. Clisis and diachrony. In Charles N. Li (ed.), *Mechanisms of syntactic change*, 539–79. Austin: University of Texas Press.

Steele, Susan, with Adrian Akmajian, Richard Demers, Eloise Jelinek, Chisato Kitagawa, Richard Oehrle, and Thomas Wasow. 1981. *An encyclopedia of AUX: a study in cross-linguistic equivalence*. Cambridge, MA: MIT Press.

Steever, Sanford B. 1981. Morphological convergence in the Khondmals: object incorporation. In Sanford B. Steever (ed.), *Selected papers on Tamil and Dravidian linguistics*, 47–63. Madurai: Muttu Patippakam.

1987a. The origins of the past negative in Koṇḍa. *Journal of the American Oriental Society* 107.71–88.

1987b. Remarks on Dravidian complementation. *Studies in the Linguistic Sciences* 17.103–19.

Stein, Dieter. 1988. Semantic similarity between categories as a vehicle of linguistic change. *Diachronica* 5.1–20.

1990. *The semantics of syntactic change: aspects of the evolution of "do" in English*. Berlin: Mouton de Gruyter.

Steinitz, Wolfgang. 1950. *Ostjakische Grammatik und Chrestomathie, mit Wörterverzeichnis*. 2nd edn. Leipzig: Otto Harrassowitz.

Steinthal, Heymann. 1860. Assimilation und Attraktion, psychologisch beleuchtet.

Zeitschrift für Völkerspsychologie und Sprachwissenschaft 1.93–179.

Stenson, Nancy. 1981. *Studies in Irish syntax.* Tübingen: Gunter Narr.

Stiernhielm, Georg. 1671. *De linguarum origine Praefatio. D. N. Jesu Christi SS. Evangelia ab Ulfila Gothorum translata.* Stockholm.

Stipa, Günter Johannes. 1990. *Finnisch-ugrische Sprachforschung.* Helsinki: Suomalais-Ugrilainen Seura.

Stockwell, Robert P. 1977. Motivation for exbraciation in Old English. In Charles N. Li (ed.), *Mechanisms of syntactic change,* 291–314. Austin: University of Texas Press.

Stoll, Otto. 1918. Die Entwicklung der Völkerkunde von ihren Anfängen bis in die Neuzeit. *Mitteilungen der geographisch-etnographischen Gesellschaft* 18.1–130. (Zurich.)

Strahlenberg, Philip Johan Tabbert von. 1730. *Das nord- und östliche Theil von Europa und Asia.* Stockholm.

Strong, David Robert. 1983. Aspects of the diachrony of the Italian causative construction. University of Michigan dissertation.

Stump, Gregory T. 1983. The elimination of ergative patterns of case-marking and verbal agreement in modern Indic languages. *Ohio State University Working Papers in Linguistics* 27.140–64.

1984. Agreement vs. incorporation in Breton. *Natural Language and Linguistic Theory* 2.289–348.

1989. Further remarks on Breton agreement. *Natural Language and Linguistic Theory* 7.429–71.

Suárez, Jorge A. 1977. La influencia del español en la estructura gramatical del náhuatl. *Anuario de Letras* 14.115–64. (Mexico.)

1983. *The Mesoamerican Indian languages.* Cambridge University Press.

Svensson, Pirkko Forsman. 1983. *Satsmotsvarigheter i Finsk prosa under 1600-talet: participialkonstruktionen och därmed synonyma icke-finita uttryck i jämförelse med språkbruket före och efter 1600-talet.* Helsinki: Suomalaisen Kirjallisuuden Seura.

Sweet, Henry. 1900. *The history of language.* London: J.M. Dent; New York: Macmillan.

Tai, James H.-Y. 1976. On the change from SVO to SOV in Chinese. In Sanford B. Steever, Carol A. Walker, and Salikoko S. Mufwene (eds.), *Papers from the Parasession on Diachronic Syntax,* 291–304. Chicago Linguistic Society.

Téné, David. 1980. The earliest comparisons of Hebrew with Aramaic and Arabic. In Konrad Koerner (ed.), *Progress in linguistic historiography* (Studies in the history of linguistics, 20), 355–77. Amsterdam: John Benjamins.

Thomason, Sarah Grey. 1980. Morphological instability, with and without language contact. In Jacek Fisiak (ed.), *Historical morphology* (Trends in Linguistics, Studies and Monographs, 17), 359–82. The Hague: Mouton.

Thomason, Sarah Grey and Terrence Kaufman. 1988. *Language contact, creolization, and genetic linguistics.* Berkeley: University of California Press.

Thurgood, Graham. 1977. Burmese historical morphology. *Berkeley Linguistics Society* 3.685–91.

1983. Morphological innovation and subgrouping: some Tibeto-Burman notes. *Berkeley Linguistic Society* 9.257–65.

1984. The "Rung" languages: a major new Tibeto-Burman subgroup. *Berkeley Linguistics Society* 10.338–49.

1986a. Lolo-Burmese subordinators from case postpositions: several partial etymologies. In Scott Delancey and Russell S. Tomlin (eds.), *Proceedings of the second Annual Meeting of the Pacific Linguistics Conference*, 449–453. University of Oregon Press.

1986b. The nature and origins of the Akha evidentials system. In Wallace Chafe and Johanna Nichols (eds.), *Evidentiality: the linguistic coding of epistemology*, 214–22. Norwood, NJ: Ablex.

Thurneysen, Rudolf. 1946. *A grammar of Old Irish*. Dublin Institute for Advanced Studies.

Timberlake, Alan. 1974. *The nominative object in Slavic, Baltic, and West Finnic.* (Slavistische Beiträge, 82.) Munich: Otto Sagner.

1977. Reanalysis and actualization in syntactic change. In Charles N. Li (ed.), *Mechanisms of syntactic change*, 141–77. Austin: University of Texas Press.

Timm, Lenora. 1989. Word order in 20th century Breton. *Natural Language and Linguistic Theory* 7.361–78.

Timmer, B.J. 1939. The place of the attributive noun–genitive in Anglo-Saxon. *English Studies* 21.49–72.

Tomanetz, Karl. 1879. *Die Relativsätze bei den ahd. Übersetzern des 8. und 9. Jahrhunderts.* Vienna: C. Gerold's Sohn.

Tomlin, Russell. 1986. *Basic word order: functional principles.* London: Croom Helm.

Toon, Thomas E. 1987. Old English dialects: what's to explain; what's an explanation? In Willem Koopman, Frederike van der Leek, Olga Fischer, and Roger Eaton (eds.), *Explanation and linguistic change*, 275–94. Amsterdam: John Benjamins.

Topuria, Varlam. 1937. Zogierti brunvis genezisisatvis megrul-čanurši. [On the origin of certain cases in Mingrelo-Laz.] *Enimk'is Moambe* 1.179–82.

1967 [1931]. *Svanuri ena*, vol. I: *Zmna.* [The Svan Language, vol. I: The Verb.] [Published as volume I of his *Šromebi* (Works).] Tbilisi: Mecniereba.

Trask, R.L. 1979. On the origin of ergativity. In Frans Plank (ed.), *Ergativity: towards a theory of grammatical relations*, 385–404. New York: Academic Press.

Traugott, Elizabeth Closs. 1965. Diachronic syntax and generative grammar. *Language* 41.402–15.

1969. Toward a grammar of syntactic change. *Lingua* 23.1–27.

1972. *A history of English syntax: a transformational approach to the history of English sentence structure.* New York: Holt, Rinehart, and Winston.

1973. Some thoughts on natural syntactic processes. In C.J.N. Bailey and R.W. Shuy (eds.), *New ways of analyzing variation in English*, 313–22. Washington, DC: Georgetown University Press.

1980. Meaning-change in the development of grammatical markers. *Language Science* 2.44–61.

1982. From propositional to textual and expressive meanings: some semantic–pragmatic aspects of grammaticalization. In W.P. Lehmann and Y. Malkiel (eds.), *Perspectives on historical linguistics*, 245–71. Amsterdam: John Benjamins.

1990. From less to more situated in language: the unidirectionality of semantic change. In Sylvia Adamson, Vivien Law, Nigel Vincent, and Susan Wright (eds.), *Papers from the fifth International Conference on English Historical Linguistics*, 497–518. Amsterdam: John Benjamins.

Traugott, Elizabeth Closs and Bernd Heine (eds.). 1991a. *Approaches to grammaticaliza-*

tion. (Typological Studies in Language, 19.) 2 vols. Amsterdam: John Benjamins.

Traugott, Elizabeth Closs and Bernd Heine. 1991b. Introduction. In Elizabeth Closs Traugott and Bernd Heine (eds.), *Approaches to grammaticalization*, vol. I: *Focus on the theoretical and methodological issues*, 1–14. Amsterdam: John Benjamins.

Traugott, Elizabeth Closs and Ekkehard König. 1991. The semantics–pragmatics of grammaticalization revisited. In Elizabeth Closs Traugott and Bernd Heine (eds.), *Approaches to grammaticalization*, vol. I: *Focus on theoretical and methodological issues*, 189–218. Amsterdam: John Benjamins.

Trumpp, Ernst. 1873. *Grammar of the Pašto or language of the Afghans*. London: Allen.

Tuggy, David H. 1979. Tetelcingo Nahuatl. In Ronald W. Langacker (ed.), *Studies in Uto-Aztecan grammar*, vol. II: *Modern Aztec grammatical sketches*, 1–140. Arlington: Summer Institute of Linguistics and the University of Texas at Arlington.

Turgot, Anne Robert Jacques. 1756. Etymologie. In Denis Diderot and Jean le Rond d'Alembert (eds.), *Encyclopédie ou dictionnaire raisonné des sciences, des arts et des métiers* vol. VI, 98–111. Paris. (New edn. 1961, introduction, annotations by Maurice Piron. Bruges: De Tempel; Facsimile edn. 1967. Stuttgart: Frommann.)

Vachek, Joseph. 1972. On the interplay of external and internal factors in the development of languages. In Bertil Malmberg (ed.), *Readings in modern linguistics*, 209–23. Stockholm: Läromedelsförlagen.

Van der Gaaf, Willem. 1904. *The transition from impersonal to the personal constructions in Middle English*. (Anglistische Forschung 14.) Heidelberg: Carl Winter.

Vendryes, Joseph. 1968 [1921]. *Le Langage: introduction linguistique a l'histoire*. Paris: La Renaissance du Livre.

Vennemann, Theo. 1973. Explanation in syntax. In John Kimball (ed.), *Syntax and semantics*, vol. II, 1–50. New York: Academic Press.

1974a. Topics, subjects and word order: from SXV to SVX via TVX. In J. M. Anderson and Charles Jones (eds.), *proceedings of the first International Conference on Historical Linguistics*, vol. I: *Syntax, morphology, internal and comparative reconstruction*, 339–76. Amsterdam: North Holland.

1974b. Analogy in generative grammar: the origin of word order. In Luigi Heilmann (ed.), *Proceedings of the eleventh International Congress of Linguists, Bologna and Florence*, vol. II, 79–83. Bologna: Società editrice il Mulino Bologna.

Versteegh, Cornelis H.M. 1983. A dissenting grammarian: Quṭrub on declension. In Cornelis H.M. Versteegh, Konrad Koerner, and Hans–J. Niederehe (eds.), *The history of linguistics in the Near East* (Studies in the History of Linguistics, 28), 167–94. Amsterdam: John Benjamins.

Vico, Giambattista. 1948 [1744/1725]. *The new science of Giambattista Vico*, translated from the 3rd edn. (1744) by Thomas Bergin and Max Fisch. (1st edn. 1725.) Ithaca: Cornell University Press.

Vincent, Nigel. 1980. Iconic and symbolic aspects of syntax: prospects for reconstruction. In Paolo Ramat (ed.), *Linguistic reconstruction and Indo-European syntax: proceedings of the Colloquium of the "Indogermanische Gesellschaft"* (Amsterdam Studies in the Theory and History of Linguistic Science, series 4, vol. 19), 47–68. Amsterdam: John Benjamins.

1982. The development of the auxiliaries H A B E R E and E S S E in Romance. In Nigel Vincent and Martin Harris (eds.), *Studies in the Romance verb*, 71–96. London: Croom Helm.

Virtaranta, Pertti and Pentti Soutkari. 1964. *Näytteitä suomen murteista.* [Samples of Finnish dialects.] (Tieto-lipas 34.) Helsinki: Suomalaisen Kirjallisuuden Seura.

Visser, F.T. 1963–73. *An historical syntax of the English language.* 3 vols. Leiden: Brill.

Vočadlo, Otakar. 1938. Some observations on mixed languages. In *Actes du quatrième Congrès International de Linguistes,* 169–76. Copenhagen: Einar Munksgaard.

Vogt, Hans. 1948. Dans quelles conditions et dans quelles limites peut s'exercer sur le système morphologique d'une langue l'action du système morphologique d'une autre langue? In Michel Lejeune (ed.), *Actes du sixième Congrès International des Linguistes,* 31–45. Paris: Klincksieck.

1954. Language contacts. *Word* 10.365–74.

1971. *Grammaire de la langue géorgienne.* Oslo: Universitetsforlaget.

Wackernagel, Jakob. 1892. Über ein Gesetz der indogermanischen Wortstellung. *Indogermanische Forschungen* 1.333–436.

1926–8. *Vorlesungen über Syntax,* vol. I 1926, vol. II 1928. (2nd edn. 1950.) Basle: E. Birkhäuser.

Wahlén, N. 1925. *The Old English impersonalia,* Part I. Göteborg: Elanders.

Wang, William S-Y. 1969. Competing changes as a cause of residue. *Language* 45.9–25.

(ed.) 1977. *The lexicon in phonological change.* The Hague: Mouton.

Wang, William S-Y. and Chin-Chuan Cheng. 1977. Implementation of phonological change: the Shuāng-fēng Chinese case. In William Wang (ed.), *The lexicon in phonological change,* 148–58. The Hague: Mouton.

Warner, Anthony R. 1982. *Complementation in Middle English and the methodology of historical syntax.* University Park: Pennsylvania State Press.

1983. Review of *Principles of diachronic syntax,* by David W. Lightfoot. *Journal of Linguistics* 19.187–209.

Watkins, Calvert. 1963. Preliminaries to a historical and comparative analysis of the syntax of the Old Irish verb. *Celtica* 6.1–49.

1964. Preliminaries to the reconstruction of Indo-European sentence structure. In H.G. Lunt (ed.), *Proceedings of the ninth International Congress of Linguists,* 1035–45. The Hague: Mouton.

1969. *Indogermanische Grammatik,* vol. III: *Formenlehre,* Part I: *Geschichte der indogermanischen Verbalflexion.* Heidelberg: Carl Winter Universitätsverlag.

1976. Towards Proto-Indo-European syntax: problems and pseudo-problems. In Sanford B. Steever, Carol A. Walker, and Salikoko S. Mufwene (eds.), *Papers from the Parasession on Diachronic Syntax,* 306–26. Chicago Linguistic Society.

Watters, J. 1979. Focus in Aghem. In L. Hyman (ed.), *Aghem grammatical structure* (Southern California Occasional Papers in Linguistics, 7), 138–89. Los Angeles: Department of Linguistics, University of Southern California.

Waugh, Linda. 1975. A semantic analysis of the French tense system. *Orbis* 24.436–85.

Weerman, F. 1989. *The V2 conspiracy: a synchronic and diachronic analysis of verbal positions in Germanic languages.* Dordrecht: Foris.

Weinreich, Uriel. 1953. Languages in contact: findings and problems. (Publications of the Linguistic Circle of New York, 1.) New York. (9th printing, The Hague: Mouton.)

Weinreich, Uriel, William Labov, and Marvin Herzog. 1968. Empirical foundations for a theory of language change. In Winfred Lehman and Yakov Malkiel (eds.), *Directions for historical linguistics,* 95–195. Austin: University of Texas Press.

Westphal, Rudolf. 1873. *Das indogermanische Verbum, nebst einer Uebersicht der einzel-nen indogermanischen Sprachen und ihrer Lautverhältnisse.* Jena: Hermann Costenoble.

Wexler, Kenneth, and Peter W. Culicover. 1980. *Formal principles of language acquisition.* Cambridge, MA: MIT Press.

Whitney, William Dwight. 1881. On mixture in language. *Transactions of the American Philosophical Association* 12.1–26.

1889. *Sanskrit grammar.* 2nd edn. Cambridge, MA: Harvard University Press (12th issue of the 2nd edn., 1971).

Windisch, Ernst. 1869. Untersuchungen über den Ursprung des Relativpronomens in der indogermanischen Sprachen. *Studien zur griechischen und lateinischen Grammatik* 1. 201–419.

Winter, Werner. 1984. Reconstructional comparative linguistics and the reconstruction of the syntax of undocumented stages in the development of languages and language families. In Jacek Fisiak (ed.), *Historical syntax*, 613–26. Berlin: Mouton.

Winters, Margaret E. 1987. Innovations in French negation: a cognitive grammar account. *Diachronica* 4.27–53.

Wojcik, Richard. 1976. Verb fronting and auxiliary *do* in Breton. *Montreal Working Papers in Linguistics* 6.259–78.

Wotton, William. 1730 [1713]. *A discourse concerning the confusion of languages at Babel.* London: S. Austen and W. Bowyer.

Wright, Joseph. 1907. *Historical German grammar,* vol. I: *Phonology, word-formation, and accidence.* London: Oxford University, Geoffrey Cumberlege.

1910. *Grammar of the Gothic language.* Oxford: Clarendon.

Wright, Joseph and Elizabeth Mary Wright. 1928. *An elementary Middle English grammar.* 2nd edn. Oxford University Press.

Wright, Larry. 1976. *Teleological explanation.* Berkeley: University of California Press.

Wundt, Wilhelm. 1900. *Völkerpsychologie. Eine Untersuchung der Entwicklungsgesetze von Sprache, Mythus und Sitte,* vol. I: *Die Sprache.* Leipzig: W. Engelmann.

Xajdakov, S.M. 1980. *Principy imennoj klassifikacii v dagestanskix jazykax.* Moscow: Nauka.

Xubua, Mak'ar. 1937. *Megruli t'ekst'ebi.* [Mingrelian texts.] T'pilisi: Ak'ademia.

Zeitlin, Jacob. 1908. *The accusative with infinitive and some kindred constructions in English.* New York: Columbia University Press.

Zwicky, Arnold. 1977. *On clitics.* Bloomington: Indiana University Linguistics Club.

Ʒiʒiguri, Šota. 1973. *K'avširebi kartul enaši.* [Conjunctions in the Georgian language.] Tbilisi: Universit'et'i.

Index of languages and language families

Index of scholars

Abesaӡe, Nia 290
Adelung, Johann Christoph 22, 25
Aitchison, Jean 178, 214, 322
Akmajian, Adrian 178
Allen, Cynthia Louise 85, 123, 226, 285, 289, 380 n. 2, 381 n. 2, 396 n. 29, 397 nn. 31, 32, 403 n. 3
Andersen, Henning 384 n. 14
Andersen, Paul Kent 211, 214
Anderson, John M. 112–13
Anderson, Stephen R. 200, 246, 279–80, 409 n. 8
Anttila, Raimo 384, n. 14
Appel, René 125, 128
Ard, William Josh 400 n. 16
Aristar, Anthony Rodrigues 210
Aristotle 16, 382 n. 5
Austin, Peter 143

Babby, Leonard H. 71, 115
Bean, Marian C. 205
Behaghel, Otto 21, 23, 24, 218
Bennett, David C. 234, 351–2
Bickerton, Derek 306
Blake, Barry J. 197, 210
Bloomfield, Leonard 375–6
Bopp, Franz 17, 18, 31
Borsley, Robert D. 158
Brown, Penelope 285–6
Brugman(n), Karl 18, 19, 26, 31, 326–7
Bruneau, C. 183–4
Brunot, F. 183–4
Bubenik, Vit 137–41
Bybee (Hooper), Joan 212, 298–303
Byrne, Brian 238

Campbell, Lyle 75–6, 98–100, 125, 126–7, 129–30, 137–41, 146–7, 147–9, 232, 306, 352–3, 361
Cercvaӡe, Ilia 187–9
Chafe, Wallace 309
Chung, Sandra 48–9, 333
Čikobava, Arnold 187–9, 342
Clark, Ross 333

Comrie, Bernard 199, 236, 420 n. 10
Condillac, Etienne Bonnot de, l'abbé 22
Coseriu, Eugenio 125–6, 384 n. 14
Coteanu, I. 132, 133
Craig, Colette 23
Curme, George O. 225–6
Curtius, Georg 17, 18

Davidson, Elizabeth 238
Delbrück, Berthold 22–3, 25–6, 27
Deroy, Louis 132
Dixon, Robert M.W. 242, 251, 279
Dryer, Matthew S. 137, 196–7, 364, 406 n. 16, 415 n. 18
Du Bois, John 251–5
Dumézil, Georges 352

Ebert, Robert Peter 62, 123, 393 n. 8
England, Nora C. 235, 419 n. 46
Esenç, T. 352

Faarlund, Jan Terje 11–12, 37, 218–20, 322–3, 402 n. 23, 405 n. 11
Fischer, Olga C.M. 108–13, 397 n. 32
Friedrich, Paul 198, 230
Fujii, Noriko 144
Fulda, Friedrich Carl 22, 25

Gair, James W. 143
Garrett, Andrew 245, 248–9, 274
Genetti, Carol 291
Gildea, Spike Lawrence Owen 246–8
Givón, Talmy 151–2, 199, 205, 210, 213, 289, 336, 419 n. 46
Greenberg, Joseph H. 137, 138, 139, 195–6, 210, 341–2, 363
Gyarmathi, Sámuel 33

Haiman, John 274, 290–1, 421 n. 15
Hale, Kenneth 23
Hale, Mark 67
Harries-Delisle, Helga 154
Harris, Alice C. 68–70, 100–1, 215, 245–6,

Index of subjects